Reach and Power

the Heritage of the United States Air Force in Pictures and Artifacts

AIR
FORCE
History
and
Museums
PROGRAM
United States Air Force
Washington, D.C. 1997

Air Vice Marshal Ron Dick, RAF

Library of Congress Cataloging-in-Publication Data

Dick, Ron. 1931–

Reach and power: the heritage of the United States Air Force in pictures and artifacts/Ron Dick.

Includes bibliographical references and index.

    1. United States. Air Force—History. 2. Aeronautics, Military—United States—History. 3. United States—History, Military—20th century. I. Title.

UG633.D53   1997.   97–26252

358.4'00973—dc21   CIP

For sale by the U.S. Government Printing Office
Superintendent of Documents, Mail Stop: SSOP, Washington, DC 20402-9328
ISBN 0-16-049271-8

Foreword

The 50th anniversary of the independence of the United States Air Force is an occasion to reflect on the application of American air power in both peace and war. In the history of American aviation, which predates the creation of the USAF in 1947, notable accomplishments and actions stand out: from the era of the Wright biplanes before and through World War I; the bold years of development between 1919 and 1941; the harrowing maturation of the force during the crucible of World War II's global fight; the creation of the service itself; its tempering during the Berlin Airlift and the Korean War; the long watch of the Cold War; the grueling conflict in Southeast Asia; the rebuilding of the force in the 1970s and 1980s; air power's triumph in the Gulf War, and its use since then for both humanitarian and combat operations.

Through all of this, the service has reflected the spirit, dedication, and teamwork of the men and women of America from every race, ethnic group, and geographic locale. Individuals of diverse backgrounds, they have made the USAF's technology work for great purpose. Too often, they have had to pay for their successes with their own blood and suffering.

In this 50th anniversary year of the United States Air Force we remember their sacrifice. We honor their accomplishments by recognizing that they transformed the nature of military and national security affairs. They brought forth the era of three-dimensional military power and gave to the world a global air force ready to defend liberty and serve the needs not only of Americans, but of our allies and friends around the globe.

RICHARD P. HALLION

Air Force Historian

Preface

The United States Air Force on its 50th anniversary as a fully independent branch of the nation's defense establishment is fortunate that it can look to a unique resource at Wright-Patterson Air Force Base to celebrate its past, its present, and its future. The United States Air Force Museum, the largest and most visited of its type in the world, contains plentiful evidence of the spectacular achievements and proud heritage of a distinguished service. This evidence, in the form of aircraft, spacecraft, hardware, personal memorabilia, artifacts, artwork, photographs, films, documents, and diaries is displayed to tell the epic story of the often explosive development of American military aviation and air power from the acquisition of the first Wright Military Flyer as Signal Corps Aeroplane No. 1 in 1909 to the building of the USAF for the 21st century. The story of the USAF and its predecessors: the Aeronautical Division of the Office of the Chief Signal Officer of the Army, the U.S. Army Air Service, the U.S. Army Air Corps, and the U.S. Army Air Forces, has involved men and women of courage and daring who endured the physical challenges of operating military aircraft in war and peace. They possessed flair and determination in the face of the often short-sighted views that have bedeviled the defense policies of the United States and other democratic nations. The story has also involved political struggle at the highest level, inter-service rivalry at its bitterest, and continuous debate on the nature and use of air power. Advances in the hugely expanded frontiers of science and technology have produced a bewildering variety of equipment with seemingly magical capabilities. The flights of imagination of prophets like H. G. Wells have been eclipsed by the reality of events in the 20th century. Above the trenches of Saint-Mihiel and the oil fields of Ploesti, from the "Hump" of the Himalayas to the beaches of Normandy, over burning German and Japanese cities and the Yalu River in Korea, in Southeast Asia and the Middle East, American air power has shaped world events. There is every reason to suppose that it will continue to do so.

Anyone wishing to learn the story told in the pages of this book could do no better than visit the USAF Museum, near the home of the brothers who brought the first chapter of aviation history to a successful conclusion—Wilbur and Orville Wright. Since their amazing feat of controlled, powered flight, the area with Wright-Patterson Air Force Base at its center has remained at the forefront of USAF research and development, expanding aeronautical science and introducing successive generations of military aircraft to operational service. The USAF Museum is, therefore, appropriately sited, a treasure house of air power history, unsurpassed anywhere in the world for the size and quality of its military aviation collection. It is also the repository for a significant piece of America's national fabric; the United States could not be the world's strongest nation without air power, and the artifacts that record the building of air power are at Dayton.

Illustrations for *Reach and Power: The Heritage of the United States Air Force in Pictures and Artifacts* are drawn, as far as possible, from the USAF Museum's historic photographs, most of which came from its archives, and a dramatic new series of color photographs of the major items exhibited in its extensive galleries. From the USAF's official art collection selected works by some of the world's leading aviation artists are featured to impart both dramatic sweep and focus to the service's story. The book also contains decriptions of what visitors might see while walking through the museum's galleries and reliving the events of the periods covered.

If there is a message behind the story told in *Reach and Power: The Heritage of the United States Air Force in Pictures and Artifacts* and revealed by the illustrations that bring it to life, it is that the USAF is an organization in which remarkable accomplishment has been and is the daily fare of those who think of themselves as typical Americans—men and women of every race, religion, and national origin. Singular personalities have commanded attention and will be remembered, but, it could be argued that the airmen who fought so hard and so well in World War II, for example, were a citizen force of youngsters who had been students, farmers, clerks, and mechanics before the war.

While this book is intended as a 50th anniversary tribute to those men and women whose combined efforts and brave sacrifices since the days of the Wright brothers have contributed to an inspiring air power story and to the building of the modern United States Air Force, a necessary selectivity may disappoint some readers who will, no doubt, feel that much valuable and interesting material has been left out. Perhaps inevitably, the exploits of the personnel and machines at the USAF's "sharp end," the operational units, have most of the space available. However, what should never be forgotten is that operatorational units cannot function without a supporting cast of technicians, armorers, logisticians, administrators, medics, air traffic controllers, meteorologists, caterers, and other specialists who combine to make the USAF an effective military organization. Even when they are not directly mentioned, their efforts are recorded between the lines.

Acknowledgments

Considerably honored, as a retired Royal Air Force officer, to put together a book to celebrate the 50th anniversary of the United States Air Force, I began reviewing the achievements of an air force other than my own with some trepidation, but the nature of the task and the encouragement I received made completing it memorable and enjoyable. If the finished work does not do justice to its subject, the fault is mine alone.

Many people helped me along the way. My colleague, Dan Patterson, an aviation photographer of rare talent whose eye for the shapes and colors of aviation technology gives the book life, contributed his original photographs, which are unique and startling in their impact.

Richard Hallion, the Air Force Historian, reviewed and commented on the book and Mary Lee Jefferson of the USAF History Support Office edited it. From USAF Media Services, Mary Walden designed the book's cover and layout with pre-press support from: Robin Conner, Stephen Gonyea, Susan Linders, Lori Crane, Nick Mosura, Evelyn Buhl, Roni Williams, Kathy Jones, Ben Sansbury, Jon Arntzen, Roxie Pangallo, Technical Sergeant Rusty Kirk, Joe Ruggero, and O.C. Carlisle. Other staff of the USAF History Support Office also assisted me: Herman Wolk, Lieutenant Colonel "Chip" Hunt, Captain Jim Gates, Cargill Hall, Jack Neufeld, Anne Johnson-Sachs, Dan Mortensen, and Roger Miller.

Staff of the USAF Museum allowed access to the institution's resources: Dick Uppstrom, Joyce Watson, Myndie Wright, Wes Henry, Dave Menard, Diana Bacher, Bob Bobbitt, Leonard DeBerry, Jim Dinsmoor, Angela Lester, David Lockhart, Teresa Jones, J.R. Pass, Mark Swigart, Gary Bays, Paul Lee, Frank McVay, Bob Patterson, Steve West, Tom Bachman, Ted Beegle, Randal Canady, Ted Chapman, Dick Daughtery, Roger Deere, Rick Dodd, Mike Douglass, Paul Lake, David Lazzarine, Myrl Morris, Ray Petrusch, David Robb, Jim Shepherd, Gil Vaillancourt, Charles Weyrauch, Bob Spaulding, Earl Beach, and Richard Tobias.

Staff of Combat Camera in the Pentagon provided current USAF photographs. John McDowell of *Airman* magazine and Colonel "Smoky" Greene contributed conventional hard-copy images. Bob Limbrick provided reproductions of works from the USAF's official art collection.

The International Foundation of Eagles in Montgomery, Alabama, a longtime supporter of aviation history projects, consistently encouraged this one. At its annual Gathering of Eagles at Maxwell Air Force Base, Alabama, I met many of the aviators whose names and exploits enrich the narrative.

Closer to home, Don Babb proofread meticulously and Mike Harbison lent his computer expertise. Finally, my family offered its patience when the book was for me the center of the universe. I owe heartfelt thanks to Gary, who also lent computer knowledge, to Peta, and to Daniel for their understanding, and particularly to my wife, "Paul," for her tolerance of this latest manifestation of my obsession with aviation. I hope she thinks the result is worth the turbulence that accompanied its gestation and birth.

Contents

Foreword iii
Preface iv
Acknowledgments vi

Part I Creation
Chapter 1 Flying Start and Lost Advantage 3
Chapter 2 Building and Fighting, 1917–1918 33
Chapter 3 Challenge and Controversy 77
Chapter 4 Strategies and Demarcations 113

Part II Victory
Chapter 5 Girding For Conflict, 1939–1941 139
Chapter 6 The European Air War, 1942–1945 179
Chapter 7 The Pacific Air War, 1942–1945 241

Part III Independence
Chapter 8 Autonomy and Constraint 291
Chapter 9 SAC and the Centuries 337
Chapter 10 Limited War Learning Curve 371
Chapter 11 Resurrection 419

Part IV Supremacy
Chapter 12 Frontiers of Flight 443
Chapter 13 Wild Black Yonder 467
Chapter 14 Air Power Master Class 489
Chapter 15 21st Century Air Force 509

Appendix A The United States Air Force Museum 527
Appendix B Leaders of the United States Air Force 533
Appendix C Medals of Honor 535
Appendix D The Mackay Trophy 537
Bibliography 541
Glossary 549

Part I

Creation

I suppose we shall soon travel by air vessels; make air instead of sea voyages; and at length find our way to the moon, in spite of the want of atmosphere.

(Lord Byron, 1822)

I said to my brother Orville that man would not fly for fifty years.

(Wilbur Wright, 1901)

Success four flights Thursday morning all against twenty one mile wind started from level with engine power alone average speed through air thirty one miles longest 57 seconds inform Press home Christmas. Orevelle Wright.

(Telegram, complete with errors, received by Bishop Wright, 17 December 1903)

. . . what they had done was a miracle . . . . Without any formal training whatsoever, two ordinary Americans from an ordinary town in the state of Ohio had not only grasped and advanced the whole known science of aerodynamics. They had become its admitted masters.

(General of the Air Force Hap Arnold)

[It is demonstrable that] no possible combination of known substances, known forms of machine, and known forms of force can be united in a practicable machine by which men shall fly long distances through the air.

(Simon Newcomb, eminent scientist, 1906)

Chapter 1
Flying Start and Lost Advantage

A Walk through Air Power History at The United States Air Force Museum

The history of man's contemplation of flight and of efforts made by people the world over to emulate the birds is mankind's common heritage. The United States Air Force Museum's first gallery offers a brief reminder of the thousands of years of human fantasies and aspirations that preceded manned flight. Its displays lead visitors from the winged figures of early religions through fable and legend to the stumbling experiments of daring men who reached for the sky. It introduces visitors to those who found success in the lighter-than-air flight of balloons and airships, and to those who tried but failed in controlled flight with various heavier-than-air contraptions. The gradual progress represented by these failures and near successes sets the scene for the final triumph of the Wright brothers and the beginning of the creation of American air power.

The Wright Approach

Museum visitors turning away from the evidence of man's early hopes and dreams are suddenly made aware that the heroic prelude is finally over and that the curtain is rising on the first act of the drama of human flight. The Wright brothers and their works are at center stage. For visitors, the thrill of seeing full-size versions of the aircraft that were among the first to carry men aloft in controlled, heavier-than-air flight is heightened by the knowledge that the adventure began in Dayton, close to where the USAF Museum now stands. The Wrights' progress from bicycle manufacturers to the world's first true aviators is traced through photographs and artifacts, and is most impressively manifested by the aircraft at the heart of the display. Some of the engines that made it possible to fly are here, too, and so is evidence that Americans were among the first to give practical consideration to the military potential of flying machines.

The letters and newspaper clippings on the museum's walls convey a sense of the satisfaction that the Wrights felt at their success and of the flying start it gave to the United States. The U.S. government, however, was slow to recognize its inherent promise and the advantage passed to Europe, where the development of aircraft for

Wilbur, left, and Orville Wright on the back porch of the family house on Hawthorn Street in Dayton, Ohio, 1910.

military purposes was hastened by the outbreak of World War I. The Wrights themselves seemed reluctant to apply their inventive genius beyond their first successful aircraft and were soon surpassed by others. The few efforts at the development of military aviation in the United States Army were limited in scope and effectiveness. As the United States became committed to entering the war in Europe,

German gliding pioneer Otto Lilienthal. Lilienthal conducted many of his successful flights from a conical artificial hill built near Berlin. From its 50-foot summit, he could launch in any direction, depending on the prevailing wind.

its air power was almost nonexistent and thus it relied on European aircraft designs as it prepared to fight. A flying start had become a stumbling run to catch up, and, having shown the world how to fly, America's aviators found themselves ill-prepared to face European airmen who had already learned the realities of war in the air.

Beginnings

For Americans, 1903 was a vintage year—one that widened their horizons. The Ford Motor Company was incorporated to produce Henry Ford's Model A; the Harley-Davidson motorcycle was introduced; and, in a 52-day epic, a Packard was driven from San Francisco to New York to complete the first successful transcontinental journey by car. Hardly noticed at the time was a far more significant feat accomplished by two brothers from Dayton, Ohio. On 17 December 1903, when the thoughts of most Americans were turning toward Christmas, Wilbur and Orville Wright braved the icy winds of Kill Devil Hills near Kitty Hawk, on North Carolina's outer banks, to achieve powered, controlled flight for the first time. Orville himself later described their accomplishment as "the first in the history of the world in which a machine carrying a man had raised itself by its own power into the air in

Samuel Pierpoint Langley, right, and his able assistant Charles Manly. In 1903, striving to become the first man to achieve sustained powered flight in Langley's Aerodrome, Manly survived two successive dunkings in the Potomac River when the cumbersome Aerodrome "slid into the water like a handful of mortar" after being launched.

Octave Chanute, the first significant aviation historian and a crucial link between the aeronautical communities of Europe and America. Perhaps even more important, Chanute was a constant source of encouragement to the Wright brothers during their experiments.

full flight, had sailed forward without reduction of speed, and had finally landed at a point as high as that from which it had started."

The Wright brothers' achievement passed almost unremarked in 1903, even though they had taken the first step along an aerial highway that would, in the course of the 20th century, change every society on Earth. Those who only heard of the event were largely skeptical, lacking the imagination to believe the Wrights' claim that human flight was possible. Indeed, they may have subconsciously rejected the idea of flight; its mystic quality was necessarily diminished if mere mortals could lift themselves into the third dimension.

The Wrights Invent the Airplane
Wilbur and Orville Wright probably became intrigued by the idea of human flight in 1894 after reading a magazine article on the exploits of Otto Lilienthal, the German gliding pioneer, but it was not until 1899 that they gave serious consideration to the problem of how man might fly. That year, after careful bird-watching, Wilbur came to an important conclusion. "My observations of the flight of buzzards led me to believe that they regain their lateral balance…by a torsion of the tips of the wings." His concern with how flight was controlled was crucial to the brothers' eventual success. Unlike earlier would-be airmen, the Wrights thought about control from the beginning. They recognized that without control in the air adequate lift and power would be meaningless.

"The first flight lasted only twelve seconds, a flight very modest when compared with that of birds, but it was,
nevertheless, the first in the history of
the world in which a machine carrying a man had raised itself by its own
power into the air in free flight, had
sailed forward on a level course without reduction of speed, and had finally
landed without being wrecked."

Wilbur & Orville Wright

THE WESTERN UNION TEL
INCORPORATED
23,000 OFFICES IN AMERICA.
CABLE SE

RECEIVED ‡‡

176 C KA CS 33 Paid.   Via Norfolk Va

Kitty Hawk N C Dec 17

Bishop M Wright
                    7 Hawthorne St

Success four flights thursday morning all against twenty one mile
wind started from Level with engine power alone average speed
through air thirty one miles longest 57 seconds inform Press
home Christmas.   Orevelle Wright 525P

Circumstances denied Wilbur and Orville Wright the benefit of the college education enjoyed by their older brothers, but their intelligence and inventive flair were undoubted. They were methodical, self-sufficient, and became moderately successful. Their bicycle shop in Dayton, Ohio, had given them a solid background as light engineers and businessmen. When they turned their attention to flying, they did so with their accustomed thoroughness, first writing to ask the Smithsonian Institution for a list of relevant literature on the subject. They read voraciously, carefully noting the results of previous researches before moving on to experiments of their own. Included in the recommended reading was Octave Chanute's *Progress in Flying Machines*, which so impressed Wilbur that he wrote to Chanute in 1900 for advice and thus began a copious exchange of correspondence that marked a close and fruitful friendship.

The Wrights approached flying very differently from most of their predecessors. Although the accumulated wisdom in the books they read provided a basis for their work, they took nothing for granted. In trials they might use figures recorded by others such as Lilienthal for wing area and camber as points of departure, but they closely scrutinized and corrected them where they varied with their own results. Their scrupulously systematic methods went hand-in-hand with frugal practicality. Building their flyer, the brothers saw no need to employ expensive materials. They used timber, fabric, and wire readily available in local stores, and they shaped spars, stitched seams, and rigged wings with their own hands. When they needed an engine, they designed and made their own from scratch. They developed and built remarkably efficient propellers as well. Their special genius was fueled by a sincere belief in the goal of human flight and an unshakeable confidence that they were capable of overcoming any difficulties in attaining it. They confronted each problem that arose with logic and worked their way through to a solution. It seems simple, yet not until the Wrights had anyone pieced the elements of the flying puzzle together and made them into a comprehensible whole. In an age when far-reaching and profound technological developments would generally be born from the sophistications of big business and great industries, the Wrights changed the world from the bench of a home workshop.

When the brothers built their first glider in 1900, they deliberately avoided the inherent stability so avidly pursued by others, seeking instead to make the machine as responsive as possible to pilot control. As Wilbur put it: "We therefore resolved to try a fundamentally different principle. We would

Wright aero-engine. Chains and sprockets on the 12-horsepower engine are evidence of the builders' background in bicycle engineering. The strut-mounted anemometer for measuring airspeed was lent by Octave Chanute.

Wright memorabilia. The USAF Museum's collection of Wright brothers relics includes fabric from the 1903 Flyer, the splintered propeller from the 1908 accident that killed Lieutenant Selfridge at Fort Myer, a wing rib made by the Wrights, an American flag given to Orville by the commander of Fort Myer in 1908, an anemometer made by the Wrights, copies of the diary entry from 17 December and of the telegram sent after the first flight, and an original drawing made by the Wrights.

Wilbur Wright, left, and Dan Tate launching Orville Wright in the brothers' third glider at Kill Devil Hills, near Kitty Hawk, North Carolina, October 1902.

arrange the machine so that it would not tend to right itself." The 1900 glider also featured what the Wrights called the "helical twisting of the wings," a system they had already tried on a biplane kite in 1899. It was a control method later described by Chanute as "wing-warping," the more common term. By introducing a capacity to alter the shape of the wings, twisting the trailing edge of one wing-tip up and the other down, the brothers correctly interpreted the flight of vultures they had observed and at one stroke overcame the problem of controlling an aircraft in roll.

The brothers built three gliders in 1900, 1901, and 1902 and flew them at Kill Devil Hills. The site, near Kitty Hawk on North Carolina's lonely and wind-swept outer banks, was chosen for its lively breezes and because the brothers preferred to conduct their trials away from the public's prying eyes. With their first two gliders, each a simple biplane with no tail and a forward control surface, which they called a "horizontal rudder," they daringly concluded that Lilienthal's figures for wing area and camber were wrong. Wilbur wrote: "Having set out with absolute faith in the existing scientific data, we were driven

to doubt one thing after another, till finally, after two years of experiment, we cast it all aside and decided to rely entirely upon our own investigations."

The Wrights' "investigations" included designing and building their own wind tunnel, capable of providing a steady wind of 30 miles per hour, in which they tested many differently shaped wings. Exhaustive researches led them to rework Lilienthal's aerodynamic tables and thereby achieve a firm basis on which to found future success. In 1902, using the figures they had derived, they built a third glider, adding vertical tail surfaces. Although wing-warping had given them the control in roll they were looking for, it introduced another problem. The warped-down wing rose as it should, but it also swung back, inducing a nasty sideslip toward the down-going wing. The twin vertical tail surfaces were designed to keep that from happening.

Once the Wrights started flying the third glider, they realized from its sharply improved performance that they had been right to doubt Lilienthal. In September and October 1902, it completed over 1,000 glides and flew splendidly, although, at first, side-slipping

The Wright wind tunnel, a 6-foot long, 16-inch square wooden box with a glass viewing window on top. The tunnel's metal honeycomb straightened out air flowing in from a large belt-driven fan. Balances measured the lift and drag of model wings placed inside the tunnel. Scraps of wallpaper are covered with the brothers' calculations.

Wright horizontal rudders, which proved extremely sensitive.

was still a problem. They eventually worked out that when a wing was warped down its drag increased markedly. They devised a solution—to convert the fixed tail surfaces into a single movable rudder interconnected with the wing-warping control. Whenever the pilot initiated a banked turn, the rudder was automatically applied to counter the "warp drag" on the rising wing.[1]

Now sure that they had a practical flying machine, the Wrights turned their attention to adding power. Automobile engines of the time proved too heavy, so, ever practical, the brothers designed and built their own. When completed, their water-cooled engine with its accessories weighed about 200 pounds and produced 12 horsepower. It turned over at 1,090 revolutions per minute and was geared down through the simple bicycle-style chains and sprockets, with which they were familiar, to drive twin propellers. If the engine was a triumph of do-it-yourself light engineering, the propellers were works of art. They were eight feet across and made of laminated spruce,

carefully shaped with a gentle twist. In the absence of any useful information on propellers other than marine, the brothers determined their form by viewing them as wings moving through the air along a helical path in the vertical plane. The concept was difficult to grasp but the finished propellers proved remarkably efficient. Mounted on the aircraft, they gave further evidence of the thoughtful logic characteristic of the Wrights' work. They were "pushers" because it was thought that the airflow over the wings should not be unnecessarily disturbed, and they counter-rotated to prevent any difficulties from torque or gyroscopic effect.

The Wrights built their first "Flyer" in the summer of 1903 and took it to Kill Devil Hills in September. By the time they had assembled it and completed all preparatory work, in December, the weather was cold and unexpectedly calm. For a while, they waited patiently for a suitably stiff breeze to improve their chances of success, but by 14 December they decided to wait no longer. They took the Flyer to the crest of a gentle rise to its portable "runway," laid to allow it to run down the slope into what little wind there was. This runway was part of a typically ingenious solution to the problem of launching. The Flyer had gracefully curved skids to ease its landings on Kitty Hawk's sand, but they would not do for takeoff. They, therefore, rested on a wooden plank which was itself lying on another board fitted with two modified bicycle wheel hubs one behind the other. These tiny wheels ran along a 60-foot-long track made of 2 x 4 planks standing on edge and covered with thin metal sheet.

Success at Kitty Hawk

The toss of a coin selected Wilbur as the pilot for the first try with the Flyer. Once the engine had been warmed up, he settled himself in the prone position on the lower wing and slipped the restraining cable. The Flyer surged away down the slope and rose into the air, but too sharply. The large horizontal rudders at the front of the machine proved extremely sensitive and Wilbur underestimated their effect. The Flyer stalled and came down after being airborne for fewer than four seconds, sustaining minor damage on impact. Wilbur was disappointed, but also sure that success was now certain. Writing to his family that night, he admitted his mistake: "…the real trouble was an error in judgement in turning up too suddenly after leaving the track…. The machinery all worked in an entirely satisfactory manner, and seems reliable. The power is ample, and but for a trifling error due to lack of experience…and this method of starting, the machine would undoubtedly have flown beautifully."

The Flyer's twin rudders, the answer to the problem of sideslipping.

Wing-warping, the key to success. The Wrights achieved control in the air by wing-warping, the essential element ignored by so many others. Multiple exposures reveal the extent of the warping.

Langley's Aerodrome *on its way into the Potomac River after leaving its houseboat launching ramp, 7 October 1903.*

A closeup of the Aerodrome breaking up during its descent.

During repairs, the wind rose and the temperature fell. On the morning of 17 December, despite a cutting, almost too strong, northerly breeze of about 25 miles per hour, the brothers decided to try again. This time the track was laid on level, hard-packed sand, and it was Orville's turn at the controls. At about 10:35 a.m., he slipped the restraint and moved forward, as Wilbur ran alongside steadying a wing-tip. After travelling along the rail for some 40 feet, the Flyer rose into the air. Orville recorded his impressions in his diary:

> I found the control of the front rudder quite difficult on account of its being balanced too near the center and thus had a tendency to turn itself when started so that the rudder was turned too far on one side and then too far on the other. As a result the machine would rise suddenly to about 10 feet and then as suddenly, on turning the rudder, dart for the ground. A sudden dart when out about 100 feet from the end of the track ended the flight. Time about 12 seconds (not known exactly as watch was not promptly stopped).

Apart from Wilbur, the audience on the beach comprised five local men. Standing there in the icy wind, they may not have realized that they were witnesses to a turning point in history. In a mere 12 seconds of undulating progress, the fulfillment of the dream of human flight had begun and the door had cracked open on the aviation century. By the end of the day, the door was significantly further open. Alternating as pilots, the brothers made four flights in all, improving their performance with each. On the last, Wilbur remained airborne for 59 seconds and travelled 852 feet. Given the strength of the wind, his actual distance through the air was about half a mile. There was no longer any question that the Flyer could fly.

For its performance on 17 December 1903, the Flyer's place in aviation history is assured, but it never flew again. Before it could be returned to its shed, it was caught by a very strong gust of wind and turned over. It was substantially damaged but the Wrights left Kitty Hawk to spend Christmas in Dayton without repairing it. The career of one of the world's most famous aircraft was over after it had been in the air for not much more than a minute and a half.

At times between 1899 and 1903 the Wrights became depressed by what they felt was a lack of progress. In later years Wilbur wrote that, after suffering some disappointments with the 1901 glider, he had confided to Orville his opinion that "man would sometime fly,

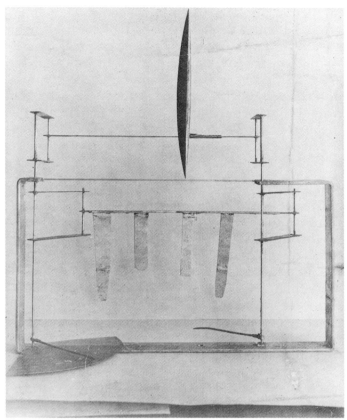

Wright wind tunnel balance. The device had an upper bar on which model wings could be mounted. The lift of a wing was compared with figures already determined for metal plates carried on the lower bar.

but…not within our lifetime." Looking back at what the brothers accomplished in those four years, however, a dispassionate observer must surely be astonished that the Wrights, starting from scratch and with their innate intelligence and talent, solved a problem of the ages in so short a time. Their achievement was immense, yet it passed almost unnoticed. The withdrawn nature of the brothers and the remoteness of Kitty Hawk combined to ensure that their activities were underreported, whereas the public failures of Samuel Langley in the heart of the nation's capital were described in some very influential newspapers.[2] Few people got to hear a true account of the events at Kitty Hawk, and most who did doubted that an obscure pair of bicycle mechanics would succeed where a distinguished scientist like Langley had failed.

Developments at Dayton

The public's disinterest had little effect on the Wrights. They knew that their first Flyer was imperfect and they set out to make it better. By the spring of 1904, they completed a second Flyer. Similar in design to its predecessor, it was sturdier and had an engine capable of producing 16 horsepower. Fully engaged in powered flying, they were no longer so dependent on the fresh breezes of the outer banks. They thus arranged with a farmer to carry out their trials in an 80-acre field near Dayton known as Huffman Prairie. To make up for the relative lack of wind in Ohio, they erected a derrick in the field and hung 600 pounds of metal weights from a rope inside it. The rope ran from the top of the derrick, under the launching rail, to the front of Flyer II's trolley. When ready, the pilot tripped a catch restraining the weights and their fall considerably augmented the thrust of the twin propellers as Flyer II surged forward to takeoff.

During 1904 the brothers made over 100 flights in Flyer II. None of them was very long and the series was bedeviled by small mishaps. Nevertheless, having learned a great deal, by the end of the year, both Wilbur and Orville had managed circling flights of more than five minutes. In 1905 they poured their experience into a third aircraft, Flyer III, which, in its final form, was more aesthetically pleasing and effective than either of its forebears. Its front and rear control surfaces were mounted farther from the wings and the link between the rudder and the wing-warping mechanism was disconnected to improve control. The result was both graceful and maneuverable. By the end of the year, Flyer III had proved capable of completing tight figure eight patterns and flying as long as its fuel lasted, which on 5 October had been

38 minutes. It was the world's first practical flying machine. No other would-be aviator had succeeded in achieving any kind of controlled, powered flight, and most authorities still flatly refused to accept that it was possible.

The Wrights had decided in 1904 to seek the legal protection of patents and in the process were unwilling to allow anyone close to their Flyers or trials. Apart from local farmers, few people realized what was going on at Huffman Prairie. By this time the brothers wanted some return on their investment, and it had occurred to them that their aircraft had military potential, principally for reconnaissance. Accordingly, they informed both the U.S. and British governments that they had produced a flying machine and could supply others like it for a contracted price. The British government appeared to accept the Wrights' offer, but refused to go further without a practical demonstration, something the brothers were not prepared to give without promise of a contract. The U.S. government firmly rejected the offer. No American official thought it worthwhile to visit Dayton. Responding to the Wrights' third approach, the Board of Ordnance and Fortification in October 1905 seemed to represent the official blind eye at its most opaque. Its letter concluded: "…the Board does not care to…take any further action until a machine is produced

First flight. At 10:35 a.m. EST, 17 December 1903, as Orville took the controls and Wilbur looked on, the Wright brothers opened the door to the aviation century. For the first time "a machine carrying a man had raised itself by its own power into the air in full flight, had sailed forward without reduction of speed, and had finally landed at a point as high as that from which it had started."

The Wright brothers with their new Flyer at Huffman Prairie, Dayton, Ohio, May 1904.

which by actual operation is shown to be able to produce horizontal flight and to carry an operator."

Frustrated and discouraged that there was little likelihood of a government contract in the foreseeable future, they closed up shop and secured themselves against possible commercial espionage. They kept the details of their Flyers secret until their patents were finally approved and governments became more amenable. They did not take to the air again for two and a half years.

In the course of this interregnum, the Wrights refined their engine and continued to build aircraft, one of which they crated and shipped to France in 1907 when the possibility of a French governmental contract arose. No contract materialized, however, and the plane sat in its box at Le Havre until the following year. A number of air-minded Frenchmen, alarmed by stories of the Wrights' success and the thought that their country might be left behind, were working on a variety of machines, but they did not fully appreciate the real problems that had to be overcome

before human flight could occur. The Wrights' basic secrets had been made available through a 1903 lecture by Chanute in Paris and by the publication of the Wrights' patents in 1906, but the vital clues contained within them were unaccountably ignored by Europeans who should have known better. They undertook no methodical program of research and did not even consider the critical problem of three-dimensional control in the air. The Wrights noted what was going on and rightly saw no serious rivals on the horizon.

There were small successes, however. In 1906 the Paris-domiciled Brazilian, Alberto Santos-Dumont, managed a few barely controlled hops of up to 250 yards in a tail-first creation that was little more than a few large box-kites strung together. Entirely impractical, it contributed nothing to the advancement of aeronautics, but its performance was well reported and wildly applauded by a French population ignorant of what the Wrights had done. Although the Wrights faced no real technological threat from

Santos-Dumont's machine and others that followed it in Europe, they did become alarmed about any prospects for aircraft contracts. Since few understood what Wright Flyers represented in terms of research and development, the very suggestion that the secrets of flight were about to become common property might be enough to complicate contract negotiations. With this in mind the Wrights renewed their efforts to attract potential customers in 1907. They met with a company interested in selling Flyers to the French government and sent a new proposal to the U.S. Board of Ordnance and Fortification after President Roosevelt, his attention drawn to the brothers through the Aero Club of America, had nudged his administration into finding out more about what they were up to in Dayton.

The U.S. Army Stirs
Meanwhile, the U.S. Army felt the tremors of growing aviation fever in Europe and decided to revive its moribund interest in the third dimension. A balloon detachment of the U.S. Army's Signal Corps had been formed in 1892 but had languished after 1898.[3] On 1 August 1907, an Aeronautical Division of the Signal Corps was established under Captain Charles Chandler to "have charge of all matters pertaining to military ballooning, air machines, and all kindred subjects." The first official step on the road to the United States Air Force had been taken.

Within months, the new Aeronautical Division had issued Signal Corps Specification No. 486 for "...the construction of a flying machine supported entirely by the dynamic reaction of the atmosphere and having no gas bag." The specification was based on the Wrights' performance estimates and issued for competitive bidding on 23 December 1907. It required the aircraft to carry two persons weighing a combined 350 pounds, reach a minimum speed of 40 miles per hour, and fly for 125 miles. It attached a 10 percent bonus or penalty on the agreed price for speeds above or below 40 miles per hour and stipulated that the machine be easily disassembled for transporting in Army wagons, with reassembly taking no more than an hour. The specification also required the aircraft to land on an unprepared field without damage and descend safely should its propulsion unit break down. Most particularly, the specification required the machine to be "sufficiently simple in its construction and operation to permit an intelligent man to become proficient in its use within a reasonable length of time." Such was the general ignorance of the Wrights achievement that the American press ridiculed the specification, claiming that it asked for the impossible. Surprisingly, no fewer than 41 bidders responded, but only 3 bids were thought worth accepting, including that from the Wrights, who set their price at $25,000. However, only the Wrights proved capable of providing an aircraft for trial.

Alberto Santos-Dumont. The rich Brazilian, living in Paris, recorded the first powered flight in Europe in 1906, coaxing his kite-like 14–bis into the air for around 21 seconds. He later turned to monoplane designs like this, the little Demoiselle, the first successful ultra-light aircraft.

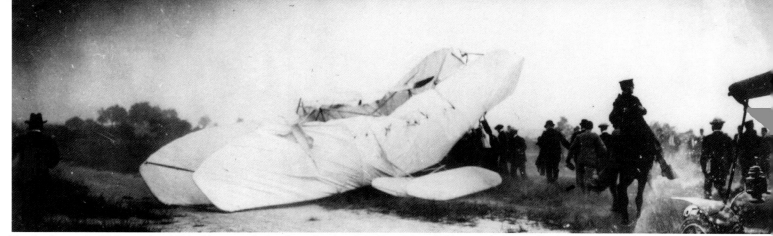

Tragic aftermath, 17 September 1908. After completing four circuits of the Fort Myer field, a cracked propeller began a series of structural failures that led to the crash of the Military Flyer. Orville Wright was the aircraft's pilot, Lieutenant Thomas Selfridge was a passenger. Amid the tangled mass of wreckage, Wright was conscious but badly injured, having broken a thigh and several ribs. Selfridge's injuries included a fractured skull. He died after surgery, becoming the world's first fatality in an aircraft accident.

Public Demonstrations

After doing some refresher flying at Kitty Hawk in the 1905 Flyer III, Wilbur set off for France in May 1908 to collect the Flyer stored at Le Havre, reassemble it at a racecourse near Le Mans, and then show off its capabilities publicly for the first time. His preparations were regarded with great skepticism by the French, and a critical audience gathered to view his first flights on 8 August 1908. Subsequent reaction to his mastery of the air was dramatic. The Flyer's easy maneuverability and soaring flight put the struggling efforts of European pioneers into perspective, and skeptics on both sides of the Atlantic were at last forced to recognize the true magnitude of the Wright brothers' achievement. The European press lionized Wilbur, calling his performances "Marvelous! Glorious! Sensational!" One French commentator remarked: "We are as children compared with the Wrights." In England, Major Baden-Powell of the Aeronautical Society reached beyond the collective European astonishments of the moment to comment: "That Wilbur Wright is in possession of a power which controls the fate of nations is beyond dispute."

While Wilbur widened European eyes, Orville stayed at home to arrange the trials of their Type A Military Flyer. They were to be carried out at Fort Myer, just across the Potomac River from Washington, D.C. Like the Flyer in France, this new biplane had upright seats for a pilot and a passenger. Orville began flying on 3 September 1908 and promptly duplicated Wilbur's success, electrifying onlookers with the sureness of his control in the air. Within the next two weeks he achieved an endurance record of more than an hour, set an altitude record of 310 feet, and carried the first military observer, Lieutenant Frank Lahm of the Aeronautical Division. The Army was impressed and local spectators were wild with enthusiasm. The trials could not have gone better, until the last day. On 17 September Orville took off with Lieutenant Thomas Selfridge. They were circling

Fort Myer's field when a crack developed in a blade of the starboard propeller. It became unbalanced and was deflected sufficiently to strike and tear loose a bracing wire supporting the rudder. The Flyer lost control and dived steeply into the ground, severely injuring Orville and killing Lieutenant Selfridge, who thus gained morbid distinction as powered flight's first aerial fatality.

The First Military Aircraft

The accident did not discourage the Army. It had seen enough in two weeks of flying at Fort Myer to be convinced that the Wrights were more than capable of meeting the specifications of their contract, which was extended to give Orville time to recover from his injuries. In July 1909, he was back at Fort Myer with a new Flyer. After a few days of false starts, he got into his stride and showed that the Flyer did indeed meet the specifications. On 27 July, as President Taft looked on, Orville and Lieutenant Lahm were airborne for 1 hour, 12 minutes and 40 seconds, a new record for a flight with a passenger. Then, on 30 July, Orville flew with Lieutenant Benjamin Foulois as navigator on a "cross-country" speed trial between Fort Myer and Alexandria, Virginia. Their average speed was 42.583 miles per hour, enough to secure the $25,000 contract price, plus a $5,000 bonus. On 2 August, the U.S. Army officially accepted the Flyer as the world's first military aircraft. Officially designated Signal Corps Aeroplane No. 1, it was reported by the *Washington Evening Star* as "Aeroplane No. 1, Heavier-Than-Air Division, United States Aerial Fleet."

Competition

While the Wrights and their aircraft undoubtedly dominated aviation during this period, a number of rivals appeared. Wilbur's performance in France had initially chastened and amazed the Europeans, but as their shock wore off they were inspired to greater things. Great men like Henry Farman, Hubert Latham, Louis Bleriot, S.F. Cody, and J.T.C. Moore-Brabazon

Signal Corps Aeroplane No. 1, the world's first military aircraft. The Wright Type A Military Flyer comfortably exceeded the Army's contract specifications and became the basis of America's "aerial fleet" for $30,000.

came to the fore, showing themselves eager to learn, adapt, and develop the Wrights' methods and ideas. As they grasped the essential nature of the Wrights' system of three-axis control, they retained the inherent stability of the largely unsuccessful European machines. Reaching for a sensible compromise between the two, they progressed rapidly and before long were producing aircraft that outperformed Wright Flyers.

On the other side of the Atlantic, the Wrights faced some home-grown competition in the form of the Aerial Experiment Association (AEA), led by Alexander Graham Bell. Among its original members, known as "Bell's Boys," were Lieutenant Thomas Selfridge, who died in Orville's crash at Fort Myer, and Glenn Curtiss, who also was at Fort Myer in 1908, involved with trials of Thomas Baldwin's airship. The airship subsequently became Signal Corps Dirigible No 1. It owed much of its success to an engine designed and made by Curtiss. A water-cooled four-cylinder engine of 20 horsepower, it was a modest beginning for a long line of Curtiss engines and derivatives that would significantly influence aviation.

Glenn Curtiss was a young motorcycle engineer and racer who turned to aviation because it combined new engineering challenges with adventure and promised excitement and speed. He was involved with the AEA's construction of four biplanes in 1908,

the third of which, the *June Bug*, he designed and flew with considerable success. On 4 July 1908, when the Wrights were otherwise occupied, Curtiss and the *June Bug* won *Scientific American* magazine's prize for the first flight in the United States of more than a kilometer by staying in the air for almost a mile in front of several hundred spectators at Hammondsport, New York. The flight was not, by the Wrights' standards, much to shout about, but it was done in public and given far more acclaim than anything the secretive brothers had done up to that time.

Perhaps piqued by all the acclaim, Orville wrote to Curtiss pointing out that since the *June Bug* had "movable surfaces at the tips of the wings, adjustable to different angles on the right and left sides for maintaining lateral balance," there appeared to be an infringement of the Wright's wing-warping patents. Before the year was out, the brothers were embarked on a long and bitter law suit against Curtiss, which set out not only to punish him for using ailerons but also to prove that their patents should be applied to all forms of lateral control on aircraft world-wide. Sadly, over the years, the implacability of the Wrights on this matter diminished their reputations. They were widely viewed as obstructions to aeronautical progress, and the strictures of their patents were largely ignored or circumvented. Rightly recognized as men of genius who had once pointed the way to the future, after 1909 they were often attacked for defending the achievements of the past as their personal property. While they expended their energies trying to hang on to what they had, others overtook them and went on to greater things. By 1911, European designs, notably Bleriot monoplanes, were being built under license in the United States and sold assembled for $1,000, complete with the proud boast, "All assembled machines guaranteed to fly!"

The U.S. Army Flies

With the acquisition of an "aerial fleet," the U.S. Army needed pilots. Under the terms of their contract, the Wrights were required to train two and it was arranged that they would do so from a cleared site just north of Washington, D.C., at College Park, Maryland. Wilbur gave Lieutenants Frank Lahm and Frederic Humphreys about three hours of dual instruction each and sent them both to solo at College Park on 26 October 1909. On 5 November they damaged the aircraft, and the Army returned both of them to their regular units. For a while, therefore, the "aerial fleet" had neither an airworthy aircraft nor pilots to fly it.

Having undergone repairs, the Military Flyer was shipped to Fort Sam Houston in Texas to escape the Washington winter, and Lieutenant Benjamin "Benny" Foulois, who had managed three brief flying lessons with the Wrights, was sent with it. As Foulois later recalled, he got his orders from the Chief Signal Officer, General James Allen, in person: "Don't worry. You'll learn the techniques as you go along.... Just take plenty of parts and teach yourself to fly." On 2 March 1910, after seeking the Wrights advice on "how to avoid basic disasters," Foulois got Aeroplane No. 1 airborne and completed his first solo intact. He continued to fly throughout the summer of 1910, suffering a number of minor accidents and repeatedly patching up his long-suffering aircraft in the course of gaining proficiency. Foulois later recalled that "...the bad bucking habits of No. 1 in gusty winds and forced landings because of the erratic temperament of the engine kept the machine in the shop more days than it was out." The Army did not seem to be all that interested. It was one thing that it had formed an Aeronautical Division and acquired a flying machine, but it was quite another that it provide the necessary operating funds. Foulois was startled to discover that his budget for the year was just $150, and more than once he was forced to reach into his own pocket to pay for fuel and repairs.

The Signal Corps made a case for operating funds, new aircraft, and an appropriation of $200,000, but

Benny Foulois, Chief of the U.S. Army Air Corps in the early 1930s, seen as a U.S. Army Air Service captain in front of a Burgess trainer.

Congress was not impressed. One of its members was driven to remark, "Why all this fuss about planes for the Army? I thought we had one." By the end of 1910 the Army's one aircraft was sadly the worse for wear and ready for retirement. The Aeronautical Division was in danger of being grounded until Robert Collier, the publisher, bought a new Wright Type B Flyer and, in February 1911, leased it to the Army for the princely sum of $1 per month. This bizarre arrangement may have helped to shame Congress into taking limited action, because, only three months later, approved appropriations for the War Department included $125,000 for military aeronautics, $25,000 of which became available immediately.

This was hardly a generous allocation, and it was indicative of the nation's apathy toward the potential of military aviation. To the American public, flying was a great new adventure in which daredevils broke records or entertained crowds at fairs. The United States was protected by vast oceans and distances, and it seemed inconceivable that flimsy aerial machines could ever be more than marginally useful to either the Army or the Navy. In Europe, the picture was quite different. Its smaller, more densely populated

Glenn Curtiss. Motorcycle racer, engine builder, and founding member of Alexander Graham Bell's Aerial Experiment Association, he became a dominant figure of American aviation's early days. Curtiss' aircraft held a place in the air forces' front line until after World War II, and his ideas influenced some of the world's most successful in-line engine designs.

countries were traditionally on guard against each other across notoriously porous land frontiers. Only the British had the luxury of a water barrier, and the effectiveness of that was questioned when Louis Bleriot flew his monoplane across the English Channel in 1909.

It was true that many European military officers sneered at the aircraft. Britain's most senior soldier regarded aviation as a "useless and expensive fad, advocated by a few individuals whose ideas are unworthy of attention." Marshal Foch of France later added: "It is good sport, but for the Army the aeroplane is useless." Nevertheless, there were enough highly-

placed Europeans concerned about the aircraft's military potential to ensure that it was not ignored. The differences in pre-World War I military aviation funding and pilot training between the United States and Europe were profound. Between 1908 and 1913 France and Germany spent well over $20 million each, Russia $12 million, and even Belgium $2 million. In the same period, the United States allocated less than $500,000. In terms of certified pilots, both civilian and military, the disparity was startling. In 1913 there were about 2,400 pilots in the world; the United States could claim fewer than 100.

America's conservative attitude toward military aviation was emphasized when it came to anything that might improve the aircraft for war. In 1911, Riley Scott demonstrated a bombsight that showed great promise, but the War Department was not interested. Discouraged, he took his device to Europe where it won a prize in international competition. Colonel Isaac Lewis produced a lightweight low-recoil machine-gun in 1912 and its airborne firing trials were so good that he was asked to produce ten more guns for intensive testing. He was prevented by the Ordnance Department because the gun had not been adopted as a U.S. Army weapon. The Army decreed that its own standard Benet-Mercie, whose weight and size made it entirely unsuitable for mounting in an aircraft, should be used in the air, in the unlikely event it was needed. Lewis promptly left for Belgium, where his gun was manufactured to become a standard air-to-air Allied weapon in World War I.

Seen in this context, Congress' first appropriations devoted to military aeronautics in 1911 were short-sightedly small and only pointed out the fact that America's lead in aviation was being allowed to slip away across the Atlantic. Even so, the appropriations were a beginning. General Allen immediately ordered five new aircraft at a cost of about $5,000 each—two Curtiss Model Ds and three Wright Type Bs. The first of these to be delivered in April 1911 was a Curtiss Model D, which became Signal Corps Aeroplane No. 2 (SC2).

Curtiss' aircraft were directly descended from his successful Golden Flyer, successor to the *June Bug*. In 1909, flying a modified Golden Flyer fitted with his 50-horsepower engine, Glenn Curtiss won the Gordon Bennet Trophy race at the world's first international air meet near Reims, France. He averaged a speed of 47 miles per hour. His Model D, which had similar performance, was a pusher biplane with only one seat; trainee pilots necessarily learned to fly it without the benefit of an instructor alongside.

USAF Museum aircraft and engine replicas. The Curtiss Model D is a replica of Signal Corps Aeroplane No. 2. Original materials were used in the reconstruction, except the engine, which is rendered in wood and plastic.

Some of America's earliest military aviators line up. From left: Lieutenant Frank Lahm, Lieutenant G.C. Sweet (U.S. Navy), Major C. McK. Saltzman, Major George Squier, Captain Charles Chandler, Lieutenant Benny Foulois, and 2nd Lieutenant Frederic Humphreys.

A student pilot trained in stages. First, he made himself familiar with the controls. Then he tried straight-line taxying with the foot throttle tied back so that he could not exceed 15 miles per hour. Comfortable with that, he was allowed to get off the ground in short hops of no more than ten feet off the ground, gradually progressing to free flight. Curtiss supervised these elementary operations at his flying school at North Island on San Diego Bay.

In April 1911 Foulois at last lost his lonely status as America's only military pilot. He was joined at Fort Sam Houston by three graduates of Curtiss' flying school, Lieutenants Beck, Kelly, and Walker. The Aeronautical Division did not have long to enjoy its newly acquired strength intact. On 10 May, Lieutenant Kelly got into trouble in SC2, crashed at Fort Sam Houston, and became the first pilot to be killed in a heavier-than-air flying accident. The local commander, General Carter, decided that he could no longer tolerate the hazard of dangerous machines using his drill field for their runways and maneuvering in the air over the heads of his troops. He forthwith prohibited all flying at Fort Sam Houston and hastened the Army into moving the Aeronautical Division back to College Park, where some of the Signal Corps' new-found funds were already being spent on a more permanent military flying school in Maryland with winter quarters in warmer Augusta, Georgia.

At College Park Captain Chandler resumed his position as Chief of the Aeronautical Division and also served as commandant of the flying school. Up to that time, even though a number of officers had been flying, none of them had been properly certified as Army pilots. In the absence of a prescribed military test, the Army decided to use the regulations of the Federation Aeronautique Internationale (FAI). Two newly arrived pilots, Lieutenants Henry "Hap" Arnold and Thomas Milling, both of whom had just completed a flying course with the Wrights in Dayton, passed the FAI tests in July 1911 and earned certificates as U.S. Army Aviators Nos. 1 and 2. Captain Chandler and his adjutant, Lieutenant Roy Kirtland, became students of Arnold and Milling and qualified soon after.

The Army now had an embryo flying school. It also had aircraft but no certainty within the Aeronautical Division of their military role. Beyond a vague idea that they might be useful as observation platforms no exact idea of their use in anger yet existed. In later years, General Hap Arnold recalled:

Without radio communications, the rapid delivery of intelligence still depended largely on horsemen. We, the airmen, were to jot down what we saw on brightly colored pieces of paper and drop the weighted paper to the ground, where a cavalryman, galloping hell for leather, would pick it up and take it back to the command post.

Army pilots, firm in their belief that they were not taken seriously by senior commanders, most of whom regarded the aircraft as little more than a toy, found the lack of positive direction from above disconcerting. They, therefore, decided to define their mission themselves and set out to discover what their machines were capable of and what devices might be hung on them to boost their effectiveness.

Arnold and Milling gradually increased their cross-country flight distances, going out as far as Frederick, Maryland, 42 miles away, and Arnold made a point of seeing how high he could coax the Wright biplanes, eventually getting one up to 4,167 feet. Milling also flew with Scott's bombsight and Lewis's gun, only to find that the Army was not interested. Earlier, in 1910, Lieutenant Jacob Fickel had fired a rifle while flying, consistently hitting a small ground target, and Glenn Curtiss, flying a pusher biplane, dropped tennis ball-sized dummy bombs on a target shaped like a battleship. Live bombs followed in January 1911, as Wright demonstrator Philip Parmalee piloted a Flyer in exercises near San Francisco while Lieutenant Myron Crissy dropped the bombs by hand.

In September 1911 Arnold became the first pilot to carry U.S. mail when he flew a small satchel of letters five miles from the Nassau Boulevard field to Hempstead, Long Island. Another pilot, delayed on his return to College Park until after sunset, was, in aviation's first, if inadvertent, night flying, guided to a safe landing by a row of burning oil puddles set afire by his anxious comrades. Arnold and Milling also experimented with air-to-ground communication by radio and found that they could dispense with horses and bits of paper by sending coded radio messages. Taken individually, such small achievements may not have seemed very significant to the Army, but they were slowly expanding the known capabilities of the Aeronautical Division and, since the press regularly reported its activities, establishing the fact of military aviation with the American public.

Unfortunately, the press reported accidents as well. Accidents were frequent, and too many of them were fatal. In the five and a half years from the date of Lieutenant Selfridge's death on 17 September 1908 to the end of February 1914, the Aeronautical Division suffered 11 flying fatalities, seemingly few,

Hap Arnold and Thomas Milling. Both men learned to fly in 1911 in a Wright Type B Flyer. As majors they flew Boeing P–12s at Mather Field, California, and later became generals. Arnold went on to be Chief of the U.S. Army Air Forces and was the only airman ever promoted to five-star rank.

Grim reminder. An unsmiling Lieutenant Thomas Selfridge seated in the Wright Military Flyer just before the crash that killed him during the Fort Myer, Virginia, test of 17 September 1908. The pilot, Orville Wright, seated at Lieutenent Selfridge's left, was injured. Flying was a dangerous business, as America's press never failed to report, and accidents and fatalities were frequent in Wright "pusher" biplanes. By 1912 they had not evolved much beyond what they had been in 1903, with rear-mounted engines, and were soon superseded by Curtiss and Burgess "tractor" types.

but the number of aircrews in those days was very small and the length of flights quite short. The truth is revealed by Signal Corps flight records. In 1911, a death occurred for every 65 hours spent in the air, or once in 372 flights. By 1914, the rate was down to one in 125 hours or 515 flights, but it was still much too high. Lesser accidents in which aircraft were destroyed or damaged and personnel injured also took their toll. Hap Arnold himself had one unpleasant incident, in a Wright Type C in 1912, which so alarmed him that he stopped flying for four years. He was not the only one to find that particular type difficult to handle, and in February 1914 the Signal Corps grounded it, noting its involvement in most of the fatal accidents. Shortly thereafter, a board of investigation found the Type C "dynamically unsuited for flying" in favor of the newer Curtiss and Burgess machines, both of which were "tractors" rather than pushers, with the engine and propeller mounted ahead of the pilot instead of behind. It may have been felt that the weight of wood and metal in front absorbed the shock of an impact more safely than it did in the rear where it could rush forward and crush anyone in its path. Whatever the reason, it was clear that the days of the Wrights' supremacy were over. When Wilbur died in 1912, Wright biplanes were still the fragile descendants of the original 1903 Flyer—pusher biplanes with no cockpit and with wing-warping for lateral control. The aviation world born of the Wright brothers' genius had passed them by.

Although painfully slow to grow and develop, American military aviation was at last granted formal recognition as a military activity. In 1912, the Army announced that qualified officers should be rated Military Aviators and awarded a badge showing an eagle in flight after they successfully completed certain flying tests. These included climbing to 2,500 feet, operating in a wind of at least 15 miles per hour, carrying a passenger to 500 feet, landing power off within 150 feet of a chosen point, and flying a 20-mile cross-country exercise at 1,500 feet.

The following year, in 1913, Congress, considering and accepting the arguments put by Army aviators on the daily hazards of military flying and the need to attract more aviation volunteers, authorized a 35 percent pay increase for officers assigned to flying duties. In 1914, it passed legislation in the form of "An Act to Increase the Efficiency of the Aviation Services of the Army, and for Other Purposes," and

> ...hereby created an aviation section, which shall be a part of the Signal Corps of the Army, and which shall be, and hereby is, charged with the duty of operating or supervising the operation of all military aircraft, including balloons and aeroplanes, all appliances pertaining to said craft, and signalling apparatus of any kind when installed on said craft; also with the duty of training officers and enlisted men in matters pertaining to military aviation.

The Aviation Section was allowed a strength of 60 officers and 260 enlisted men and ratings of Military Aviator and Junior Military Aviator. Both would grant entitlement to flying pay, but neither was expected to be conferred on other than unmarried lieutenants of the line.

As military aviation became an established element of the U.S. Army, it spread to very distant outposts. For a time between 1912 and 1914, there were flying schools in Hawaii and the Philippines. The Army eventually closed down both, mainly due to difficulties in keeping aircraft serviceable under local conditions and lack of replacement aircraft. The schools were notable if only because they were Army units regularly engaged in operating from water. At Kamehameha, Hawaii, and in Manila Bay, Army flying was done with floatplanes, which struggled on until they were destroyed or rendered useless by repeated accidents. Having gotten its feet wet, the Army continued to flirt with the water, going so far as to order three Curtiss F Type flying boats in 1912.

The year 1913 was a turbulent one for the Army's fledgling air arm. On 25 February, as the bulk of the Aviation Section endured unexpectedly unfriendly weather at its southern base near Augusta, Georgia, Captain Chandler received orders to move the unit to Texas City, Texas, on the Gulf coast. Relations between the United States and Mexico had become strained and aircraft were dispatched for possible border patrol. As the year moved into spring, tensions with Mexico eased, but others within the Aviation Section did not. Chief Signal Officer, Brigadier General George Scrivens undertook corrective measures to

ease dissatisfactions and raise morale. Recognizing that flying units needed to be properly organized to operate in the field, he established the 1st Provisional Aero Squadron on 5 March 1913. It consisted of a headquarters staff and two aero companies with a total strength of 9 officers and 51 enlisted men, plus 9 aircraft.

Scrivens instituted more improvements as the Aviation Section established more flying schools, drew up requirements to force manufacturers to make safer aircraft, and began installing radios and rudimentary flight instruments. He was occasionally irritated by the impatience of the young airmen and once described them as "deficient in discipline and a proper knowledge of the customs of the service and the duties of an officer." Hap Arnold later recalled seeing a letter from them to Scrivens that demanded changes in the senior personnel controlling military aviation; it is perhaps not surprising that the Chief Signal Officer was irritable.

The need for aircraft on the Mexican border having passed, the 1st Provisional Aero Squadron got ready to leave, but was not ordered back to College Park. The lease on the Maryland field had expired and was not renewed. Instead, most of the squadron moved on to North Island, San Diego, which now became the Army's principal flying school and a center for Army

Foulois and officers of the 1st Aero Squadron in front of a Curtiss JN–3. Left to right: Lieutenant T.S. Bowen, Lieutenant J.E. Carberry, Lieutenant C.G. Chapman, Captain B.D. Foulois, Lieutenant T.D. Milling, and Lieutenant I.A. Rader, San Antonio, Texas, 1915. All were among the squadron's first participants in U.S. Army operations during the Punitive Expedition into Mexico.

The Signal Corps' center for Army aviation and flight training at North Island, San Diego, California, 1916. The closeup shows Burgess trainer aircraft .

Curtiss aircraft at a primitive and hastily established 1st Aero Squadron base at Colonia Dublan, Mexico, 1916.

aviation. Many famous airmen, including Carl Spaatz, were taught to fly at North Island.

Mexican Adventures

Although the border alarm came to nothing in 1913, the turbulence of the Mexican revolution continued to effect the use and deployment of the U.S. Army and its Aviation Section. Tensions flared again early in 1914, by which time War Department General Order No. 75, dated 4 December 1913, had set out formal tables of organization for flying units. The word "provisional" was removed from the title of the 1st Aero Squadron. Once again, aircraft were deployed to Texas but the danger passed and they saw no action. The struggle between the three Mexican factions of Venustiano Carranza, Emiliano Zapata, and Francisco "Pancho" Villa raged on, however, and early in 1916 it spilled across the border into the United States. In October 1915, the United States had recognized the government of Carranza, and Pancho Villa, angry at being denied American supplies for his forces, crossed into New Mexico on 9 March 1916, killing residents of the town of Columbus. President Wilson reacted by sending a force of 15,000 men under General Pershing to punish the raiders and to capture or kill their leader. The 1st Aero Squadron accompanied the expedition.

Captain Benny Foulois at an Aviation Section field near Casas Grandes, Mexico, 1916.

Major H.A. Dargue and a Curtiss JN–3, after having been attacked by angry mobs in Chihuahua City, Mexico, during the Punitive Expedition, 1916. Alone at the time, he tried to repair his damaged aircraft and posed for this picture, keeping the photographer occupied and surrounding crowd quiet as long as he could until help arrived.

In the absence of landing fields and fuel depots on the way, the 1st Aero Squadron sent its aircraft to Columbus by rail. They arrived on 15 March, only six days after Villa had left. The squadron, with eight aircraft and now under the command of Captain Benny Foulois, deployed with 10 pilots and 84 enlisted men, and increased to 16 officers and 122 enlisted men by May. The squadron was tasked with assisting the Army's ground forces, but it soon became apparent that it was the airmen who were in need of help. Operating from a desert strip 100 miles south of Columbus, the eight Curtiss JN–3s (Jennies) proved inadequate. Extreme temperatures, penetrating dust, and boisterous mountain winds combined to take their toll of aircraft that were already well-worn from a year of training pilots. Even when fully serviceable, the JN–3s could not get across the area's ranges of 10,000 feet and more, and they were vulnerable to the violent weather of the mountains.

Relegated to the ignominy of carrying dispatches in good weather, the squadron still got into difficulty. Foulois and Lieutenant Herbert Dargue took two aircraft to Chihuahua City in Mexico to deliver dispatches to the American consul and were fired on when they arrived. Foulois was arrested and jailed. An angry mob burned one aircraft's fabric with cigarettes and slashed it with knives. When Foulois was released, the two tattered JN–3s took off, but a section of Dargue's fuselage, loosened because the crowd had removed some bolts, blew off and damaged the tail. He landed and was set upon by a stone-throwing mob for his trouble. Holding his own until Mexican soldiers arrived to stand guard, he hurriedly completed basic repairs and left.

By 20 April, after little more than a month of operations, the 1st Aero Squadron was reduced to two flyable JN–3s, just serviceable enough to be flown back to Columbus and condemned for scrap. The squadron collected four new Curtiss N–8s to replace the JN–3s, but they proved to be equally unsuited to the harsh conditions of the border and were junked within a year. One way or another, the unit struggled on until 1917, but it was never able to offer anything of much value to the military expedition it was supposed to support. General Pershing, while unimpressed with the operational performance of his air arm, recognized where its shortcomings lay. Acknowledging that Foulois and his men had done their best, he said: "They too often risked their lives in old and often useless machines, which they have patched up and worked over in an effort to do their share of the duty this expedition has been called upon to perform."

American Aerial Shortcomings

The limited capabilities of American military aviation were brutally exposed during the Mexican Punitive Expedition. The First Aero Squadron represented the best that the Aviation Section had to offer, and by any measure it suffered in comparison with European air forces. By 1916, all major combatants of World War I were engaged in aerial reconnaissance, air-to-air combat, and tactical support of ground forces. Heavy bombers for strategic operations were being produced by Russia, Italy, France, and Britain, and air fighting tactics had been well developed in the hard school of combat experience. High explosive bombs and machine guns synchronized to fire through propeller arcs had been evolved. This effort

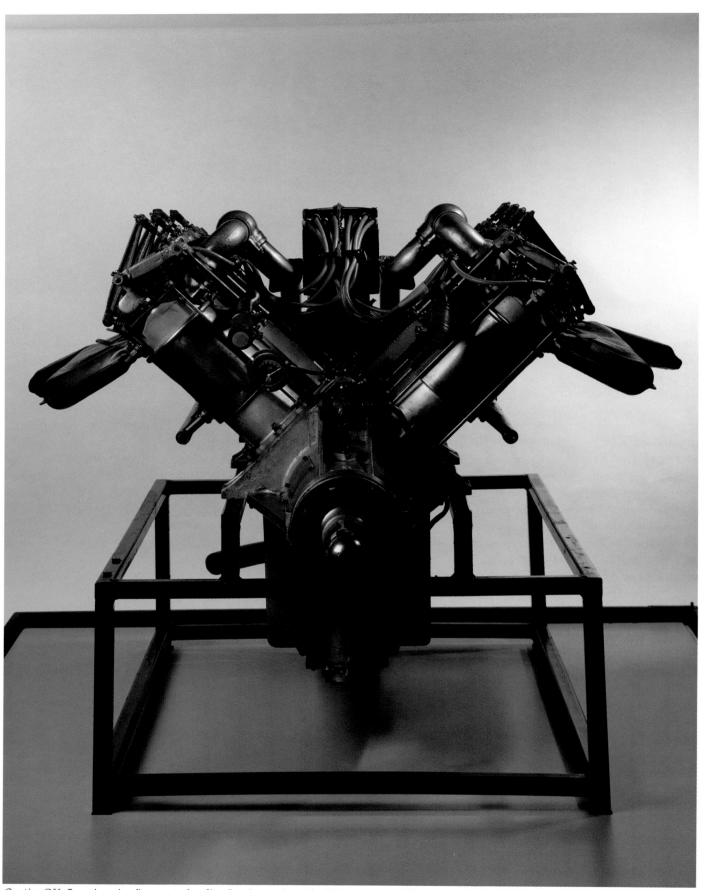

Curtiss OX–5 engine. A refinement of earlier Curtiss engines, the 90-horsepower OX–5 powered the Curtiss Jenny. Its V-shape dominated liquid-cooled engine design, and a later Curtiss engine, the D–12, inspired Rolls-Royce to develop the line of V–12s that led to the famous Merlin.

Curtiss Jenny. The first aircraft to be built in quantity for the Signal Corps, the Curtiss Jenny was the nearest thing to a combat aircraft owned by the U.S. Army before World War I. It proved sadly inadequate for the task of supporting ground operations during the Mexican Punitive Expedition in 1916. High temperatures, strong winds, and rugged terrain exposed its operational shortcomings, and any maintenance facilities were rudimentary at best.

was backed by large training organizations and industries producing air force equipment in vast quantities. Confronted by the alarming shortcomings of American military aviation and the news of the air war in Europe, Congress was finally spurred into action, authorizing in August 1916, $13,281,666 for military aeronautics. The sum was still inadequate, but seen against the fact that less than $1 million had been allocated since the Wright brothers first flew, it indicated that attitudes in Washington were changing. The Aviation Section was to be increased to seven front-line squadrons and three flying schools spread among six bases in the United States, including the Philippines and Hawaii. With America's involvement in Europe imminent, the fact was that its air power remained shockingly unimpressive.

Early in 1917, the U.S. Army Signal Corps' Aviation Section had only one front-line squadron, with a second working up. They were equipped with Curtiss R–2s and R–4s , little more than upgraded Jennies and quite unsuitable for aerial combat. At a time when the British and French each had more than 1,700 combat aircraft available, the total strength of the Aviation Section was 131 officers, 1,087 enlisted men, and fewer than 250 aircraft, only half of which were serviceable. None of the machines could be classified as other than a trainer, and many were obsolete even in that role. No bombers or fighters were even being procured. Worse still, America's aircraft industry was then incapable of supplying the equipment needed to support an operational air

force. In the eight short years since the purchase of the first Wright Military Flyer, the United States had fallen to fourteenth in the world's ranking of aviation powers. With war on the horizon, it had to start catching up.

Notes

1. On later aircraft the term became aileron drag.
2. Langley, a distinguished engineer and astronomer, became Secretary of the Smithsonian Institution. He believed that in the development of a flying machine, power and lift came first. He largely ignored control problems. A $50,000 War Department subsidy for the construction of a man-carrying airplane followed his flying of steam-powered models. His *Aerodrome* was ready for trials in 1903, and two attempts were made in early December to launch it from a houseboat on the Potomac. Both intended flights became plunges into the river.
3. Even earlier was the Balloon Corps of the Army of the Potomac, formed in 1861. Although it proved its usefulness on more than one occasion, it was disbanded in 1863.

When my brother and I built and flew the first man-carrying machine, we thought we were introducing into the world an invention which would make further wars practically impossible.

(Orville Wright, 1917)

Rick (Rickenbacker) wasn't the best pilot in the world . . . but Rick rarely missed. He even pulled the wing off an Albatros one time—with his tail skid.

(Major Reed Chambers, 94th Aero Squadron)

If you see a steady line of tracers coming near you, remember that the quickest way to change your relative position is a jerk on the stick—not too strong or you will disconcert the observer.

(Captain Stephen Noyes, Corps Observation Group, First Army)

Aerial observation is neither a bed of roses nor the path to glory that the man on the ground some times imagines it to be. The wind behind a Liberty [engine] is terrific, and it taxes the strength of the strongest to fight it three hours. If the ship is rolled and tossed about very much, either by bumps or purposely to avoid shell and shrapnel, the occupants sometimes get sick . . . you lose your lunch and the wind places it in a neat layer on your goggles. The wind has blown your handkerchief from your pocket. You wipe it off on your teddy bear [airman's fur coat] sleeve. You start to write your messages and of your three pencils you have one left. You break the point on it and your knife is in your pocket under your teddy bear . . . but I like it.

(2nd Lieutenant W. Rogers, Observer, 50th Aero Squadron)

Chapter 2
Building and Fighting, 1917–1918

War in the Air

In a famous poster of 1914, a stern, pointing figure of Britain's General Kitchener welcomes museum visitors to the World War I gallery of the USAF Museum. Wall displays include brief reminders of the vast strides made by military aviation in Europe while the U.S. Aviation Section languished in the shadow of America's isolationist policy between 1914 and 1917. More significant evidence of America's general unpreparedness for large scale aerial conflict when war came is all around; the combat aircraft standing on the museum floor and those suspended overhead in simulated flight are all of European design.

The exhibit's themes begin with the unrealistic expectations of America's military aviation following its awakening in 1917, move on to the struggles of its industry and the Aviation Section to create a powerful air force, and climax with the first successful applications of its air power that marked the closing months of the war. Attention is drawn to American airmen whose impatience for combat led them to join the British and French Air Forces before 1917, and there are displays which single out those who particularly distinguished themselves in Europe—Lufbery, Vaughan, Rickenbacker, Luke, Bleckley, Goettler and Mitchell.

Their stories, together with small collections of their memorabilia—uniforms, flying helmets, log-books, medals, and awards—provide fascinating details and bind the World War I display together, but inevitably the eye is first caught and held by the aircraft, their engines, and armament. A Fokker Dr1 Triplane soars inverted over Allied fighters—a Sopwith Camel, a SPAD VII and a Nieuport 28—while the massive shape of an observation balloon floats in the background. The birth of strategic air power is represented by a Caproni Ca 36 bomber, and a Halberstadt CL IV illustrates an early stage in the development of close air support for ground troops. Hovering nearby are examples of famous American trainers, including the Standard J–1 and the legendary Curtiss Jenny. But the pride of the World War I fleet is a two-seat reconnaissance aircraft, the SPAD XVI flown by Billy Mitchell when he commanded the American air forces on the Western Front in 1918.

Captain Edward "Eddie" Rickenbacker (1890–1973). Eddie Rickenbacker commanded the 94th (Hat-in-the-Ring) Aero Squadron in France during 1918. He became America's World War I ace of aces, with 26 confirmed victories in the air.

Curtiss Jenny. Regarded with affection for its viceless handling qualities, the Curtiss Jenny was the Army's primary flying trainer during World War I and the early 1920s.

As visitors leave the World War I gallery they can be in little doubt that the United States made extraordinary advances in military aviation during 1917–1918 while acknowledging serious shortcomings in the way it built its air strength. Its achievements eventually recorded were remarkable by any standards. In less than two years its aircraft industry grew from almost nothing, and a burgeoning air arm with a hard core of experienced airmen had more than held their own against determined adversaries. Through this single gallery visitors have moved from the depressing inadequacies of 1916 to a point where the United States has all that is necessary to become a formidable power in the air. It has met the challenges of aerial warfare; it will meet very different post-war challenges in days to come.

The Air War in Europe

When the United States declared war on 6 April 1917, few realized just how far it had fallen behind European combatants in the development and application of air power. In 1914 the European powers had faced each other with the most rudimentary of air arms. They had no truly military aircraft. For them, and certainly their respective armies, the airplane had little use beyond reconnaissance or artillery spotting. Three years later, aerial warfare had grown to encompass a wide range of specializations and was taking up more than its share of space in national newspapers. Air forces were using aircraft designed for roles as diverse as air defense, interception, interdiction, ground attack, reconnaissance, and strategic bombing. The tactics for each were highly developed. Large training organizations had been created, both for air and ground crews, and industries had arisen which, in France and Britain, produced the almost incredible number of 50,000 aircraft for each nation in the course of the war.

Germany, having already laid the foundations of strategic bombing, notably by attacking London, was operating heavy bombers, as were Russia, Italy, and Britain. The horrors of aerial warfare predicted by such writers as H.G. Wells had begun to be realized with attacks on civilian populations, yet, in the public eye, the new dimension seemed to restore a kind of chivalry to a war in which men lost their identities in the mass and were dominated by the unfeeling efficiency of barbed wire and machine guns. Aerial combat was compared to the knightly tournaments of an earlier age, the opponents facing each other as individuals in fair contest, mounted on brightly decorated, propeller-driven steeds, their silk scarves fluttering like banners in the wind. The reality of men trapped in burning machines or falling thousands of feet to their deaths was glossed over, and the names of national champions like Richthofen, Immelman, Boelcke, Guynemer, Fonck, Ball, McCudden, and Mannock became as familiar as those of celebrated actors or sporting figures.

The airmen themselves were often caught up in the chivalrous imagery of their profession, saluting each other's prowess and honoring fallen enemies. Guynemer once fought a long battle with Ernst Udet until the German's guns jammed; seeing his enemy disarmed, the Frenchman waved gallantly and flew away.[1] When Boelcke was killed, Royal Flying Corps (RFC) aircraft flew over his grave and dropped a wreath with the message: "To our brave and chivalrous foe." If they came to see themselves as airborne knights, however, they also accepted the fact that they were poor insurance risks. Loss rates were high and death was no respecter of reputations; few of the famous survived the war. Major John Slessor, later a Marshal of the Royal Air Force (RAF), of No. 80 Squadron, RFC, remembered:

> "The squadron's average [aircrew] strength was 22 officers, and in the last ten months of the war no less than 168 officers were struck off strength from all causes—an average of about 75% per month, of whom a little less than half were killed."

The air war, by 1917, had become an enterprise of unforeseen scale. It had a rapacious appetite for men and machines. It was demanding an increasing share of national resources and beginning to change the way the generals thought about strategy and tactics. By its very nature, it stood much of military tradition on its head. It was breeding a force in which officers were fighting men and enlisted men were skilled technicians rather than cannon fodder. Its public figures were junior officers rather than

generals, and in its attacks on civilian populations it was opening the door to a modern concept of total war.

American Commitments

When America entered the war, most of its leaders and military men had not grasped the extent to which the air war had developed, nor did they fully understand the art of the possible as they proposed that the Aviation Section join the fray on an equal footing. Nor did the European Allies appreciate how far behind America had lagged. They saw only the immense potential of its resources in terms of manpower and industrial capacity. French Premier Alexandre Ribot opened the bidding on 24 May 1917 with a message to President Wilson in which he suggested a program "to enable the Allies to win supremacy of the air." A target date of spring 1918 was set and the United States was asked to send to the front by then a total of 4,500 aircraft, 5,000 pilots, and 50,000 mechanics, plus supporting services. Using the French request as a basis for planning, a group of officers headed by Major Benjamin Foulois proposed an even more ambitious program—22,625 aircraft (12,000 of them intended for combat) supported by 80 percent spares, plus 45,000 engines. The thousands of aircrews to man this armada were to be graduated from flying schools which did not then exist. The estimated cost of this astonishing program was a massive $640 million.

Given that the United States had produced a total of fewer than 1,000 aircraft of all types in the 14 years since Kitty Hawk, and that the combat capability of the Aviation Section in 1917 was non-existent, these were startling figures. They did nothing, however, to dampen the sudden enthusiasm of the American public for military aviation. The air war had glamorous appeal and the building of an air force was seen as the quickest way to bring the power of America's industry to bear. The newly formed Aircraft Production Board burst into print with a confident statement including the passage:

> …manufacturing capacity can easily be doubled in the first year. A prominent British general has asserted that America's greatest contribution to the war will be aircraft and aviators. We believe that once started upon quantity production, American mechanical genius will overcome any present obstacles to the progress of the art.

The link between quantity production and art may not have been entirely clear, but the general euphoria was emphasized by the words of the Aircraft Production Board's chairman, Howard Coffin:

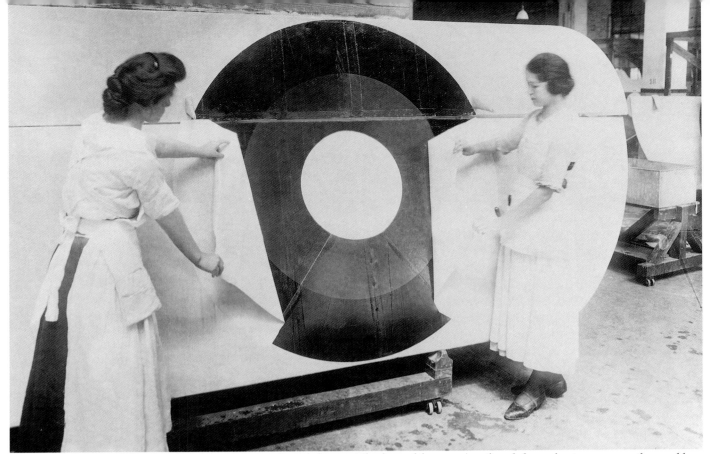

American industry and the war, 1918. Manufacturers struggled to meet the demand for new aircraft and churned out as many as they could. A newly painted Air Service insignia roundel decorates a wing.

"The road to Berlin lies through the air. The eagle must end this war." An emotive outburst from the U.S. Army's Chief Signals Officer, General George Squier, spoke in glowing (if archaic) terms of putting "Yankee punch into the war by building an army in the air; regiments and brigades of winged cavalry on gas-driven flying horses." Secretary of War Newton Baker announced that military aviation "furnishes our supreme opportunity for immediate service." Carried along by the fervor of the moment, Congress passed a bill authorizing $640 million for the Aviation Section almost without dissent, and it was signed into law by President Wilson on 24 July 1917.

With promises made, production goals set, and money available, it was time for the United States to start facing facts. It did not have an aircraft industry capable of building the required numbers of combat aircraft in the time specified. Even under the pressure of contracts already issued and war newly declared, American aircraft builders had delivered just 78 airplanes during the month of July 1917. After the war, Secretary Baker acknowledged that eagerness for the idea had overcome reason when the aviation program was approved. He wrote:

> The airplane itself was too wonderful and new, too positive a denial of previous experience, to brook the application of any prudent restraints which wise people would have known how to apply to ordinary industrial

and military developments. As a consequence, the magicians of American industry were expected to do the impossible for this new and magical agency, and this expectation was increased by the feverish earnestness with which all Americans desired that our country should appear speedily, worthily, and decisively in the war.

While industry wrestled with impossible problems, the Aviation Section broke the original plan down into more detailed figures. In August 1917 it announced that 345 combat squadrons would be formed (plus supporting services), 263 of which were to join the front line in France by 30 June 1918, a mere ten months away. Plans could specify what they liked, but, as soon became obvious, good intentions, even when backed by unlimited money, could not make up for years of neglect. The difficulties were staggering. In the United States aircraft manufacturers were dwarfed by the size of their task. They could not rely on the nation's lumber industry, which, although huge, was unable to meet the vast increase in demand for the spruce needed in aircraft construction. Nor could they rely for the design of combat-capable aircraft on the expertise of the nation's technicians; it was non-existent. At any rate, the U.S. Army had no officers serving who had much idea of the kind of aircraft needed. In part, this was the fault of the European Allies, who had exercised strict censorship of aeronautical information

The Dayton-Wright Airplane Company. A DH–4's engine is tested outside; a DH–4's wooden fusilage panel rests next to a metal jig inside the plant.

Liberty engines awaiting installation as aircraft take shape behind them.

throughout the war, but the fault was compounded by the complete absence of any Aviation Section plans for building an air force capable of combat.[2]

To solve their most pressing problem, air and industrial leaders decided to make use of already proven European designs. A mission under Major Raynal Bolling went to Europe in June 1917 and recommended four types for production in the United States—the SPAD single-seat fighter, the Bristol two-seat fighter, the DH–4 reconnaissance/light bomber, and the Caproni Triplane heavy bomber. It later added the Handley-Page 0/400 heavy bomber. During the latter part of 1917, the government awarded contracts to a number of companies, including Curtiss, Dayton-Wright and Fisher Body, to build these aircraft in the thousands necessary to meet the commitments so freely given for an air force in the front line by the summer of 1918.

The contracts were complicated by the government's decision to modify those combat aircraft built in the United States to carry a standard American engine, if possible. It was reasoned that although the United States might lag in aircraft design, it was among the world's leaders in engines for automobiles and

would, therefore, be able to provide new ones suitable for combat aircraft without much difficulty. Starting on 29 May 1917, prodigies of design and construction were achieved and the first 8-cylinder Liberty engine was test running by 4 July. A 12-cylinder version followed on 25 August and was soon delivering 440 horsepower. The Liberty was rushed into production with the major automobile manufacturers and, despite some early teething troubles and the complaint that it was too heavy for fighter aircraft, it proved to be an American success. When the war ended in November 1918, the United States had provided a total of 13,574 Liberty engines, its production rate eventually rising to 150 per day. Modified Liberty engines continued to provide power for American military flying for more than a decade.[3]

Bitter Realities

If America's engine production was something of a triumph, most other aspects of its air arm program continued to disappoint. The aircraft industry, expanding dramatically as it tried to reach its planning goals, faced too great a task, and its efforts were not helped by the confusion of constant changes of plan and uncertainty over who was responsible for what. Until the end of the war the problem of poor coordination of ideas and activities among the War Department, the American Expeditionary Force (AEF) Headquarters, the Aircraft Production Board, and the Air Service was severe, despite a number of reorganizations and changes of command intended to alleviate it.

By the end of 1917, a summer of unbounded confidence had become a winter of discontent. Widespread public disillusion at the apparent failure of the Air Service program led to some reassessments and, in light of badly lagging aircraft production, more realistic goals. A new program both reduced the number of operational squadrons promised for the front line and delayed the date of their arrival. Soon, 263 squadrons became 120, to be in action by January 1919, not June 1918. After Herculean efforts, even these sensible targets were unrealized. When the war ended in November 1918, there were 45 squadrons assigned for combat, 12 of which were operating DH–4s, manufactured in the United States. The DH–4 was the only combat aircraft made in any numbers in American factories; 3,431 had been delivered. Of these, 1,200 had arrived in France, but only 417 had reached the front.

Looking back on his experiences many years later, General Hap Arnold could not hide the bitterness he felt over the way the Air Service program had been handled in 1917–1918 when he wrote:

No American-designed combat plane flew in France or Italy during the entire war. The foreign planes built in this country failed to arrive in Europe on schedule or in the promised numbers, until what had started out as a triumphant exhibition of American know-how turned into a humiliating series of Congressional and other investigations.

Eddie Rickenbacker, the celebrated American fighter ace, was equally harsh in his judgement:

> None of us in France could understand what prevented our great country from furnishing machines equal to the best in the world. Many a gallant life was lost to American aviation in those early months of 1918, the responsibility for which must lie heavily on some guilty conscience.

Sentiments like these are understandable, especially from those who went to war, and endless stories and statistics emphasize the shortcomings of America's air effort in World War I. However, in 1917 the United States was being invited to accelerate from a standing start to the hectic pace of an air war that had been in progress for three years. What it actually accomplished, therefore, is more creditable. Its industry in 1917 was negligible, but by 11 November 1918 it had grown to a size which had provided over 11,000 aircraft of all types, including nearly 8,000 trainers, and its production rate had risen to no less than 21,000 aircraft per year.

DH–4s of the 168th Aero Squadron. Arriving at the front at the end of September, 1918, the squadron's DH–4s were in time to take part in the Meuse-Argonne campaign. The name Mary Alice on the aircraft in the foreground also appears on a B–17G displayed at Duxford, the Imperial War Museum's airfield in the United Kingdom.

Training Explosion

The expansion of aviation training was remarkable by any measure. There was no shortage of willing volunteers, inspired by stories of the air war in Europe, wanting to fly. When the United States entered the war, thousands of young Americans clamored for flight training and the Air Service embarked on a program that brought about a 150-fold expansion by the end of the war, a period of just 19 months. A force of 1,200 grew to one of over 190,000. The numbers of airfields grew from 3 to 43. In all, 4,872 officers, 46,667 enlisted men, and 16 airfields were overseas, and 45 operational squadrons were manned by 767 pilots, 481 observers, and 23 gunners.

At the heart of the program at the primary flying schools was the Curtiss JN–4 Jenny powered by the 90-horsepower OX–5 engine. The Standard J–1 trainer was produced in smaller numbers to supplement the Jenny, but it was a more temperamental beast and never matched the popularity of its celebrated Curtiss rival, which proceeded to dominate primary training for years to come. The Jenny was neither powerful nor very quick, being flat out at 75 miles per hour, but it was durable and it was not so forgiving that a student could afford to develop bad habits or be careless. Thousands of American and Canadian pilots, including many who would later make their mark on the world of aviation, flew their first solos in the Jenny and later recalled the biplane with affection.

Jimmy Doolittle, who was not very tall, trained in the Jenny in 1917, finding that his greatest difficulty was seeing over the edge of the high-sided cockpit. He was sent solo after only six hours of dual instruction and later proved himself one of the world's greatest airmen in peace or war. The Jenny went on to a life after the Armistice, too, principally as aircraft of choice for the barnstormers of the 1920s. Many surplus Jennies were sold off as training wound down and were flown by their ex-military pilots to fairgrounds and cow pastures all over the United States. Americans who had never seen an airplane could watch the thrills of aerobatics or wing walking, and, if they had the nerve and a few dollars, they could climb into a cockpit and fly. The foundations of America's air power were laid with the help of the Curtiss Jenny. It may not have been a sensational performer, but it trained the first generation of American combat airmen, and, to the great future benefit of the United States, it played a large part in making Americans air-minded.

Expanded primary training in the United States was underway by 1917, but not the advanced training that new pilots would need before being committed to combat. It was obvious that early waves of American volunteers would reach their squadrons in Europe all the quicker if they trained there at already functioning schools; only the European Allies had the necessary aircraft and experience. It was equally obvious that American-built combat aircraft could not be available for some time. The United

OX–5 engine. The 90-horsepower OX–5 engine powered the Jenny and led the way to a Curtiss family of V-shaped, liquid-cooled engines used by American fighters during the inter-war years. Curtiss engines were studied by other manufacturers, including Rolls-Royce, designers of World War II's famous Merlin.

Aircraft in various states of repair in the hangar at Issoudun, home of an American flying school in France.

States, therefore, reached agreements with Britain, France, and Italy for flying training facilities and the purchase of suitable aircraft.

In common with all other aspects of America's entry into the air war, almost nothing about the first phases of the training build-up went smoothly. Administrative shortcomings, language difficulties, failures of communication, and clashes in priorities all contributed to a series of delays and disappointments. Places held open at European schools in the summer of 1917 went unfilled and most were unavailable when American cadets arrived in the autumn. The cadets accumulated in their hundreds and were misemployed as guards or as construction workers for new American airfields. The backlog was not fully cleared until the summer of 1918, by which time a number of American schools were operating in France, notably those at Issoudun and Tours. Issoudun in the winter of 1917–1918 was not remembered with affection by the cadets. One of them described it as "a sea of frozen mud." He described "waiting shivering in line before dawn for the spoonsful of gluey porridge slapped into outstretched mess kits, cold as ice. Wretched flying equipment. Broken necks. The flu. A hell of a place, Issoudun."

Americans in Combat

While this was going on, a number of Americans were already in action, having found a quicker way to the war. Since 1915 American volunteers had been flying with the French and British, and several became legendary figures. Among the first was the French-born American, Raoul Lufbery, who reached a French squadron after being a U.S. Army soldier in the Philippines, a mechanic for a barnstormer in India and China, and a French Foreign Legionnaire. He transferred to the French Air Service as a mechanic and inveigled his way into pilot training. By October 1915 he was flying bombing sorties in French two-seaters. He got the opportunity to make his name with the formation of the Escadrille (squadron) Americaine, the inspiration of a Harvard graduate named Norman Prince.

Norman Prince. A founding member of the Lafayette Escadrille and a five-victory ace, Norman Prince is shown in the unusual Voisin Avion Canon fitted with a huge 47-mm cannon. The effect on so slow and apparently fragile a biplane of the firing of such a weapon can only be imagined.

Lafayette Escadrille memorabilia. The USAF Museum has a number of items that recall the days when American airmen flew with the French Air Service in World War I as members of the Lafayette Escadrille. Shown are Robert Rockwell's jacket, William Thaw's helmet and pocket altimeter, Thomas Hitchcock's service cap and log-book, and a pilot's badge of the French Air Service.

After tortuous governmental negotiations between the Americans and the French in 1915, the Escadrille Americaine was formed as a pursuit (or *chasse*) squadron equipped with Nieuports on 21 March 1916. By that time several of the original American aviators of fortune, impatient at the bureaucratic delays, had already joined French squadrons. Once established, the Escadrille Americaine attracted many more Americans after a chance to engage in "the knightly combat of the air," and it was not long before the unit began to build itself a reputation. Its public recognition drew a formal complaint from the German ambassador to the United States, and the name of the squadron was changed to the Lafayette Escadrille so that diplomatic niceties might be observed.[4]

So many Americans were eager to join the squadron that a larger organization was introduced—the Lafayette Flying Corps. It functioned as a headquarters, arranging for American volunteers to enter French flying schools and for graduates to be sent forward as replacements, as necessary, to the Lafayette Escadrille, but also to French combat units. Frank Baylies was one who served with a French squadron and scored 12 victories before being shot down on 18 June 1918. Of 224 Americans awarded French wings, 51 were killed in action. Between them, they were credited with destroying 199 enemy aircraft.

The First Aces

Early members of the Lafayette Escadrille included Norman Prince, William Thaw, Elliott Cowdin, Bert Hall, James McConnell, Victor Chapman, and the brothers Rockwell—Kiffen and Robert. Kiffen Rockwell scored the first victory for the squadron on 18 May 1916, but it was Raoul Lufbery who became its most celebrated airman. He recorded his fifth kill on 12 October 1916 to become America's first ace and added steadily to his score in the following months, reaching a total of 17 before transferring to the U.S. Air Service and becoming a major in the 94th Aero Squadron in February 1918. Lufbery led the first patrol of three aircraft from the 94th over the front line on 6 March 1918, choosing as his wingmen Lieutenants Douglas Campbell and Eddie Rickenbacker, both of whom later became aces in their own right. Astoundingly, they flew in unarmed aircraft; although the Nieuports had been delivered, their guns had not!

Lufbery's personal victory score remained at 17, but he exerted considerable influence on the way the untested American squadron approached its combat initiation, continuing to lead patrols of the 94th, with and without guns, for another two months. On 19 May 1918 he took off alone in pursuit of a German two-seater. He was seen to open fire and then to pull away, apparently to clear a jammed gun. When he

attacked again the German gunner got off an accurate burst and set the Nieuport ablaze. The little fighter dropped for some distance before Lufbery either fell from the cockpit or jumped to his death to avoid the flames.

Lufbery flew Nieuport 17s and 28s during most of his combat career. They came from a line of fighters that had challenged the Germans effectively when introduced to the front line in 1915, and they became the favorite mount of many great aces—Ball, Guynemer, and Fonck among others. Nieuport 17s had the advantages of being small, very agile, and fairly fast for their time, but they had disadvantages, too. The upper wing had the reputation of disassembling itself in a high-speed dive, and the engine was a large rotary, which led to other problems. One was the rotating engine mass, which had a considerable effect on the handling of such a small aircraft. One pilot said it was "like trying to fly a gyroscope." Another was the absence of a throttle, the rotary being controlled only by a "blip" switch, which allowed the pilot to have the engine running flat out or stopped; there were no half measures. As 1st Lieutenant Louis Simon of the 147th Aero Squadron reported: "...the Nieuport 28 has the rotary motor and is the hardest to fly formation with because you can't regulate your speed.... In those with stationary motors, formation flying is easier because of not having to "S" so much..."

American links with the French Air Service—through training, aircraft acquisition, provision of bases, service with French units, and so on—were generally more extensive than those with the other European

Raoul Lufbery, a French-born American who flew with both the Lafayette Escadrille and the 94th Aero Squadron. He recorded 17 aerial victories before his death in combat on 19 May 1918.

Douglas Campbell, typical of the young Americans eager to experience "the romance" of aerial combat in Europe. He took part in the 94th Aero Squadron's first flight over enemy lines. By war's end he had become an ace and had lost most of an arm. He is shown in front of a Nieuport 28.

American pilot Emil Zadmais and his Nieuport 28 in 1918.

Stalwarts of the Lafayette Escadrille, a squadron of American volunteers flying with the French Air Service before America's entry into the war. From left to right: *James McConnell, Kiffen Rockwell, Georges Thenault (the French commanding officer), Norman Prince, and Victor Chapman.*

Nieuport 28 guns. Standard armament for the Nieuport 28 was two Vickers .303-inch machine guns, offset to the left, firing through the propeller.

Nieuport 28 cockpit. To keep the aircraft's weight as low as possible, the pilot's seat in the Nieuport 28 and other scouts was made of basketwork.

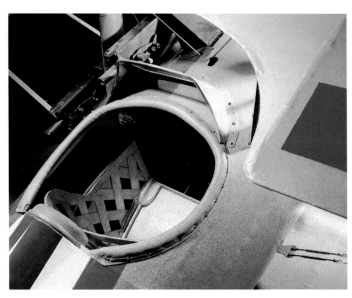

Nieuport 28. The aircraft was a later version of a successful fighter introduced in 1915. The U.S. Army Air Service took delivery of 297 Nieuport 28s in 1918, but they were no match for Fokker D VIIs and were withdrawn from operations after only four months in the front line.

Nieuport nose. The Nieuport 28 was the first scout flown in combat by American pilots in World War I and by Lieutenants Winslow and Campbell of the 94th Squadron when they scored the first U.S. Army Air Service victories on 14 April 1918. It was no match for the Fokker D VII, however, and had an unfortunate tendency to shed wing fabric at high speeds.

48

Luke's Nieuports. In the early days of his meteoric career, Frank Luke flew the Nieuport 28. He is seen here leading in a flight after a balloon-busting mission.

Nieuport repairs. As pursuit aircraft Nieuport 28s were aesthetically pleasing, but they had worrying structural problems. In high-speed dives their upper wings could be stripped of fabric or removed from their bodies altogether. Airframe riggers are shown re-skinning one after such over-stressing.

Allies. The scale of this association is best exemplified in aircrew training and aircraft programs. More than 8,000 American pilots and observers received training of some sort in France, and the French delivered over 4,800 aircraft to the American Air Service during the last year of the war. The bulk of these were out-dated types used for advanced training, but French machines, principally SPAD fighters, Breguet bombers, and Salmson observation aircraft, still constituted the lion's share of America's front-line strength of 740 aircraft in November 1918.

RFC Connections
Cooperative arrangements between the United States and Britain were equally diverse if not so large. A few individuals had joined the Royal Flying Corps before 1917, but it was not until the United States entered the war that a trickle became a flow of both air and ground personnel. Agreements between the two countries reached in December 1917 provided for the United States to build up a force of 15,000 mechanics in the United Kingdom to train on

front-line aircraft and to release British mechanics for posting to France. As the American mechanics gained proficiency they were to become available for France and replaced with newcomers to maintain the 15,000 total. In addition, a labor force of 6,200 was to work on British bases. Because of insufficient shipping space the 15,000 figure for mechanics was not reached until August 1918, and no more than half of the 6,200 workers were ever employed. Nevertheless, at the Armistice there were over 20,000 Air Service personnel in Britain, and at least 15 American squadrons in France were manned by British-trained mechanics. Yet another sizeable force was working on an ambitious program to equip 30 U.S. Air Service squadrons with Handley-Page 0/400 night bombers for a strategic campaign against Germany in 1919.

The first American cadets bound for Britain docked at Liverpool on 2 September 1917. Quickly assimilated into the RFC's program, they began their training on aircraft like old Farmans (known as Rumptys) or DH–6s, and moved on through Avro 504s to

SE–5 cutaway. Compare the bare essentials—the simple wire-braced, box-girder wooden construction and the empty spaces of the fuselage of this typical World War I scout with the features of the F–86 cutaway shown in Chapter 8.

single-seat Sopwith Pups and Camels. In contrast, student pilots in France began what Hap Arnold described as "the gradual absorption of the knowledge of the art of flying…[as each was]…transferred from one machine to another until he finally reached the best of its particular type." Arnold did not fully reflect the caution of the French approach. Handling exercises were begun in "rouleurs" (planes with wings clipped so that they could not fly) and progress was made in a series of carefully controlled steps through aircraft with increasingly demanding characteristics until a combat type was reached. The lengthy process was justified, the French insisted, because it saved lives. Even so, 78 Americans were killed at Issoudun in the course of pursuit training.

The RFC's approach was more robust. Cadets often flew combat types like the Sopwith Pup only a

month after they started training. Arguably, it was too robust, since 34 of a little more than 500 American airmen trained by the British died in flying accidents, most of them in single-seaters at the most advanced stage of pursuit training. By modern standards, this is a horrifying statistic, but during World War I it was accepted as one of the hazards of doing business. In his final report at the end of the war, Major General Mason Patrick, Chief of Air Service, AEF, acknowledged the dangers of flight training, wherever it was carried out. Recording the deaths of 218 pilots and observers at training centers in Europe, he wrote: "…a great many can be fairly ascribed to engine failure and lack of judgement or poor flying on the part of the pilot," and he drew particular attention to "…the fundamental failure to maintain sufficient flying speed." He also stressed the dangers of

Sopwith Camel. For many pilots, the Sopwith Camel was the supreme combat aircraft. Although not very fast, it was extremely maneuverable and a good gun platform. By the end of the war the Camel was the most victorious aircraft of either side, destroying a total of 1,294 enemies.

single-seat pursuit training in his findings on the proportion of fatalities to graduates—1 to 90 in preliminary training, 1 to 50 in advanced observation training, and a startling 1 to 9.2 in pursuit training.

American Squadrons in Action

By March 1918 the first British-trained Americans were joining their units in France, and, at the end of the war, 216 of them had served either with RFC squadrons or two American squadrons fighting on the British front, the 17th and 148th. The two American squadrons flew their first operations closest to the Channel coast in July 1918. As was usual with newly formed units, they patrolled a relatively quiet sector for their introduction to the battle area. Even so, before long they had some success. On 13 July 1918, Lieutenant Field Kindley of the 148th shot down an Albatross D3 over Ypres, and one week later the 17th opened its score when Lieutenant Rodney Williams downed a Fokker. A natural rivalry developed between the squadrons that led them to compile two of the most illustrious combat records in the history of the American Air Service.

The 17th and the 148th flew Sopwith Camels on the British front. By the summer of 1918 the Camel was not quite the dominant fighter it once had been. With a top speed of 115 miles per hour, it was among the slowest of the fighters. It sometimes proved an embarrassment on escort duty, because the RFC's DH–9 bomber was faster when flying level and in the dive. One pilot asserted: "A Camel pilot had to shoot down every German plane in the sky in order to get home himself, as the Camel could neither outclimb nor outrun a Fokker." It was also tricky to fly because of its small size and the considerable

torque from its rotary engine. In a sharp turn to the left the nose rose abruptly and had to be checked by coarse use of the rudder, or the Camel would quickly spin without warning. On the other hand, it was extremely maneuverable in the hands of a competent pilot and had the quickest right turn in the air. Many of its pilots came to think of it as "unquestionably the greatest plane on the front." Between the time of its introduction in July 1917 and the end of the war, it was the victor in more aerial combats than any of

Le Rhone engine. The solution to the problem of cooling early aircraft engines was keeping the crankshaft still and spinning the finned cylinders around it. The Le Rhone rotary weighed 308 pounds and generated 110 horsepower. The torque of the whirling engine helped a small aircraft like the Sopwith Camel to achieve quick right turns.

Sopwith Camel guns. Two Vickers .303-inch machine guns mounted close together and synchronized to fire through the propeller helped to make the extremely maneuverable Camel World War I's deadliest combat aircraft.

52

Sopwith Camel. The slightly humped shape of the Camel's fuselage, from which the name derived, was masked by the two Vickers .303-inch machine guns mounted over the engine cowling.

Sopwith Camel cockpit. The aircraft's instrumentation was not complex. Compare fighter cockpits illustrated at the end of Chapters 10 and 11.

Fokker D VII nose. The nose's blunt shape hid either a 160-horsepower Mercedes or a 185-horsepower BMW 6-cylinder liquid-cooled engine.

Fokker D VII cockpit. The area is typically uncluttered, with two Spandau machine guns close at hand.

its contemporaries on either side, destroying a total of 1,294 enemy aircraft. In spite of its shortcomings, it has some claim as the fighting scout supreme.

The pace of combat picked up rapidly for the 17th and the 148th as their victories and losses rose steadily, although the balance was always markedly in their favor. Of the two, the 17th had the most fluctuating fortunes. On 13 August 1918 it took part in a devastatingly successful raid on a German airfield in Belgium, destroying 14 aircraft and killing more than 30 pilots on the ground. Just two weeks later it was ambushed by several Fokker formations and had six Camels shot down, three pilots killed, and three taken prisoner. The shattered squadron withdrew from the line to refit and wait for replacements.

One of those taken prisoner was Lieutenant Robert Todd, who had shot down his fifth enemy just moments before. One of his combat reports is typical in its description of the aerial fighting of the time—brief, violent, and terribly final—and offers an object

Fokker D VII. The most famous of all of Germany's World War I fighters, the Fokker D VII was often painted in exotic color schemes. The lavender finish on this one was favored by Lieutenant Rudolph Stark of Jasta 35 *in October 1918.*

Fokker D VII. Its often flamboyant appearance reflected the confidence felt by the Fokker D VII's pilots. A good all-around performer and a delightfully sensitive aircraft to fly, it proved a formidable opponent for the Allies in the closing months of World War I.

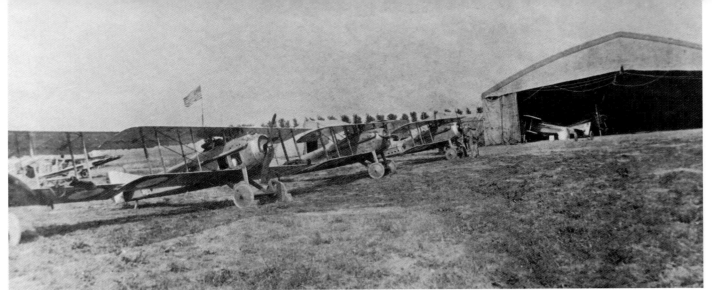

SPAD VIIs of the Lafayette Escadrille lined up near their hangar, 1916. Americans were still flying SPAD VIIs when the unit was transferred to the U.S. Army Air Service in February 1918, but they soon moved on to larger and more powerful SPAD XIIIs.

lesson in the dangers to a pilot concentrating so hard on his opponent that he loses track of his own position:

> While on offensive patrol, 8 to 10 a.m., August 1, 1918, our formation met three triplanes and one Fokker biplane at 14,000 to 16,000 feet. The leading three of our formation dived on the EA [enemy aircraft] and when the EA turned, I dove on the nearest triplane, opening fire at about 100 yards range. The triplane pulled up, allowing me to get within 25 yards of him, and my next burst sent him down out of control. While watching him, I went into a spin accidentally and pulled out of it at about 6,000 feet. While still diving, I saw the triplane crash into a wood near Provin.

Near war's end on 28 October 1918, the 148th, catching a German formation in a carefully prepared ambush, decided to exact revenge for the rough treatment suffered by the 17th in August. Four Camels led by Field Kindley, flew over no-man's land at 3,000 feet to act as bait. Eight more aircraft from the 148th flew 7,000 feet higher and hung back in the shadow of some clouds. Seven Fokkers duly attacked Kindley's flight from above. Timing their interception perfectly, the 148th's high cover tore into the Germans as Kindley's Camels turned to meet their enemy. Within seconds the fight was over. Seven Fokkers littered the ground within a radius of 1,000 yards and the 148th had not lost a single pilot.

At war's end, the 148th was officially credited with 66 victories in the air, the 17th with 52, despite taking time behind the lines to refit in late August. Casualties (killed, wounded, or taken prisoner) were 25 for the 17th and 11 for the 148th. Both squadrons had several pilots who finished the war as aces, notably George Vaughan (13), Lloyd Hamilton (9), and Howard Burdick (8) of the 17th, and Field Kindley (12), Elliott Springs (12), Henry Clay (8), and Jesse Creech (8) of the 148th.[5] Including those airmen who flew only with RAF units, American pilots on the British front had destroyed 200 enemy aircraft at a cost of 84 casualties. (Different sources claim as many as 225 destroyed for as few as 71 casualties.)

In November 1918 the 17th and 148th Squadrons finally went to the U.S. Air Service. They moved to the American sector of the front near Toul and began their conversion to the SPAD XIII, but the war ended before they could return to combat. On their departure from the British front, General John Salmond, the RAF's commander in France, sent a letter to General Mason Patrick of the AEF:

> Now that the time has come when Nos. 17 and 148 Squadrons return to you, I wish to say how magnificently they have carried out their duties…. Every call has been answered by them to the highest degree, and when they have arrived with you, you will have two highly efficient squadrons filled with the offensive spirit.

Americans in Italy

The program between the United States and Italy was smaller than those in France and Britain, but it was significant because it gave American airmen combat experience of a quite different character. Training for American fliers was centered in Foggia, near the spur on Italy's heel, and was managed by a U.S. Congressman who had volunteered for the Air Service—Fiorello LaGuardia, later mayor of New York. As an Italian-speaking politician with family roots in Foggia, he was a natural choice for the job.

Just over 400 Americans were graduated from the Italian school between September 1917 and the end of the war. Preliminary training was done in old Farmans, and it did not progress very quickly. An American cadet, Claud Duncan, later offered his comments on it. Some of them reflected the frustrations of an eager young man being taught to fly by an instructor with whom he had no common language:

> The Italians had a belief that you couldn't absorb more than ten minutes flying in a day, so you would go out and get your ten-minute hop and that was all for the day. Of course, you stayed out on the line, observed, listened, and picked up what you could. It took a long time at ten minutes a day to get any time in…. In our particular set-up the motor mechanic was the one who spoke English. We would go up and fly around with the instructor and come down. He would tell the mechanic what he wanted to tell us and the mechanic would say it to us in English…. I think we got as much information out of talking with each other as we did out of the instructors.

Duncan got his first flight with an instructor on 10 October 1917 and was graduated on 22 February 1918 with only 18 hours of flying. Advanced training began in the SIA7, until it was condemned as too fragile, and continued in the gigantic Caproni heavy bomber. The Caproni was among the world's earliest aircraft built specifically to attack strategic targets beyond the battlefield. The huge biplane was twin-boomed with a wingspan of over 70 feet, powered by three engines, two pulling and one pushing. Initially its total available power was 450 horsepower, in later models, 600 horsepower. Given the weight of a fully loaded Caproni (between 8,000 and 12,000 pounds), the unreliability of its engines, and the enormous drag of its angular airframe, it was not abundantly powerful. As one American pilot said:

> The principal trick to flying a Caproni was getting off the ground. You had three throttles and would start opening the two side motors little by little until the plane had good speed on the ground. Sometimes the rear motor would stop without your knowing it while you were getting the side motors open, which could of course be mighty serious if you had a load of bombs in a small field.

For all its limitations, the big Caproni was an effective first step on the road to strategic bombing. It could carry almost 2,000 pounds of bombs and had a range of nearly 400 miles. Its crews acknowledged

Major Fiorello La Guardia and Count Gianni Caproni, July 1918. Caproni was a pioneer builder of large, multi-engined aircraft, and La Guardia, an Italian-speaking U.S. Congressman with family roots in Foggia, was an ideal manager of the training program for the U.S. Army Air Service in Italy. American airmen flew Caproni bombers on strategic missions toward the end of World War I.

that it was slow and not very sophisticated. It was flat out at 85 miles per hour and, in the absence of any trimming controls, exhausting to fly and tail-heavy. One pilot reported: "You had literally to jam your elbow into your stomach and hold the stick forward with one hand while you operated the ailerons with the other." The instruments were pretty basic, too. Another remembered:

> The air speed indicator was a rough and ready affair consisting of what we called a penny on a string, a little round disc on a spring on one of the struts outside the cockpit. When the wind was blowing on it, it [went] backwards, and when the wind wasn't so strong, it came forwards. Behind it was a plate on which were the two words Minima

and Maxima. If you let it get below Minima you stalled, and if you got above Maxima the wings fell off.

From June 1918 American pilots were assigned to Italian squadrons where they were integrated to fly bombing missions against Austrian targets. Almost 100 Americans served in the battle area and took part in 65 raids, mostly at night. In the course of a raid on 27 October 1918, a Caproni flown by Lieutenants Dewitt Coleman and James Bahl was attacked by five enemy fighters. The bomber put up a terrific fight and shot down two of its attackers before being itself destroyed. The Caproni's crewmen were killed, and Coleman and Bahl were awarded respectively gold and silver Medals of Valor, Italy's highest decoration for courage in combat.

It had been intended that the Caproni should be acquired in large numbers for the U.S. Air Service, and if the war had lasted into 1919 it probably would have been. The aircraft was to be built in the United States and powered by Liberty engines, but only one

Ca 36 engine. The Caproni Ca 36 was powered by three 6-cylinder, 150-horsepower Isotta-Fraschini engines. Two engines pulled and one pushed from its mount between the aircraft's twin booms.

Caproni Ca 36 nose. Two pilots sat side by side in the open cockpit nose of Caproni bombers from 1914 onward. A gunner was exposed to the elements even farther forward with a single Revelli machine gun.

Caproni Ca 36. A variant of the Ca 33 fitted with five-section wings for easy disassembly, the Ca 36 was, like other Caproni bombers, stable and pleasant to fly but was not a lively performer, its maximum speed being less than 90 miles per hour. It carried a useful bombload of nearly 2,000 pounds and had a range of almost 400 miles.

was completed before the end of the war brought about its cancellation. Although small and brief, the Italian program provided the U.S. Air Service with its first combat experience in strategic bombing.

Enter Billy Mitchell

The greater part of America's air effort in World War I was necessarily concentrated in France and with the French. It had begun with the arrival in Paris of Major William "Billy" Mitchell only a few days after the United States declared war. Until the arrival of U.S. headquarters under General Pershing in June 1917, Billy Mitchell used his initiative and visited French combat units, headquarters, airfields, and supply depots. He borrowed French aircraft and flew reconnaissance flights over the battle area. He then reported to Washington, commenting on everything he saw, and included copious personal observations and recommendations. His hand could be seen behind the text of the cable from the French premier to President Wilson on 24 May 1917, which suggested the scale of America's involvement in the air war.

One of Mitchell's visits was to the British front, where he met the Commander of the RFC in France, Major General Hugh Trenchard. Years later, Trenchard was to become the first Chief of Staff of the Royal Air Force and a noted advocate for strategic air power. Mitchell was profoundly influenced by Trenchard, who held that aircraft were primarily offensive weapons, that they should be used for the deep penetration and bombing of enemy territory, and that they should be operated under unified command. These ideas took root in Mitchell's fertile mind and grew into the concepts with which he later so forcefully sought to shape the development of American air power.

For 15 months after the United States declared war, the Air Service of the American Expeditionary Force was first formed and then reorganized as General Pershing searched for the best way to provide his Army with air support. As chains of command and areas of responsibility changed, disagreements among staff officers were frequent and often acrimonious. Pershing remarked that the Air Service was "a lot of good men running around in circles." Always prominent at the center of the turbulence was Billy Mitchell. By June 1917 he was promoted to lieutenant colonel and made Aviation Officer on Pershing's AEF staff. While in that appointment, he recommended that the Air Service be composed of two distinct forces, the first for strategic operations and the second for support of the ground troops. Pershing appointed a board of examining officers, which included Mitchell. It essentially rubber-stamped Mitchell's ideas, recommending an Air Service with a strategic force of 30 bombardment and fighter groups, plus a second air force of a size determined by the strength of ground forces it was to support. Pershing, an old Army warhorse, was unready for such revolutionary views and accepted only the second recommendation. Later, the formation of specialized bombardment and pursuit squadrons was authorized, but a separate strategic force was never accepted, much to Mitchell's disappointment.

In the months after his initial appointment as Aviation Officer, AEF, Mitchell became successively Air Commander, Zone of Advance (front-line areas), and Chief of Air Service for 1st Corps, 1st Army, and finally Army Group. In the process he rose to brigadier general and managed to annoy most of his superiors at one time or another. After a particularly difficult period, General Foulois went so far as to write to Pershing on 4 June 1918 requesting that Mitchell "be immediately relieved from duty as Chief of Air Service, 1st Corps, and sent to the United States." Pershing recognized that Mitchell's prickly temperament made him difficult to live with but also knew his potential as a combat commander and calmed things down by imposing a truce. Faced with such aggressively independent behavior in the Air Service, senior soldiers tried to make the chain of command quite clear. General Patrick said: "The units of the Air Service are organized as integral parts of larger [Army] units…. They are therefore commanded in the full sense of the word by the commanding generals of these larger units…. There is no separate chain of tactical command in the Air Service." Despite the official position, Mitchell insisted on exercising considerable independence in his use of Air Service squadrons during the closing weeks of the war.

First Blood

Although flying in unarmed aircraft during their first patrols in March 1918, American airmen saw no combat until 14 April, almost a year after the United States entered the war. On that day, Lieutenants Alan Winslow and Douglas Campbell of the 94th Squadron (Hat-in-the-Ring) were standing by on alert duty at Gengault Aerodrome. The day was misty with low clouds and they were not expecting much to happen, particularly in the relatively quiet Toul sector where American squadrons were operating. However, at 8:45 a.m. the alarm was given and Winslow and Campbell in their Nieuports roared into the air. Clearing the airfield, they took two German single-seaters emerging from the fog, a Pfalz D3 and an Albatros D5, completely by surprise. They shot them down in rapid succession within sight of the cheering men

Billy Mitchell with staff officers in the latter stages of World War I. Once appointed Chief of the U.S. Army Air Service in France, Mitchell sought to use air power overwhelmingly at selected points, rather than thinly along the front. Air offensives launched under his command made decisive contributions to the success of the Allied ground forces as the war entered its final phase.

of the 94th, giving a sensational start to the American air campaign and a wonderful boost to the newcomers on the front line.

Building Combat Strength

In following weeks the American buildup gathered pace as more squadrons arrived at the front and became operational. The 94th was paired with the 95th, and these two were later joined by the 27th and 147th. As more squadrons became available they were formed into pursuit groups until, by November 1918, 4 groups controlled 12 pursuit squadrons. One of these was the 185th Night

Pursuit, operating as the 5th Squadron in the 1st Pursuit Group. At the same time, others were taking their place in the line. The 1st Aero Squadron, which not so long before had been dragging its Curtiss Jennies over the unfriendly terrain of northern Mexico in search of Pancho Villa, was the first to arrive in France from the United States in September 1917. Commanded by Major Ralph Royce, its airmen endured a lengthy conversion to the art of battlefield observation in obsolete Dorand AR1s and finally reached the front line in April 1918. They were not very happy that their operational aircraft was the SPAD XI, a two-seat variant of the excellent SPAD fighter that never

Salmson 2A–2. The 91st Aero Squadron used the Salmson 2A–2 for observation duties. Powered by a 260-horsepower water-cooled radial engine, it was reliable and relatively fast and had an advantage over most German pursuit aircraft at its usual operating altitudes above 10,000 feet.

matched its single-seat cousin. It had an unreliable engine and was uncomfortably unstable in the air.

Because the DH–4s expected from the United States were still months from delivery, American observation squadrons had to make do with cast-offs from the French and the British. Units arriving after Ralph Royce's 1st suffered aircraft which were, frankly, obsolete. The 12th had to use Dorand AR1s—"Antique Rattletraps" to their crews—while the 88th was issued French-built Sopwith 1½ Strutters designed in 1915. It was helpful that the Toul sector of the front was quiet and that the German air strength facing the Americans there was weak. Fortunately, before long, new French Salmson 2A2s arrived. They were fast, rugged two-seaters powered by reliable 260-horsepower radial engines and were each well armed with two Lewis guns for the observer and a forward-firing Vickers. They were maneuverable enough to give their crews a fighting chance against German fighters. As was later recorded:

"At the altitudes at which the 91st Squadron worked [5,000 meters], the Salmson had a decided advantage over [Pfalz and Albatros scouts] both in climbing and in horizontal speeds."

Like pursuit squadrons, observation squadrons were formed into groups as their numbers grew, with Major Royce moving up to command the 1st Corps Observation Group on 8 May 1918. At war's end, 16 observation squadrons in eight groups served 1st Army and seven army corps, and over 700 Salmson 2A2s had been delivered to the U.S. Air Service.

The number of bombardment squadrons was much slower to build up. The 96th was first into the fray on 12 June 1918; that it was able to get into action by then was a tribute to the ingenuity of its mechanics. Its aircraft were Breguet 14–B2s, in use at a training school since late 1917, and they were worn out. Spare parts were impossible to obtain. Master Sergeant James Sawyer and his men scavenged the local area for pieces of discarded farm machinery, putting them to imaginative use: "Part of a weather-beaten harvester was used for a tailpost for one of the planes; wagon tires were cut up and used for tail skids, and pieces of an ox-cart tongue were employed to reinforce wing spars. One of the planes carried brace wires which had once served on the telephone line…"

The determination of the 96th to join the battle and its valiant efforts to fight on with dilapidated equipment were brought to a temporary halt by one of the most embarrassing episodes of the American campaign. On 10 July 1918, the squadron's "press-on" spirit was much in evidence as its commander led his six available Breguets on a late evening raid against German railway yards. Flying conditions were poor, with heavy clouds, and an unexpectedly strong wind blew the aircraft deep into Germany. After a fruitless search for a break in the weather, the squadron commander turned for home and eventually let down through clouds. Their fuel almost exhausted, the six Breguets landed successfully. All of the airmen were captured, and their aircraft were taken intact. At one stroke, the only operational American bombardment force had been lost. The Germans were quick to send Air Service Headquarters a message: "We thank you for the fine airplanes and equipment you sent us, but what will

we do with the Major?" Billy Mitchell was furious. He wrote in his diary: "I know of no other performance in any air force in the war that was as reprehensible as this. Needless to say, we did not reply about the major, as he was better off in Germany than he would have been with us."

August saw the delivery of new Breguets to the 96th; September saw the arrival of more bombardment squadrons equipped at last with Liberty-engined DH–4s. The Breguet was almost universally popular with American aircrews, but the Liberty DH–4 got mixed reviews. Opinions varied widely, but in general the bomber crews disliked the DH–4 more than the observation crews. When loaded with bombs, the DH–4 became sluggish; its top speed dropped and it did not climb well. The length of fuselage between the pilot and observer made communication between them difficult. Unprotected fuel tanks occupied the space between the cockpits. Some aircrews referred to the DH–4 as "two wings on a hearse" or "the flaming coffin." They believed it was more susceptible than other aircraft to bursting into flames when hit by enemy fire. Observation squadrons were not always so critical. The commander of the 50th Squadron, Captain Daniel Morse, admitted that his airmen would have preferred protected fuel tanks, armored seats, and better visibility, but he concluded

Breguet 14–B2. Big and boxy, it was a reliable workhorse bomber and was popular with its American crews. It had dual controls and such advanced features as an aluminum tube framework and automatic flaps that extended at speeds below 70 miles per hour. As can be seen, servicing facilities on most French airfields were rudimentary.

DH–4. Known by some aircrews as "two wings on a hearse," the Liberty-engined DH–4 was the only aircraft built in the United States to see combat in World War I. Of 3,431 made, only 417 reached the front line before the end of the war.

that: "…the Liberty plane was considered the best on the front, and its excellent speed and combat power were well demonstrated in actual combat with enemy planes…. The Liberty, at low altitude could outdistance and outclimb any plane the Germans had."

Serious Opposition

The Americans' acclimatization to the battle area in the relatively quiet sector of Toul came to an end in the summer of 1918. On 29 June the 1st Pursuit and 1st Observation Groups moved to airfields near Chateau-Thierry, on the Marne River east of Paris. These groups, together with French squadrons, formed the 1st Air Brigade under Mitchell, positioned to help in countering German thrusts along the Aisne and Marne Rivers. As they soon found out, the opposition in their new area of responsibility was far harsher than anything they had experienced. The Germans had concentrated 46 of their 78 squadrons, including all three of the celebrated "Flying Circuses," on the Western Front. Inexperienced American squadrons, still equipped at first with outdated aircraft, were outnumbered four to one by battle-hardened German *Jagdstaffeln* units.

As American squadrons moved to Chateau-Thierry, the Chief of the Air Service established a marking system by which a leader's aircraft could be easily identified; new pilots had to be able to keep track of their leader in the maelstrom of a dogfight, or even

in the excitement of their first patrols, in the presence of the enemy or not. There were to be streamers on the wingtips and rudder, and red, white, and blue diagonal bands behind the cockpit. Units could mark their aircraft with distinctive badges, but only after they had proved themselves under fire. Several squadrons already met the combat requirement, and their aircraft soon wore their emblems, among them the 94th's Hat-in-the-Ring, the 95th's Kicking Mule and the 103rd's Indian Head.

During July the Allies first stopped and then drove back the German Army's offensive in a series of bloody battles that presaged its final defeat. Although the Allies were successful, the Germans had generally held the advantage in the air. American casualties mounted as their small formations were often overwhelmed by masses of enemy fighters. Even so, they usually gave as good as they got. By the time the Aisne-Marne campaign had run its course, the 1st Pursuit Group had lost 36 pilots, the 1st Observation Group, 11 aircrews. Thirty-eight enemy aircraft were claimed destroyed. The unsung members of the Air Service balloon companies had gone through their baptism of fire, too. Eight balloons were lost to enemy aircraft and 12 observers were forced to use their parachutes.

Although the airmen may seem to have gotten off lightly in comparison with the ground forces, who suffered appalling casualties, there was no doubt that their losses were deeply felt by the squadrons, small groups of men with close personal relationships. Within weeks most of the original faces had gone, to be replaced by others fresh from the flying schools and just as eager and unknowing as the founding members had been such a short time before. The concern of squadron commanders at the young newcomers' brash confidence could be heard in the welcoming remarks given to nine of them by Major Harold Hartney of the 27th Squadron:

> You are going to be surprised in the first, second, or third trip over the line and, despite all I can say right now, you will never know there is an enemy ship near you until you notice your windshield disintegrating or until a sharp sting interrupts your breathing.

Hartney's prophetic warning was made fact on 1 August when the 27th lost six aircraft in a whirling dogfight with four Fokker *Jagdstaffeln* and a number of two-seat Rumplers and Hanoveraners.[6] In the same fight, Lieutenant Donald Hudson experienced to the full the bedlam and blazing intensity of air combat. In just a few minutes of confusing action in a sky full of airplanes, he escaped an attack by four Fokkers, had a near collision with a stricken SPAD, spun and recovered three times, dealt with a boiling engine, and shot down a Fokker and two Rumplers.

Mitchell in Command

As the local air commander, Billy Mitchell grasped the opportunity to make his mark. At an early stage of the campaign, on 15 July, with the Allies uncertain of where the German blow would fall, Mitchell borrowed a SPAD and set off on a lone dawn reconnaissance. The clouds were as low as 300 feet and he followed the Marne River, flying between its steep banks. As he rounded a turn in the river near the town of Dormans, he came upon five pontoon bridges carrying masses of German troops, and saw at once the point of the German assault. He ordered a continuous air attack on the bridges, forewarning the Allied armies. Later in the day, Mitchell made a decision which significantly affected the battle. He shifted the weight of air attack from the bridges to the enemy supply base behind the front to destroy essential supplies and compel the German air units on to the defensive to protect their stockpile. The plan worked. Mitchell afterwards commented that it was:

> …the first case on record where we, with an inferior air force, were able to put the superior air force on the defensive and attack whenever we pleased, without the danger of the Germans sending great masses of pursuit aviation over to our side of the line.

The German assault blunted, the initiative passed to the Allies, who began preparations for a major

Bobby Soubiran and a SPAD XIII. The commanding officer of the 103rd Pursuit Squadron was Bobby Soubiran, shown with his personal SPAD XIII.

offensive involving American forces. General Pershing had the job of removing the St. Mihiel salient to shorten the front line for a subsequent general Allied offensive. Mitchell was appointed Chief of Air Service, 1st Army, and successfully argued for the assembly of the greatest concentration of air power ever in a single operation. Hap Arnold later said: "The air offensive which Mitchell laid on in September 1918 was the greatest thing of its kind seen in the war…the first massed air striking power ever seen." Units of American, French, British, and Italian air forces were gathered on 14 airfields, bringing together a total of 1,481 aircraft—701 fighters, 366 observation aircraft, 323 day bombers, and 91 night bombers. Facing them on the other side of the line, the Germans had between 200 and 300 aircraft of all types. The air superiority boot was on the other foot.

Mitchell planned to use his massive air force to overwhelm the opposition. He would dedicate one third to ground support and split the remaining two thirds to attack installations, communications, and troop columns behind the lines, as well as the flanks of the St. Mihiel salient. Not just intent on defeating the enemy's air force, he wanted also to use his fighters for "attacking [the enemy's] troops on the ground, and protecting our own air and ground troops." This commitment was something new in warfare. Fighters had been used before in attacking ground targets, but mostly randomly and not in large numbers. This time the air force would influence the ground war in a big way.

The attack was launched on 12 September 1918 in foul weather. Major Hartney, now Commander of the 1st Pursuit Group, noted the conditions and drew attention to the change in policy:

> …the weather was atrocious—pouring rain, with low-hanging clouds. This, however, was perfect for part of our plan—low flying. The pilots certainly flew low that day; they could not do otherwise; and the success of this new system (low-altitude strafing and bombing attacks on troop convoys and trenches) pointed the way we followed until the end of hostilities. And by low I mean low. The clouds at times formed a solid mist at 100 feet and everything had to be done below that. This low flying by an entire group was a revolution in war-time flying.

Pilots were now exposed to the horrors of the ground war. Eddie Rickenbacker was among those who described the carnage that followed a single-seat fighter's attack on a column of troops:

Billy Mitchell and a SPAD XVI. In the closing months of World War I, Brigadier General Billy Mitchell often used a SPAD XVI as his observation and command aircraft. This aircraft is now on display at the USAF Museum.

> Dipping down at the head of the column I sprinkled a few bullets over the leading teams. Horses fell right and left. One driver leaped from his seat and started running for the ditch. Half way across the road he threw up his arms and rolled over on his face…. All down the line we continued our fire—now tilting our aeroplanes down for a short burst, then zooming back up for a little altitude in which to repeat the performance. The whole column was thrown into the wildest confusion. Horses plunged and broke away. Some were killed and fell in their tracks.

Lieutenant Walter Case's account was equally graphic:

> At one time we flew over a small town where there were, to my judgement, about

3,000 troops…. I fired on the troops in the street, which caused utter confusion, a great many of them trying to enter one door at once. I concentrated my fire on that door, killing and wounding many of them, I am sure, for I could see them fall…

Poor weather persisted and necessarily limited air activity for the first two days, but the efforts made by Mitchell's command contributed significantly to the success of the whole operation. Losses were high on both sides[7] but the Germans were kept on the defensive by the aggressiveness of the Allied air forces and most of the action took place on the German side of the front. During the four-day Allied armies' assault, American airmen flew 3,300 combat sorties, fired 30,000 rounds of ammunition, and dropped over 75 tons of explosives. General Pershing was

suitably appreciative. In a letter of congratulation to Mitchell he commented:

> The organization and control of the tremendous concentration of air forces…which has enabled the 1st Army to carry out its dangerous and important mission is as fine a tribute to you personally as is the courage and nerve shown by your officers a signal proof of the high morale which permeates the service under your command.

The final act of World War I began on 26 September 1918 with the start of the Meuse-Argonne offensive. American troops had the task of penetrating several defensive lines lying across the broad valley between the heights of the Argonne forest to the west and the bluffs of the Meuse River to the east. Both areas of high ground were studded with German guns, and

French SPAD XIII. Robust and fast, the SPAD XIII was the principal pursuit aircraft used in World War I by the U.S. Army Air Service, which took delivery of 893 in 1918.

the defensive lines took advantage of rugged features in the valley. Pershing's hopes for a rapid advance and breakout were not realized and the American Army, which rose to more than one million men, was forced to grind its way forward in the face of determined resistance.

On 2 October soldiers of the 308th Infantry Regiment broke through the German line only to be surrounded and pinned down by heavy fire in a deep ravine. Their exact position was unknown and the 50th Aero Squadron was asked to find what the press was calling the Lost Battalion. In atrocious weather, several crews took their DH–4s through the area at low level without success, and by 6 October the soldiers' plight was desperate. On that morning, Lieutenants Harold Goettler and Erwin Bleckley flew through a number of ravines so low that German gunners fired down on them. They returned to base with more than 40 holes in their aircraft. Later in the day they volunteered to try again, aiming to draw enemy fire and so home in on where the battalion might be. Repeatedly flying at tree-top level through the most likely ravine, they were raked with gunfire again and again. Mortally wounded, Goettler lifted the shattered DH–4 out of the ravine and crash-landed in front of the French. He was dead and Bleckley was dying when help arrived. Bleckley's mission notes were intact and the search for the Lost Battalion was narrowed to a small area. A rescuing American force reached it the next day. Of 554 men who had entered the ravine, only 194 walked out.[8] Lieutenants Goettler and Bleckley were both awarded the Medal of Honor.

Billy Mitchell, promoted to brigadier general during the campaign, continued to trust the tactical principles that had worked at St. Mihiel. This time, however, his relative superiority in numbers was not so great. On 26 September he had more than 800 aircraft at his disposal, three-quarters of which were available to operate. The Germans began the battle with 300 aircraft but, as the offensive progressed, they reinforced their air strength, and by early November closed the ratio to 700 against 500. Whatever the circumstances, Mitchell steadfastly refused to compromise. He would not spread his forces thinly in an attempt to cover the whole area, but wherever possible operated strong formations and kept after the German rear. He agreed to protect the forward American troops by flying patrols of five aircraft assigned to six-mile fronts. These patrols were flown at low level by the 1st Pursuit Group and were responsible for breaking up any enemy formations attacking American soldiers. At the same time they took every opportunity to strafe German soldiers and shoot down observation balloons.

Aces Extraordinary
Attacking balloons was a dangerous business, as they were heavily guarded by anti-aircraft guns and fighters and a gauntlet of fire from the infantry. The most successful and celebrated practitioner of this hazardous art was Frank Luke. Between 12 and 29 September, Luke, flying a SPAD XIII of the 27th Squadron, shot down the incredible total of 14 balloons and 4 aircraft. His meteoric and often undisciplined career ended on the evening of 29 September when he subjected the Germans on

SPAD XIII. The favored fighter of the U.S. Army Air Service, the SPAD XIII was fast and had an excellent rate of climb. The USAF Museum's example is finished in the 1921 colors of the 95th Pursuit Squadron.

SPAD tail. The aircraft's powerful rudder once allowed Eddie Rickenbacker to bring his guns to bear from almost alongside an enemy.

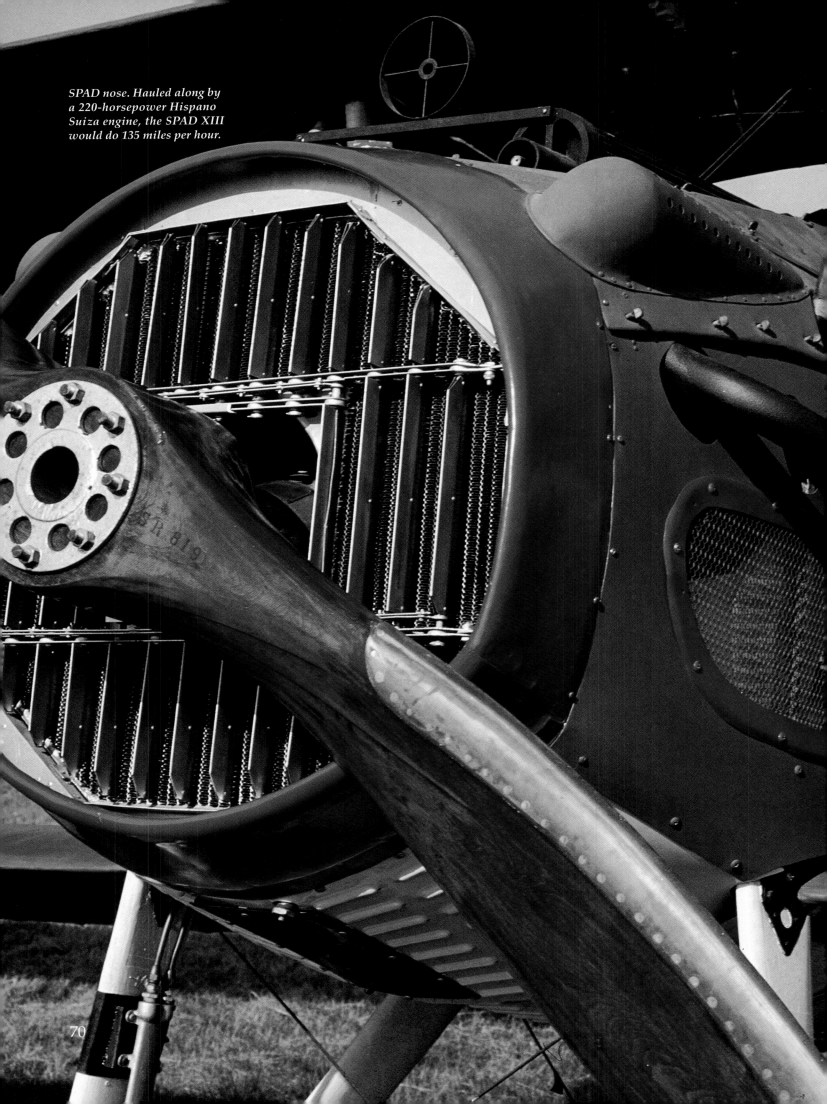

SPAD nose. Hauled along by a 220-horsepower Hispano Suiza engine, the SPAD XIII would do 135 miles per hour.

Lieutenant Frank Luke with a SPAD XIII fighter, France, 1918. A tenacious aerial "dogfighter," Luke shot down 14 enemy balloons and 4 aircraft during a two-week period in September 1918. He destroyed 4 more enemy balloons before he was brought down over Germany, but he was killed returning fire while resisting capture. Luke was the only Air Service member awarded a Medal of Honor (posthumously) before the war ended.

SPAD cockpit. Still simple, the SPAD XIII's cockpit was, nevertheless, more complex than that of its predecessors. Its pilot's field of vision could not have been helped by the framing of the small windscreen.

Medal of Honor
and lapel rosette

Rickenbacker memorabilia. The USAF Museum's display on Eddie Rickenbacker includes his Sam Browne belt, watch, war diary, and Medal of Honor, set against a World War I airman's uniform jacket.

the front near Verdun to a lone assault worthy of a Wagnerian epic. As the sun set he flew over the American 7th Balloon Company and dropped a note with the warning: "Watch for burning balloons." Luke sent his first German balloon down in flames at 7:05 p.m. and another rapidly afterward. He was momentarily diverted by harassing Fokkers and disposed of two of them before claiming his third balloon. At some point he was hit by ground fire and seriously wounded, but he turned to strafe German troops before crash-landing his SPAD. Once on the ground, he dragged himself from his cockpit and died nearby, pistol in hand. He was posthumously awarded the Medal of Honor.

Another prominent figure to feature in the war's closing battles was Eddie Rickenbacker. He had six victories in the Toul sector before a severe ear infection grounded him for much of June, July, and August. He returned to action with the 94th in mid-September and became squadron commander a few days later. Older than most fighter pilots at 28, he was a mature and thoughtful leader, much respected by his men. In the air, he was nerveless and calculating, taking time to maneuver the tactical situation in his favor rather than rushing headlong into combat. Like all of the great aces, he believed in getting in close to his enemy, firing one solid burst, then breaking away, ever watchful for the surprise attack from behind.[9]

At the opening of the Meuse-Argonne offensive, Rickenbacker's personal score had risen to ten enemy aircraft. On his first day as squadron commander he demonstrated his skill. He set off on a "hunting" expedition over the front and sighted two LVG observation aircraft escorted by five Fokkers. Placing himself above them and into the

Eddie Rickenbacker, in flight suit standing by his SPAD XIII. He described it as "…the ultimate aircraft in the war in which aviation developed."

sun, he dived onto the last Fokker and dispatched it with one burst. As the other escorts broke up in confusion, Rickenbacker kept his dive going for the LVGs. After exchanging spirited fire with their rear gunners and avoiding the attempt of one LVG to get behind him, he slipped to one side of the pair, ruddered his SPAD, and put the nearer LVG into his line of fire. As Rickenbacker himself so colorfully described: "It burst into flames and tumbled like a great blazing torch to earth, leaving a streamer of black smoke against the blue sky." He went on to take his score of kills to a total of 26 (22 aircraft and 4 balloons) and became America's leading ace of World War I. In 1931 his exploits were finally recognized formally and, belatedly, he became the fourth airman to be awarded the Medal of Honor.

Although Rickenbacker achieved his early kills flying the Nieuport, both he and Luke were linked with the SPAD XIII. Heavier and not nearly so maneuverable as the Nieuport or its formidable adversaries the Fokker Dr1 and D VII, the SPAD had signal advantages. It was powerful and so robustly built that it easily stood the strains of combat flying. Its sturdy airframe was a rock steady gun platform, but its controls were light and its rate of roll was excellent. It climbed well, reaching over 20,000 feet, but above all, it was fast, capable of over 130 miles per hour in level flight, and it could outdive any of its contemporaries. The fighter suited Rickenbacker's aerial combat style perfectly. He described it as "…more impressive than any other airplane, any automobile, any other piece of equipment I had ever seen…the ultimate aircraft in the war in which aviation developed."

Armistice and Aftermath
It was perhaps appropriate that the 94th Squadron, having led the American Air Service into combat, should bring the fighting to a close with the last American aerial victory of World War I. On 10 November 1918 one of its officers, Major Maxwell Kirby, flying a SPAD, shot down an unsuspecting Fokker near the village of Maucourt. The guns fell silent on the following day.

In seven months of combat, American airmen claimed 781 enemy aircraft destroyed, plus 73 balloons.[10] They had taken part in over 150 bombing raids and dropped more than a quarter of a million pounds of bombs. There were 289 American Air Service aircraft and 48 balloons lost in the struggle and 569 battle casualties (164 killed, 200 missing, 103 wounded, 102 captured). Another 319 American airmen were killed in accidents, and 335 died of other causes, such as influenza. It is beyond doubt that many Allied flyers killed in action could have been saved had they been issued parachutes. However, although these life-savers were being used by balloon observers and, in the latter stages of the war, by German airmen, Allied aviators irrationally spurned them as an implied insult to their courage and skill.

Although American airmen fought well in World War I, given the chance, they were never able to fulfill the promises made in the euphoric days following their entry in 1917. As 1918 drew to its close, American manpower flooded forward and the great wheels of American industry finally shifted into top gear. Had the war lasted into 1919, the U.S. Air Service might have provided the legions of aircraft predicted at the outset, including the squadrons of strategic bombers intended for deep strikes against targets in Germany. Such overwhelming air power might then have become a decisive factor in the struggle, but what might have been necessarily takes second place to what was.

As things stood on 11 November 1918, air power had not played a decisive part in the victory. However, many strategists understood that it had permanently changed the face of war and that a defining principle was emerging. In effect, the experiences of 1918 suggested that, even if air power could not itself procure victory, its absence could ensure defeat. The most reactionary of Army commanders was beginning to see that the achievement of air superiority over the battlefield was essential to success. At the strategic level, the evidence was thin, but there was enough to support the revolutionary idea that air forces could leap over armies and navies, attack an enemy's heartland and bring about national collapse—all without incurring the awful carnage resulting from the clash of ground forces. The air power debate that raged between the wars was beginning.

World War I had roused American air power from its slumber. Inevitably, with the coming of peace the U.S. Air Service would feel the pain of contraction as the great American military machine went into reverse. Airmen like Billy Mitchell might secretly regret that the fighting had stopped before the United States could "darken the skies," but the "genie" of air power was "out of its bottle" and could not be replaced. Many future leaders of American military aviation—Mitchell and Spaatz among them—had been in aerial combat and had strong views on how America's air power should develop. America's aviation industry had been jerked out of its lethargy and forced to think about matching Europe's. Even more important, perhaps, American airmen generally had begun to develop pride in their service and to nurture the roots of a service tradition. They had proved themselves in battle and some were already charting a course toward an independent air force. They had won the war; now they had to face the lengthier challenges of the peace.

Notes

1. This may not have been a wise move. Udet survived the war with 62 aerial victories and went on to become one of Hitler's generals who built the Luftwaffe during the 1930s. He was given responsibility for aircraft development and production programs and committed suicide in 1941 when they began to fail.

2. To Americans in the early part of the 20th century the concept of planning for war was alien. President Wilson himself was reported to have been outraged by the idea that the War Department was considering war plans in 1916. He believed it should be concerned only with the mobilization of manpower.

3. Between July 1917 and November 1918, the United States built over 32,000 aircraft engines, among them 10,000 Hall-Scott A7A and Curtiss OX–5 engines for trainer aircraft. The engine of the famous Curtiss Jenny, the 90-horsepower OX–5 led the way to a Curtiss family of V-shaped, liquid-cooled engines that powered American fighters of the 1920s and influenced Rolls-Royce designs for the Merlin, the most successful engine of World War II.

4. In February 1918 the Lafayette Escadrille was transferred to the U.S. Air Service and became the 103rd Aero Squadron, commanded by Major William Thaw. The squadron continued combat operations without interruption and remained under French command for five more months before joining the 3rd Pursuit Group on the American front in August.

5. The question of aerial victories claimed and officially recognized is vexing. National authorities had different rules for keeping score. For instance, if more than one pilot had shared in shooting down an enemy aircraft, each would be awarded a fraction of the victory on the British front, but a whole kill on the French front. This explains the sometimes wide discrepancies between squadron and individual scores. (The 95th Squadron's official victories total 48, but its individual pilots' scores added together total 70.) It is equally the case that historians find it difficult to agree on true figures. While the 148th Squadron's official victories total 64, in various histories its totals are 71, 66, and 63.

6. One of the Americans missing in the fight was Lieutenant Charles McElvain, who experienced a little of the chivalry still in evidence even in the late stage of the air war. He was unable to disengage from a lengthy duel with Lieutenant Alfred Fleischer of *Jasta* 17 and ran out of fuel. As he glided down with his engine dead, Fleischer held his fire and landed close by. Their meeting led to a close friendship and, eventually, to Fleischer's son's becoming an American citizen and working in McElvain's company.

7. American bombardment squadrons were particularly hard hit. On one raid, the 11th Squadron launched 17 DH–4s. One crashed shortly after becoming airborne and ten failed to reach the primary target. Of the six that bombed the primary, only one survived. Ten officer casualties included the squadron commander, two flight commanders, and the lead observer. The squadron was withdrawn from operations to replenish its strength. Also driven from the battle was the bedeviled 96th, still flying its Breguets. The 96th lost 16 officers and 14 aircraft in 5 days to record the highest AEF loss rate of the war.

8. It was during this rescue that Corporal, later Sergeant, Alvin York singlehandedly defeated a German battalion, killing many in it and bringing in 132 prisoners and 35 machine guns. He was subsequently awarded the Medal of Honor.

9. After World War II the Luftwaffe's "Bubi" Hartmann (the supreme ace of aces, with 352 aerial victories) revealed that he regarded dogfighting as a waste of time. He, too, took care to get the tactical situation clearly in his favor before committing himself to an attack, and he usually opened fire from 100 yards or less. It was his opinion that 90 percent of those he shot down never even saw him.

10. Although a victory claim was allowed even when a single enemy was attacked and shot down by more than one American flyer, in every air war claims usually outnumber actual kills by at least two to one. Accurate German records from World War I are not available, but Allied victory claims are probably similarly inflated. On the other hand, the claims of leading aces like Rickenbacker and Luke are well documented and can be assumed to be close to accurate.

The most necessary thing now is to educate the people as to what may be expected in aeronautics and how it affects the well-being of every citizen of this country.

(Brigadier General Billy Mitchell, 1919)

People have become so used to saying that Billy Mitchell was years ahead of his time, that they sometimes forget that it is true.

(General Hap Arnold, after Mitchell's death)

Pilots will not wear spurs while flying.

(U.S. Air Service regulation, 1920)

We wouldn't do it again for a million dollars — unless we were ordered to.

(Lieutenant Lowell Smith, after completing the first global flight, 23 September 1925)

The insatiate United States Army won the race for the world's premier seaplane trophy, the Schneider Cup, on Chesapeake Bay " . . . it must have been a grievous sight to sailors when Lieutenant James H. Doolittle, U.S. Army, putting pontoons on his landplane, romped away with the cup . . . "

(New York Times, 27 October 1925)

Chapter 3

Challenge and Controversy

Higher, Faster, Farther

World War I is left behind and, as USAF Museum visitors move toward the promises of peace, they are first reminded that war has its aftereffects. Wall displays tell of Americans who, once the armistice was signed, could not go home and of some who went on fighting. Photographs show that American forces were needed for occupation duties in Germany, and that American pilots, in the spirit of the Lafayette Escadrille, formed the Kosciuszko Squadron and fought for Poland against the Bolsheviks.

The atmosphere created in the 1920s collection suggests a period of continuous struggle and achievement. As the Air Service sought to build on the lessons of World War I, it tried to overcome its peacetime problem of drastically reduced manpower and money. New equipment was scarce; most of the aircraft displayed reflect their World War I ancestry. Although it had made its mark in combat and changed the face of war, military aviation was still a minor element of America's armed forces. Some of the exhibits recall the furious arguments over its role in future conflicts, particularly those led by Billy Mitchell to gain pride of place for air power.

As they bent their efforts to create an effective air force, leading American airmen recognized the importance of progressing as much as possible in research and development and of keeping the Air Service in public view through heralded achievements. Exhibited among the museum's fruits of invention from the laboratories at Dayton's McCook and Wright Fields are the McCook wind tunnel, an often dangerous 37-mm cannon, parachutes, landing lights, propellers, instruments, gyro controls, retractable landing gear, and Wright Field research records.

The public face of the Air Service is here displayed everywhere. In the 1920s American aviators were pushing hard at the frontiers of flight, and military airmen were often in the vanguard. Around the museum's walls are stories of men who dedicated themselves to climbing higher, staying airborne longer, travelling farther, and flying faster than before. Tales are told of many who reached their goals only through feats of remarkable endurance or while suffering severe hardship. Others tell of those who died in their attempts. Great names are here—Doolittle,

Brigadier General William "Billy" Mitchell (1879–1936). Returning from World War I covered in glory, Billy Mitchell was thought by many (including himself) to be ideal for appointment as Chief of the Air Service. The General Staff was not so sure it wanted such an unquiet spirit in the post, and he had to be content as Deputy Chief. Disappointment did not quiet him, however. He became "the gadfly of the General Staff and the hero of the Army's flyers," never ceasing to promote his ideas on the primacy of air power.

Bettis, Harris, Macready, Schroeder, Spaatz, Eaker, Quesada, Maitland, Hegenberger, and those of the men who flew the 1924 Douglas World Cruisers.

Events that captured fewer headlines but were, perhaps, just as significant to ordinary Americans are also recalled. Military aviators were encouraged to involve themselves *in humanitarian aid wherever needed and they were only too keen to help, dropping food supplies to flood victims, dusting crops, and putting the destructive capacity of bombardment squadrons to good use against ice jams and lava flows.*

The museum's 1920s exhibit closes showing that, although the Air Service has gained in status with a new designation— the Air Corps—and that most Americans know that the nation's military airmen are capable of great achievements, the promise of air power is a long way from fulfillment. The Air Corps of 1930 is still struggling to leave the shadow of World War I and is doing its best to meet its burgeoning responsibilities with less-than-adequate resources.

Post-War Problems

The signing of the armistice on 11 November 1918 left American airmen glad to see the end of World War I but convinced that their potential had been unfulfilled. They had fought hard with what they had and won some notable victories, but they had not darkened the skies with fleets of American warplanes nor had they decisively proved the strategic promise of military aircraft. Their disappointment led to recriminations and a series of hearings and investigations from which criticisms liberally spread. The U.S. government, industry, and military were all blamed to some degree for lack of organization, indecision, and poor judgement. The Air Service defended itself and spoke up with vigor on its future. Billy Mitchell was his usual forthright self on the subject of air power, but he was not the only prominent airman to voice a strong opinion. In 1919 Benny Foulois went so far as to tell a Senate Committee:

> The General Staff of the Army—either through lack of vision, lack of practical knowledge, or deliberate intention to subordinate the Air Service's needs to the needs of other combat arms—has utterly failed to appreciate the full military value of this new weapon, and, in my opinion, has failed to accord it its just place in our military family.

Whatever their convictions and aspirations, the Air Service's firebrands had first to cope with the sobering realities of peacetime. America's war machine had only just shifted into high gear, but went into reverse as demobilization began immediately. An air arm that had grown from 1,200 to nearly 200,000 men in only 18 months experienced pains of contraction as it reached fewer than 10,000 by mid-1920. Airframe and engine orders—the life-blood of America's newly risen aircraft industry—were summarily cancelled. By 1920 nearly 90 percent of the industry was gone,

remaining companies hung on without military contracts. Worse still, a glut of cheap surplus military aircraft depressed the civil market.

Reflecting the post-war attitude of the country toward military spending, Congress budgeted parsimoniously. The $460 million of fiscal year 1919 fell to no more than $25 million for fiscal year 1920. Politicians could scarcely imagine any nation's posing a credible threat to the United States, a winner in "the war to end all wars." Military expansion had provided the Air Service with thousands of aircraft and spares and Congress believed that until they were used up, there was little need to spend much money on more. American military airmen could look forward to little more than a good many years in DH–4s and Curtiss Jennies.

Likewise, they could look forward to little more than discouraging prospects for a change in the status of the Air Service. In 1919 bills presented in both the Senate and the House proposed the creation of a separate U.S. Air Force. A commission under the Assistant Secretary of War proposed the creation of a separate Department of Aeronautics to control an independent air force. The bills died and the War Department's generals and Secretary, Newton Baker, rejected the recommendations of the commission. Baker warned the Air Service against building a bomber force for attacking cities, and General Pershing delivered himself of the opinion that "...an air force acting independently can of its own account neither win a war at the present time nor, so far as we can

tell, at any time in the future." In what was seen as a crushing defeat for their cause by many airmen, particularly Mitchell and Foulois, Congress agreed with the Secretary of War and authorized the Air Service as a combatant unit of the Army, limited to only 1,500 officers and 16,000 enlisted men. But Congress also raised the rank of the Chief of the Air Service to major general; allowed the Air Service control of its own research, development, procurement, personnel, and training; authorized flight pay; and put tactical units under the command of flyers.

Despite these welcome advances, the size and shape of the Air Service gave the apostles of air power many reasons to preach. In the front line of 27 squadrons just 4 were devoted to pursuit and 4 to bombardment; only 1 was devoted to heavy bombardment. The remaining 19 squadrons were all concerned with observation, as were 32 balloon companies. This emphasis reflected the long-held belief of most senior Army officers that aircraft should be used primarily for close support of troops on the battle-field. Control of tactical squadrons went to Army corps commanders, and the Chief of the Air Service was left with training schools and depots.

The Unquiet Spirit

Many Air Service officers, Hap Arnold among them, hoped that Billy Mitchell would be Chief of the Air Service when he returned from Europe. As he said later: "Above all others, [Mitchell] had the background, the reputation, the personal courage, the knowledge of air operations to do the job." However,

Mitchell's fiery reputation preceded him and the General Staff was not ready for his radical ideas on air power, even though some had proved remarkably successful in France. The first peacetime Chief was, from the U.S. Army's standpoint, a sensibly conservative choice—Major General Charles Menoher—an infantry officer, *not* a pilot. Mitchell had to be content as number two.

The General Staff, hoping to keep Billy Mitchell quiet by making him a subordinate, would be disappointed; he became its "gadfly…and the hero of the Army's flyers." Central to Mitchell's vision of an independent air force was his conviction that air power could become a decisive strategic instrument. The total war concept inherent in his ideas was popular in neither military nor civilian circles. In suggesting that future wars could be decided by airmen before soldiers got involved, Mitchell was attacking the Army's arguments to bolster its diminishing budget for ground forces, and his belief that navies were made largely redundant by air power had the sailors apoplectic. His view that modern war could no longer exclude women and children horrified almost everyone. "The entire nation," he said, "is, or should be, considered a combatant force." In the face of considerable opposition, Mitchell was persistent. He continued to speak in public frequently, testified regularly before Congressional committees, and wrote articles and a book[1] spelling out his air power gospel.

At the same time, Mitchell attacked the day-to-day business of the Air Service relentlessly in papers on

"Kelly Field, Texas, 1925," Willard Fleming, 1982, USAF Art Collection.

countless proposals—very long range bombers, amphibious aircraft, all-metal bombers, troop-carrying aircraft, armor-piercing bombs, large-caliber cannon, aerial torpedoes, civil defense against air raids, private flying as the provider of a pilot reserve and so on, without pause. He also encouraged news-making events to generate favorable publicity for the Air Service and, wherever possible, test its potential. At first, these involved no more then military aircraft performing at county fairs and other public gatherings, but soon they involved cross-country flights and aerial competitions. Sometimes this exhibitionism led young pilots to forget the bounds of good sense and show off with low-level flying and aerobatics. Some indulged high spirits by hunting wildfowl with their machine guns. Their accident rate rose until it was higher than it had ever been during the rapid expansion of World War I, and it stayed high.[2]

Cross-country Hazards

Even controlled exercises had their excitement. In the Air Service's first transcontinental flight, Major Albert Smith led five Curtiss Jennies from Rockwell Field, San Diego, California, on 4 December 1918. In the course of a flight in which Major Smith reached

Jacksonville, Florida, on 18 December and returned to Rockwell on 15 February 1919, via Washington and New York, two aircraft crashed, two more wrecked in bad weather, and several got major overhauls. Forced landings were common, and pilots became accustomed to landing in any field or flat area that appeared and accepting the accompanying hazards. One pilot sent a message that he was delayed "...due to cow eating wing." In a later report, he wrote that "...some unprincipled bovine with a low sense of humor and a depraved appetite had eaten large chunks out of the lower wing panels and stabilizer."

At about the same time, Major Theodore Macauley of Taliaferro Field, Fort Worth, Texas, flew a DH–4 west to Rockwell and then across the continent to Jacksonville before returning to Fort Worth. His first aircraft was seriously damaged twice in landing accidents and was replaced by another DH–4 in Alabama during the return trip. The second aircraft needed lengthy repairs after being flown through heavy rain in Mississippi. Not at all discouraged by the trials of this attempt, Macauley did it again in April 1919, this time without any serious problems, completing the round trip across the United States in 7 days with a flying time of 44 hours and 15 minutes.

In July 1919 a more ambitious exercise tested the long-range capabilities of the Martin MB–2 (NBS–1) bomber and the reliability of its Liberty engines. Lieutenant Colonel Rutherford Hartz and his crew left Bolling Field, Washington, D.C., on 24 July for a flight around the rim of the United States to chart air routes and locate possible landing fields. After a marathon effort in which they coped with seven forced landings, numerous repairs and the challenges of social occasions in 18 of the outermost states, Hartz and his crew completed the circuit by returning to Bolling on 9 November 1919, having covered 9,823 miles in 108 days with a flying time of 114 hours and 25 minutes.

As men like Smith, Macauley, and Hartz discovered in the pioneering days of the Air Service, lengthy absences of aircraft and aircrews did not seem to be a problem, and fact-finding adventures were deemed at least as important as routine training. Local commanders had a great deal of latitude and waved the Air Service's flag as they saw fit. Accidents and outlandish escapades led to the curtailment of this freedom of action in September 1919. From that date, authorization for special flights had to be obtained from Air Service Headquarters in Washington, and participation was organized into fewer and larger events.

The Air Service's most important exercise of 1919 under the new rules was Mitchell's "transcontinental reliability and endurance test." It was meant to be a "...[field maneuver] calculated to yield a far greater profit to the Air Service and the cause of aeronautics in general than any field maneuver ever did before." Personnel, equipment, communications, and organization would be subjected to the pressure of an extended exercise as would navigation, meteorology, landing fields, and other matters bearing on operations. Mitchell's underlying goal was to gather facts on the operational problems of an air force that had suffered savage cuts and was flying obsolete aircraft over country with inadequate facilities. To check on a participants' ability to respond to a challenge, Mitchell did not announce the exercise until 18 days before its start.

Any local commander could enter an aircraft and pilot, and Mitchell's test rapidly took on the character of a race, which excited the interest of the American public. Its route lay between New York and San Francisco and could be flown either way, but all aircraft had to pass through 29 control stations on the 2,700-mile flight. No night flying was allowed. Winners would be announced for the shortest elapsed time, the shortest flying time, and the fastest flying time based on a handicap system for various machines. Fifty-eight aircraft entered to start from New York, 16 from San Francisco. Fifty-two DH–4s dominated the lineup. They were joined by 1 DH–9, 7 SE–5s, 5 Fokkers, 3 LUSAC 11s, 2 Martin bombers, 1 Ansaldo SVA–5, 1 Thomas-Morse MB–3, 1 SPAD, and 1 Bristol Fighter. A number of them failed to reach the starting line for one reason or another, including two fatal

An upended Curtiss Jenny. While docile, the aircraft sometimes trapped the unwary student pilot. The Jenny continued to be used as the primary trainer for American military pilots until the late 1920s.

accidents. In the event, 46 aircraft started from Roosevelt Field, Long Island, on 8 October 1919, and another 15 set out from San Francisco's Presidio.

Lieutenant Belvin Maynard's DH–4 was the first to arrive at San Francisco, and an SE–5 flown by Major Carl "Tooey" Spatz[3] led the west-east group into New York. Eventually, 26 of the New York starters reached the west coast, and there were 7 finishers from San Francisco. Seventeen of these 33 set off immediately in a hastily-authorized extension of the race into a round trip. Six made it back to New York and two to San Francisco. The double crossing was completed by 5 DH–4s, 2 SE–5s and 1 Fokker.

As the survivors were only too ready to attest, it had been a grueling ordeal for both men and machines. They contended with rain, snow, ice, fog, and long stretches of severe cold. They got lost, which was hardly surprising, given the weather, the guidance of very basic magnetic compasses, and their Post Office and Rand McNally state maps. They battled mechanical problems—engine failures, broken landing gear, splintered propellers, frozen water pumps, blown tires, leaking radiators, and damaged wings. The overall winner, Lieutenant Maynard, survived a forced landing after breaking a crankshaft, and, with his mechanic, successfully changed the Liberty engine overnight for one retrieved from a crashed Martin bomber. Fifty-four accidents marred the exercise, and these added seven deaths and two serious injuries to the two fatal accidents suffered before the outset.[4]

Mitchell's exercise had proved costly but had revealed glaring needs, the most obvious being more landing fields and improvements to those that existed. Reliable servicing facilities, communications, airfield lighting, navigation aids, and weather information were also essential. Mitchell drew comfort from the newsworthiness of such competitive events and endeavored to keep the Air Service in the public eye to better build his case for a large and powerful air force. Fifty-four accidents and nine fatalities in the transcontinental exercise were not good, but even they helped to draw attention to the challenges of military flying in obsolete aircraft.[5]

Mitchell Versus the Navy
If the Army found Mitchell hard to live with, the Navy saw him as its mortal foe. It carried out one of its principal duties—guarding the nation's coasts against hostile approaches—with the heart of its defensive might—the battleships it considered almost invulnerable. Mitchell scathingly attacked them as outdated, declaring the day of the dreadnought over. He asserted that aircraft could sink any ship afloat and that the country would be safer leaving its coastal defense to the Air Service. Some in the Navy recognized that the aerial threat to their ships was real and were keen to develop naval air power as the proper response, but many others sneered at

Belvin Maynard and a DH–4. The winner of the Air Service's 1919 trans-continental reliability and endurance test, Lieutenant Maynard was known to the press as "the flying parson." He overcame the handicaps of a forced landing and an impromptu engine change during his epic flight.

Mitchell memorabilia. The USAF Museum's collection includes Billy Mitchell's binoculars, spectacles, medals, the pennant flown from his aircraft during the battleship trials, and his uniform jacket, believed to have been worn at his court martial.

*"General Mitchell's Bombers
Sink the Ostfriesland, 1921,"
Robert Lavin, 1958, USAF
Art Collection.*

*The Ostfriesland before sinking
into the waters off the coast
of Virginia.*

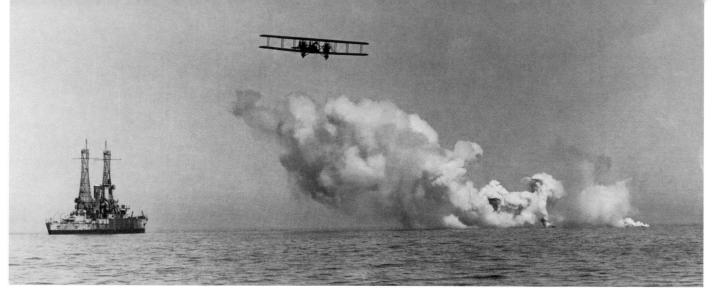

Martin B–2 bombers and the USS Alabama. *During the first phase of Billy Mitchell's exercises against the old battleship in September 1921, Martin MB–2 bombers laid smokescreens. Later aircraft attacked with increasingly large bombs, finally sinking the ship with one weighing 2,000 pounds dropped close alongside.*

aircraft in any form. The Chief of Naval Operations actually wanted to disband the small naval air arm, saying; "I cannot conceive of any use that the fleet will ever have for aircraft." Faced with Mitchell's assault, he added: "Aviation is just a lot of noise." The Secretary of the Navy was even more intemperate. He went so far as to say that he would be prepared to stand bareheaded on the deck of any capital ship under attack from the air.

The Ostfriesland, *a target in General Mitchell's ship-bombing tests of July 1921.*

Since joining General Menoher's staff in 1919, Mitchell had been asking for a test of aircraft against ships. In 1921, after several newspapers had picked up his theme to argue that battleships were indeed relics of the past, his campaign finally bore fruit. A number of ex-German warships, acquired under terms of the Versailles Treaty, were available for tests, as were some old American ships. The Navy agreed to have them ready for trial by air attack 50 miles off the mouth of Chesapeake Bay in June.

A special unit known as the 1st Provisional Air Brigade was assembled for the trials at Langley Field, Virginia, and Mitchell made sure they got as much training in the techniques of ship attack as possible. Air Service airmen began testing against an ex-German destroyer, the G–102, in mid-July. First, a wave of SE–5s dropped 25-pound anti-personnel bombs and simulated strafing the ship from 200 feet. Sixteen Martin bombers followed, dropping two 300-pound bombs each from 1,500 feet. After the Martins' first pass, the G–102 sank. On 18 July the cruiser *Frankfurt* got similar treatment and was sunk by Martins carrying 600-pound bombs. A more serious challenge came on 20 July in the shape of the 27,000-ton battleship *Ostfriesland*. With a four-layered hull and watertight compartments end to end, the ex-German warship was thought unsinkable. The Martins struck on 21 July, this time delivering the *coup de grace* with two 1,000-pound bombs and sinking the *Ostfriesland* in just 21 minutes.

By 29 July Mitchell drove home more air power points by leading his bombers in mock raids on New York City, Philadelphia, Wilmington, Baltimore, and Annapolis. The final report on the naval tests and city attacks reached General Menoher on 29 August. Mitchell's conclusions were uncompromising. Bombers had demonstrated that any ship could be sunk and that American cities were vulnerable from the air. Aircraft could provide the only proper defense and these should be operated by an independent air force. "Aviation," he insisted, "can only be developed to its fullest extent under its own direction and control. An efficient solution of our defensive needs will not exist until a Department of National Defense is organized."

A joint Army-Navy Board acknowledged the added dangers of the air threat, stating that it was imperative "as a matter of national defense to provide for the maximum possible development of aviation in both the Army and the Navy." However, the board concluded that battleships "were still the backbone of the fleet and bulwark of the nation's sea defense." The certainty of that assertion seemed dubious after later bombing attacks on the battleship *Alabama* in September 1921, and on two more, the *Indiana* and the *Virginia*, in 1923. All three were sent to the bottom by Mitchell's bombers. On the far side of the world, Japanese naval officers took note.

General Menoher forwarded Mitchell's report to the Secretary of War, adding his profound disagreement with its conclusions. The matter might have died had the report not been leaked to the press on 13 September 1921. In the ensuing furor, General Menoher decided that he had had enough and resigned. Mitchell, still viewed warily by the Secretary of War, was passed over again. The new Chief of the Air Service was General Mason Patrick, a reliable member of the old Army

Major General Mason Patrick, Chief of the U.S. Army Air Service and first Chief of the U.S. Army Air Corps, with Major Ralph Royce and a Curtiss Jenny.

The USAF Museum's DH–4. The aircraft is painted in the colors of General Mason Patrick, Chief of the Air Service during the early 1920s. Note the wing structure clearly revealed by the translucent fabric covering.

DH–4 cockpit. The layout of the post-World War I DH–4's cockpit retains the essential simplicity typical of wartime aircraft. Since most people are right-handed, such controls as the throttle and the elevator trim wheel are placed to the left. The right hand grasps the stick and maneuvers the aircraft.

DH–4 engine. The De Havilland DH–4 was selected for large-scale production in the United States primarily because of its capacity to mount the American Liberty engine. The combination did not produce startling performance, but the aircraft was very reliable and remained in service in a number of roles until the late 1920s.

Wreck of the Shenandoah Airship, near Ava, Ohio, September 3, 1925.

establishment. He had been Air Service commander in France, and had dealt with Mitchell before. Patrick was aware of Mitchell's single-mindedness on the subject of air power and knew that he could be a difficult subordinate, but he respected Mitchell's originality, having seen some of his ideas succeed in the heat of combat.

While not the uncompromising, flamboyant advocate for air power that Mitchell was, Patrick agreed with his number two about the need to build up the Air Service. He called attention to the improper balance among front-line squadrons, urging fewer observation and more pursuit and bombardment types. Ideally, he said, observation squadrons should constitute no more than 20 percent of combat strength. In 1923 Patrick's persistence led to the appointment of a board, headed by Major General William Lassiter, to study his plans. The Lassiter Board accepted many of Patrick's arguments, finding that the shape of the Air Service bore "no relationship to war requirements." Disagreements between the Secretaries of War and Navy later doomed the findings, but the essence of Patrick's case for air power was better understood.[6]

Air Power Prophet on Trial

Mitchell was not prepared to be as patient as his chief. In 1924 he resumed his outspoken personal campaign with more speeches, articles, and Congressional testimony.[7] As he grew more strident, he gained something of a public following but his efforts were counterproductive in the most important places. He had not only angered the Secretaries of War and Navy and senior officers, he antagonized President Coolidge as well. When his tour of duty as Assistant Chief of the Air Service expired in April 1925, Mitchell was not reappointed. He reverted to his permanent rank of colonel and was "exiled" to Texas. From there, his frustration burst the bounds of reason. On 5 September 1925 Navy losses of an aircraft and the airship *Shenandoah* within days of each other prompted the Secretary of the Navy to announce that the accidents had proved that aircraft could not attack the United States. Mitchell issued a reaction to the press which indicted "…the incompetency, criminal negligence, and almost treasonable administration of our national defense by the Navy and War Departments." The court-martial which Mitchell appeared to seek was duly ordered by the President and held in Washington during the closing months of 1925.

Mitchell and his supporters—including such future leaders as Arnold, Spaatz, Olds, and Eaker—knew that the verdict of the court was a foregone conclusion, and they treated the trial as a public hearing on the case for air power. Mitchell was found guilty of "conduct of a nature to bring discredit upon the military service," and sentenced to suspension from the service for five years without pay. On 1 February 1926 he resigned from the Air Service to continue the fight as a civilian. Unfortunately, the onset of the depression diverted the public's attention from defense matters, and Mitchell died almost a forgotten man in 1936. Ten years later, when many of his predictions had proved all too accurate, the farsightedness and courage, if not the diplomacy, of his principled stand were belatedly recognized when President Truman authorized the posthumous award of a special Medal of Honor to Billy Mitchell, air power prophet extraordinary.

Aircraft and Engines of the 1920s

During his tenure as Assistant Chief of the Air Service, Mitchell had continued to encourage well-publicized activities and the research and development spearheaded by the Engineering Division at McCook Field. Much valuable work was done on ancillary equipment—bombsights, cannons, propellers, engines, and so on—and a number of experimental aircraft were built at McCook in the early 1920s with the help of a wind tunnel capable of providing an airstream of 450 miles per hour. Funds were limited, however, and by 1923 experimental activities declined and aircraft manufacturers took on the work of designing new machines to meet Air Service specifications. They made progress, but slowly. Many of their products proved disappointing as ideas ran ahead of available technology.

Efforts to develop aircraft with strategic reach were particularly disappointing. The Barling bomber (XNBL–1) was an impressive monster that seemed to tackle the problem by being bigger and having more of most things than its contemporaries. In the words of one observer, it looked "more likely to antagonize the air than to pass through it." A triplane with a 120-foot wingspan, the Barling had two tailplanes and four fins and weighed more than 42,000 pounds. It first staggered into the air on 22 August 1923 from Wright Field, next to the present-day site of the USAF Museum. Powered by six Liberty engines, it could lift its bombload off the ground but was then incapable of carrying it farther than 170 miles or of dragging its mass of struts and wires along at more than 95 miles per hour. Finally, the Barling proved incapable of crossing the Appalachians to reach the east coast. It was hardly the creature of Billy Mitchell's air power dreams.

For the remainder of the 1920s, American bombers followed more conventional lines, but none came close to matching Billy Mitchell's vision. The Martin MB–2

Keystone bomber. The Keystone aircraft series captured over 90 percent of the U.S. Army's bomber procurement funds in the late 1920s and early 1930s. As Adolf Hitler rose to power in Europe, the U.S. Army Air Corps' strategic bombers had open cockpits, a maximum speed of 120 miles per hour, and a range of under 1,000 miles. They were armed with three .303-inch machine guns and a 2,500-pound bombload.

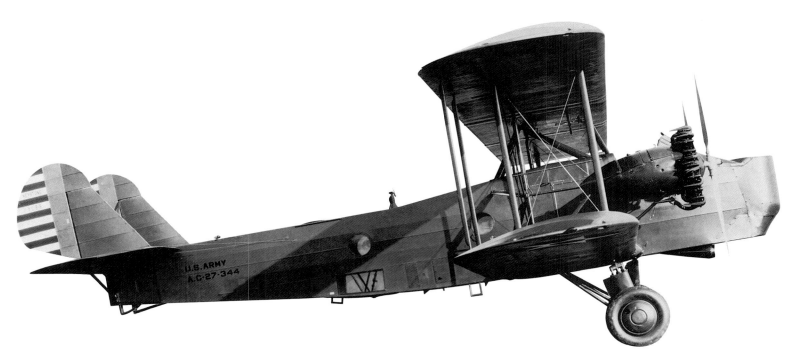

of 1920 was joined by the first of the Keystone bombers in 1923. Keystones monopolized Army bomber procurement at the time, apart from a dozen Curtiss Condors ordered in 1927. Neither the Keystone nor the Condor differed significantly from the World War I style of the MB–2. All three were open-cockpit, twin-engined biplanes capable of carrying bombloads of 2,500 pounds or so over ranges of up to 800 miles. Engines improved and service ceilings rose to the 17,500 feet of the Condor, but maximum speeds remained stubbornly low at no more than 130 miles per hour. Inadequate as strategic bombers, the Keystones and the Condors kept the force and its expertise alive while aeronautical technology struggled to catch up with strategic theory.

With bombers in the United States and elsewhere threatening no great improvements in performance, fighters remained framed almost as badly as they had been in World War I. The Air Service entered the 1920s still relying on SE–5As designed in Britain in 1916 and on Thomas-Morse MB–3s. The Thomas-Morse fighter was later developed into the more powerful MB–3A, built under contract by a little-known manufacturer in the Pacific northwest called Boeing. In those days, the government commonly bought the rights to aircraft designs and then put a production contract up for bids rather than arranging a deal with the original designer. In the case of the MB–3A the low bidder was Boeing, and the Thomas-Morse Company lost its aircraft. In the long run,

P–6 formation. The Curtiss P–6E was one of the most attractive biplanes ever built and was much loved by its pilots. Here the 17th Pursuit Squadron from Selfridge Field, Michigan, shows off its formation skills and Snowy Owl emblem. By the time the squadron took delivery of its P–6Es in 1932, bombers like the Martin B–10 were already flying and achieving higher maximum speeds.

P–6 engine. The 12-cylinder 600-horsepower Conqueror engine powered the Curtiss P–6E Hawk. The Conqueror was splendid, but it could not haul the P–6E through the 200 mile-per-hour barrier in level flight.

"Winter Maneuvers," Nixon Galloway, 1978, USAF Art Collection.

although it helped companies like Boeing get established, this policy had adverse effects. Companies generally were discouraged from expending time and effort on new designs for the military since they knew they stood a good chance of failing to get a production contract even if their designs were accepted.

By the end of the 1920s the fighter had advanced, but not by much. Boeing and Curtiss had cornered the market, producing some single-seaters that, while very agile and attractive, still bore a family resemblance to the biplanes of the Western Front in 1918. The Curtiss Hawk series had begun with the P–1 in 1925, which by 1929 had become the P–6E, an elegantly classic design affectionately remembered as a worthy symbol of the golden age of flight. Besides being photogenic, the P–6E had a top speed of 197 miles per hour and could reach 25,000 feet. It was, however, still an open cockpit biplane armed with just two 3-inch machine guns firing through the propeller arc.

As the decade drew to a close, Boeing provided a fighter with a 500-horsepower Pratt & Whitney radial engine. It was the P–12, and it proved reliable and popular. (Over 350 were delivered to the U.S.

Army Air Corps.) But it represented an alternative to the Curtiss fighter rather than a noticeable improvement. Its performance was similar to that of the P–6 and it was the last of the biplane fighters flown by the Army. Rapidly overtaken by technological advances in the 1930s, the last of the P–12s, nevertheless, managed to hang on until 1941 before being retired.

For all of their obvious links with a bygone era of air warfare, the Army's biplane fighters projected a glamorous image of military flying to the American public. Gaudily decorated in bright color schemes and unit insignia, they were a glorious sight at air shows. Their pilots wore leather helmets and silk scarves and called forth memories of Rickenbacker and Luke. Biplanes were creatures of the past, but the Curtiss Hawk pointed one way to the future. Its cowlings hid the 450-horsepower Curtiss D12 engine or its 600-horsepower successor, the V–1570 Conqueror. The D12 was a true technical watershed, an aluminum monobloc V-shaped engine that would influence aviation until the advent of jet propulsion. Over the years, refinements were designed to raise overall power and the ratios of power-to-weight and power-to-frontal area, but essential elements of the engine remained unchanged. Rolls-Royce studied D12 before it began the series of V–12s which culminated in the Merlin, the engine that powered such famous World War II fighters as the Hurricane, Spitfire, and Mustang.

A D12 derivative was also fitted to an aircraft specifically designed for ground attack. The Curtiss A–3 was a two-seater born of low-level troop-strafing in 1918 and the thought (perhaps even hope) that the DH–4 could not last forever. It first appeared in 1926 bearing a distinct family resemblance to the Curtiss Hawk. Armored and fitted with bomb racks, it carried four forward-firing machine guns plus two for the observer. Noticeably heavier than the Hawk, it was not very quick at 140 miles per hour and would probably have been hazardous to the health of its crews if operated as intended in any major conflict. Even the A–3, however, was a marked improvement on the first attempt at a ground-attack aircraft to come out of the Engineering Division at McCook Field. The GA–1 was a large, heavily armored triplane with two Liberty engines driving pusher propellers. Its three crew members directed the fire of eight machine guns and could drop a variety of bombs. There was even provision for fitting a 37-mm cannon. It flew, but not very well, and the Army changed its mind about an extended contract for its production. The ubiquitous DH–4, hung about with extra guns, filled in until the A–3 came along.

Remaining Army aircraft during the 1920s included a plethora of observation, cargo, and training types. Notable among the observation aircraft were Douglas biplanes, beginning with the O–2 in 1925 and continuing until the O–38 of the early 1930s, in the process developing from open cockpit Liberty engined two-seaters not much different from a DH–4 into more sophisticated machines, each with a cockpit canopy and Pratt & Whitney radial. As engine power increased so did weight. Improvements in performance were minimal, none of the aircraft ever exceeded more than 150 miles per hour.

Even slower but more intriguing was the Loening OA–1. An amphibian built for the Army, it was a single-engined biplane dominated by a huge central float containing retractable landing gear and was the foundation for a slab-sided fuselage. To raise the propeller clear of the protuberant float, the inescapable Liberty engine was inverted. Forty-five of these eccentricities were ordered between 1924 and 1928, primarily for deployment in Hawaii and the Philippines, but used wherever lakes and rivers outnumbered airfields.

Cargo aircraft of the 1920s were mostly civilian airliners adapted for military use. Prominent among them were two designs by the Dutchman, Anthony Fokker. The T–2 was a high-wing monoplane built in 1921 that seemed much too large for its power plant. Eighty-one feet across the wing and nearly 50 feet long, its uncompromisingly angular shape was hauled by a single Liberty engine. In 1927 the T–2 was joined by the Fokker C–2, more reasonably provided with three Wright Whirlwind radials; other trimotors in the stable were the Fords, C–3, and C–4. In the extraordinary category sesquiplane[8] was another amphibian, the twin-engined Sikorsky C–6, in which ten passengers were carried in a large hull, tenuously suspended beneath twin booms trailing an impossibly high wing.

Trainer aircraft were not nearly so exotic. Until the mid-1920s, primary flight training took place in the Curtiss Jenny. From 1926 on the Jenny was replaced by the Consolidated PT–1, so solid and dependable that it earned the nickname "Trusty." It was perhaps too easy to fly and so allowed some students of dubious capability to pass on to their next stage of training. The transition from primary training to operational aircraft was handled principally in DH–4Ms. (M for modernized by Boeing).

Winning Airmen

While outstanding aircraft were few and far between in the 1920s, the U.S. Army's aircrews waved the air power flag as much as possible and recorded outstanding performances in the process. Faster, farther, higher, longer—American airmen were prominent among those who struggled to push back the frontiers of flight.

Speed was always exciting and a race, even if bizarre, was guaranteed to attract the press. In 1921 Hap Arnold, who commanded Crissy Field at the Presidio in San Francisco at the time, challenged a flock of homing pigeons to beat his DH–4 back from Portland to San Francisco. Since Arnold neglected to warm up his engine beforehand, the result was nearly a fiasco. Forty-five minutes elapsed after the pigeons had been released before he induced the cranky Liberty to start. Saving the Air Service's pride, Arnold overtook the pigeons en route and was hailed the winner.

More serious Army races began in 1920. Billy Mitchell fervently believed that competition and record achievements benefitted the air power cause. They garnered good publicity and helped to drive the development of better aircraft and engines. He encouraged McCook's engineers to design an Army aircraft specifically for air race competition. The result,

The Loening OA–1A. The aircraft merged fuselage and hull as a single structure to gain the qualities of a small flying boat, but added retractable wheels to become an amphibian. The need to keep the propeller clear of the hull meant that the inevitable Liberty engine was inverted.

The Loening OA–1A San Francisco, *one of five amphibians sent on the 22,000-mile Pan American Goodwill Tour of 1926 and 1927. Its pilots were Captain Ira Eaker (shown here) and Lieutenant Muir Fairchild. Both officers became generals in World War II, Eaker rising to command first the Eighth Air Force and then the Mediterranean Allied Air Forces.*

a chunky little biplane powered by a hefty Packard engine of 600 horsepower, was designed by Alfred Verville and designated VCP–R. On Thanksgiving Day 1920, the biplane, flown by Lieutenant Corliss Moseley, won the first Pulitzer Trophy race at the disappointingly low average speed of 156.54 miles per hour. However, the Army had tasted success and would set a pattern. After missing the 1921 Pulitzer because of insufficient funds, its flyers became regular entrants and were successful more often than not, winning in 1922, 1924, and 1925. In the 1922 race, Curtiss R–6s flown by Lieutenants Russell Maughan and Lester Maitland finished first and second, and afterwards Billy Mitchell used Maughan's racer to set a new world's speed record of 222.97 miles per hour. On the strength of that showing, Curtiss became the prime contractor for the next Air Service fighter, and the R–6 parented the Hawk series.

The 1925 Pulitzer race, held at Mitchel Field, New York, was the Army's last because after that year Billy Mitchell was no longer on the scene, and research and development funds were spent elsewhere. The Air Service exited with a flourish, Lieutenant Cyrus Bettis winning with a Curtiss R3C–1 at 248.98 miles per hour. Waiting in the wings as backup was a man who became one of the country's greatest military aviation figures—Lieutenant James "Jimmy" Doolittle. In the days preceding the race, he and Bettis had advertised it by flying over and through New York City. As Doolittle recalled later: "It was a rare thrill to fly down the city streets and look up at the tall buildings. It was also interesting to do it inverted."

Doolittle Belies his Name

Twelve days after Bettis won in the Pulitzer, it was Jimmy Doolittle's turn. Much to the U.S. Navy's

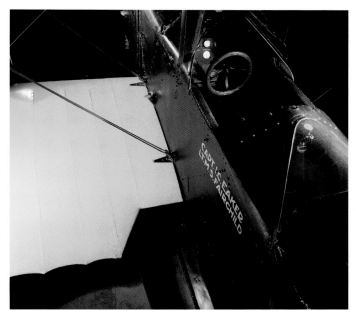

Loening OA–1A cockpit. San Francisco, the USAF Museum's Loening OA–1A, was flown by Ira Eaker and Muir Fairchild on the Mackay Trophy winning Pan-American Goodwill Tour of 1926 and 1927.

chagrin, he flew the same Curtiss racer, now the R3C–2 because it had been fitted with floats, to leave the opposition in his wake in an over-water race, the 1925 Schneider Trophy. Winning over the Chesapeake Bay course, Doolittle, who had never flown a seaplane before, set world seaplane closed-course speed records for 100 and 200 kilometers; the next day he took the outright world seaplane speed record at 245.71 miles per hour. Returning to home base at McCook Field,

Doolittle was dressed in a naval uniform by insistent colleagues and paraded through the streets of Dayton in a boat bearing signs saying: "Admiral James H. Doolittle."

It was not the first time Jimmy Doolittle had been in the news, and it was a long way from being the last. Although he could be an inspired and wonderfully disciplined pilot, he himself admitted to being something of a mischief maker. He had bent a few rules and had wrecked a few aircraft in his early years and been disciplined for misbehavior several times. Once, he reminisced: "I made a $5 bet with some friends that I could sit on the axle between the wheels while [McCullough] made a landing." He won the bet but was promptly grounded for a month when his commander, Colonel Burwell, found out. Burwell, nevertheless, had an eye for talent and was generally tolerant of Doolittle's high spirits. A short time later, Doolittle amply repaid such understanding, becoming one of the outstanding aeronautical engineering students of his day. Entering the Massachusetts Institute of Technology in October 1923, he was awarded a master's degree in June 1924, and was a Doctor of Science one year later.

In the air, Jimmy Doolittle made his mark in many ways. In September 1922, after several months of preparation during which his DH–4 was extensively modified to extend its range, he became the first man to cross the United States in less than a day, flying from Pablo Beach, Florida, to San Diego in 22 hours

Jimmy Doolittle in the cockpit of the Consolidated NY–2. To test blind flying instruments and radio aids, on 24 September 1929, Doolittle took the NY–2 through a flight from takeoff to touchdown on instruments alone. They included three new devices—which he helped to develop—an accurate altimeter, a directional gyro, and an artificial horizon.

Fokker T–2. The first non-stop aerial crossing of the United States was achieved in May 1923 by Lieutenants John Macready and Oakley Kelly in a Fokker T–2. Powered by a single 400-horsepower Liberty engine, the slab-sided T–2 covered the 2,520 miles between Long Island and San Diego at a less-than-brisk average of 94 miles per hour.

and 35 minutes, including a stop of 85 minutes at San Antonio. In 1927 flying a Curtiss P–1, he became the first pilot to complete an outside loop. In 1928 he headed a blind flight laboratory at Mitchel Field, New York, at the start of a year in which he carried out test flying of immense value to aviators everywhere. By September 1929 he had evolved a cockpit layout which included three new instruments—an accurate altimeter, a directional gyro, and an artificial horizon. Radio aids had been developed to home an aircraft onto a runway. On 24 September Doolittle succeeded in flying a specially equipped Consolidated NY–2 through a complete flight, from takeoff to landing, while "under the hood" and unable to refer to anything outside the cockpit. "It was," he said, "the first time an airplane had taken off, flown over a set course and landed on instruments alone." The *New York Times* greeted the achievement with prematurely euphoric headlines: "Blind Plane Flies 15 Miles and Lands, Fog Peril Overcome."

Around-the-World Flight passing over Grants Tomb, New York City, September 8, 1924.

Fokker T–2. After World War I, Fokker T–2s were among the aircraft used by the newly-formed Air Reserve and aviation units of the Reserve Officer Training Corps and the National Guard in training programs throughout the nation.

Premature certainly, but the achievement was real enough. Jimmy Doolittle's work had shown the way to a reliable method of defeating the weather or flying at night, and aviation had become safer because of it.

Range and Endurance

After Doolittle's coast-to-coast success, long-distance flying by military aircraft grew ever more ambitious. Establishing routes, it provided vital information for the rapid deployment of aircraft within and beyond the limits of the continental United States. In 1922 Lieutenants Oakley Kelly and John Macready set out in the coffin-shaped Fokker T–2 across the continent non-stop. On their first attempt, they took off from Rockwell Field, San Diego, but could not coax the heavily laden T–2 over the hills. Not wishing to waste the occasion, they settled down to break the world's endurance record. They landed over 35 hours later, having surpassed the record by almost nine hours. After modifying the aircraft at McCook Field, they tried again in April 1923, and set a new world mark of 36 hours, 4 minutes, and 34 seconds. The following month, they took off on another transcontinental flight, this time in the opposite direction, from Roosevelt Field on Long Island. A little less than 27 hours later, they touched down in San Diego, exhausted but jubilant. The Air Service acclaimed the accomplishment and the aviators showed that moving men, ammunition, and supplies during a national emergency from one coast to the other in one day was feasible. Of course, the Air Service exaggerated slightly. The crossing was achieved by two carefully prepared pilots, and the specially modified T–2 they flew had so much trouble just lifting its own fuel it could not have carried any cargo, but at least it held a vision of the future.

The T–2's record did not last long. The problem of lifting enough fuel to stay airborne for long periods had been exercising airmen for some time and

Hap Arnold's engineering officer at Rockwell Field believed he had a solution. As Arnold himself reported: "There were no precedents to follow. The idea itself was simple—send up one plane and send up another when needed, carrying gas, oil, water, or food to be transferred to the duration plane." After a couple of false starts, Lieutenants Lowell Smith and John Richter did just that in a DH–4B on 27 August 1923. The servicing aircraft, a second DH–4, flew above trailing fuel or oil hoses, or a rope for food and messages. Richter grabbed the hose or rope and received what they transferred while Smith steadied the aircraft. It was all very crude, but it worked and the DH–4B stayed in the air for 37 hours and 15 minutes. They had earned the endurance record, but, more important, they had demonstrated the basics of a technique that would be essential to the future of military aviation.

In another year for epic distance flights, 1924, Lieutenant Russell Maughan, inspired by Doolittle's coast-to-coast crossing in 1922 and his own victory in the Pulitzer later that same year, flew a Curtiss aircraft to beat the sun across the continent from east to west. Preparatory work and false starts out of the way, he left Mitchel Field, New York, half an hour after official twilight on 23 June 1924 and, with stops at Dayton, St. Joseph, North Platte, Cheyenne and Salduro, passed over Crissy Field, San Francisco, with just one minute to spare before official dusk.

Around the World

As Maughan battled his way west, an even greater epic was in the making. Once the U.S. Navy's NC–4 and the Vickers Vimy of Alcock and Brown conquered the Atlantic, airmen the world over considered the possibility of flying around the world. The competition to be first was international. In the United States, both the Navy and the Army had thought about it, but it was the Army that prevailed, better able to find out about operating over long distances in

Douglas World Cruiser flight montage. The USAF Museum has commemorated the achievement of the first around-the-world flyers in a display of artifacts left by some of the U.S. Army Air Corps men who took part in that epic 1924 flight. Among items displayed are Leigh Wade's jacket, helmet, and gloves, and John Harding's bible, diary, and cigarette case. Erik Nelson is represented by a pennant given to him by a rival around-the-world airman, Antonio Locatelli of Italy.

100

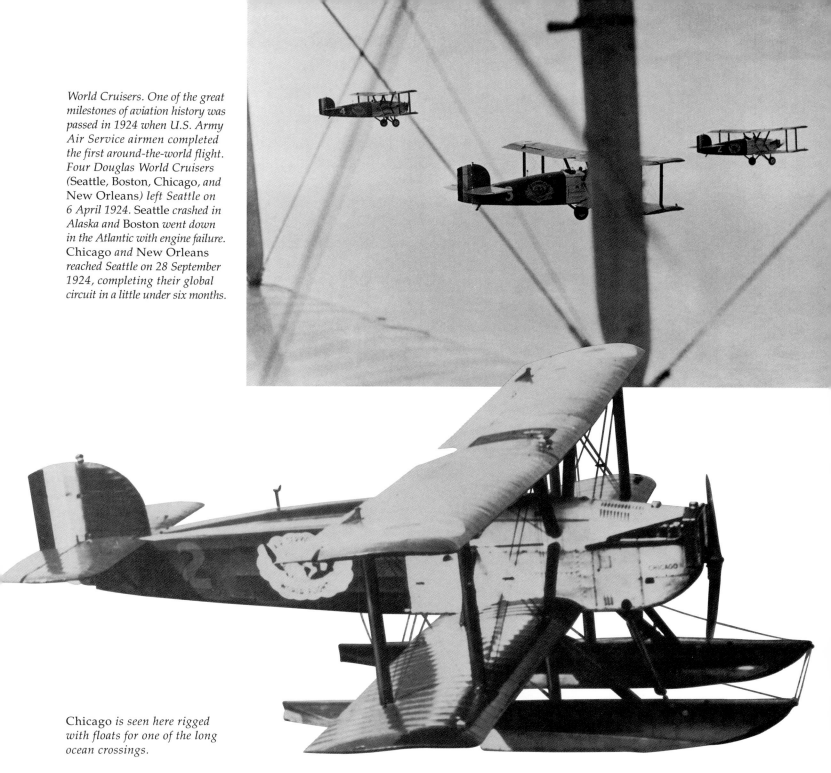

World Cruisers. One of the great milestones of aviation history was passed in 1924 when U.S. Army Air Service airmen completed the first around-the-world flight. Four Douglas World Cruisers (Seattle, Boston, Chicago, *and* New Orleans) *left Seattle on 6 April 1924.* Seattle *crashed in Alaska and* Boston *went down in the Atlantic with engine failure.* Chicago *and* New Orleans *reached Seattle on 28 September 1924, completing their global circuit in a little under six months.*

Chicago *is seen here rigged with floats for one of the long ocean crossings.*

different climates. Unspoken was the obvious point that success in such a venture would produce wonderful publicity for the Air Service.

The Air Service prepared for the flight by shipping all manner of spare parts and tools to various points along the proposed route, getting clearances from the foreign governments involved, positioning rescue ships and dispatching officers to collect local information and arrange for supplies. It also obtained aircraft capable of getting the job done—the Douglas World Cruiser (DWC), designed by Donald Douglas and based on his rugged Liberty-engined DT–2 Navy floatplane. The DWC was a big, two-seated,

open-cockpit biplane with a fuel capacity of 450 gallons, enough for well over 1,000 miles in still air. Since its cruising speed was not much more than 80 miles per hour, the Army was prepared to take time in the venture, ordering five DWCs, four to make the flight plus one spare.

Led by Major Frederick Martin, a formation of four DWCs—christened *Seattle, Chicago, Boston,* and *New Orleans*—left Seattle on 6 April 1924 and headed for Alaska. There they suffered a serious blow when Martin crashed *Seattle* into a mountain obscured by fog on the long Alaskan Peninsula. He and his mechanic survived, and the flight continued with

The Loening OA–1A Detroit *during the U.S. Army Air Corps' Pan American tour of 1926 and 1927. Beset by problems, including the loss of two of five participating aircraft in a mid-air collision over Buenos Aires, the tour, nevertheless, won the Mackay Trophy for the most meritorious U.S. Army Air Corps flight of the year.*

The Fokker C–2 trimotor Bird of Paradise. *In June 1927 the* Bird of Paradise, *flown by Lieutenants Lester Maitland and Albert Hegenberger completed the first aerial crossing from California to Hawaii. Maitland and Hegenberger overcame the hazards of a 2,400-mile over-water flight to a small island with the help of radio beacons, meticulous pre-flight planning, and precise navigation.*

three aircraft, now led by Lieutenant Lowell Smith, the aerial refueling pioneer. Their route took them from Alaska via Japan, China, India, Iraq, Turkey, and across Europe to the United Kingdom. After refitting for the Atlantic crossing, Lieutenant Leigh Wade lost *Boston* through engine failure on the way to Iceland. Rescued by the USS *Richmond*, Wade and his mechanic were able to rejoin the flight in Newfoundland, where a spare DWC, now named *Boston II*, was waiting. On 28 September 1924, Lieutenants Lowell Smith and Erik Nelson succeeded in closing the circle with *Chicago* and *New Orleans*, arriving in Seattle 175 days and over 360 flying hours

after they began. Meticulous preparation combined with professionalism and determination had brought the U.S. Army Air Service the honor of being the first to fly around the world.

Flag-waving and Fuel-burning

In the late 1920s most of aviation's glory and headlines went not to Army flyers but to civilian trailblazers like Charles Lindbergh (a Reserve officer), Amelia Earhart, Wiley Post, and Charles Kingsford-Smith. Even so, the Air Corps had its achievements. In December 1926 five Loening OA–1A amphibians, led by Major Herbert Dargue, went on a goodwill

The Fokker C–2 Question Mark. *On New Year's day 1929 a crew including three men destined to be among the great names of World War II—Spatz, Eaker, and Quesada—took off from Los Angeles to see how long they could stay airborne. In a Fokker C–2 emblazoned with a large question mark, they flew for over 150 hours, undergoing 37 refuelings by a team of DH–4Bs. The exercise demonstrated that range and bomber payload could be increased by air-to-air refueling.*

tour of South America. It was not trouble-free. Two crew members were killed in a midair collision over Buenos Aires in which Dargue bailed out to survive, and in more than one place the flyers met anti-American demonstrators. Dargue struggled on through break-downs and diplomatic crises to complete the tour in May 1927, having visited most of the countries in Central and South America plus a host of Caribbean islands. It was his misfortune that he reached the United States in time to be overshadowed by Lindbergh after his Atlantic crossing.

Two other Air Corps exploits did attract headlines. In June 1927 Lieutenants Lester Maitland and Albert Hegenberger flew a Fokker C–2 tri-motor, *Bird of Paradise,* in a 2,400-mile trip over 25 hours and 50 minutes from San Francisco to Oahu. They enjoyed the benefit of several advances in aviation since 1924— radios and radio beacons at departure and arrival points, an earth indicator compass, magnetic compasses, and drift sights for aircraft. Lindbergh

commented that the trip was "the most perfectly organized and carefully planned flight ever attempted." The Fokker C–2 also figured in a return to endurance flying in 1929. On New Year's Day, the extraordinarily talented crew of Major Carl "Tooey" Spatz, Captain Ira Eaker, Lieutenant Harry Halverson, Lieutenant Elwood "Pete" Quesada, and Staff Sergeant Roy Hooe, got airborne from Los Angeles in a C–2A with a large question mark painted on its fuselage. The question was: How long could they stay in the air? Using crude techniques developed for the DH–4s in 1923, they completed 37 contacts with their refueling aircraft, staying aloft for 150 hours and 40 minutes, and landing on 7 January 1929. They were well satisfied, and Spatz noted in his report that, with aerial refueling, a bomber's radius of action "has scarcely any limit at all." The *New York Post* reported that the flight had opened "a new chapter in the history of aviation." The *Washington Star*, with great foresight, predicted an eventual non-stop flight around the world.[9]

The crew of the Question Mark, *fresh from their record-breaking endurance flight, 1929. The Army airmen braved fog, cold, darkness, fatigue, and a difficult aerial refueling technique. To keep their Fokker trimotor light they sacrificed radio communications with the ground, leaving the necessary heavy equipment behind.* Left to right: *Unknown person, Major Carl Spatz, Captain Ira Eaker, Lieutenant Harry Halverson, Lieutenant Elwood Quesada, and Staff Sergeant Roy Hooe.*

An immediate result to all the publicity for the *Question Mark* was a rush of competitors, over 40 by the end of 1929, and the year closed with a small private aircraft, the *St. Louis Robin,* in the prime spot after a flight of 420 hours and 21 minutes. The contest had assumed the status of a circus act, and the Air Corps was no longer interested. Tooey Spatz and the *Question Mark* had told them all they needed to know and offered a glimpse of the future for military aviation.

Into the Stratosphere
The efforts of American military airmen to fly faster, farther, and longer were matched by those of others to fly higher. This proved unusually hazardous, as McCook test pilot Major Rudolph Schroeder found

out on 27 February 1920. Flying a LePere LUSAC 11 with a supercharged Liberty engine, he ran out of oxygen above 30,000 feet and collapsed. The aircraft fell over five miles before he revived sufficiently to land at McCook Field, but his eyes were frozen open. Recovering in a hospital, he learned that he had reached the world's record altitude of 33,143 feet for his pains. Lieutenant John Macready, known for his part in the first non-stop coast-to-coast flight, took over from Schroeder and in 1921 pushed the record to 34,508 feet. At the time, the press speculated seriously that Macready might climb high enough to escape into Earth orbit![10]

In 1927 the Air Corps' pursuit of altitude research by balloon ended in disaster. Captain Hawthorne Gray

Triple Mackay Trophy winner John Macready bundled up in high-altitude clothing before taking the LePere LUSAC 11 to unheard of heights. In 1921 Macready pushed the world altitude record to 34,508 feet. A worrying public feared he might actually escape into Earth orbit!

made a number of very high ascents in an open balloon basket. On one occasion he bailed out after collapsing at more than 40,000 feet, coming to with the balloon falling rapidly. Although his instruments showed that he had attained 42,470 feet he was denied an international record because he was not with the balloon when it came to earth. Trying again, his instruments showed that he once more rose to 42,470 feet, but this time he died from lack of oxygen as he descended. Sadly, he was refused the world's record a second time because, as the Federation Aeronautique Internationale explained, the aeronaut "was not in personal possession of his instruments" when he landed.

In the late 1920s the Air Corps continued high-altitude research flights in aircraft, but seemed to learn the lessons of upper air slowly, if at all. Reaching altitudes of more than 35,000 feet several times, its pilots still flew in open cockpits bundled up ineffectively against the extreme cold, and they quite often collapsed,

reviving only when they descended into thicker air. (Jimmy Doolittle estimated being unconscious for 30 minutes on one occasion.) A thoroughly systematic method of investigation into the physiological and psychological effects of low pressures and temperatures on human beings still lay some years ahead.

Safety Measures

At the beginning of the 1920s, airmen simply shrugged off the hazards of flying open-cockpit biplanes with unreliable engines over all sorts of country in every kind of weather and viewed safety improvements like the turn-and-slip indicator with suspicion. Pilots proud of their ability to "fly by the seat of their pants" resisted trusting instruments more than their senses. They spurned parachutes, too, as less than manly. Reacting to a 1921 press report that 30 percent of airmen killed in accidents could be saved by parachutes, Major Follett Bradley wrote: "To require a pilot to wear a parachute and encourage him to employ it would foster faintheartedness." The issue came to

a head late in 1922 when, within a period of three weeks, two pilots at McCook Field, Lieutenants Harold Harris and Frank Tyndall, became the first Air Service airmen to escape from disintegrating aircraft by using parachutes. As a consequence, the Air Service issued regulations requiring anyone flying an Army aircraft to have a parachute, and the McCook Field Parachute Unit was formed. It preceded a new association that would grow into an international brotherhood. It was called the Caterpillar Club, for people who had saved their lives by using a parachute.

Patrols and Good Works

Behind newsmaking events, Army airmen were kept busy in exercises and maneuvers for gunnery, bombing, and unit mobility. Army aircraft were routinely used to move men and supplies between bases, and the growing cross-country traffic led to the establishment of airways, additional landing grounds, and weather stations. Operating from basic facilities in rough country, squadrons flew regular patrols along the Mexican border, an experience remembered by one pilot as "a life of hardship, possible death, starvation pay, and a lonely life without social contacts, in hot barren wastes, tortured by sun, wind and sand." Some airmen joined the Forest Service patrolling western woodlands, looking for forest fires and directing fire-fighters, and others were pioneer crop sprayers, helping the Department of Agriculture to combat threats like the boll weevil. Air Service aircraft were detached to assist several U.S. government agencies by mapping surveys, photographing in days areas that might have consumed years if tackled on the ground.

Billy Mitchell was particularly enthusiastic about mapping, estimating that the Air Service could conduct it aerially at one-tenth the cost and in one-hundredth the time required by any other method. He also encouraged the Air Service to promote its public image while helping in emergencies. As a result, its aircraft bombed ice jams and lava flows, flew search and rescue missions, dropped emergency food supplies to flood victims, or delivered medical supplies wherever most needed. These and more personal efforts by the Air Service were much appreciated. One pilot flew over a house where a fire was developing. Since nobody appeared to be reacting, he landed in a nearby field, ran to the house, and knocked on the front door. The owner was surprised but grateful to be told by this ministering angel: "Mister, your house is on fire!"

Army aerial photography. The Army allowed its airmen to engage in what was proving to be an invaluable service—aerial photography for survey and mapping. General Mitchell tirelessly promoted the practice as spectacularly efficient and cost effective.

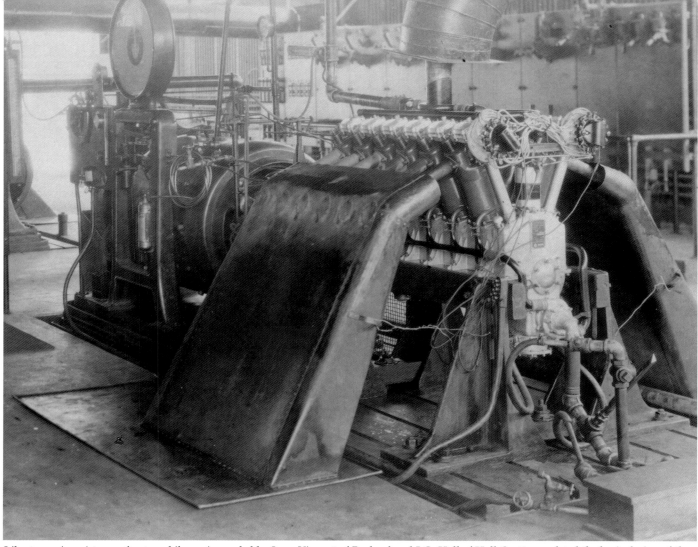

Liberty engine. A team of automobile engineers led by Jesse Vincent of Packard and J.G. Hall of Hall-Scott completed the basic design of the Liberty engine in a Washington hotel suite during an intensely active week in May 1917.

Changing an engine on a P–12 in the field—simply a matter of putting a block and tackle in the right place.

Hap Arnold seen here with one of the more than 20,000 Liberty engines produced. While stocks lasted, the Liberty found its way into most American military aircraft designs, eventually becoming something of a drag on technological progress.

Originally conceived as an eight-cylinder engine, the Liberty went into production as a V–12, producing 400 horsepower. Enough Libertys were built—20,478—to remain the backbone of American military aviation until the late 1920s. The USAF Museum's example is the last Liberty to have served with the U.S. Army Air Corps.

109

Orville Wright and a DH–4. Although quiet and reserved, Orville Wright remained involved in aviation until his death in 1948. He is shown, left, in the early 1920s before flying in a DH–4 with pilot Howard Rinehart.

Air Power Debated

Mitchell, the fiery war leader and strident air power prophet, was a hero to most Army airmen, but even his closest admirers wished he could advance his cause less abrasively. Many came to believe that his no-holds-barred approach had been counterproductive, making more enemies than friends, and that his sacrifice in the heat of political battle had occurred when he had little to show for it. While there may be some truth in that belief, it is equally true that Mitchell's persistence kept the air power debate alive. By the time he resigned in February 1926, many of the air power seeds he had helped to plant were on their way to at least partial fruition.

During 1924 and 1925, the Lampert Committee of the House of Representatives investigated the operations of all U.S. air services, taking up where the neglected Lassiter Board had left off as far as military aviation was concerned. After 11 months of hearings, the Lampert Committee found for an independent air force and increased spending on new flying equipment. However, to draw the Lampert Committee's sting and offset its supposed sympathy for Mitchell's arguments, President Coolidge ordered an inquiry of his own. Appointed by the President in September 1925, the Morrow Board reached its conclusions in less than three months and published its findings two weeks before the Lampert Committee. It did not agree that air power was a decisive instrument of war and did not recommend the formation of a separate air force. The President, and eventually Congress, generally accepted more of Morrow's ideas than Lampert's. Some of the news, but not all, was bad from the airmen's point of view. Superficially, by amending the name of the Air Service to Air Corps and creating an additional Assistant Secretary of War to foster military aeronautics, the Air Corps Act of July 1926 improved the status of Army aviation, but not much had really changed in terms of how air power was to be used. On the other hand, the Act authorized a five-year Air Corps expansion program.

However, there was no money immediately available to begin the expansion, so it was delayed, to run from July 1927 to June 1932. Its goal was to reach a level of 1,650 officers, 15,000 enlisted men, and 1,800 serviceable aircraft from a starting point of 919 officers, 8,725 enlisted men, and a total aircraft strength of less than 1,000. The Air Corps drew up hopeful plans, but money shortages persisted throughout the five year program. Americans were not inclined to increase military spending at a time when they held isolationist and pacifist views strongly and were convinced that no foreign power posed a threat to national security. With the onset of the Great Depression, federal revenues declined and with them adequate Air Corps funds. When June 1932 arrived, it was no surprise that the goals set in 1927 had not been achieved. Shortfalls were substantial—396 more officers and 1,940 enlisted men were needed. Throughout the period, politicians, the Army General Staff, and the Air Corps argued endlessly about what "1,800 serviceable aircraft" really meant. Did that figure include trainers, aircraft for the National Guard and Reserve, obsolete aircraft, those being used for research or held to cover annual wastage, or those undergoing major servicing? There were no easy answers, and in June 1932 the politicians and the Army General Staff reached a figure of 1,814 "serviceable aircraft" over Air Corps objections, counting those on hand for the Army, National Guard, and Reserve, and including 210 aircraft being overhauled. However, they made some progress, altering the balance of the front line to 16 pursuit, 12 bombardment, 4 attack, and 13 observation squadrons. The alteration was not quite what the Air Corps had been after, but it was noticeably better than before.

Dispassionately viewed, the Air Corps was much better off than it had been at its beginning, but was a long way from the air force the Army's airmen had hoped to create. Disappointed by the past, they looked to the uncertain future. New politicians, new commanders, and new, exciting aircraft were on the horizon, all of which could change the character of the air power debate. Perhaps the 1930s would see the promise of air power fulfilled.

Notes

1. *Our Air Force, the Keystone of National Defense* by William Mitchell, 1921.
2. During the last year of the war, the Air Service suffered one death per 3,072 flying hours. In the first six months after the armistice, the rate increased to one death every 2,208 hours.
3. The original spelling of the name was Spatz, with the "a" pronounced "ah." It was legally changed in 1938 to Spaatz to ensure correct pronunciation.
4. One death in particular drew attention to one of the basic design flaws in the DH–4 and to the growth of very dangerous unofficial practices developed to overcome the aircraft's shortcomings. Its main wheels were set too far back and the aircraft, therefore, had a tendency to nose over when landing, especially on soft ground. To overcome this, some regular rear seat passengers had taken to unfastening their safety belts during landing and sliding back over the fuselage to reach the tail and hold it down. Two passengers did this in the course of the transcontinental exercise, and one was killed when thrown off.
5. In the absence of funds for new aircraft and improved equipment, the accident rate of the Air Service continued to run at an appallingly high level. Between July 1920 and June 1921, there were 330 major accidents resulting in the deaths of 69 aircrews out of a total strength of only 900.
6. Even so, lack of funds and reactionary attitudes opposed change. In 1924 the Air Service had a total of 1,364 aircraft on strength. Only 754 were in commission, and 457 of these were observation aircraft. In all, 59 bomber, 78 pursuit, and 8 attack aircraft were serviceable.
7. On 24 October 1924, after a tour of the Far East, Mitchell submitted a report to the War Department in which he stated that war with Japan was almost inevitable. In a prediction of startling accuracy, he suggested that the Japanese would strike first at Pearl Harbor: "…that is where the blow will be struck," he said, "on a fine, quiet Sunday morning."
8. A biplane in which one wing has half the area, or less, of the other.
9. Thirty years later, in February 1959, a Boeing B–50 named *Lucky Lady II* circled the globe in 94 hours, refueled by KB–29 tankers four times on the way.
10. John Macready is a largely unsung hero of the air force story whose achievements in the early 1920s were unique. He is the only man to have been awarded the Mackay Trophy three times. The trophy was established in 1912 for the most meritorious military flight of each year. Macready won his in three consecutive years: 1921 for high altitude flights; 1922 for a T–2 endurance record; and 1923 for a transcontinental non-stop flight. He also represented the Air Service in the Pulitzer races, made the first emergency parachute jump at night, was the second man to fly in a pressurized cabin, the first pilot to demonstrate crop dusting, and a pioneer of American aerial photographic survey.

I will not attempt to predict what advancements will be made in the next fifty to sixty years, but I will say that I believe that in aerospace nothing, absolutely nothing, is impossible. We'll just keep moving ahead.

(Major General Benny Foulois, First Chief of the Air Corps)

The best protection [for the United States] is to accept and build upon American tradition and not try to purchase freedom with gadgets.

(Secretary of War George Dern on the Air Corps' bid for strategic bombers, 1933)

Independent air missions have little effect on the issue of battle, and none upon the outcome of war.

(Findings of the Baker Board, 1934)

If [President Roosevelt] is in office when war comes he'll want to be the strategist. If he's not air-minded by that time, then God help the country.

(Billy Mitchell, 1935)

Air power is as vital a requirement to the military efficiency of a great nation as land power or sea power, and there is no hope for victory in war for a nation in which it is lacking.

(Major General Frank Andrews, 1938)

Chapter 4
Strategies and Demarcations

The Changing Shapes of Air Power

Covering the years of the 1930s, the USAF Museum shows that great changes lay ahead for American military aviation. A beautifully restored Martin B–10 dominates the end of the gallery and contrasts sharply with all that has gone before. The lingering images of World War I, so evident in aircraft like the P–6E, are erased in the shape of this all-metal monoplane with closed cockpits, internal bomb stowage, and retractable landing gear. Here is a machine that is linked with the future, not with the past. The Air Corps' enthusiasm for its splendid new weapon is readily apparent in an account given nearby of the flight of a B–10 formation to Alaska in 1934.

In contrast is a display on the Air Corps' ill-fated 1934 involvement in carrying the U.S. mail with inadequate equipment in the teeth of appalling winter weather. Eighteen airmen were killed in four months, but their deaths drew public attention to the parsimonious funding of the Air Corps and the resulting lack of many important capabilities.

More encouraging wall displays cover the formation of GHQ Air Force in 1935, a significant step on the road to an independent air force, and the saga of the B–17 Flying Fortress. Various early adventures with the B–17 are shown, especially two involving the young Curtis LeMay—a goodwill flight to South America in 1938 and the celebrated interception of the Italian steamship Rex in mid-Atlantic that same year. Mention is made also of the first of the super-bombers, the XB–15 and XB–19. A main-wheel from the XB–19 gives an idea of the aircraft's immense size. Other technological achievements covered include the first auto-land equipment, the first pressure cabin, and the mounting of a 75-mm cannon in a B–18. At the end of the 1930s, the United States was once again preparing to recover from years of neglecting and misunderstanding military aviation and getting set to catch up with other nations in the air. Reference is made to President Roosevelt's concerns and to the approval given by Congress in 1939 to a program for building an air force of 5,500 aircraft.

American fighters of the late 1930s are represented in the chubby, gleaming shape of the only surviving Seversky P–35A. It was the first American single-seater with metal

Hap Arnold at the controls of a B–10. He would soon be at the controls of the entire U.S. Army Air Corps as it geared up for its most grueling challenge ever in the skies over Europe and Asia during World War II.

skin, closed cockpit, and retractable landing gear. The P–35 was, nevertheless, soon overtaken by events, but its connection with its illustrious offspring, Republic's P–47 Thunderbolt, can be seen at a glance.

As the museum's inter-war story closes, another opens. The explosive beginnings of the bloodiest war in history lie just around the corner.

Decade of Change

The 1930s came to America's military airmen in several conflicting guises. An Aladdin's Cave of new developments in aviation offered a promising air power future where the predictions of prophets like Billy Mitchell might come to pass. Barring the way, however, was a slough of despond. It hid in its depths the realities of major economic depression and the stultified attitudes of the "old soldiers" of the U.S. Army, either of which could crush the growth of American air power. Even if such a slough were traversed, a threat of appalling proportions loomed—war shaped by Japanese militarism in Asia and Hitlerian fascism in Europe. It seemed that aviation's Aladdin's Cave held at least part of the answers to this global holocaust, but American airmen would not find pulling clear of the slough's drag to reach the treasures very easy.

In 1931 General Foulois, who in 1910 had been the U.S. Army's only pilot and who had since been a forthright advocate for independent air power, was made Chief of the Air Corps after General Fechet. His ardor for independence was in no way diminished, but he had begun to see that "half a loaf was better than none." It seemed to him, and to a number of his senior Air Corps colleagues, that the GHQ Air Force, an interim arrangement, might be an acceptable compromise for a while. At the same time, it had occurred to the U.S. Army General Staff, whose resistance to giving the airmen a longer leash was beginning to crumble, that the creation of a GHQ Air Force might subdue the clamor for independence in the continuing and wearing struggle over air power. The seeds of the idea had taken root, but it would be some years before they would bear fruit. Some of that fruit, to the airmen, would be quite sour.

In November 1930 General Douglas MacArthur became Chief of Staff and almost immediately sought a way to end the bickering of the Army and Navy over the responsibility of operating military aircraft. On 9 January 1931 MacArthur and the Chief of Naval Operations, Admiral William Pratt, reached an agreement. A press release stated:

> The naval air forces will be based on the fleet and move with it as an important element in performing the essential missions of the forces afloat. The Army air forces will be land based and employed as an element of the Army in carrying out its mission of defending the coasts, both in the homeland and in overseas possessions.

MacArthur felt that the arrangement enabled "the air component of each service to proceed with its own planning, training, and procurement activities with little danger of duplicating those of its sister service." He may indeed have believed that his imposing presence had been all that was necessary to remove a long-standing thorn in the side of interservice relationships, but the events of later years would prove his satisfaction premature.

In mid-1933 Admiral Pratt retired and his successor, Admiral Standley, could hardly wait to repudiate the agreement. The Navy proceeded to develop land planes of its own for the defense of America's coastline while the General Staff went on planning for an Army role in airborne coastal defense. The Air Corps built its case for long-range, reconnaissance-capable aircraft for missions over water, insisting that they were needed to intercept and destroy attacking enemy ships. The airmen hoped that the remarkable similarity between aircraft, essentially defensive, and their Holy Grail of a strategic bomber force, unquestionably offensive, would not be too obvious.

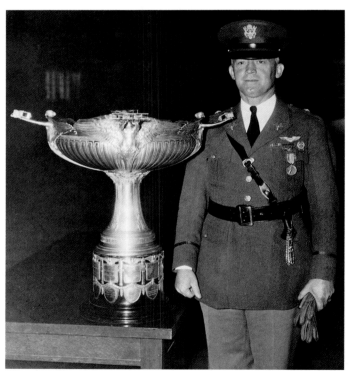

Hap Arnold and the Mackay Trophy, 1934. Brigadier General Arnold was awarded the trophy for the Air Corps' outstanding aerial achievement of the year—the 6-day, 4,000-mile Alaska flight. He lead a squadron of 10 B–10s from Washington. D.C. to Fairbanks on an unprecedented trip that proved that aircraft could be deployed quickly to far-away destinations and resulted in the photographic survey of huge tracts—over 20,000 square miles—of the Alaska Territory.

B–9 and P–26 escort. The Boeing B–9 was a private-venture development of the Monomail freight carrier. With an all-metal stressed skin and retractable undercarriage, it had a top speed of 188 miles per hour and was a notable advance in bomber design when it first flew in 1931. It was, however, overshadowed by the Martin B–10, which flew only months later.

Metal Monoplanes

Strategic air power had been hampered in the 1920s by the state of the art in bomber design and construction, but the introduction of techniques that were little short of revolutionary in the 1930s promised dramatic advances in aircraft performance and the steady eclipse of the biplane. Aircraft could go higher, faster, and farther than ever before. The Boeing B–9 in 1931 was a foretaste of things to come, but even this remarkable aircraft was overshadowed by the appearance only a few months later of the Martin B–10. The B–10 embodied so many new techniques and devices that it stands out as one of the most significant single advances in the history of military aircraft. Here for the first time was a cantilevered, all-metal monoplane of stressed-skin construction with wing flaps, retractable landing gear, enclosed cockpits, a glazed gun turret, variable pitch propellers, low-drag engine cowlings, and an internal bomb bay with power-driven doors. Even the underpowered prototype outran every fighter in service. Its bombload of a little over one ton could have been bigger, and its combat range was only 700 miles, but the B–10 was rightly seen as the harbinger of an American air power spring. It quickly became the Air Corps' front-line bomber for aggressive long-range reconnaissance.

It had no sooner entered service than it was used in a series of exercises to demonstrate the flexibility of air power in a deployment to Alaska. On 19 July 1934, ten B–10s commanded by Colonel Hap Arnold left Bolling Field, Washington, D.C., and flew in easy stages to Alaska. They landed at Fairbanks six days later, but they had covered more than 4,000 miles in just over 25 hours of flying time without any problems. After conducting a 20,000-square-mile photographic

General Henry "Hap" Arnold (1886–1950). In 1934, as a colonel, Hap Arnold put on a heavy flight suit and led a squadron of B–10s to Alaska. By 1938 he was Chief of the U.S. Army Air Corps, and in 1949 he became the only airman ever to be promoted to five-star rank.

survey of Alaska, they flew back to Bolling Field—without any problems. More than half a century later, when air travel to Alaska is commonplace, the B–10 flight remains a considerable achievement. Hap Arnold was awarded his second Mackay Trophy and

Martin B–10s. Delivery of B–10 bombers went on until 1936 and they continued to serve with U.S. Army Air Corps squadrons for several years thereafter. These pictured were photographed near San Francisco, California, in January 1940.

Martin B–10. One of the most significant advances in the history of military aircraft, the B–10 combined for the first time all-metal stressed skin construction, cantilever monoplane wings, flaps, and retractable landing gear. Its cockpits and rotating gun turret were fully glazed. During trials in 1932, the new bomber proved too fast for pursuing U.S. Army Air Corps fighters and it was immediately ordered into production, first reaching squadron service in 1934. The USAF Museum's B–10 is the only surviving example.

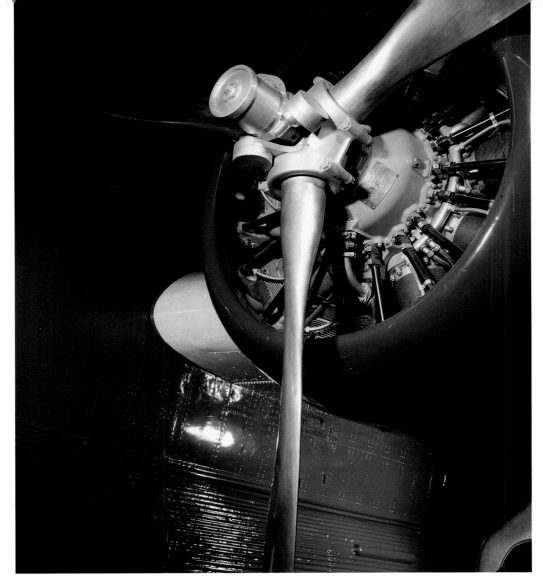

B–10 engine. The Martin B–10 was powered by two Wright R–1820 Cyclone engines of 775 horsepower each. Note the variable pitch propellers and advanced engine cowls.

B–10 bomb doors. Among the B–10's innovations was an internal bomb-bay with power-driven doors.

Air Mail. Hap Arnold's cheerful smile for the camera could not have lasted long. Instructed to take over responsibility for delivering air mail in February 1934, the U.S. Army Air Corps suffered 66 crashes in three months. The uproar that followed was instrumental in forcing Congress to find the funds for much needed improvements in Air Corps equipment and training.

a citation that singled out the overwater leg from Juneau to Seattle for "...linking the Territory of Alaska with the United States by air, without a stop on foreign territory, for the first time."[1]

Such bright spots aside, the Air Corps was hit hard by the depression of the early 1930s and was forced to abandon its annual maneuvers, reduce flying hours sharply, stop live weapons training, and cut pay. Accident rates went up. On the other hand, the government's public relief programs provided money and labor for major works, such as building or improving military airfields.

Against these problems, the GHQ Air Force began to take shape. In 1933 the U.S. Army reorganized its land forces into four field armies, to which, it believed, the combat units of the Air Corps could respond more effectively if they answered directly to the General

Staff, instead of to individual field commanders. As General Foulois formed a headquarters unit for GHQ Air Force in Washington in October of that year his and the Air Corps' attention were drawn in another, temporarily more pressing, direction.

Flying the Mail

Irregularities in air mail contracts with the commercial airlines led to their cancellation by President Roosevelt in February 1934. While new contracts were being drawn up, he asked the Air Corps to step into the breach and fly the mail, giving General Foulois ten days to create the necessary organization, assign and position men and equipment, prepare aircraft, and begin training pilots on the routes they would follow. Foulois divided the United States into three zones, setting up commands at Salt Lake City under Hap Arnold, and at Chicago and New York under

Lieutenant Colonel Horace Hickam and Major Byron Jones. This rush prompted a number of dire predictions, including some from Eddie Rickenbacker, then vice president of North American Aviation. He pointed out that commercial airlines employed experienced and well-trained pilots in aircraft specifically designed for their job. He warned: "Either [Air Corps pilots] are going to pile up ships all the way across the continent, or they're not going to be able to fly the mail on schedule."

The words were hardly out of Rickenbacker's mouth before the first accident was reported. On 20 February 1934 the Air Corps was to take over as the official U.S. mail carrier, but on 16 February two pilots leaving California in a Curtiss A–12 attack aircraft to position themselves at Salt Lake City, were killed when they flew into a snowstorm-hidden mountain in Utah. A few hours later, the pilot of a Douglas B–7 died when he hit the ground in Idaho at night. Rickenbacker was not reticent about saying he had told them so. The next day he called what had happened "legalized murder!"

The weather that winter was the worst in many years, and Air Corps pilots took it on in open cockpits with poor instrumentation, inadequate navigation aids, and almost inevitable results. A little more than three months after having been assigned the burden of carrying the mail, the Air Corps was relieved of it on 1 June 1934. During that time 66 crashes had killed 18 men—12 on mail routes and another 6 on training or ferrying flights. Fifteen others were hospitalized for injuries.

The Air Corps' air mail fiasco caused an uproar and focused the attention of everyone, including President Roosevelt. Foulois later recalled that at one stage he and General MacArthur had been summoned to the President's bedside to endure "…a tongue-lashing which I put down in my book as the worst I ever received in all my military service." When the whole unpleasant adventure was over, recriminations dragged on for months and eventually led, in December 1935, to Benny Foulois' resignation. There were, however, other more positive effects. Foulois himself felt that both the President and Congress were compelled by public outcry to face the need to improve the Air Corps, basing the provision of additional funds on the report of the 1934 Baker Board. The board had readily acknowledged the shortcomings of the Air Corps' equipment but praised the valiance with which the Air Corps' pilots had tackled an inappropriate task. It suggested major improvements in all forms of equipment and

In 1931 General Foulois, who in 1910 had been the U.S. Army's only pilot and who had since been a forthright advocate for independent air power, was made Chief of the Air Corps after General Fechet.

recommended that aircrews should receive more training in night and bad weather flying and radio navigation and that they should average a minimum of 300 hours of flying a year. Foulois saw the board's report as "…the first comprehensive outline of War Department policy with respect to aviation that the Army has ever had." He felt strongly that the air mail pilots had not died in vain. Without their sacrifice, Foulois believed, the United States would have been as unprepared in the air in 1941 as it had been in 1917.

GHQ Air Force
Although the Baker Board's report was helpful to the Air Corps, overall, it expressed little conviction on the importance of air power. Noting "…the limitations of the airplane," it stated: "The idea that aviation, acting alone, can control the sea lanes, or defend the coast, or produce decisive results…are all visionary, as is the idea that a very large and independent air force is necessary to defend our country." A lone board member recorded a dissenting view. Jimmy Doolittle, then with Shell Oil, told the world that most of the members of the board knew "…as much about the future of aviation as they do about the

B–15 and P–26 escort. The accompanying P–26 accentuates the fact that Boeing's XB–15 was very large, with a wingspan of 149 feet. It proved too large for the engines of the 1930s and was a lumbering performer, but it was invaluable in paving the way for the later B–29.

sign writing of Aztecs." More formally he asserted: "I believe that the future security of our nation is dependent upon an adequate air force," and he reaffirmed his view that such an air force would be more effective if developed as a separate arm of the military.

Boosted by the Baker Board's findings, the move to create a GHQ Air Force resumed where it had been interrupted by the requirement to fly the mail. Other currents in the wider world spurred the building of a more powerful and responsive air arm. By 1933 militarism was rampant in both Japan and Germany. The Japanese were flexing their military muscles in China and Hitler had pulled Germany out of the Disarmament Conference in Geneva. Although understandably concerned with domestic issues and essentially isolationist, many Americans recognized that the United States could not afford to ignore the implications of what was happening in Europe and Asia.

On 1 March 1935, one week before Hitler announced the existence of the Luftwaffe, Brigadier General Frank Andrews assumed command of the GHQ

Air Force and set up his headquarters at Langley Field, Virginia. On the face of it, the new command and that of the Chief of the Air Corps were of equal status, both answering directly to the General Staff. GHQ Air Force oversaw operational affairs. Training and logistics remained under the Air Corps. Administrative jurisdiction over the airmen's bases was given to local Army corps commanders. Base commanders confronted the predicament of reporting to several different chiefs. This arrangement was severely flawed and created wrangling about responsibilities and chains of command, which continued throughout the tenure of Major General Oscar Westover, Foulois' successor as Chief of the Air Corps. It was not until Frank Andrews left GHQ Air Force in March 1939 that the organization was finally changed to unify U.S. Army aviation under a single chain of command.

Troubles with Strategic Bombers

Arguments over the way they should be organized never diverted military airmen from their goal of building a strategic bomber force. In 1934 the War Department agreed to an Air Corps project to

121

not too concerned that a strategic bomber might be hiding behind the screen of long-range reinforcement and reconnaissance.

The new project, undertaken by Boeing, grew into a monster of an aircraft—the XB–15–with a 149-foot wing span and 70,000-pound gross weight. Its sheer size made it an experimental enterprise in every sense of the word. Boeing engineers had new problems to solve at each stage of the aircraft's construction. They spent three and a half years finishing it, then found that their design had outrun available engine technology. The XB–15 was underpowered and, therefore, doomed. Only one example was ever built. Nevertheless, it was enormously helpful in paving the way for two other Boeing bombers that would leave their mark on aviation history in World War II.

On the heels of the XB–15 contract came another, sweeping Boeing into another competition. With the B–10 only recently in service, the Air Corps was already looking toward its replacement, a multi-engined bomber able to carry at least a ton of bombs over a range of 1,020 miles at a speed of 200 miles per hour (although a range of 2,500 miles and a speed of 250 miles per hour were preferred). Adding spice to its challenge in August 1934, the Air Corps required prospective bidders to provide their aircraft in time to compete at Wright Field in exactly one year.

Three companies complied. Martin appeared with the B–12, little more than an updated B–10. Douglas offered the DB–1, a twin-engined bomber developed from the successful DC–2 airliner. Boeing, however, stole the show with a completely new four-engined aircraft. Its Model 299 flew in non-stop from Seattle, averaging 232 miles per hour on the way. Two months

develop a larger, longer-range aircraft than the B–10. It would be designed to reinforce either coast of the United States or its overseas possessions without refueling. Surprisingly for an old soldier, General MacArthur encouraged the move, calling "…the bombardment airplane…the most important element of the GHQ Air Force." He added that the heavy bomber "…makes it possible to inflict damage on an enemy in the rear areas of his armies and his zone of interior, which no other weapon can do." MacArthur, unlike the rest of the General Staff, was apparently

B–17 Flying Fortresses intercepting the Italian liner, Rex, *776 miles at sea, May 12, 1938. The B–17s had departed from Mitchel Field near New York City.*

later, after exhaustive tests, the 299 was leading the competition. Then, on 30 October 1935, just after taking off for its final test flight, the 299 reared up, stalled, and crashed. Its control locks had been left engaged and the pilot could not lower the rising nose when the 299 left the ground. Boeing's hopes went up in smoke as the DB–1, now the B–18, won by default. Douglas received an immediate production contract for 133 aircraft.

GHQ Air Force, however, had seen enough of the 299 to know what it wanted—the accident, after all, was not the aircraft's fault—and approved the acquisition of thirteen 299s for flying evaluation, plus one more for static tests. This first series was designated Y1B–17 by the Air Corps[2] but the press had already coined the name by which the public would always recognize the aircraft. A Seattle reporter had been so amazed at the sight of the bomber and its five gun positions that he called it a Flying Fortress. Bitter combat experience would reveal that the name, at least for early versions, was a considerable exaggeration of the truth, but it sounded good and it stuck.

The B–17 was the answer to the Air Corps' prayers. It was well-mannered in the air, and easily exceeded military specifications. General Andrews embarked on a persistent campaign of support, insisting that his bombardment squadrons should be equipped only with four-engined aircraft. In a letter to General Oscar Westover in 1937 he observed, "The Air Corps until recently prided itself in securing the best equipment obtainable regardless of expense, but the recent procurement of bombers [B–18s]…is the first time that an inferior airplane has been produced when a superior one was available." The Army General Staff, however, was not so easily convinced. The Deputy Chief of Staff, Major General Stanley Embick, insisted that "…our national policy contemplates defense, not aggression." This shortsighted policy, adhered to slavishly since 1919, continued to stand as a barrier to the building of effective U.S. armed forces at a time when Japan was waging total war in China and Hitler had repudiated the Versailles Treaty and declared general conscription. As German troops rolled into the Rhineland, the U.S. Army General Staff could still say that in its preference for the B–17, the Air Corps had been led astray by "…a quest for the ultimate in aircraft performance at the expense of practical military need." The B–18 remained the Army's bomber of choice.

Utterly sure of their faith in the B–17, airmen took every opportunity to show off its capabilities. Between March and August 1937 the 2nd Bombardment Group at Langley Field, commanded by Lieutenant Colonel Robert Olds, received 12 Y1B–17s. Soon after, they began appearing at conventions and expositions. They flew over a number of cities in formation and their speeds were always published. In January 1938 one of them, piloted by Colonel Olds, broke the American transcontinental record flying from Langley to March Field, California, in 12 hours and 50 minutes and back in 10 hours and 46 minutes. Others flew two extensive goodwill tours of South America, both without serious incident, in a blaze of favorable publicity.

Y1B–17. By May 1937, when this photograph was taken, the Boeing Y1B–17 test program was well underway, and the U.S. Army Air Corps was taking every opportunity to show off its new bombers over cities across the country, proudly announcing their point-to-point flight times.

Even as these impressive feats were unfolding, it appeared that the death knell of the four-engined bomber might be sounding. In May 1938 a memorandum from the Adjutant General to the Assistant Secretary of War included the passage:

> The Chief of the Air Corps has been informed that experimentation and development for the fiscal years 1939–1940 will be restricted to that class of aviation designed for the close-in support of ground troops, and for the production of that type of aircraft such as medium and light aircraft.

The note went on to emphasize that the Air Corps had no military requirement for four-engined bombardment aircraft and would place no orders for B–17s in 1938.

In some ways, the airmen had only themselves to blame. GHQ Air Force had compounded its problem in August 1937 by thumbing its nose at the Navy. Colonel Olds' B–17s succeeded in intercepting and hitting (with water bombs) the USS *Utah*, a target ship in an exercise off the California coast in poor weather and despite what the airmen believed was deliberately misleading information from naval sources. An unauthorized leak to the press on the B–17s accomplishment did not improve the Navy's temper. Its irritation became outrage in May 1938 when General Andrews decided to use the Italian trans-Atlantic liner *Rex* to represent an approaching enemy fleet. Three B–17s set off from Mitchel Field, New York, to intercept a single ship 700 miles out in the ocean. The day was cloudy and rainy but General Andrews, gambling on success, took along reporters

from the *New York Herald Tribune* and the *New York Times*, and the lead aircraft carried a commentator from NBC radio and his transmitters. The commentator was to begin a national broadcast from the B–17 at precisely 12:25 p.m. To the eternal relief of the airmen, the three aircraft burst out of a squall just before the appointed time to find the *Rex* dead ahead.[3] Their splendid achievement was reported on the front pages of newspapers all across the United States. The *New York Times* declared the B–17's performance "…one from which valuable lessons about the aerial defense of the United States will be drawn." Glowing from the success of the exercise, and protesting modestly that the flight had been no more than routine for B–17 crews, the airmen were unprepared for what happened next.

The morning after, GHQ Air Force, celebrating the success of the B–17s, received a telephone call from the Army Chief of Staff, General Malin Craig. He was not amused. As Hap Arnold put it: "Somebody in the Navy apparently got in quick touch with somebody on the General Staff and, in less time than it takes to tell about it, the War Department had sent down an order limiting all activities of the Army Air Corps to within 100 miles from the shoreline of the United States."

There is no evidence that this remarkably restricting order was ever written down, and its origins are hidden in hazy memories and oblique references. Almost certainly the Navy, perhaps at the level of the Secretary or senior naval staff, protested that the Army had usurped the Navy's blue water prerogatives. It may be, also, that General Craig was irked after

B–18A. The shark-like appearance of the B–18A was the result of a grotesquely modified nose that projected the bombardier's position out, above and ahead of the front gunner. Slow and poorly defended, the B–18 was obsolescent almost as soon as it reached its squadrons. It is sobering to think that this was the U.S. Army Air Corps' front-line bomber when Hitler's troops crossed the Polish border in 1939. The B–18A at the USAF Museum belonged, according to its markings, to the 38th Reconnaissance Squadron.

125

Curtiss P–36 of the 18th Pursuit Group commander, over Oahu in February 1940.

The business end of a Boeing P–12E, the U.S. Army Air Corps' most successful biplane fighter. Powered by a 500-horsepower Pratt & Whitney R–1340–17 radial engine, P–12E-series aircraft had a maximum speed of 189 miles per hour and a service ceiling of 26,300 feet. Introduced in 1929, P–12s were in service until 1941.

receiving a naval broadside when he had not been fully informed of GHQ Air Force's intentions. What-ever the case, the verbal order restrained air exercise planners even though it was never spelled out or properly understood. Months later, General Andrews sought clarification of the order because it "…took a 1,000-mile weapon and reduced its operating range to 100 miles." He was told that General Craig did not object to maneuvers more than 100 miles offshore provided the Air Corps requested proper authority (General Staff agreement) well in advance. Many airmen believed that the order had been issued in a momentary fit of pique. Nevertheless, because it was never formally issued, it was never properly rescinded, and its effects bedeviled Army aviation for many months.

While the Navy's objections were real enough, underlying the 100-mile restriction was the fact that many Army officers saw no justification for developing long-range heavy bombers. They believed that Army aviation should primarily support the land battle and would, therefore, not require expensive four-engined

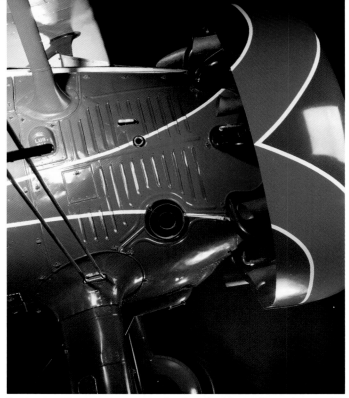

P–12 nose. The P–12E was an early aircraft with an all-metal stressed-skin fuselage. Its wings were still wooden with fabric covering. The P–12E at the USAF Museum is finished in the bright colors of the 6th Pursuit Squadron, based in Hawaii during the 1930s.

aircraft. Twin-engined medium and light bombers were more than adequate. More to the point, two or even three of them could be bought for the price of one heavy bomber. That argument certainly appealed to politicians. In 1938, the year of the Munich crisis, the B–17's future did not look bright.

The Problem of Pursuit

Bombers were pushed into controversy by aeronautical progress in the 1930s. They threatened to eliminate the performance gap between bombardment and pursuit aviation. By 1933 General Westover was reporting that bombers had enough speed and fire-power to operate without support. He expressed doubts that pursuit aircraft could intercept and engage at such high speeds. General Andrews and Colonel Arnold believed bombers capable of penetrating any defensive system. Seeking an answer to the pursuit problem, the Air Corps considered a number of solutions, including large multi-seat fighter aircraft armed with outsized cannon and bombs. Arnold actually used Martin B–12s as fighters during a 1934

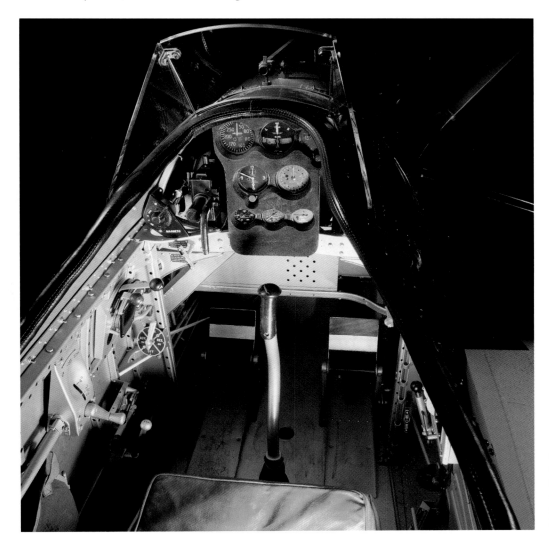

P–12 cockpit. The pilot, despite evidence that his needs had been considered in the P–12's separately designed instrument panel, still sits in an open cockpit, protected by only a small windscreen.

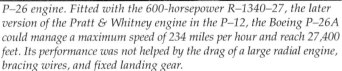

P–26 engine. Fitted with the 600-horsepower R–1340–27, the later version of the Pratt & Whitney engine in the P–12, the Boeing P–26A could manage a maximum speed of 234 miles per hour and reach 27,400 feet. Its performance was not helped by the drag of a large radial engine, bracing wires, and fixed landing gear.

exercise, but without much success. Somewhat less outrageous were the Berliner-Joyce P–16 and Consolidated P–30 two-seaters, but neither remained long in squadron service. The multi-place idea flowered fully in the Bell XFM–1 Airacuda, a twin-engined heavy fighter for a five-man crew, armed with two .30- and two .50-caliber machine guns, two 37-mm cannon, and twenty 30-pound bombs. Sanity prevailed after extensive testing and the Airacuda never saw operational service.

More conventional development led to the Boeing P–26 as the standard Air Corps fighter for most of the 1930s. A chubby little monoplane with spatted, fixed undercarriage, braced wings, and an open cockpit, the P–26 could manage 235 miles per hour in level flight, but it was soon exceeded by Boeing's

P–26. Although it was the first U.S. Army Air Corps fighter with Boeing's all-metal low cantilever wing, the P–26, when it was first delivered late in 1933, was destined to be little more than an interim aircraft. As important as its advances were and as pretty and delightful to fly as it was, the P–26 was soon overtaken by other monoplane designs on both sides of the Atlantic.

P–26 cockpit. His instruments had improved, but the pilot of a P–26 still braved the elements in an open cockpit.

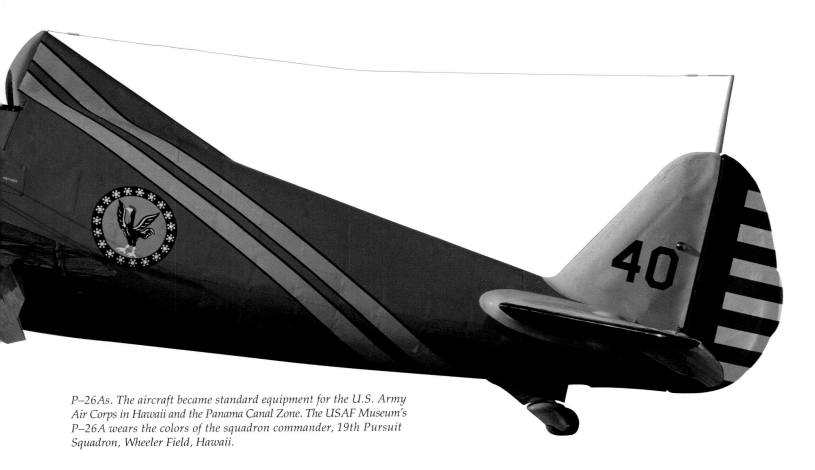

P–26As. The aircraft became standard equipment for the U.S. Army Air Corps in Hawaii and the Panama Canal Zone. The USAF Museum's P–26A wears the colors of the squadron commander, 19th Pursuit Squadron, Wheeler Field, Hawaii.

Seversky P–35. The aircraft was the first single-seat, all-metal fighter with enclosed cockpit, right, and retractable landing gear to see service with the U.S. Army Air Corps. Seventy-five were assigned to the 1st Pursuit Group at Selfridge Field, Michigan, in 1937. The chubby lines of the P–35 reveal the ancestry of a later and most significant combat aircraft— the P–47 Thunderbolt.

P–35 fuselage. The USAF Museum's P–35A is the only known survivor of the type. It carries the insignia of the 19th Pursuit Squadron based at Selfridge Field.

own B–17 and by the bombers of Mitsubishi and Heinkel. In the late 1930s, pursuit aviation advanced more obviously with the Seversky P–35 and the Curtiss P–36, both radial-engined, single-seaters with closed cockpits and retractable undercarriages. Maximum speeds for both were close to 300 miles per hour for the first time and, although both aircraft were rugged and agile, neither could match the performance of fighters being produced in Europe. As World War II drew closer, uncertainty about the role of the fighter and the lack of a powerful in-line engine left the United States with no aircraft capable of superiority in the air.

Other Roles

Attack aviation was similarly in the doldrums. Although the standard attack aircraft, the Northrop A–17, was beautifully constructed and popular with its crews, by the late 1930s it was clearly obsolescent and being phased into training and support roles. In transport, the Air Corps fared better. The United States led the world in transport aircraft design, and the Air Corps benefited with three—the Douglas DC–2— designated the C–33, the C–34, and the C–39. However, observation aircraft of the 1930s still resembled

Close-up view of the Seversky
P–35 cockpit.

P–35 undercarriage. Only
partially retracted, the P–35's
wheels swung backward into
recesses, where they hid behind
their streamlined fairings.

A North American BT–9, the forerunner of the more famous AT–6, winging over above the distinctive circular pattern of Randolph Field, Texas. In 1939 Randolph was the most modern of the U.S. Army Air Corps' Training Centers, which turned out the modest total of 300 pilots per year.

the multi-role machines of World War I. The high-wing Douglas O–46 and elephantine North American O–47 were too slow and cumbersome to avoid enemy fighters and too heavy to operate from unprepared fields. Both were moved to less demanding duties after brief duty with operational squadrons.

In flying training the United States could not have been better served. In the mid-1930s the Stearman PT–13 and the North American BT–9 appeared; the latter was the forerunner of a famous and enduring line that would train the pilots of over 50 nations through the remainder of the century. The Link Trainer, the grandfather of all flight simulators, also appeared. Invented in 1928, it had been ignored by the Air Corps until the air mail debacle of 1934. After that and the introduction of blind flying training,

Link's little blue instrumented box, sporting stubby yellow wings, made pilots sweat in increasing numbers as they struggled to master its jerks, groans, and other idiosyncrasies. Whatever its shortcomings as a flight simulator, the Link raised the standard of instrument flying wherever it was used.

Throughout the 1930s the Air Corps' lighter-than-air branch became less and less relevant, except to a few Army officers who trusted balloons more than aircraft when advising the artillery. However, the branch, a rump of just 10 officers and 350 enlisted men, did not let the decade pass without the flourish of a final launch, even though in a balloon funded by the National Geographic Society. The Goodyear Company built two balloons, *Explorer I* and *Explorer II* in 1935 to gather information about the stratosphere and to

Explorer II. As its gas escapes, the balloon lowers Captains Stevens and Anderson to the ground.

break the world's altitude record. *Explorer II*, with Captains Albert Stevens and Orvil Anderson on board, succeeded in doing both, reaching 72,395 feet over South Dakota in November 1935.

The Arnold Era Dawns

In September 1938 Major General Hap Arnold became Chief of the Air Corps after the death of General Westover. On an inspection tour of western facilities, Westover had been flying alone in an A–17. Approaching Lockheed's airfield at Burbank, California, the A–17 stalled and spun into the ground, where it burst into flames on impact. Arnold inherited an air force that was full of promise, but still suffering from its subservience to traditional Army ways and from limited funding. The United States, still inclined toward isolationism, was no higher than sixth in the world ranking of nations with combat aircraft, and other major powers, unlike the United States, were already building their war machines with air power very much in the fore. Change was on its way, however, and was supported from what the airmen would have believed was an unlikely source.

President Roosevelt had a particularly soft spot for the Navy. After his meeting on military aviation with the President in 1935, Billy Mitchell declared: "Everything on his desk bore some relation to a ship…. If only I could have seen one model airplane among those mementoes, I'd feel a lot better about the safety of the country." It may be that the President took note of Mitchell's pleas, which were certainly reinforced by events in China and Spain in 1937, and by Hitler's threat to use air power to get his way in Europe the following year. Whatever the case, air power became prominent in the President's mind by 1938. As his adviser, Harry Hopkins, remarked after the Munich crisis: "The President was sure then that we were going to get into a war and he believed that air power would win it." When the meaning of the Hitler-Chamberlain meeting in Munich became clear, Roosevelt called a meeting of his senior military advisers and announced that the United States must immediately increase military aircraft production and build a much more powerful American air arm.

General Arnold could hardly believe it. He later wrote: "…a battle was won in the White House that day that took its place with—or at least led to—the victories in combat later." Determined to pursue his new enthusiasm, Roosevelt announced that he intended to ask Congress for 20,000 military aircraft and for facilities to support the production of 24,000 per year. Such amazing figures overjoyed the airmen, and they were diminished in light of reasoned assessments later. After the President's State of the Union address in January 1939, in which he stated bluntly that America's air forces were utterly inadequate, Congress agreed to raise the Army's aircraft authorization to 6,000 and to fund over a two-year period 3,251 new models and additional manpower and construction. None of this was achieved without considerable opposition and charges of wastefulness but, viewed in the knowledge of what followed later, such fiercely debated figures seem pitifully small.

The Air Corps planned to commit 3,300 of its authorized aircraft to combat. They were to include a host of new types. Four-engined bombers rose from the dead as 39 B–17Bs and 7 Consolidated B–24s, still at the prototype construction stage. Fighters included 524 Curtiss P–40s, 13 Lockheed P–38s, 12 Bell P–39s, and 13 Republic P–43s. Douglas would provide 186 A–20s to give the Air Corps an attack bomber worthy of the name. North American and Martin had new medium bombers on the way—the B–25 and the B–26.

The Goodyear balloon Explorer II, *which carried Captains Albert Stevens and Orvil Anderson to a world altitude record of 72,395 feet in 1935.*

As a brighter future opened for the Air Corps and American military aviation and the realities of air power would begin to be faced, accommodating changes in organization and policy occurred. In March 1939, with the departure of General Andrews from his command, GHQ Air Force lost its apparently equal status with the Air Corps. No longer answering directly to the Army General Staff, GHQ Air Force was placed under the Chief of the Air Corps. For the first time, the enormously heavy responsibility for all Air Corps activity would rest with one man— Hap Arnold. In 1939 even he did not fully appreciate the weight that would rest on his shoulders, a weight resulting from the most dramatic expansion of military capability ever undertaken in the history of warfare.

The President had made it clear that Air Corps missions would expand beyond the nation's coastline to the broader horizons of hemispheric defense. The case for the long-range four-engined bomber had been made by presidential mandate. The strategic bomber and other aircraft needed to make U.S. Army aviation into a major player on the stage of world air power were on their way. In the meantime, it was Arnold's job to begin building an air force capable of using them. After Munich, the Air Corps proposed a goal of 24 combat-ready groups by mid-1941, by which time personnel strength should have risen to 48,000 officers and enlisted men. More training facilities would be needed to turn out not just 300 but 1,500 pilots per year.

(B–18s, A–17s, and P–36s) were no match for their counterparts in European air forces.

Under the circumstances, it was providential that the United States was spared immediate direct involvement in the conflict. The Air Corps had begun to grow, acquiring more capable aircraft as soon as they became available, but it would, as Hap Arnold and his colleagues now knew, have to keep growing to an unprecedented degree. Its goal for a 24-group air force was seen as far too modest in the face of Hitler's rampages and Japan's intensifying military belligerence. The Air Corps had to start planning for an air force that could project massive power on a global scale.

"The Night Before," Wesley McKeown, 1965, USAF Art Collection.

Expansion had hardly begun when the blow fell. On 1 September 1939 Hitler's forces invaded Poland. As the world gathered itself before the most destructive war in history, the U.S. Army Air Corps had just 26,000 officers and enlisted men, of whom 2,000 were pilots. The Luftwaffe stood at almost half a million strong with over 50,000 aircrews. American squadrons in the continental United States were operating, according to Frank Andrews, "…only slightly over 400 fighting planes" compared to the Luftwaffe's more than 4,000. More sobering than that numerical disparity was the fact that standard front-line American aircraft

Notes

1. Arnold won the first Mackay Trophy ever awarded when, near Washington in 1912, he used a Wright Flyer to demonstrate the reconnaissance capabilities of aircraft. His 1934 flight was not the first to link the Alaska Territory with the United States by air. In a perhaps even more remarkable achievement, Captain St. Clair Streett led the Black Wolf Squadron of DH–4s from New York to Nome in 1920, refueling several times in Canada and covering the 9,000-mile round trip in 112 flying hours without serious incident.

2. Aircraft designations can be confusing. In the case of the Flying Fortress, Model 299 was a Boeing number. When a prototype is accepted for flying, it gets a military designation that it carries throughout its service life, plus the letter X for experimental. The 299 should have become the XB–17, but it crashed before the designation could be changed. Test series aircraft are given the letter Y, and the first fourteen B–17s delivered to the Air Corps were YB–17s. The figure 1 was inserted merely to indicate the source of funds used to buy the aircraft and made them Y1–B17s. Production aircraft lose their prefixes and gain series letters after the numbers B–17A, B–17B, B–17C, etc. All B–17s were Flying Fortresses.

3. It is worth noting that the successful lead navigator on the first South American tour and for the interceptions of the *Utah* and the *Rex* was Lieutenant Curtis LeMay. Transferred from pursuit aviation, he did not then have sufficient flying hours to become a B–17 pilot, and so began his career in four-engined aircraft as a navigator.

We must be the great arsenal of democracy.

(President Franklin Roosevelt, December 1940)

[Americans] can make cars and refrigerators, but not aircraft.

(Reichsmarshal Hermann Goering, August 1941)

In order to achieve . . . superiority, it is plain that we shall need the greatest production of aircraft which the United States of America is capable of sending us.

(Winston Churchill to President Roosevelt, December 8, 1940)

Part II
Victory

We must be the great arsenal of democracy.

(President Franklin Roosevelt, December 1940)

[Americans] can make cars and refrigerators, but not aircraft.

(Reichsmarschal Hermann Goering, August 1941)

In order to achieve . . . superiority, it is plain that we shall need the greatest production of aircraft which the United States of America is capable of sending us.

(Winston Churchill to President Roosevelt, December 8, 1940)

. . . at eight o'clock . . . a great fleet of Japanese bombers bombed our ships in Pearl Harbor and bombed all of our airfields . . . casualties, I'm sorry to say, were extremely heavy.

(President Franklin Roosevelt to his Cabinet, 7 December 1941)

Chennault's U.S. flyers in China fight unfairly. They zip into target areas, drop their bombs and zip right out again before we have a chance to fight back. Unless Chennault changes his tactics, the Japanese Government has warned we will take stern measures.

(Tokyo Radio, 1941)

Chapter 5
Girding for Conflict, 1939–1941

Weapons and Warriors

The USAF Museum's World War II collection, reflecting the scale and impact of the most destructive war in history, confronts visitors with an almost overpowering embarrassment of riches. Among them are P–36 and P–40E fighters flown by Americans in the early days of the war, and a gleaming but portly Douglas C–18A Bolo that, with all its limitations, was the standard front-line American bomber when Hitler's blitzkrieg broke across the Polish frontier.

Wall displays cover the beginnings of the European air war, the establishment of the U.S. Army Air Forces (USAAF), and the Day of Infamy, 7 December 1941 at Pearl Harbor. Others tell of those Americans who, unable to wait for the United States to get into the war, went to fly with the Royal Air Force (RAF) in Britain or with the American Volunteer Group (AVG) in China. Special mention is made of AVG leader Claire Chennault and of America's first World War II aces, Albert Baumler, who scored aerial victories against three Axis powers; William Dunn, the first American ace of World War II; and Don Gentile, one of the most celebrated of American fighter leaders. An extensive display on the Eagle Squadrons of the RAF is set off by a magnificently restored Hawker Hurricane IIA in the markings of No. 71.

More wall displays cover the unprecedented expansion of the USAAF's training programs which fed the appetite of its rapidly growing front line. During the war they produced nearly 200,000 pilots, over 50,000 navigators, 45,000 bombardiers, and 21,000 glider pilots. Some of the program's aircraft stand nearby—a Stearman PT–13, a Fairchild PT–19, a Ryan PT–22, a Vultee BT–13, a North American BT–14, and a Schweizer glider. Posters encourage their readers to "Remember December 7th!"; "Fly! For her liberty and yours!"; "Do your part for Duty, Honor, Country!" The Tuskegee Airmen get special mention, as do women in the WASPs (Women Airforce Service Pilots), and the nation's burgeoning aircraft industry, which, we are reminded, between 1 July 1940 and 30 August 1945, produced the almost incredible total of nearly 300,000 aircraft and over 800,000 engines.

A War on the Home Front section covers such diverse topics as radar, the Observer Corps, civil defense, ration

Two of World War II's greatest leaders discuss progress in the European air war, April 1944. General Hap Arnold, right, met Major General Jimmy Doolittle at Bassingbourn, home of the 91st Bombardment Group in England, not long after Doolittle had taken command of the Eighth Air Force.

books, and Japanese balloon bombs. Advanced trainers in the shape of the North American AT–6 and the Beech AT–11 stand with such famous devices as the Norden Bombsight and the Link Trainer. Around a corner, the immortal poem "High Flight" by Pilot Officer John Gillespie Magee is inscribed on the wall, and, nearby, the Air Force song can be heard at the push of a button.

PT–22 and cadets. The U.S. Army, to tackle the immense task of expanding its flying training from 300 to 30,000 pilots per year, contracted with civilian flying schools for primary training. Their students flew 65 hours in aircraft like the Ryan PT–22 before moving on to the BT–13, the AT–6, and the AT–9.

PT–22 cockpits. Like other primary trainers of the 1930s and 1940s, the PT–22 Recruit was a simple aircraft. With all-metal construction, it was robust but forgiving, as a machine that suffered continually from the ministrations of student pilots had to be.

Fins of cousins. The Fairchild PT–19 Cornell nestles behind the PT–22.

were led to believe that the Luftwaffe in its size and configuration was ideal as an instrument of conquest. It had seemed well suited for fighting tactical battles in support of the army, for engaging in short, fierce campaigns, and for terrorizing city populations to gain speedy surrender and victory. Not so obvious at the time were the lack of a strategic bomber and limited aircraft production plans. They would, with many other problems, come to haunt the Luftwaffe when it was forced to face the consequences of endless combat on several very different fronts at once.

In 1939 the Luftwaffe appeared all-powerful. Its success in Poland was evidence enough for most international onlookers. Luftwaffe squadrons outnumbered their Polish counterparts by almost four to one, and highly experienced German aircrews flew vastly superior aircraft. Nevertheless, by the end of September, the Luftwaffe had lost 285 aircraft. Its stocks of spares and armaments were dangerously low. These relevant facts were ignored by jubilant German leaders and largely escaped the attention of their worried neighbors to the west.

Urged by his generals to pause for breath, Hitler reluctantly shelved a plan for an immediate westward assault and allowed his forces to regroup during the winter months of the "phony war." By the spring of 1940 they were ready. In April, spearheaded by the Luftwaffe, the Germans occupied Denmark and Norway, and on 10 May began sweeping through Holland, Belgium, Luxembourg, and France. On 4 June the last survivors of the British Army's expeditionary force were driven off the continent at Dunkirk, and on 22 June the French surrendered. German forces controlled Western Europe from North Cape to the Franco-Spanish border, and Britain stood alone against Hitler's ambitions. Germany's success had come quickly, but its air losses had been grievous. The *blitzkrieg* had cost nearly 1,500 aircraft, over 1,000 in combat. The French and British had lost 750 and 950 respectively, many of them abandoned as airfields were overrun. Once again, the Luftwaffe's pain was forgotten in the euphoria of victory.

American Reactions
News of the fall of France stunned the United States. Most Americans had assumed that the combined forces of the French and British would be a match for those of the Germans. Since the attack on Poland, the United States had viewed the European conflict with concern, generally sympathetic to the Franco-British cause, but desirous of detachment. On 3 September 1939 President Roosevelt announced: "This nation will remain a neutral nation, but I cannot

Hermann Goering. *When the Battle of Britain began in 1940, Reich Marshal Hermann Goering,* left, *was a swaggering figure at the height of his powers. His Luftwaffe had been crushingly effective as an element of the German* blitzkrieg *on the continent of Europe and was poised to lead the invasion of Britain. At this stage, the Nazi war machine was considered unstoppable and Goering belittled the capacity of the United States to intervene effectively in the war.*

ask that every American remain neutral in thought as well." With France defeated and Britain vulnerable, the United States began to look more closely at the Nazi threat. German soldiers stood on the southern shore of the English Channel singing: "Today England, Tomorrow the World!" Americans began to realize that they would have to take Hitler's global ambitions seriously, even though they lay across the natural barrier of the Atlantic.

The possibility that British resistance could be overcome concentrated American minds. It raised the specter of a Germany in complete control of French and British industrial, naval, and colonial assets and, in concert with Japan and Italy, in a position to challenge the United States. It raised the further possibility that many other countries, perhaps those in Latin America, would follow the Nazis in what they would perceive to be their own interests. President

Roosevelt's commitment of January 1939 to protect the western hemisphere in a reaffirmation of the Monroe Doctrine now assumed greater significance. In May 1940, when France verged on collapse, the President, reemphasizing the concept of hemispheric defense, proclaimed that "the American people must recast their thinking about national protection." To give substance to his rallying cry, he issued a call for 50,000 military aircraft supported by a production capacity of that same number annually.

The Air Corps immediately revised its expansion program from 24 to 41 groups, and, within two months, to 54 groups. The 54-group program (The First Aviation Objective) proposed an Army air force of over 21,000 aircraft and more than 200,000 men by April 1942. In an atmosphere of national emergency, it received its authorization, but it would not achieve such a vast increase overnight. For once in its history, the Air Corps suffered the frustration of having more money than time. By December 1940 impatient airmen chafed at the fact that the aircraft industry was producing only 800 aircraft per month, up from 250 since January but still not enough. To complicate matters, Hap Arnold's staff was already raising its sights. In March 1941 it produced its Second Aviation Objective, an 84-group air force with a personnel strength of over 400,000 by June 1942.

As sensible as these proposals were in terms of the nation's security, they faced a number of seemingly insurmountable hurdles connected with the goals to increase aircraft production, expand training facilities, and support the British in their hour of need. Prime Minister Winston Churchill pressed the point when he addressed President Roosevelt in a radio broadcast, saying: "Give us the tools and we will finish the job!"

Churchill's appeal did not fall on deaf ears. As Germany's conquests mounted, more and more Americans came both to sympathize with the British and to understand that the first line of American defense lay in the United Kingdom. As early as November 1939, an American embargo on arms sales to belligerents had been lifted by the Cash and Carry Act under which Allied nations could buy and collect armaments in the United States. Increasingly liberal release policies followed, culminating in the Lend-Lease Act of March 1941. It allowed the United States to transfer military equipment to an ally, requiring only that it be returned after the war. President Roosevelt likened this act of generosity to lending a neighbor a garden hose to "help him put out a fire." Although the legislation had been framed primarily with Britain's difficulties in mind, it had implications for the Chinese, and within months, during Hitler's

imperious lunge to the east, it would apply to the Soviet Union, too. The trouble was that, given the increasing requirements of the American services, the garden hose was needed at home as well.

By mid-1940, as American industrial production struggled to a higher gear, the Air Corps' 54-group program was calling for 21,470 aircraft. The British had outstanding orders for 14,000 more. Because Britain was then in desperate need, the Air Corps had to defer the delivery of 8,586 aircraft in its favor. The offer of the hose to a friend in the European fire, however generous, threatened to deny the Air Corps the flow of nourishment so essential for its growth.

The Luftwaffe Rebuffed

In mid-1940 the British did seem in desperate need. Beginning in July the Luftwaffe launched a campaign against the Royal Air Force, a prerequisite for an invasion of the United Kingdom by the German Army. In a savage air battle lasting until October, the Luftwaffe suffered its first defeat, losing over 1,700 aircraft to RAF Fighter Command's 950. Luftwaffe leader Hermann Goering had revealed the limits of his strategic vision when he compared the planned invasion to "a big river-crossing." By October the Germans had discovered that the English Channel was no river and that, whatever its tactical capabilities, the Luftwaffe was an air force neither equipped nor trained for a strategic campaign on the scale of the Battle of Britain.

If anything, Americans became more enthusiastic about helping Britain as prospects for its survival improved. Their fears that military aid might be going to a lost cause were dispelled by the Joint Aircraft Committee (JAC), established in September 1940 to ensure the more systematic and equitable distribution of aircraft and engines. The JAC was made up of representatives from the three principal customers of America's aircraft industry—the U.S. Army Air Corps, the U.S. Navy Bureau of Aeronautics, and the British Purchasing Commission. When Lend-Lease became law, the JAC was integral to its administration.

Anglo-American Cooperation Begins

At the same time, representatives of America's and Britain's service staffs were studying how their two countries could best collaborate if the United States eventually joined the war. They issued two reports known as ABC-1 and ABC-2 in March 1940. ABC-1 was later judged to be one of the most important military documents of the war. It concluded that in a global conflict, "the Atlantic and European area is considered to be the decisive theater." Especially significant were comments that U.S. Army air

B–24 production line. The Ford plant at Willow Run, Michigan, was typical of the huge factories erected to produce war material. A mile long, it churned out B–24s at a rate that astonished doubters of American industry's ability to meet huge planned production figures. Overcoming the problems of adapting automobile mass production methods to large aircraft, Ford reached a peak monthly production rate of 428 B–24s in August 1944. Between September 1942 and June 1945 Willow Run completed a total of 6,791 B–24s, plus a further 1,893 "kits" for assembly elsewhere.

bombardment units would "operate offensively in collaboration with the Royal Air Force, primarily against German military power at its source," and that the joint powers should achieve as rapidly as possible "superiority of air strength over that of the enemy, particularly in long-range striking forces." ABC-2 essentially recommended that aircraft production in the United Kingdom and the United States be accelerated. New estimates to satisfy contingencies discussed in the report suggested that American industry would need to increase its output to the undreamed of total of 60,000 aircraft per year. Skeptics were to find that American mass production techniques could accomplish almost anything, particularly with government support.

Federal money built new factories for aircraft manufacturers, who also got tax advantages and an easing of restrictions on excess profits. The expertise of the automobile industry was harnessed to aircraft and components manufacture with startling results. Ford, for example, confounded those who claimed that large aircraft were too complex to mass produce. At Willow Run, Michigan, in the largest factory in the world at a mile long by a quarter of a mile wide, Ford established a line which churned out B–24 Liberators at a rate to rival family cars. The

achievements speak for themselves. From a total military aircraft production figure of just over 900 in 1939, industry reached the astonishing number of more than 96,000 warplanes for 1944. Such an output, whose rate kept rising, allowed the air arm to replace the wastage of combat losses, accidents, and obsolescence and still increase the number of aircraft on strength from about 12,000 in 1941 to almost 80,000 in 1944.

The U.S. Army Air Forces

Such planning and production shook the structure of American air power to its foundations. The old organization, with responsibilities divided between the Air Corps and General Headquarters, Air Force (GHQ Air Force), was incapable of managing the vast increases in machines, manpower, and facilities underway. A series of organizational jugglings led, in March 1941, to the appointment of Robert A. Lovett as Assistant Secretary of War for Air, a post which had been vacant since 1933. Lovett was given the job of promoting aircraft production and streamlining Army aviation. His efforts resulted, on 20 June 1941, in the creation of the U.S. Army Air Forces (USAAF), which had the Air Corps and Air Force Combat Command (replacing the old GHQ Air Force) as subordinate elements. Hap Arnold wore two hats

Eagle Squadron memorabilia. The USAF Museum's Eagle Squadron collection includes Don Gentile's Royal Air Force (RAF) cap, his flying jacket, and his uniform jacket with its RAF wings and Eagle Squadron shoulder badge. Dog tags are shown resting on the wing-tip of a Luftwaffe aircraft shot down over England.

Eagle Squadron pilots scrambling for their Hurricanes. "Red" Tobin, leading the charge, was one of the seven Americans to fly with the Royal Air Force during the Battle of Britain. Sam Marillo and Luke Allen run to his left.

as Chief of the USAAF and as Deputy Chief of Staff to General George C. Marshall, the Army Chief of Staff. It was not a perfect arrangement, and other major changes would follow within the year, but it marked a considerable advance toward air force autonomy. Advocates of independent air power were far from satisfied, but Arnold was content to make progress one step at a time. He worked well with Marshall and thought it unwise to press for more while the USAAF was expanding and preparing for war.

Arnold's Air Staff was soon hard at work. America's war tasks set out in ABC-1 were finalized in Joint Army and Navy War Plan RAINBOW 5. The Air Staff's Air War Plans Division took account of this in producing a document known as AWPD/1. AWPD/1 reflected the accepted view that the USAAF had an offensive role and estimated that its war mission would require 239 combat groups. For a front line of that size it would need a personnel strength of nearly 2.2 million to operate a total of 26,416 combat and 37,051 training aircraft. The manpower figure included 135,000 aircrews. Among combat aircraft were almost 7,500 heavy bombers. Prepared in less than a week by a team of brilliant young staff officers, AWPD/1 proved a remarkably accurate estimate.[1]

Americans in Britain
The United States and the United Kingdom, increasing their collaboration, exchanged military missions to London and Washington. American observers had been in London for some time and had been present during the Battle of Britain, but the arrangement was regularized in May 1941 by the formal opening of a

headquarters for the American mission in the American Embassy. The Army section was known as the Army Special Observer Group (SPOBS) and was commanded by Major General James Chaney, whose chief of staff was Brigadier General Joseph McNarney. Significantly, both officers were airmen. The neutral status of the United States notwithstanding, Chaney's principal responsibility was to prepare for the establishment and control of American forces in the United Kingdom as laid down in RAINBOW 5.

Other Americans had been in the United Kingdom ignoring American neutrality for some time under less formal arrangements, but they, too, were leading where many would follow. When the war began, a number of them had concluded that their country's eventual involvement was inevitable, but they were not prepared to wait for it. At least one, Jimmy Davis, managed to join the RAF before the war began. He flew Hurricanes with No. 79 Squadron and was awarded a Distinguished Flying Cross before being killed in combat in June 1940. Seven others are listed among the famous few who fought in the Battle of Britain. This small group flew and fought initially with regular RAF squadrons, and it was the vanguard of many more American volunteers. Only one of the seven survived the war.[2]

American airmen crossed the Atlantic in increasing numbers in 1940, all seeking the adventure of flying fighters. Many were touched by an unadmitted idealism. As Chesley Peterson, later an Eagle Squadron commander, recalled:

> Everyone wanted to fly big, fast airplanes, and the only way to do that was in one of

the services. Since most…did not have the necessary qualifications to join the U.S. Army or Navy, the only answer that readily presented itself was the RAF.

Peterson also remarked that most Eagles would not admit to being influenced by ideals, but he noted that no Americans ever volunteered to fly for the Luftwaffe.

By the time the Battle of Britain was ending, the number of Americans flying with the RAF was sufficient to justify the formation of a separate unit, No. 71 Eagle Squadron. Two more Eagle Squadrons, Nos. 121 and 133, followed in May and August 1941. These three compiled a distinguished record with the RAF and the pilots who fought with them gained considerable combat experience against the Luftwaffe. It was to prove invaluable when they became the 4th Fighter Group, USAAF, in September 1942, forming the nucleus of the fighter force that would later dominate the skies over Europe.

Training Challenges

Meanwhile, back in the United States, the USAAF suffered serious growing pains. The challenge of its aircrew training program alone was daunting. Having heard the President's statement on the need for greatly increased air power in November 1938, General Arnold foresaw problems and began to take action. He contracted with nine of the nation's largest civilian flying schools to take on a primary flight training program for the Army. It got underway in 1939 when on average only 300 pilots per year were graduated. As one USAAF plan succeeded another during the following months, the training programs's task grew by leaps and bounds. The First Aviation Objective raised the requirement to 30,000 pilots per year, a staggering one hundred-fold increase, but even that was dwarfed by the Second Aviation Objective, which proposed 50,000 per year by mid-1942, little more than three years after the Air Corps' explosive growth began. At wartime's peak, no fewer than 56 civilian primary flight schools would be among those training pilots.

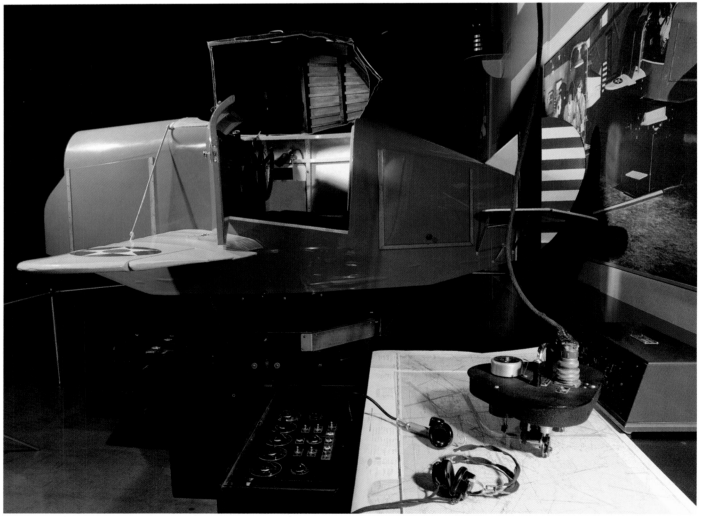

Link trainer. Often known as the "torture chamber," the Link trainer allowed pilots to practice instrument flying procedures while fastened firmly to the floor. In the foreground is the map table and the "crab," a device that traced the pilot's wanderings during navigation exercises.

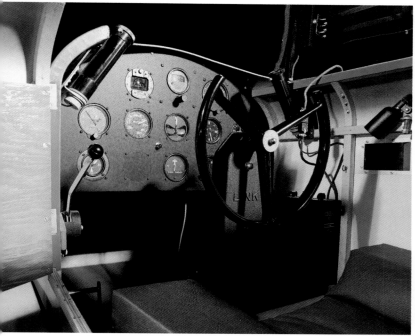

Link cockpit. The Link trainer's wheezing noises were hardly typical and its movement was often jerky, but once its hood was down its cockpit reproduced the basic instruments and controls necessary to simulate flight so effectively that the pilot could quickly become immersed in the problems he was given.

PT–13D. The Stearman Kaydet was one of the world's most significant training aircraft. A total of 10,346 were ordered for the United States and the Allies in the ten years following 1935. (Boeing acquired the Stearman company in 1938.) The PT–13D at the USAF Museum carries a 220-horsepower Lycoming radial engine, but other variants were differently powered and given separate designations—PT–17 with a Continental engine and PT–18 with a Jacobs.

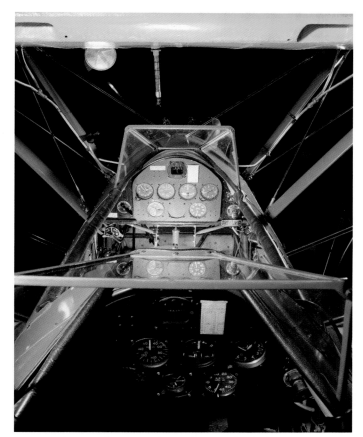

PT–13 cockpit. In the PT–13 the student sat ahead of his instructor. Note the basic fuel gauge over the aircraft's front cockpit, and the small mirror which allowed the instructor to monitor expressions of fear or delight as they appeared in the student's eyes.

In these primary training schools cadets spent about 65 flying hours in a biplane such as the Boeing PT–13 or 17 (the Stearman) or a monoplane such as the Fairchild PT–19. They completed their first solos, became accustomed to simple maneuvers, and learned the basics of airmanship. They then progressed to basic training in a closed cockpit aircraft such as the Vultee BT–13 (known universally as the Vibrator) with 75 hours of aerobatics, formation, navigation and instrument flying. In advanced training, potential fighter pilots went on to the North American AT–6 for 70 hours, practicing more of everything plus aerial gunnery. Future heavy pilots went on to twin-engine types such as the Curtiss AT–9 and were introduced to the delights of asymmetric handling. At the end of advanced training, cadets received their wings and commissions as 2nd lieutenants. Between 1 July 1939 and 31 August 1945, the civilian training program graduated 193,440 pilots, but the true magnitude of its scale is indicated by the number of trainees who failed to complete its course—124,000.

AT–6. One of the world's great aircraft, the North American's AT–6 Texan was powered by a 600-horsepower Pratt & Whitney R–1340 engine and had a maximum speed of 210 miles per hour and a range of 770 miles. In later life the AT–6 was used as a combat aircraft, notably in the forward air controller role during the Korean War, and it remains the most popular of the world's "warbirds" at air shows more than half a century after its birth.

AT–6 formation. The AT–6 Texan is perhaps the most famous trainer ever produced. Over 15,000 were built in various forms between 1938 and 1945. More than 10,000 went to the U.S. Army Air Forces. They were used for advanced flying training, when a pilot polished his formation, instrument, gunnery, and bombing skills before being awarded his wings and going on to combat aircraft.

AT–6 cockpits. The AT–6's tandem seating helped to give a student the feeling of being master of his fate even when an instructor was sitting behind him.

AT–6 front cockpit. The pilots of over 20 countries got their wings by sitting in the AT–6's front seat. As a trainer for introducing pilots to the art of pure flying, the AT–6 has probably never been surpassed.

AT–9. More often called the Jeep, the Curtiss AT–9 Fledgling was a bridge between single-engined trainers and multi-engined combat aircraft. It was not easy to fly, but its idiosyncrasies prepared pilots to take on the challenges of high performance twins like the B–26 or P–38. Two 295-horse-power Lycoming R–680–9 radial engines gave it a maximum speed of nearly 200 miles per hour.

AT–9 and crew. The bridge between basic trainers and multi-engined combat aircraft was the Curtiss AT–9.

AT–9 cockpit. Control wheels, side-by-side seating, and central console introduced pilots to a big aircraft environment.

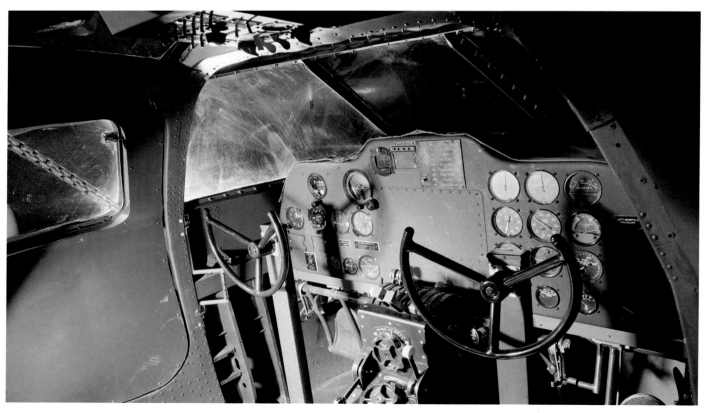

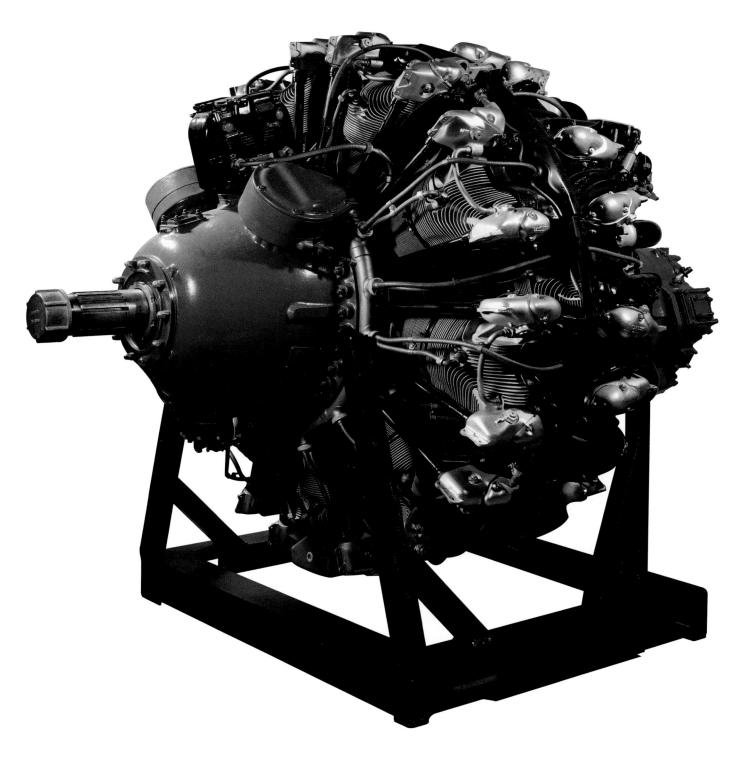

Pratt & Whitney R–2800. The Double Wasp was one of World War II's great engines. Various forms of the 18-cylinder twin row radial were mounted in several U.S. Army Air Forces combat aircraft, including the Martin B–26, Northrop P–61, Douglas A–26, and Curtiss C–46. The Republic P–47D's R–2800–59 developed 2,430 horsepower at takeoff power.

Rolls-Royce Merlin. If any engine deserves singling out for having done more than any other to "win the air war" it is probably the V–12 liquid-cooled Merlin. Besides powering several major Royal Air Force aircraft (the Hurricane, Spitfire, Mosquito, and Lancaster, among others), it served the U.S. Army Air Forces P–51 Mustang. Designed by Rolls-Royce, the Merlin was modified and built in the United States by Packard. Mounted in the P–51D, it provided 1,695 horsepower.

New pilots then undertook transition training in combat types such as older-model P–40s or B–18s. Paul Tibbetts described the B–18 as "...a gentle airplane," having "little value except as a trainer," but Don Lopez (23rd Fighter Group) viewed the P–40 as more of a challenge. Of his first takeoff in one he remembered: "It was fortunate that the runway was very wide, or I would have run off both sides of it." If pilots survived transition training, they were assigned to operational units in the United States for combat training before going overseas. Over about a year they had at least 400 hours in the air before they met the enemy. Their likely opponents were less thoroughly prepared. By 1944 Luftwaffe pilots were entering combat with about 150 hours; the Japanese were managing fewer than 100.

Matching steps ensured that the USAAF had sufficient aircrews trained with equal thoroughness in categories other than pilot. The service had in all, 50,000 navigators and 45,000 bombardiers before the end of the war. In 1939 technical school graduates numbered 1,500. Two years later, they numbered 42,000. The rise kept growing annually but did not come easily. Schools were forced by equipment shortages to improvise as best they could. To achieve results many moved to shift-working a 24-hour day seven days a week.

To accommodate the prodigious need, new training facilities sprang up all over the United States. The 1939 Air Corps operated 76 installations (including 21 major bases). During World War II the USAAF came to control a total of 2,252 at one time. Established bases were greatly expanded, often with solid brick construction, but newer facilities contained more temporary buildings, even tarpaper shacks. Some airfields were generously supplied with concrete, while others made do with hastily laid turf. By December 1941 these efforts had created a USAAF of 70 combat groups, but that was only a beginning. The USAAF continued to grow from 350,000 to over 2.25 million people in uniform by war's end.

In such a huge and increasingly autonomous air force, the old Air Corps principle, that officers should be pilots, could no longer apply. Besides other aircrew specialties, the USAAF needed professional administrators, engineers, lawyers, public relations executives, doctors, communicators, meteorologists, educators, and many more. Arnold bowed to the inevitable and authorized the founding of an Officer Candidate School to impose minimum standards of military training on applicants for commissions and to sort the "wheat from the chaff."

WASP and P–38. The WASPs (Women Airforce Service Pilots) numbered little more than 1,000, but they were invaluable as ferry pilots and instructors. During World War II WASPs became qualified on every kind of U.S. Army Air Forces aircraft, including the most demanding operational types. Louise Thompson stands in front of a new P–38 awaiting delivery.

Gender and Race

The pressures of a rapidly growing Air Corps soon forced Arnold to face two other issues—the employment of women and black Americans within the ranks. Neither group was put to its best use, despite the national emergency of World War II. The strictures of American society and the conservatism of the U.S. Army at the time erected too many formidable social barriers. The maximum wartime strength of the Women's Army Corps (WAC) with the USAAF was less than 30,000. Women were confined primarily to clerical duties, although some managed to break away and become mechanics. They also performed in their traditional role as nurses, but some shattered convention in a small group known as the WASPs (Women Airforce Service Pilots). Only 1,074 WASPs flew for the USAAF. They served as ferry pilots, flight instructors, and target tug pilots, but they qualified in every type of USAAF aircraft, including such demanding machines as the P–47, B–26, and B–29.

Racial segregation was even more difficult to overcome. In 1941 there were only five black officers in the whole of

Benjamin Davis. Racial segregation was a problem for America's services in World War II. A relatively small number of black men were selected for flight training at Tuskegee, Alabama, and just over 1,000 reached squadrons as aircrews. Their leader was an inspiring young man named Benjamin Davis, who eventually rose to three-star rank. He is shown, left, *during primary flight training.*

the American military, and three of those were chaplains. The vast majority of black enlisted men in the USAAF maintained roads and buildings or manhandled supplies at depots. A select few were accepted for flight training at the Tuskegee Institute in Alabama. Inspired by the example of their leader, a young man named Benjamin Davis, Jr., these black airmen overcame the handicaps of racial segregation. The Tuskegee program eventually graduated 673 fighter pilots, 253 medium bomber pilots, and 132 navigators. Davis had a distinguished career in the service during and after the war and rose to the rank of lieutenant general.

Changes in USAAF Size and Shape

To ease the problems of controlling its changing and continually growing force, the USAAF established four numbered and three overseas air forces—the Far East in the Philippines, the Caribbean (later Sixth) in Panama, and the Hawaiian. It created other new organizations, including Technical Training Command to direct the vast training program for mechanics and technicians, Maintenance Command to manage maintenance and supply, and Air Service Command to concentrate on procurement, research, and

development. The growing task of delivering aircraft to the RAF generated yet another new organization in Ferrying Command, and before long the growth of aircrew training programs compelled the creation of Flying Training Command.

In 1941 the USAAF's growing material power was becoming obvious, as was its change in status. In August, President Roosevelt met Winston Churchill on board the battleship HMS *Prince of Wales* off the coast of Newfoundland. Accompanied by their political and military staffs, they discussed the war and, to a great extent, the application of air power. Because a senior RAF officer was present as the representative of his independent service, Hap Arnold was there to speak for the USAAF. In this way, Arnold was accepted as a member of the Combined Chiefs of Staff, even though he was still subordinate to the U.S. Army's Chief, General Marshall.

Expanding Frontiers

As the prospect of war loomed larger every day for the United States, the USAAF looked to the outer limits of its defensive responsibilities in the western hemisphere. In September 1940 President Roosevelt announced an agreement with the United Kingdom that transferred 50 World War I destroyers to the hard-pressed Royal Navy in exchange for 99-year leases on airfield and base sites in Newfoundland, Bermuda, British Guiana, and a number of Caribbean islands. Other agreements with the Danish and Icelandic governments in mid-1941 allowed American forces to establish bases on Greenland and Iceland. The defining purpose of these measures was defensive, but it was implicit that their existence secured the firm links with the United Kingdom that would in time be vital to the Allied cause.

The sense of urgency that marked the strengthening of American defenses on the Atlantic side was not so evident at outposts in the Pacific. As its relations with Japan deteriorated the United States tried to make up for lost time, but it had to weigh every action against Atlantic needs. Its policy was to deter Japan without disrupting activities to keep the door to Europe open. Most of its planned improvements were either incomplete or mere paper proposals by December 1941, but it had authorized some reinforcement of bases on Hawaii and the Philippines and the provision of landing strips on several islands—Midway, Johnston, Palmyra, Canton, and Christmas. Many American military leaders were less than confident about conducting an effective defense of the Philippines or other farther flung outposts.

The reinforcement of Clark Field in the Philippines included the deployment of 35 B–17Ds. They were intended to attack Japanese bases on Formosa and blockade the China Sea from the air. The United States also hoped that the Soviet Union might agree to allow B–17 shuttle operations between Luzon and Vladivostok and put the Japanese home islands within Allied bombing range. The air defense force at Clark had 100 P–40s and 68 obsolete fighters—a mixture of P–35s and P–26s. The forward deployment of so many B–17Ds at this early stage left Hawaii with only 12, along with 12 A–20s, 33 B–18s, and a fighter force of 99 P–40s, 39 P–36s, and 14 P–26s.

Defensive preparations in Alaska, too, were "eleventh hour." Although the Air Corps had been pointing out the area's strategic value for years, the USAAF did not begin constructing a major base at Anchorage until 1939 or establish Air Field Forces, Alaskan Defense Command, until May 1941. (Air Field Forces, Alaskan Defense Command became Air Force, Alaska Defense Command four months later.) It did install several rough forward airstrips in 1941, the westernmost on Umnak Island in the Aleutians to provide cover for the naval base at Dutch Harbor, but its overall readying of the Alaska Command was

not impressive. The USAAF deemed the locale too remote and the weather and geography too awful for any priority over others more readily accessible. By early December 1941 the command's front-line aircraft strength stood at 12 B–18s and 20 P–36s. Against a determined enemy the region's fierce storms seemed a more realistic deterrent.

When the Japanese fleet put to sea on 26 November 1941 and set course for Hawaii, determined to strike the U.S. Navy a crippling blow, the United States was a long way from being ready for war. In the two years and more since Hitler's forces had attacked Poland, American leaders had appreciated the dangers and had taken a great many steps toward preparedness. However, any real benefits remained in the future. The nation's human and industrial capacities had not yet made themselves felt. Their vast potential was there and machinery was in motion, but in 1941 few people on either side realized just how awesome American power would become in the months ahead.

In the short term, 7 December 1941 was not a propitious day for the Western democracies. Japanese aircraft wreaked havoc at Pearl Harbor and Hitler's troops stood at the gates of Moscow. The future did not look promising. But the Japanese attack and Hitler's subsequent declaration of war had finally released the United States from the shackles of neutrality and dedicated it to relentlessly prosecuting a global war, the result of which would never again be in doubt. The realities of American power and the inevitability of the course of events had escaped the leaders of the Axis powers. Not long before his careless decision to declare war on the United States, Hitler wrote to Benito Mussolini: "Whether or not America enters the war is a matter of indifference, inasmuch as she is already helping our enemy with all the power she can muster." He must later have thought his breezy assessment a little hasty.

Pacific Surprise, Pearl Harbor
As early as 1924 Billy Mitchell declared that war between the United States and Japan was almost inevitable. He cannot have been too surprised that his forthright views did little to concentrate Americans on the intentions of a potential enemy. In the 1920s the horrors of the war just ended had rendered the idea of global conflict nearly unthinkable, and the broad reaches of the Pacific lent an air of unreality to the prospect of a military confrontation involving such widely separated nations. Americans of that time dismissed defense issues and soon forgot Mitchell's somber prediction that the Japanese would strike first at Pearl Harbor. The awful precision of his prophecy was revealed on 7 December 1941, 17 years after his

Wheeler airfield burning, 7 December 1941. A Japanese photograph shows Wheeler Field, Oahu, Hawaii, under Japanese air attack. The virtual absence of anti-aircraft defenses and the compactness of the rows of aircraft in front of their hangars made the destructive task of the delighted enemy all the simpler.

Mitsubishi A6M, Type 0. Otherwise known as the Zero, the aircraft came as a shock to the Allies. It was a formidable, highly maneuverable fighter, and in the Pacific War's early stages it seemed almost unbeatable. Later, when such weaknesses as its lack of armor and self-sealing fuel tanks became apparent, Allied pilots learned to defeat it by using the superior speed of their fighters and avoiding turning dogfights.

visionary warning, when the blow fell "...on a fine, quiet Sunday morning," just as he had said it would.

Launched from six aircraft carriers 200 miles north of Oahu, Japanese airmen attacked Pearl Harbor in two waves of more than 350 aircraft. Surprise was total. Repercussions of the shock felt by Americans at the news from Pearl Harbor have never ceased to reverberate. How could the United States have been caught so completely off guard? How could American forces have been so thoroughly crushed while their attackers escaped almost unscathed? The answers to these questions are complex, but, in essence, they reflect America's general lack of readiness to fight a Pacific war and local convictions in Hawaii that Pearl Harbor was too remote from Japan to be a likely target.

As the principal victim of the perfectly executed strike, the U.S. Navy suffered heavily. Most notably, all eight of the U.S. Pacific fleet's battleships were either sunk or badly damaged. Luckily, its aircraft carriers were at sea. Japanese airmen made equally damaging attacks on Oahu's shore installations, including the airfields. Here, they found ideal targets. Reacting to a message from Washington on 27 November warning of deteriorating relations between the United States and Japan, General Short, U.S. Army Commander in Hawaii, had judged the most serious threat to be sabotage. He, therefore, ordered all Army aircraft moved out of protective revetments and massed in the open or in hangars, where, he believed, they could be better protected. Many aircraft were unarmed and defueled. Standing in neat rows or huddled together under cover, they could hardly have been better arranged by the enemy.

By the time the raid was over, Oahu's airfield buildings and support facilities had suffered widespread damage by bombing and strafing, and only 83 of 234 U.S. Army aircraft on strength were flyable. Among local survivors were 12 B–17s that had left California the night before on their way to the Philippines. They and their tired aircrews arrived over Oahu in aircraft fitted for ferrying, with neither guns nor armor in place, to find themselves in the midst of a major battle. Short of fuel and being shot at by both enemy and thoroughly aroused "friendly" anti-aircraft gunners, the B–17s scattered and landed where they could. One ended up on a golf course; one was destroyed; and another three were badly damaged.

America's defensive reaction had been at times courageous, but pitifully ineffective and occasionally indiscriminate. Angry anti-aircraft gunners fired at any planes they saw, some American, and shot down the P–40 of Lieutenant John Dains. The U.S. Army Air

Forces flew only 25 sorties against the raiders and claimed 10 enemy aircraft destroyed, 4 of them by Lieutenant George Welch's P–40. Altogether, the Japanese lost 29 aircraft in combat, plus a few more in accidents during recovery to their carriers. Given the scale of their victory, they paid a small price. Japanese felt exultation, and Americans felt anger and a desperate need to avenge the humiliation of defeat. Emotions ran high, but beyond agony and ecstasy lay hidden ironies. Seeking to secure the eastern flank of its southerly expansion, Japan had managed to end America's isolationism and so ensured its own eventual defeat. Attacking American battleships, it had demonstrated the effectiveness of air power against naval vessels while failing to destroy any enemy aircraft carriers.

Debacle in the Philippines
To the west, a combination of human failings and the vagaries of the weather brought the United States another military disaster. News of the Pearl Harbor attack reached General MacArthur in the Philippines shortly after 3 a.m. local time. Exactly what happened in the next few hours is not entirely clear because the recollections of the principal officers involved differ considerably. It does seem, however, that MacArthur's capacity for decisive action temporarily deserted him, and that his chief of staff, General Richard Sutherland, denied direct access to him to the air commander, General Lewis Brereton. Brereton's request for permission to launch a B–17 strike against Japanese airfields on Formosa was passed through Sutherland but was not immediately approved.

Shortly after 7 a.m., General Brereton was contacted by General Arnold from Washington and warned not to let his aircraft get caught on the ground. When Brereton received a report that unknown aircraft were approaching Manila, he scrambled 36 P–40s to intercept and ordered the B–17s at Clark Field into the air as a precaution. When it appeared that the alarm was false, the P–40s landed to refuel, but the B–17s remained airborne. Later in the morning, Sutherland called Brereton to authorize both a photographic reconnaissance of Formosa and a late afternoon attack on the Japanese bases there once the photographs had been evaluated. Accordingly, the B–17s were recalled to be refueled and loaded with bombs.

Brereton was understandably anxious. He had been living in constant expectation of a Japanese attack on Clark Field since first light, and his instincts were correct. Japanese airmen had planned to strike Clark at dawn but had been frustrated by thick fog covering their airfields on Formosa. They in turn had suffered agonies of apprehension as they waited for the fog to disperse, expecting the B–17s to arrive overhead

Wright Cyclone R–1820. The 9-cylinder engine developed 1,200 horsepower. A typically oil thirsty but rugged radial, the Cyclone was reliable and resistant to battle damage. Many times it continued to run with shattered cylinders. Hamilton Standard constant-speed three-bladed propellers could drag the B–17 to well over 30,000 feet.

163

at any moment. When the skies cleared, 108 bombers and 84 fighters took off, setting course for the Philippines. One formation reached Clark soon after midday and could hardly believe its good fortune. American aircraft were still on the ground, bunched together as they took on fuel and armaments. Mitsubishi G3M Nells and G4M Bettys bombed without opposition, and Zero fighters dropped down to strafe at will, leaving a smoking shambles. All of the hangars were destroyed and most of the aircraft, including two squadrons of B–17s, were reduced to scrap. Similarly catastrophic damage was done to other American air bases on Luzon. At a stroke, American air power in the Philippines, insufficient for its tasks anyway, had lost over half of its strength.

Sixteen B–17s were deployed at Del Monte on Mindanao out of reach of the Japanese, and on subsequent days they and a motley collection of other aircraft did their best to counter the invasion of the Philippines. They were courageous but many of their efforts did little more than annoy the enemy. The hard facts of America's lack of preparedness for war were now revealed. Aircraft were too few and often obsolete; communications facilities were unsatisfactory; airfield defenses were poor; and intelligence was inadequate. As a result, a bitter air power lesson was administered to American forces

on the first day of the conflict: air superiority is fundamental to successful military operations. Within a week, it was clear that the Japanese already controlled the air over Luzon, and that their capture of several airfields made the extension of that control over the whole of the Philippines merely a matter of time.

Shocked by the defeats in Hawaii and the Philippines, and the prospect of more, Americans needed a hero, a symbol of defiance and fighting spirit. On 10 December a suitable figure emerged. Captain Colin Kelly was a pilot whose B–17C had bombed Japanese ships off the northern Luzon coast. According to early reports, his attack had sunk the battleship *Haruna*, but it subsequently emerged that the warship was most probably the cruiser *Ashigara*, which may have been damaged, not sunk. On the return flight, the B–17 was attacked by enemy fighters and set on fire. Ordering his crew to abandon the aircraft, Kelly remained at the controls to allow its escape. He died when the B–17 exploded in the air before he could parachute from it. His was the first B–17 to be shot down, and he was awarded a posthumous Distinguished Service Cross.[1]

On 13 December Americans had more to cheer about when, during a reconnaissance sortie, Lieutenant "Buzz" Wagner's P–40 ran into a formation of obsolescent

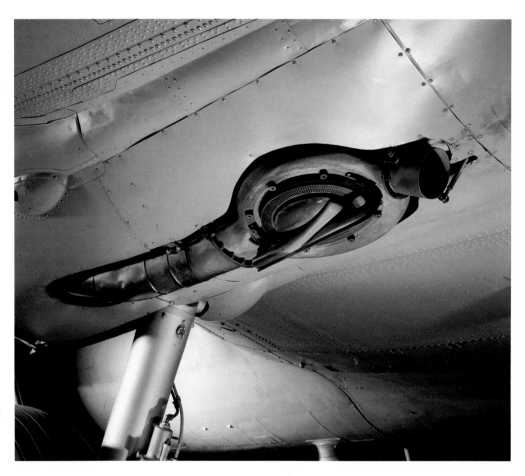

Supercharger. Maintaining engine power at high altitude would not have been possible without supercharging. The turbo-supercharger shown here is fitted to one of the Wright Cyclones on the B–17 Shoo Shoo Baby.

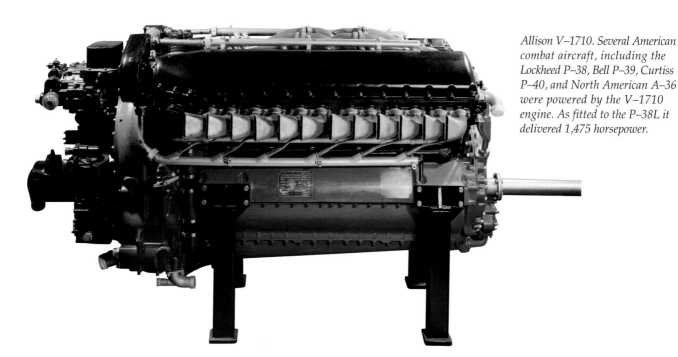

Allison V–1710. Several American combat aircraft, including the Lockheed P–38, Bell P–39, Curtiss P–40, and North American A–36 were powered by the V–1710 engine. As fitted to the P–38L it delivered 1,475 horsepower.

Nakajima Ki–27s. He shot down four of them and went on to strafe other Japanese aircraft on the airfield at Aparri. Three days later he scored another aerial victory to become the USAAF's first ace.

Apart from these brave efforts, Americans did not have much to savor in the Pacific. Japan's advance was irresistible and by 18 December the last of the B–17s in the Philippines had been withdrawn to Darwin, Australia. General MacArthur talked stubbornly of the needs for reinforcements and 200 fighters and 50 dive bombers were delivered to the Philippines by aircraft carrier. He was too late with too little, however, as Japanese forces pressed speedily through the islands. MacArthur withdrew his troops into the Bataan peninsula and made his headquarters on the fortress island of Corregidor. American resistance there was dogged, but final surrender came at last in May 1942. The experience of defeat convinced American ground forces commander General Jonathan Wainwright, of "…the futility of trying to fight a war without an air force."

The Capable Enemy
The Japanese Air Force was a revelation to its opponents. Its aircrews were well trained; its tactics were sound; and its aircraft were formidable. Its Zero fighter in particular could outfly anything the Allied air forces had. First proven over China in 1940, the Mitsubishi A6M, Type O, known as the Zero, should have been no surprise to the Allies, who disbelieved early reports of its performance. In fact, it was a remarkable fighter. Powered by a 950-horsepower radial engine, the Zero had a maximum speed of 330 miles per hour and was slower than some of its competitors, but it had an excellent rate

of climb and was incredibly maneuverable. Saburo Sakai, the Japanese ace who scored 64 victories, described it as "…a dream to fly. The airplane was the most sensitive I had ever flown, and even slight finger pressure brought instant response." Its range, too, was extraordinary—nearly 2,000 miles with a drop tank—allowing it to appear in areas thought to be unreachable by Japanese fighters.

Such outstanding performance came at a price, however. The Zero's weight was kept as low as possible, at not much more than 5,000 pounds fully loaded. Japanese fighter pilots wanted unencumbered, light, agile aircraft made like "…master craftsmen's Samurai swords." The Zero's designer, Horikoshi Jiro, later wrote: "As a result of our pilots' figurative demand for the blades and the arts of the old masters, Japanese fighters were the lightest in weight and among the most maneuverable in the world." They had no armor plate or self-sealing fuel tanks. Once American fighter pilots learned to use their own aircrafts' superior speed and diving ability to advantage and to avoid being drawn into low-speed turning dogfights, they soon exposed the Zero's shortcomings in brutal fashion.

During the first six months of their campaign to create a Greater East Asian Co-prosperity Sphere, Japan ran riot. Weaknesses in the Zero or in any other element of its military machine were not readily apparent. Its successes at Pearl Harbor and in the Philippines were reflected in similar victories elsewhere. By May 1942 its combat record was impressive. Japan had crippled the U.S. Pacific fleet, conquered the Philippines, Hong Kong, Indochina, Malaya, Singapore, the Dutch East Indies, and Burma, and

P–40. The USAF Museum's Curtiss P–40E was originally a Kitty Hawk, the export model produced for the Royal Air Force. It has been restored as a Warhawk and finished in the markings of Chennault's American Volunteer Group in China, the Flying Tigers. P–40s fought on every combat front in World War II.

"Duke" Hedman in front of his American Volunteer Group (AVG) P–40 in China. Hedman flew with the AVG's 3rd Squadron, which styled itself Hell's Angels. In accordance with the complex rules of air combat, Hedman was credited with 4.83 victories during his time with the AVG.

had spread out across the Pacific to seize a host of islands, including Wake, Guam, the Gilberts, and the Solomons. It seemed only a matter of time before it would add Australia and India to its list. Trying to halt the avalanche, Allied forces in Southeast Asia had been consistently outfought and, most important, had suffered the consequences of facing superior air power forcefully applied.

Chennault's Flying Tigers

Despite the prevailing gloom, two remarkable efforts were emerging to brighten the Allies' spirits in the first half of 1942. The first was led by Claire Chennault, a man who had left the Army Air Corps in 1937 because his uncompromising views on the uses of fighter aircraft ran counter to the bomber-driven doctrine of the generals. Hired by the Chinese to

improve their air force, he recruited and organized the American Volunteer Group (AVG), later known as the Flying Tigers, to fly for China. The AVG was equipped with P–40s and Chennault made sure that his pilots knew how to take advantage of their aircraft's level flight speed, diving ability, and rugged construction. The Flying Tigers generally operated in pairs and used hit-and-run tactics whenever possible. On 20 December 1941, the Japanese got their first taste of the AVG in action when ten Kawasaki Ki–48 Lilys attacked Kunming. Four were shot down, and a Japanese history records that the survivors turned for home, having "...realized that P–40 fighters were prevailing."

In following months, the Flying Tigers continued to harass the Japanese Air Force at every opportunity,

P–40 cockpit. The new-fangled gunsight in the P–40 cockpit was apparently not so trusted that the external ring and bead could be removed.

A field of P–40 Flying Tigers. The Flying Tigers generally operated in pairs and used hit-and-run tactics whenever possible.

P–40. The celebrated tiger shark's teeth on any Flying Tiger P–40 are a prominent feature.

B–25. Most versatile of the U.S. Army Air Forces twins, the North American B–25 Mitchell made significant contributions in both the Pacific and European theaters and was flown by several Allied air forces. Heavy on the controls and something of a challenge when engines failed, the B–25 was well regarded because of its resistance to punishment. The glazed nose carried a single .303-inch machine gun. Other .303s were in the waist positions, and twin .50s fired from dorsal and ventral turrets. The USAF Museum's Mitchell was rebuilt by North American to B–25B configuration and marked as the aircraft used by Jimmy Doolittle on his 1942 Tokyo raid.

Doolittle Raiders launching. Soon after 0800 on 18 April 1942, Doolittle's 16 B–25s took off from the USS Hornet. *Tokyo was 824 miles away. All 16 B–25s bombed Japan. Fifteen crashed in China and the sixteenth was impounded by the Soviets when it landed at Vladivostok.*

consistently recording a markedly favorable victory-to-loss ratio in combat. They were among the first to show that the Japanese military could be successfully opposed. When the AVG was disbanded in July 1942, many of its pilots transferred to the USAAF, taking with them the experience of fighting the Japanese in the air and winning.

The Doolittle Raid

The second raiser of Allied hope came from what might best be described as a gesture of defiance. Americans were impatient to hear that the United States had taken the offensive by striking back at Japan. President Roosevelt wanted the home islands attacked to remind the Japanese people that they were not beyond the reach of the war and to bolster American morale. In an operation fraught with risk, 16 modified B–25 Mitchell medium bombers led by Lieutenant Colonel Jimmy Doolittle were to be

Jimmy Doolittle, Marc Mitscher, and Tokyo Raiders. Captain of the USS Hornet, *Mitscher has just handed Doolittle some Japanese medals (presented to U.S. Navy personnel during a 1908 goodwill visit) with the instruction from Secretary of the Navy Frank Knox that they be returned to Japan "with interest." They were attached to the fin of the nearby bomb. (Navigator Tom Griffin is standing behind Mitscher's left arm.)*

launched from the aircraft carrier *Hornet.* To some, such daring seemed beyond reason; it did to the enemy. As the American task force ploughed through rough seas in the Pacific, the Japanese listened to an English language news report from Radio Tokyo describe as "laughable" the idea that American bombers could attack the home islands. "It is absolutely impossible" the announcer told her audience "for enemy bombers to get within 500 miles of Tokyo."

On 18 April the task force was seen by Japanese picket boats 650 nautical miles east of Tokyo. The decision to launch Doolittle's aircraft immediately put them 200 miles farther from their targets than intended. They would have minimal fuel reserves for their planned recovery to Chinese airfields. All 16 B–25s took off successfully, Doolittle in the leading bomber having only 467 feet of deck available. Thanks to the *Hornet's* 20-knot speed into a 30-knot wind, he

Doolittle raid memorabilia. The USAF Museum's Doolittle raid collection includes a small piece of a crashed B–25, a simple bombsight, a flight jacket (belonging to Tom Griffin, navigator, aircraft no. 9), the camera used to take the only strike photographs of the mission (belonging to Richard Knobloch, co-pilot, aircraft no. 13), and part of a parachute canopy used to supply a sleeping bag, raincoat, and bandages (belonging to Ross Greening, pilot, aircraft no. 11)

Two of the photographs taken over Japan during the Doolittle raid by Richard Knobloch, co-pilot in B–25 no. 13. The camera he used is among the items in the USAF Museum's Doolittle raid collection.

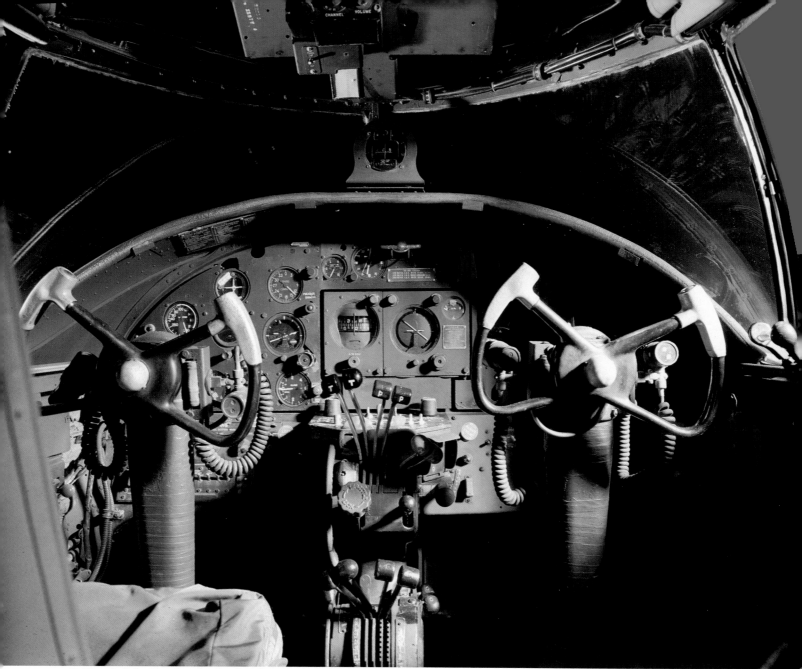

B–25 cockpit. Looking functional and ready to go, the B–25's basic flight instruments are duplicated between the pilots' panels. Engine instruments are clustered to the right behind the co-pilot's control column.

later said that he was "off the deck with feet to spare." During the subsequent flight, the B–25s passed many Japanese ships and aircraft and were engaged by numerous anti-aircraft guns, but all dropped their bombs at various points in Tokyo, Kobe, and Nagoya. Fifteen of the force were helped to China's coast by a providential tailwind, but in falling darkness and foul weather, their fuel low, and unable to make radio contact of any kind, all of them were lost when their crews were forced to either crash land or bail out. Three men were killed, several were injured, and eight were captured by the Japanese. Three of the eight captured were later executed as war criminals, and another died in captivity. The 16th B–25 landed without damage near Vladivostok, where it was appropriated and its crew interned by the Soviets.

Depressed by the sight of his aircraft's wreckage the next day, Doolittle convinced himself that the raid had failed and that he would face court-martial for the loss of his and the other B–25s when he returned to the United States. As the President had believed it would, the raid deeply shocked the Japanese and tremendously cheered the Americans at a difficult time. Jimmy Doolittle was rewarded for his efforts with a promotion to brigadier general and the award of the Medal of Honor.

The raid appears to have initiated a series of strategic disasters for Japan. The Imperial Japanese Navy had suffered a crushing loss of face. The sacred soil of Japan had been desecrated by the enemy. In an immediate and emotional reaction, the Japanese brushed aside the cautions of the High Command and demanded retaliation. Operations which might

175

Doolittle raiders—half a century later. Tom Griffin, left, and Travis Hoover shown in the USAF Museum's B–25 more than 50 years after their epic raid on Tokyo. Hoover was the pilot of no. 2 aircraft and Griffin the navigator of no. 9.

better have been separated in time were brought quickly to fruition in what was intended to be a massive four-pronged expansion around the extremities of Japan's huge empire. The four prongs pointed at Port Moresby in New Guinea, Guadalcanal in the Solomons, Midway Island, and the Aleutians. The prospects for success in four such widely separated and challenging campaigns at once might have suggested the delay of at least one of them, but the Japanese people were in no mood for delay. In any case, most were infected with "victory disease." They had accomplished so much so easily that failure seemed only a remote possibility. The Japanese Navy, in particular, needed to expunge its feeling of shame.

It began a tremendous flurry of activity following the Doolittle raid and, in so doing, proved a considerable boon to American intelligence analysts who were able to break into its code using thousands of intercepted coded radio transmissions. They read perhaps 5 percent, enough to learn that the Japanese

One of the most surprising sights of the Pacific War—B–25 bombers parked on the deck of the Hornet *while on their way to launch a "one-way ticket" attack on the Japanese mainland in April 1942.*

were dispersing their superior forces in a way that would allow the United States to concentrate its then limited strength against them individually. American commanders became hopeful.

It was perhaps understandable that Jimmy Doolittle was depressed by the thought that he had done no more than deliver a pinprick to the enemy, that he had lost all of his aircraft doing it, and that the Chinese people were suffering terrible retribution as a result; but his raid also accomplished a great deal. It was the first small offensive step on the road that led to the eventual defeat of Japan.

Notes

1. The four authors of AWPD/1 were Lieutenant Colonels Harold George and Kenneth Walker and Majors Laurence Kuter and Haywood Hansell, Jr.

2. The RAF fighter pilots of the Battle of Britain were immortalized by Churchill in the words: "Never in the field of human conflict was so much owed by so many to so few." The seven American citizens listed as having fought in the Battle are Billy Fiske, Art Donahue, Ken Haviland, "Shorty" Keough, Philip Leckrone, Andy Mamedoff, and "Red" Tobin. Only Ken Haviland survived the war. He became a professor of aeronautical engineering at the University of Virginia in Charlottesville.

3. After the war, it was discovered that Kelly's B–17 was shot down by one of Japan's greatest aces, Saburo Sakai. In his book, *Samurai,* Sakai wrote of his surprise at the ruggedness of the B–17. After a succession of firing passes from ten Zeros, the bomber seemed unharmed and full of fight: "I decided to try a close-in attack directly from the rear. Greatly to my advantage was the fact that the early B–17s lacked tail turrets…. Pieces of metal flew off in chunks from the bomber's right wing, and then a thin white film sprayed back…. The bomber's guns ceased firing; the plane seemed to be afire within the fuselage."

To have the United States at our side was to me the greatest joy. Hitler's fate was sealed. Mussolini's fate was sealed. As for the Japanese, they would be ground to powder. All the rest was merely the proper application of overwhelming force.

(Winston Churchill, December 1941)

North American Aviation had kept their word and given us the best fighter ever designed.

(Pete Hardiman, P–51 pilot, Eighth Air Force)

Allied bombing was the dominant factor in the success of the [Normandy] invasion.

(General Feldmarschall Hugo Sperrle, Luftwaffe, 1945)

If I didn't have air supremacy, I wouldn't be here.

(General Dwight Eisenhower, Normandy, June 1944)

Chapter 6

The European Air War, 1942–1945

Death and Glory

The USAF Museum's European combat exhibits follow the USAAF to England, North Africa, Sicily, Italy, and through the Allied invasion of the continent, describing every aspect of the air assault on Germany and ground forces support. Displays are liberally supported by historical photographs, maps, newspaper clippings, and assorted memorabilia that recreate the atmosphere of a monumental struggle. Among American airmen given special mention are George Preddy, a 26.83 victory ace who once shot down six enemy aircraft in one day and was himself killed by American ground fire, and John Meyer, who scored 24 in the air and 13.5 on the ground (plus two more in Korea) and rose to wear four stars as Commander in Chief, Strategic Air Command. High above is a massive painting of Luftwaffe senior officers in conference. Goering, Sperrle, Kesselring, Udet, and Molders are recognizable in discussion, while Galland stands in the background, peering pensively out a window.

As visitors reach the end of the wall display gallery they find the main hall of the museum hangar and World War II aircraft. On one side is a Lockheed P–38 Lightning, on the other a Bell P–39 Airacobra over PSP airfield matting. Suspended above are two Grasshopper spotter aircraft from Taylorcraft and Aeronca. Farther on, the pugnacious silhouette of the Consolidated B–24 Liberator dominates the end of the hall. This one is **Strawberry Bitch**, *which flew 59 combat missions with the 376th Bombardment Group.*

Arranged between aircraft are various engines, armaments, and war relics. An engine, nose-wheel, and propeller recall the B–24 **Lady Be Good**, *which disappeared into the Libyan desert in 1943. Contrasting exhibits suggest the sufferings of prisoners of war at the hands of Japanese captors and the delights of a Glenn Miller band concert. The well-known faces of Ronald Reagan, Jimmy Stewart, Clark Gable and Joe Louis appear as Celebrities in Uniform.*

Much admired is a perfectly restored Boeing B–17G of the 91st Bombardment Group, the famous **Shoo Shoo Shoo, Baby**. *Its partners are on every side—Republic's P–47 Thunderbolt, Martin's B–26 Marauder, Northrop's P–61 Black Widow, and North American's B–25 Mitchell, P–51D Mustang and only surviving A–36. Allied aircraft*

Lend-Lease aircraft. The Lend-Lease Act of March 1941 allowed the United States to "lend" war equipment to an ally. It also optimistically stipulated that the equipment be returned after the war. Lockheed Hudsons were among the aircraft awaiting shipment to Britain.

are exhibited, too, in American markings—a Supermarine Spitfire and a De Havilland Mosquito. Luftwaffe aircraft include two Messerschmitts—a 109G in the markings of Gerhard Barkhorn (301 aerial victories), and a 262, the first jet aircraft to see combat. A Fiesler Storch hangs overhead. The Italians are represented by a Macchi 200 in desert camouflage, and the Japanese by a Kawanishi George from the last year of the war.

Enlivening the museum's hall is an assortment of contemporary vehicles, weapons, some early guided bombs, the feared German 88-mm flak gun, and engines such as a Rolls-Royce Merlin, which powered the P–51D, the Spitfire, and the Mosquito to their successes. More wall displays draw attention to the Lend-Lease program by which aircraft were delivered to the Soviet Union, to the history of enlisted pilots in the U.S. Army, and to glider pilots.

Overhead is Little Girl, *a Waco CG–4A glider used in the D-Day assault on Normandy.*

The USAF Museum is continually acquiring more air power history artifacts and the World War II collection has long since overflowed its original home. In other halls or on the old Wright Field taxiways outside the main buildings are World War II aircraft and displays just as worthy of attention as those in the principal exhibit. Among them are wonderful transports (a Curtiss C–46 Commando and a Douglas C–47 Skytrain), rare aircraft (a Douglas C–23), forgotten observers (a Douglas O–46 and a Curtiss O–52 Owl), enemies (a Junkers 52 and an 88), air-sea rescuers (a Consolidated OA–10 Catalina), attackers (a Douglas A–20 Havoc), and many more. On the approach to the museum is a replica of a typical World War II air traffic control tower in England; to one side stands a group of Nissen huts of the kind so closely associated with life on an operational airfield of the U.S. Army's Eighth Air Force.

Germany First

At Pearl Harbor and in the Philippines, American forces had suffered ignominious defeat. In the early months of 1942 the Japanese, in the grip of "victory disease," were sweeping all before them. Naturally, the United States focused on the Pacific, wanting badly to stop Japan and avenge early defeats. However, Adolf Hitler's impulsive declaration of war, four days after Pearl Harbor, committed the nation to battle on two fronts. American military leaders necessarily turned to the provisions of the Joint Army-Navy War Plan RAINBOW 5, which established the principle of "Germany First."

The War against the U-Boats

For the first few months, most U.S. Army Air Forces activity to the east of the United States was limited to countering the depredations of German U-boats. By the end of 1941 enemy submarines had moved closer to the mainland and were enjoying rich pickings, often attacking at night when ships were silhouetted against the brightly-lit cities along the Atlantic coast. Before long, they were sinking ships at a rate that exceeded the capacity of America's shipyards to replace them and were seriously threatening Allied cargo-carrying capability. Because the U.S. Navy was ill-prepared to deal with an assault of this magnitude, the USAAF carried out anti-submarine patrols. At first, a motley collection of B–18s, B–25s, and older model B–17s was made available, but they could manage only a limited number of daily patrols between them. These were augmented by Civil Air Patrol pilots in private aircraft based all along the east coast. Few patrolling aircraft were armed, and those that were did not carry depth charges. Nor were many crews

trained in overseas navigation, anti-submarine attack, or ship recognition. On one memorable occasion, a USAAF bomber crew aimed four bombs at a USN destroyer, mistaking it for a surfaced submarine. Luckily, their delivery was as wide of the mark as their identification.

Matters improved as the USAAF gained experience and its aircraft were fitted with radar in March 1942. However, for all of the thousands of hours the USAAF flew on monotonous searches, its recognizable successes were few. Not until 7 July 1942 did a Lockheed A–29 record the first confirmed sinking of a U-boat. The combat report leaves no doubt that the submarine was destroyed:

> [Lieutenant Harry Kane of the 396th Bombardment Squadron] attacked from fifty feet at 220 miles per hour, releasing three Mk XVII depth charges in train about twenty seconds after the target submerged. The submarine was still visible underwater as the bombs fell. The first hit short of the stern, the second just abaft the conning tower, and the third just forward of the conning tower. Fifteen seconds after the explosions, large quantities of air came to the surface, followed by seventeen members of the crew.

The rarity of attacks on U-boats was not, however, a true indication of patrolling aircrafts' effectiveness. Submarines were keenly aware of them and U-boat commanders were forced to keep their heads down more than they would have liked. In 1942 air patrollers became more persistent and forcibly drove the U-boats from the east coast first to the Gulf of Mexico, then to the Caribbean, and finally out into the Atlantic. In October 1942 the USAAF activated the Army Air Forces Anti-Submarine Command (AAFAC), and, as months went by, the war against the U-boats intensified from steadily improving technology. Besides microwave radar, aircraft were equipped with magnetic anomaly detectors, sonobuoys, radar altimeters, LORAN (Long Range Aid to Navigation), and improved depth charges. Obsolete aircraft were replaced by B–24s with powerful offensive capability, and the force grew to 286 aircraft. After the war the radar-equipped B–24 was singled out by Admiral Karl Doenitz as a decisive factor in the defeat of his U-boats.

Operating in concert with the USN and Canadian and British forces, the AAFAC helped turn the tide in the Battle of the Atlantic. By July 1943 the nature of the threat had changed to such an extent that the USAAF could withdraw from anti-submarine

A–29. Developed from the L–14 civil transport, the Lockheed A–29 Hudson was designed to meet British requirements for a maritime patrol aircraft. In 1942, as the United States faced a serious U-boat threat along its east coast, a number of Hudson's were delivered to U.S. Army Air Forces (USAAF) squadrons. It was an A–29 of the 396th Bombardment Squadron that scored the first USAAF success against a U-boat on 7 July 1942.

operations. The AAFAC was disbanded and its equipment handed over to the USN. Its units had flown 135,000 hours on patrol, making only 100 direct attacks, but the considerable effort that they expended (and the mind-numbing boredom that their crews endured) had been worthwhile. The submarines had been robbed of their freedom of action and had been so hounded from the air that they were at last rendered operationally ineffective.

The USAAF Arrives

Meanwhile, the USAAF had been preparing for what it believed would be the main event. In February 1942 it sent Brigadier General Ira Eaker to the United Kingdom to establish a bomber command headquarters and prepare for the arrival of combat units. At that time General Arnold had ordered the formation of a new air force, the Eighth, to take part in Operation GYMNAST, a proposal for the occupation of French North West Africa. When GYMNAST was abandoned as impractical at that stage, Arnold reassigned the Eighth Air Force to the United Kingdom, selecting Major General Carl "Tooey" Spaatz to command it.

During the early part of 1942 Eaker and his staff moved into a large manor house, formerly a girl's school, near Royal Air Force Bomber Command Headquarters at High Wycombe, 30 miles west of London. With the RAF's assistance and encouragement, they set about the daunting process of acquiring and building airfields, establishing a logistics chain, and planning a training program. From the beginning, American and British airmen recognized the need for cooperation, and the RAF did its utmost to help its potentially powerful new neighbor settle in as quickly as possible. Excellent relations between the two air forces were in no small part due to the character of Eaker himself. He was generally well liked, endearing himself to the British

on his arrival with the pointed brevity of his first speech: "We won't do much talking until we've done more fighting. After we've gone, we hope you'll be glad we came."

For the first few months, the infant Eighth Air Force relied on the battle-hardened RAF for help and advice as it was readied for the fight. The British assumed initial responsibility for the defense of American airfields, arranged transportation and administrative support, shared intelligence, provided communications and weather services, trained American intelligence officers and photographic interpreters, and allocated training airfields in Northern Ireland. Eaker and his staff attended the daily operations conference held at RAF Bomber Command, where it was agreed that the two forces would cooperate in the selection of targets and in the issuance of press releases. Amid so much activity, which went remarkably smoothly, there was much goodwill. In June, Eaker reported: "We are extremely proud of the relations we have been able to establish between the British and ourselves..." Even so, there were still some notable differences of opinion.

To begin with, the RAF proposed that Eighth Air Force fighter units cover some of the air defense sectors in England. The Eighth was not very enthusiastic about such a heavy responsibility since the USAAF preferred to concentrate its forces for the air assault on Germany. Spaatz clarified the American position when he stated that USAAF fighters were primarily "to support [Eighth Air Force] bombers in an effort to secure air supremacy and not for the defense of England." Nevertheless, he compromised, adding that American fighter squadrons could be trained for air defense and used in an emergency.

More fundamentally, the two air forces disagreed about how heavy bombers should be used. In the first few months of the war in Europe, the RAF had tried daylight operations and had been badly mauled. Furthermore, its fighters had defeated Germany's day offensive in the Battle of Britain, but had been unable to stop Luftwaffe bombers from operating at night during the ensuing *blitz*. The British concluded that if they were to succeed in carrying the war to Germany, they had to do it at night. The Eighth Air Force, on the other hand, was determined to bomb by day. It was an article of faith with the USAAF, built on interwar air power theories, that formations of fast, well-armed bombers could fight their way through to their targets, unescorted if necessary, and see, hit, and destroy those targets most effectively by day. Initially, the British sought to dissuade the Americans by pointing out the hazards of the practice and offering the alternative of being integrated into the night offensive. The USAAF, however, was determined to do what it was trained and equipped to do. As events were to prove, neither air force in 1942 was capable of undertaking a strategic air offensive to match the hopes of its leaders, nor would they be for many months to come. The difficulties of building an overwhelming bomber force would be overcome only with the help of bitter experience and a host of developments, both technical and operational.

During May 1942 ships carrying Eighth Air Force ground elements began docking in the United Kingdom, and on 18 June General Spaatz assumed command. The first B–17 landed in Scotland on 1 July, bringing with it the hope that daylight heavy bomber operations were not far behind. The distinction of being the first American bomber to drop bombs on a European target, however, had already been claimed. A detachment of B–24s, originally en route to the Far East via Africa, was halted in Egypt and ordered to strike a blow in Eastern Europe to help the hard-pressed Soviets against Hitler's invading armies. Its target was the immense Ploesti oil refinery complex in Rumania. A blow by only 12 B–24s could never have been more than a gesture, whose effects were even more limited by cloud cover on the day of the raid, 10 June 1942. Although it was ineffective, it offered a small sample of greater things to come.

The Eighth in Action

The first Eighth Air Force airmen to see European action were Captain Charles Kegelman and his crew from the 15th Bombardment Squadron. Flying a Douglas Boston (A–20) borrowed from the RAF, they were quietly added to a force striking the Hazebrouck marshalling yards in France on 29 June 1942. USAAF crews entered the fray more formally a few days later, marking 4 July by joining a British squadron in low-level attacks against German airfields in Holland. It was not an auspicious start. Enemy flak was as fierce as any RAF veterans could remember and two American aircrews were shot down. A third, Kegelman's, survived through gritty determination and superb airmanship. On the run-in to De Kooy airfield, Kegelman's aircraft was hit in the right engine. The propeller flew off and flames erupted beneath the cowling. As the low-flying Boston slewed

Boston (A–20). The first Eighth Air Force airmen to take part in active operations against German forces were Captain Charles Kegelman and his crew from the 15th Bombardment Squadron. On 29 June 1942, they flew with the Royal Air Force in a borrowed Douglas Boston to attack French railway marshalling yards.

B–17Es over France. Aircraft such as these B–17s equipped the first U.S. Army Air Forces heavy bomber units in England. Their first mission in Europe was against the Rouen marshalling yards on 17 August 1942.

to the right, its right wing-tip and rear fuselage scraped the airfield's surface. Dragging his crippled aircraft back into the air, Kegelman got rid of his bombs and blasted a flak tower with gunfire. The engine fire went out and he succeeded in struggling back across the North Sea to base. His thoroughly deserved Distinguished Service Cross was the first of many awards for gallantry won by the Eighth Air Force.

As the year wore on into August, American leaders grew impatient for the main Eighth Air Force bombing campaign to begin. Even with their first wave of bombers in place, they were frustrated by the seemingly endless and laborious creation of their new air force, the minimal training level of some arriving aircrews, and an ever-present obstacle—the fickle weather of northwestern Europe. At last, on 17 August, the skies cleared sufficiently to allow 12 B–17Es of the 97th Bombardment Group to fly their first operational mission. Escorted by RAF Spitfires, they attacked the marshalling yards at Rouen in France. Opposition was light, visibility was good, and the bombing from 23,000 feet was reasonably accurate. The 97th's aircraft returned to base almost untouched to find that British monitors had heard a German voice reporting "12 Lancasters heading inland." The error was perhaps understandable at that stage, but the German controllers would have every opportunity to grow familiar with the shape of the B–17 over time.

The first B–17 raid raised American morale considerably. The Eighth was in action, even if only on a small scale,

and the smoothness of the operation hinted at great things for the future. Several prominent (or soon to be) air force figures were involved. The mission was led by Colonel Frank Armstrong, with Major Paul Tibbetts in the other pilot's seat. General Eaker was in the leading aircraft of the second flight, a B–17 appropriately bearing the name *Yankee Doodle*. Congratulations to Eaker came immediately from the Commander in Chief of RAF Bomber Command, Air Marshal Sir Arthur Harris, in a message that read: "*Yankee Doodle* certainly went to town and can stick another well-deserved feather in his cap!"

The early promise of the Rouen raid seemed confirmed by eight more missions flown against other targets in France or the Netherlands between 19 August and 5 September. None was large in scale; none went very far into enemy territory; and all were heavily escorted by fighters. Nevertheless, no B–17s were lost and their bombing was quite accurate. The growing confidence of the bomber crews and their commanders received its first check on 6 September during a raid on aircraft factories at Meaulte in France. For the first time, Luftwaffe fighters pressed home their attacks on the bomber formation and two B–17s were shot down. Several others were damaged and came back with casualties.

Weather restricted operations in the following weeks, but on 9 October Eighth Air Force bombers again faced serious opposition. On that day General

"Fortresses Engaged,"
Keith Ferris, 1985,
USAF Art Collection

B–17 nose. The aircraft was originally named Shoo Shoo Baby *after a World War II popular song. The third* Shoo *was added by a crew flying later combat missions.*

B–17 nose. The plexiglass nose of the B–17 was a spectacular and often frightening place from which to view the air war. Pilots had the impression of sitting in front of rather than inside it as four churning radials close behind them roared on. The compartment was home to the navigator, with a table just below the left cheek gun, and the bombardier, who fired the remotely controlled chin turret guns when not using the Norden bombsight.

Eaker issued his first mission tasking for over 100 bombers—84 B–17s and 24 B–24s taking off with fighter escort to attack targets near Lille. Mechanical failures forced 15 B–17s and 14 B–24s to turn back, reducing the force to 79. Over northern France the Luftwaffe harried the bombers continually, shooting down four and damaging most of the rest. Bombing results were poor, but gunners claimed that they had destroyed 56 fighters, probably destroyed 26 more, and damaged another 20 (in intelligence officer's shorthand: 56-26-20). Since this total almost equalled the number of Luftwaffe fighters thought to have been in the area it was welcomed, but with some

skepticism. Further investigation eventually reduced the figures to 21-21-15, but even that was probably excessive. Inevitably, in the confusion of battle, as many gunners fired at the same fighter, they exaggerated claims. While those claims complicated the assessment of enemy losses, they at least boosted aircrew morale.[1]

Another problem that would bedevil the Eighth Air Force throughout its time in England first arose on the Lille mission. Large aircraft flying in close proximity introduced an obvious collision hazard that had to be accepted. In 1942 the problem was relatively minor since the number of USAAF aircraft in the United

The USAF Museum's B–17G Flying Fortress, Shoo Shoo Baby. *The aircraft led an adventurous life. Delivered to the 91st Bomb Group at Bassingbourn, England, in March 1944,* Shoo Shoo Baby *survived 23 combat missions before flak damage forced a diversion to neutral Sweden. After the war she served as a Danish airliner and then as a photographic survey aircraft for both Denmark and France, suffering Arctic cold and tropical heat in the process. Abandoned and left to rot in France in 1961, the B–17G was recovered by the U.S. Air Force in 1972. Her restoration began at Dover Air Force Base, Delaware, in 1978, and a reborn* Shoo Shoo Baby *flew to her permanent museum home at Wright-Patterson Air Force Base in October 1988.*

B–17 tail. The top of the B–17G's tail stands 19 feet from the ground, but the space reserved for the tail gunner is remarkably cramped. The white triangle with the capital A identifies this as an aircraft belonging to the 91st Bombardment Group, Eighth Air Force.

Kingdom was still quite small. Even so, two B–17s of the 92nd Bombardment Group on their way to Lille collided over the English Channel. One was stripped of its rudder and part of its fin. The other lost two engines and ruptured a fuel tank. On this occasion, both aircraft managed to get back for emergency landings, but future incidents would not always end so happily. As the Eighth grew in strength, its aircrews often met disaster as they tried to operate thousands of aircraft in the uncertain weather and restricted airspace over eastern England.[2]

With four B–17 and two B–24 groups available and the force tested in combat, Eaker was looking forward to

the Eighth's further growth and missions into the German heartland where his bombers could strike with real power. His crews had gained valuable experience but he had limited them to small, fairly ineffectual attacks. Unfortunately for Eaker, higher authorities were about to make it impossible for him to develop the bomber offensive as he would have wished.

Operation TORCH
President Roosevelt and Prime Minister Churchill had originally agreed that first priority be given to the preparation of plans for an Allied invasion of Europe, principally to ease pressure on the hard-pressed Soviet Union. While an invasion seemed impractical in late

1942, a plan (codenamed SLEDGEHAMMER) for one was drawn up to be carried out if the Soviet Union appeared on the brink of defeat.

Much firmer was the proposal to launch an invasion of France in the spring of 1943. This operation was codenamed ROUNDUP, and its preparatory phase was BOLERO. The Eighth Air Force figured in both, as a strategic weapon and an ensurer of air superiority for Allied forces, and Spaatz and Eaker worked to build up its strength and capability as quickly as possible. Believing as they did, with other air leaders, that the future status of air power within America's military depended largely on the strategic bomber, they were keen to show the skeptics, who claimed that there were better ways to use national resources, that the Eighth could use the aircraft successfully. In 1942 so many other battles had to be fought; it was by no means certain that the air war over Germany would remain a high priority. The U.S. Joint Chiefs of Staff (JCS) needed convincing, and it was up to the Eighth to provide the proof.

As the summer of 1942 progressed, tension eased somewhat in the Pacific and the Japanese advance to the gates of India was slowed by the monsoon, but the German Army still hammered at the Soviets, and the British suffered a series of defeats at the hands of Rommel in North Africa. By July, Rommel's army stood within reach of the Suez Canal and there was talk among the Allies of reviving the GYMNAST plan for an American invasion of North Africa, much against the wishes of the JCS. They still believed that ROUNDUP should take pride of place, but Roosevelt and Churchill concluded otherwise, and decided that an invasion of North Africa, under the new codename, TORCH, should take precedence. The promised second front in Europe to help the Soviets would have to take the form of an intensified air assault against Germany. In that, of course, the Eighth Air Force chiefs were only too ready to take part, but at that stage the force's resources were insufficient to mount a strategic air offensive and provide air support for a major invasion simultaneously. Spaatz wrote to Arnold in August:

> Regardless of what operations are conducted in any other theater, in my opinion, [England] remains the only base area from which to launch aerial operations to obtain air supremacy over Germany, and until such air supremacy is established there can be no successful outcome of the war.

Arnold's chief of staff did his best to reassure Spaatz in his reply, suggesting that Operation TORCH was to be carried out at the expense of anything *but* the

L–4 cockpit. Reflecting the L–4's role, sufficient instruments are fitted for safe flight but not so many as to distract the crew from looking outside.

bombing offensive from the United Kingdom, but his promise was soon seen as an empty one. The forces were just not available for both offensives at once. On 8 September Spaatz had to order that all air operations in the European theater be subordinated to preparations for the invasion of North Africa. The Eighth Air Force was to lose a large part of its existing strength to a new air force, the Twelfth, being created for the invasion, and for some time to come the Twelfth would be given priority for men and machines. Answers to the strategic bombing question would have to wait.

The Allied landings in North Africa took place on 8 November 1942, under the overall command of Lieutenant General Dwight Eisenhower. TORCH was the first Allied combined operation, and it was as complex and potentially dangerous as any that followed. Over 500 ships from the United States and United Kingdom made their way through the dangerous waters of the Atlantic to land more than 100,000 men on the North African coast, at Casablanca, Oran, and Algiers. Aircraft operating from carriers and from RAF bases at Gibraltar and Malta provided initial air cover, but it was not long before Twelfth Air Force units joined the battle against the French colonial forces resisting the landings.

L–4. Simple and cheap, thousands of Piper L–4A Grasshoppers were delivered and saw service in every World War II combat theater. This one is marked as an aircraft flown during Operation TORCH, the Allied invasion of North Africa.

L–4. The military version of the Cub, the Piper L–4A Grasshopper was typical of the small liaison and observation aircraft used by the U.S. Army Air Forces in World War II. Fitted with a 65-horsepower Continental engine, it cruised at 75 miles per hour. Its slow speed, combined with a high wing and generous greenhouse windows, allowed the crew to pay close attention to details on the ground, report what they saw, and call in artillery fire or aircraft strikes.

The commander of the Twelfth, Major General Jimmy Doolittle, arrived at Gibraltar on the afternoon of 6 November, his B–17 bearing the scars of a brisk encounter with four Ju 88s over the Bay of Biscay. He was, therefore, on hand on 8 November to order the 31st Fighter Group, waiting on the crowded airstrip, to fly its Spitfires into Tafaraoui airfield near Oran. Their arrival there was eventful. Before landing, some Spitfires managed to silence French artillery shelling the airfield. Others took on four and destroyed three Dewoitine fighters that had shot down one of the 31st's aircraft during its approach. Within hours

Supermarine Spitfires. The U.S. Army Air Forces obtained hundreds of Supermarine Spitfires from the British for operations in the European and Mediterranean theaters. Among the first Twelfth Air Force units to land in North Africa in support of Operation TORCH were Spitfire squadrons of the 31st and 52nd Fighter Groups. Spitfire 5Bs of the 31st Fighter Group shown here stand ready for action in Tunisia.

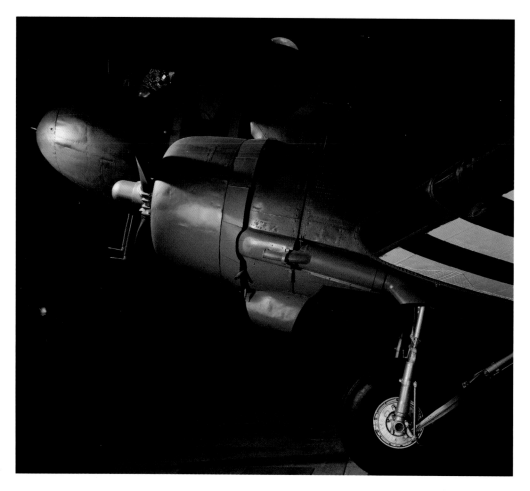

C–47 nose. The Douglas C–47 Skytrain was usually called the Gooney Bird. Over 9,000 C–47s were delivered to the U.S. Army Air Forces. They were used in every wartime theater as general transports and for taking troops into battle, either carrying them as paratroops or towing them in gliders. In later years, C–47s played their part in the Berlin Airlift and Korea and added to their roles in Vietnam as gunships. The Gooney Bird in the USAF Museum is a C–47A in the markings of the 88th Troop Carrier Squadron, 438th Troop Carrier Group, in June 1944.

C–47 tail. The Allies painted black and white stripes on their aircraft before the Normandy invasion in the hope that ground and naval forces would recognize them as friendly. Added at the last minute, the stripes were often slapped on with brooms or mops and their edges were anything but even. The museum's restoration has reproduced this ragged appearance faithfully.

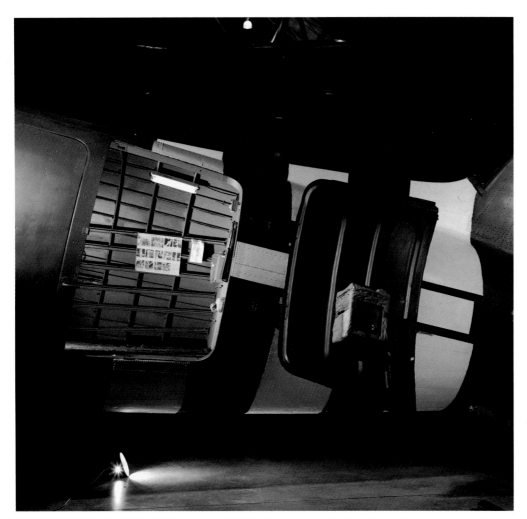

C–47 door. The strengthened floor and large double doors of the C–47 turned the civilian DC–3 into the jack-of-all-trades needed by the military. Rugged, reliable, and adaptable, C–47s served with distinction in every corner of the world.

the 52nd Fighter Group's Spitfires and the 33rd Fighter Group's P–40s were added to the Twelfth's strength ashore. The 60th Troop Carrier Group's C–47s also arrived carrying paratroops from the United Kingdom, although bad weather and communications failures bedeviled their efforts and scattered them over the northwest shoulder of Africa.

By 10 November the French Air Force in North Africa had been destroyed or captured. The Twelfth Air Force had lost six Spitfires (two to friendly fire) and three C–47s. In the next ten days, the Twelfth's strength in Algeria grew to include four fighter groups (the 1st and 14th with P–38s, and the 31st and 52nd with Spitfires), a light bomber squadron (the 15th with A–20s), the B–17s of the 97th Bombardment Group, and two troop carrier groups. In Morocco the build-up went more slowly, but there were still the P–40s of the 33rd Fighter Group, some B–25s of the 310th Bombardment Group, and parts of the 62nd Troop Carrier Group.

Once established ashore, the Allied forces turned east to move on Tunisia and crush Rommel's army between themselves and the British 8th Army under General Montgomery, which was now driving the Axis armies westward out of Egypt. The Germans reacted quickly, pouring reinforcements into Tunisia and checking the forward Allied units. Worse, heavy winter rains were bogging down the Allied armies' inadequate transport and turning their dirt airfields to soup. The Luftwaffe, operating from hard surfaces, was not affected. The winter months were a testing time for the Allied forces and the Luftwaffe generally had the upper hand in the air. Nevertheless, Allied bombers continued to harass the enemy whenever possible, attacking airfields and port facilities with B–17s, B–26s, A–20s, and RAF Blenheim Vs. They were joined by RAF Wellingtons based in Malta and the western desert and by B–17s and B–24s of another recent arrival in the Mediterranean theater, the U.S. Ninth Air Force.

New Command Arrangements

Late in June 1942 Major General Lewis Brereton arrived in Cairo from the Pacific to command a hurriedly organized U.S. Middle East Air Force. In November it became the Ninth Air Force, operating principally in support of General Montgomery's 8th Army as it pursued Rommel in his westward retreat. By February 1943 the Axis armies had been driven back into Tunisia, and the campaigns of the British 8th Army and the Allied TORCH armies merged. After interim arrangements the Allied air forces combined as part of a sweeping reorganization in the Mediterranean. Air Marshal Sir Arthur Tedder became Commander,

Mediterranean Air Command, which had three elements—the Malta and Middle East Commands, and the Northwest African Air Forces (NAAF). The NAAF was given to Carl Spaatz in a shuffle that still left him with the responsibility of commanding American air forces in the European theater while accompanying Eisenhower to Africa. Ira Eaker was moved up to command the Eighth Air Force in the United Kingdom.

The NAAF was functionally divided into three elements—the Northwest African Strategic Air Force (NASAF) commanded by Jimmy Doolittle; the Northwest African Tactical Air Force (NATAF) under Air Marshal "Maori" Coningham; and the Northwest African Coastal Air Force (NACAF) led by Air Marshal Hugh Lloyd. The new arrangements placed the two officers who had been most closely involved with the development of army-air force cooperation during the war in the desert, Tedder and Coningham, in command positions, and their record of success profoundly influenced their USAAF colleagues. The NAAF was a new experience for American airmen. USAAF and RAF officers were intermingled at every level and constantly reminded of the importance of eliminating interservice rivalries and working closely with their army opposite numbers. Functional divisions also became common as whole air forces were designated strategic or tactical. Also, the placement under a single air commander of closely cooperating air forces fighting in the land battle was firmly established.

The Luftwaffe Struck Down

As the winter weather eased, Coningham issued a directive to the NATAF, in which he stressed the necessity of achieving air supremacy before becoming heavily engaged in the land battle. His priorities were: first, "a continual offensive against the enemy in the air," and second, "sustained attacks on enemy airfields." He emphasized that "the inculcation of the offensive spirit is of paramount importance." With concentrated Allied offensive operations unleashed in March 1943, the days of Luftwaffe superiority were over. German aircraft losses rose rapidly, both in air combat and on the ground. Much to the relief of Allied troops, but probably to the regret of the fighter pilots, the notorious Ju 87 Stuka had to be withdrawn from combat in Africa after crippling losses, notably on 3 April, when the 52nd Fighter Group intercepted 20 and, brushing aside their escort, destroyed 14 for the loss of one Spitfire.

From March 1943 until the end of the North African campaign in May, Allied air forces put constant pressure on enemy airfields, ports, and troop

B–26s. Among the medium bombers operated by the Twelfth Air force in the Mediterranean theater was the Martin B–26 Marauder. The 319th Bombardment Group was one of the first to see action with the B–26 in North Africa.

concentrations. Tactical aircraft, including P–40s of the 57th and 79th Groups, after a relentless thrashing, broke the principal Axis line of defense in Tunisia—the Mareth Line. Luftwaffe fighters became hunted creatures, moving continually from one airstrip to another and adopting extreme dispersal measures. The B–17s introduced themselves to Italy, achieving an impressive success in sinking the cruiser *Trieste* at its anchorage from 19,000 feet. Additionally, they destroyed 30 acres of Palermo's docks and several ships in an explosion felt at 24,000 feet.

In April the Allies took measures to sever the Axis lifeline across the straits between Sicily and Tunisia. As many as 500 enemy transports (Ju 52s, SM 82s, and Me 323s) were being used to ensure the survival of the Axis armies in North Africa. Offensive sweeps against Sicilian airfields mounting the enemy airlift destroyed dozens of transports on their bases, and strong fighter patrols made the straits a killing ground. Among a number of memorable days for the Allied fighters was 18 April, the day of the Palm Sunday Massacre. Four squadrons of P–40s (of the 57th and 324th Fighter Groups) with a top cover of RAF Spitfires intercepted a huge formation of about 100 Ju 52s, escorted by MC 202s, Bf 109s, and Bf 110s.

The Allied fighters shot down 51 transports and 16 of their escorts for the loss of 6 P–40s and 1 Spitfire. Four days later, more Allied fighters caught and obliterated a formation of 21 giant Me 323s, each carrying 10 tons of fuel, and effectively ended the Axis airlift. They destroyed over a period of only 17 days of the North African campaign a total of 435 enemy transport aircraft, breaking the back of Luftwaffe airlift capability.

Under incessant pressure from Allied ground and air forces, Axis resistance crumbled, and by 7 May the German air commander in Tunisia was ordering his squadrons to fly to safety. Serviceable aircraft left for Sicily immediately, but because of the effectiveness of the Allied campaign against Axis airfields, more than 600 aircraft were unable to escape and had to be left behind. The final surrender of all Axis units in North Africa came on 13 May, when over a quarter of a million troops capitulated and passed into captivity.

The USAAF had no enthusiasm for Operation TORCH, seeing it as an unwelcome diversion from the principal objective—the development of a bombing offensive against Germany. Nevertheless, the North African adventure had proved invaluable. The Allies had gained combat experience at relatively little cost and had absorbed the basic principles of air-ground cooperation. Lessons learned were quickly incorporated into Field Manual 100-20, which forthrightly declared:

> Land power and air power are co-equal and interdependent forces.... The gaining of air superiority is the first requirement for the success of any major land operation.... The inherent flexibility of air power is its greatest asset.... Control of available air power must be centralized and command must be exercised through the air force commander if this inherent flexibility and ability to deliver a decisive blow are to be fully exploited.

These principles, established in North Africa, would give rise to the overwhelming tactical air power that proved so vital to the overthrow of Hitler's Fortress Europe.

The Air Assault on Germany

In January 1943 Roosevelt, Churchill, and their Combined Chiefs of Staff met in Casablanca to discuss the future direction of the war. Daylight strategic bombing was among the operations subjected to their scrutiny. The claims of its USAAF advocates were still unproven, and not a single Eighth Air Force bomb had yet fallen on Germany. The British still believed that the Eighth should become part of the night bombing offensive. The USN wanted the resources needed to build up a bomber force in England expended in the Pacific.

At this stage of the war the USAAF could produce little supporting evidence to defend its position. Since being ordered to support Operation TORCH, the Eighth Air Force had accomplished nothing of great significance. The shortages of aircraft and crews and the appalling winter weather in northwestern Europe had placed tight limits on both the strength and frequency of its operations, most of which, worse still, had to be diverted against U-boat pens in France. These were nearly impervious to attack and well defended. From almost every point of view, the Eighth's results were discouraging. Between mid-October 1942 and mid-January 1943, of just over 1,000 bomber sorties, over 400 had failed to attack. In September 1942 the number of aircraft returning from raids with repairable battle damage was 13.3 percent of the

Me 323. In the early months of 1943 Allied aircraft effectively destroyed the enemy's capability to supply his forces in North Africa by air. Enemy transport aircraft venturing over the Mediterranean did so at their extreme peril. This giant Me 323 was caught and shot down near Corsica by a passing B–26.

attacking force; by December, it was up to 42.1 percent. The Eighth's total losses had risen from 3.7 percent in November to a disturbing 8.7 percent in January.

One factor affecting these worrying figures was a change in Luftwaffe fighter tactics. On 23 November 1942, during a mission against St. Nazaire, fighters led by *Oberleutnant* Egon Mayer began to attack the bomber formations head on. At that time neither the B–17 nor the B–24 was heavily armed in the nose, and there were blind spots which the guns of the aircrafts' upper and lower turrets could not reach. The rapid closing rates of frontal attacks made the fighters into small-area targets, which, at high crossing speeds, were more difficult for defending gunners to hit. Luftwaffe pilots began to score consistently against Eighth Air Force bombers as frontal attacks became a feature of the struggle throughout the air war in Europe. Almost immediately the Eighth sought countermeasures, adding more forward-facing guns to the B–17s and B–24s and devising new formations to allow each bomber to make the most of mutual protection. At first, bomber formations had flown in elements of no more than three loosely coordinated aircraft. By 1943 the Eighth's bombers were going to war in combat boxes of 18 to 21 aircraft, with two or three boxes flying together in a defensive pattern.

Only too well aware of the Eighth's problems, Hap Arnold summoned Ira Eaker to the Casablanca Conference to present the case for strategic daylight bombing. Eaker brushed aside past and present difficulties and concentrated on future prospects, winning over Churchill by describing an offensive in which the USAAF by day and the RAF by night would subject Germany to a steady pounding, to "soften the Hun for land invasion and the kill." Churchill's imagination was caught by Eaker's pledges, particularly one that became a slogan—to bomb the Third Reich "around the clock." As a result of Eaker's persuasions, Allied leaders were able to agree that a coordinated bombing offensive, by day and night, was the only way immediately available to carry the war to Germany, and that it was indispensable preparation for the eventual invasion of Europe. A directive was issued calling for a combined bomber offensive aimed at "…the progressive destruction and dislocation of the German military, industrial, and economic system, and the undermining of the morale of the German people to a point where their capacity for armed resistance is fatally weakened."

Less than a week after the end of the Casablanca Conference, on 27 January 1943, the Eighth Air Force opened its long campaign against Germany with a raid on Wilhelmshaven. Fifty-five aircraft out of 91 bombed their targets, but clouds and fighters spoiled their aim and effectiveness. A B–17 and two B–24s were lost, but the gunners had a good day, claiming 22 fighters shot down. (The actual score was 7.) The first step having been taken, the offensive against German targets did not build up as hoped. Between the first Wilhelmshaven raid and mid-August 1943, more than six months later, the Eighth was able to take advantage of only 20 days within which to penetrate German airspace, although it carried out raids in France and Holland. Eaker's superiors in Washington had difficulty grasping the reasons for the force's slow progress, although their policies were in large part responsible for it. Eaker had to withstand a continual stream of criticism as the Eighth battled the enemy, European weather, the diversion of assets to other theaters, shortages of spares, and inadequately trained new aircrews. Sometimes half of his meager force was grounded because neither spares nor qualified aircrews were available.

The Eighth's missions flown into Germany included its first attacks on Kiel, Hamburg, and the Ruhr. With them came an inkling that unescorted daylight bombing might not be feasible after all. The Eighth suffered notable losses on 13 June (22 B–17s of 60 attacking Kiel), 25 July (15 B–17s of 100 against Hamburg), and 12 August (23 B–17s of 133 over the Ruhr). On these days, and a number of others, the air force felt the absence of escort fighters severely. The P–47 Thunderbolts tasked for escort duty could not accompany the bombers past Aachen on the German border, after which the Luftwaffe took over. Not content with swarming in on the bombers head-on (at least one head-on collision was reported between a B–17 and an FW 190 in this period), German fighter units tried new tactics—aiming bombs and salvoes of rockets at formations—among others.[3] The Luftwaffe would grow more and more determined to oppose the USAAF, most obviously in the latter half of 1943.

The significance of high loss rates was not lost on the bomber crews, who in 1943 needed 25 missions to complete a tour of combat duty. A mere 4 percent loss rate meant that no crew would finish a tour. Double figure percentages suggested that all bomber crews would quickly reach a point where they were living on borrowed time. As the months went by, the slow pace of the bomber offensive stretched out the accumulation of combat missions into an agony of waiting, and the number of aircrews who reached the end of their tours seemed frighteningly small. It was June 1943 before a crew of the 91st Bombardment Group, together with its B–17F, became the first in the Eighth Air Force to complete a combat tour and

A B–17F of the 569th Bombardment Squadron, 390th Bombardment Group, at Framlingham awaiting its lethal cargo. The 390th was involved in one of the war's most concentrated air battles on 10 Oct 1943 over Munster. The group lost 8 B–17s and claimed 60 Luftwaffe fighters, a record for a bomber group on one operation.

return to the United States. It was a sufficiently notable event that Captain Bob Morgan's crew and their B–17, *Memphis Belle*, were sent on a publicity tour of the United States to promote the sale of war bonds.[4]

Ploesti

The directive governing the Combined Bomber Offensive, derived from plans drawn up after the Casablanca Conference, was issued on 10 June 1943 and code named POINTBLANK. Among its primary targets were ball bearings and oil. In August 1943 the USAAF turned its attention to both of these vital products and launched two daylight raids that penetrated more deeply into Europe than ever. The first, in Rumania, against the Ploesti oil refineries, producers of almost two-thirds of Axis oil, was made by B–24s operating from North Africa. Two groups from the resident Ninth Air Force (the 98th and 376th) joined two deployed from the Eighth (the 44th and 93rd) and a new group from the United States (the 389th) in sending 177 B–24s across the Mediterranean on 1 August 1943. For maximum impact, waves of B–24s flew at extremely low level through the target area, almost nose to tail.

On the face of it, the B–24 was not an ideal low-level aircraft in close proximity to others. Weighing 60,000

pounds and spanning 110 feet across the wing, it was often likened to a truck. Pilot Carl Fritsche said: "To fly formation for several hours in a B–24 required endurance. The controls took so much strength to move that you didn't have to worry about getting to sleep after a long mission." The B–24's great advantage was its range. It was sent to Ploesti because in 1943 it was the only bomber capable of getting there and back. The round trip to the refinery from Libya covered about 2,700 miles, and some aircraft were in the air for more than 16 hours.

To succeed over Ploesti the B–24s needed the best navigators, good weather en route, light enemy defenses, and the element of surprise. Unfortunately, they got none. As the leaders approached the coast of Greece on the outbound leg, the B–24 *Wingo Wango*, carrying the mission's lead navigator, suddenly dived steeply into the sea. A second aircraft, with the deputy lead navigator, circled to investigate and was left far behind. Over Albania severe weather disrupted the formations, splitting them into two main groups. Approaching the target area, the aircraft carrying the mission commander, Brigadier General Uzal Ent, turned too early and took the leading groups (the 376th and 93rd) toward Bucharest instead of Ploesti.

Both Major Ramsay Potts of the 93rd and Major Norman Appold of the 376th broke radio silence to warn of the mistake, but by this time the cohesion of the raid was lost. The two groups finally turned to approach Ploesti from the south instead of the northwest, their crews on the lookout for targets of opportunity. Adding to their problems was inaccurate information on the strength of area defenses. By August 1943 Ploesti was one of the most heavily defended sites in Europe, bristling with anti-aircraft guns and supported by fighters based nearby. Nor were the B–24s blessed with the advantage of surprise, having been seen by German radar before crossing the Greek coast.

Their ordered ranks gone, the raiders attacked in ragged flocks from several directions, few finding their allocated targets and all heavily engaged in a running battle with German gunners in flak towers, on freight trains, or in haystacks. Within minutes, Ploesti was covered in flame and smoke as bombs found oil storage tanks and aircraft fell to the defenders' guns. B–24s hurtled between refinery chimneys and dodged other bombers coming at them head on. Aircraft attacked whatever targets presented themselves among the dense clouds of oily smoke, and other B–24s flew through the blast of the resulting explosions. Colonel Leon Johnson, leader of the 44th Bombardment Group, said it was "…indescribable to anyone who was not there. We flew through sheets of flame, and airplanes were everywhere, some of them on fire and some of them exploding." Countless acts of heroism and grim determination marked the battle. One of the more memorable was that of Lieutenant Lloyd Hughes. The tanks of his B–24 punctured and, streaming fuel, Hughes pressed home his attack at the Campina refinery through a wall of flame. His aircraft's liquid fuze of leaking fuel ignited and fire enveloped the aircraft, but Hughes held it

Ramsay Potts. As a 26-year-old major he took part in the low-level Ploesti raid. More than 50 years later he renewed his acquaintance with the B–24's cockpit at the USAF Museum.

B–24s over Ploesti. Consolidated B–24 Liberators of "Killer" Kane's 98th Bombardment Group fly through the smoke and flame of the 93rd Bombardment Group's earlier attack on the Ploesti oil refineries. Kane was awarded the Medal of Honor for his determined leadership on this raid.

level and delivered his bombs before attempting a crash landing. Two gunners survived the impact. Hughes died and was one of five airmen to be awarded the Medal of Honor for the raid.[5]

Escaping the fires of Ploesti, surviving B–24s were harassed by fighters all the way to the Ionian Sea. Several bombers diverted to Malta and Cyprus, and others struggled to Turkey, where their crews were interned. Still others crashed into the Mediterranean, leaving just 88 to reach their home base in Libya. In all, 54 B–24s were lost, 41 of them in combat; 532 airmen never returned, including more than 100 taken prisoner or detained. The damage sustained by surviving aircraft was such that only 30 of 177 were fit for combat the following day.

The aircrews paid a high price for their valiant effort but were disappointed by its results. They had inflicted

severe damage on Ploesti and reduced its total refining capacity by 40 percent. However, that capacity had been much less than full before the raid. Within days, idle plant had been brought on line to replace lost production. The Allies did not follow up the costly mission, deciding that another would be impractical. They could not have borne loss rates of over 30 percent. The USAAF would no longer attempt any unescorted long range, low-level attacks by heavy bombers against defended targets.

Schweinfurt

On 17 August 1943, the Allies turned their attention to Germany's ball-bearing industry, planning a maximum effort by B–17s of the Eighth Air Force against Schweinfurt and Regensburg, site of a Messerschmitt aircraft factory. At that time Schweinfurt's factories produced half of the bearings needed by the Nazi war machine. Regensburg was the deeper of the two into

Lady Be Good. *On 4 April 1943, the airmen of* Lady Be Good, *a B–24 of the 376th Bombardment Group, left Soluch, Libya, to attack Naples. It was their first mission—and their last. Pushed on by a tailwind during their night return, they overshot Soluch by 400 miles. Sixteen years later, the wreckage of* Lady Be Good *was discovered in the desert, and the bodies of her crew were found at intervals of up to 100 miles to the northwest. A member of the 1959 investigating team is shown preparing to examine the interior of the aircraft's fuselage.*

B–24 cockpit. A challenge for any pilot, the B–24's cluttered cockpit was complicated; because of frequent modifications its instrument panels were not standardized. Constants were the red buttons on the coaming that were used to destroy secret equipment if a forced landing was made in enemy territory. The red buttons at the top of the windscreen are feathering controls, turning failed engine propellers knife-edge to the wind to reduce drag.

The twin .50s in the tail turret of a B–24. With more room than his B–17 counterpart, the tail-gunner was still the loneliest man in the crew, physically separated from his colleagues and unable to see the hazards into which his aircraft was heading.

B–24 nose. The deep greenhouse nose of the B–24D was modified in later marks to accept a turret firing twin .50-caliber machine guns. The navigator's astrodome remained in place.

B–24. The USAF Museum's B–24D Liberator, Strawberry Bitch, *arrived at Soluch, Libya, in September 1943 to join the Fifteenth Air Force. With the 512th Bombardment Squadron of the 376th Bombardment Group,* Strawberry Bitch *flew 59 missions against targets in Italy.*

Germany, and it was planned that the 4th Bombardment Wing groups allocated to the target lead the way for the whole force and continue to North Africa after bombing. The idea was to time the 1st Bombardment Wing's raid on Schweinfurt so that Luftwaffe fighters opposing the Regensburg mission would be on the ground refueling when the second force arrived. Unfortunately, on the morning of 17 August, fog blanketed the Eighth's airfields and prevented its aircraft from taking off at dawn, as planned. The 4th Bombardment Wing's airfields began to clear first and the Regensburg mission got airborne, but thick fog persisted over the 1st Bombardment Wing, delaying the Schweinfurt force for more than three hours.

Fog also disrupted the 4th Bombardment Wing's intended fighter escort of P–47s. Only one group made contact with the bombers, and even they had to turn back as they neared the German border. Colonel Curtis LeMay, leading the Regensburg attack with the 96th Bombardment Group, later remarked that the only escorts he saw "had black crosses on their wings." The 4th Bombardment Wing began its journey across Europe with 139 B–17s, but that number began falling before they reached Germany. Both Luftwaffe fighters and flak left their mark while the B–17s were still over Belgium. By the time they reached Regensburg, 14 had been shot down, and 3 others had been forced to jettison their bombloads; 122 B–17s were left to attack the Messerschmitt factory. The two leading groups had never come under serious attack and were intact, but some of those farther back had taken a severe beating, particularly the 100th Bombardment Group, which had lost 6 of its original 21 aircraft and had several others damaged. Looking back from near the front of the aerial armada, Staff Sergeant Earl Spann (390th Bombardment Group) had a grandstand view:

> The trip into Germany was a bloody battle all the way. It was mostly fighter planes but also heavy flak at times…. From our position, I could see behind us and there were planes falling everywhere, a lot of ours and a lot of theirs. Many trails of smoke could be seen coming up from crashed planes. A lot of brave men had died…

Lieutenant Colonel Beirne Lay (100th Bombardment Group) captured the intensity of the struggle in the phrase: "Each second of time had a cannon shell in it."[6]

The final approach to Regensburg met few fighters and little flak. Visibility was generally excellent. Bombing was accurate and tightly grouped. No B–17s were lost in the target area (although three were badly damaged and would not reach Africa) and the Messerschmitt factory was heavily hit. LeMay's Wing could hardly have done a better job. At the time it was thought that factory production would be severely curtailed, and there is no doubt that several weeks' worth was lost, later estimated at perhaps the equivalent of 1,000 fighters. What was not then realized was that the bombs being used (500 pounders, plus incendiaries) were powerful enough to knock down buildings but not to destroy machine tools. Within weeks the Germans had dispersed their production facilities and were on their way back to business. Nevertheless, the raid achieved one great success that was hidden from the Allies at the time. Among the items destroyed were jigs for a revolutionary new fighter—the jet-propelled Messerschmitt Me 262.

The 4th Bombardment Wing landed in North Africa five hours later, having faced little further opposition. Its not turning back from Regensburg appeared to have taken the Germans by surprise. Attrition took its toll, however, as damaged aircraft continued to fall from formation. Of 139 B–24s that had crossed into Europe, 24 were lost. Of those, 9 had come from the 100th Bombardment Group, a crippling unit loss rate of over 40 percent.

Shortly before midday, the 1st Bombardment Wing was finally ordered into the air. Having long since abandoned the original plan of mutual support with the 4th Bombardment Wing, it realized that the long flight to Schweinfurt and back would be hazardous. As it crossed the Dutch coast, 222 B–17s faced a reinforced Luftwaffe fighter force prepared to meet what it believed would be the Regensburg force on its way back to England. Almost 300 Luftwaffe fighters were ready and waiting to fight along the route into southern Germany.

Up to the German border, first Spitfires and then P–47s did a good job of holding the Luftwaffe at bay. Things changed dramatically as the last Allied fighters left. Lieutenant William Wheeler (91st Bombardment Group) recalled the scene:

> The thing I remember most vividly is that the Germans started making their initial attack almost exactly at the same time as the P–47s above us made their 180-degree turn to return to base…. Looking back at it now, I think that very moment…was the major turning point when the Air Force had it proved to them that their idea of sending B–17s unescorted on a deep penetration was

P–47 cockpit. Everything about the P–47 was large, but even in such a spacious cockpit the throttle lever could seem unreasonably prominent. Compare the cockpit of this World War II Thunderbolt with that of the World War I Camel and with that of the A–10 Thunderbolt II shown at the end of Chapter 15.

P–47 canopy. To begin with, P–47Ds were built with a sliding framed cockpit canopy. Not until a bubble canopy from a Hawker Typhoon was tested on a P–47 airframe in mid-1943 were clear canopies generally adopted for all P–47s. The simple bucket pilot's seat in the P–47D was backed by armor plate that reached from the floor to behind the headrest.

P–47 nose. The enormous bulk of the 2,430-horsepower Pratt & Whitney R–2800–59 radial engine is the dominant feature of the rugged Republic P–47D Thunderbolt. It determines the portly shape of the fuselage and is a large part of the aircraft's high all-up weight of 17,500 pounds, unprecedented in a single-engined fighter. The Museum's P–47D carries the markings of the 56th Fighter Group, in terms of enemy aircraft shot down the most successful Group in the Eighth Air Force.

not valid. It broke the back of the theories of those who were convinced that the Flying Fortress could protect itself if you had good formation discipline and that excellent 50-caliber gun…

This time it was the leading groups of the 1st Bombardment Wing that bore the brunt of the Luftwaffe assault. The German fighter leaders deployed their *Staffeln* well ahead of the B–17s in line abreast, as many as 15 fighters at a time, in waves of head-on attacks, each one following relentlessly after another. The B–17 aircrews who experienced it testified to the ferocity and determination with which the German airmen pressed home their attacks. Staff Sergeant John Thompson (waist gunner, 384th Bombardment Group) spoke for many of his comrades when he recalled the battle:

> I witnessed something that mankind will never see again. It was rare to see hundreds and hundreds of aircraft in the sky at once. On one occasion our formation made a small turn and I was able to look back. It looked like a parachute invasion of Germany…. Planes were going down so often that it became useless to report them.

Lieutenant Donald Rutan (co-pilot, 381st Bombardment Group), was mesmerized by what was he saw:

There wasn't much sense in calling out fighters that day; everything was at twelve o'clock level for what seemed like an eternity. Each time they came in you thought it would be our turn to get it. So many of our planes had gone. This was the fiercest we ever had.

While the 1st Bombardment Wing suffered grievous combat losses and savage battle damage on its long flight across Germany, 184 of its B–17s reached and bombed Schweinfurt. Shaken and somewhat scattered by the ferocity of the running fight, many aircrews became confused by the dust and smoke that soon covered the target area. Later groups, unable to identify the ball-bearing factories, followed their briefing instructions to aim at the center of the city. As a result they were unable to concentrate their bombing and left the factories damaged, not destroyed. Some aircrews were only too well aware of their limited success; one navigator complained that they had suffered so much "only to come this far and miss the damned target."

By the time the 1st Bombardment Wing fought its way back across Germany to the haven of its English bases, 36 of its B–17s had gone down. From the combined force of 361 heavy bombers that had crossed into Europe during the day, 60 had been lost. At least 11 more were so badly damaged that they never flew again, and 162 others had lesser damage. Over 550 men had been killed or were missing. In one day, the Eighth Air Force had suffered losses equal to those of its first six months of operations.

Such alarming figures were thought at the time to have been offset by the successes of the B–17's gunners who claimed no fewer than 288 Luftwaffe fighters destroyed. Post-war research revealed that the Luftwaffe lost 47 fighters on 17 August 1943—21 to B–17s, 21 to escorts over Belgium, and 5 to accidents. Given the disappointing Allied results over Schweinfurt, the laurels of the day belonged to its defenders. They took precautions against future air attacks by more than doubling the number of anti-aircraft gun batteries around the Schweinfurt factories, withdrawing more fighter units from duties elsewhere to cover the approaches to southern Germany and giving thought to dispersing ball-bearing production. Despite their defensive successes, the Germans were beginning to worry that they would be badly hurt by the persistence and growing strength of the Eighth Air Force.

In the remaining months of 1943, the hard lessons of Schweinfurt and Regensburg were driven home whenever the Eighth struck at targets within Germany. On 6 September in a depressing fiasco, 262 B–17s scattered bombs in the Stuttgart area through clouds, doing little damage and losing 45 aircraft. Of 1,074 B–17s launched between 8 and 10 October against various German targets, 855 bombed; the rest were lost. As always, these figures told only part of the story. On these raids, well over 600 aircraft were damaged, many never to fly again.[7] Grimly determined that the Eighth Air Force should continue the battle of attrition and defeat the Luftwaffe, General Eaker sent his bombers back to Schweinfurt on 14 October. A force of 291 B–17s set out to be met with a Luftwaffe performance described by the official USAAF history as "unprecedented in its magnitude, in the cleverness with which it was planned, and in the severity with which it was executed." In the face of such powerfully determined opposition, the Schweinfurt mission was remarkable. This time, highly accurate bombing severely damaged the factories, but at an unbearably high price—another 60 B–17s were shot down, 7 more were destroyed returning to England, and a further 138 were damaged to some degree. As many as 288 Luftwaffe fighters were claimed destroyed (German records suggest only 35, although many more were damaged), but even that exaggeration could not obscure the fact that the Eighth Air Force was taking a beating. Over Germany, the Luftwaffe was consistently imposing losses of well above 10 percent, a rate

that would lead inexorably to the Eighth's destruction. It was ever more apparent that the daylight bombing offensive could not be continued in the absence of escort fighters with the range to accompany the bombers over Germany.

Changes at the Top

The year 1943 had been a testing time for the Eighth Air Force, and, as it drew to a close, the daylight offensive was in the balance. Experiments in which some B–17 units joined the RAF's night offensive to gain experience in case daylight bombing failed had to be abandoned altogether. Unpromising as things looked, however, the Eighth's persistence was about to be rewarded; 1944 would bring great changes and see the scale and intensity of the air war over Europe raised to levels unimagined in pre-war years.

Among them was the replacement of General Ira Eaker as the commander of the Eighth Air Force. Hap Arnold's impatience with what he perceived as the slow pace of the air assault on Germany led him to initiate a shakeup among his senior leaders. Eaker was to take over command of the Mediterranean Allied Air Forces (MAAF) from Tedder, who, with Eisenhower, would move to England to prepare plans for the invasion of northwestern Europe. Spaatz would command the U.S. Strategic Air Forces (USSTAF) in Europe (coordinating the operations of the Eighth and Fifteenth Air Forces), and Doolittle would be the new commander of the Eighth Air Force. Eaker was not happy at this turn of events. Having seen the Eighth through its worst days, he had been looking forward to future triumphs. His vigorous protests were brushed aside, however, and he duly packed his bags and moved south. Although resentful of the change, he found his new command much changed from its days in North Africa. It was now an immense force of over 200 Allied squadrons, and it included two numbered U.S. air forces—the Twelfth, which had evolved into a tactical force, and the Fifteenth, which had a strategic role.

Sicily and Italy

At the Casablanca Conference in January 1943 the Allies agreed that the defeat of the Axis forces in North Africa would be followed by an invasion of Sicily and then of Italy. In a preliminary step, their air forces began to strike at Pantelleria during the latter part of May and early June 1943. This heavily defended island in the middle of the Sicilian Straits boasted a usable airfield from which to provide air cover for the Allied landings on Sicily. Over 5,000 Allied sorties were flown against Pantelleria, the bulk of the bombing being done by USAAF squadrons.

Eighth Air Force commanders. In the months before D-Day in 1944 Colonel Ramsay Potts was commanding officer of the B–24-equipped 453rd Bombardment Group, with movie star James Stewart as his group executive officer. Potts is shown here in illustrious Eighth Air Force company: Left to right: *Lieutenant General Carl Spaatz, Potts, Major General Jimmy Doolittle, and Major General William Kepner.*

As assault forces approached the island on 11 June, the defenders ran up a white flag. Pantelleria had been conquered by air power alone.

A continuous air campaign had also been carried out against Axis airfields and ports in Sicily and southern Italy, and its tempo rose as D-Day for the Sicilian invasion drew nearer. During June and the first ten days of July, about 1,000 Axis combat aircraft were destroyed by the Allied air campaign. Many were caught on the ground, strafed and bombed when they diverted from damaged bases into one or two airfields left untouched by the Allies. These became killing grounds where Allied fighter-bombers took full advantage of a generous selection of targets.

Allied troops invaded Sicily on the night of 9–10 July 1943. They were massively supported by Allied air forces, who encountered only negligible opposition from enemy aircraft. Allied air supremacy had been imposed over Sicily and the surrounding area for the invasion. Nevertheless, aspects of the air operation went sadly awry, notably those concerned with paratroop operations and air-naval cooperation. "Friendly fire" instances were numerous, as naval gunfire forced covering Allied fighter patrols up to higher altitudes and shot down some of the 23 C–47s lost during paratroop operations. Alarmed by the gunfire and dispersed by bad weather, the C–47s scattered their paratroops widely. Sixty-nine Horsa and Hadrian gliders fell into the sea. On 13 July, when 124 C–47s once more flew through friendly fire to drop their paratroops, 11 were destroyed and another 50 were damaged. Investigations after these bungled affairs led to specific recommendations that benefited later airborne operations. In particular, they emphasized that plans for such operations should be drawn up in one nominated headquarters and that associated ground and naval forces should be informed of those plans well ahead of time.

By mid-August 1943 the Allies had overcome all enemy resistance in Sicily by depriving Axis forces of air cover and slowly strangling their supply lines from the north with incessant air attacks. The defeat and the constant pressure of air power on targets as far away as Rome helped to bring down dictator Benito Mussolini and drive Italy out of the war. By early September all Italian forces had laid down their arms and surrendered to the Allies.

American commanders were less than enthusiastic about a campaign against the "soft underbelly of Europe" after North Africa had been secured. They had feared that involvement in southern Europe might detract from preparations for an invasion of France in 1944. Now, with the fall of Mussolini, General Eisenhower pressed for immediate landings on the Italian mainland. He wanted to complete a rapid occupation of Italy and acquire the bases from which to attack Germany from the south. In this the Allies would be only partially successful. Troops deposited in the toe of Italy and at Salerno, near Naples, early in September had fought their way north to occupy Naples on 1 October. Soon after, worsening weather and determined German resistance stabilized the front on the prepared defenses of the Gustav Line, about half way between Naples and Rome. For more than six months the Allied armies, their movement hampered by mountainous terrain and severe winter weather, battered themselves against the line and were denied. In the air, results were more positive. The continuous Allied air assault drew Luftwaffe squadrons south and so benefited the Eighth Air Force's bomber offensive from England. Without substantial Luftwaffe combat losses in Sicily and Italy, the near defeat of the Eighth over Germany might have been a disaster.

Equally significant was the capture of a number of Italian airfields around Foggia on the Adriatic coast. From there, after the end of 1943, heavy bombers of the newly formed Fifteenth Air Force, commanded by Major General Nathan Twining, could cover strategic targets all over northern Italy, southern Germany, Austria, and Rumania. The oil complex at Ploesti was now within easy reach, and it was visited regularly by USAAF bombers in high-level raids. Before being overrun by the Red Army in August 1944, it had been attacked by nearly 7,500 heavy bomber sorties and its oil production had almost dried up. At the cost of about 350 aircraft, Germany's capacity to fuel its forces during the final year of the war was seriously reduced. Heavies from Foggia also delivered telling blows on the German aircraft industry, particularly the Messerschmitt factory at Wiener Neustadt.

Although they were important, strategic operations did not typify the air war in Italy the way ground support operations did. True to FM 100-20, the Allies gave priority to achieving and maintaining air supremacy, then, interdicting enemy supply lines, then, directly supporting ground forces. At the heart of these operations were the fighters and medium bombers—in USAAF squadrons principally A–36s,

The P–40 and the C–47—air support workhorses for the war in Italy, September 1943.

P–38s, P–39s, P–40s, Spitfires, B–25s, and B–26s—although heavy bombers also flew tactical missions as necessary. The introduction of forward air controllers (Rover Joes) and improvements in air-ground communications allowed the calling of precise strikes, even from medium altitudes, on enemy positions immediately in front of friendly troops, within the area between the front line and the normal bomb line.

To break the impasse in central Italy, Allied troops landed at Anzio, north of the Gustav Line, on 22 January 1944. Despite having achieved complete tactical surprise, largely because the Luftwaffe had been denied the ability to fly reconnaissance or to operate any aircraft in strength in the battle area, the troops were unsuccessful. The Allies flew thousands of sorties against enemy airfields and road-rail communications before the assault. The troops reached Anzio almost unopposed, but the Germans reacted swiftly and quickly sealed off the Allied beachhead. At the same time, a major Allied offensive had stalled on the Gustav Line and, as the Germans there consolidated their position, they began to move more troops to Anzio. A series of heavy attacks on the Allied bridgehead might well have succeeded in bringing about its collapse had not the Allied air forces held such marked air superiority. During this critical period, the Luftwaffe was able to fly about 150 sorties per day over the front lines, whereas the Allies consistently managed to put up ten times that many.

A–36s were among the most effective harassers of German troops. The A–36 was the ground attack dive bomber version of the P–51, and had all of the advantages of the Mustang's clean design. Although fitted with dive brakes, it was seldom used as a dive bomber, shallow dives and strafing runs being its usual attack profiles. Unlike most other aircraft considered for a dive bombing role, it was both fast and maneuverable, and, once it unloaded its bombs, could engage enemy fighters on equal terms at low level. Unfortunately for the aircraft's reputation, A–36 squadrons seemed to be involved in more than their share of friendly fire incidents. General Omar Bradley recorded his own experience when several attacked a column of American tanks:

> The tankers lighted their yellow smoke bombs in a prearranged recognition signal. But the smoke only caused the dive bombers to press their attacks. Finally, in self defense, the tanks turned their guns on the aircraft. A ship was winged and as it rolled over, the pilot tumbled out in a chute. When he landed nearby to learn that he had been shot down by American tanks, he bellowed in dismay. "Why, you silly sonuvabitch," the tank commander said, "didn't you see our yellow recognition signal?" "Oh,——!" the pilot said. "Is that what it was?"[8]

At the heart of the Gustav Line was the town of Monte Cassino, dominated by the abbey of St. Benedict. Convinced that the enemy was directing its defensive operations from the abbey, Allied commanders ordered it bombed. On 15 February 1944, it was destroyed by B–17s, B–25s, and B–26s, which dropped

A–36A. Flown by the squadrons of the 27th and 86th Fighter-Bomber Groups, the A–36 was heavily involved as a ground attack aircraft during Allied campaigns in Sicily and Italy.

A–36 nose. Beneath the cowling of the North American A–36 Apache was a liquid-cooled Allison V–1710 engine of 1,675 horsepower. This was the first version of the Mustang airframe to see service with the U.S. Army Air Forces. It was in action in North Africa as early as June 1943. Its high-altitude performance was disappointing but it proved effective as a ground attack aircraft. The A–36A in the USAF Museum is painted as Margie H, *flown by Captain Lawrence Dye of the 522nd Fighter-Bomber Squadron, 27th Fighter-Bomber Group, in Tunisia, Sicily, and Italy. Aerial victories are marked by swastikas, ground attack missions by bombs.*

A–36. Prominently featured in the A–36 were dive brakes, much needed restraints on an aircraft that accelerated eagerly during dive-bombing attacks. Unfortunately, because of frequent malfunctions, they were kept wired shut.

nearly 600 tons of bombs in daylight operations. One month later, the stalemate still unbroken, the town itself was flattened by over 1,000 tons of bombs. The record of B–26 squadrons in this attack was remarkable. Close to 90 percent of their bombs fell within a target area of 1,400 by 400 yards.[9] Less impressive were the B–17s. Several of their bombs fell among Allied troops, who were positioned only 1,000 yards from the edge of the town.

Although the tremendous Allied attack effectively destroyed Monte Cassino, its wielding of close-support aircraft as a club against dug-in enemy troops was a two-edged sword. Concentrated bombing created obstacles—craters and masses of rubble—which impeded advancing infantry and tanks alike. It deluded ground commanders into believing that enemy

resistance in the face of tremendous destruction would be negligible, but that was seldom the case.

Denied by the tenacity of the Germans both on the Gustav Line and at Anzio, Allied commanders launched STRANGLE, an interdiction operation to sever supply lines in northern Italy, so starving the German war machine and forcing a withdrawal. Between 19 March and 11 May 1944, aircraft under General Eaker's command flew over 50,000 sorties against railway lines, tunnels, bridges, and ports. It was a massive effort, but STRANGLE did not achieve the results its proponents predicted. The Germans were not forced to withdraw by the use of air power alone. However, their capacity to maintain stocks of ammunition and food (or to move at all behind the front) was seriously diminished.

When STRANGLE gave way to DIADEM, a combined Allied air-ground offensive begun in May, the Germans could no longer resist. The Gustav Line crumbled and Allied forces swept forward, entering Rome on 4 June 1944 and joining up with troops breaking out of the Anzio beachhead.

The quick Allied occupation of Italy originally hoped for had not materialized nearly a year after the invasion of Sicily, and the Italian campaign was far from over. German resistance in Italy would persist until the last days of the war while the Allies concentrated their efforts on other fronts. By the time General Mark Clark's Fifth Army took Rome, Allied forces in Italy had already had to accept the diversion of many units needed for the build-up of the Normandy invasion force in England (OVERLORD). Other units would follow for an invasion of southern France (ANVIL). France now featured at center stage, while Italy was almost forgotten in the background.

The reassuring presence of their own air cover little more than a distant memory, the German Army retreated northward to form another defensive line, the Gothic, in the mountains south of the Po River valley. There, opposing armies faced each other through the miseries of a second Italian winter. Whenever the weather allowed, the Allied air forces pressed their interdiction campaign, smashing transport routes until rail networks were a shambles and daylight travel of any kind, even by bicycle or mule, was unsafe. In the spring of 1945, when the Allied armies resumed their offensive, the Germans in Italy were no longer capable of effective resistance. They fell back across the Po, hounded unremittingly by air power, and finally surrendered on 2 May 1945.

The lessons of the USAAF's experience in the Mediterranean were not forgotten. The uses of air power to influence the land battle had been thoroughly absorbed and the priorities laid down in FM 100-20 confirmed. Allied air superiority had allowed the ground forces the maximum possible flexibility. Strong medium bomber forces, notably of B–25s and B–26s, had been at the heart of an interdiction campaign that had subjected enemy supply lines and airfields to incessant battering and had seriously limited German Army and Luftwaffe action. The dramatic impact of the fighter-bomber directly supporting troops in contact with the enemy and harassing any movement behind the front had been repeatedly demonstrated. As General Ira Eaker wrote in February 1945: "The Mediterranean theater has been the primary crucible for the development of tactical air power and the evolution of joint command between Allies." Hard-learned lessons were to be carried forward and applied in World War II's climactic year, a year that began with the Allied invasion of Normandy.

The Tide Turns

As 1944 dawned, the Eighth Air Force began to see "light at the end of the tunnel." The dark days of 1943 were over and changes were occurring that would make the Eighth the mightiest instrument of air power ever assembled. American industry and the air force training system were both in high gear; new aircraft and crews were pouring across the Atlantic in an ever increasing flood. At the same time, new command structures were in place, designed to take advantage of the experience being gained by senior commanders as they applied the lessons of air power. Tactical procedures and combat techniques had been tested in battle and changed to be used to the best possible effect. New equipment was improving the force—H2X, an airborne radar that allowed bombing through clouds, and, at long last, fighter aircraft capable of escorting bombers to their targets and engaging the Luftwaffe on equal terms when they got there.

In the latter months of 1943 the burden of escort over enemy territory had been borne by P–38s and P–47s. Extra fuel in drop tanks had made a difference, but the shorter-range P–47s had still been used principally to cover the outbound and inbound legs of a bomber mission, while the P–38s had reached as far as Bremen and Ludwigshaven in Germany. For all of their advantages in range, however, the P–38s had some problems, too. Below 18,000 feet they were a match for Luftwaffe fighters, but above, where they needed to operate as escorts, they were outclassed by Bf 109s and FW 190s. The extreme cold of high altitudes induced frequent failures in their Allison engines and strained pilot endurance in cockpits almost devoid of heating. Even so, a P–38 was the first USAAF combat aircraft to fly over Berlin. On 3 March 1944, Lieutenant Colonel Jack Jenkins, leading the 55th Fighter Group, unaware that the bombers had turned back because of weather, reached the German capital in P–38J *Texas Ranger IV*. He recorded: "I got so cold that my crew chief had to help lift me out of the cockpit."

A solution to the long-range fighter problem was already at hand, although not recognized at first. The outstanding qualities of the P–51 airframe had been evident from the time of its earliest flights, but performance limitations at high altitudes destined it for ground attack. Even when the Rolls-Royce Merlin replaced its original Allison engine and transformed P–51 performance at all altitudes, the penny did not immediately drop. Although the Eighth Air Force was eager to get them, the first P–51s in England went to

General Brereton's Ninth Air Force, whose head-quarters had moved from the Mediterranean and reformed in England in October 1943. The Ninth was thenceforth to be exclusively tactical, its principal role that of supporting the Allied armies in the invasion of Europe. General William Kepner, commanding VIII Fighter Command, deplored the arbitrary assignment of P–51s as tactical aircraft, insisting that "…developments in Germany [made the P–51] the only satisfactory answer." The situation was remedied and the P–51 got its chance when in October 1943 all fighter units in the United Kingdom were tasked to support the bombers engaged in Operation POINTBLANK until further notice.

The first Merlin-engined Mustang to arrive in England was the P–51B. It was given to the 354th Fighter Group, which began operations on 1 December 1943 under the temporary leadership of Lieutenant Colonel Don Blakeslee. A highly experienced fighter pilot,

Blakeslee had flown 120 fighter sweeps with the RAF before transferring to the USAAF to become deputy commanding officer of the 4th Fighter Group, the unit he would return to command after seeing the 354th through its P–51 conversion. The 354th was soon in the thick of things, shooting down 16 enemy fighters without loss during a mission to Kiel on 5 January 1944. On 11 January it repeated the performance. Major Jim Howard was awarded the Medal of Honor for his protection of a B–17 wing in an hour-long solo battle with 30 Luftwaffe fighters. He was credited with three confirmed killed and a number of others damaged. His Mustang had a single bullet hole in the left wing.

Blakeslee rejoined the 4th Fighter Group and was delighted when its P–47s were replaced by P–51s in February 1944. On 4 and 6 March 1944, he led a P–51 escort with the first American bombing missions against Berlin. Neither raid was particularly auspicious.

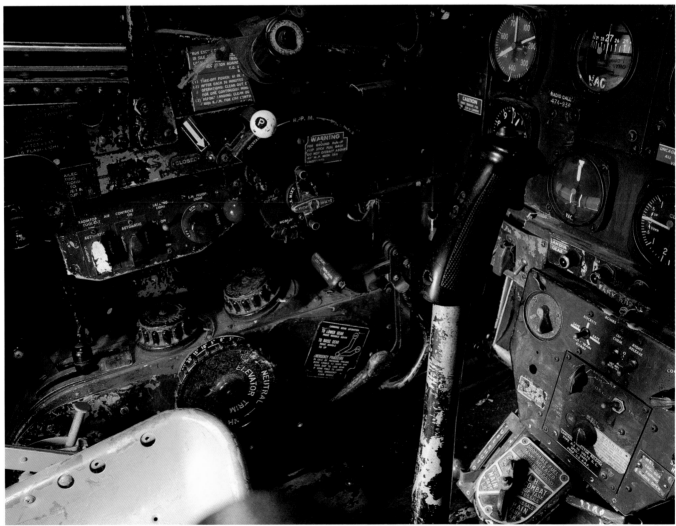

P–51 cockpit. The USAF Museum's P–51D is marked as Shimmy IV, *flown by Colonel C. L. Schluder, commanding officer of the 325th Fighter Group, Fifteenth Air Force, in Italy during 1944. This particular airframe was also the last propeller-driven fighter in service with American forces. Below the throttle quadrant are the trimming controls. On takeoff, the rudder trim was set six notches to the right to help counteract the Mustang's tendency to swing to the left.*

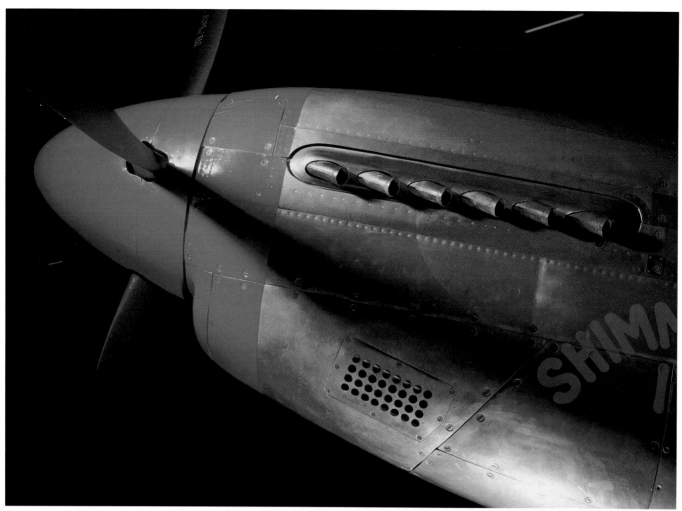

P–51 nose. A classic symbol of the Anglo-American alliance in World War II was the P–51 Mustang. The superb aerodynamics of North American's P–51 were wrapped smoothly around Rolls-Royce's Merlin engine in a combination that gave the U.S. Army Air Forces the instrument it needed to achieve victory in the air war against the Luftwaffe.

P–51 drop tank. Pressed paper drop-tanks carried the additional fuel that took P–51s to Berlin and back. The barrels of the three .50s in the port wing are clearly visible.

P–51 gun-bay in the port wing. Belts of .50-caliber ammunition fed three guns in each wing. Information on loading the bays and harmonizing the guns is given on the underside of the covering panel.

On 4 March bad weather scattered the formations; only one bomber group reached Berlin; and no fewer than 16 of the new Mustangs were lost, 11 of them from the inexperienced 363rd Fighter Group. On 6 March the Eighth tried again and bombed Berlin with 672 heavies in one of the fiercest running air battles of the war. A total of more than 800 USAAF fighters performed escort at various points in the course of the mission, but even their strong showing could not prevent the Luftwaffe from taking its toll. Fifty-three B–17s, 16 B–24s, and 11 fighters were lost. Between them, the bombers and their escorts claimed 179 attackers, a figure later reduced to 66 from German records. The Eighth realized that raiding Berlin would never be easy, even with the help of long-range fighters, but it was at last capable, as it had not been in 1943, of putting more than 500 heavy bombers over a target deep inside Germany and hurting the Luftwaffe in the process. Despite its agony, the Eighth Air Force knew that losses would be replaced and that more units would be formed. By contrast, the Luftwaffe was finding replacement increasingly difficult, particularly of experienced pilots.

The weight of fire from a well-organized B–17 group was impressive and no Luftwaffe pilot ever relished attacking a heavy bomber formation. The appearance of USAAF fighters over the Reich was disturbing. A Mustang flying interference came as a considerable shock. Here was a fighter that could accompany the bombers to Berlin, and yet was superior to the Bf 109 and FW 190 in speed and turning ability. Although German aircraft had better rates of climb, they could not match the P–51's zoom climb or dive. The FW 190's only noticeable advantage was its rate of roll, and even that diminished at high speeds. To quote Major Robert Riemensnider, Commander of the 55th Fighter Squadron: "[The P–51] had speed, range, and an all-round versatility that was unsurpassed by any of its contemporaries in combat service."

Adding to the Luftwaffe's problems, the long-range fighters had been let off the leash. Soon after General Doolittle took over the Eighth Air Force, he visited General Kepner, his fighter commander, who had been urging a more aggressive fighter policy. Fresh in Doolittle's mind was his New Year message from General Arnold: "Destroy the enemy air forces wherever you find them, in the air, on the ground, and in the factories." On Kepner's office wall was a sign reflecting previous commanders' concerns. It read: "The first duty of Eighth Air Force fighters is to bring the bombers back alive." Doolittle ordered the closing phrase changed to read "…is to destroy German fighters." Escorting bombers was still important, but close escort, which confined the fighters to the vicinity of the bomber stream, became a thing of

Gentile group. 4th Fighter Group pilots in front of one of their P–51s are, from left: John Godfrey, Don Gentile, Peter Lehman, Jim Goodson, and Willard Millikan. Gentile was withdrawn from combat in June 1944; Lehman was killed in action; Godfrey, Goodson, and Millikan were all shot down and became prisoners of war.

Don Gentile. An American, Don Gentile got into the air war early by joining the Royal Air Force and becoming a member of No. 133 Eagle Squadron. Later, he flew both the P–47 and P–51 with the 4th Fighter Group, Eighth Air Force. He was most successful in the P–51B when teamed with John Godfrey. The partners were described by Winston Churchill as "a latter-day Damon and Pythias." Officially credited with 21.83 victories in the air and 7 on the ground, Gentile is also remembered for the spectacular destruction of his P–51B Shangri-La as it buzzed the field at Debden after his last mission. Don Gentile was killed in the crash of a T–33 near Andrews Air Force Base on 28 January 1951.

the past. Strong fighter forces would now range ahead of the bombers as hunters, and escorts would pursue enemy fighters aggressively, not merely to chase them away but to destroy them. Released from close escort, fighters would seek targets of opportunity on the way home, descending to ground level and strafing enemy airfields that presented themselves.

Doolittle regarded his freeing of the fighters as "…the most important and far-reaching military decision that I made during the war." The bombers, in effect, became not only the droppers of high explosives on German targets, they became the bait that lured the Luftwaffe into battle with USAAF long-range fighters. Luftwaffe General Adolf Galland acknowledged the dramatic effect of the change:

> Only now did the superiority of the American fighters come into its own. They were no longer glued to the slow-moving bomber formation, but took action into their own hands. Wherever our fighters appeared, the Americans hurled themselves at them. They went over to low-level attacks on our airfields. Nowhere were we safe from them, and we had to skulk on our own bases. During takeoff, assembly, climb, and approach to the bombers, when we were in contact with them, on our way back, during landing, and even after that, the American fighters attacked with overwhelming superiority.

Big Week

In concert with the new fighter-escort policy, the Allies, intent on ensuring air supremacy for the invasion of France, hatched a plan to cripple Germany's aircraft industry. Known as Operation ARGUMENT, its principal objectives were factories engaged in final aircraft assembly and aircraft component and ball-bearing manufacture. Terrible weather prevented ARGUMENT's launch during the early weeks of 1944, but the skies over Europe began to clear in mid-February. Between 20 and 25 February, in what came to be called Big Week, over 3,300 Eighth Air Force bomber sorties punished Germany's aviation industry. They were joined by 500 more from the Fifteenth Air Force in Italy. RAF Bomber Command added another 2,750 nighttime raids. Nearly 4,000 fighter sorties were dispatched to accompany the daytime raids. By the time weather closed in to end Big Week, the USAAF had lost 226 bombers (6.8 percent) and 41 fighters; the RAF's losses from four major raids totaled 141 aircraft (5.1 percent).

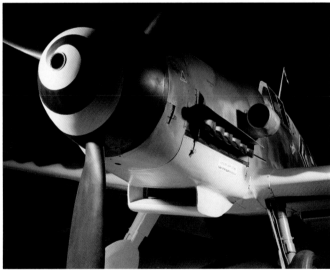

Bf 109. Between 1936 and the end of World War II, more than 33,000 Messerschmitt Bf 109s were manufactured. The 109 was a classic fighter—small, fast, maneuverable, and well armed. The USAF Museum's 109 was originally a Spanish-built HA–1112–MIL. In 1982 and 1983, its Merlin engine was replaced by a Daimler Benz 605 and it was restored as a 109G in the markings of Gerhard Barkhorn, the world's second ranking ace with 301 aerial victories. From the front, the aircraft reveals both strengths and weaknesses. The 20-mm cannon firing through the propeller boss gave the 109 a hefty punch, but the stalky, narrow-track undercarriage made it tricky to handle on the ground and, therefore, prone to landing accidents throughout the war. Other features are the wide oil cooler intake beneath the fuselage and the supercharger intake above the exhaust stubs of the DB 605 12-cylinder inverted V engine.

Bf 109 cockpit. Although anything but standard, Messerschmitt Bf 109 cockpits had two things in common—a cramped interior and a heavily framed canopy—shortcomings that were never overcome.

FW 190D–9. The D–9 was a formidable variant of the Focke-Wulf 190 fighter. The lengthening of its nose to hold a more powerful engine led to a compensating extension of its tail and a noticeably stretched appearance compared to earlier 190s. The Jumo 213A–1 12-cylinder liquid-cooled engine, misleadingly housed under an apparently radial cowling, was rated on takeoff at 1,776 horsepower, but this could be increased to 2,240 horsepower with methanol-water injection. The FW 190D–9's maximum speed was 426 miles per hour at 21,000 feet, and it could reach that height in just over seven minutes.

In the fierce fighting of Big Week's first day, three Medals of Honor were awarded to B–17 crew members, two of them posthumously. 1st Lieutenant Walter Truemper and Staff Sergeant Archie Mathies, the navigator and the flight engineer in a B–17 of the 351st Bombardment Group, were killed trying to land their damaged aircraft at base. Their co-pilot was dead, but they refused to bail out and abandon their badly wounded pilot, who survived the crash but died soon after. In a second incident highlighting the hazards of head-on attacks, a B–17 of the 305th Bombardment Group straggled when its bombload failed to release over the target. It was heavily hit by fighters. Cannon shells set an engine on fire and

shattered the cockpit, killing the co-pilot and wounding eight other crew members. The pilot, 1st Lieutenant Bill Lawley, seriously hurt and bleeding profusely, held the dead co-pilot off the controls with one hand and recovered from a steep dive with the other. Electing not to bail out because of serious injuries to his crew, Lawley made for the English Channel, surviving another fighter attack, which set fire to a second engine. Shock and loss of blood caused Lawley to suffer a temporary collapse on the way home, but by the time he crossed the French coast, his bombs had been jettisoned and both engine fires had been extinguished. Over southern England a third engine died and Lawley, by now at very low altitude, managed

FW 190D cockpit. The space afforded in the FW 190D–9's cockpit was typically small, but the pilot had the advantage of sitting under a blown clear vision hood.

A German 88-mm flak gun. In World War II the German 88-mm was the gun most feared by the Allies, whether used in land battles or as an anti-aircraft gun. The pivoting gun mount, resting on four arms, allowed a 360-degree traverse and vertical travel from +85 to -3 degrees. The rate of fire was 15 to 20 rounds per minute, and shells could reach a maximum altitude of 48,000 feet.

Mosquito, rear view. The U.S. Army Air Forces's need for a fast reconnaissance aircraft was met by reverse Lend-Lease De Havilland Mosquitos acquired from the British. The USAF Museum's example is marked as a PR Mk XVI of the 653rd Bombardment Squadron, 25th Bombardment Group.

Mosquito. Known to the press as the "wooden wonder" because of its principally plywood construction, the Mosquito was powered by two Rolls-Royce Merlin engines of 1,690 horsepower each. The combination of lightness, clean lines, and great power made the Mosquito a formidable performer. It could achieve well over 400 miles per hour and reach altitudes above 40,000 feet. In the reconnaissance role it was unarmed, relying on performance alone for protection.

A P–47 of the 78th Fighter Group. Group identification markings were introduced generally in March 1944. On this P–47 the 78th Fighter Group at Duxford adopted a striking black and white checkerboard pattern for the engine cowling.

to belly-land his B–17 on the grass airfield at Redhill, south of London, without further injury to his crew.

Big Week had been costly to the bombers, but far from fatal. The Luftwaffe, however, staggered under repeated blows. The material injury to its aircraft industry and the losses of its fighter aircraft—355 fighters destroyed and 155 damaged—were serious but not disastrous in themselves. Under the organizational leadership of Albert Speer, German industry proved wonderfully resilient, dispersing its assets and actually increasing aircraft production after Big Week's conclusion. The Luftwaffe's real problem was not replacing fighters but replacing flyers—its lifeblood. In February 1944 it lost well over 400 fighter pilots. In March, over Berlin, it lost nearly 500, among them a dozen of the greatest German aces, including Egon Mayer, the man who, in November 1942, initiated the massed head-on attacks against the B–17s. During the five months before the D-Day invasion, no fewer than 2,262 German fighter pilots died. All of the aircraft

in the world were of little use without competent pilots to fly them.

During this period, when the Eighth Air Force began to impose its will on the Luftwaffe, P–47 Thunderbolts still bore the lion's share of fighter-escort duty, flying over 3,000 of all fighter sorties supporting Big Week. An unusually big fighter for its time, the P–47 was powered by the huge Pratt & Whitney R–2800 radial engine of over 2,000 horsepower. The aircraft was heavier than its rivals by several thousand pounds and could not match them as a dogfighter. However, it was fast, ruggedly built, and heavily armed. It was almost impossible to escape because it could outdive any of its likely opponents (until the coming of the Me 262 jet), and a burst from its eight .50-caliber machine guns was usually decisive.

The P–47's toughness was attested to by its capacity to withstand battle damage. Its combat loss rate was a remarkably low 0.7 percent, compared with the P–51's 1.2 percent. As a pilot in the 362nd Fighter Group said: "For the low-level job we had to do, where you couldn't keep out of the light flak and small arms fire, there wasn't a better plane than the P–47. It would keep going with damage with which other types would have fallen out of the sky."

These characteristics endeared the Thunderbolt to its pilots, among whom were some of the great USAAF aces of World War II. The leading P–47 fighter group was the 56th, commanded initially by Colonel "Hub" Zemke, one of the war's outstanding fighter leaders. By the end of the war, the 56th had destroyed 664.5 enemy aircraft in aerial combat, more than any other group in the Eighth Air Force. Many leading aces scored their victories while on its roster, among them Fred Christensen (21.5), "Gabby" Gabreski (28), Gerald Johnson (27), "Bud" Mahurin (21), and David Schilling (22.5).

The V–weapons

The Eighth Air Force might have directed its assaults on German air elements more intensely had its assets not occasionally been diverted and employed in an Allied effort to counter a new and initially puzzling enemy threat. Aerial reconnaissance had revealed that the Germans were building large concrete structures, including several ramps, in northern France. Photographs gave substance to other intelligence on the development of two German "vengeance" weapons— the first, a small pilotless aircraft (the V–1) powered by a pulse-jet, the second, a large ballistic missile (the V–2). Both were armed with warheads weighing about a ton. By December 1943 the Allies had formally titled their campaign against these weapons Operation CROSSBOW and identified a chain of over 70 probable launch sites near the Channel coast of France, in an area 10 to 20 miles deep and 300 miles long. Most of the ramps appeared aimed at London, but the Allies feared that the weapons could disrupt the planned invasion of Normandy.

During the first six months of CROSSBOW, the Allied air forces between them dropped over 36,000 tons of bombs on V–1 and V–2 installations. The USAAF's Eighth and Ninth Air Forces delivered most of them, seriously damaging all but a small number of sites. General Doolittle and Air Marshal Harris grumbled about having to repeatedly divert their heavy bombers from the assault on Germany, but the effort was not in vain. It was later estimated that CROSSBOW

56th Fighter Group pilots. The highest scoring group in the Eighth Air Force was the 56th Fighter Group flying P–47s. Among its pilots were, standing, from left to right, *Francis "Gabby" Gabreski, Robert Johnson, Walker "Bud" Mahurin, Robert Landry;* on the wing, *Walter Cook and David Schilling.*

probably delayed the V–weapon program by three to four months. By the time the first V–1 landed in England on the night of 12–13 June 1944, Allied armies had already secured their Normandy beachheads.

Once under way, V–weapon attacks soon increased in intensity, the V–2 joining the V–1 in the offensive against England on 8 September. The V–1 (known as the buzz-bomb because of the distinctive note of its engine) was small, fast, and not easily intercepted. The V–2, approaching from the stratosphere at supersonic speed, was immune from interception. Both weapons were impressively destructive in built-up areas, but neither could be aimed accurately and were essentially indiscriminate. Given the scale of the German offensive, Operation CROSSBOW had to be continued. It was not entirely successful and when it ended with the Allied armies' advance in March 1945, over 3,000 V–1s and 1,000 V–2s had fallen on British soil. Nearly 2,000 more V–weapons fell on Allied-held territory on the continent, mostly in and around Amsterdam. Although they were destructive, they ate up immense amounts of scarce German resources and achieved little of military value. They did, however, divert a considerable amount of Allied air power from targets with a more direct bearing on the outcome of the war.

By April 1944 the tide in the daylight bombing offensive had turned. Operations POINTBLANK and ARGUMENT had largely achieved their objectives, leaving the Luftwaffe incapable of holding back the flooding Allied air assault. German fighter pilot loss rates were running at 25 percent per month. Replacements had a life expectancy in a front-line squadron of no more than 30 days. As the Luftwaffe declined, Allied air power grew until it was irresistible. By day, USAAF armadas operated over Europe at will, carving out an aerial victory that had seemed only a remote possibility in the dark days of 1943.

To most airmen's surprise, it was a victory being won because of an aircraft they had thought an impossible dream—an agile single-seat fighter with the range of a strategic bomber.

The Coming of the Ninth
As the air war tipped in the Allies' favor, the newcomer to northern Europe's skies—the Ninth Air Force— became an increasingly significant participant. Drawing up plans for the USAAF in the Allied invasion of France, the air force staffs had originally suggested that the Eighth Air Force Air Support Command be enhanced to provide tactical capability. By August 1943 General Arnold had decided that the scale of air operations for the invasion was such

that a separate tactical air force was warranted and that the tactical air commander should be Lieutenant General Lewis Brereton, who had proved himself in the Mediterranean theater. Accordingly, when Brereton moved to the United Kingdom in October 1943, his Ninth Air Force Headquarters staffs went with him, leaving their combat and support units behind to be absorbed by the Twelfth Air Force. The nucleus of the new Ninth was formed from tactical and support units transferred from the Eighth Air Force, which from then on concentrated on operating its burgeoning front line of heavy bombers and escorting fighters.

The Ninth's primary mission, and the reason for its formation, was to support the Allied armies' invasion of Normandy and their subsequent drive to defeat the enemy and occupy Germany. As its strength increased in late 1943 and first months of 1944, the Ninth was tested against CROSSBOW targets and in operations supporting the combined bomber offensive. By the date of the invasion, it had become the most powerful tactical air force in the world, with three combat commands—IX Fighter Command[10] (under the outstanding brigadier general, Elwood "Pete" Quesada, who in 1929 had joined with Ira Eaker and Tooey Spaatz for the endurance flight of the *Question Mark*) with 13 groups of P–47s, 3 of P–38s, and 2 of P–51s; IX Bomber Command with 11 groups of B–26 medium and A–20 light bombers; and IX Troop Carrier Command with another 14 groups. In all, the Ninth could, with a personnel strength of 170,000, field about 4,500 combat aircraft plus about 2,700 gliders. The Ninth, with some justification, claimed that it could, by itself, project more power than the entire Luftwaffe.

From the time of its formation in the United Kingdom until the end of the war in Europe, the Ninth Air Force was continually engaged in fierce combat. In little more than a year and a half, it flew almost 370,000 sorties and lost over 2,900 aircraft, 2,139 of them fighters. In the course of its labors, it dropped 240,000 tons of bombs, expended 75 million rounds of ammunition, and claimed as destroyed 4,200 enemy aircraft— contributing immensely to the eventual Allied victory in Europe.

Preparing for Invasion
In the tasking for the Normandy invasion (Operation OVERLORD) the Allied air forces were primarily responsibility for preventing the Luftwaffe from interfering with the amphibious assault. In a very real sense, the strategic bombing offensive had been working toward this end for some time. Losses inflicted by the Eighth Air Force during the first half

B–26s over Charleroi. U.S. Army Air Forces medium bombers pounded targets in France in the weeks before the D-Day invasion of Normandy. Smoke rises from Charleroi behind B–26s of the Ninth Air Force.

B–26 nose. The high wing-loading of the B–26 gave it an unjustified reputation as a "widow maker." In its early days apprehensive units were sometimes cured of their fears when the new aircraft was delivered by a member of the WASPs. By the end of the war the Marauder had recorded the lowest loss rate of any U.S. Army Air Forces bomber and had proved itself a most effective combat aircraft. Its tubular fuselage was beautifully streamlined, and its high wing design left almost the whole mid-section available as a bomb-bay. The B–26 became the chief medium bomber used by the Ninth Air Force in its European operations.

B–26 engine. Pratt & Whitney R–2800–43s developing 2,000 horse-power each were the engines for the B–26. Four bladed propellers soaked up the power, and huge radials were neatly cowled in giant nacelles that matched the fuselage shape.

B–26 tail. The upright fin of the B–26 looked out of place on such a smoothly contoured airframe. This one carries the stripes of the 387th Bombardment Group, Ninth Air Force.

B–26 cockpit. As they were in most bombers of the time, control wheels were preferred to sticks for the B–26.

223

of 1944 had effectively broken the Luftwaffe's capacity to take the offensive. Nevertheless, the Allies were not complacent. The USAAF would keep pressuring the Luftwaffe to prevent its making difficulties and, with the RAF, perform a great many other necessary tasks in preparation for an amphibious operation of unprecedented scale against a heavily defended coastline. As D-Day drew nearer, these other tasks—reconnaissance, destruction of coastal defenses, and isolation of the invasion area—became increasingly important.

If there was one thing the Allied leaders agreed on, it was that the invasion would be impractical without overwhelming strength in the air. In only a few years, even the most critical of pre-war skeptics had grown to realize that air power was a dominant factor in modern warfare. Whether air power alone could defeat an enemy had yet to be proved, but there was no denying that victory, on the battlefield or, finally, in war, could not be won without it. Any disagreements concerned how best to apply it. As invasion plans were laid, the Allied commanders split into two camps over how the heavy bombers of the Eighth Air Force and the RAF would be used. Their debate did not easily divide along national or service lines. The bomber men, led by General Spaatz and Air Marshal Harris, wanted to weaken Germany's opposition by pounding away at its industrial heart, particularly at the oil industry. Those ranged against them included Air Marshal Tedder (Eisenhower's deputy), Air Marshal Leigh Mallory (Allied Expeditionary Air Forces [AEAF] commander), and General Brereton (Ninth Air Force commander). They wanted to paralyze the enemy's ability to move by destroying as much of its rail network as possible in Belgium and northern France. After a protracted and often passionate argument, General Eisenhower decided in favor of a campaign against transportation targets to further the invasion's success.

On 14 April 1944, to the discomfort of Spaatz and Harris, the Combined Chiefs of Staff placed the Eighth Air Force and RAF Bomber Command under Eisenhower's direction until the Allied armies successfully established themselves on the continent. From 14 April, in addition to huge naval and ground forces, Eisenhower directed the AEAF (the Ninth Air Force, the RAF's 2nd Tactical Air Force, and the Air Defense of Great Britain), USSTAF (the Eighth and Fifteenth Air Forces), and RAF Bomber Command. On D-Day this formidable combination had available for operations from the United Kingdom 3,467 heavy bombers, 1,645 medium and light bombers, 5,409 fighters, and 2,316 transports. The Luftwaffe had a front line that included 3,200 combat-ready fighters and bombers to cover demands on several fronts. From the numbers, it had been clear to the Supreme Commander for some time that his air forces should have no difficulty providing the required air supremacy over the Normandy beaches. He was encouraged to find that they were equally effective meeting other challenges.

In the weeks leading to D-Day, Allied air forces concentrated on a wide variety of targets near the Channel coast, taking care to mislead the Germans as much as possible by hitting two targets outside Normandy for every one in the invasion area and pulverizing and rendering almost untenable airfields within 130 miles of the proposed beachhead. The Eighth Air Force persisted in mounting at least some raids against strategic targets in Germany to discourage the Luftwaffe from moving fighters forward into France and to continue with the battle of attrition that had been so effective.

The enemy's coastal defenses were heavily fortified and, therefore, not particularly profitable targets, with the notable exception of radar stations. By D-Day, the Allies had destroyed more than 80 percent of the radar coverage along the Channel coast, leaving some sites near Calais deliberately intact and ingeniously misleading observers as to the objective of the main Allied landings. In effect, the enemy defenders were blinded and left vulnerable to the confusion that engulfed them over Allied intentions on the morning of 6 June 1944.

The Allies began attacking transportation targets, rail centers, and repair facilities to cripple Germany's entire rail network and render its transport problems unmanageable. An intense campaign involving every type of offensive aircraft, from heavy bombers to fighters, achieved impressive levels of destruction. A German Transport Ministry report of 15 May admitted: "Large scale strategic movement of German troops by rail is practically impossible at the present time, and must remain so while attacks are maintained at their present intensity." Even so, the campaign was not producing the results expected by the Allied commanders; and German ingenuity was countering the effects of much of the damage it caused. On 20 May the campaign escalated with wide-scale fighter sweeps against railways. The most spectacular of these were the "Chattanooga Choo Choo" missions that began on 21 May. They involved 763 AEAF and 500 Eighth Air Force fighters that went after locomotives, wagons, signal boxes, and maintenance sheds whenever they found them and

P–38 shadow. During the build-up to the D-Day invasion, the Allies kept a close watch on German activities along the Atlantic Wall. F–5Es (photographic reconnaissance versions of the P–38) were among the aircraft that photographed enemy defensive preparations on the beaches of northern France. Sometimes their cameras brought back evidence of water obstacles and of how low the reconnaissance missions were being flown.

"Chattanooga Choo-Choo" sortie victim. A German military train's final journey is registered in a U.S. Army Air Forces fighter's gun camera. The transport was hit during one of many strafing sweeps against enemy rail traffic conducted shortly before the Allied invasion of Normandy in June 1944.

hounded moving trains, usually betrayed by a tell-tale stream of smoke, unmercifully. The fighters mounted similar missions on following days, bringing sharp reductions in daylight train traffic.

The culminating blow to transportation targets fell on the bridges over the Seine. Until early May they had appeared too unrewarding. One estimate suggested that heavy bombers would have to drop more than 1,200 tons of bombs against each bridge to destroy them. However, on 7 May 1944, a dramatic demonstration of fighter-bomber power offered a much cheaper solution. Eight of Pete Quesada's P–47s delivered two 1,000-pound bombs apiece on a steel railway bridge across the river and demolished it. Thereafter, "bridge-busting" became primarily a Ninth Air Force responsibility. During the last few days before D-Day its B–26s and P–47s conducted a spectacular series of low-level strikes and destroyed every crossing of the Seine, rail and road, between Paris and the Channel coast. As General Spaatz, a reluctant participant against transportation targets, confessed to General Arnold: "[The campaign] opened the door for the invasion."

Operation OVERLORD

The story of Allied air operations flown on 6 June 1944 in support of the D-Day landings points largely to the value of victories already won and emphasizes the rewards of careful preparation. Against combat sortie totals of 8,722 for the USAAF and 5,676 for the RAF, the Luftwaffe managed to send fewer than 100 in opposition. It was a far cry from the day, only four years before, when Goering had stood on the coast of France and, confident of victory, gloried in the power of the Luftwaffe's bomber fleets as they roared overhead on their way to England. Now Eisenhower, from the other side of the Channel, could tell his waiting troops with certainty: "If you see a plane, it will be one of ours."[11]

In the darkness preceding the first Allied landings, RAF Bomber Command pummeled the German defenses along the Normandy coast, and the transports and gliders of Brereton's Ninth Air Force assembled for the largest troop carrier operation ever undertaken. Over 800 C–47s, plus others towing over 100 gliders, set out to drop the troops of the 82nd and 101st Airborne Divisions on the Cotentin Peninsula, behind Utah Beach on the right flank of the Allied assault. RAF transports and gliders were similarly engaged with the British 6th Airborne Division on the left flank. Most participating C–47 pilots were on their first combat mission. The challenge of flying at night in large numbers through low clouds and intense flak led the inexperienced pilots to separate the troop carrier formations and widely scatter the American divisions during the drop. However, what could have been a disaster was redeemed by the initiative of individual American paratroopers. Lost in the darkness, their unit organization hopelessly disrupted, they engaged the enemy wherever they encountered him, spreading confusion and alarm among German forces defending the peninsula. As the Supreme Commander's report later stated: "…the success of the Utah assault could not have been achieved…without the work of the airborne forces."

As dawn broke over Normandy, it was the Eighth Air Force's turn. Over 1,000 B–17s and B–24s attacked Omaha and the British beaches in waves, crossing the coast at right angles and dropping almost 3,000 tons of bombs against coastal defenses. Unfortunately, clouds forced the bombing to be done on radar and, to ensure that friendly forces would not be hit, pathfinder bombardiers deliberately delayed their drops for several seconds after the indicated release points. The apparently crushing bombardment, therefore, proved disappointing. Most of it fell inland from the beaches, leaving enemy defenses largely untouched, although it disrupted their communications and incidentally cleared a number of mine fields.

Bombardment was not disappointing on Utah beach, however, or in the area immediately behind it. The Germans there suffered the attentions of B–26s, A–20s, and P–47s of the Ninth Air Force, all of them finding ways to attack their targets visually. As a result, Utah's bunkers and blockhouses were severely dealt with, and the defenders' capacity to resist was much reduced. Not that the American airmen had it all their own way. A B–26 crew-member reported that the flak was: "…the most withering, heavy, and accurate we ever experienced." At least, however, the Luftwaffe was not a factor. One German officer, dragging himself from the ruins of his concrete gun emplacement after the shattering experience of a B–26 attack, was driven to exclaim: "It looks as though God and the world have forsaken us. What has happened to our airmen?"

German soldiers tired of asking the question. By the close of D-Day, as the Allied armies were tightening

A–20s. Before, during, and after the D-Day invasion, the Ninth Air Force's light and medium bombers were heavily involved in attacking such point targets as gun emplacements, bridges, and road junctions. Clearly marked with black and white Allied invasion stripes, these A–20s leave the hedgerows of Normandy behind and head for their base in England after a mission.

their grip on the beachheads, the Allied air forces were demonstrating their awesome power. Perceptive Germans must have realized that the pattern of the war in the West had been set as 171 squadrons of Allied fighters ensured that the Luftwaffe would be conspicuous by its absence and that anything moving among the hedgerows of Normandy would be strafed.[12] German soldiers grew to accept their grim lot—fighting on under incessant Allied air force harassment, without hope of significant help from the Luftwaffe, which, although it had moved over 1,000 additional fighters from Germany by early July, accomplished relatively little. The reality of Allied air supremacy would be apparent in the weeks and months following the Normandy invasion.

Tactical Air Rampant

The days immediately following the invasion were critical for the Allies. The assault forces were ashore, but the beachheads were far from secure, and it was vital that the speed of any German reinforcement should be slower than that of the Allied build-up across the Channel. Fighters of the Ninth Air Force and the RAF's 2nd Tactical Air Force had to make it as difficult as possible for German units to move forward into the battle area. On D-Day itself, the Allies were greatly helped by the indecision of the German High Command. Until late afternoon, poor flying weather prevented Allied tactical aircraft from operating freely, and three *Panzer* divisions which might have intervened in the battle were prevented from doing so by the hesitancy of Hitler and his general staff. By the time the armored divisions were released, the skies had cleared and an opportunity was lost. *Panzer Lehr* division, needing to cover only 130 miles to the front, found it impossible to make progress at more than six or seven miles per hour under aerial attack. As Major General Fritz Bayerlein, division commander, has recalled: "By the end of the day [7 June] I had lost 40 tank trucks carrying fuel and 90 others. Five of my tanks were knocked out, and 84 half-tracks, prime movers, and self-propelled guns."

The Allied air forces intensified their interdiction of the German Army's rear areas after D-Day. Since the need to disguise their intentions no longer obtained, they hit bridges more frequently, adding the crossings of the Loire River to those of the Seine, continued attacking rail centers, and systematically bombed German supply dumps.[13] The fighters of the Ninth Air Force and the 2nd Tactical Air Force undertook a massive and even more rewarding campaign of armed reconnaissance over Normandy and the surrounding region. In daylight, almost nothing could move anywhere in the area without attracting their attention.

One German officer observed that: "…the effect of Allied air superiority on the Normandy front and as far as Paris is so great that…even single vehicles are used by day only in the most extreme emergencies." As early as 10 June, Field Marshal Erwin Rommel was reporting: "Every traffic defile in the rear areas is under continual attack and it is very difficult to get essential supplies of ammunition and petrol up to the troops."[14]

As the Allies' battle for Normandy dragged on and the provision of close air support to the troops became ever more important, soldiers and airmen cooperated in developing methods to increase its effectiveness. They incorporated radars originally designed for air defense into a system for the control of air strikes, and, at Quesada's instigation, IX Tactical Air Command began flying armored column cover missions. An air support party in a tank equipped with VHF radio accompanied each tank column, over which IX Tactical Air Command aircraft flew from dawn to dusk on call and looking for trouble. As a command operation order of the time put it:

> Each of the rapidly advancing columns will be covered at all times by a four-ship flight…which will maintain a close armed "recce" in advance of the column. They may attack any target which is identified as enemy, directing their attention to the terrain immediately in front of the advancing column.

The contrast in the opposing armies' behavior with the Allies' aggressive use of their dominant air power could hardly have been more complete. By day, German troops were forced to keep their vehicles hidden from the searching eyes of roving fighter pilots. Allied tanks and trucks often moved openly in tightly spaced columns, confident that the Luftwaffe was incapable of offering any threat worth bothering about. Later in the campaign, the Luftwaffe occasionally concentrated its forces and managed to strike back, usually ineffectually. Allied ground troops, used to nothing less than complete protection, invariably protested such leaks in the air umbrella. They had grown accustomed to the warmth of the air security blanket. Their German counterparts could only shiver in their nakedness.

If the aircraft of IX Tactical Air Command were considered integral to the Allied armies' daily operations, Eighth Air Force heavy bombers in direct troop support were more controversial. Although they had been effective during the pre-invasion campaign to seal off Normandy, they had been less successful during the invasion itself, when much of the immense weight of their bombardment had fallen on empty fields. Their subsequent efforts to break the impasse on the Allies' left flank, in front of Caen, were also disappointing. Their short bombing had caused casualties among forward Allied troops, and, although they pounded German defenses savagely, they did not break them. Nevertheless, the Eighth would take part in Operation COBRA, a massive blow intended to break the U.S. First Army out of the miseries of Normandy's *bocage* country.[15]

COBRA got off to a false start on 24 July because of bad weather. Only part of the force attacked and erratic bombing caused casualties on both sides of the line. The USAAF committed its aircraft to a maximum effort on the following day; 1,508 heavies, 380 mediums, and 559 fighters struck at the German defenses immediately to the west of the little town of St. Lô. The very sight of such massive formations inspired awe in both friend and foe, and the three-hour bombardment they unleashed was terrifying in its concentrated ferocity. The organization of many German units was broken by an experience most frequently described by survivors as "shattering." General Bayerlein of *Panzer Lehr* found that 70 percent of his personnel were "dead, wounded, crazed, or dazed," and, under interrogation after the war, Field Marshal Gerd von Rundstedt called the St. Lô bombing "the most effective, as well as the most impressive tactical use of air power" in his experience. Unfortunately, as before, there were some gross bombing errors and the U.S. 30th Infantry Division was the principal sufferer. Over 100 American soldiers died, among them Lieutenant General Lesley McNair, the highest ranking American officer killed in World War II. Although distressed by friendly losses, U.S. ground forces were not discouraged for long. They surged forward, breaking through the crumbling barrier of German resistance and throwing off the straitjacket of Normandy's *bocage* at last.

COBRA confirmed the obvious truth that the heavy bomber force was more akin to an indiscriminate bludgeon than a precise rapier, especially when used tactically. Of course, there were bitter reactions from the troops who had suffered from the waywardness of the friendly bombardment. Many Army ground commanders began to believe, along with Spaatz and Harris, that heavy bombers were better left to strategic tasks, but they, nevertheless, had to concede that the aircraft had been the keys that unlocked the German defenses at St. Lô. The U.S. VII Corps admitted: "Our losses would have been infinitely greater, and our success would perhaps never have materialized, if it had not been for the overall effectiveness of this heavy bombardment." General Eisenhower

later declared that, despite the problems, it was impossible "to convince the Army that the battle of St. Lô had not been won as a result of the direct support given by the Eighth Air Force."

As the number of American troops in France approached the million mark and control became too unwieldy for one headquarters, the ground forces split into two separate armies, the First (under Lieutenant General Courtney Hodges) and the Third (under Lieutenant General George Patton). Quesada's IX Tactical Air Command continued its old association with the First Army, and the newly activated Third Army was allocated an air force of its own, XIX Tactical Air Command commanded by Major General Otto Weyland. As the airmen of XIX Tactical Air Command would find out, they had "a tiger by the tail." Swinging at the outer edge of the Allied armies' opening door under Patton's forceful leadership, the Third Army moved across France at great speed. XIX Tactical Air Command had to keep up, moving its headquarters and squadrons forward continually and operating from hastily repaired or improvised airfields to ensure air cover when and where needed. These were Herculean labors, achieved with remarkable skill and timeliness by the Ninth's engineers and logistical units. As time went by Patton came to rely increasingly on this responsive tactical air arm, and revealing the level of trust and cooperation reached between air and ground commanders, he asked XIX Tactical Air Command to take on the responsibility of protecting the Third Army's long, exposed southern flank during its headlong advance.

By the end of the first week of August 1944, the U.S. Army had burst out of the Cotentin Peninsula at Avranches. Its spearheads were sweeping west across Brittany and east toward the Seine. In a desperate attempt to stem the hemorrhage, Hitler ordered a counterattack through Mortain to the sea to sever the head of the American advance from the body of its support. This formidable enemy thrust was built around five *Panzer* divisions and backed by a rare concentration of Luftwaffe fighters; but it was denied in one of the war's best demonstrations of interservice and inter-Allied cooperation. Slowed by stubborn resistance from American infantry, German armored columns were savaged from the air. Rocket-firing Typhoons of the RAF's 2nd Tactical Air Force took on the *Panzers* while IX Tactical Air Force fighters flew interdiction sorties and kept the Luftwaffe from interfering. To the *Wehrmacht*'s dismay, not one Luftwaffe fighter appeared over the battlefield. The *Panzer* spearhead stopped in its tracks with heavy losses. When the German generals finally accepted that their counterattack had failed, they began a withdrawal that soon degenerated into a headlong rout. As a consequence of Hitler's reluctance to abandon Mortain, their retreat was too late, and the stage was set for one of the most destructive demonstrations of tactical air power ever seen.

As the British and Canadians drove south toward Falaise and the U.S. Third Army raced to take Argentan from the south, the German Seventh Army and Fifth *Panzer* Army became almost completely encircled in an oval pocket, which, by 14 August, was less than 50 miles long and not more than 30 miles across at its widest point. The one remaining path of escape to the east was then only ten miles wide and being squeezed shut under Allied pressure. The interior of the Falaise Pocket and the narrow neck of its exit became classic killing grounds for tactical aircraft as German troops struggled to find a way out. Tanks and guns were destroyed in their hundreds, soft-skinned vehicles in their thousands. Although as many as 40,000 German soldiers escaped the Falaise trap, they left most of their equipment behind, as well as 60,000 of their colleagues—50,000 prisoners and 10,000 dead.

The campaign in northern France represented the heyday of tactical air power. The operational statistics of XIX Tactical Air Command alone for the month of August 1944 give some idea of the effort involved:

Flown: 12,292 combat sorties

Claimed: 4,058 motor vehicles, 466 tanks, other armor, 598 horse-drawn vehicles, 246 locomotives, 2,956 railroad cars, 155 river craft, 26 sea-going vessels, attacks on artillery, supply dumps, radars, airfields, barracks, troops, etc., 229 aircraft (163 in the air, 66 on the ground)

Lost: 114 aircraft

Allowing for the inevitable exaggeration associated with combat claims, these are impressive figures. It is hardly surprising that Patton felt moved to commend Weyland's XIX Tactical Air Command, calling its operations: "the best example of the combined use of air and ground troops I have ever witnessed."

While these heady days were passing into history in the north, Allied forces struck at Hitler's fortress from yet another direction. On 15 August 1944, they invaded the south of France and, profiting from lessons learned in previous amphibious operations, were quickly ashore. Opposing German forces were inferior to the invaders both in quality and quantity,

but ground Allied commanders were quick to acknowledge that air supremacy saved them a great many lives and a great deal of time. XII Tactical Air Command, commanded by Brigadier General Gordon Saville, operated with the bombers of the Mediterranean Allied Air Forces at the heart of the air campaign. Persistent interdiction before the landings had disrupted enemy supply lines, and counterair activity had effectively removed the Luftwaffe threat. Most of the coastal defenses were neutralized, and both the airborne assault and the landings went in under a powerful air umbrella and plenty of close support. With effective air-ground cooperation Allied forces swept forward and joined the right wing of Patton's Third Army west of the Swiss border in early September. At that point, having proved its combat capabilities after destroying tactical targets by the thousands in the Italian campaign and the drive through southern France, XII Tactical Air Command left the operational control of the MAAF to add its strength to the already formidable power of the Tactical Air Commands controlled by Ninth Air Force.[16]

Wehrmacht Defiant

By mid-September 1944, the Allies had freed most of France, Belgium, and Luxembourg, and they were ready for the next great challenge—reaching and crossing the Rhine. General Eisenhower ordered a main thrust to the north, with the First Allied Airborne Army (FAAA) participating.[17] On 17 September the Allies launched an ambitious operation codenamed MARKET/GARDEN. In this valiant, but ill-fated, attempt they planned to drive a 60-mile-long salient through the German lines and, by seizing bridges in the Netherlands near Eindhoven, Nijmegen, and Arnhem, open the way to a crossing of the lower Rhine. Aircraft of the Eighth and Ninth Air Forces and the RAF prepared the way by attacking flak defenses and German troop concentrations. Assaulting airborne forces were dispatched in an armada of 1,546 transports and 478 gliders and reinforced the following day with another 1,306 transports and 1,152 gliders. Unfortunately, the Allies faced strong, well-placed German forces, especially at Arnhem. Even worse, the airborne troops, because of bad weather were deprived of the level of close tactical aircraft support they had counted on. After a week of bitter fighting, during which armored spearheads struggled forward through Eindhoven and Nijmegen to relieve the beleaguered paratroops, the Allies realized that Arnhem was "a bridge too far," and abandoned the operation.

The European winter of 1944 was one of the worst in living memory. Storms and leaden skies combined to keep the Allied tactical air forces grounded at least half of the time. Taking advantage of the situation, Hitler gathered together his reserves and ordered a massive counterattack against thinly held U.S. Army positions in the Ardennes. On 16 December eight *Panzer* and ten infantry divisions punched through the U.S. front to split the Allied armies and drive on to the coast, retaking the port of Antwerp and cutting the logistics chain. The Battle of the Bulge was on. For once, it seemed, the Luftwaffe was prepared to offer the *Wehrmacht* real support, although for a week bad weather hampered both side's air forces in their attempts to intervene. In that time, the enemy penetrated another 60 miles, although a number of U.S. Army units held out in surrounded strong points, notably the 101st Division at Bastogne.

On 23 December the skies cleared at last and the enemy felt the full fury of Allied air power as it descended over him in the bulge. Medium bombers attacked roads and railways behind German columns repeatedly and struck at Luftwaffe airfields. Transports parachuted supplies into Bastogne. Fighters swarmed over *Wehrmacht* units, strafing and bombing guns, vehicles, and enemy-held buildings throughout the salient. In supporting operations on Christmas Eve, Eighth Air Force heavies pulled out all the stops and launched their largest effort of the war to that point. Over 2,000 B–17s and B–24s took off to hit German airfields and communications and greatly hampered the German offensive.[18]

Somewhat to the surprise of Allied airmen, the Luftwaffe had gathered its reserves together, too, and it rose in strength, flying as many as 800 sorties on 23 December, challenging Allied fighters to combat, and inflicting the highest losses ever on the Ninth's medium bombers. From a force of 624 B–26s and A–20s, 35 were shot down and over 180 were badly damaged. On 1 January 1945, the Luftwaffe did even better, launching nearly 900 aircraft for a sweep against Allied airfields. It achieved considerable success, destroying over 150 Allied aircraft and damaging many others, but at a cost; it lost almost a third of its strength—237 pilots killed, missing, or taken prisoner, and another 18 wounded, among them a number of experienced leaders.

While German industry might be able to supply new aircraft, men were irreplaceable. Hitler's Ardennes offensive was disastrous for the Luftwaffe, which suffered catastrophic pilot losses in the course of the Battle of the Bulge and was nearly at its last gasp. Among several bad days was 17 December, when 79 pilots were killed or wounded. On Christmas Day 62 more were killed, and on New Year's Eve, another 41, besides smaller numbers on other days. In its struggle with the Allied air forces, the Luftwaffe was bleeding to death.

By the end of January 1945 the Battle of the Bulge was over and German Army units were back where they had started, and considerably worse off than before. USAAF claims for ground targets destroyed during the period were staggering—11,378 motor vehicles, 1,161 tanks and armored vehicles, 507 locomotives, 6,266 railroad cars, 472 guns, 974 rail cuts, 421 road cuts, and 36 bridges. If claims were exaggerated by the smoke of battle, effects were not. The enemy offensive had been defeated, and the evidence for the air's part in that defeat was plain to see on every side.

They Also Served

The overwhelming scale of the strategic and tactical air campaigns often tended to obscure the activities of smaller, but nonetheless important, air force roles, two of which were significant to the advance through France and the Battle of the Bulge. Night fighters had, throughout the campaign in Europe, intercepted occasional Luftwaffe forays and operated as intruders over enemy-held territory. By 1944 the Northrop P–61 Black Widow had added its considerable firepower (usually four 20-mm cannon and four .5-inch machine guns) to the Ninth Air Force. Fast and maneuverable despite its size, the P–61 was a fearsome night fighter, but it also kept the enemy under the pressure of tactical air attack around the clock. German supply columns moving at night could not be sure that darkness would shield them, nor could repair crews working on bridges destroyed or damaged during the day. Trains, barges, factories, warehouses, and troop concentrations all felt the sting of P–61 weapons by night.

At the other end of the scale were the Grasshoppers, tiny aircraft like the Piper L–4 which proved indispensable for rapid liaison between senior commanders and their units. They served as airborne observation posts, assisted in controlling ground forces, and even functioned as "horseflies," pointing out selected targets to the fighter-bombers. Occasionally, their presence could be decisive. One hard-pressed U.S. Army unit in the Battle of the Bulge did not have the radio channels to talk to the only tactical aircraft nearby, which were RAF Typhoons. A Grasshopper intervened and led the Typhoons into action. As Major General Ernest Harmon of the U.S. 2nd Armored Division recalled: "It was like a butterfly leading a squadron of buzzards. The Typhoons…left devastation in their wake. What was left of the German column retired with our troops in hot pursuit."

L–4. Although unsung, the ubiquitous Piper L–4 was an essential part of the Allied drive across France in 1944. Its pilots, apart from their usual liaison and observation duties, found themselves reconnoitering new airfield sites from the air as battle lines raced forward and being "horseflies" to guide fighter-bombers to their targets.

The USAAF also engaged in leaflet dropping and clandestine operations known as carpetbagger missions. In black-painted B–24s fitted with special radio aids, the 492nd Bombardment Group flew nighttime low-level sorties to parachute agents into Europe and to supply resistance groups with arms and ammunition. In the course of hazardous operations, the carpetbaggers delivered over 20,000 containers, 11,000 packages and 1,000 agents for the loss of 25 B–24s. Their job in France done, many of the group's B–24s were used as flying fuel trucks to deliver much-needed gasoline to the racing columns of Patton's Third Army.

Final Offensive

Although cognizant that their forces were contributing significantly in direct support of the Allied armies in France, the strategic bomber commanders remained impatient with any task deflecting them from what they viewed as their primary responsibility—the destruction of Germany's war-making capacity.

Fortunately for their peace of mind, Eisenhower understood the nature of the strategic campaign, and he was quite prepared for Spaatz and Harris to continue operations against German industry in the absence of more pressing requirements on the battlefields or the V–weapon sites. After the tense early days of the Normandy invasion, he gave the "bomber barons" ample scope to develop their strategic bombing campaigns as they thought best.

Spaatz had no doubts about the way he should deploy his bombers. On 8 June, only two days after D-Day, he issued an order to the Eighth and Fifteenth Air Forces that established their primary strategic aim—to starve the enemy's armed forces of their oil. His clear strategic vision was never more in evidence than on this issue. Spaatz correctly assessed that his oil plan could accomplish several things at once, all of them important in pursuit of Allied victory. Oil restrictions directly affected transportation, factories, the German Army's mechanized and armored units, and the Luftwaffe. Thus, oil facilities were targets that the Luftwaffe had to defend. Doing so, it committed itself to an ever downward spiral. The Luftwaffe would suffer heavy losses from the battle of attrition with the USAAF; it would then demand more replacements from a flying training system already inhibited by lack of fuel; its experience levels would fall and it would become less and less effective. As the USAAF struck more and more fuel targets the Luftwaffe's capacity to respond would be hampered by shortages of fuel and pilots. Before long, Spaatz was convinced, the Luftwaffe would be forced to its knees and the whole German war machine would grind to a halt.

Spaatz had begun his assault on German oil even before D-Day. In May 1944 the Fifteenth Air Force hit Ploesti's refineries three times and the Eighth Air Force hit various synthetic oil plants in Germany. The assumption that the Luftwaffe would fight for oil was proved right. It strongly opposed the raids and inflicted considerable losses on the attacking bombers, but it suffered as well, and the oil plants were hit hard. Ultra intelligence intercepts soon revealed the level of German concern over the raids. Fighter squadrons badly needed elsewhere were

retained to meet them, and large numbers of flak units were being moved into positions from which they could defend the oil industry. Albert Speer warned Hitler: "The enemy has struck at one of our weakest points. If [he persists] at this time, we will soon no longer have any fuel production worth mentioning." The enemy did indeed persist, with major blows falling on the oil industry unceasingly until the end of the war.

An offshoot of the USAAF's strategic offensive was a belated agreement that its aircraft would be allowed to use bases in the Soviet Union for "shuttle" bombing missions. Aircraft operating from England and Italy would attack targets in Eastern Europe and fly on to refuel and rearm in the Soviet Union before striking at other targets on the way back. By May 1944 three bases were ready in the Ukraine, and the first of the FRANTIC missions, as they were called, was flown by the Fifteenth Air Force on 2 June. The Eighth Air Force joined in on 21 June, when 145 B–17s, escorted by 70 P–51s, bombed oil plants south of Berlin on their way to the Ukraine. Their bombing was excellent, but disaster followed. Unseen by the B–17s, a Heinkel 177 trailed them to Poltava airfield; that night the Luftwaffe surprised them on the ground,

B–24s over Ploesti. Surrounded by heavy flak, B–24s of the Fifteenth Air Force attack the Ploesti oil complex from high altitude on 31 May 1944. By the time the Soviet Army arrived in August 1944, oil production at Ploesti had dwindled to a trickle.

233

Soviet officers watching Lieutenant General Ira Eaker's 97th Bombardment Group B–17G arrive at Poltava on the first of the Operation FRANTIC shuttle bombing missions on 2 June 1944.

destroying 44 B–17s and damaging 26. USAAF aircraft made sporadic attempts to use FRANTIC bases in succeeding months, but their missions were not outstandingly successful. Soviet enthusiasm for the idea was never very great, and the results achieved did not match the cost. USAAF aircraft flew their last FRANTIC mission on 13 September 1944, by which time the Soviet Army had advanced so far that bases in the Ukraine were too distant from likely targets to be of much help.

The Allied armies' advance in the West had brought all of Germany within reach of tactical as well as strategic aircraft by the beginning of 1945. In a bid to tear out its remaining sinews and perhaps to stun its population with a massive display of air power before launching troops across the Rhine, the Allies devised Operation CLARION. It called for every available Allied aircraft to attack transportation targets—rail, road, canal, and river—all over Germany on the same day. On 22 February 1945, the weather was favorable and the skies above Germany were filled with more than 6,000 Allied aircraft, fighters hunting and strafing at low level, and bombers attacking targets from as low as 10,000 feet or less. The Luftwaffe reacted feebly; its few enemy fighters that did get airborne were brushed aside. Allied losses were minimal and their results so promising that they repeated the operation the next day. CLARION's dust finally settled on a badly crippled enemy transport

system. Having so disrupted Germany's life lines and clamped so tight an aerial tourniquet on its oil supply, Allied airmen believed, with some justification, that the Third Reich's collapse was imminent.

The changing fortunes of the USAAF and the Luftwaffe in the space of one year had been dramatic. At the end of 1943 the Eighth Air Force had gritted its teeth as it struggled to overcome the impact of heavy losses—45 bombers out of 262 sent to Stuttgart (17.2 percent); 60 out of 229 at Schweinfurt (26.2 percent); 29 out of 440 at Bremen (6.6 percent); 24 out of 281 at Solingen (8.5 percent); and so on.... In stark contrast, as 1944 drew to its close, the Eighth was nearing omnipotence in German skies. Its operations involved huge numbers of bombers and escorts, and American airmen had begun to feel that they could go where they wished without fear of serious Luftwaffe opposition. Flak could still be intense, but loss rates among bomber crews were not nearly as demoralizing as they had been just a year before. As the final offensive gathered pace in 1945, the statistics told their own story—1 bomber lost from a force of 1,094 sent to Kassel; 5 out of 1,310 at Chemnitz and Magdeburg; 0 of 1,219 at Nurnburg.

Even losses that climbed into double figures, as on 3 February 1945—25 out of 1,370 bombing Berlin—were low enough to seem bearable. Twenty-four out of 281 at Solingen had been nearly 9 percent, dismaying to aircrews hoping to complete their combat tours unscathed. Twenty-five out of 1,370 was well under 1 percent and much more reassuring, since in 1945 it was a rate that was uncharacteristically high.

As the tide of war turned irrevocably, the Luftwaffe was left wondering what might have been. It had neither the trained fighter pilots nor the fuel with which to oppose the Allied aircraft filling the skies, even with the introduction of new aircraft types, which, had they been available in the winter of 1943–1944, could have tipped the balance of the air war in the Third Reich's favor. Although wounded, the German aircraft industry, operating under the dispersal policies of Albert Speer, produced over 40,000 combat aircraft in 1944, almost five times more than in 1939.[19] However, after an encouraging, but brief, period when front-line squadrons benefited from the glut by reequipping, the relentless attrition of combat took its toll and pilot strengths began to fall. By 1945 fighters sat in rows waiting to be delivered,

but their tanks were empty and they outnumbered the end product of the Luftwaffe's flying training program. Even those that did arrive on front-line bases could not always join the battle immediately. In many cases, Luftwaffe engineers found it no longer worth their while to repair aircraft with even minor battle damage. It was easier for them to push a damaged fighter to one side and pull out a new one.

The Coming of the Jets

While Speer's production miracles had little apparent effect on Allied airmen, Germany's visionary aircraft designers managed to take them by surprise. Turbo-jet engines had been under development in Britain and Germany since the 1930s, but progress toward the production of operational jets was slowed in both countries by a combination of technical problems and official skepticism. The first jet to fly was German, the Heinkel 178 on 27 August 1939, but it was in the summer of 1944 before the first jet squadrons became operational. The Germans introduced the remarkable

Me 262. Nazi Germany's first operational jet aircraft, the Messerschmitt Me 262 began intercepting high flying Allied reconnaissance aircraft in the spring of 1944. The 262 was much faster than any Allied aircraft, being capable of well over 500 miles per hour at all altitudes. With four 30-mm cannon grouped together in the nose, its weight of fire, too, was superior. Power was supplied by the world's first successful axial-flow jet engines, two Junkers Jumo 004B engines of 1,980 pounds of thrust each. Operating at the outermost limits of engine technology, such an early jet demanded very gentle handling by its pilot, who could, by carelessly handling the throttle, induce damage or destruction.

Me 262 cockpit. Besides normal flight instruments, the Me 262's cockpit included unfamiliar gauges, like those measuring critical exhaust gas temperatures, and others capable of recording RPM figures as high as 9,000.

Messerschmitt Me 262[20] to the Luftwaffe's front line in July 1944, initially as a high-speed bomber. The RAF's No 616 Squadron started chasing V–1 flying bombs with its Gloster Meteor jets later the same month.

Boasting swept wings and two axial-flow jet engines, the Messerschmitt Me 262 *Schwalbe* (Swallow) could reach 540 miles per hour and climb to 30,000 feet in seven minutes. This marked superiority in performance over any Allied aircraft was impressive, as was the Me 262's heavy armament of four closely grouped 30-mm cannon, which could destroy a heavy bomber in one short burst. At a time when the air war seemed all but over, it promised to confront Allied airmen, and particularly those in the B–17s and B–24s, with a very real threat. As it was, because of problems with the Junkers Jumo engine and Hitler's initial insistence that it be brought into service as a fast bomber against the Allied invasion force, the first unit of Me 262 interceptors was not operational until October 1944. Jets were seen by American aircrews only rarely and managed to fly more than 50 sorties in one day just once, on 7 April 1945, when the Eighth Air Force alone flew 1,261 bombers and 830 fighters over Germany.

A host of problems combined to ensure that the Me 262 would never play a major role in the air war. There were the teething troubles, which were only to be expected with so revolutionary a design. For example, the running life of the Junkers Jumo engine never exceeded 25 hours, and the aircraft's poor-quality tires were inclined to burst under the impact of 120 mile-per-hour landings. Flying training, particularly at the reduced levels of 1944–1945, was soon recognized as inadequate for such an aircraft. Operational units were, therefore slower in forming. Then there were the incessant attentions of the Allied air forces. Me 262s and their spares were often stranded in the ruins of the German transport system, and jet airfields became prime targets for the bombers and fighters of both the Eighth and Ninth Air Forces.[21]

Knowing that the jets were at their most vulnerable during takeoffs and landings, American fighter pilots took to patrolling over their airfields. Lieutenant Urban Drew of the 361st Fighter Group showed the way in his P–51 as early as 7 October 1944 when he caught two Me 262s just after they had taken off and shot them both down before they could accelerate away. Once up to speed, the Me 262 was a more difficult proposition and an experienced pilot could bank on being allowed to choose or refuse combat because of his jet's superior performance. Despite that advantage, even the best of them got caught by persistent and ever-present USAAF fighters. The redoubtable Walter Nowotny, a Luftwaffe ace with 258 aerial victories, was killed on 8 November 1944 after attacking a B–17 formation and tangling with its P–51 escort. On 26 April 1945, the celebrated fighter leader Adolf Galland was caught napping by Lieutenant James Finnegan's P–47 and forced to put his badly damaged Me 262 down on an airfield being heavily attacked by other P–47s. This was Galland's last operational sortie and it offered sharp commentary on the Luftwaffe's problems in the closing days of the war. Even Galland, one of the world's most seasoned fighter pilots, flying the most advanced fighter aircraft in existence, could not escape the USAAF's relentless pursuit, either in the air or on the ground.

Mission Accomplished

During the final weeks of the air war in Europe, Germany was hit by a series of hammer blows from massive formations of Allied aircraft. Berlin, Hamburg, and Dresden were among cities crushed under immense bomb tonnages intended to complete the dislocation of Germany and its war machine. On 16 April 1945, General Spaatz sent a message to the Eighth and Fifteenth Air Forces that began: "The advances of our ground forces have brought to a close the strategic air war waged by the United States Strategic Air Forces and the Royal Air Force Bomber Command." In fact, it was not quite over. Strategic missions continued until 25 April, when RAF Lancasters bombed Hitler's redoubt at Berchtesgaden and Eighth Air Force heavies attacked targets in Czechoslovakia and southeastern Germany. The last bombs of the 696,450 tons dropped by the "Mighty Eighth" fell from the bomb-bays of the 384th Bombardment Group. That done, the battle-worn B–17s and B–24s took on the quieter occupations of dropping leaflets and delivering food to the starving people of the Netherlands.

Since the ground forces were necessarily in action until all fighting stopped, the tactical air forces retained their combat responsibilities into the last day of the war, and at least some Luftwaffe units were ready to oppose them to the end. As late as 26 April 1944, Adolf Galland, on his last sortie, led his Me 262s against a First Tactical Air Force formation in which four B–26s were shot down. The last Eighth Air Force fighter pilot victory was claimed the day before by Lieutenant Hilton Thompson in a P–51 of the 479th Fighter Group, and, again, it involved a jet. Thompson caught an unsuspecting Arado 234 jet bomber near Salzburg and sent it down in flames. These skirmishes concluded, the European air war was over. It had been a vast enterprise, too complex to allow easy summary or glib assessment. Its operations lent themselves, however, to the cold science of statistics. Figures cannot hope to tell the stories or capture the feelings of the millions of individuals who endured the ferocity of aerial combat first hand, but they give some idea of the scale of the conflict and its awful cost in the European and Mediterranean theaters, from 1942 to 1945:

Total USAAF casualties (dead, wounded, missing, captured).............94,565

Total USAAF personnel dead (all causes) 30,099

USAAF combat sorties 1,693,565

Bomb tonnage dropped..................1,554,463

Enemy aircraft claimed in aerial combat 29,916

USAAF aircraft lost (all causes out of 41,575 worldwide) 27,694

Behind the figures lay the facts. From the first, the Allied air forces took the war to the enemy. Until 1945 combat aircraft were the only offensive instruments capable of striking directly at Germany. Although at first its effects were not great and its costs were sometimes grievous, the air offensive steadily gained the initiative and forced the Germans to divert more and more resources to the defense of the Reich. German manpower, aircraft, guns, and scientific effort, which could have made a difference to the front lines, were devoted increasingly to countering Allied bombers. At the same time, the German people were constantly reminded that they were in a war of their own making, and that their opponents were not about to give up.

As the Allied air forces grew in strength and capability they had more influence on the course of the war. They heavily damaged the German aircraft industry and compelled it to disperse. Over time, they comprehensively wrecked the transportation system, so essential for the efficient movement of troops and supplies. By April 1945, in perhaps their most effective campaign, they reduced German oil production to no more than 5 percent of its original capacity. Taken together, there could be no doubting that the Allies' various bombing campaigns had crippled the German war effort and had fatally weakened the enemy's capacity for resistance.

Equally important was the Luftwaffe's defeat, a victory that can be attributed largely to the long-range fighters of the Eighth Air Force. Their efforts over Germany broke the Luftwaffe's back and led directly to Allied air supremacy. That achievement made the invasion of Normandy possible. Subsequently, it gave the Allied tactical air forces the necessary freedom of action to relieve the ground forces of Luftwaffe harassment and give them the air support they needed as they drove forward to occupy what was left of Hitler's thousand-year Reich.

If confirmation were needed of air power's decisive role in Germany's defeat, it came from those who had been on the receiving end. Field Marshal Gerd von Rundstedt, Commander in Chief West until March 1945, listed air power first of the factors that led to Allied victory. Field Marshal Albert Kesselring, Commander in Chief Italy and then Commander in Chief West after March 1945, stated: "It was your air force that decided the conflict." General Alfred Jodl, German High Command Chief of Staff, believed that air supremacy decided the war. Field Marshal Wilhelm Keitel gave principal credit for the victory in the West to the Allied air forces, and General von Vietinghoff commented similarly about the campaign in Italy. Albert Speer, Hitler's Minister for Armaments Production, repeatedly stated that, even though there were ways in which the air offensive could have been more effectively conducted, Allied air power had been the principal reason for Germany's defeat.

Even before the final aerial dramas were played out, Americans were preparing an exhaustive evaluation of the air war in Europe by an impartial body known as the United States Strategic Bombing Survey (USSBS). By April 1945 teams of trained investigators were following close behind the Allied armies, collecting documents, and interviewing prisoners to assess the contribution of air power to the defeat of Nazi Germany. The findings of the USSBS report were detailed and comprehensive. They brought out many of air power's achievements, and they were sometimes sharply critical of the way the air war had been conducted. In later years, some of these criticisms were used selectively by those who wished to deprecate air power's role in World War II, but it should be remembered that the final paragraph of the USSBS report begins with an emphatic conclusion:

Allied air power was decisive in the war in Western Europe. Hindsight inevitably suggests that it might have been employed differently or better in some respects. Nevertheless, it was decisive.

Notes

1. Post-war researches showed that gunners' claims were generally about three times Luftwaffe losses. The battle of 9 October 1942 is perplexing because only two Luftwaffe losses can be traced. Equally baffling was a running battle in which "Wild Bill" Casey and his crew defied a succession of fighter attacks on 23 November 1942. Casey's gunners described shooting down seven FW 190s in 12 minutes. They "disintegrated" or "hit the sea," and more than one pilot was seen to bail out. German records for that day indicate that one FW 190 was lost. None of this suggests that the gunners' claims were anything less than genuine, but it does highlight how the stress of combat can affect mood and memory.

2. The collision on the Lille raid was the first of more than 100 between Eighth Air Force heavy bombers during the war. The vast majority were fatal to aircrews.

3. On 28 July 1943, a B–17 of the 385th Bombardment Group was struck by a rocket and broke up, its pieces crashing into two other B–17s, which were also destroyed.

4. *Memphis Bell* survived the war and is now exhibited in a special museum on Mud Island, Memphis, Tennessee.

5. Posthumous Medals of Honor were awarded to Lieutenant Lloyd Hughes (389th Bombardment Group), Lieutenant Colonel Addison Baker, and Major John Jerstad (93rd Bombardment Group). Surviving recipients were Colonel Leon Johnson (44th Bombardment Group) and Colonel John "Killer" Kane (98th Bombardment Group).

6. Beirne Lay subsequently wrote the screen play for the epic film about Eighth Air Force operations—*Twelve O'Clock High*.

7. Curiously, one of the most celebrated examples of daylight precision bombing took place during this period, and with minimal loss. On 9 October 1943, 96 B–17s from the 94th, 95th, 100th, 385th and 390th Bombardment Groups attacked the Focke Wulf factory at Marienburg. Eighty-three percent of their bombs dropped fell within 2,000 feet of the aiming point. Only two B–17s failed to return.

8. See Richard P. Hallion, *Strike from the Sky* (Smithsonian Institution Press, 1989), pp. 177–178 for descriptions of several other instances in which A–36s attacked their own troops.

9. Air Marshal Sir John Slessor was General Ira Eaker's deputy in the Mediterranean Allied Air Forces. In a letter to the RAF's Chief of Air Staff in April 1944 he commented on: "…the astonishing accuracy of the medium bomber groups, particularly the Marauders [B–26s]; I think that the 42nd Bombardment Group…is probably the best day bomber unit in the world."

10. Through IX Fighter Command, Quesada controlled two further burgeoning commands, IX and XIX Tactical Air Commands, both of which would feature significantly in the Allied sweep through France and into Germany.

11. Eisenhower's prediction may have been accurate, but to minimize risks to friendly airmen from trigger-happy soldiers and sailors, the Allies painted their aircraft with prominent black and white stripes on the wings and fuselage and employed distinctive twin-boomed P–38 fighters, aircraft unlike any operated by the Luftwaffe, to give close cover to the invasion fleet.

12. Fifteen squadrons were allocated for shipping cover, 54 patrolled the beaches, 33 escorted the bombers and conducted offensive sweeps, 33 undertook interdiction of the areas inland from the beaches, and 36 were available for direct support of the assault forces.

13. The selection of these was driven by intelligence from Ultra, which often revealed the whereabouts of significant targets and indicated which attacks were most effective. An Ultra-inspired air strike on 10 June 1944 destroyed *Panzergruppe* West Headquarters and killed many of its staff, thus removing the vital armored forces control center from the battle.

14. On 17 July 1944, Rommel experienced the implacable ferocity of Allied fighters first hand when his staff car was strafed by two Spitfires. Their sweep, which killed his driver and fractured his skull as the car plunged off the road, effectively ended his career.

15. The *bocage* was Norman farming country made up of small fields bounded by thick hedgerows and sunken lanes. It provided ideal defensive positions.

16. In effect, by the end of 1944, each of the armies had its own air force. First Army had IX Tactical Air Command (Quesada); Third Army had XIX Tactical Air Command (Weyland); and Ninth Army had XXIX Tactical Air Command (Nugent). In the north 21st Army Group was supported by the RAF's 2nd Tactical Air Force, and 6th Army Group to the south had the services of XII Tactical Air Command (Saville) and the First French Air Force. XII Tactical Air Command and the French joined together to become the First Tactical Air Force (Major General Ralph Royce, a celebrated figure from the early days of American air power).

17. The FAAA was formed on 8 August 1944 under the command of Lieutenant General Lewis Brereton. It included the U.S. 17th, 82nd, and 101st Airborne Divisions; the British 1 and 6 Airborne Divisions; and the Polish Independent Parachute Brigade. Air elements were the USAAF's IX Troop Carrier Command, and the RAF's 38 and 46 Groups. Major General Hoyt Vandenberg commanded the Ninth Air Force after Brereton.

18. Leading the Eighth on this raid was Brigadier General Fred Castle, a former commanding officer of the 94th Bombardment Group, revered by his men. His B–17 was shot down on the way to the target and he was killed in the crash, having stayed at the controls to give his crew time to escape. He is the only general officer in American history to die while directly involved in a specific act to save the lives of his subordinates. His was the last Eighth Air Force Medal of Honor to be awarded.

19. American aircraft production figures rose from 2,100 in 1939 to 96,300 in 1944. The latter figure, startling enough in itself, includes such large, complex aircraft as the B–29, whereas German industry was driven to produce more and more single-seat fighters.

20. The Messerschmitt Me 163 was equally remarkable, but flawed in concept. Powered by a rocket engine, it was very fast but its fuel supply was so limited that it ran at full power for only four minutes, after which it became a glider. It was limited to an operational radius of no more than 25 miles and rendered helpless during its recovery to base.

21. It is interesting to speculate on the possibilities if the Me 262 had reached the Luftwaffe just one year earlier, before the appearance of the P–51 as an escort fighter. It is conceivable that the Eighth Air Force would have had to halt its strategic campaign, and that Allied air superiority would then not have been won as it was. In that event, an invasion in 1944 would not have been possible and the war would probably have dragged on for at least another year, with who knows what long-term consequences for Europe.

Our airplane was maneuverd into position. My crew was in place. I ran both engines up, tested them, and gave the thumbs-up signal to the officer holding the checkered signal flag. I glanced at my watch. It was 8:20 a.m. ship time.

(Lieutenant Colonel Jimmy Doolittle on Tokyo raid launched from carrier USS *Hornet*, 18 April 1942)

The B–25 is most terrifying!

(Survivor of an Army Air Forces attack on Japanese shipping)

. . . I myself, on the basis of the B–29 raids, felt that the [Japanese] cause was hopeless.

(Premier Kantaro Suzuki, testifying in 1945)

The outstanding and vital lesson of [World War II] is that air power is the dominant factor in this modern world, and it will remain the dominant factor as long as power determines the fate of nations.

(Marshal of the RAF Lord Tedder, General Eisenhower's deputy, speaking in 1947)

Chapter 7
The Pacific Air War, 1942–1945

Perseverance and Destruction

The USAF Museum's story of the Pacific war starts with Pearl Harbor and moves through the Philippines, Java, New Guinea, the Solomons, the Aleutians, the island hopping campaign, Burma, and the devastation of Japan, singling out special people and events on the way—among them the Doolittle raid on Tokyo, the Hump flights into China, and Medal of Honor recipients Richard Bong and Thomas McGuire.

The main exhibit closes with the bombing campaign against the Japanese home islands. The huge shape of the Boeing B–29 **Bockscar**, which ended World War II with an atomic bomb on Nagasaki, takes up one corner of the hangar. Visitors can wander beside the shining silver fuselage and gaze up into the bomb-aimer's position. Near the B–29's tail stand copies of the atomic bombs **Little Boy** and **Fat Man**. The dying spasms of Japanese militarism are remembered in the ultimate kamikaze machine suspended to one side of **Bockscar**—a piloted glider bomb boosted by rockets. The Japanese called it Oka (Cherry Blossom); Americans named it Baka (Fool).

Taken together, the USAF Museum's collection offers visitors an unrivaled opportunity for remembering or learning about the scale and power of the U.S. Army Air Forces in World War II. We are continually reminded that this was a citizens' air force, built up from modest beginnings to awesome proportions, in which ordinary Americans combined to accomplish extraordinary feats. With their achievements very much in mind, visitors can turn away from **Bockscar** and begin to examine the post-war world. As the museum's telling of the tale of American air power unfolds, they will see how, for America's military airmen, that world held the promise of an independent air force, the challenges of the jet era, and the unwelcome prospect of having to confront an international opponent in a nuclear armed standoff.

P–40 in the Aleutians. In the latter part of 1942 the 11th Fighter Squadron, 353rd Fighter Group, in the Aleutians was operating P–40Es. The commander was Jack Chennault, son of Claire Chennault, the celebrated leader of the American Volunteer Group in China. As a tribute to his father and the Flying Tigers, the 11th adopted a stylized tiger design for their aircraft and became known as the Aleutian Tigers.

Japan on the Move

Stung beyond endurance by the Doolittle raid of April 1942, Japanese military leaders launched into the next phase of their imperial expansion with more haste than good sense. To consolidate and rationalize the perimeter of their empire, they proposed a four-pronged offensive. In the south, they intended to capture Port Moresby in New Guinea. From there they could threaten Australia. At Guadalcanal in the Solomons they planned to build an airfield as a base for further island conquests to interdict the United States–Australia trans-Pacific lifeline. Farther north, they wanted Midway Island, which would give them a grip on the Central Pacific and plug a worrying gap in their far-flung defensive screen. In part as a diversion from the attack on Midway, they also proposed an invasion of the Aleutians. Afflicted by "victory disease," Japanese military leaders did not seem to realize that their forces, already involved over an immense portion of the globe, might be overstretched. Their enforced return to rationality was to prove painful in the extreme.

In early May the hazards of the Tokyo raid and his B–25 bail-out still fresh in his mind, newly promoted Brigadier General Jimmy Doolittle began the long journey back to the United States via India and Egypt. He had hardly left China before a Japanese invasion force was on its way to Port Moresby. The ensuing Battle of the Coral Sea, the first ever fought between aircraft carriers, was judged a tactical draw, as both sides suffered serious losses. However, since the Japanese fleet was forced to abandon the invasion and retreat, the vital strategic victory belonged to the U.S. Navy.

Before May was out, the Imperial Japanese Navy was embarked on the most ambitious of its operations, committing its considerable strength to the achievement of three goals—the capture of Midway, the invasion of the Aleutians, and the destruction of the U.S. Pacific Fleet's aircraft carriers. In the epic Battle of Midway on 4 June 1942, USN airmen wrested victory from what had seemed certain defeat by sinking four Japanese carriers for the loss of the *Yorktown*. Once again, the enemy fleet was forced to retreat, but this time its Imperial Japanese Navy had sustained a blow from which it would never recover. It lost four large carriers, aircraft, and many experienced naval pilots in pivotal action. From then on, the initiative in the Pacific passed to the United States and the Japanese found themselves almost continually on the defensive.

U.S. Army Air Forces aircraft played a part at Midway, but not a particularly distinguished one. B–17Es of the Seventh Air Force made the principal effort, flying 55 sorties against the Japanese, bombing their ships mainly from high-level and scoring at most one hit on a transport. Worse yet, on 6 June six B–17s attacked what they reported was an enemy cruiser, claiming two direct hits and sinking it "in fifteen seconds." As remarkable as that seemed, the B–17s' crews would have preferred that their target unsink itself after they departed. Later that day, an indignant signal from the USS *Grayling* asked why an American submarine should have to crash-dive to avoid being plastered by the USAAF. It begged the question. Was it reasonable to expect heavy bombers, flying at high level, to identify and attack small moving targets, like ships, with any hope of success?

Aleutian Adventure

Meanwhile, far to the north, the Japanese had secured a foothold in the Aleutians, establishing troops on the islands of Attu and Kiska. Given their circumstances, the troops may have come to regret their achievement. Aleutians weather is invariably appalling, with gales, rain, blizzards, and low clouds. As one air force officer wrote: "During April and May, the weather for air operations is bad. For the rest of the year, it is worse." Camp sites and airstrips were either buried in snow and ice or immersed in mud and water.

The geography and climate of the Aleutians and the North Pacific were too harsh to allow the development of a major campaign by either side, and the region was never considered more than a secondary theater of war. The Japanese had not intended to launch a major action, like an assault on Alaska, from Attu and Kiska. Their detachments were purely defensive, placed there to block any possible American advance toward Japan down the Aleutian chain. Nevertheless, the Japanese occupation of American territory could not be treated lightly. Instead of settling for a mutual standoff, the United States undertook an air campaign to make things as uncomfortable as possible for the occupying troops. The Eleventh Air Force under Brigadier General William Butler, strengthened with P–38s, B–24s, and B–25s, persistently attempted to bomb and strafe Japanese positions in always hazardous and often unrewarding raids, such as one described in the USAAF official history:

> On the 18th [January 1943]…seven heavy and five medium bombers flew out of Adak with a six-fighter escort. Before they reached the target, the fog closed in and the planes turned back. The mediums and the fighters were fast enough to reach Adak before the base was completely "souped in." Four of the

slower Liberators had to seek an alternate landing field; the nearest possibility was Umnak, two and a half hours east of Adak. Two B–24s disappeared into the fog and were never heard from. A third, crash-landing on Great Sitkin, was damaged beyond repair. One reached Umnak and landed by the light of flares, but overshot the runway and crashed into two P–38s, destroying them. Six planes were lost, no bombs were dropped, and no enemy was encountered—save fog. Bad luck continued. On 21 January two B–17s, out of Umnak for Adak, collided in mid-air; one disappeared, the other landed, badly hurt. A P–40, out of control, crashed into Kuluk Bay the same day. On the 23rd two B–25s tangled in a fog and went down.

As bad as they were, these losses only continued a pattern. During a five-month period in the latter half of 1942, the Eleventh Air Force lost 72 aircraft, only 9 of them in combat. Between the beginning of June and the end of September 1943, it lost 40 aircraft in combat, but wrote off 174 more to "operational hazards." The Eleventh gained only partial consolation knowing that the Japanese were suffering similar problems.

Compared to other theaters of war, the losses were insignificant—the Eleventh Air Force was never capable of operating more than 200 or 300 aircraft— and the American military in the Aleutians had every

right to feel clamped in the icy grip of a "forgotten war." Besides flying operations in weather that would have grounded air forces elsewhere, the airmen of the Eleventh Air Force endured poor food, miserable living quarters, inadequate airfields, and rudimentary navigation aids while going after the Japanese whenever possible. Much of their agony eased in 1943, during what passed for the Aleutian summer. American forces retook Attu after a bloody struggle in which the Japanese defenders fought to the last man. American commanders did not look forward to attacking Kiska, but the Japanese did not contest and quietly withdrew.

Having restored America's territorial integrity, the Eleventh Air Force shrank until, by September, it had only two bombardment squadrons (one heavy, one medium), a fighter group, and one troop carrier squadron. Its operations then consisted of patrolling the frigid northern waters and harassing Japanese bases in the distant Northern Kurile Islands. These activities seemed thankless at the time, but they forced Japan to watch its back door. In 1944 it had over 70,000 troops and more than 400 aircraft in the Hokkaido-Kuriles region, held there by the Eleventh's constant reminder that Americans posed a threat to the home islands from the north.

If Americans were frustrated by the fighting in the Aleutians, they were consoled by the one priceless jewel that fell into their laps during the campaign. One of the war's great surprises had been the

Mitsubishi A6M fighter, known to the Allies as the Zero. It was outflying everything it met and almost nothing was known about it. After a raid on Dutch Harbor in the Aleutians, one Japanese pilot elected to put his failing fighter down on land rather than crash into the icy sea. He saw what he took to be a flat grassy area on Akutan Island and attempted a normal wheels-down landing. He dug his wheels into boggy ground, turned the Zero over, and broke his neck. A month later, the aircraft was seen by a patrolling Catalina and recovered practically undamaged. It was shipped to California, rebuilt, and test flown, giving results that led to countering tactics and directly influenced the design of later American fighters, particularly naval.

New Guinea

After his escape from the rampaging Japanese in the Philippines, General Douglas MacArthur assumed command of the South West Pacific theater in April 1942, setting up his headquarters in Australia, initially at Melbourne and later at Brisbane. His appearance on the scene complicated command responsibilities and the appointment of a Supreme Allied Commander in the Pacific. The Combined Chiefs of Staff decided that the Pacific should be an American strategic responsibility. The U.S. Joint Chiefs of Staff (JCS) reconciled differences between the Army and the Navy by selecting two principal lines of advance against the Japanese and, therefore, two commanders. MacArthur would rule in the South West Pacific Area and Admiral Chester Nimitz in the Pacific Ocean Area. They would be responsible for developing a two-pronged assault, through New Guinea and the Solomons, to envelop the Japanese main base at Rabaul on New Britain.

MacArthur's air commander was Lieutenant General George Brett, whose assets during the summer of 1942 were a scattered collection of American and Australian aircraft, described as "pitifully inadequate for their task." The few USAAF bombardment squadrons on hand were equipped with A–24s and early models of the B–25, B–26, and B–17. Available fighters were for the most part P–40s and P–400s, the latter an inferior model of the P–39 developed for export. Despite shortcomings, the Americans made efforts to maintain an offensive posture, flying their bombers unescorted over very long distances against forward Japanese bases, often suffering significant losses to both the enemy and the elements. For their part, American fighters tackling Japanese raids found themselves consistently outclassed, particularly in their P–400s, by escorting Zeros.

Many American airmen facing these discouraging operational realities were already war-weary from painful campaigns in the Philippines and the Dutch East Indies, and they knew that their circumstances were not likely to improve very soon. The policy of Europe First would keep them at the end of the priority list for some time. Their aircraft, most of them recognizably inferior, were also poorly maintained, afflicted by perpetual shortages of spare parts and trained mechanics. Worse, their units were generally deployed to remote areas of Australia to endure primitive and uncomfortable bases, inadequate medical facilities, and unpalatable food. Naturally, their commanders found it difficult to maintain a high level of morale.

Conditions for the airmen had not improved when, in July 1942, the Japanese, who were already established elsewhere in New Guinea, beat the Allies to the punch and landed at Buna on the north coast of Papua, only 100 miles from Port Moresby. From there they launched an overland offensive through the Owen Stanley Range, fighting their way forward in a bloody and relentless campaign until, in late August, overcome as much by the terrain, the jungle, and disease as by the desperate opposition of the Allies, they reached the end of their tether and began to fall back.

At about the same time, Major General George Kenney, one of the most gifted combat commanders of World War II, arrived to take over the Allied Air Forces in the South West Pacific Area. Widely regarded as an air power visionary, he encouraged imagination and initiative in his subordinates. Under his leadership, Allied air power in the South West Pacific was markedly strengthened. American industry gathered pace and made more and newer aircraft available, but that was not the whole story. Kenney's energetic influence pervaded his command. He inspired enthusiasm and determination where none had been before.

Kenney first tackled the maintenance muddle, talking to the men on the line and finding out what their real problems were first hand. Always prepared to be unconventional if necessary, he quickly improved matters and raised the number of aircraft available to the squadrons. He insisted, too, that maintenance facilities be kept as close to the front line as possible. He found jettisonable fuel tanks to extend the range of his fighters, and he fostered the development of hard, aggressive low-level attack techniques, including skip-bombing and he gave one of his proteges, Major Paul "Pappy" Gunn, a free hand to experiment with fitting heavier armament to A–20s and B–25s. Gunn's modifications turned moderately effective attack

B–25 nose. The B–25H head-on was a fearsome sight. Inspired by Major Paul "Pappy" Gunn's ideas in the Fifth Air Force, many B–25s were modified as strafers with a variety of forward firing options. This B–25H carries eight .50-caliber machine guns and a 75-mm cannon. The strengthened skin around the guns allowed the B–25 to withstand the destructive effects of its own firepower.

aircraft into deadly weapons. To further improve and better protect them from damage by their own ordnance, Kenney himself suggested attaching parachutes to the fragmentation bombs that they used in low-level attacks. Before long, Kenney had molded his air force into a fearsome instrument of war. He was also man enough to stand up to the imperial MacArthur and win his confidence.

In September 1942 American air force units in the South West Pacific were organized as the Fifth Air Force, Kenney assuming command at his headquarters in Brisbane. A small forward headquarters, tasked with the day-to-day conduct of operations during the New Guinea campaign, was set up at Port Moresby under Kenney's deputy, Brigadier General Ennis Whitehead. Soon after the Fifth Air Force was established, Kenney wrote to General Hap Arnold, setting out his views on the use of air power in the special circumstances of the South West Pacific. Extracts from his letter emphasize his need for close cooperation with the ground forces and include some of the forceful imagery illustrative of his colorful personality:

> "Tanks and heavy artillery can be reserved for the battlefields of Europe and Africa. They have no place in jungle warfare. The artillery in this theater flies.

> The Air Force is the spearhead of the Allied attack in the South West Pacific. Its function is to clear the air, wreck the enemy's land installations, destroy his supply system, and give close support to troops advancing on the ground.

> Clearing the air means more than air superiority. It means air control so supreme that the birds have to wear our Air Force insignia.

> Wrecking the enemy's ground installations does not mean just softening them up. It means taking out everything he has—aerodromes, guns, bunkers, troops. Destroying his supply system means cutting him off the vine so completely and firmly that he not only cannot undertake offensive action but, due to his inability to replenish his means to wage war, he cannot even maintain a successful defense."

Kenney's actions were as good as his words during the New Guinea campaign. Allied infantry slogging up the Kokoda Trail through the Owen Stanley Range was supported whenever possible by low-flying attack aircraft, the unloved P–39 Airacobras coming into their own as strafers with their 37-mm cannon. The rapid forward movement of troops by air, urged on MacArthur by Kenney, was immensely successful. C–47s shuttled back and forth between Australia and Port Moresby and forward into areas from which Allied soldiers could surprise the Japanese and threaten their communications and main bases. By the end of 1942 the Japanese had been driven back to the north coast of New Guinea and were desperately defending Buna. Allied ground forces were able to maintain their offensive because of the C–47 life line over the mountainous interior and because the Fifth was growing steadily more effective as a fighting air force. B–24s were arriving to take the load as the region's principal heavy bomber; Pappy Gunn's modified A–20s and B–25s were in action; and P–38 Lightnings were replacing tired out P–39s and P–40s.

In Europe the P–38 was not much admired, but it came into its own in the Pacific. Its twin engines were reassuring to pilots who had to operate over wastes of jungle and ocean, and, with external tanks, it had legs long enough to cope with the scale of the Pacific theater. It was no match for the Zero as a dogfighter,

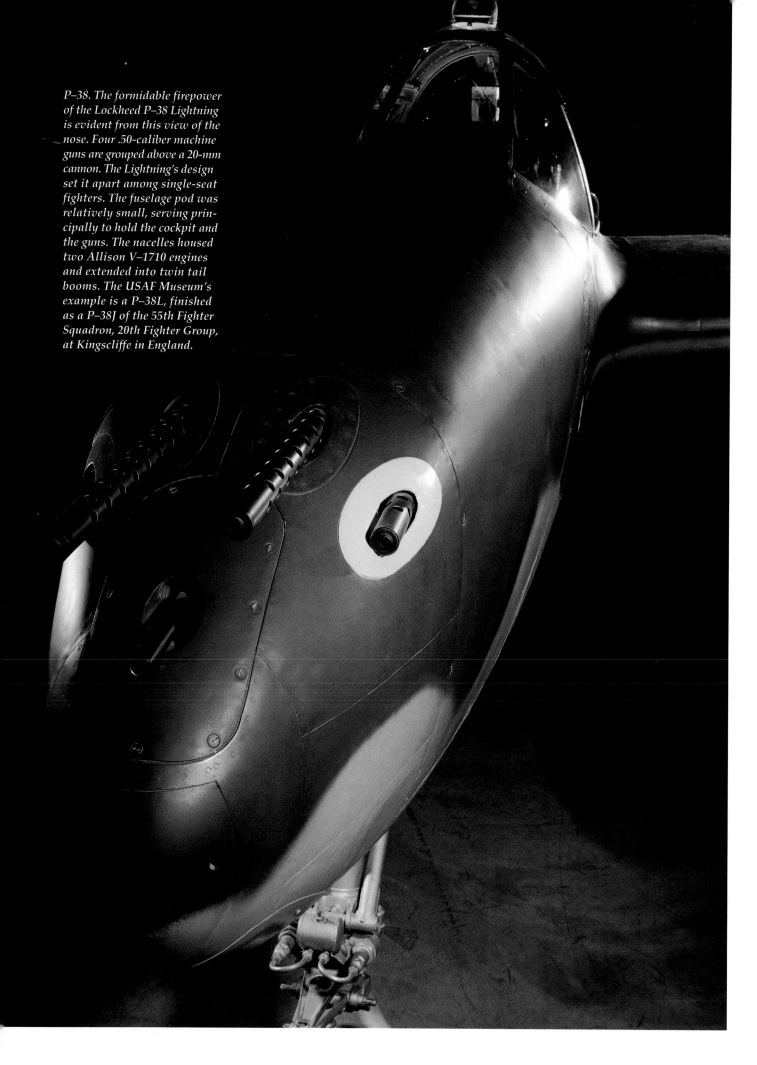

P–38. The formidable firepower of the Lockheed P–38 Lightning is evident from this view of the nose. Four .50-caliber machine guns are grouped above a 20-mm cannon. The Lightning's design set it apart among single-seat fighters. The fuselage pod was relatively small, serving principally to hold the cockpit and the guns. The nacelles housed two Allison V–1710 engines and extended into twin tail booms. The USAF Museum's example is a P–38L, finished as a P–38J of the 55th Fighter Squadron, 20th Fighter Group, at Kingscliffe in England.

P–38 cockpit. The Lightning was large for a fighter, and the impression of size was enhanced by the spectacle grip provided for the pilot's flying controls, an arrangement which might have been more normally associated with a bomber or a transport.

but it was much faster, and it could outclimb and outdive its Japanese opponent. The P–38 also had an armored cockpit and self-sealing fuel tanks, and its heavy armament of a 20-mm cannon and four .5-inch machine guns made short work of the more lightly built Zero. When American pilots made the most of these advantages, they outclassed the Zero.

Organized Japanese resistance in and around Buna came to an end on 22 January 1943. By that time the Fifth Air Force had long since established air superiority over the Papua region of New Guinea, assuring, among other things, that vital air transport operations into airstrips on the north coast were never seriously threatened by Japanese aircraft. It also assured the ground forces of their supplies and gave them the added comfort of rapid medical evacuation. Allied soldiers suffered over 10,000 casualties in bloody struggles with the enemy, but, thanks in large part to the tireless efforts of the C–47 squadrons, only 7 percent died.

An entry in a Japanese soldier's diary, written in December 1942, graphically describes the Fifth Air Force aircrafts' Papuan success: "They fly above our position as if they owned the skies." General MacArthur, who had freely criticized the Fifth Air Force's capabilities at the time of Kenney's arrival, now just as freely praised them in a statement of some architectural confusion:

> To the American Fifth Air Force and the Royal Australian Air Force [RAAF] no commendation could be too great. Their outstanding efforts

in combat, supply, and transportation over both land and sea constituted the keystone upon which the arch of the campaign was erected.

Driven out of Buna, the Japanese determined to strengthen their position to the west on the north coast of New Guinea, began to move reinforcements from their main base at Rabaul to the Huon Gulf port of Lae. On 30 December 1942, a Lockheed F–4 Lightning reconnaissance aircraft discovered 21 warships and 70 merchant ships assembled at Rabaul. In a first attempt, the Japanese successfully got a small convoy through to Lae and landed about 4,000 troops, but they lost 2 troop transports and over 50 escorting fighters doing it. The Allies lost 10 aircraft. In his drive to "make the birds wear our Air Force insignia," Kenny welcomed this sort of exchange rate. He knew that more convoys would be coming to Lae and that, since enemy fighters had to escort the ships, combat between the air forces was inevitable. The Japanese were caught in a war of attrition that Kenney was sure he could win.

At the end of February 1943, 5,000 troops of the Japanese 51st Infantry Division set out for Lae from Rabaul in a convoy of seven merchant ships, eight destroyers, and a special service vessel. On 1 March a B–24 spotted the convoy and, over the next three days, the Fifth Air Force and the RAAF hit it in a series of attacks that became known as the Battle of the Bismarck Sea.

B–17s and B–25s bombing from medium altitude claimed early successes in the battle, but aircraft strafing and bombing from low-level did most of the

A P–38 of the 475th Fighter Group parked on steel matting in the Philippines. Note the two sizes of drop tanks carried—310 and 165 gallons.

Douglas A–20. Not an attack aircraft to be taken lightly, the A–20 Havoc was armed with six .50-caliber machine guns in its nose and could carry up to 4,000 pounds of bombs. The A–20G on display at the USAF Museum is marked as an aircraft of the 89th Bombardment Squadron, 3rd Bombardment Group, in the Southwest Pacific.

A–20s of the Fifth Air Force undergoing servicing at Eagle Farm depot in Australia.

damage on 3 March. Those modified by Pappy Gunn to carry much heavier forward-firing armament came into their own and proved especially destructive. Gunfire from the B–25s, A–20s, and Beaufighters swept the decks of the Japanese ships, and 500-pound bombs skipped across the sea to smash into their sides. The Allied attacks, coordinated at first, soon developed into free-for-alls as aircraft separated and maneuvered to take on one ship and then another. They criss-crossed through the convoy and competed for victims, flying at mast-head height and sometimes lower. One A–20 finished off a run by shortening a ship's radio mast with its right wing. Inevitably, the attackers wound up aiming at the same target. Out of the corner of his eye, an Australian saw something flying alongside him as his Beaufighter steadied for a strafing run. It was a B–25's 500-pound bomb mid-skip, heading in the same direction.[1]

As low-level attackers approached the convoy, they were startled to find themselves passing through a shower of long-range fuel tanks. Above the smoke and flame of the surface battle, the P–38s of the 35th and 49th Fighter Groups had lightened their load before keeping the covering Zeros occupied. Their efforts were eminently successful. By the end of the battle, they had shot down more than 50 enemy aircraft, at a cost of three P–38s and one B–17, plus one B–25 in a landing accident. More important, they had sunk 12 ships, including all of the troop transports. Over 3,000 Japanese soldiers died, and the 51st Division was effectively destroyed.

General MacArthur later spoke of the Battle of the Bismarck Sea as "the decisive aerial engagement" in his theater of the war. Kenney's airmen had demonstrated their ability to obliterate a convoy with aircraft, and had created an aerial blockade of Japanese forces around the Huon Gulf. Never again did the Japanese attempt to run large ships into Lae, and the troops there were left to subsist on a meager resupply from the few submarines and barges that managed to break through. In effect, the Japanese had to accept that their hold on the eastern half of New Guinea was broken, and that, in the face of growing American air power, their stay on the rest of the island would be of limited duration.

As he turned his attention to the New Guinea campaign's next phase, Kenney believed he could count on greatly increased air strength, and, in the summer of 1943, several more groups joined the Fifth Air Force. Among their new aircraft were the 348th Fighter Group's P–47s and examples of another Mitchell variant, the B–25G, equipped with a ship-busting 75-mm cannon. As good as these were,

Kenney was always impatient for more. To emphasize his need for troop carrier replacements, he told Hap Arnold: "The figures show that between weather and Nips a man lives longer in a P–39 than he does in a C–47 flying troop carrier supply runs in New Guinea." He added a reminder about the scale of

A–20 cockpit. The area was neatly and conveniently arranged, with the exception of a few instruments hiding behind the control column. Like many Douglas models, the A–20 was considered to be very much a pilot's aircraft. Note the way in and out of the A–20 pilot's seat—through the roof.

C–47s. On 5 September 1943 the 54th Troop Carrier Wing's C–47s dropped the U.S. 503rd Paratroop Regiment and some Australian units onto the kunai-grass plains of Nadzab in New Guinea.

the South West Pacific theater, pointing out that the P–47s were not much good without long-range tanks, since they had no more range than was needed "to defend London or to make a fighter sweep across a ditch no bigger than Chesapeake Bay."

Whatever the limitations of their equipment, Kenney's air force did wonders with it. MacArthur now understood that New Guinea's geography defied even rudimentary maneuvers on the ground, and that victory depended on gaining and holding air superiority. The campaign settled into a pattern. The Allies used air power to hammer and neutralize enemy forces before bypassing them with troops moved forward by sea or air transport. The infantry then held the ground while airstrips were constructed, after which the process could begin again. Gradually overcome by the endless attrition of combat, Japanese

air forces in New Guinea finally succumbed in March and April 1944, when the Fifth Air Force carried out heavy attacks on three air bases in the Hollandia area. The Allies wrecked them and, counting those destroyed in the air and on the ground, the Japanese lost more than 450 aircraft. The loss ratio in aerial combat often favored the American pilots by ten to one or more, and it was clear that the caliber of the Japanese pilots had noticeably declined. Even so, the Fifth Air Force had not escaped lightly. In the two years following September 1942, it had lost 1,374 aircraft to all causes, and more than 4,100 airmen killed or missing.

By mid-1944 the Thirteenth Air Force in the Solomons found itself underemployed and was moved to join the Fifth Air Force as part of Kenney's command in the South West Pacific Area. Kenney became

Commander, Far East Air Forces (FEAF), as Whitehead moved up to take over the Fifth. The Thirteenth's original commander, Nathan Twining, had long since left for Europe, after surviving six uncomfortable days in a life raft when his B–17 got lost and ran out of fuel. The new commander, Major General St. Clair Streett, set up his headquarters initially at Los Negros in the Admiralty Islands, northeast of New Guinea, seized as part of the Allied encirclement of Rabaul. The Japanese ground forces continued to resist in New Guinea until September, by which time the Fifth and Thirteenth Air Forces were preparing for the next big step—MacArthur's return to the Philippines.

The Solomons

As the Japanese were landing troops at Buna to start their offensive against Port Moresby, they were also building an airfield on Guadalcanal in the southern Solomons. The Allies immediately drew up plans to counter these actions, which represented a major threat to their trans-Pacific lifeline. It was clear that, since Guadalcanal was in the USN South Pacific Area, any USAAF action would be supporting.

B–25 parafrag bombs. After the 3 April 1944 attack on Japanese airfields in Hollandia, the Fifth Air Force effectively owned the air over New Guinea. B–25s of the 38th and 345th Bombardment Groups strafed the airfield at Dagua and sowed parafrag bombs among the parked aircraft with deadly effect.

P–39. Because its Allison V–1710 engine was mounted behind the pilot and a long drive shaft ran through the cockpit to the propeller, the Bell P–39 Airacobra was unusual for the 1940s in being a single-seat fighter with a tricycle undercarriage. Lacking a supercharger, the P–39 was not a good performer at altitude, but it was powerfully armed with two .50-caliber machine guns and a 37-mm cannon firing through the propeller boss. It was, therefore, most suitable for ground attack operations and particularly popular with Soviet pilots.

P–39 cockpit. Among other P–39 peculiarities was the car door entry to its cockpit. Inside, the layout was reasonably typical for a fighter of the period.

P–39 tail. The USAF Museum's Airacobra is a P–39Q painted as the P–39J flown by Lieutenant Leslie Spoonts of the 57th Fighter Squadron in the Aleutians during 1942.

To safeguard Army interests in an essentially naval sphere, the War Department agreed to the appointment of an airman, Major General Millard Harmon, to command U.S. Army forces in the South Pacific. Operationally, Harmon's USAAF units served under Rear Admiral John McCain, who controlled all air assets in the region. Harmon arrived at his headquarters at Noumea, New Caledonia, in late July 1942, just a week before the U.S. Marines landed on Guadalcanal. At that time, the USAAF's presence in the South Pacific was small and widely scattered. Isolated units operated a total of 33 B–17s, 22 B–26s and 79 P39/400s deployed on airstrips as far apart as New Caledonia, the New Hebrides, Fiji, and Tonga—an area not much smaller than the United States.[2]

During the early stages of the long struggle for Guadalcanal, the USAAF's B–17s struck Japanese bases and ships as far away as Rabaul and flew long-range reconnaissance to watch for any movement of enemy warships and convoys throughout the Solomons. By the end of August the P–400s of the 67th Fighter Squadron had been moved forward to Guadalcanal's Henderson Field. Because of their poor performance they were incapable of joining in the daily air battles with Japanese bombers and fighters over the island, but they proved useful in close support, using their cannon to good effect to harass enemy troops engaging the Marines.

Only too well aware of USAAF shortcomings in the South Pacific, General Harmon badgered headquarters for more and better aircraft, only to be reminded of his low position on the war's priority list. Fearing that the Japanese would make every effort to evict the Marines from an only tenuously-held Guadalcanal, he also urged Admiral Robert Ghormley, Commander, South Pacific, to reinforce the troop lodgement there and to develop Henderson Field as quickly as possible into an air base capable of handling B–17s. As weeks went by, Harmon's apprehensions were justified. In a series of spectacular naval operations involving heavy losses to both sides, the Japanese succeeded in building up their forces on Guadalcanal to 30,000 men. Henderson Field's defenders withstood ferocious ground assaults, constant air attacks by day, and frequent naval bombardment by night, but they hung on. Any doubts about their determination were eliminated in October 1942, when Ghormley was replaced by the fiery Admiral William "Bull" Halsey.

P–39. The 347th Fighter Group was assigned to the Thirteenth Air Force in January 1943 and sent to Guadalcanal, from where it used its P–39s in attacks against Japanese ground forces and shipping.

Catalina. The Consolidated OA–10 was the U.S. Army Air Forces's version of the PBY Catalina operated extensively by the U.S. Navy. OA–10s were used principally for air-sea rescue work and long-range reconnaissance. Slow and cumbersome, the Catalina was, nonetheless, a welcome sight to downed airmen. The USAF Museum's OA–10 is finished as Snafu Snatchers, *an aircraft of the 2nd Emergency Rescue Squadron as flown in the Southwest Pacific.*

Catalina gun blister. Bulging like frog's eyes from the fuselage, the Catalina's gun blisters each carried a single .50-caliber machine gun.

It was a close run thing, but by the end of the year, the Japanese were forced to accept as too costly their attempt to recover Guadalcanal from a main base over 600 miles away. Their ships were finding it impossible to break through the stranglehold of the U.S. naval and air blockade, and their troops on the island were suffering greatly from enforced isolation. Combat deaths, injuries, sickness, and malnutrition had, by November 1942, reduced the original force of 30,000 to little more than 13,000 fit for duty. Early in February 1943 the Japanese bowed to the inevitable, acknowledged the growing imbalance of power, and withdrew the remnants of their army. The grinding six-month struggle for Guadalcanal was over.

American naval losses at sea were severe and certainly attracted attention, but the aerial conflict had been severe, too, even though the numbers involved in combat on any one day were never very great. In six months both the USN and USAAF had lost over 600 aircraft each. The USAAF's share, which reflected its relatively minor role, had included 27 B–17s, 5 B–26s, 10 P–40s, 6 P–38s, and 33 P–39/400s.

In the course of the campaign for Guadalcanal, the USAAF in the South Pacific changed and developed. Its pilots, although limited by the inadequacies of their P–400s, had, nevertheless, integrated their operations successfully with their Navy and Marine counterparts

at Henderson Field. The Cactus Air Force, as it was known, was a splendid example of interservice cooperation under fire, and it laid the foundation for further collaborative efforts later on. As the year ended, a few P–38s were available at last and had both high-altitude and long-range capability. B–24s, too, had appeared, and one radar-equipped squadron had demonstrated that it could strike Japanese shipping through clouds or from low-level at night.

For his part, General Harmon remained upset about having so little say in the operational employment of his aircraft, especially when more and better models were becoming available. He was particularly concerned that naval commanders, seeing the B–17 primarily as a patrol aircraft, diverted it too often from its role as a bomber. As things were, he found "too little imagination being exercised in the employment of our air force." In December 1942 his pleas bore fruit when General Marshall decreed that a new air force would be formed in the South Pacific. On 13 January 1943, the Thirteenth Air Force was activated under the command of Brigadier General Nathan Twining and headquartered on the island of Espiritu Santo. The USAAF gained little beyond the added status of a numbered air force. General Harmon retained administrative responsibility for USAAF units, but operational control of his aircraft in the South Pacific still rested with an admiral.

Catalinas. Used extensively for reconnaissance and as a mine-layer and bomber, the adaptable Catalina is still remembered most for its air-sea rescue work in the Pacific. Hundreds of Allied airmen were saved from capture or a watery grave by the appearance of a lumbering "Cat."

In most theaters of war, the services, one from the other could distinguish their responsibilities clearly. They had difficulty doing so in the Solomons where an odd mixture of units and aircraft had come together on Henderson Field almost by accident. Sheer necessity had driven them to work together for mutual survival, and after the fighting had ended on Guadalcanal they took time to formalize their situation by creating a headquarters known as Air Command Solomons (COMAIRSOLS). Admiral Halsey and General Harmon agreed that unity of command was essential and the new organization was tasked to employ USN, Marine, USAAF and RNZAF (Royal New Zealand Air Force) units operating varied types, including P–39s, P–40s, P–38s, B–25s, B–17s, B–24s, PBYs, C–47s, Lockheed Venturas, and a mixture of naval aircraft. Naval officers filled the COMAIRSOLS chair until mid-1943, when Thirteenth Air Force's General Twining took over.

Faced with the fact of defeat in Papua and on Guadalcanal, Admiral Isoroku Yamamoto tried to regain the initiative for his forces in the Solomons with a series of air raids in April. They were roughly handled and the ratio of losses greatly favored American fighters. With the momentum of victory building against him, Yamamoto decided to put some steel into the Japanese units by visiting them

in person. Unfortunately for him, American intelligence officers were reading his mail.

The code breakers had determined that Yamamoto would be visiting Ballale, off the southern tip of Bougainville, on 18 April 1943. They knew his detailed itinerary, complete with timings. Since Ballale was just within the reach of P–38s fitted with drop tanks, Major John Mitchell of the 339th Squadron had the job of planning an interception and an assassination. From every point of view, his operation was a long shot. The P–38s assigned would have to follow a curving track for nearly 500 miles over water, flying at low level the whole way to avoid detection. Without radio aids, they would have to navigate by dead reckoning, relying on notoriously suspect aircraft compasses and primitive weather forecasting. Even if they made an accurate landfall and got to Ballale on time, they would not be certain that Yamamoto's aircraft would be there. Mitchell had made a number of assumptions about the route and the airspeed of the Japanese formation from the decoded itinerary, but there were no guarantees.

Eighteen P–38s and pilots of the 339th, 12th, and 70th Fighter Squadrons were detailed for the operation. Sixteen actually set course. Four were selected as an attack section to concentrate on Yamamoto's transport,

Three of the P–38 pilots from the attack section that shot down Admiral Isoroku Yamamoto's Betty over Bougainville on 18 April 1943—Thomas Lanphier, Besby Holmes, and Rex Barber. The fourth, Raymond Hine, was lost.

P–61 silhouette. In late 1944 P–61 Black Widows were deployed on Saipan, covering the build-up of the B–29 force in the Marianas.

while the rest took on his escort and whatever other fighters appeared from the nearby base. Much to the jubilation of the Americans and the shock of the Japanese, the 16 P–38s ran into 2 Betty bombers and 6 Zeros at exactly the appointed time and place. In the ensuing melee, Lieutenants Thomas Lanphier and Rex Barber between them managed to shoot down both Bettys. The body of Japan's premier admiral, architect of the attack on Pearl Harbor, was found in the jungle the following day.

Throughout 1943, as Marine soldiers forced their way up the chain of the Solomon Islands toward Bougainville and Rabaul, the aircraft of COMAIRSOLS moved with them and maintained relentless pressure on the enemy. Wherever possible, they pounded Japanese strongholds that had been bypassed and left behind to become prisons for their isolated garrisons. In November American troops landed in a lightly held area of Bougainville, established a perimeter, built airfields, and did their best to ignore 60,000 Japanese elsewhere on the island. Cut off and over-matched, enemy units struggled on fitfully, some soldiers persisting until the end of the war and beyond.

Just over 200 miles away, on their airfields near Rabaul, the Japanese steeled themselves to oppose the American buildup on Bougainville, denuding

several carriers and main bases to gather together a force of 550 aircraft. American airmen welcomed these developments, relishing the chance of bringing large numbers to battle. Heavy bombers from Kenney's Fifth Air Force joined the Thirteenth Air Force in raids against Rabaul, and fighters harassed the Japanese unceasingly on the ground and in the air. By March 1944 both American air forces had wrecked Rabaul harbor, effectively destroying Japanese air forces there and sinking many ships. They left few ground installations intact and reduced most of the town's buildings to ruins. They rendered Rabaul, with its 100,000-man garrison, helpless. American commanders left it behind, cocooned in its uselessness, and turned their attention toward the Philippines.

Central Pacific

While the Fifth and Thirteenth Air Forces were building their combat reputations far to the southwest, Major General Willis Hale's Seventh Air Force had remained quietly in Hawaii, regularly being asked to release units for service with its more heavily engaged cousins. In the fall of 1943 the Seventh's decline was halted by an infusion of fresh units as American forces prepared for their offensive in the Central Pacific, and, by November, Hale's B–24s were striking Japanese strongholds in the Gilberts and Marshalls from forward bases in the Ellice Islands.

P–61 cockpit. The Northrop P–61 Black Widow was the first American aircraft designed from the outset as a night fighter. It, therefore, did not follow in the typical fighter tradition. It is a large, heavy twin-boomed aircraft with a crew of three—pilot, gunner, and radar operator.

The Seventh's combat record is possibly the least well known of any numbered air force. In the Central Pacific theater, the stars were USN carriers. Nevertheless, the Seventh Air Force played an essential role for Admiral Nimitz as he drove his forces forward in a series of huge leaps, taking some islands and bypassing others. Nimitz knew that local air superiority was essential to his success and he used the Seventh's bombers to batter enemy air bases in a targeted island's area before an assault. He also made it a priority to set up new bases as soon as possible for the USAAF's long-range aircraft, which, once established, could begin reaching out to soften up the enemy for the next jump ahead. The Seventh also paid regular visits to bypassed Japanese garrisons, keeping them powerless to intervene in a war that had left them behind, frustrated and impotent.

In the three months following November 1943, American amphibious forces swept forward through the Gilberts and the Marshalls, taking such key atolls as Tarawa, Kwajalein, and Eniwetok in fierce fighting against fanatical Japanese defenders. Moved to bases on Kwajalein and Eniwetok, the Seventh's bombers then joined the USN in the reduction of Truk, one of the strongest Japanese naval bases in the Pacific, in a task that lasted until the end of the war. However, before then Truk had been rendered ineffective by constant battering from the air. Meanwhile, the Seventh also took part in the capture of the Marianas, supporting assaults made on Saipan, Tinian, and Guam in June and July 1944. The first wave of Marines hit Saipan's beaches on 15 June, and only a week later, with savage fighting going on close by, aircraft of the Seventh were ashore, too. In a first for the USAAF, P–47s of the 19th Fighter Squadron were catapulted from the light carriers *Manila Bay* and *Natoma Bay* to land at Aslito (Isley) Field. Within days, they were joined by a second P–47 fighter squadron, the 73rd, and the 6th Night Fighter Squadron, newly equipped with P–61 Black Widows. The 333rd Fighter Squadron of P–47s arrived the following month, bringing the 318th Fighter Squadron up to full strength.

By day P–47s were fully occupied with standing air patrols, close support missions, and fighter sweeps over neighboring Tinian and Guam, while P–61s filled in by night. This was the first

Central Pacific operation that used land-based fighters for close support of the ground troops and they proved particularly versatile. From the outset, they could strafe with their .5-inch machine guns, drop 500-pound bombs, and launch 4.5-inch rockets. In the latter stages of the struggle they introduced a new weapon of fearful effect. Wing tanks filled with a petroleum mixture (napalm) dropped from 50 feet could each clear an area 200 feet long by 75 feet wide.

As the Marines began the first phase of the Saipan operation, the Japanese made a major effort to stop the American advance toward Japan once and for all. They gathered a formidable fleet around three large and six smaller carriers with a total of 450 aircraft between them. In addition, they fielded a supporting force of over 500 land-based aircraft in the Marianas. An enormous confrontation between Admiral Jisaburo Ozawa's Mobile Fleet and Admiral Raymond Spruance's Fifth Fleet, later known as the Battle of the Philippine Sea (or more colloquially by Americans as the Great Marianas Turkey Shoot), finally broke the back of

Japanese naval air power, destroying 3 carriers and nearly 500 carrier and land-based aircraft.

Although the last Japanese outpost on Guam did not fall until early September, the Americans declared the Marianas secure by mid-August. Airfield construction crews were already at work building unusually long runways. New B–29s were on the way and, from bases in the Marianas, these very heavy bombers would be able to raid the home islands of Japan. Strategic air power theorists would have another opportunity to test whether an enemy nation could be bombed into submission and defeated.

MacArthur's Return

To prepare for MacArthur's next move, American forces established themselves on islands to the south and southeast of Mindanao, the southernmost main island of the Philippines. By October 1944 USAAF aircraft were operating from both Morotai and the Palaus. These bases were to support MacArthur's invasion of Mindanao, but intelligence reports suggested that the weakest point in the Japanese defense of the

*P–61 nose. Because the nose was reserved for the disc antenna of an AI radar, heavy armament was located in a remotely controlled top turret with four .5-inch machine guns and a belly pack of four 20-mm cannon. The USAF Museum's Black Widow is a P–61C, **Moon Light Serenade**, marked as a P–61B of the 550th Night Fighter Squadron as flown in the Pacific in 1945.*

Philippines would be Leyte, in the center of the archipelago. Admiral Halsey, mixing metaphors in his enthusiasm, called the Japanese air force in the Philippines "a hollow shell operating on a shoestring." He recommended that MacArthur drop all intermediate plans and go straight for Leyte. MacArthur seized the opportunity to bypass the large Japanese forces in Mindanao, and American troops went ashore in Leyte Gulf on 20 October.

Although the USN had gathered an awesome armada,[3] General Kenney was not entirely happy. For the first time his Far East Air Forces were based too far away to offer direct support to the Leyte Gulf landings. Air cover was provided by the carriers of the U.S. Third and Seventh Fleets, and their presence set the scene for the largest naval battle ever fought. Committing themselves once more to the "decisive battle" they had sought since Midway, the Japanese threw their ships into a desperate attempt to defeat the invasion. In the Battle of Leyte Gulf, which was actually a series of actions sometimes hundreds of miles apart, the Imperial Japanese Navy lost 4 carriers, 3 battleships, 6 cruisers, 12 destroyers, and all of its remaining front-line carrier-borne aircraft. As a significant fighting force, it had ceased to exist.

On land, however, the Japanese were still a serious threat. At the time of the Leyte Gulf landings, they had 450 combat aircraft on the island of Luzon, and awaited reinforcements being rushed forward from bases on Formosa and in Japan. Even after American troops were ashore the first few days, the beachhead was anything but secure. U.S. naval aircraft were there to provide air cover, but a horrifying new development made them understandably anxious about the protection of their own ships. Pilots from specially formed *kamikaze* units had begun to sacrifice themselves, deliberately crashing their bomb-laden aircraft into American ships. In initial operations they had already sunk one escort carrier and damaged several more, seriously reducing the USN's capacity to provide its promised air cover over the troops. Aware of the problem, engineers opened a 2,800-foot airstrip at Tacloban by 27 October. Thirty-four P–38s of the 49th Fighter Squadron flew in that day and to immediate action.

Other units arrived as the days went by, but until well into December 1944, when more airstrips became usable, the situation around Leyte Gulf had USAAF men gritting their teeth. Japanese air raids on Tacloban were frequent, and they often caught American aircraft on the ground. Losses to strafing attacks were distressingly high and requests for replacements were commonplace. Combat also took its toll and, for a while, FEAF's front-line strength declined as losses from all causes exceeded replacements. In three

Richard Bong, American ace of aces, and his P–38 Marge. *He was withdrawn from combat after scoring 40 aerial victories. Bong was killed in a P–80 crash near Burbank, California, on 6 August 1945.*

months from 1 September P–38 holdings fell from 497 to 398; P–47s began with 429 in September, a figure which had become 257 plus 95 P–51s by the end of the year.

The Japanese were much worse off. Loss rates in aerial combat invariably favored the USAAF, and FEAF fighters often wreaked havoc at enemy air bases. On 1 November, for example, 42 P–38s of the 8th Fighter Squadron swept over three airfields, shooting down 7 enemy fighters in the air and destroying 75 more on the ground for the loss of 3 of their own. Pacific fighter pilots added dramatically to their scores, P–38 pilots leading the pack. Before the end of October the 49th Fighter Squadron had claimed its 500th aerial victory, and by Christmas their leading ace, Richard Bong, had raised his personal total to 40.[4] Major Tommy McGuire of the 475th Fighter Group, who claimed 38 before crashing during low-level combat over the Philippines, scored multiple victories on a single mission 11 times, and he was by no means unique. Robert Aschenbrenner, John Dunaway, William Dunham, and Gerald Johnson[5] were among those who shot down 4 enemy aircraft in one sortie. Even more remarkable were the achievements of Captain William Shomo and Lieutenant Paul Lipscomb of the 82nd Reconnaissance Squadron. Flying P–51s as a pair on 11 January 1945, they attacked a formation of 12 fighters escorting a Betty bomber. Neither had been in combat before, but when the fight was over Shomo had shot down the Betty and 6 fighters, and Lipscomb had added 3 more.[6]

After FEAF established units on Leyte, MacArthur next moved to the island of Mindoro in mid-December 1944, following the reassuring pattern of the New Guinea campaign in which the ground forces fought under the umbrella of their own air forces. Even so, the Japanese still operated ships and aircraft in the area and were occasionally able to make things difficult. Indeed, on 26 December they would have seriously jeopardized the American beachhead on Mindoro but for the determination of the 310th Wing squadrons, which had just arrived on rudimentary strips nearby. As night fell, a Japanese naval unit comprising two cruisers and six destroyers appeared offshore to sink Allied transports and shell the beachhead area. The Americans hurled every aircraft on strength into a low-level assault on the ships—13 B–25s, 44 P–38s, 28 P–47s, and 20 P–40s. Nighttime attacks were necessarily uncoordinated, and in the glaring confusion of gunfire and bomb-bursts, pilots flashed navigation lights in the hope of avoiding collisions. By morning the badly mauled Japanese force was withdrawing, minus one destroyer, having sunk one transport, but

it failed to disrupt the landing operations. The airmen had won a victory and had protected the troops, but at considerable cost—they lost 3 B–25s, 7 P–38s, 10 P–47s, and 6 P–40s. A grateful Brigadier General William Dunckel, commander of the task force, wrote: "The action of our air units on that night will stand forever as one of the most gallant deeds to be established in the traditions of American fighting men."

Mindoro was a staging post for the later invasion of the main island of Luzon. The landing was the largest American amphibious operation of the war, with 175,000 men covering a beachhead 20 miles wide. Aircraft of the fleet's escort carriers did their best to counter the threat from the *kamikazes*. Even so, many got through, sinking an escort carrier, a destroyer, 10 other vessels, and damaging 67 more. The onslaught eased only when the Japanese ran out of resources. Their own self-destructive methods, together with a combined American air and naval campaign against airfields on Luzon, reduced Japanese air power in the Philippines to impotence.

MacArthur's troops went ashore in Lingayen Gulf on 9 January 1945, reassured by Kenney's fighters overhead. In the long and bloody struggle for Luzon, American soldiers were never again unduly bothered by Japanese aircraft. FEAF was able to concentrate on providing the ground forces with the support they needed to win the land battle. The Luzon campaign was characterized by overwhelming American air power. B–24s hammered strong points; B–25s, A–20s, P–38s, P–40s, P–47s, and P–51s strafed, rocketed, bombed, and napalmed Japanese troops; L–5s marked targets; P–61s harassed by night; C–47s kept forward units supplied and dropped paratroops to speed the ground offensive. They gave a virtuoso performance, later singled out for comment by the JCS: "Of the many Pacific tactical air operations, we think the most striking example of the effective use of tactical air power…to achieve decisive results at a minimum cost in lives and material was the work of the Far East Air Forces in the Lingayen Gulf-Central Luzon campaign."

The embers of Japanese resistance smoldered on in the Philippines until the end of the war, and many of MacArthur's troops were kept occupied in operations which, in terms of the strategic aim of defeating Japan, were not strictly necessary. Bypassing many enemies and leaving them isolated, American and Australian troops now found themselves engaged in bitter battles to crush the Japanese dug in on the outer islands of the Philippines and on Borneo. Although they were savage, they were sideshows. The curtain-raisers to the main event were being prepared to the north, where strategic air power was moving toward center stage.

CBI Affairs

For reasons both geographical and political, the Allies did not assign the China-Burma-India (CBI) theater of the war the same priority as Europe and the Pacific. It was the most difficult theater to reach and supply. In addition, Allied leaders did not always feel entirely comfortable dealing with Chiang Kai-shek or involving themselves in a struggle that seemed likely to return a number of colonial territories to their former European rulers. Nevertheless, they generally agreed on the importance of keeping China in the war and of preventing the Japanese from pursuing their expansionist ambitions into India.

The fall of Burma, and particularly the loss of the northern base of Myitkyina in May 1942, effectively cut China off from the Western Allies. It could only be supplied by transport aircraft flying from bases in India across the Himalayas to Kunming. With Myitkyina in enemy hands, China's aerial supply line was forced farther north over much higher mountains. Heavily-laden aircraft often wallowed along at heights of up to 18,000 feet. The contrast between the steamy heat of the Indian plains and the freezing temperatures of high altitudes was hard on both men and machines, and, for much of the year, they faced violent storms, heavy rain, and ice along their route. They sometimes flew blind for hours with only the most basic of instrument panels and radio aids. Icing or loss of power spelled disaster, and even a successful crossing could precede a perilous arrival if, as was frequently the case during the monsoon, the destination airfield was covered with water.

Flying the "Hump" was among the most hazardous of military air occupations. The China airlift was handled by a few transport aircraft organized into the Assam-Burma-China Ferry Command, the last stage in the longest supply chain in the world. The airlift started in Miami and travelled via the Atlantic, North Africa, and the Middle East to Karachi and Assam. By the end of 1942 the responsibility for controlling its increasing numbers of aircraft crossing the Hump had passed to Air Transport Command (ATC). The CBI theater lacked all but the most basic systems of communication, yet it exceeded by a considerable margin the size of the United States.

Meanwhile, Major General Lewis Brereton had been ordered to India in March 1942 to establish the Tenth Air Force, in the latest stage of his westward progress. He had spent the war retreating through the Philippines and the Dutch East Indies in front of the victorious Japanese and he must have felt a little discouraged at the scale of the problems he faced in his new command. The Tenth was intended to supply the Chinese (until ATC assumed responsibility at the end of 1942), defend the Hump route and its airfields, and help the British fight the Japanese in Burma. To tackle this monumental task he had an air force only on paper—a few aging B–17s and P–40s—and little prospect of getting more in the near future. Brereton wrestled with the problem until June, when he was told to pack his bags again and move to Egypt, this time to take command of U.S. air forces in the Middle East and help the British against the Germans. He duly left, taking his B–17s with him. The Tenth became, again, an air force without teeth.

In July 1942 Brigadier General Chennault's American Volunteer Group was transformed into a regular element of the USAAF, joining the Tenth Air Force. However, the ex-Flying Tigers added to its bite in name only. They remained, in effect, independent, forming the core of a new organization called the China Air Task Force (CATF). Commander of the CATF was the AVG's Chennault, recalled to duty with the USAAF. A few of his pilots had elected to join him in the move, and they brought their battered P–40s and the benefit of their combat experience to the newly arrived 23rd Fighter Group. Seven B–25s of the 7th Bombardment Group provided a little striking power.

The CATF was never very big, but the challenges and hardships it faced must have developed remarkable characters, because it seems to have had more than its share. The 23rd Fighter Squadron was commanded by Colonel Bob Scott, author of the book *God is my Co-pilot*. Two of the squadrons were commanded by aces from the AVG, "Tex" Hill and Ed Rector. In 1943 Tex Hill, then commander of the 23rd Fighter Group, led one of the most successful raids of the war in China, striking Shinchiku airfield on Formosa with a force of 14 B–25s, 8 P–38s, and 8 P–51s and destroying over 40 Japanese aircraft without loss. Later members of the 23rd included Don Lopez, who gained his first aerial victory over a Zero by surviving a head-on attack driven through to collision, and John Alison, who decided to experiment with night interceptions in his P–40 and succeeded in destroying two bombers and damaging another at his first attempt. Badly shot up and his P–40 on fire, he lived through a night ditching in a river and swam ashore.

Chennault lost no opportunity to promote air power as the only practical weapon with which to fight the Japanese in China. He, thus, put himself at odds with the senior American officer in the theater, Lieutenant General "Vinegar Joe" Stilwell, an infantryman, who insisted on concentrating a ground offensive into northern Burma. As the Allied chiefs preferred to continue with both options, they split any limited resources between the two, and neither was given what he considered adequate for the tasks at hand. However, Chennault's persistence, and his unabashed use of political channels through Chiang Kai-shek, led to the formation of the Fourteenth Air Force from the elements of the CATF—at the direction of President Roosevelt and against the advice of Generals Marshall and Arnold. In the process, Chennault advanced to the rank of major general.

Following the constitution of the Fourteenth Air Force in March 1943, the fortunes of American airmen in China gradually improved. Combat units, equipment, and supplies began to flow more generously across the Hump. Even so, apart from the Eleventh in Alaska, the Fourteenth remained the smallest of the American numbered air forces throughout the war, reaching a maximum strength of a little over 700 combat aircraft early in 1945. As the Fourteenth grew in size, it acquired P–38s, P–51s, B–24s, and more and newer B–25s. Chennault established a series of bases in southern China and adopted an aggressive operational policy. The Fourteenth struck at Japanese ports and bases in China and Indo-China, harassed shipping

Hap Arnold and Claire Chennault. Hap Arnold visited China in January 1943 and met Claire Chennault. He judged the prickly Flying Tiger to be a formidable fighting man but a poor administrator and too often a representative of the interests of Chiang Kai-shek rather than the United States.

along the Asian coast, mined harbors, attacked enemy airfields, supported Chinese troops, interdicted Japanese supply lines, and fought the Japanese Air Force for air superiority over China. Badly hurt by these efforts and fearing further expansion of American air power, the Japanese launched a massive assault into southern China in 1944 to deny the Fourteenth its airfields and open up internal communications between Southeast Asia and Japan. By the end of the year they had rolled over demoralized Chinese armies and taken 13 of the American bases, forcing the Fourteenth Air Force back toward Kunming and limiting its operations in eastern China. Japanese troops had suffered badly under air attack, but never enough to stall their advance.

Seriously concerned, Chiang Kai-shek appealed for help to Stilwell, who was heavily occupied with his campaign in Burma. The general, reluctant to leave, became intransigent and was recalled to Washington. He was replaced as Commanding General, U.S. Forces, in the China theater by Lieutenant General Albert Wedemeyer, who took over at the end of October 1943, and soon agreed to return Chinese troops from Burma in preparation for a counteroffensive in the spring of 1945. From May 1945 the reorganized Chinese Army, closely supported by American tactical aircraft, first checked the Japanese and then drove them back, using napalm and the concentrated fire of .5-inch caliber machine guns most effectively to reduce enemy strong points. By the end of July central China and the coast were virtually free of Japanese forces. The Allies then considered continuing their offensive to the north. Within days, however, they had no need to; Japan surrendered. As the fighting in China ground to a halt, the men of the Fourteenth were left feeling that they had fought on the fringes of the war. Hard as they had struggled to overcome the enemy, the elements, their living conditions, the convoluted command chain, and the low priorities accorded them by their friends and Allies, they clearly had not occupied center stage. The core of the Allied victory over Japan was in the Pacific. Their satisfaction came from the knowledge of a job well done and in an accolade from an enemy general who said that, but for the Fourteenth Air Force, "we could have gone anywhere we wished."

Chennault was not there to celebrate the victory with his airmen. General Arnold's patience with his unconventional subordinate had come to an end. In June 1945 he wrote to General Wedemeyer:

> General Chennault has been in China for a long period of time fighting a defensive air

war with minimum resources. The meagerness of supplies and the resulting guerilla type of warfare must change to a modern type of striking, offensive air power. I firmly believe that the quickest and most effective way to change air warfare in your theater, employing modern offensive thought, tactics, and techniques, is to change commanders. I would appreciate your concurrence in General Chennault's early withdrawal from the China theater.

At the same time, Arnold offered a plan for reorganizing the air forces in China. Chennault entered a vigorous protest against the whole idea, but the die was cast and he grudgingly put forward his request for retirement on 6 July.

While Chennault had been creating his own air force and fighting his own kind of war, the Tenth Air Force had been wrestling with equally challenging problems. Shortly after the CATF was formed as an element of the Tenth to give Chennault his freedom of action, Brigadier General Clayton Bissell, the Tenth's new commander, created a similar organization for the India-Burma region, the India Air Task Force, activated on 3 October 1942. Bissell had to face the fact that not one of its nine allocated squadrons was capable of combat operations. Several either had no aircraft or were not yet even in the theater. Matters, particularly those of supply, improved very slowly. Throughout their time in the CBI, USAAF commands and units operated under a tangled web of national and service rivalries and were handicapped by being at the bottom of a long priority list. Chains of command were duplicated and tasks complicated to a degree unknown in other theaters. In 1943 Generals Marshall and Arnold decided that a senior airman should be appointed to the CBI to straighten things out. Almost immediately, Chiang Kai-shek objected to what he viewed as interference in his direct relations with Chennault. He had his way; the new commander would have only advisory responsibility toward the Fourteenth Air Force.

In August 1943 Major General George Stratemeyer assumed command of all USAAF units in the India-Burma Sector (IBS) of the CBI. At the time, this amounted to little more than the Tenth Air Force, then commanded by Brigadier General Howard Davidson. Recognizing the limitations of the position and the complexity of overlapping organizational arrangements and regional politics, Arnold warned Stratemeyer:

> This new command setup and your relationships...are somewhat complicated

An Air Commando B–25H after attacking Wunto, Burma, on 18 March 1944.

and will have to be worked out to a great extent among yourselves…. If a true spirit of cooperation is engendered throughout this command, it will work. If the reverse is true, it is doomed to failure.[7]

As 1943 drew to a close, more organizational changes occurred. USAAF and RAF units in the IBS merged under a new headquarters called Eastern Air Command (EAC), under General Stratemeyer. All Allied air force combat units in the IBS having been joined together, he separated them again, this time functionally, under strategic, tactical, troop carrier, and reconnaissance headings. Davidson of the Tenth drew the strategic force, while tactical aircraft, as the Third Tactical Air Force, went to his RAF opposite number, Air Marshal Baldwin. Addressing his new command, Stratemeyer emphasized their need to: "…merge into one unified force in thought and

deed—a force neither British nor American, with the faults of neither and the virtues of both."

During the latter half of 1943 the number of combat units available to the Allies in the IBS increased markedly. America's contribution in 1943 had risen to include five complete groups—the 80th Fighter Group, the 311th Fighter-Bomber Group, the 7th Bombardment Group (H), the 341st Bombardment Group (M), and the 5306th Photo Reconnaissance Group—and four troop carrier squadrons. More groups joined them in 1944. As Allied air power grew, so did its determination to wrest the initiative from the enemy. Bombers struck at transportation targets, military airfields, ports, and supply dumps; fighters strafed Japanese forward airfields and began to inflict serious losses in the air. The struggle in the air shifted in the Allies' favor in early 1944, and by the spring their air superiority was an accomplished fact.

Without Allied air superiority, two major ground force campaigns in March 1944 would probably have concluded very differently. On 10 March a Japanese offensive threatened to overwhelm the British Army near Imphal and Kohima on the India-Burma border. Large numbers of British and Indian troops were surrounded and were able to hold out only because reinforcements and essential supplies were flown in daily for weeks. The air transport force was augmented by troop carriers from as far away as the European theater, and more than 20,000 tons were delivered, plus the better part of two divisions of infantry. By June the British Army was strong enough to go over to the offensive. With the constant support of Eastern Air Command (EAC) tactical aircraft, the British Fourteenth Army under General Sir William Slim broke out and, inflicting a decisive defeat, drove the enemy into a retreat that degenerated into a rout. Before his assault, Slim announced that he based his whole plan of battle on Allied air support. Japanese

radio broadcasts later openly attributed their difficulties in Burma to Allied "air supremacy" and to the work of the troop carrier squadrons.

As the Japanese struck at Imphal the Allies launched a very different offensive of their own. In early 1943 Brigadier General Orde Wingate, a British officer who specialized in unconventional operations, had led a force of 3,000 men into the jungles behind Japanese lines, causing confusion and disrupting communications for four months. He wanted to repeat the experiment, but on a much larger scale and this time supported by aircraft. The Allied leaders accepted the proposal for Wingate's Long Range Penetration Group (the Chindits) at the Quebec conference in August 1943 and General Arnold had agreed that the USAAF would provide the necessary air power. Colonels Philip Cochran and John Alison were given a free hand to form a special air task force, and they put together the First Air Commandos to operate under the control of General Stratemeyer's EAC.

C–46 detail. The USAF Museum's C–46D is painted as an aircraft that flew the Hump in 1944. The circular insignia is that of Air Transport Command, U.S. Army Air Forces.

C–46. With two Pratt & Whitney R–2800 radial engines of 2,000 horsepower each, the Curtiss C–46 Commando could carry 12,000 pounds of payload almost a thousand miles. The transport gained its reputation during operations to supply China from India over the Hump of the Himalayas.

The First Air Commando Force was carefully tailored for the task with a remarkably varied collection of aircraft—13 C–47s, 12 C–46s, 150 CG–4 gliders, 75 TG–4 gliders, 100 L1/L5s, 6 YR–4 helicopters, 30 P–51As, and 12 B–25Hs. The operation began on the evening of 5 March 1944 when the transports and gliders took off to deliver the first soldiers to a large jungle clearing, codenamed Broadway, over 100 miles deep into Japanese-held territory. Each transport had to act as tug for two gliders and soon had problems. The gliders were overloaded and the C–47 tugs had to struggle up to 10,000 feet to haul them over the rugged Naga Hills. Turbulent conditions compounded the difficulties and several gliders parted from their tugs, having broken their tow ropes or been cast adrift by alarmed pilots. Less than half of the 67 gliders dispatched arrived at Broadway, and most of those crash landed after dark on a very rough surface. Of the men who got there, 31 were killed and 30 were injured. Nevertheless, 539 men, 3 mules, and nearly 66,000 pounds of stores arrived safely, enough to get things started. Among those ready to go was John Alison, who had set aside his fighter background to become a glider pilot for the operation. His cargo included the flying control equipment he needed for handling later flights and a bulldozer, which leveled

an airstrip by the following night. L–5s came in the next morning for the casualties, and a procession of C–47s began flying in with many more men and much more equipment. On a second strip, named Chowringhee, which opened a few miles away for a while, by 11 March, the Air Commandos had delivered over 9,000 men, nearly 1,400 mules, and almost 260 tons of stores to set Wingate's offensive in motion.

By any standards, Wingate's achievement had been extraordinary, but one which he did not live to see rewarded. On 25 March he was killed in the crash of a B–25 flying from Broadway back to Imphal. For the next few weeks, his Chindits roamed the jungle in a number of columns and, supplied by air, harassed and confused the Japanese, cutting their supply lines to forward units. Cochran's P–51s and B–25s operated on call for close support and raided Japanese forward airfields, taking a heavy toll of aircraft on the ground. The B–25Hs were impressive, firing their 75-mm cannon and dropping parafrag bombs on Japanese soldiers in close contact with British troops. A British patrol found a message written by a Japanese officer that recorded his despair over the relentless attentions of the Air Commandos. Unless something was done about the American aircraft, his operation

C–46 and the P–40–two potent symbols of the Fourteenth Air Force in China. A C–46, mainstay of the aerial supply line over the Hump, lands near a P–40 of the 23rd Fighter Group, the unit that inherited the mantle of the American Volunteer Group Flying Tigers.

was doomed. Flesh and blood, he insisted, could not stand up to them.

Meanwhile, Stilwell had driven his "New China Army" down the Hukawng Valley into northern Burma and a unit of American special forces, "Merrill's Marauders," had accomplished an astonishing forced march through jungles and over mountains to take the airfield at Myitkyina. For their success, both advances had relied heavily on air supply, a luxury not available to their often starving and poorly equipped enemies.

By mid-1944 the Japanese armies in Burma were reeling back on all fronts. Monsoon weather and the stubborn endurance of Japanese soldiers prolonged the war there into 1945, but the final result was never again in doubt. In the end, the campaign was a triumph for Allied foot soldiers, who overcame appalling hardships to defeat the enemy. However, their victories had been built on air power, most notably on the achievements of the air transport force. Nowhere else had C–47s and C–46s so obviously turned the tide of battle. Allied commanders began to realize that even large forces, isolated by geography or cut off by the enemy, could survive if supplied

by air. When counterair operations denied the enemy the same facility, victory was only a matter of time. An entry in a Japanese officer's diary put it most succinctly:

> "Enemy aircraft are over continuously in all weather. We can do nothing but look at them. If we only had air power! Even one or two planes would be something. Superiority in the air is the decisive factor in victory."

The Destruction of Japan

In the late 1930s a few visionary air planners were already thinking of a strategic bomber that would be a generational improvement over the B–17 and the B–24. In November 1939 General Arnold formally proposed the development of such an aircraft, and in September 1942 two contenders took to the air. The Consolidated XB–32 was the first to fly, but an early crash and design difficulties prevented its type from seeing combat until the closing days of the war, and then only in very small numbers. The other prototype was Boeing's XB–29, which had problems enough, but was nevertheless the first step toward the production of the B–29 Superfortress, one of the war's most significant aircraft.

Boeing B–29 Superfortresses of XXI Bomber Command passing Mt. Fuji on their way to Japanese targets.

Great urgency surrounded and forced a compression of its development program, with the result that the B–29 went into production with more than its share of teething troubles. Before the XB–29 even flew, the USAAF ordered 1,664 on the strength of blueprints and a wooden mock-up. Pressurized crew compartments, new construction techniques, remotely controlled guns, and, most important, new radial engines of unprecedented power were rushed into front-line service but harbored problems for aircrews and mechanics to overcome in the field.

In 1940 air force planners believed that VLR (Very Long Range) bombers would be primarily engaged against Germany by 1944. Positive developments in Europe and the relatively poor situation of the Allies in the CBI brought about a shift in policy by late 1943. Japan became the more likely target for the B–29, situated as it was in a region of few bases and vast distances. As the date of the B–29's operational debut drew nearer, USAAF Headquarters was besieged by requests from commanders who believed that the new bomber's capabilities would be best exploited in their theater. To avoid argument and recrimination, and to prevent the B–29s being wasted on missions for which they were not designed, General Arnold decided to form a new air force specifically for them and to keep it under his own command. Accordingly, the Twentieth Air Force came into being on 4 April 1944.

The organization of the B–29 front line began somewhat earlier, in June 1943, with the formation of the 58th Bombardment Wing (VH)[8] at Salina, Kansas. XX Bomber Command followed in November, with Brigadier General Kenneth Wolfe, the officer responsible for the B–29 production program, its commander. The command's operational deployment had to wait a while for solutions to training and logistical problems. The sheer size of a B–29 unit was daunting. A wing had 180 B–29s; 1 B–29 had a crew of 11. With a double crew allocation and its full maintenance establishment, the total personnel in a wing reached 11,112, including 3,045 officers. When XX Bomber Command went to war, it moved with more than 20,000 officers and men. It accommodated and fed them on the far side of the world, which was difficult enough; it had the added challenge of operating and maintaining over a hundred very large and untried bombers from a deployment base. Its task was truly monumental.

MATTERHORN, the codename of the bombing offensive against Japan, planned for the use of B–29s based in India and operating through forward airfields in China. The first of the big bombers arrived at its base near Kharagpur, India, on 2 April 1944. There followed long weeks as XX Bomber Command prepared the Chinese airfields near Chengtu for operations. It pre-positioned fuel, armaments, and spares, and, since transport aircraft were scarce, the crews of the 58th Bombardment Wing (VH) found themselves doing their own airlift. On average, they flew eight B–29 "freighter" flights into Chengtu to support one operational sortie. When all was ready, they flew their first combat mission on 5 June—but not through China. The target was a railway repair shop in Bangkok.

The Bangkok mission was a dress rehearsal for what followed. It was not a polished performance. Of 98 B–29s that set out at dawn, 1 crashed on takeoff, 14 aborted, and several others failed to find the target. Clouds prevented formation flying, thus, many aircraft made their way separately. One hour and 40 minutes went by between the passage of the first and last of the 77 crews claiming to have bombed the target, 48 of which did so by radar. Japanese defense was feeble and there were no combat losses. On the return trip, however, mechanical failures took their toll before bad weather and fuel shortages scattered the B–29s over a wide area—2 in the Bay of Bengal and more than 40 at airfields other than their own. XX Bomber Command lost 5 B–29s and 15 crewmen, paying dearly for placing fewer than 20 bombs within the target area. It put on a brave face over the results, saying that its crews had gained a great deal of experience from operating the B–29 under combat conditions. XX Bomber Command did not have much time for reflection as it received an urgent message from Arnold. A maximum effort was required for a raid on Japan. It was time for the B–29 to get on with the real war.

All who participated in MATTERHORN made strenuous efforts to turn it into a success, but the conditions under which the operation labored were too difficult. The first B–29 raid on Japan was indicative of some of them. Eighty-three bombers were gathered together at Chengtu for a mission to strike the Yawata steel works. Sixty-eight got airborne on the evening of 15 June, intending to be over the target close to midnight. Forty-seven of them bombed Yawata and 7 more unloaded elsewhere. Seven B–29s were lost, only 1 of them to enemy activity, and 55 men died. Just one bomb hit the target area, and that was over half a mile from the aiming point. Although its concrete results were poor, the mission cheered the Americans enormously. Their bombs had fallen on Japan for the first time since the Doolittle raid more than two years before. If their strident reaction was anything to go by, the Japanese were deeply concerned. In the United States the B–29s competed with the Normandy beachheads for the front pages of the newspapers.

MATTERHORN struggled on for the rest of the year, the B–29s striking at Japan and a number of targets in Southeast Asia. Wolfe, an excellent logistician and engineer, returned to the United States to sort out B–29 production problems, and, in September, Major General Curtis LeMay arrived from Europe to grip the problem of making XX Bomber Command more effective. He reorganized squadrons and changed tactics, occasionally getting good results, but aircraft losses continued and there were times when results were abysmal. By October 1944 the preferably located airfields in the Marianas were ready for the B–29s. Operations through Chengtu had given a poor return on the investment of men and materials, limiting the 58th Bombardment Wing (VH) because of bad weather, geography, and logistics to just 49 missions, less than half of them against Japan, and an average of only two sorties per aircraft per month. Of course, MATTERHORN had provided operational lessons. Its crews had become familiar with the B–29, which had been refined and relieved of its many "bugs." On the other hand, MATTERHORN's support costs had been prohibitive, and so, by the end of the year, had the loss of 147 B–29s—the majority *not* to enemy action.[9]

On 12 October 1944, Brigadier General Haywood "Possum" Hansell brought the first B–29 into the Marianas, landing *Joltin' Josie, the Pacific Pioneer* on the vast new Saipan base. Hansell had been one of the principal planners of the air assault on Japan, and he was now to lead XXI Bomber Command, which was being formed to spearhead the offensive. The 73rd Bombardment Wing (VH) provided XXI Bomber Command's cutting edge. It flew training missions against Truk and other Japanese-held islands, and, after some preliminary photographic sorties by F–13s (a strategic reconnaissance version of the B–29), it aimed its first bombing mission at Japan on 24 November. The target directive from the JCS put aircraft assembly and engine plants at the top of the priority list, and the Nakajima engine factory in Tokyo was the first. As had been the case with the raids by the 58th Bombardment Wing (VH), weather and mechanical problems had their effects and the results were disappointing. Only two B–29s were lost, but, ominously, one of them went down after what appeared to be a deliberate ramming by a Japanese fighter pilot.

With few exceptions, the B–29 raids followed strategic bombing's conventional wisdom for the next three months, generally occurring in daylight from high altitude as precision strikes on specific targets, usually in the aircraft industry. Reconnaissance revealed that they were doing very little damage. XXI Bomber Command reported a now familiar list of shortcomings, among them the slow build-up of the B–29 force,

"Pacific Pioneer," James Dietz, 1985, USAF Art Collection.

Curtis LeMay and Haywood Hansell. Major General Curtis LeMay, left, moved to Guam and took over XXI Bomber Command from Brigadier General Haywood Hansell in January 1945. Brigadier General Roger Ramey, right, who had been serving as Hansell's chief of staff, moved to India to take LeMay's place at XX Bomber Command.

A B–29 heading for the island sanctuary of Iwo Jima with its No. 4 engine feathered and smoking heavily. B–29 raids on Japan were not unopposed.

bad weather, poor bombing accuracy, mechanical problems leading to a high abort rate and to aircraft losses, and a lack of escort fighters. Nevertheless, the raids had disturbed the Japanese sufficiently that they struck back at Isley Field on Saipan with aircraft from Iwo Jima, destroying several B–29s on the ground.

Impatient for better results, Arnold intervened, sending LeMay to replace Hansell as commander of XXI Bomber Command in January 1945. LeMay brought his usual energy to making changes aimed at improving aircraft maintenance and aircrew training, but initially the operational pattern remained the same. Daylight precision attacks continued to be made dropping high explosive bombs from above 20,000 feet and the results were little better than before. At the request of Twentieth Air Force, a couple of experimental raids were made with the B–29s

B–29s being serviced on Guam between missions. Their 18-cylinder Wright R–3350 engines generated 2,200 horsepower but were temperamental, suffering repeated fires.

274

B–29s in tight formation for mutual protection during a daylight raid on Japan. Curtis LeMay introduced attacks by night and from much lower altitudes.

carrying only incendiaries. These were also from high altitude and did not produce much more encouraging results, although a few promising fires were started. By the time February arrived XXI Bomber Command was nearing a crisis. Two things happened to deflect it. The first was another island assault by the U.S. Marines 725 miles north of Saipan, and the other was a radical change in B–29 bombing tactics.

Japanese aircraft on Iwo Jima had posed a threat to American bases in the Marianas from the start against B–29s on the ground. Iwo's fighters intercepted the bombers on their way to Japan or forced them to dogleg—use more fuel and reduce bombloads. If no interception took place, radar on Iwo still gave early warning to the Japanese mainland of the B–29s' approach. Even taken together, these threats did not amount to much and hardly justified Iwo's capture. To the American forces that took the island, however, the benefits were considerable. Iwo's airfields would allow the B–29s to operate over Japan under escort, and its runways would be available for emergency use by bombers either damaged or struggling home with a mechanical failure. Equally important, Iwo would be a forward base for air-sea rescue units, which had already proved to be essential to B–29 missions against Japan.

The Marines went ashore at Iwo Jima on 19 February 1945, setting off a bloody battle that raged until the island was declared secure in the middle of March. On 6 March P–51s of the Seventh Air Force's[10] 15th Fighter Squadron began arriving on Iwo's South Field and were soon in action, often taking off under fire to give close support to the nearby Marines. Later in the month, they were followed by the 21st Fighter Group and by the P–61s of the 548th and 549th Night Fighter Squadrons. As it happened, the fighter squadrons did not contribute as much as had been expected as escorts for the B–29s. By the time they were ready to fly, the air defense of Japan was already deteriorating, and, in any case, the B–29s were operating much more frequently by night. Iwo's true value proved to be as an emergency way station for ailing bombers, and as such it was in frequent use.

Early in March, LeMay made a decision that stood conventional strategic bombing theory on its head. The B–29 had been designed for daylight precision bombing and its planned employment against Japan had naturally been based on classic USAAF doctrines. LeMay himself had fought under those doctrines in Europe, but his mind was not closed to other ways of doing things, and his observations since taking

275

B–29s bombing. Bombs cascade from B–29 bomb-bays during an attack on a Japanese target. One Superfortress was capable of loading up to 20,000 pounds of bombs internally.

command of XXI Bomber Command convinced him that B–29 operations had to change if they were to play a decisive part in the defeat of Japan. In his view, the B–29's ineffectiveness was the result of several factors, most of them attributable to high-altitude flying in daylight. Low-level flying he reasoned, would save fuel, which was heavy and required in climbing, and would thus increase bomb-carrying capacity. It would also save wear and tear on the engines and perhaps cure the fires that tended to ignite them. Japan's day defenses had been improving and the B–29 loss rate was rising. Japan's night defenses were thought to be poor, and LeMay believed that even flak would not offer a serious threat. He also felt that, in spite of the inconclusive results from the experimental raids flown so far, Japan's wood and paper cities would be susceptible to incendiary attack. The quickest way to destroy many of the Japanese

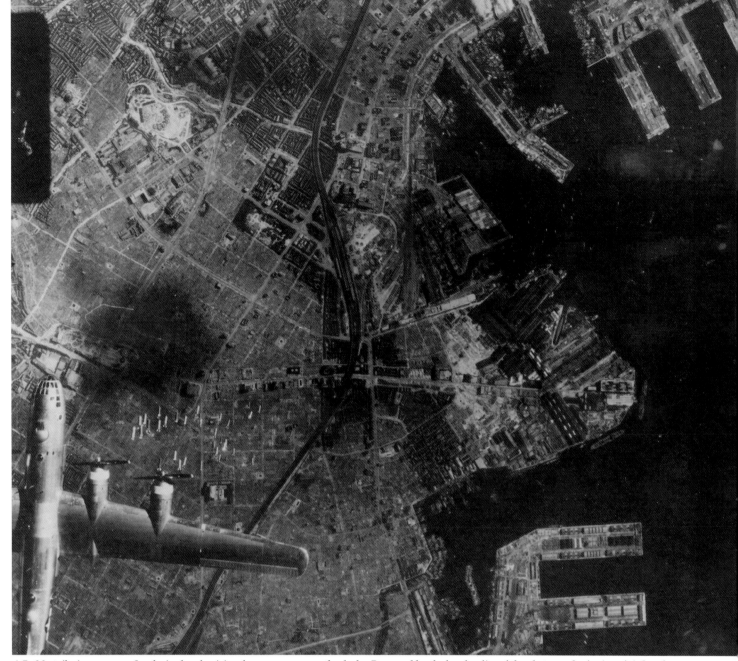

A B–29 strike in progress. Smoke is already rising from an area near the docks. Presumably, the bombardier of the photographer's aircraft is keenly aware of the one below.

war industries would be to burn them out, since most of them were integral parts of built-up areas.

LeMay then showed his decisiveness. He issued a field order for an operation to take place on 9 March. His B–29s were to conduct a maximum effort, at night, at low level. They would limit their fuel to take account of their new flight parameters and would carry no gun ammunition so that their bombloads (exclusively incendiary) would increase to about six tons per aircraft. LeMay's order raised expectations and pulse rates throughout his command. Even he must have felt a tremor of nervous excitement. He had turned the B–29 world upside down and would bear the responsibility for the risks of the operation squarely on his own shoulders. LeMay did not consult General Arnold of his intentions; he merely had him informed of them the day before the raid.

By this time three wings of B–29s were operating from Saipan, Tinian, and Guam—the 73rd, 313th and 314th Bombardment Wings. A force of 334 bombers assembled and attacked Tokyo from altitudes between 4,900 and 9,200 feet. Their first bombs fell just after midnight, starting fires at once. The flames spread quickly in a brisk surface wind. As the B–29s fanned out to cover unburned areas, new fires sprang up and merged with those already blazing. Later aircraft reported difficulties flying through the dense smoke and severe turbulence generated by the intense heat. The fire grew into one of the greatest urban conflagrations in history, consuming almost 16 square miles of the city and destroying over a quarter of a million buildings. For the Japanese, the scale of the catastrophe defied belief. More than a million people became homeless and over 80,000 died. It was the most destructive air raid of the war, unsurpassed in the European or Pacific theaters.

Fourteen B–29s were shot down and 42 were damaged by flak over Tokyo. LeMay, remembering the severity of his European experience, regarded their sacrifice as a moderate price for such a heavy strike. Given its results, he immediately ordered a similar strike against the city of Nagoya and, before the end of March, more against Osaka and Kobe. Such was the damage inflicted by his scorching raids that LeMay knew he had been right. He had in his hand a weapon capable of realizing the apocalyptic strategic air power theories of Douhet, Mitchell, and Trenchard, one which could indeed destroy the fabric of an enemy nation.

The systematic burning of Japan would continue. The need to defeat Japan as quickly as possible was paramount and, since precision bombing had failed, it was, for the time being, set aside in favor of area attack. LeMay was impatient to get it done, and he proposed driving his crews harder than ever, raising their combat flying hours to 80 per month, a far greater rate than had ever been attempted in Europe. He was eager to prove that his B–29s could ensure victory over Japan and the detractors of strategic air power. In a letter to Brigadier General Lauris Norstad, Chief of Staff, Twentieth Air Force, he wrote:

> I am influenced by the conviction that the present stage of development of the air war against Japan presents the [US]AAF for the first time with the opportunity of proving the power of the strategic air arm. I consider that for the first time strategic air bombardment faces a situation in which its strength is proportionate to the magnitude of its task.

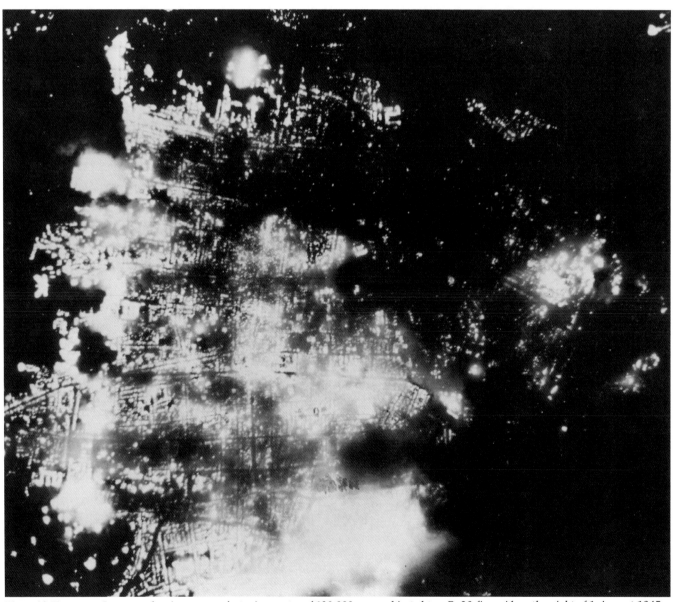

Fire raid. Toyama, a Japanese aluminum manufacturing center of 130,000, was subjected to a B–29 fire raid on the night of 1 August 1945. It was one of the war's most punishing attacks, destroying more than 90 percent of the city.

During April 1945 a pause in the fire-bombing campaign was forced on LeMay. His B–29s were diverted to support of the invasion of Okinawa, attacking Japanese airfields from which *kamikaze* missions were being flown against the American fleet. B–29s of the 313th Bombardment Wing also began the specialized work of laying mines, sowing thousands in harbor approaches and in the waterways most used by Japanese shipping. Although it was unheralded, the mine-laying was a conspicuous success, accounting for approximately half of the Japanese tonnage sunk in this closing stage of the war.

In May the incineration of Japan resumed. Until mid-June, the B–29s worked their way through its major cities, and then started on a list of smaller urban areas with populations between 100,000 and 200,000. Toward the end of July, by means of leaflets dropped from aircraft over the dozens of cities slated for attack the next day, LeMay began warning his intended victims. The leaflets advised the inhabitants to leave or suffer the consequences. Then the bombers struck some, not all, of the cities. Such warnings proved effective and were later characterized by a high Japanese official as "a very clever piece of psychological warfare, as people in the affected regions got extremely nervous and lost what faith they still had in the army's ability to defend the mainland."

By August the B–29s, running out of large places to burn, turned to towns with populations of less than 40,000. They left many of Japan's urban areas in ruins; the cities of Namaza and Fukui were almost 90 percent destroyed, and Toyama, with a pre-raid population of almost 130,000, had effectively ceased to exist. In all, the B–29s attacked 66 urban centers. About 178 square miles of Japan's built-up area had literally gone up in smoke.

Even in the face of so much destruction the bombing offensive continued with no reduction in scale. On the contrary, an extensive build-up of the USAAF's striking power in the Pacific and the restructuring of command arrangements to take account of a massive increase in strength were imminent. General Arnold advocated the appointment of a supreme commander for the final offensive against Japan, with senior and equal ground, air, and naval commanders responsible to him for operations in their own spheres. Given the sensibilities of the individual services, the question of a supreme commander was unresolved, but the JCS agreed that General MacArthur should command all land operations and that Admiral Nimitz should be the commander at sea. They further agreed that an air commander should take charge of land-based strategic aviation and have broad administrative and logistical responsibilities for all USAAF forces in the theater. The senior airman they selected to be Commander, U.S. Army Strategic Air Forces (USASTAF), Pacific was General Carl Spaatz.

Spaatz arrived from Europe to set up his new headquarters on Guam at the end of July 1945. With Germany defeated, the "Mighty Eighth" was already on its way from Europe to strengthen the air forces facing Japan. In a letter to Spaatz in May 1945 General Arnold explained his plans to build up strategic air power in the Pacific and gave some indication of the politics lurking behind the command appointment. The Eighth would operate from Okinawa with 720 B–29s, and the Twentieth would remain in the Marianas with another 720, a combined striking force more than twice as powerful as that ranged against Japan so far. In nominating Spaatz for command of USASTAF, Arnold wrote: "I believe we need somebody who can work more nearly on parity and have more influence with MacArthur and Nimitz …. I can see nobody else who has the chance to save for us a proper representation in the air war in the Pacific.…" As Arnold and others pondered these ideas and the arrangements they necessarily entailed, a revolutionary event changed the nature of global war for-ever and rendered any such activities superfluous.

The Coming of the Apocalypse

On 11 June 1945, specially modified B–29s began arriving at Tinian's North Field. They belonged to the 393rd Bombardment Squadron, the combat element of the 509th Composite Group. Externally, they were distinguished by a lack of gun turrets, apart from the two-gun position in the tail. They were parked in their own part of the airfield, a complex of heavily guarded buildings and hard stands. Once settled in, their crews followed normal practice and completed a few training missions to well-visited islands like Truk before flying several more to selected targets in Japan. The other B–29 units became curious because the 393rd never flew as part of a wing operation. They went off in small formations of their own, sometimes only two or three aircraft at a time, apparently following the discredited practice of penetrating Japanese airspace in daylight at high level. Over the targets, however, their tactics were anything but standard. At the release point the lead aircraft dropped a single bulbous bomb and immediately broke into a steep diving turn, aiming to get as far away as possible before the bomb exploded. Even to the crews performing these maneuvers, it was all very strange.

During the training period, the commander of the 509th was the only member of the unit who knew

Mushroom cloud over Nagasaki. The second atomic bomb, Fat Man, was dropped on Nagasaki on 9 August 1945 from the B–29 Bockscar when clouds obscured the primary target, Kokura. A mushroom cloud rose rapidly toward the stratosphere, and the B–29 shuddered under the impact of five separate shock waves as it turned toward Okinawa.

that his group had been formed for the specific purpose of dropping the first operational atomic bomb on Japan. He was Colonel Paul Tibbetts, an exceptional pilot with a distinguished B–17 record in Europe and North Africa, who had recently been testing B–29s in the United States. On 18 July he received a coded message which told him that an atomic bomb had been detonated at Alamagordo, New Mexico. He was pretty certain then that his months of preparatory work had not been in vain, and that the next atomic explosion would take place over Japan with himself and his crew as witnesses.

The Allied powers issued an ultimatum on 26 July calling for the Japanese to surrender or suffer "prompt and utter destruction." President Truman had decided that the "special bomb" would be used if the Japanese refused to comply, and the anticipated rejection came from Premier Suzuki on 28 July. General Spaatz had already received a directive on 25 July in the expectation that the Japanese would refuse to cooperate. In it, Spaatz was instructed that the 509th was to deliver its first special bomb, visually aimed, on or after 3 August 1945 "on one of the targets: Hiroshima, Kokura, Niigata, and Nagasaki." The field orders for the attack were signed on 2 August by Lieutenant General Twining, who in the reorganization of the Pacific air forces had become commander of the Twentieth Air Force. Hiroshima was selected as the primary target.

The fissionable material for the core of the bomb arrived at Tinian on board the cruiser *Indianapolis* on 26 July, and by 1 August both the weapon and the 509th were ready to go. Weather forecasts for the period after 3 August were promising and led to final briefings being given. On 4 August the crews of the 509th at last learned that their special bombs

Devastation at Nagasaki. The atomic bomb Fat Man *at Nagasaki yielded 23 kilotons, more than* Little Boy *at Hiroshima, which was close to 15 kilotons. Destruction was just as complete near ground zero, but the area totally destroyed (2.3 x 1.9 miles) was less than that at Hiroshima, being confined by the natural bowl in which Nagasaki was built. The U.S. Strategic Bombing Survey estimated casualties at 35,000 dead, 5,000 missing, and 60,000 injured.*

The crew of **Bockscar** on 9 August 1945. Charles Sweeney stands at far right.

The B–29 Bockscar *approaching Nagasaki, 9 August 1945.*

were expected to explode with a force equal to 20,000 tons of TNT.

At 0245 on 6 August 1945 Paul Tibbetts lifted his B–29, *Enola Gay*, off the Tinian runway and headed north. Two other B–29s, *The Great Artiste* and *No. 91*, followed with official observers on board. Approaching Japan, Tibbetts received a report from weather reconnaissance aircraft indicating that the skies over Hiroshima were almost clear of clouds. By then the weaponeer had made the bomb live and all was ready for the drop. Navigator "Dutch" van Kirk brought the *Enola Gay*

accurately to the initial point for the attack and, at 0911, Tibbetts steadied at 31,600 feet on the final heading for the target and handed the aircraft over to bombardier Tom Ferebee. At 0915 the bomb, a uranium device known as *Little Boy*, fell from the bomb bay toward the aiming point of Hiroshima's Aioi Bridge. Tibbetts immediately broke hard right and dropped the nose, gathering speed to escape the coming blast. Fifty seconds after release *Little Boy* detonated and Hiroshima was transformed into a scene of utter devastation.

Bockscar *nose. It was from this position in* Bockscar, *the USAF Museum's Boeing B–29 Superfortress, that Captain Kermit Beahan saw a hole in the cloud over Nagasaki and dropped the atomic bomb* Fat Man *on 9 August 1945.*

Bockscar *cockpit. The pilot's seat in a B–29 seems almost too exposed. The area's general roominess is emphasized by the huge expanse of glass on every side.*

B–29 engineer's panel. The flight engineer's position of a B–29 was comprehensive in its coverage of the aircraft's systems. Note the throttle, pitch, and mixture control levers which duplicate those between the pilots.

Inside the forward bomb-bay of Bockscar looking toward the nose. Fat Man was carried here. The crew compartment hatch is in the center.

The official Japanese communiqué after the raid minimized the disaster at Hiroshima. It mentioned a new bomb which had caused "considerable damage" and "should not be made light of," but it gave no hint of a Japanese surrender. Therefore, the United States decided to drop the second of the two atomic bombs, *Fat Man*, which had a plutonium core. On 9 August Major Charles Sweeney in a B–29 called *Bockscar*,[11] headed for the primary target, Kokura, but that city was saved by the weather. Complete cloud cover defied Sweeney over Kokura and he turned *Bockscar* toward the secondary target, Nagasaki. He approached the target, in persistent cloud cover, on radar, but at the last moment the city appeared through a break and the bombardier released *Fat Man* visually. The blast from its explosion caught up with the aircraft about a minute later. The crew felt "as if the B–29 were being beaten by a telephone pole."

At Hiroshima, the area destroyed covered nearly five square miles. Almost 80,000 people died and those injured numbered about the same. Nagasaki was to some extent protected by its hilly terrain and the area destroyed was less than one and a half square miles. The dead and injured figures could not be precisely determined, but they were approximately 35,000 and 60,000 respectively.

The Japanese were in desperate straits. Their armies had been defeated, their navy and air forces destroyed, their sea lanes closed, their cities burned, and their nation shocked by the impact of two frightful new

Charles W. Sweeney, pilot of Bockscar *over Nagasaki on 9 August 1945. More than 50 years later he once more took his place in the left hand seat.*

weapons. As if that were not enough, on 8 August the Soviet Union had declared war on them and its armies were sweeping into Manchuria. Yet Japan's militarism remained strong and there were still those among its leaders who vehemently opposed any move for peace. Deadlocked, the Japanese government turned to Emperor Hirohito, and on 10 August he gave his view that "the time has come when we must

Looking aft through the hatch at the rear of the forward crew compartment of Bockscar. *Commander Frederick Ashworth (U.S. Navy), climbed through this hatch to arm the atomic bomb* Fat Man *on the way to the target.*

bear the unbearable." Papers flew between Japan and the Allies, but it was 14 August before the Emperor's will prevailed. While intense internal struggles were going on in Tokyo, the USAAF resumed its conventional operations, culminating in a "1,000 plus" grand finale on 14 August, when 828 B–29s and 186 escorts attacked various targets. Before the last B–29 landed, President Truman was at last able to announce the unconditional surrender of Japan.

Formalities ending the Pacific War were concluded by General MacArthur on board the battleship *Missouri* in Tokyo Bay on 2 September 1945. The Army's senior soldier and the Navy's battlewagon occupied center stage, but overhead the Air Force made its point with a flypast of 462 B–29s. In view of recent events, it was a display of strength which could hardly fail to draw the eye.

With Hindsight

Generally speaking, air power served the Allied cause even more effectively in the Pacific and CBI theaters than in Europe. This was possible because, for one thing, the discrepancies in strength between the two major combatants were more obvious. In terms of population and industry, Japan was greatly inferior to the United States. That became obvious in the air as the Japanese air forces were increasingly outnumbered and unable to keep up in the race to produce not only more aircrews and aircraft, but better versions of both. What was extraordinary was the speed with which the United States mobilized and organized its forces in the Pacific while still committing huge resources to the Allied policy of Germany First. In 1942 the USAAF in the Pacific was an operator of small, scattered collections of outdated aircraft. Little more than three years later, its six Pacific-CBI air forces had grown into a mighty assembly of air power capable of dominating any confrontation anywhere in the world. American air power was emphasized as truly overwhelming when it was able to mount an aerial offensive against the main islands of Japan. The emphasis was marked because Japan's air defenses were found to be relatively poor and the cities housing its principal industries proved particularly susceptible to incendiary attack. In Europe, on the other hand, the Luftwaffe was always a ferocious adversary and German industry was more robust.

Vast distances and frequently rudimentary national infrastructures put a premium on the reach and flexibility of air power, and the United States employed its assets far more effectively than did its enemy. Japan understood the importance of air power, but had a limited view of how to use it. It was primarily for the support of ground and naval units, and

Japan generally kept the efforts of its air forces well separated. The USAAF used its aircraft in every role imaginable—strategic bombing, interdiction, close support, artillery spotting, reconnaissance, air defense, fighter escort, ship attack, maritime patrol, air-sea rescue, troop and freight transport, glider assault, casualty evacuation—and became highly effective at each. The USAAF did all these things, usually did them very well, and still found time to cooperate in operations alongside the USN.

At war's end, it became clear that the immense amount of destruction effected during the fire-bombing campaign had reduced Japan's already declining industrial capacity dramatically. By mid-1945 Japan's production was down to about one third of that reached during the previous year, and this was the result of both the loss of factories and a lowering of the morale of the Japanese people, who had become noticeably more defeatist and less willing to work. Their evacuation in large numbers into the countryside was also having an effect.

The first series of incendiary attacks on its major cities in March 1945 shocked some of Japan's leaders into initiating peace negotiations. Indeed, well before the dropping of the atomic bombs, members of the "peace party" in the government were predicting that the bombing would force an end to the war by September and they were arguing that further resistance was pointless. Their reaction to the immediate aerial threat was understandable, but, in its post-war examination of the air war against Japan, the United States Strategic Bombing Survey took care not to attribute Japan's defeat to any single factor, preferring to mention "the numerous causes which jointly and cumulatively were responsible for Japan's disaster." The USSBS report pointed out that the final air assault on Japan had not been feasible until bases had been secured within reach of the main islands and that the history of the war in the Pacific was largely one of surface forces seizing territory with the support of air forces. It went without saying that the surface campaigns would have been unlikely to succeed in the absence of air support.

Of course, the USSBS's comments were justified. By the time the B–29 offensive began, Japan was in decline as a result of calamitous defeats for its armed forces and the strictures of a relentless naval blockade. Nevertheless, it is interesting to speculate on how the war might have gone had there been no strategic bombing campaign. Given the nature of their society in 1945 and the military domination of their government, the Japanese would probably have endured the sufferings of total isolation and would have fought to the death against invasion. The B–29s made such stoicism impossible by bringing the war home in a form so irresistible and so horrifyingly destructive that increasing numbers of Japanese lost the will to fight on. Even military fanatics, who could not think of surrender, no longer talked of victory but of "finding life in death."

By the time they felt driven to seek the intervention of their Emperor, Japan's leaders would undoubtedly have been keenly aware that they faced inevitable defeat. Their military reverses and the naval blockade had created that situation, but had not forced them to consider surrender. They were unequivocal in testifying later that the bombing campaign had done that. Prince Konoye said: "Fundamentally the thing that brought about the determination to make peace was the prolonged bombing by the B–29s." Premier Suzuki agreed: "It seemed to me unavoidable that in the long run Japan would be almost destroyed by air attack so that merely on the basis of the B–29s alone I was convinced that Japan should sue for peace."

Suzuki and others mentioned the atomic bombs and the Soviet declaration of war as additional factors, but seemed to suggest that, although these events were significant, they were not the real roots of Japan's drive to end the war. Their catastrophic nature served to bolster the arguments of the members of the peace party, who had already decided to face the terrible disgrace of surrender. At that stage they had no idea what kind of bomb had destroyed Hiroshima and did not particularly care. B–29s had shown that they could eradicate cities just as effectively with incendiaries and the distinction between one kind of bomb and another seemed insignificant.

By 1945 the inevitability of Japan's defeat, with or without a strategic bombing offensive, was not in doubt. The fact remains that the blows which precipitated the end of the war and obviated the need for a costly invasion of Japan were delivered by the USAAF's B–29s. It was their demonstrated destructive capacity that most affected the states of mind of Japan's leaders in 1945 and led them to sue for peace. Early air power strategists who had theorized that bombing an opposing nation's heartland would, among other things, "destroy the enemy's will to fight" might at last have claimed justification for the thought.

In 1947 General Carl Spaatz looked back on World War II and delivered the airmen's verdict on the role of air power in the Pacific:

> In our victory over Japan, air power was unquestionably decisive. That the planned invasion of the Japanese home islands was unnecessary is clear evidence that air power has evolved into a force co-equal with land and sea power, decisive in its own right and worthy of the faith of its prophets.

The views of General Spaatz were hardly unbiased but they were founded on a rock of solid achievement by the USAAF, and they were a rallying call for the faithful who believed that the time had come for the creation of an independent United States Air Force.

Notes

1. The 90th Squadron's aircraft had been modified with forward-firing armament of eight .5-inch guns grouped in the nose, plus two more in the upper turret. Almost equally effective were the A–20s of the 89th Squadron, with four .5-inch guns in addition to their original armament of four .303-inch machine guns, and the RAAF's Beaufighters, which carried four 20-mm cannon in the nose and six .303-inch machine guns in the wings.

2. In the New Hebrides, five B–17s of the 26th Bombardment Squadron operated from Efate and six B–17s of the 98th Bombardment Squadron operated from Espiritu Santo. Operating from New Caledonia were 10 B–17s of the 42nd Bombardment Squadron; 10 B–26s of the 69th Bombardment Squadron; and 38 P–39/400s of the 67th Fighter Squadron. Operating from Fiji were 12 B–17s of the 431st Bombardment Squadron; 12 B–26s of the 70th Bombardment Squadron; and 17 P–39/400 of the 70th Fighter Squadron. Twenty-four P–39/400s from the 68th Fighter Squadron operated from Tonga.

3. The Third Fleet, under Admiral William Halsey, had 106 warships. The Seventh Fleet, under Admiral Thomas Kinkaid, had 157 combat ships and 581 other vessels.

4. Major Richard Bong was presented with the Medal of Honor by General MacArthur at Tacloban on 12 December 1944. After his 40th victory, he retired from combat and returned to the United States. Bong was killed only eight months later while testing the new P–80 jet fighter in California.

5. Major Gerald Johnson was credited with 22 victories and survived the war. Shortly afterward, on 7 October 1945, he was in a B–17 on his way to Japan when it was damaged in a violent storm. He gave up his parachute to a passenger and was lost with the aircraft.

6. Shomo was awarded the Medal of Honor and Lipscomb the Distinguished Service Cross.

7. The limitations of his position having been revealed to him, Stratemeyer also discovered that, in time, no fewer than seven lines of command had found their way to his chair from above. Roosevelt, Marshall, Arnold, Stilwell, Chiang Kai-shek, Mountbatten (Supreme Commander, Southeast Asia), and Peirse (Air Commander, Southeast Asia)l were entitled to give him orders.

8. VH means Very Heavy.

9. At least three B–29s survived emergency landings in the Soviet Union. The aircraft were not returned but were copied as the Tu–4 bomber and the Tu–70 transport.

10. During the latter part of 1944 the USAAF, Pacific Ocean Area, had been formed under the command of General Harmon, who was also Deputy Commander, Twentieth Air Force. Harmon's new headquarters provided the necessary support services for XXI Bomber Command while serving as the superior headquarters for the Seventh Air Force, the latter nearing the end of its island-hopping progress across the Pacific. Harmon himself disappeared without trace into the Pacific on 25 February 1945 while on a flight to Washington. He was succeeded by Major General Willis Hale.

11. Sweeney's own B–29, *The Great Artiste*, was the principal observation aircraft and was loaded with monitoring instruments. On the Nagasaki mission Sweeney exchanged aircraft with Captain Fred Bock, whose usual B–29 was the appropriately named *Bockscar*. It is preserved as an exhibit in the USAF Museum, Dayton, Ohio.

Part III
Independence

Air power has been developed to a point where its responsibilities are equal to those of land and sea power, and its contribution to our strategic planning is as great.

(President Harry Truman to Congress, December 1945)

Anyone who is capable of understanding, who is aware of even the most basic truths upon which World War II was prosecuted, is fully aware that the first line of defense and the last frontiers of America lie in the sky.

(General Jimmy Doolittle to the Senate Naval Affairs Committee, 1946)

… the real barrier wasn't in the sky, but in our knowledge and experience of super-sonic flight.

(Chuck Yeager, after flying faster than sound in the Bell X–1, 14 October 1947)

They thought they were pretty good … so my first chore was to convince them they weren't.

(Lieutenant General Curtis LeMay, on taking over Strategic Air Command, November 1948)

It is hereby declared to be the policy of the President that there shall be equality of treatment and opportunity for all persons in the Armed Services without regard to race.

(President Harry Truman, Executive Order 9981, 26 July 1948)

Walnut Ridge, Arkansas. The site was typical of the huge aircraft parks set up to deal with the problem of 50,000 surplus U.S. Army Air Forces aircraft once World War II was over. Once essential B–17s, some of them factory fresh, were among the aircraft waiting in rows for scrap metal merchants.

everyday vocabulary. Events built toward the climactic year of 1947 and the declaration of the Truman Doctrine as the foundation of American foreign policy. The President's words were unequivocal:

> I believe that it must be the policy of the United States to support free peoples who are resisting attempted subjugation by armed minorities or by outside pressures.... If we falter in our leadership, we may endanger the peace of the world, and we shall surely endanger the welfare of this nation.

President Truman's speech formally committed the United States to bearing the responsibilities of an international power. It cleared the way for the announcement of the Marshall Plan for European recovery and gave Americans notice that they would have to provide the considerable resources necessary for promoting the Truman Doctrine. Not least among them would be military forces based outside the United States and capable of "containing" the Soviet Union.

When Carl Spaatz took over from Hap Arnold as Commanding General, U.S. Army Air Forces, in February 1946, he was already working on the problems of how best to cope with force contraction and how

to reorganize the USAAF for the future. Convinced by his own experience, Spaatz saw air power in global terms and believed that long-range bombers should form the core of American air power. He was also an advocate of a strong Air National Guard and Air Force Reserve, and he argued for the importance of a well-funded research and development program. He worked with the confidence that independence for the air forces could not be long delayed. In March 1946 he proposed a new framework for the service that took his convictions into account. At the heart of his reorganization were three new functional commands to provide the air forces' teeth—Strategic Air Command, Tactical Air Command, and Air Defense Command. In support were Air Materiel, Air Proving Ground, Air Transport, and Air Training Commands, plus Air University. Overseas combat strength, deployed from the functional commands, would be controlled primarily by the United States Air Forces in Europe (USAFE) and the Far East Air Force (FEAF). Smaller overseas elements were the Alaskan, Caribbean, and Northeast Air Commands. Between them the combat commands would field 70 front-line groups. At a time when defense spending was not popular, a 70-group air force seemed over-ambitious.

While Spaatz's restructuring was going on, so were even greater things. Independence for the air arm was not a new idea; it had been a subject for discussion since before World War I. As early as 1916 Congress had considered legislation for an independent department for aviation, and, in following years, it revisited the topic on Capitol Hill on more than 50 occasions, even during World War II. However, senior airmen were then rightly wary of taking such a major step with so much on their minds. Even so, as the war progressed and the importance of air power was more clearly recognized, the USAAF enjoyed what was very close to independence and General Arnold was accorded the privileges of a member of the Joint Chiefs of Staff (JCS). Ideas of reorganization persisted in the background, however. A 1943 War Department paper concluded that there was a need for a single Department of National Defense, and in 1944 the JCS ordered a study to examine alternative systems for national defense management. This study agreed with the earlier paper in recommending the creation of a single department of government controlling three service branches.

In the latter stages of the war and the months immediately thereafter, a rash of studies issued from a number of committees seeking the ideal arrangement. However, they generally reflected the bias of their members. Those from the War Department generally favored a Department of the Armed Forces with three single service divisions, while those from the Navy Department, although conceding the need for a separate air force, were strongly opposed to placing the services under a superior authority. Congressional hearings drew endorsements for a single department not only from air force men like Arnold and Spaatz, but also from such eminent soldiers as Marshall and Bradley. Always opposed were the admirals—King, Nimitz, Halsey, and Leahy. In December 1945 President Truman intervened and requested that Congress introduce legislation to combine the War and Navy Departments. Arguments dragged on into 1946, but the President persisted, returning to the charge repeatedly as several proposed bills failed. Eventually, a compromise bill entitled the National Security Act of 1947 went to Congress at the end of February 1947. It provided for a single Secretary of National Defense and a separate Department of the Air Force, but it was careful to stipulate that the Navy would retain control of its own aviation units and the Marine Corps. President Truman signed the bill into law on 26 July 1947 after prolonged hearings and many amendments. Immediately after approving the National Security Act, he signed an executive order setting out the functions and roles of what were now three independent services. Appropriately enough, he received the papers as he waited to leave for Missouri from Washington's National Airport, and signed them on board his official aircraft, the C–54 *Sacred Cow*.

President Truman's C–54, Sacred Cow, *on board which the bill creating the USAF was signed.*

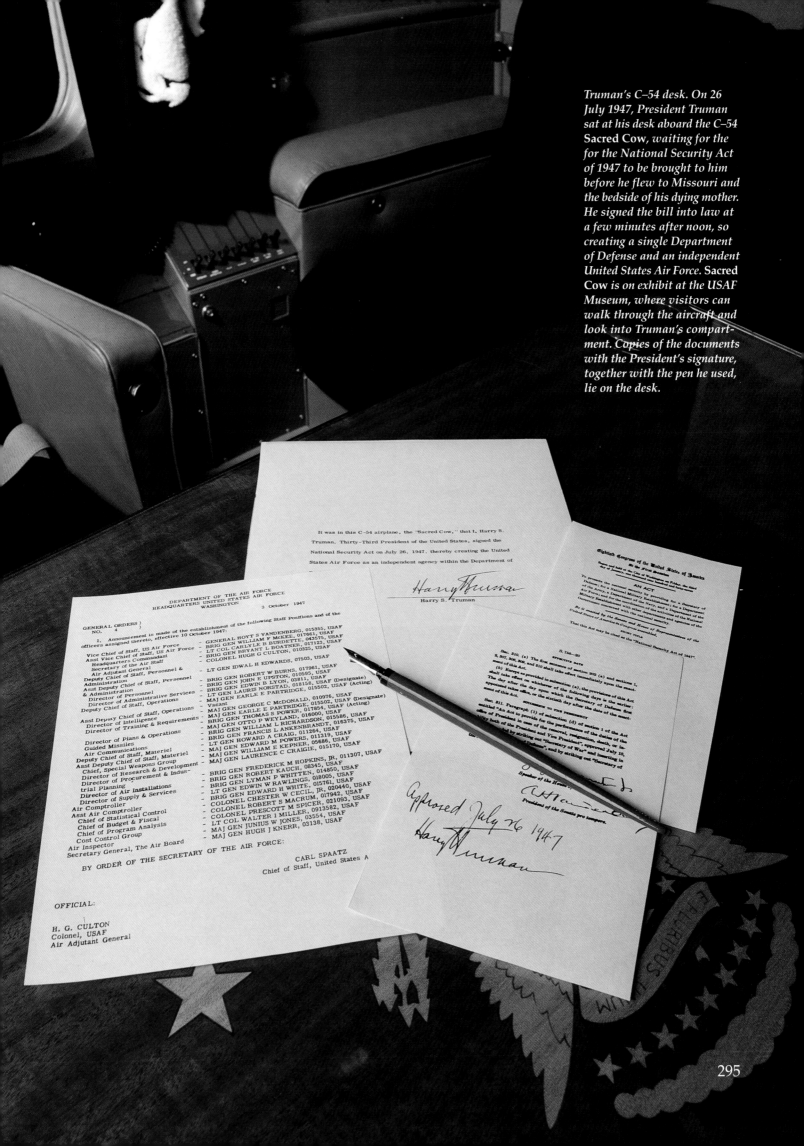

*Truman's C–54 desk. On 26 July 1947, President Truman sat at his desk aboard the C–54 **Sacred Cow**, waiting for the for the National Security Act of 1947 to be brought to him before he flew to Missouri and the bedside of his dying mother. He signed the bill into law at a few minutes after noon, so creating a single Department of Defense and an independent United States Air Force. **Sacred Cow** is on exhibit at the USAF Museum, where visitors can walk through the aircraft and look into Truman's compartment. Copies of the documents with the President's signature, together with the pen he used, lie on the desk.*

Stuart Symington and Carl Spaatz, the first leaders of their newly independent service seen together soon after Symington had been sworn in as the first Secretary of the Air Force on 18 September 1947. That day is recognized as the official birthday of the United States Air Force.

Billy Mitchell's vision had at last been given substance. The U.S. Air Force was legally an independent service, officially tasked with performing a number of functions for the nation—gaining and maintaining general air supremacy, establishing local air superiority, operating strategic air forces, supporting land and naval forces, supplying airlift for airborne operations, and providing air transport generally for the armed services. Consummating the act was the formal appointment of officials—Stuart Symington as the first Secretary of the Air Force, and General Carl Spaatz as

the new service's first Chief of Staff. Symington was sworn in on 18 September 1947 and that date was established as the official birthday of the United States Air Force.

Jet Turbulence

If the size, shape, and structure of the USAF as a whole were adapting to the march of organizational evolution, what was beginning to happen on air force bases was closer to revolution. In the late 1940s the familiar sights, sounds, and smells of hangars

P–59. America's first jet aircraft, the Bell P–59 Airacomet was not good enough to be a front-line fighter, but it was a useful introduction to the jet age. The aircraft illustrated had shorter wings and fins than earlier models and was one of 30 P–59Bs built.

P–59 in flight. This head-on view of the P–59 shows how the engines were buried in the wing roots and suggests a small frontal area and clean lines. However, the wings are quite thick, and the picture reveals neither the aircraft's considerable weight nor the limitations of its first generation jet engines.

P–59 jet pipes. The combined thrust emerging from the P–59's jet pipes at full throttle was no more than 3,300 pounds, but it was sufficient to push the straight-winged Airacomet along at a maximum speed of 410 miles per hour at 30,000 feet. (In 1944 the Me 262 was achieving well over 500 miles per hour at any height above 20,000 feet.)

P–59 nose. On 1 October 1942 the Bell P–59 Airacomet became the first American jet aircraft to fly. It was powered by two General Electric I–16 (J31) engines constructed from designs by the British jet pioneer, Frank Whittle. Since each engine produced only 1,650 pounds of thrust, the conventionally-shaped P–59 was not a spectacular performer. Nevertheless, it paved the way to the jet age in the United States and provided the foundation of experience on which more dramatic advances developed.

and flight lines began to change dramatically. Jet engines had arrived and they had their effects in varying degrees on everything the USAF did. Operational and training concepts, engineering practices, logistics, equipment design, and other administrative functions were remolded by the hot breath of jet propulsion. Pilots had to adjust their mental gears to take account of aircraft that flew faster and higher than their piston-engined predecessors, and guzzled fuel at frightening rates, especially at low level.

American interest in developing a jet aircraft began before the United States entered World War II. In September 1941 the U.S. Army Air Forces asked Bell Aircraft to design a jet fighter. Just one year later, the XP–59A was ready to fly. It was a large aircraft weighing over 13,000 pounds and was powered by

F–80. The first U.S. Air Force aircraft to exceed 500 miles per hour in level flight and, in the Korean War, the first to see combat was the Lockheed F–80 Shooting Star. On 8 Nov 1950 Lieutenant Russell Brown, flying an F–80C, shot down a Soviet MiG–15 in the world's first all-jet air battle. The F–80C on display at the USAF Museum flew combat missions in Korea with the 35th Fighter-Bomber Squadron, 8th Fighter-Bomber Group.

F–80 intake. As can be seen from the warning sign, the exterior of the F–80's sculpted intake was delicate. A custom-made ladder was provided to allow heavy booted pilots to reach the cockpit.

298

P–59 cockpit—seemingly almost as conventional as the airframe. However, the throttle lever needed very careful handling. First generation jet engines were intolerant of rapid throttle movements.

two General Electric-built Whittle engines of a modest 1,100 pounds of thrust each. It was not the answer to a fighter pilot's dream. Production variants, delivered from August 1944 onward, had General Electric engines of 2,000 pounds of thrust, but they were never lively performers. Nevertheless, the P–59 opened the door to the jet age for the USAF, imparting many useful lessons. Much better aircraft were not far behind.

Among the earliest was one from "Kelly" Johnson and his design team at Lockheed. They had toyed with the idea of a jet aircraft in 1939 but had abandoned it for lack of an engine and in the face of bureaucratic indifference. In 1943 the USAAF asked them to try again, replacing indifference with urgency and stipulating a time limit of 180 days between request and first flight. Lockheed had the XP–80 ready in 143 days. It first flew on 8 January 1944 and inspired enthusiasm from the start. It was a delight to fly and, even though powered by a de Havilland engine of only 2,460 pounds of thrust, it was capable of exceeding 500 miles per hour. Production P–80s were larger and heavier but also stronger and faster. In April 1944 the USAAF placed orders for 1,000 P–80As, and 4 reached Europe before World War II was over, but

Lockheed's P–80A Shooting Star, the first jet fighter ordered in large numbers by the U.S. Army Air Forces. Deliveries of 677 P–80As began in December 1945.

F–80 cockpit. Befitting an operational aircraft, the F–80's cockpit was more complex and well organized than that of the earlier P–59. Note the ejection seat handle at lower left and the pad on the gunsight, placed there in the hope of protecting pilots' good looks during accidents.

T–33 cockpit. The T–33A Shooting Star advanced trainer had, by a little over three feet, a longer fuselage than the aircraft from which it was derived—the P–80. The two cockpits were arranged in tandem and covered by a long, very heavy single-piece canopy, hinged at the rear to ensure clean separation if it was jettisoned. The ejection seats protruded well above the cockpit rails. Warning signs left no doubt that explosive seats should be treated with respect.

F–89 cockpit—well-ordered compared with that of the F–94. The radar scope has been assimilated into the layout and flight and engine instruments are in their proper places. Note the comprehensive warning signs drawing attention to the horrors of explosive seats and high pressure pistons.

too late to see any action. Lockheed's basic design would prove one of the most enduring of the jet age. The two-seat T–33 version, universally known as the T-Bird, became the world's best known jet trainer and was still in service with more than a dozen air forces more than 50 years after the XP–80 first flew.

Few early bids in the jet race were nearly so successful as the P–80 and its offspring. Jet engines with limited thrust were often married with airframes from the piston-engined era and performed disappointingly. Bomber designs like the XB–46 and XB–48 were essentially conventional aircraft hung with jet engines. So was the North American B–45, which the USAF ordered into production as an interim measure. Orthodox airframes persisted in the fighter world, too. Republic produced the F–84 Thunderjet, a tough and reliable single-seater which later led to greater things, and Northrop followed up the successful P–61 with the F–89 Scorpion, another large, heavily armed night fighter with a shape seemingly made to encourage drag.[2]

The jet engine, while full of promise, was beset by a host of aerodynamic problems, some answers to which were already on the way. Among the most important were those revealed at the end of World War II when the results of research done by German aerodynamicists and engineers fell into the hands of the Allies. Particularly significant was the use of swept wings to delay and diminish compressibility drag. Designers at Boeing and North American were the first to bring the fruits of these discoveries into service with the Air Force. Both companies had been working on jet designs with straight wings, but moved quickly to incorporate sweepback. The results were Boeing's B–47 Stratojet and North American's F–86 Sabre, two of the best military aircraft ever built.

The modernization and reorganization of the USAF in the post-war period made little impact on the general public. With the war won, the average American was content to let someone else worry about military affairs. Only days after the USAF became independent, however, an event occurred that excited public interest and pride in the accomplishments of America's professional military airmen. It was the first major achievement of the new service and it could hardly have been more auspicious for the future.

Brittle Barrier

During World War II, high performance piston-engined aircraft, like the P–51 and the Spitfire, sometimes reached very high speeds in dives and their pilots then encountered severe buffeting and control problems. To explore the unknown aerodynamic territory close to the speed of sound where these phenomena occurred,

F–89. Northrop's F–89 Scorpion was not the prettiest aircraft ever built. Its bulky airframe could reach maximum weights of over 45,000 pounds, a startling amount even for an all-weather interceptor in the 1950s. However, two Allison J35 engines offering 7,200 pounds of thrust in afterburner could coax the F–89 to 45,000 feet or better. Several variants were equipped with nuclear-tipped Genie missiles and were thus formidable propositions for any aircraft attempting to penetrate American airspace with evil intent. The USAF Museum's F–89J is marked as an aircraft of the 449th Fighter-Interceptor Squadron, Ladd Air Force Base, Alaska.

"Chuck" Yeager and the Bell X–1. On 14 October 1947, Chuck Yeager became the first man to fly faster than sound. His rocket-powered Bell X–1, Glamorous Glennis, *reached Mach 1.06 at 43,000 feet after being launched from a B–29 mother-ship.*

Bell Aircraft developed the X–1, a small, bullet-shaped aircraft with thin, straight, laminar-flow wings. It was powered by a four-chamber liquid-fuel rocket motor, whose maximum thrust was 6,000 pounds with all four chambers burning. Its four tons of fuel disappeared in only two and a half minutes. The X–1 was carried aloft in the belly of a B–29 and launched into free flight at 20,000 feet or higher. It was thus able to get the most out of each flight.

A Bell company test pilot conducted the X–1's initial proving flights but when the aircraft had performed satisfactorily up to Mach 0.8, the USAF took over the program. The pilot selected to fly the X–1 into unknown regions was Captain "Chuck" Yeager, a man who had already built himself a considerable reputation with the P–51 in Europe.[3] On 14 October 1947 the X–1 was dropped from a B–29 over the California desert and Yeager fired up all four rocket

chambers to climb away. At 36,000 feet he switched two chambers off again. The following is his description of what happened next:

> Leveling off at 42,000 feet, I had 30 per cent of my fuel, so I turned on rocket chamber three and immediately reached .96 Mach. I noticed that the faster I got, the smoother the ride. Suddenly the Mach needle began to fluctuate. It went up to .965 Mach, then tipped right off the scale…. We were flying supersonic!

For being the first man to fly faster than sound Chuck Yeager won both the Mackay and Collier Trophies. He had confirmed that the "sound barrier" was no barrier at all, and he pointed the way for whole families of aircraft to follow the X–1 and make supersonic flight an everyday occurrence. For the USAF it was an inspiring start to life as an independent service.

Operation VITTLES

In the wider world, where the services functioned as instruments of international politics, the USAF's post-war decline was causing its leaders concern. Implicit in the Truman Doctrine was the need for an air force that could project power globally, but at the moment of its birth in 1947 the USAF's ability to do so was severely limited. Strategic deterrence of Soviet expansionist ambitions seemed to depend solely on America's nuclear monopoly and on the B–29 as a means of delivering a nuclear weapon. Respecting the weight of such a big stick, the Soviet Union chose to challenge the Western nations in ways that emphasized its strengths and minimized the risk of America's nuclear threat. In February 1947 Czechoslovakia's government was overthrown in a communist coup and the country became a Soviet satellite. A month later the Soviet Union raised the stakes in Berlin. By so doing, it ensured that the USAF's

first operational test would not feature its front-line fighters and bombers. The stars of this show were to be haulers of food and fuel.

Berlin, the pre-war German capital, was deep inside the Soviet zone of occupation in Germany from 1945 on. Itself divided into Soviet, American, British, and French zones, Berlin was connected to the West by a number of air and surface corridors over and through Soviet-held territory. The Soviets refused to cooperate with the Western Allies in encouraging Germany's economic revival. The Western Allies thus decided to proceed with proposals affecting only their occupation zones. In March 1948, angered by what they saw as an attempt to build up West Germany into a resurgent threat against them, the Soviets began harassing Allied road and rail traffic into Berlin, causing all surface deliveries to cease entirely by 24 June. On that day the Allies received a teletyped message from the Soviet zone which read: "The

"Yeager's Quest," Stan Stokes, 1947, USAF Art Collection.

Transport Division of the Soviet Military Administration is compelled to halt all passenger and freight traffic to and from Berlin tomorrow at 0600 hours because of technical difficulties."

Since blocking surface routes was a simple matter, and forcing the issue on the ground was likely to be unacceptably dangerous, the Allies were left with two alternatives—withdrawing from Berlin or supplying it by air. They had never contemplated an airlift on the required scale before. They doubted that West Berlin, with a population of nearly two and a half million, could be sustained by aircraft alone. The Allies estimated that once the city's reserves had been depleted, they would have to supply about 4,500 tons of essentials per day, a figure that included not only food, but also large quantities of fuel, much of it coal.

The USAFE commander in 1948 was Major General Curtis LeMay. Soon after the Soviet blockade began, he was called by the American Military Governor in Germany, General Lucius Clay, and asked a simple question: "Curt, can you transport coal by air?" Understandably confused, LeMay asked for the question to be repeated. His answer was confident, if a little sweeping: "Sir, the Air Force can deliver anything!"

Scraping together every aircraft he could lay his hands on, LeMay managed to have 80 tons of supplies flown into Berlin on 26 June. It was a pitifully small amount compared with the requirement, but it was a start. The Allies did not have many aircraft immediately on hand. LeMay had about 100 C–47s and a couple of C–54s. The Royal Air Force (RAF) had a few more Dakotas (C–47s). Berlin needed the equivalent of 1,500 C–47 sorties per day. Even if it got that many, it had only two airfields available—Tempelhof in the American zone and Gatow in the British zone. Its task seemed almost impossible, but by mid-July LeMay's transport force had increased to 54 C–54s and 105 C–47s with a daily lift of 1,500 tons. RAF Yorks and Dakotas added 750 more tons. The force was a long way from meeting the long-term need, but it was improving steadily, and it had certainly irritated the Soviets, who encouraged their fighter pilots to "buzz" Allied aircraft following the air corridors in and out of the city.

The Western Allies determined to meet the Soviet challenge and the USAF reacted strongly. General Hoyt Vandenberg, who had taken over as Air Force Chief of Staff on 30 April, deployed three B–29 groups to the United Kingdom to send the Soviets an unmistakable message. He followed up by ordering F–80s to Germany from bases in the United States and the Canal Zone. On 23 July the Military Air

General Curtis LeMay in typical cigar-chewing pose at Tempelhof, Berlin, 1948. Commander of USAFE when the Soviets blockaded Berlin, he initiated the airlift that saved the city.

Transport Service detached eight squadrons of C–54s (72 aircraft with three crews apiece) to join the airlift. Aircraft flew in from as far away as Guam and Alaska. To ensure that the growing number of transports was used as effectively as possible, the USAF formed an Airlift Task Force, which at the end of July, came under command of Major General William Tunner, a veteran of the Hump airlift into China. By October Tunner was running a Combined Airlift Task Force, which merged American (U.S. Air Force and two squadrons of U.S. Navy R5Ds) and British efforts.

To get the most out of his resources, Tunner standardized everything—training, crew briefing, in-flight procedures, ground handling, aircraft maintenance, loading, and unloading. What he called "a real cowboy operation" was turned into an endless conveyor belt of aircraft delivering supplies with metronomic efficiency. Besides improving the organization, Tunner also pressed for bigger aircraft. He got the C–47s replaced as rapidly as possible by larger-capacity C–54s, an average of 300 of which became the airlift's front line. Usually around 225 were available to fly, while another 75 underwent maintenance. The British had more than 100 aircraft in operation on any given day.

The airlifters became specialized, the USAF concentrating on coal and the British on liquid fuels.

Flights inbound to Berlin entered the air corridors 3 minutes apart, 24 hours a day, maintaining precise heights and speeds from one radio beacon to the next. Interspersing arrivals with departures, an aircraft moved every 90 seconds of the day or night from both Gatow and Tempelhof. Careful planning and accurate flying were essential. Aircraft that missed an approach, which they occasionally did in bad weather, were not permitted a second try. They were committed to taking their cargo back to base. Once landed and parked on the ramp in Berlin, aircrews stayed with their aircraft. They were briefed for the return flight while their aircraft were unloaded, keeping the average turnaround time to 30 minutes.[4]

Aircrews exercised tight control of their aircraft both in the air and on the ground. As check pilots ensured adherence to procedures, ground controlled approach operators monitored aircraft separation, "Follow Me" jeeps marshaled arrivals after landing and operations officers allocated slots for each flight.

A meticulous program of aircraft maintenance was vital to the continued success of the airlift. The C–54 had been designed by Douglas as the DC–4, an airliner intended to fly for long periods at cruising power and to land at relatively light weights. On the airlift, they were operating overloaded, flying short legs and, therefore, spending more time each day at takeoff power. They carried such difficult cargos as coal or salt, which spread corrosive particles into every corner, and landed at well over their designed

C–54s unloading. Almost two-thirds of the cargo carried during the Berlin Airlift was coal. A C–54 carried over six tons of coal, but an energetic team could unload the aircraft in under six minutes.

C–54s at Tempelhof. By mid-winter 1948–1949, the Allied airlift into Berlin had reached a daily total of 5,500 tons. As many as 300 C–54s formed the backbone of the relentless delivery schedule, night and day, in all weather.

weight. Engines, brakes, and tires suffered excessive wear and tear. Ground crews worked wonders to keep their aircraft on the line, and ex-Luftwaffe mechanics, so recently the enemy, were hired to help out. Besides normal servicing, one of the more onerous jobs done at base was aircraft cleaning with brooms and mops to keep the grit down as much as possible. Bearing the residual scars and grime of their unexpected calling, the C–54s were withdrawn to the United Kingdom for major inspections every 200 flying hours. At 1,000 hours they went back to the United States for a complete overhaul.

With growing confidence and experience, airlift aircrews went on without pause throughout the winter of 1948–1949. The daily tonnages they delivered rose above the 4,500 originally estimated in September 1948. A third airport, at Tegel, became usable in December, and by January 1949, the daily figure was averaging more than 5,500 tons; in May it reached over 8,000. On one spectacular day of deliveries, 15 April 1949 (known thereafter as the Easter Parade), 1,398 aircraft landed in Berlin and off-loaded 12,941 tons of supplies.

Impressive as the Berlin airlift was, it contained a smaller, unofficial activity, known as Operation LITTLE VITTLES, which generated almost as much publicity and at least as much affection. C–54 pilot Lieutenant Gail Halvorsen sympathized with Berlin's children and brought them candy whenever he could. There were always a few children watching the aircraft on the approach to Tempelhof, and it occurred to him that he could drop them candy as he flew by. He and his crew chief made small parachutes from handkerchiefs, hung candy beneath them, and began throwing them out his aircraft's cargo door on finals. The small groups of children soon grew into crowds and Operation LITTLE VITTLES made news. People in the United States contributed handkerchiefs; American servicemen gave candy; and safety equipment personnel cut time-expired parachutes into smaller editions. The operation was both a great kindness and a public relations success. Bringing a much-loved and light-hearted touch to a serious business, it was watched with despair by the Soviets. If the Americans could take the time to think about throwing candy to kids, were they likely to find it difficult to keep the airlift going?

Several relics of the Berlin Airlift at the USAF Museum—coal and flour sacks, bags of beans, and packets of dehydrated POM (potatoes one minute).

"C–54s on Ramp at Tempelhof Airport," Randolph Advertising Art, 1948, USAF Art Collection.

On 12 May 1949, the Soviets called it a day and lifted the blockade. The Allies continued the airlift until 30 September to help build up Berlin's stocks against possible future emergencies. On that day, a USAF C–54 completed the last of the 277,804 flights which comprised the airlift. In all, the Allies flew 2,325,000 tons of supplies into Berlin, or almost exactly one ton per inhabitant. Over 1,783,000 tons of the total were lifted by American aircraft, no less than one and a half million tons of which was coal. Given the intensity of the operation, accidents were almost inevitable, and there were losses. The USAF lost four C–47s and six C–54s; the USN lost one R5D; and the British lost another nine transports. However, the Soviets had been made to back down and had been given a graphic illustration of Allied resolve and capability. The losses were sad, but relative to the immense total of sorties flown they were a small price to pay for such a triumph.

In monetary terms, the Berlin airlift had given extremely good value. For $200 million the opposition had been seen off and the USAF had gained immeasurably in experience and from lessons learned. Interservice and international teamwork could not have been better. The Allies had tried and proved the feasibility of extended and intensive transport operations by day and night in all weather. They had developed air traffic and freight handling procedures to new levels of excellence. Aircrews had become expert flying accurately on instruments for long periods and had come to trust the guidance of radio aids and approach controllers. Major General Tunner had his enthusiasm for large aircraft reinforced. As he pointed out, a daily lift total of 4,500 tons into Berlin would have required a fleet of almost 500 C–47s flying three sorties per day. About 180 C–54s had done the same job, with others adding a bonus. If C–74s (later C–124s) had been available, only 68 could have handled the same lift for fewer flights, fewer men, less maintenance, and a cheaper, less hazardous operation. For their part, the Soviets had learned that the West was prepared to be stubborn in Europe. It seemed that communism would have to try elsewhere. It was not long before it did just that.

Confronting the Bear

The continued intransigence of the Soviets and their openly threatening behavior in Czechoslovakia and Berlin alerted the Western powers to the marked disparity in conventional military capability that had arisen in Europe since the end of World War II. The Soviet Army had, if anything, increased in strength, while the West had effectively disarmed. The only clear Western advantage lay in American nuclear weapons and it was by no means certain that they would be enough to deter a westward march of Soviet influence, either through political blackmail or direct military action. To counter the threat and provide a mutual support system within which individual nations might build prosperous democratic societies, the Allies formed the North Atlantic Treaty Organization (NATO) in 1949. Twelve Western nations agreed to develop their capacity to defend themselves and to regard an attack on one as an attack on all. There was no doubt, particularly in 1949, that the alliance depended heavily on American military power, and that the USAF was a vital element of that power. The problem was that the USAF was "but a shadow of its former self," the USAAF.

Of the combat commands, TAC suffered most from the post-war shortage of funds. By 1949 TAC had withered to a small planning headquarters under Continental Air Command (CONAC), a new organization designed to absorb the sadly diminished rumps of ADC and TAC, allocating their resources to air defense or tactical missions as situations demanded. Those previously mighty tactical air forces, the Ninth and Twelfth, could muster only 11 groups between them. The first jet fighters, F–80s and F–84s, were starting to appear, and there were twin-boomed C–82s on the troop-carrier squadrons, but the USAF's tactical air strength was generally far below what was needed for an air force with global responsibilities.

ADC was hardly any better off than TAC. The knowledge that the Soviet Union possessed a B–29 look-alike in the Tu–4, which could at least make one way attacks on the United States, concerned USAF leaders and led them to seek funds for the construction of a North American early warning radar system. By 1949 Congress had authorized only an interim measure (known as Lashup), but the fact was that the United States was practically defenseless against air attack. Radar coverage was almost non-existent, and available fighters were inadequate for maintaining a day and night continental air defense. The piston-engined F–82 Twin Mustang, armed with .5-inch machine guns, served on night fighter squadrons until well into the 1950s.

SAC of all the commands had benefitted from the allocation of the USAF's scarce funds, and by 1949 changes and improvements that those funds had permitted were beginning to show. Perhaps the most notable of these came in the person of General Curtis LeMay, who assumed command of SAC in October 1948. In the course of a remarkable nine-year tenure, LeMay imposed his steely will to a degree rarely equalled in military history and built SAC into an awesome instrument of war, the annihilating weapon he believed a strategic striking force should be. When he took over, he was appalled by the command's lack of strategic capability and poor performance standards. He took an early opportunity to administer a sharp shock and ordered a bombing exercise at altitudes vastly greater than SAC crews were used to. The results were, as he expected, abysmal. His remarks to commanders were typically blunt: "What a sorry operation. I've been telling you we were in bad shape. We *are* in bad shape. Now let's get busy and get this fixed."

LeMay began by establishing the highest possible performance standards for every aspect of life in SAC. He was an unforgiving master and a relentless perfectionist, demanding only the best from aircrews, maintenance men, administrators, and everyone else. It was clear, however, that he demanded the best *for* them, too. Better aircraft began to arrive and the living standards on SAC bases soon became the envy of the rest of the service. Under the driving impulse of LeMay's personality, SAC grew steadily in power and in self respect.

If LeMay needed added fuel to stoke the fires of SAC's expansion, it came in August 1949, when the Soviet Union detonated its first atomic bomb. The short-lived American nuclear monopoly was broken and SAC's significance as an element of national security surged overnight. At this stage, its position as the nation's primary strategic military instrument was still a matter of ardent discussion and debate, which had intensified in 1948. In the competition for limited funds, the USN and the USAF argued over the respective merits of carrier task forces and long-range bombers for conducting strategic air operations. Meetings held by the Secretary of Defense, James Forrestal, at Key West, Florida, and Newport, Rhode Island, led to formal allocations of primary responsibility for strategic air warfare to the USAF and for control of the seas to the USN. The overall military requirement for procuring both aircraft carriers and large aircraft from the funds available, however, necessarily affected the USAF's long-term plans for building to seventy groups. By 1949

President Truman's proposed defense budget contained provision for only 48 groups.

Well aware of the running controversy over funds and missions, Forrestal's successor as Secretary of Defense, Louis Johnson, ordered a review of major programs. It led Congress to cancel the USN's proposed supecarrier during 1949. It further led Congress to hold hearings on the USAF's new bomber, the Convair B–36. In testimony, those who favored the funding of the supercarrier questioned the B–36's ability to carry out its strategic mission, likened it to an expensive obsession that was having a damaging effect on the USAF's other roles, and suggested that there had been corruption in the aircraft's selection process. Beyond that, in debating the aircraft's merits, they broadened their criticism into an indictment of the USAF's strategic bombing doctrine as a whole. When the dust had settled, the USAF had successfully defended both its procurement of the B–36 and its doctrine, and naval leaders had to accept that long-range bombers

B–36. The last version of SAC's first global bomber, the Convair B–36J was originally conceived during World War II for trans-Atlantic attacks on Germany should they become necessary. At the outset of the Cold War the B–36 was the only American combat aircraft capable of reaching Soviet targets from American bases.

were going to take a large share of the defense budget in the years ahead.

The B–36, impressive as it might be, was a holdover from World War II. It had been planned originally to attack Germany from the United States in the event that Britain was overrun by the Nazis. It operated over a 5,000-mile radius of action carrying a 10,000-pound bombload. Since it did not fly until 1946 and was not in regular squadron service until 1948, its intended purpose was overtaken by events, but, with the onset of the Cold War, it was the only aircraft capable of reaching strategic targets in the Soviet Union from American bases. It was gigantic, measuring 230 feet across the wing and weighed, with an eventual maximum load, 410,000 pounds (the B–36J). Its power came from six 3,500-horsepower Pratt & Whitney radial engines, later augmented by the addition of four General Electric jet engines of 5,200 pounds of thrust each. Over a radius of 2,300 miles, the B–36 could deliver the incredible total of 72,000 pounds of bombs—far more than the B–17.[5]

Such startling figures aside, however, the B–36 was something of a dinosaur. Although it was heavily armed with multiple cannon in turrets, such a lumbering monster could hardly have penetrated Soviet airspace with impunity; fighters could hardly have escorted it on intercontinental missions. Only the capacity to deliver nuclear weapons made it a credible threat. The USAF did attempt to provide an escort by hanging one on the B–36 itself. The McDonnell XF–85 Goblin was a tiny parasite fighter designed to be carried in one of the B–36's bomb-bays and released when needed. The XF–85's instability and limited endurance doomed the project, although a few reconnaissance versions of the B–36 (GRB–36F) later succeeded in operating for a while with RF–84Ks carried in a cradle. Staying in international airspace, the aircraft launched the RF–84K on a high-speed dash mission and then retrieved it for the ride home.

By the end of 1949 there were three heavy bombardment wings of B–36s in service. Their arrival had demoted the existing B–29s to the medium bomber category, where they were joined by newly delivered B–50s, essentially greatly improved B–29s. There were 11 B–29/50 wings, plus 2 fighter and 3 reconnaissance wings. SAC organized these assets into three numbered air forces—the Eighth (heavy-medium bombers); the Fifteenth (medium bombers); and the Second (reconnaissance). With well over 1,000 aircraft, SAC set about making itself into a strategic force to be reckoned with, working on professionalism and readiness, and looking for ways to improve its global reach.

Overseas bases in the United Kingdom and Greenland began the process of constructing a worldwide network, and, in a return to ideas pioneered for DH–4s in 1923, SAC undertook to make all of its bombers capable of in-flight refueling. In an early demonstration of this force-multiplying technique, the B–50A *Lucky Lady II* remained airborne for 94 hours between 26 February and 2 March 1949, covering almost 24,000 miles and completing the first non-stop flight around the world. It was refueled four times from B–29 tankers based in the Azores, Saudi Arabia, the Philippines, and Hawaii. With the passage of time, in-flight refueling would become ever more important to USAF operations, and the tanker force would grow to impressive proportions, employing, at first, only flexible hose systems but soon moving to the more efficient Boeing flying boom system. With tankers, SAC could reach targets anywhere in the world.

As the USAF prepared itself for the long confrontation of the Cold War, it was changing in several ways. President Truman's Executive Order 9981 of 26 July 1948 attacked discrimination and fostered the principle of equal opportunity in the armed services. The USAF had already conducted some studies on the problem, but it was still a segregated service in 1948. The USAAF had deactivated the celebrated 332nd Fighter Group at the end of World War II, but it had retained the 99th Fighter Squadron and assigned it to the 477th Composite Group at Lockbourne, Ohio, equipped with B–25s and P–47s. Later, this all-black unit lost its B–25s and regained its number as the 332nd Fighter Wing. Following the President's order, the USAF led the way in writing an integration plan and was the first of the armed services to issue revised rules and procedures for training, employing, and accommodating personnel. Air Force Letter 35–3 of 11 May 1949 set out the new policy and included the sentence: "It is the policy of the United States Air Force that there shall be equality of treatment and opportunity in the Air Force without regard to race, color, religion, or national origin." Just three weeks later, on 1 June 1949, the 332nd Fighter Wing was disbanded and its personnel reassigned to a variety of units throughout the Air Force.

Almost as significant was the USAF's step to most visually symbolize its separation from its parent service. On 25 January 1949 it said an official goodbye to its Army uniform. From then on, Air Force blue would be the dress of the day. On 2 June there was a powerfully symbolic gesture of another kind. President

F–82s and F–80Cs sharing the ramp at Itazuki, Japan. The first American fighters to see action in Korea, on 27 June 1950, just two days after the communist invasion of South Korea began, both types were involved in air battles with the North Korean Air Force. Three Yak–9s and four IL–10s were destroyed without loss to the U.S. Air Force.

Truman recognized Hap Arnold's achievements as "Father of the Air Force" by awarding him the permanent rank of General of the Air Force. It was just reward for a man who, more than any other living, embodied American military aviation. Six months later, the only USAF officer ever raised to five star rank was dead. General Arnold died of a heart attack in Sonoma, California, on 15 January 1950.

Surprise Attack
In the closing days of World War II, Soviet forces invaded Korea and accepted the surrender of the Japanese in the northern half of the country. Ignoring prior agreements with the Allies, the Soviets refused to allow the North to take part in the free elections of 1948. Instead, they created the Peoples' Democratic Republic of Korea, dividing the country into two states at the 38th parallel. It was across this arbitrary partition that communism next chose to challenge democracy. At first light on 25 June 1950, in the wake of several border incidents, North Korean armed forces swept across the frontier, intent on conquering the South and reuniting Korea under a communist government.

The attack achieved complete strategic and tactical surprise. Ten communist divisions, with ample armor and artillery, brushed aside the inadequately armed Republic of Korea (ROK) Army and raced

southward. During these early hours of the war, the North Korean Air Force (NKAF) was active and effective. It operated almost 200 aircraft, mostly Russian of World War II vintage, including 70 Yak–9 fighters and 62 IL–10 ground attack bombers. Unimpressive by Western standards, the NKAF's inventory was formidable compared to the ROK's—a pitifully few T–6 trainers.

The United States led the world's response to North Korea's incursion. Reacting to pleas for help from South Korea, President Truman pledged support, and the United States took the matter to the Security Council of the United Nations (UN). In the fortuitous absence of the Soviet Union, whose delegation was boycotting the Security Council at the time, member nations voted to support the South against the aggression of the North. Member nations were encouraged to "render such assistance to the Republic of Korea as may be necessary to repel the armed attack...." General MacArthur was appointed Supreme Commander, Allied Powers, and the United States set about rallying democratic nations to the flag.

As a first step, MacArthur was instructed to ensure the evacuation of American citizens from Korea, covering it with fighter aircraft flying from bases in Japan. Once again, American transport aircraft were to lead the charge in meeting an emergency. The first

MiG–15. In the Korean War, principal opposition in the air came in the shape of the MiG–15. Lighter and more maneuverable than the F–86, it was also more heavily armed with three cannon—two 23-mm and one 37-mm. It was powered by a 6,000-pound thrust centrifugal-flow engine copied from a Rolls-Royce Nene. The MiG–15 in the USAF Museum was flown to South Korea on 21 Sep 1953 by Lieutenant Kim Sok No, a defector from the North Korean Air Force.

MiG–15 cockpit. Despite its familiar look, the cockpit of the MiG–15 was different from those of its Western counterparts. Some instruments are marked in Russian, but a Chinese message written in red can be seen over the top of the stick. The English word fuel is taped to the gauge near the bottom of the stick, and an American G meter sits on top of the coaming, presumably added during trials by Western test pilots. The protective pad on the gunsight is a dome rather than a cushion.

F–51s. At the beginning of the Korean War, F–51s, overdue for retirement but better able to cope with the primitive conditions of Korean airfields in 1950, were hastily restored to front-line service. Two 18th Fighter Group F–80C squadrons transitioned back to the F–51. One of them was the 12th Fighter-Bomber Squadron at Chinhae, near Pusan, its Mustangs recognizable from their grinning sharks' mouths.

USAF aircraft lost in the Korean War was a C–54, strafed and burned by a Yak–9 on the first day at Seoul's airfield, Kimpo. On 27 June the NKAF hit Kimpo again, but this time it met F–82Gs from the 8th Fighter-Bomber Wing overhead. They destroyed three out of five Yak–9s, Lieutenant William Hudson of the 68th Fighter Squadron claiming the first American air victory. Later that day, eight IL–10s tried their luck and were met by F–80Cs of the 35th Fighter-Bomber Squadron. Four IL–10s were destroyed, and the rest fled. Although these encounters suggested the superiority of USAF aircrews and aircraft, the NKAF did pose a threat best countered at its source. On 30 June President Truman authorized the USAF to strike targets above the 38th parallel and, within a month, its attacks on airfields in the north by B–26s[6] and B–29s had helped to reduce the NKAF to a handful of aircraft and impotence.

With the USAF's easy establishment of air supremacy over the whole of Korea, Allied army commanders may have hoped that the situation there would come to resemble that in Western Europe after the Normandy invasion. If so, they were to be disappointed. The two conflicts were vastly different. Most significant was the fact that the resources committed to the Korean War were never on the unlimited scale of World War II, nor could they be used as unrestrainedly.

By the time of the D-Day landings in Normandy, the United States had been fighting an all-out war for over two years, committed to a maximum effort, its supplies of both men and material seemingly endless. It was virtually unrestricted by political or other considerations in the way it and the Allies fought the enemy and, whenever possible, it applied its massive force using the best available equipment. The United States and the Allies had achieved and maintained air supremacy over Western Europe. Free of effective opposition, the Allied air forces were able to inflict severe damage on German industry and to disrupt the sophisticated system of road and rail communications on which the enemy heavily depended.

In Korea, American forces went into action without preparation at a time when their military was at a low ebb, surviving on minimal funding and with its units often understrength and poorly equipped. Their condition would improve, but massive force, as it was understood in Europe, was never available. They achieved air supremacy over Korea at the outset but it would not last, even though the USAF was invariably able to gain local air superiority when necessary. What was perhaps most significant was that political restrictions seriously limited the way American forces fought the war, reducing the effectiveness of air strikes and offering the enemy safe

315

havens. Enemy industries supplying the war from outside Korea were permanently out of reach, and the effective interdiction of surface communications proved almost impossible, given the USAF's restrictions and the undeveloped nature of Korea. The enemy was always ready to use pack animals and manpower to keep supplies flowing over trails to the front. In short, the United States found itself involved in a limited war, a phenomenon that was to become disturbingly familiar as the twentieth century progressed.

Gaining air supremacy in the first month of the war was one thing; checking the onrushing North Korean Army was quite another. Neither the soldiers of the broken ROK Army nor the lightly equipped U.S. Army infantry units were capable of imposing anything more serious than temporary delays on their rampant opponents. By the end of July the Allies had been driven back into a small pocket no more than 70 miles across in any direction, centered on the port of Pusan. Here, General Walton Walker, U.S. 8th Army commander with responsibility for UN ground forces, took his stand, warning his troops: "There will be no more retreating, withdrawal, readjustment of lines or whatever you call it." Until early September the Allies hung on, enduring an almost endless series of crises as the North Koreans hurled themselves against the defenses of the Pusan perimeter. During the desperate weeks of August, American and ROK soldiers withstood numerous fierce assaults, buying time for reinforcements and supplies to build up through Pusan. At times, the North Koreans broke through the lines, but were stopped by judiciously used reserves and air power. On 3 September Major General William Kean of the 25th Division reported: "The close air support strikes rendered by the Fifth Air Force again saved this Division, as they have many times before."

At the heart of the Allied air effort in Korea was the USAF's Far East Air Force, commanded by Lieutenant General George Stratemeyer. The largest of its subordinate commands was the Fifth Air Force, described by its commander, Lieutenant General Earle Partridge, as "a small but highly professional tactical-type air force." It comprised three F–80C wings, one understrength light bombardment wing of B–26s, and two all-weather fighter squadrons with F–82s. One wing of FEAF B–29s was drawn from the Twentieth Air Force in Okinawa, and a further two wings were detached from Strategic Air Command. The three B–29 wings formed FEAF Bomber Command under Major General Emmett O'Donnell.

Initially, the F–80Cs were something of a problem. Their combat radius was limited and there were no airfields in Korea capable of handling jets. Thus, many F–80 pilots found themselves reconverting to F–51s taken from storage. The Mustangs could be based in South Korea, had the endurance to fly extended armed reconnaissance sorties, and could carry bombs and napalm, which the F–80Cs could not. At a time when the ground forces were so hard pressed and close air support was vital, the "born-again" F–51s proved invaluable, repeatedly blunting enemy thrusts until Army reserves could be brought into action.

Throughout August the airmen's top priority was close support of the beleaguered Allied troops. They flew 7,397 close support sorties, compared to 2,963 interdiction, and 539 strategic bombing sorties. They sometimes used the B–29s against battlefield targets, counter to Stratemeyer's advice and with disappointing effect. For the most part, however, Bomber Command's B–29s pounded industrial and transportation targets north of Seoul, and did a good job. By September there was little left of the North's steel plants, oil depots, railway yards, and harbor facilities.

The Fifth Air Force tackled more difficult interdiction targets south of Seoul. It caught some enemy convoys in the open in daylight and dealt with them severely; however, after a few days the North Koreans learned to move at night. Thereafter, FEAF's lack of an adequate night tactical capability proved something of an embarrassment. The night intruder role fell to the B–26s, but they were far from ideal since they were not fitted with radar altimeters, short-range navigation radar, or blind-bombing radar. Nor were they particularly maneuverable, which was a distinct disadvantage for an aircraft that sometimes needed to operate at low level by night through Korea's rugged terrain. Although the B–26s tried to overcome their failings by operating in pairs, one aircraft dropping flares and the other strafing, they were not often successful. The enemy was too elusive in the darkness.

Interdiction of static targets by daylight was much more rewarding. By mid-September, FEAF claimed that, with the help of naval aircraft, its airmen had destroyed 140 bridges between Seoul and the Pusan perimeter and had made and maintained 47 cuts in rail lines. They had rendered another 93 bridges around Pusan unusable, and destroyed hundreds of locomotives, railway cars, and motor vehicles. Even so, they were never entirely able to stop the flow of North Korean supplies. Pack animals, including humans, helped to keep them trickling through. Nevertheless, it is clear that the interdiction campaign against the lengthening enemy logistic chain played

A C–119 of the 314th Troop Carrier Group dropping four tons of supplies to United Nations troops in Korea.

an important part in the eventual defeat of the North Korean offensive. Enemy records show that North Korean infantry divisions received 166 tons of ordnance between 25 June and 15 July, but only 17 tons from 16 August to 20 September. They also show that, at the same time, the average daily ration of a soldier fell from a mixed diet of 800 grams to 400 grams, almost all rice. It is significant that North Korean prisoners taken in September admitted that the morale of their units, extremely high at the start of the offensive, plummeted significantly. Their two greatest fears had been shortages of food and aircraft.

MacArthur Strikes Back

When it came, the collapse of the North Korean Army came rapidly. On 15 September General MacArthur loosed his master stroke, landing the 1st Marine Division at Inchon, close to Seoul and 150 miles behind the fighting around Pusan. Strongly supported by Allied carrier aircraft, the Marines advanced rapidly and within two days had recovered Kimpo airfield. The day after the Inchon landing, the 8th Army broke out of the Pusan pocket and drove north under a Fifth Air Force umbrella. No longer capable of withstanding American firepower and hounded from the air, the North Korean Army disintegrated and by the end of the month had been driven from South Korea.

MacArthur made it clear that he intended to seek the enemy army's final destruction by continuing to advance beyond the 38th parallel. He was quite sure that the risk of Chinese intervention was minimal. On 7 October 1950, the UN, buoyed by success, encouraged its General Assembly to approve a resolution that: "...all necessary steps be taken to ensure conditions of peace throughout the whole of Korea." Under this thin cloak of authority, UN troops set off for the Yalu River, the boundary between Korea and China.

If anything, Fifth Air Force support of UN soldiers was better than ever. With the utility of forward air controllers (FACs) on the ground limited by the terrain, North American T–6s drew an unexpected and often hazardous combat role, flying close to the battle lines with FACs on board. Known as mosquitoes, they kept in radio contact with both ground units and supporting fighters, marking targets with 2.75-inch rockets and controlling air attacks as necessary. Air transport came into its own, too, as C–119s and C–47s of General Tunner's new Combat Cargo Command dropped 2,860 paratroopers across enemy escape routes north of P'yongyang, in North Korea, in one of the most

Bombed up F–84Es of the 8th Fighter-Bomber Squadron on their way to a target in Korea.

effective paratroop operations ever carried out. It sealed the fate of the enemy forces leaving the city.

North Korean resistance quickly crumbled all along the front and, by the end of October, some UN units had reached the banks of the Yalu. MacArthur was triumphant, believing that the war would soon be over and that he had brought about the unification of Korea, giving the communists a bloody nose in the process. Such unbounded confidence was sharply checked in November, when the Chinese showed that they were not prepared to sit idly by while North Korea was forcibly gathered to the bosom of democracy.

Chinese Intervention

China, angered by this turn of events, intensified the heat of its anger against American forces toward the end of October. Its troops overran some forward positions and, on 1 November, shot down a patrolling F–80C with anti-aircraft guns, firing across the Yalu. Its MiG–15s began "trailing their coats" over North Korea and, on 8 November, in the world's first

all-jet combat, jumped F–80Cs of the 51st Fighter Interceptor Wing. In a brief exchange, the USAF scored first blood, Lieutenant Russell Brown shooting down one of the attackers. That early American success did not indicate relative capabilities, however. It was quickly apparent that F–80Cs were no match for MiG–15s. Designed with the benefit of German swept-wing aerodynamics and powered by a copy of a British jet engine, the MiG–15 was approximately 100 miles per hour faster than the F–80C, could climb to 50,000 feet, and was heavily armed with one 37-mm and two 23-mm cannon.

By the end of November Chinese ground forces, estimated at more than half a million men, had crossed the Yalu and thrown the UN forces into a disorderly retreat. Overwhelmed by sheer numbers, many units broke and ran under the shock of the massive Chinese assault. In the air, the UN air forces had nothing to match the MiG–15 and thus could not guarantee air supremacy close to the Yalu River. It was fortunate that during this period, as the USAF moved to meet the threat, the Chinese Air Force was not particularly aggressive.

By mid-December the arrival in Korea of the 4th Fighter-Interceptor Wing, equipped with North American F–86A Sabres, brought a measure of balance to the air war. A classic fighter, beloved by its pilots, the F–86 was not quite as good in the climb or at very high altitude as the lighter MiG–15, nor did its six .5-inch machine guns have the hitting power of its opponent's cannon, but it was just as fast and was more stable as a gun platform at higher speeds. It also had the advantage of being fitted with a radar-ranging gunsight. Just as important, the Sabre was a joy to fly and had no vices, whereas the MiG–15 had a tendency to flick savagely if driven too hard in high-G turns.

Another, less glamorous American jet arrived in Korea in December. The 27th Fighter Escort Group brought its F–84E Thunderjets to the war. The F–84 inspired more respect than affection in its pilots. It was a rugged, workmanlike machine, but it was underpowered for the fighter-bomber job it had to do and it was not very lively. Fully loaded with bombs, rockets, and fuel tanks, the F–84 weighed over ten tons. Its spidery, wide-stanced undercarriage had to

F–86A Sabres of the 4th Fighter-Interceptor Squadron arriving at Kimpo, South Korea, December 1950. The aircraft shown, gun panels open, is the mount of Glenn Eagleston, the 4th's commander in 1951, who went on to add two MiGs to his World War II total of 18.5 aerial victories.

cope with punishingly long takeoff runs on the rough airfields of Korea and the J35 engine of the earlier models was apt to shed turbine blades when shaken too hard. Nevertheless, for all its minor shortcomings, the F–84 proved a fearsome fighter-bomber and the champion hauler of bombs and napalm in the Korean War. For the hard pressed UN soldiers its heavy punch inspired every bit as much affection as respect.

It was not long before the new American arrivals were in action. On 17 December Lieutenant Colonel Bruce Hinton of the 4th Fighter-Interceptor Wing gained the first F–86 victory over a MiG–15, the first of four achieved by his unit that day. The welcome intervention of the F–86 in the air war was short-lived, however. The Chinese ground offensive forced the

UN armies back south of Seoul, thereby denying airfields to the F–86s, which retreated temporarily to the safety of Japan. With his demoralized troops facing an apparently inexhaustible Chinese Army, MacArthur suggested that Korea could not be held unless mainland China was attacked, and he advocated the use of nuclear weapons. During this unpromising phase of the war, the F–84s imposed themselves on the battle, hammering advancing Chinese troops incessantly and giving desperate units of the 8th Army the chance to escape destruction. In the eastern half of Korea, salvation for the Marines also came with wings—their own close air support aircraft and FEAF transports. Cargo aircraft kept the troops supplied during their fighting withdrawal from the Chosin

J33. Producing 4,600 pounds of thrust, the Allison J33 jet engine was used to power the Lockheed P–80 and T–33. It was directly descended from Frank Whittle's original centrifugal flow design.

F–86 cutaway. The dense construction of jet combat aircraft is demonstrated by the USAF Museum's F–86H Sabre, displayed without its skin and with its internal organs nakedly revealed. Among the most recognizable items are the H-model's 20-mm cannon and their ammunition bays. Compare these features with the emptiness of the SE–5 cutaway in Chapter 2.

"F-86 Sabre Dance," Harley Copic, 1986, USAF Art Collection.

Reservoir, flew out their wounded from hastily prepared landing strips, and dropped a 16-ton, 8-section Bailey bridge to aid their escape across a deep gorge. Eventually, the transports completed an aerial evacuation of over 4,000 men from the Hamhung area right under Chinese noses.

As the bleak winter days of January 1951 passed into history, UN ground forces' resistance stiffened under the inspiring new leadership of General Matthew Ridgway. By the middle of the month, facing a more determined foe and with extended supply lines relentlessly attended by Allied aircraft, the seemingly irresistible Chinese Army slowed to a halt. UN counterattacks recovered Seoul, and the F–86s were back in Korea by the end of February to resume their confrontation of the MiG–15s.

Although American pilots were probably better trained than their Chinese counterparts, they were still at a disadvantage operationally. Based near Seoul, their F–86s had to fly up to "MiG Alley"—the region of northwestern Korea between the Yalu and Ch'ongch'on Rivers—to meet their enemy. There they were close to their range limit and could not spend long in combat. They were forbidden to cross the Yalu into Manchuria. Their opponents, on the other hand, often operated within sight of their bases and could stay on their side of the Yalu until they chose to engage, timing their attacks to advantage. The F–86s were also heavily outnumbered. During 1951, the number of MiGs available rose to over 500, as opposed to 100 or so F–86s, although only about half of either force might be combat ready at any one time. The figures made little difference to the consistent

The North American F–86 Sabre was the U.S. Air Force's first swept-wing jet fighter. It was a delight to fly and could be supersonic in a dive. During the Korean War it was the only Allied fighter that met the MiG–15 on equal terms. The USAF Museum's F–86A bears the markings of the aircraft flown by Bruce Hinton of the 4th Fighter Group when, on 17 Dec 1950, he became the first F–86 pilot to shoot down a MiG.

F–86 cockpit. As in the typical 1950s jet fighter, the F–86's flight instruments in the center and to the left of the panel included, clockwise *from the vertical speed indicator in front of the stick on the bottom row:* turn and slip, altimeter, Mach meter (reading from 0.5 to 1.5), radio compass, airspeed, compass, and artificial horizon (with gyros toppled). The white handle to the right of the stick is an emergency hand-pump for the hydraulic system.

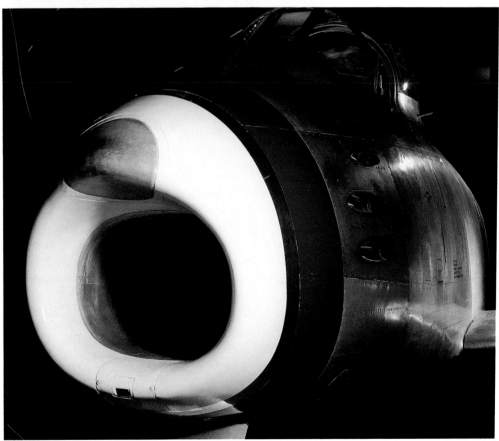

F–86 nose. The small beak over-hanging the engine intake on the F–86A housed the antenna for the radar gunsight. Six .50-caliber machine guns were mounted in the fuselage. A gun camera recorded the action through the small hole visible beneath the intake.

325

A MiG–15 shot down. Fast, maneuverable, and heavily armed, the MiG–15 nevertheless proved no match for the F–86 during the Korean War. One major reason for the claimed ten-to-one kill ratio in favor of the Sabre was the superior training of U.S. Air Force pilots.

combat superiority of the F–86. As the air superiority war resumed in 1951, the Sabres hit their stride, shooting down 3 MiGs in March and 14 in April. In May, Captain James Jabara became the first jet ace when he downed his fifth and sixth MiGs.[7] June saw the appearance in combat of Soviet instructors, but they had little effect on the trend. The Americans claimed 42 MiGs destroyed in the month for the loss of 3 F–86s.

The Chinese Army realized that it could not succeed against UN forces without effective air support. It set about preparing airfields in North Korea which would allow it to move fighters south of the Yalu. American reconnaissance aircraft kept an eye on the airfields until they neared completion in April 1951. The USAF then launched its B–29s on a series of raids against the Chinese that destroyed their airfield facilities and cratered their runways. The USAF repeated this exercise at intervals to such an extent that the Chinese never did succeed in operating MiGs regularly from North Korea. Important as this achievement of the B–29s was, it was not without cost. On 23 October 1951, for example, about 100 MiGs kept the escorts busy, while 50 more broke through to attack eight B–29s on

their way to bomb the airfields. Three of the bombers were shot down and the rest were so severely damaged that they never flew again.

The B–29s had experienced similar problems attempting to destroy the Yalu bridges earlier in the year. Heavy flak kept them above 20,000 feet and prohibitions against their entering Chinese airspace confined them to the river itself. Thus, their bombing runs, which became predictable, could target only the narrowest possible sites. MiGs made the B–29s' situation very much worse. On 12 April as many as 100 attacked all three bombardment groups sent against bridges at Sinuiju. They destroyed three B–29s and damaged seven.

Soon after the series of losses in October, the B–29s finally undertook only night operations to escape the attentions of the MiGs. The loss of the daylight option reduced their sortie rate and limited the weight of their effort against the Chinese transportation system. Restrictions of this kind, forced by enemy action, convinced the USAF that air supremacy was beyond its reach over North Korea.

A dramatic shot of an F–80C attacking North Korean positions at low level.

327

F–94. The Lockheed F–94 Starfires were essentially completely redesigned. The F–94C had a higher thrust engine (a Pratt & Whitney J48 engine giving 8,750 pounds of thrust with afterburner), redesigned wing, swept tail surfaces, radar, new fire control and navigation systems, and air-to-air rockets instead of guns. Some of the rockets were carried in wing pods, and 24 were mounted in a ring around the radome, protected until fired by retractable shields. The F–94 in the USAF Museum has the shield retracted to show the rocket tubes.

F–94 fin. A clue to the F–94C's increased power over that of the F–80 lies in the girth of their respective tail-pipes. The contrasting swept tailplane and upright fin are also evident, as are the markings of the 60th Fighter-Interceptor Squadron, Otis Air Force Base, in the 1950s.

F–94 cockpit. The arrival of a radar scope left the F–94 cockpit looking less well organized than many others. Two engine instruments are stranded at the top of the panel, randomly surrounded by assorted warning lights. The flight instruments are in anything but a standardized arrangement. Windscreen wiping and de-icing has been relegated to a spot near the floor. Note the red canopy rails; the F–94 canopy could crush careless fingers on closing.

Stalemate

On the ground, the war congealed into stalemate by mid-1951. Both sides, resigned to the fact that there could be no easy victory, considered armistice. After a false start in July at Kaesong, negotiations settled into a tedious and frustrating pattern at Panmunjom in October. The chief North Korean delegate, General Nam Il, paid the UN air forces a bitter tribute:

> Without the support of the indiscriminate bombing and bombardment of your air

and naval forces, your ground forces would have long ago been driven out of the Korean peninsula by our powerful and battle-skilled ground forces.

As negotiations assumed the character of a propaganda war and UN delegates found themselves embroiled in endless argument over minor details, the fighting continued.

Although the ground war had frozen into an almost static confrontation at about the 38th parallel, the aerial struggle carried on much as before. High on FEAF's list of priorities was the interdiction of the enemy's supply lines to prevent the Chinese Army from building up stocks for a future offensive. Efficiently done, interdiction might even force it to withdraw northward to shorten its logistics chain and put its front line within range of MiG–15 cover. Starting with Operation STRANGLE in May, and continuing with the Rail Interdiction Program, UN aircraft kept up a persistent day and night assault on roads and railways in North Korea throughout 1951. That the assault discomforted and inconvenienced the communist forces is certain. It did not, however, accomplish either of its main aims. It did not prevent the enemy from accumulating supplies or spark a withdrawal. On 28 December an intelligence summary from Fifth Air Force acknowledged defeat: "The enemy's highly developed repair and construction capability of both bridges and rail lines has broken our blockade of P'yongyang and has won for him the use of all key rail arteries."

There were a number of reasons for the failure of the interdiction campaigns. First, the daily consumption of Chinese divisions was small, perhaps only a tenth of that needed by their Western counterparts, particularly when they were not on the offensive. Second, the enemy's many laborers repaired damaged routes quickly and could carry supplies over primitive tracks. Third, the USAF's global commitments ensured that FEAF would never have sufficient aircraft for its tasks. Just as serious was the USAF's inability to replace losses quickly, especially once the enemy's defenses improved and FEAF's fighter-bomber loss rate rose to more than 20 a month.[8] Fourth, increasing flak forced the fighter-bombers to resort to dive-bombing, which halved the effectiveness of any strikes. Fifth, the USAF's lack of aircraft capable of effective night interdiction, especially in an underdeveloped country like Korea, severely hampered its effectiveness.

The USAF's frustrations trying to fight an enemy so ready to use low-technology countermeasures grew. Communist air forces, unable to launching a major campaign against UN airfields, began night nuisance raids using Polikarpov Po–2 biplanes to drop small bombs or hand grenades. Only occasionally did these "Bedcheck Charlies" cause any real damage, but they were intensely irritating. No sensible answer was ever found to their nightly raids, although a few were brought down, usually more by luck than judgement. Modern aircraft found it hard to cope with a wood and fabric biplane flying at under 90 miles per hour in the dark. One was shot down when it happened to fly in front of a B–26 preparing to land, and another was flown through by a pursuing F–94; since both aircraft were destroyed, it was a poor exchange. F–94s, only recently arrived to replace the F–82s, were equipped with the most advanced airborne radar then in existence. The Po–2 incident appeared to confirm the radar's accuracy, but it carried a warning about radar interception involving an aircraft whose maximum speed was less than the interceptor's landing speed.

At the other end of the performance scale, the MiG–15s changed tactics and began to impose themselves more forcibly on the air war. Now fitted with drop tanks, they expanded their area of operations and were seen as far south as P'yongyang. "Trains" of MiGs, 60 to 80 strong, crossed the Yalu at high altitude and flew down the center of the peninsula, elements peeling off at intervals to challenge patrolling F–86s. The main body continued south, converging over P'yongyang with a similar formation coming from the east coast. The resulting force of 100 or so then dropped down to medium altitude and searched for UN fighter-bombers on interdiction sorties. Their losses to the MiGs were few, but the fighter-bombers often had to jettison their weapons under attack and, by September 1951, they were forced to restrict their hunting to areas south of the Ch'ongch'on River.

Toward the end of 1951 another pattern of MiG–15 activity surfaced. Large groups of MiGs maneuvered south of the Yalu, staying at maximum altitude and keeping well clear of F–86s. Over a six-week period, MiG formations became steadily bolder. Then the cycle started again. It appeared that courses were being run to provide a gentle introduction to combat for new pilots. The fighter strength in Manchuria rose to over 1,000 MiG–15s. Neither the increase nor the innovations seemed to make much difference to the outcome of aerial battles. It remained true that USAF pilots were better prepared. During 1952 MiG losses averaged one per day. F–86 losses averaged one per week. The introduction of the F–86F with a redesigned wing and more powerful engine widened the disparity even further. The F–86F left the MiG–15 (even the improved 15) without any real advantages. In the last months of the war, from March through July 1953, there were 225 claims for MiGs shot down, while FEAF lost just 10 F–86s.

In mid-1952 FEAF bombers conducted a show of UN air power to break the stalemate at the Panmunjom talks. They undertook what was known as the Air

C–124s. Combat Cargo Command's trans-Pacific supply line kept the United Nations effort in Korea going. Three of the types involved are pictured at a Japanese base in June 1952—a C–47, a C–54, and a C–124. The C–124 Globemaster proved capable of operating into basic landing strips and could off-load five times the cargo of any other aircraft in the theater.

Pressure campaign against selected targets in North Korea. On three days at the end of June, they concentrated on North Korea's capacity to generate electricity, destroying 90 per cent of the system and crippling industry all over the country. For the rest of 1952 and the first part of 1953, FEAF bombers continued to pound at military and industrial targets, but, although North Korea was badly hurt, the peace talks remained deadlocked.

Two events, one political and one military, then exerted their influence. In March 1953 Joseph Stalin died in Moscow, after which Chinese Premier Chou En-lai let it be known that he wished to bring the talks to an end. Progress remained glacial, however, until UN aircraft attacked North Korea's irrigation system. Lieutenant General Otto Weyland, commander of FEAF since June 1951, declared that he felt morally compelled to rule that North Korean dams could not be attacked for the sole purpose of destroying rice crops. He permitted strikes against only those

dams which, when breached, would release waters to wash away railways and military supplies.

On 13 and 16 May fighter-bombers struck and breached several dams. General Mark Clark, the new UN commander, reported that the effects were "as effective as weeks of interdiction." The communists were suitably impressed and responded with vitriolic propaganda statements. Within two months, however, negotiators agreed on a ceasefire at Panmunjom. During those two months, the communists strove to improve their position and inflict military defeat on the UN. They launched and repulsed major ground offensives under the cover of massive air support. As the ground fighting subsided, FEAF bombers hit the North Korean airfields hard to render them unusable. Under the terms of the ceasefire, Chinese aircraft were forbidden to enter North Korea, and Weyland wanted to make sure that there could be no last minute move across the Yalu.

They Also Served

The fighter and bomber units bore the greater part of the USAF's burden during the Korean War, but the conflict was an all-roles effort. Reconnaissance played a vital part and it involved a wide variety of aircraft, beginning with the RB–17G and the RF–80A.[9] However, the RB–17G was outclassed and replaced by the RB–29, but it, too, was inadequate for the more dangerous missions. Improvements came with the arrival of the 91st Strategic Reconnaissance Squadron, whose units operated six different types of aircraft—RB–29s, RB–50s, and RB–36s for assorted strategic tasks, WB–26s for weather reporting, and RB–45Cs for reconnaissance over the Yalu. The sixth type was the KB–29 tanker, which offered flight refueling support to various missions.

After a poorly organized start, tactical reconnaissance was centralized under the control of the 67th Tactical Reconnaissance Wing at Taegu. Although results improved, the limitations of the RB–26 and RF–80 remained, and it was not until F–86As, and later F–86Fs, were modified to carry cameras that photographic coverage of Manchurian bases could be guaranteed.

The UN could not have sustained the war without the transport force. Initially using the C–54 and C–47, the fleet expanded to include the C–46, C–119, and, from mid-1952 on, the huge C–124 Globemaster. They flew critical supplies all the way from the United States throughout the war, and supported the troops by continuously resupplying into forward airstrips and airdropping to units in combat. Their inbound flights carried replacement personnel; those outbound took troops on leave and evacuated casualties. By the end of the war, Combat Cargo's aircraft had carried 2,650,000 passengers, evacuated 314,500 wounded, lifted 697,000 tons of freight, and airdropped 18,000 tons. By any standards, theirs was a monumental effort.

Aircraft of the Air Rescue Service (ARS) undertook the evacuation of wounded personnel from forward areas, although their principal task was the recovery of downed airmen. The waters of the Yellow Sea and the forces of the communists could be almost equally unfriendly. The presence of the ARS gave a considerable boost to the morale of UN aircrews. ARS aircraft were as varied as their operations. SB–17Gs and SB–29s covered the coasts and the open sea, carrying lifeboats instead of bombs. L–5s and SC–47s managed evacuation from the front lines. Grumman SA–16 Albatross amphibians went almost anywhere to recover airmen, including over rivers deep behind enemy lines. H–5 and H–19 helicopters, first introduced to the Korean War on a large scale, went everywhere on rescue missions. Two celebrated USAF aces, "Boots" Blesse and "Mac" McConnell, were returned to combat after being rescued from the Yellow Sea, Blesse by an Albatross and McConnell by an H–19. Helicopters often engaged in clandestine operations, too, recovering agents parachuted into enemy territory from VB–17Gs.

Ceasefire

The Korean War ended at 2200 hours on 27 July 1953. In the final acts of the air war, a 4th Fighter-Interceptor Wing F–86 shot down an IL–12 transport at twilight on the last day, and a B–26 of the 3rd Bombardment Wing dropped its bombs just 24 minutes before the ceasefire went into effect. These minor events brought to a close a struggle that had begun as President Truman's "police action" and developed into a dangerous and punishing conflict between major powers.

UN air forces flew over one million sorties during the Korean War and lost 2,670 aircraft on operations. The USAF's contribution was an impressive share of that total. It flew more than 720,000 sorties of all kinds, including over 340,000 by fighters and a quarter of a million by fighter-bombers. It delivered nearly half a million tons of ordnance. In aerial combat, it claimed 954 enemy aircraft destroyed, 792 of them MiG–15s. Compared to those of World War II, the air forces in Korea were never very large, but, at the end of more than three years of warfare, the cost to the USAF, often described as "amazingly light," was certainly not negligible. FEAF lost 1,466 aircraft of all types and 1,144 aircrew in air operations. Of the aircraft total, 605 were fighters lost to enemy action, including 78 F–86s downed in aerial combat. The MiG vs. Sabre combat ratio favored the F–86. Only 17 B–29s were recorded as shot down, but perhaps ten times that many either crashed on landing or were damaged beyond repair as a result of combat.

Those who fought in the Korean War were left with feelings of deep dissatisfaction and disquiet when it was over. The battle had raged from the tip of the peninsula to the Yalu, but all of their effort and sacrifice had left the combatants facing each other across the 38th parallel, close to where the struggle began. Many bitter lessons came out of confronting the communist powers in a limited war. Unfortunately, most of them would have to be learned again in Vietnam. One fact was driven home, however. The position of the United States as a global power was now unquestioned, and Americans realized that strong armed forces were essential elements of the Cold War policy of the containment of communism. For the first time in their history, Americans accepted that, during a period when they were technically at peace, they would have to raise and maintain a large military establishment. This time, at war's end, the services would not be run down, and the future would bring increases in the military and for improvements in equipment and professionalism. For the USAF, in particular, these improvements would often be dramatic.

The Sikorsky H–5 Dragonfly (originally R–5 for Rotorcraft), one of the earliest really practical helicopters. The example shown at the USAF Museum is a YH–5A, one of 26 ordered in 1944.

H–5 cockpit. The seating arrangement in the YH–5A was, from the pilot's point of view, less than ideal. The crew of two sat in tandem, the observer ahead in the clear bubble of the nose and the pilot behind, with far less visibility. Through the starboard door, the pilot appears hemmed in by the control panel and instruments in front of him.

H–5 side view. The H–5 gained a considerable reputation during the Korean War, despite its limitations, when it was involved repeatedly in rescuing downed pilots and evacuating wounded personnel from the front line.

"Casualty Evacuation," David Hall, 1953, USAF Art Collection.

Notes

1. Peak figures were as follows: Personnel—2,411,294 in March 1944; Combat Groups—243 in May 1945.

2. The USAF replaced the P for Pursuit designation with F for Fighter on 10 June 1948.

3. Yeager's first few flights in the X–1 took him up to Mach 0.94 where his observations on elevator control difficulties led to the discovery that a "flying tail"— a moving solid slab horizontal stabilizer— offered greatly improved control at high Mach numbers. That development later gave the F–86 Sabre a marked advantage in combat.

4. Unloading could be remarkably rapid. One German team of 12 men managed to unload 6.25 tons of coal from a C–54 in only 5 minutes and 45 seconds!

5. Reporting their aircraft type to air traffic controllers, B–36 pilots took to announcing: "Six a-turning, four a-burning!" A contemporary piece of doggerel left no doubt about the B–36's purpose: "How dare Convair try to scare the bear, with this colossus which crosses the globe to probe those gremlins in the Kremlin".

6. These aircraft were the Douglas A–26 Invaders introduced toward the end of World War II. In 1948, when the original B–26, the Martin Marauder, was phased out, the A–26 inherited the designation B–26, to the eternal confusion of aviation historians.

7. Jabara went on to become the second ranking ace of the Korean War, registering 15 victories. (He also had one and a half in World War II.) The leading scorer in Korea was Captain Joseph McConnell with 16. Eleven pilots reached double figures.

8. In August, Fifth Air Force lost 30 fighter-bombers and had another 24 damaged. In September, the figures were 33 and 233; in October, 33 and 239; and in November, 24 and 255.

9. On 28 June 1950, 1st Lieutenant Bryce Poe flew the first jet reconnaissance mission over Korea in an RF–80A. His 90 combat sorties of the war included coverage of Inchon before MacArthur's landings and of the Yalu River bridges in "MiG Alley." He later flew over 200 combat reconnaissance missions in Vietnam and rose to the rank of general to command Air Force Logistics Command.

We must secure our nation by developing and maintaining those weapons, forces, and techniques required to pose a warning to aggressors in order to deter them from launching a modern, devastating war.

(General Hap Arnold to General Marshall, 1943)

I am unable to distinguish between the unfortunate and the incompetent.

(General Curtis LeMay on his intolerance of failure to meet his standards)

We must impress Mr. Khrushchev [with the fact] that we have [an airborne alert] and that he cannot strike this country with impunity.

(General Thomas Power testifying before Congress, February 1959)

We intend to have a wider choice than humiliation or all-out nuclear action.

(President John Kennedy, 25 July 1961)

Chapter 9

SAC and the Centuries

Supersonic Progress

Up to the time of the Korean War, the museum's telling of the Air Force story takes an easily followed path through the display galleries. From then on, visitors may find themselves searching more widely in the museum's newer halls or annexes to pick up the thread. Restrictions imposed by floor space or by recent acquisitions have placed some artifacts of the 1950s and 1960s among their much younger successors. This arrangement offers visitors the chance to see and easily compare the leaps in technology made between one generation and another.

After Korea, the wall displays cover the explosive growth of Strategic Air Command into a mighty instrument of Cold War deterrence, and the initially slower build-up of Tactical Air Command. Photographs show the deployment of TAC's Composite Air Strike Force in response to emergencies in the world's trouble spots and recall the complete mobilization of the command during the Cuban Missile crisis of 1962. Shots of Soviet missile sites in Cuba emphasize the importance of good reconnaissance. The hazards of the reconnaissance task are demonstrated by tales of a few of those aircraft shot down during the Cold War—an ERB–47 over the Barents Sea and U–2s over Cuba and Sverdlovsk.

The hunt for the hardware of the period begins in the shadow of the B–36. The ubiquitous Lockheed T–33 Shooting Star trainer stands next to Convair's F–102A Delta Dagger, this one among the first to intercept and escort a Soviet Tu–95 Bear inside the Arctic circle. Nearby are two aircraft that formed the backbone of TAC from the mid-1950s—a Republic F–84F Thunderstreak and a North American F–100 Super Sabre, the world's first combat aircraft capable of exceeding the speed of sound in level flight; the one displayed, a C model, participated in a ceremony in England commemorating the 350th anniversary of the founding of Jamestown, Virginia. The F–100's streamlining contrasts with the angularity of a Sikorsky H–19 painted in the colors of one called Hopalong which, in five easy stages from Massachusetts to Scotland, made the first trans-Atlantic helicopter flight in 1952.

The trail now leads to the museum's newest hangar, known as the Modern Flight Gallery. The aircraft exhibited here

"General Curtis E. LeMay," Sandor Klein, 1962, USAF Art Collection. U.S. Air Force Chief of Staff from 1961 to 1965, LeMay was one of the service's most innovative and dynamic leaders. He became famous for heading World War II strategic bombing forces in the Pacific and for building Strategic Air Command.

show facets of air power history from World War II to the Gulf War, but selective viewing reveals the exciting story of the 1950s. The somber tone of the older galleries is gone, their dark walls and shaded illumination replaced by a brilliant overarching whiteness under which the aircraft gleam and glisten, every detail sharply etched. Here is the revolutionary Boeing B–47 Stratojet, the one on display having served as a

Wright-Patterson test bed for fly-by-wire controls. The Convair B–58 Hustler in the corner was a record breaker, earning the Bendix and MacKay Trophies for a blistering round-trip between Los Angeles and New York in 1962. Appropriately hung high above is a U–2A, the "spy in the sky" created by the genius of Lockheed's "Skunk Works."

Among the most impressive indoor exhibits is the several-storied Douglas C–124 Globemaster, known colloquially as Old Shaky. Its great jaws agape to receive visitors the way it swallowed tanks, its slab sides tower over its smaller World War II cousins. By contrast, the little Kaman H–43 Huskie rescue helicopter is less than visually dominant, but in the 1960s the one on display established seven world helicopter records for rate of climb, altitude, and distance traveled.

Scattered about the Modern Flight Gallery are representative fighters of the 1950s. The North American F–86D Sabre introduced radar fire-control systems to single-seaters, and the Convair F–106A Delta Dart so advanced the concept that the pilot became almost unnecessary. When the pilot of the museum's F–106A, for example, ejected during a flat spin in 1970, the aircraft took over and survived a gentle belly landing in a snowy Montana field.

A North American F–100D is shown in the stars and stripes of the U.S. Air Force aerobatic demonstration team, the Thunderbirds, with whom it flew in the mid-1960s. Not far away is "the missile with a man in it," the Lockheed F–104C Starfighter. A dramatic performer, the F–104 was not the fighter the USAF was looking for, but the museum's aircraft did its best by winning the William Tell Fighter Weapons Meet competition in 1962. The McDonnell RF–101C Voodoo was another star. Before the B–58 stole them away in 1962, this RF–101 held the round-trip records between Los Angeles and New York. More important, it also flew some of the low-altitude reconnaissance sorties over Cuba in 1962 that confirmed the presence of Soviet missiles on America's doorstep.

The Modern Flight Gallery also houses the trainers of the new jet age. The piston-engined Beechcraft T–34 Mentor and North American T–28 Trojan are complemented by two later jets—Cessna's T–37, commonly called the Tweety-bird, and the supersonic Northrop T–38 Talon, a two-seat cousin of the F–5 Freedom Fighter.

Further research into aircraft of the 1950s leads away from the museum's main buildings. The hangars known as the Annex, on the other side of Wright Field, are a treasure house often overlooked, but they are well worth visitors' excursions, packed as they are with artifacts of all kinds. Here is the little-known L–17A Navion, designed by North American, built by Ryan and flown in the Air Force Reserve Officers Training Corps (ROTC) program. A rarity is the

Vertol H–21 Workhorse, a twin-rotor helicopter shaped like a banana, used by the USAF for rescue and a 12-stretcher carrier. In complete contrast is a McDonnell F–101B decorated with the markings of the 142nd Fighter Interceptor Group, Oregon Air National Guard (ANG).

Outside, braving all weathers, are some larger aircraft. A Boeing KC–97 Stratotanker, the "flying gas station," which transformed Strategic Air Command, stands in the colors of the Ohio ANG. This one is a powerful L model, fitted with two additional podded jet engines. It carries the name Zeppelinheim, having been named by the mayor of that German town in 1973. Dwarfing almost everything in sight is a Douglas C–133A Cargomaster, the first transport capable of taking ballistic missiles in its hold. The museum's C–133 is another world record holder; on 16 December 1958, it carried the then astonishing load of 117,900 pounds to a height of 10,000 feet. A different kind of celebrity belongs to the Lockheed EC–121D Constellation a little farther on. Named Triple Nickel because of its airframe serial number, this "Connie" was the first aircraft ever to direct an interception which led to a USAF fighter destroying an enemy. On 24 October 1967, over the Gulf of Tonkin, a MiG–21 fell victim to the beams of the EC–121's radar.

The EC–121's success reminds visitors that the next stage of the Air Force story involves further conflict, a return to armed confrontation with a communist regime that would bedevil America for most of the 1960s and 1970s and would lead the USAF down altogether new paths of development and doctrine.

From Groups to Wings

Before America's involvement in the Korean War, the USAF had been caught between newly-won independence and shrinking defense budgets. Senior airmen wanted to build a global air force but never had enough money to do it. With Chinese intervention in Korea, USAF strength increased rapidly and America generally accepted that confrontation with communism had become a fact of life. USAF expansion continued even after the shooting stopped, albeit at a slower pace.

In 1950, before the North Koreans surged across the 38th parallel, the USAF's front line consisted of 48 combat groups. In 1951 a reorganization began that phased out the group level in the chain of command and left the wing as the principal combat unit. By June 1951 the USAF had 87 wings, an increase made possible by the recall of many reservists to duty. It set a target of 143 wings for mid-1955. At the end of the Korean War the front line was up to 106 wings, and policy discussions followed that eventually led to a new target of 137 wings by mid-1957. Although

B–47. When it appeared in the late 1940s, the Boeing B–47 Stratojet was a herald of the future. Sleek and elegant, the Stratojet shattered preconceptions of what bombers should look like with its dramatically futuristic design. Thin, swept surfaces, podded axial-flow engines, and a fighter-type cockpit were the most obvious evidence of a break with the past.

numerically less ambitious than the earlier aim of 143 wings, 137 wings amounted to almost three times the size of the force in 1950 and would be accompanied by substantial improvements in capability.

LeMay's Air Force

If any command exemplified the face of the new Air Force transformed by technological advances and determined leadership, it was Strategic Air Command. In 1950 SAC's personnel strength stood at 71,490 and its aircraft totaled 868. The backbone of its striking force consisted of 390 B–29s. Five years later its personnel strength was 196,000, and it had 3,068 aircraft, including well over 1,000 B–47s backed by a tanker fleet of more than 700. At the same time, its standards of performance rose dramatically, driven by the implacable Curtis LeMay. Besides the impact of his steely personality, he brought fresh ideas to encourage his command to new heights. He established SAC's bombing and navigation competitions as annual events, and he introduced a system of spot promotions to reward outstanding achievement. Temporary promotions could be awarded to ranks between technical sergeant and lieutenant colonel, but a return to previous grade followed failure to measure up. Failure by one member of a "select" crew could mean loss of rank by all.

SAC's force had inherited practices learned the hard way in World War II when heavily armed piston-engined bombers with large crews operated in formation, preferably with fighter escort. The command received the first of its Boeing B–47s in October 1951. The B–47 brought with it revolutionary changes in operational doctrine and aircrew attitudes to the bombing mission. It was an extraordinary technical achievement, bearing almost no resemblance to its predecessors and pointing the way to the future for large aircraft in both military and civil aviation. The loaded weight of a B–47 was half again as great as the B–29's, but its size was disguised by slender lines and the novelty of a fighter-type cockpit. The B–47 had a normal crew of only three—two pilots in a tandem cockpit and a navigator hidden in the nose. Its shoulder-mounted wings were razor-edged, remarkably thin, and swept back at the then startling angle of 35 degrees. The B–47's engines, fuel, and wheels, contrary to conventional practice, were not housed in its wings. Their placement allowed the aerodynamic advantages of thin aerofoil. The aircraft's axial flow turbo-jets were in pods hung below its wings; fuel was stored in the fuselage, above and at each end of the bomb-bay. Its landing gear was a pair of two-wheel trucks placed fore and aft on the fuselage centerline, with small outriggers under the inner

KC–97 and B–47. Air-to-air refueling gave the B–47 a much longer
reach, but it was not easy when the tanker was a KC–97. Usually the
tanker had to be in a descent at high power to hold an acceptable speed
for the B–47.

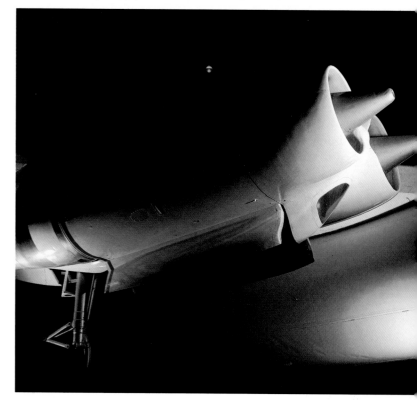

B–47 engine pod. The B–47E was
powered by six General Electric
J47 engines of 7,200 pounds of
thrust each. The podded engine
installation was novel in 1947.

B–47. Boeing's B–47 Stratojet was a revolutionary design. It was the world's first swept-wing bomber and the first developed specifically to deliver nuclear weapons. A crew of three was carried; in tandem under the canopy were the pilot and co-pilot (who fired the tail guns by remote control); the navigator-bombardier occupied a dark space beneath in the nose. The B–47E at the USAF museum was the first service aircraft used for trials of a fly-by-wire flight control system.

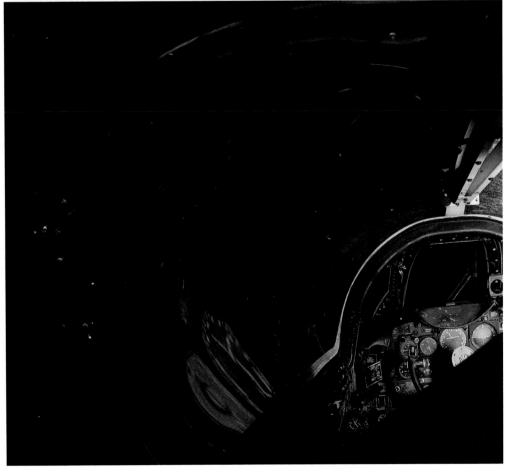

B–47 cockpit. A peek over the B–47's cockpit rail reveals a typical bomber wheel control in a fighter-sized space.

engine pods which provided stability on the ground. A large brake chute helped slow the landing speeds associated with the B–47's high wing-loading (which was twice that of a B–29). Defensive armament was limited to a remotely controlled tail turret housing a pair of .5-inch or 20-mm guns.

The B–47's principal limitation was its practical radius of action on internal fuel, about 1,500 miles, not enough for adequate coverage of targets in the Soviet Union. Again, Boeing had the answer. Three months before the first B–47 joined the 306th Bombardment Wing at MacDill Air Force Base, the 306th Air Refueling Squadron on the same base took delivery of its first KC–97 tanker. The KC–97 could fly fast enough, if necessary in a slight dive, to match a throttled back B–47, and its efficient flying boom refueling system turned the bomber into an inter-continental weapon. Each B–47 wing had a comple-ment of 45 bombers and was supported by a KC–97 squadron of 20 tankers.

The capabilities of the B–47 were amply demonstrated in a series of record flights in the 1950s. On its first overseas deployment, the 306th Bombardment Wing recorded a best time of 5 hours and 22 minutes from Maine to Fairford, England, an average speed of 575 miles per hour. During an intercontinental bombing trial, a B–47 flew non-stop from Hunter Air Force Base, Georgia, to Morocco and back in 24 hours and 4 minutes, refueling four times from KC–97s. Even more remarkable, a B–47 flown by Colonel Edward Burchinal of the 43rd Bombardment Wing was caught in the air by bad weather blanketing the whole of Western Europe and North Africa. Burchinal elected to wait between the United Kingdom and Morocco until the weather cleared and then he called for tanker support. He finally landed at Fairford after nine refuelings, having been airborne for 47 hours and 35 minutes. These and other demonstrations left no doubt that the B–47 was a strategic weapon to be reckoned with.

Although it was remarkable, the B–47 was only an intermediate step toward SAC's long-term future. In 1955 the command took delivery of the aircraft that would come to symbolize American strategic air power for generations of bomber aircrews—Boeing's B–52 Stratofortress, commonly known as the Buff. (In genteel translation: Big Ugly Fat Fellow.) In 1946 Boeing had begun work on a very large bomber, in effect, a stretched B–29 with six engines, which by 1948 had evolved to include four turbo-prop engines hung on swept back wings.[1] The USAF wanted higher performance, however, and Boeing finally produced the immense B–52, powered by eight jet

engines hung in four under-wing pods. Originally intended to penetrate enemy defenses at high subsonic speeds and altitudes above 50,000 feet, the B–52 has shown enormous capacity to absorb technological developments and to adapt to changes in role and tactics. Its unrefueled radius of action of well over 4,000 miles becomes almost unlimited with flight refueling support. Over the years its maximum loaded weight has risen to nearly half a million pounds as it has taken on more internal fuel, increased its weapon carrying capacity, and accumulated various navigation and electronic defensive systems.

As it had with the B–47, before long SAC showed the world what the B–52 could do. In 1956, within a year of its arrival in the front line, a B–52 dropped a thermonuclear weapon with a yield of almost four megatons at Bikini Atoll. The global reach of the huge bomber was demonstrated in January 1957 when three B–52s of the 93rd Bombardment Wing, supported by KC–97 tankers along the way, flew

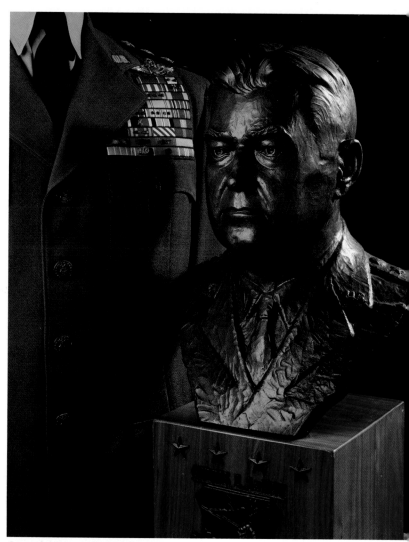

General Curtis LeMay's impressively decorated jacket, fronted by his bronze image, its severe gaze challenging USAF Museum visitors as they pass.

KC–135 and B–52D. The partnership between the KC–135 Stratotanker and the B–52 Stratofortress was the basis for the air-breathing element of America's deterrent triad. The jet-powered KC–135 eliminated problems associated with the earlier KC–97. It could operate at the same speeds and altitudes as jet bombers and could carry three times more fuel than the piston-engined tanker.

KC–97 flying boom. At the business end of a KC–97 tanker Boeing's flying boom allowed greatly increased rates of fuel transfer to thirsty combat aircraft.

from California via Labrador, Morocco, Ceylon, the Philippines, Guam, and Hawaii to complete a non-stop, around-the-world flight of 24,325 miles in 45 hours and 19 minutes. Captain of the leading B–52, *Lucky Lady III*, was Lieutenant Colonel James Morris, who had been the co-pilot of the B–29 *Lucky Lady II* on SAC's 1949 global epic. In just eight years, Morris had seen the around-the-world record reduced by better than half.

As General LeMay approached the end of his nine-year reign at SAC, the imminence of his departure did not signal any slowing in the command's expansion of its capabilities, nor was there a change of pace in July 1957 when General Thomas Power took over as its commander in chief. Responsibilities and challenges grew with every year. In 1955 SAC had been directed to work closely with Air Research and Development Command (ARDC) in establishing an operational capability for intercontinental ballistic missiles (ICBMs) and, from then on, it was clear that SAC was assured of a primary role in the USAF's increasingly important missile program. SAC extended its reach in another way when it acquired the newly-formed Sixteenth Air Force in 1957 to control bases in Spain and Morocco. In the same year SAC Head-quarters moved into its permanent home, a massive building at Offutt Air Force Base, Nebraska, that included an underground control center built to with-stand anything but a direct hit by a high-yield nuclear weapon. In 1957, too, alarmed by the Soviet Union's progress in missile development, SAC started working toward a system of ground alert duty in which one third of its strategic force would be maintained at readiness, with weapons loaded and crews standing by.

After a surprisingly short operational career, certain B–47 force elements began phasing out in 1957, but B–52s arrived at a rate of more than ten a month during the year and the command took delivery of its first jet tanker, the Boeing KC–135. In November LeMay, now USAF Vice Chief of Staff, returned to the cockpit to show off the new aircraft, flying it to Buenos Aires for Argentina's Aeronautics Week and establishing world point-to-point records in the process. The non-stop return flight from Buenos Aires to Washington, D.C., averaged 471 miles per hour over 5,204 miles. In the months that followed, KC–135s compiled impressive world records for point-to-point speed, closed circuit speeds with payload, weight lifting, and straight-line distance flown without refueling. The KC–135 proved a powerful force multiplier for the USAF, offering greatly improved tanker performance and growing into an indispensable part of everyday operations world-wide for aircraft in a wide variety of roles.

Other SAC records followed when the Consolidated B–58 Hustler made its appearance in 1960. The B–58 was about as different from previous bombers as it was possible to be. It was a true delta, with a slim area-ruled "Coke bottle" fuselage, and the USAF's first supersonic bomber, capable of Mach 2.1 at over 60,000 feet. Beneath its slender body hung a 62-foot-long payload pod, part fuel tank and part weapons bay, which was expendable when empty. The three man crew—pilot, radar navigator-bombardier, and electronics officer—sat in separate escape capsules. Within its first year of operations, the B–58 set numerous world records and suffered a very public tragedy, indeed. On 10 May 1961, a B–58 of the 43rd Bombardment Wing flew 670 miles in just over half an hour, setting a new mark for sustained speed at an average 1,302 miles per hour. On 26 May a B–58 covered the 4,612 miles from New York to Paris in 3 hours, 19 minutes and 41 seconds, about a tenth of the time taken by Lindbergh. Sadly, the aircraft was destroyed in an accident at the Paris air show only a week later. Although in many ways it was the most advanced bomber of its time, the B–58 had a short operational career. Expensive to operate and maintain, it claimed too large a share of SAC's budget and its

B–58 jet pipe. Four podded General Electric J79–5 after-burning turbo-jets of 15,600 pounds of thrust each powered the B–58. The streamlined shape of the finned under-fuselage payload pod is visible between the stalky undercarriage legs.

B–58 alert force. From 1957 on, Strategic Air Command maintained a ground alert system to allow for rapid reaction to emergencies. Here, an aircrew abandons its car and runs for its already cocked and bombed-up B–58.

B–58 cockpit. Besides its other unconventional features, the B–58 defied bomber tradition in having a fighter-type stick for the pilot. The cockpit was also equipped with the most effective air conditioning system yet designed for an aircraft.

high-altitude penetration role was overtaken by events. The B–58 was phased out of service at the end of 1969.

Under General Power's leadership between 1957 and 1964, SAC continued to enhance its capabilities. In 1958 it established airborne alert force trials, which led to the arming and flying of part of its fleet at all times, and the following year saw the creation of special air corridors in the United States where SAC bombers could fly low-level training missions. The growing nuclear strength of America's armed services brought with it the need for closer coordination of target planning, which in 1960 led to the formation of the Joint Strategic Target Planning Staff (JSTPS), under the direction of SAC's commander in chief, and the preparation of a Single Integrated Operational Plan (SIOP). That same year, SAC, using specially modified KC–135s, tested the feasibility of maintaining

an airborne command post that could assume control of combat forces if ground command centers were destroyed. In 1961 SAC went to a ground alert posture for 50 percent of its force, and airborne command post operations (codenamed Looking Glass) began, each EC–135 equipped with comprehensive communications and carrying a staff headed by a general officer. Looking Glass shifts remained on watch in the air for eight hours before handing over to another team, ensuring 24-hour coverage every day of the year.

TAC and ADC—Born Again
While SAC was making such marked progress in the strategic arena, tactical aircraft were not entirely forgotten. At the end of 1950 TAC and ADC were reestablished as separate commands, and TAC made major efforts thereafter to enhance the capabilities of its fighter-bombers and to establish them overseas.

B–58. Convair's B–58 Hustler was the first supersonic bomber to go into production and was capable of exceeding Mach 2. Among its many astonishing features was a payload pod carried beneath the slim fuselage. Pilot, navigator, and defense systems operator were sealed in separate cockpits, and each could be ejected in a capsule in an emergency. The B–58A at the USAF Museum is a record breaker, its exploits earning the Bendix and Mackay Trophies for 1962.

347

F–84F. Developed when defense budgets were tight, the Republic F–84F Thunderstreak put swept surfaces on what was essentially a re-engined version of the straight-wing F–84. Although it had several problems, including occasionally unpleasant handling characteristics, the F–84F filled the fighter-bomber gap until the F–100 arrived. The USAF Museum's Thunderstreak is one of 200 that deployed trans-Atlantic in November 1961. It bears the markings of the 178th Tactical Fighter Group, Ohio National Guard.

Even as it prepared to send F–84s to Korea, it deployed a large contingent of F–84Es in the opposite direction. In September and October 1950, 180 fighter-bombers were ferried in two huge waves from Bergstrom, Texas, to Furstenfeldbruck, Germany, stopping five times en route for fuel. Within two years, fighters equipped for in-flight refueling were making similar deployments to Europe and Japan much more quickly with the aid of tankers. As tactical aircraft gained in global flexibility they became far more powerful offensive weapons. Nuclear science had advanced rapidly and produced warheads small enough to be carried by fighters. Each weapon had a yield approximating that of *Fat Man*, the bomb that leveled Nagasaki. Thus, the deployment of a fighter-bomber wing represented a fearsome projection of potential destructive power.

These fighter-bomber developments were not entirely the result of natural evolution. Even as war raged in Korea, Air Force leaders were looking to the future, working to improve tactical aircraft and ready them for a "hot" war against the Soviet Union. The limited Korean struggle was widely regarded as not at all

typical as an air power experience, and USAF Headquarter's attention continued to focus primarily on deterring the Soviet Union by preparing for a large-scale war in Europe.[2] With that in mind, some tactically minded officers saw a need to emphasize global deployment and nuclear weapons for tactical aircraft as the only way to challenge SAC for a bigger share of the Air Force budget. Others feared that the U.S. Navy would usurp the overseas tactical air mission by promoting the claims of its own nuclear-armed fighters. Whatever the reason, from the mid-1950s on, straight-wing F–84Gs and swept-wing F–84Fs began waving the USAF's tactical flag by crossing the Atlantic as a matter of routine and standing nuclear alert on European bases. TAC, it was said, had come to resemble a sort of bush league SAC.

The nuclear emphasis continued as the next generation of tactical aircraft appeared. Agility, particularly at high altitude, might have been desirable for fighting MiGs in Korea, but it was not a notable characteristic of the North American F–100 Super Sabre and the other Century-Series fighters. The F–100 was not agile. Although ostensibly designed as an air superiority

F–84 cockpit. Note the yellow emergency handles on either side of the F–84F's seat. One jettisons the canopy and the other fires the ejection cartridge.

349

The F–100 Super Sabre, the first U.S. Air Force fighter to reach supersonic speeds in level flight. Designed as a replacement for the F–86, it proved an outstanding ground attack aircraft. This one stands under guard at Tan Son Nhut, Saigon, in May 1966.

fighter to replace the F–86, the F–100 was built in the mold of a rugged ground attack aircraft. It was heavy and very fast, the first production fighter to be supersonic in level flight. On 20 August 1955, Colonel Horace Hanes took the F–100C beyond the speed of sound for an official world record of 822 miles per hour. The F–100C, with its strengthened wings and points for external stores, confirmed the USAF's intention to use the aircraft primarily in the ground attack role, and the F–100D, the definitive variant, added the capacity to deliver nuclear weapons.

Later Century-Series fighters continued in the fast and heavy mode, and most variants, including those used as interceptors, were nuclear-capable. McDonnell's F–101 Voodoo was originally conceived as a long-range escort fighter for SAC, but became an ADC interceptor and served in TAC both as a fighter-bomber and a reconnaissance aircraft. Powered by two afterburning Pratt & Whitney J57s of nearly 15,000 pounds of thrust each, its considerable size did little to slow it down. On 12 December 1957, Major Adrian Drew raised the world speed record to 1,207 miles per hour in an F–101A.

Two other members of the Century-Series were so unashamedly fast that Lockheed's F–104 Starfighter was referred to as the "missile with a man in it." Supposedly the result of talks with fighter pilots in Korea, the F–104 was offered as an air superiority fighter, but it proved unsuitable in that role. Its dimensions were outrageous, 55 feet long and only 22 feet across the wing, and it was powered by a 15,000-pound-thrust General Electric J79, which gave it a startling performance—Mach 2.2; a 50,000-foot-per-minute rate of climb; and zoom capability to over 90,000 feet. The Starfighter was the first aircraft to be supersonic in the climb, and the first to hold world records for speed and height simultaneously.[3] Unfortunately, its tiny, razor-edged wings restricted both weapon load and maneuverability, problems which limited both the F–104's production run and its operational life with the USAF.

No such reservations were applied to Republic's F–105 Thunderchief. It was proposed in 1951 as a high-speed, long-range hauler of conventional or nuclear weapons, and it did just that extremely well. It had an internal bomb-bay, which could accommodate an extra fuel

The North American F–100 Super Sabre, the U.S. Air Force's first fighter capable of becoming super-sonic in level flight. Its extra fuel tanks and flight refueling capability allowed it trans-oceanic deployment.

F–100 tail. The sharply swept surfaces of the F–100 set the pattern for subsequent Century-Series fighters. The USAF Museum's F–100C is marked as an aircraft of the 452nd Fighter-Day Squadron, 322nd Fighter-Day Group, and was named Susan Constant in a 1957 ceremony celebrating the 350th anniversary of the founding of Jamestown.

Century-Series cockpits. The F–100 Super Sabre's cockpit left, demonstrates the conventional fighter layout established post-World War II. Principal flying instruments are in the center; engine instruments are to the right. Radios and navigation aids are along the right console, while red warning indicators are fitted at odd points, roughly at eye level. The control stick is shaped to the hand, and a number of services are operated by the pilot's fingers. Buttons transmitted radio messages or dropped weapons or fuel tanks. The trigger fired guns or rockets, and the coolie hat on top of the stick set the aircraft's trim. The cockpit of a later Century fighter, the.F–101 Voodoo is relatively uncluttered because its radar fire-control system is entrusted to the radar operator behind. In all aircraft fitted with ejection seats prominent red tags warn that safety pins must be removed before flight. This second of the USAF Museum's Voodoos is the two-seat all-weather interceptor variant, the F–101B.

An RF–101 Voodoo of the 363rd Reconnaissance Squadron flying over Shaw Air Force Base, South Carolina. Low-level reconnaissance by RF–101s in 1962 proved the siting of Soviet missiles in Cuba.

F–101 tail. The broadly expansive RF–101C's tail is topped by sharply swept tail surfaces and sits above the heavy shielding designed to protect the aircraft's skin from the blast of after-burning J57 engines.

RF–101 nose. The distinctively flat camera nose identifies this McDonnell Voodoo as an RF–101C. This particular aircraft used its cameras to good effect during the Cuban missile crisis, keeping an eye on Soviet missiles and helping to confirm their dismantling.

F–104 cockpit—snug and well arranged. The throttle lever of this F–104C is vertical rather than horizontal, and a rear view mirror clings to the open canopy rail. A yellow handle beside the foot well jettisons the canopy, and a larger handle at the front of the seat initiates ejection (including canopy jettison).

F–104 tail. Tactical Air Command's winged sword decorates an F–104C's fin. This particular Starfighter, 60914, was the mount of the winning pilot in the 1962 William Tell fighter meet.

tank, and five pylons for a variety of external stores. Known colloquially as the Thud, the F–105 was the largest single-seat, single-engined combat aircraft made, the loaded weight of later variants reaching 54,000 pounds. From the beginning it was an outstanding performer; the YF–105A exceeded the speed of sound on its first flight. Development problems held up the Thud's arrival in the front line until 1958, but it eventually proved itself operationally invaluable. The F–105D had all-weather capability and an impressive external load for combat sorties, typically eight 750-pound bombs, an ECM (electronic countermeasures) pod, and an external fuel tank. It could accommodate a 20-mm rotating-barrel cannon, and other armaments, which could include "Bullpup" air-to-surface missiles, rocket pods, napalm, and AIM–9 air-to-air missiles.

The remaining pair of Centuries originated from the urgent need to improve the defense of the United States. At the time of the Soviet takeover in Czechoslovakia, North America was essentially undefended against air attack. During the 1950s the USAF became involved in strenuous efforts to rectify matters by building immense trans-continental radar screens facing north across the Arctic and by acquiring jet interceptors equipped with air-to-air radar. Interim designs, such as the F–86D, F–94C, and Northrop's

F–104 intake. A sleek, almost wingless aircraft—the missile with a man in it—the Lockheed F–104 Starfighter was a dramatic performer. Fed by enormous quantities of air through cheek intakes, its after-burning J79 engine produced up to 15,800 pounds of thrust and could propel the F–104 to speeds well above Mach 2. In the center of each intake is a fixed shock cone, surrounded farther back by a boundary layer bleed slot.

F–102 and B–57. An F–102 Delta Dagger of the 317th Fighter-Interceptor Squadron is accompanied by an EB–57 Canberra of Alaskan Air Command near Mt. McKinley. EB–57s were used to provide electronic countermeasures training.

F–89D Scorpion served well enough for a while but were clearly inadequate as long term solutions to the problem. The Convair F–102 Delta Dagger and F–106 Delta Dart were almost identical twins designed to meet a 1949 request for a "1954 interceptor." Aerodynamic problems and performance shortcomings delayed their introduction to service until 1956 and 1959 respectively, but both eventually performed well, the F–106 in particular proving itself a formidable Mach 2 interceptor for ADC, armed as it was with both conventional and nuclear-tipped air-to-air missiles. The F–106 almost literally deserved to be called a missile with a man in it. It was the closest thing to a manned robot flying. Fitted with the Hughes MA–1, a radar developed as an automatic fire control system that could be coupled to an auto-pilot, it could be flown hands off to interception and missile launch.

As air defense squadrons received their Convair deltas, supporting ground organizations became operational. By the end of the 1950s three vast radar chains stretched across North America to provide warning in depth of air attack—the Pinetree Line in southern Canada, the Mid-Canada Line, and the Distant Early Warning (DEW) Line inside the Arctic Circle. Lockheed RC–121 Constellations acted as airborne radar stations and added wings to the system to the east and west. The Semi-Automatic Ground Environment (SAGE) system was the first computerized method of handling air defense information, and a joint North American Air Defense Command (NORAD) was functioning at Colorado Springs to control all American and Canadian air defense forces. The Ballistic Missile Early Warning System (BMEWS), with radar sites in Greenland, Alaska, and the United Kingdom, was added in 1961.

Whatever the merits or shortcomings of individual Century-Series fighters, as a group they marked a dramatic expansion of the combat aircraft's performance envelope. The P–51D made its first appearance less than ten years before the first flight of the F–100. In the following decade, fighters moved from the limitations of 40,000 feet and subsonic speed to

F–106. A natural progression from the F–102 Delta Dagger, the Convair F–106 Delta Dart first flew in 1956. It was an extremely powerful and sophisticated interceptor for its day. Its Pratt & Whitney J75 engine produced 24,500 pounds of thrust in afterburner and it could accelerate to Mach 2. Fitted with a Hughes MA–1 guidance and fire control system, it could carry out "hands-off" interceptions, firing its nuclear-tipped air-to-air Genie missiles when required and recovering to base afterwards.

50,000 feet plus and Mach 2. Despite their having done so at the expense of some maneuverability, which the USAF learned to live with until the next generation of fighters arrived, they were growing in other ways. Almost all fighters would accommodate such developments as radar, recognized as increasingly essential to fighter effectiveness, guided missiles, and the additional role of ground attack.

Although Tactical Air Command was popularly associated with its fighter squadrons, it performed many different kinds of vital duties. At the end of the Korean War, TAC controlled more than 1,100 aircraft, no less than 60 percent of which were transport types, with the Fairchild C–119 steadily replacing the aging C–46. By the mid-1950s tactical airlifters were beginning to feature the practical forms that would predominate for the rest of the century—high wings, cavernous box-shaped interiors, unobstructed flat floors, and full fuselage rear doors, which lowered to become ramps. Lockheed's incomparable C–130

F–106 tail. The F–106 was a true delta, with no separate tail surfaces. The eagle's green tail partly covers the air-brake panels, and the two small tubes on the fin's leading edge are the pitot intakes for the aircraft's artificial feel system. The USAF Museum's F–106A is an aircraft that took its hands-off capabilities to extremes. During a sortie from Malmstrom Air Force Base, its pilot ejected when he found himself locked in a flat spin. The F–106 subsequently recovered and made a gentle belly landing in a snow-covered Montana field. It was later put back into service.

Hercules and its smaller cousin, Fairchild's C–123 Provider, transformed the business of hauling military cargo and later proved to be superbly adaptable multi-role aircraft.

The rebirth of TAC might be said to have been largely accomplished by 1957. By then, the Centuries were either established or on the way, as were the new transports, and Martin B–57 Canberras rather than B–26s were flying interdiction. The Douglas B–66 Destroyer was also being introduced as a light bomber. Strategic Air Command had finally relinquished its remaining fighter squadrons to Tactical Air Command. To manage its remarkably wide range of capabilities, TAC controlled three numbered air forces—the Ninth, Eighteenth (primarily troop carrier), and Nineteenth (mobile headquarters for Army support). The Nineteenth Air Force was headquarters for what was known as the Composite Air Strike Force (CASF), a combination of fighter, light bomber, tanker, and transport units ready at any time to move overseas. The CASF deployed to cover such emergencies as America's 1958 intervention in Lebanon, the Chinese threats to Quemoy in the mid-1950s, and the Berlin Wall crisis in the early 1960s.

The Haulers

The turbulent currents of technological change began reaching out to other USAF commands, too, in the 1950s. Halfway through the decade, the Military Air Transport Service (MATS) fleet of over 1,400 aircraft included 610 four-engined transports. Most were still C–54s, but the Douglas C–124 Globemaster, known to its crews as Old Shaky, had added significantly to the lifting capacity of the command. Huge clam-shell doors in its nose allowed it to carry such bulky cargo as tanks or bulldozers, and it was capable of taking 200 fully-equipped troops in its double-decked cabin. However, it was not very speedy, and long-range deployments depending on its support and what it was transporting needed the luxury of patience. The solution to that failing was in sight, since the C–124 was the last piston-engined transport ordered for MATS. Douglas sought to retain its prime position as supplier of large military transports with the C–133 Cargomaster, a four turbo-prop monster capable of swallowing Atlas and Titan ICBMs through its rear-loading door. As useful as it was, the C–133 was never a great success, principally because of unexpected engine and fatigue problems. A little later, the

"Arabs near a C–119 at Wheeless AFB, Tripoli," Robert Handville, 1956, USAF Art Collection.

C–133. The monster Douglas C–133 Cargomaster added new dimensions to the U.S. Air Force's airlift capacity. It was capable of swallowing both Atlas and Titan ICBMs.

Boeing C–135 and the Lockheed C–141 Starlifter added pure jet speed and much greater reliability.

Besides the operation of its global route system, MATS was responsible for such specialized functions as the Air Weather Service (AWS), whose aircraft tracked and penetrated severe weather areas, and the Air Rescue Service (ARS), which carried out world-wide search and rescue activities over both land and water. The ARS of the 1950s was equipped with a broad range of aircraft—SB–17Gs, SB–29s, SC–54s, SA–16 Albatross amphibians, and helicopters like the Kaman H–43A, Sikorsky H–19 Chickasaw, and Vertol H–21 Workhorse.

The Teachers

The demands of the "New Look" USAF, emphasized by the Korean War and the accelerating shift to a jet-powered front line, created considerable problems for Air Training Command. After World War II, the USAF had as much difficulty as the other services when it came to recruiting and attracting suitable candidates into a declining military. In 1950 the flying training machine was designed to produce 3,000 pilots, but managed only 2,200. Numbers increased with the Korean War, causing ATC to create two subordinate organizations, Flying Training Air Force (FlyTAF) and Technical Training Air Force (TechTAF). With the approval of 143 wings, the USAF set a goal for pilot training at 12,000 per year by 1956, but the number graduated was actually less than 7,000, an adequate figure for the slower buildup envisaged after the Korean War was over. To do the job, ATC was operating ten primary, eight basic, and nine advanced flying schools, and using aircraft like the Beech T–34 Mentor, North American T–28 Trojan, and Lockheed T–33 Shooting Star. By the end of the 1950s these had been joined by a new twin-jet primary trainer with side-by-side seating, the Cessna T–37; the more advanced Northrop T–38 Talon was on the horizon to replace the T–33.

"Marching to Mess,"
Frank Germain, 1970,
USAF Art Collection.

The addition of increasingly sophisticated electronic equipment to USAF aircraft continually raised performance standards required in other crew members and made the training more complex. In the early 1950s ATC created another organization, the Crew Training Air Force (CrewTAF), to mold newly graduated aircrews into effective combat teams. Besides the Convair T–29 "flying classroom," ATC owned a sampling of front-line aircraft from the operational commands, which it used to ease the passage of the inexperienced newcomers on to their squadrons.

If the USAF's training of aircrews was increasingly difficult, its problems with ground technicians often seemed worse. It found its efforts to turn recruits into skilled men far from simple as competition with civilian industry for those who were expensively trained led to a turnover that was discouragingly high. In 1956 nearly 126,000 airmen failed to reenlist after serving only one four-year term. To keep the front line properly manned in the mid-1950s, the USAF's technical schools were consistently graduating over 100,000 technicians per year.

Rows of T–33 jet trainers on the ramp at Reese Air Force Base, Texas. Nearly 4,000 T–33s were delivered to the U.S. Air Force alone and they formed the backbone of USAF pilot training during the 1950s and 1960s.

From the beginning, USAF leaders were aware of the need for a solid foundation of professional training for officers. Before the Korean War most new USAF officers came from aviation cadet or officer candidate schools, the Air Force Reserve Officer Training Corps (AFROTC), or were drawn from a 25 percent allocation from each graduating class at West Point or Annapolis. It was not until 1954 that the USAF obtained authorization for its own academy. As a temporary measure, the USAF Academy opened its doors in 1955 at Lowry Air Force Base, near Denver, Colorado, and moved the cadets to its magnificent 18,000-acre permanent site in the foothills of the Rocky Mountains near Colorado Springs, Colorado, in 1958. The first graduates were commissioned in 1959. The USAF established post-graduate education at such schools as the Air Command and Staff College (ACSC) and the Air War College (AWC), at the Air University at Maxwell Air Force Base, Alabama.

Eyes in the Sky

The American military's provision of trained personnel and adequate combat power for the containment of communist expansion were vital aspects of its preparation for Cold War confrontation, but its knowledge of what the other side was doing was equally important. There was a continual need for strategic reconnaissance of potential enemies and their activities. Immediately after World War II, America's surveillance of the Soviet Union began with modified B–29s (the F–13A and B–29F) of the 72nd Reconnaissance Squadron at Ladd Field, Alaska; it continued as other units later contributed RB–50s, RB–36s, RB–45s, and RB–47s. Surveillance was a risky occupation. It involved a limited number of high-altitude overflights for photographic coverage but soon included sorties using electronic sensors to derive information from the opposition's radio and radar transmissions.

To gain maximum value from electronic surveillance, the USAF flew "ferret" aircraft close enough to Soviet airspace to provoke a reaction. At first, Soviet search and height-finding radars would sweep the ferret. If the "threat" persisted, missile guidance and ground-controlled interception radars joined in, accompanied by increased radio transmissions and message traffic, all monitored and recorded by the ferret. Occasionally, Soviet reaction to the ferret was aggressive and the information hunter became the hunted. In the decade of the 1950s about two dozen aircraft of the Western powers were lost on strategic reconnaissance missions, and several others were attacked and damaged.[4] At least eight of the losses were suffered by the USAF,

B–36 jet pod. From the D-model on, B–36s carried the extra power of four podded General Electric J47 engines of 5,200 pounds of thrust each. On the wing's trailing edge were six 3,800-horsepower Pratt & Whitney R–4630s driving 19-foot pusher propellers.

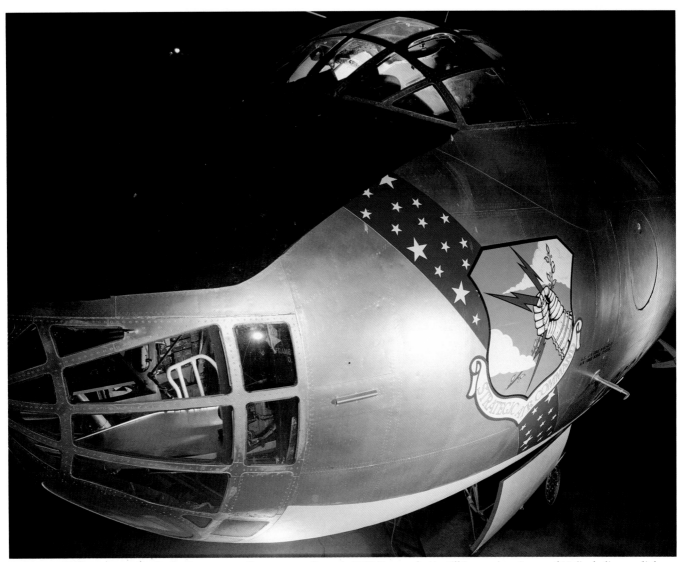

B–36 nose. Half a century after its first appearance, the enormous Convair B–36 Peacemaker is still impressive. A crew of 15 (including a relief team of four) was housed in two pressurized cells in the nose and tail, connected by an 85-foot tunnel. Those in the nose compartment worked on three levels, the pilots 20 feet above the nose wheel. The USAF Museum's B–36J was the last of the giants to fly, arriving at Wright-Patterson Air Force Base in April 1959. It is prominently marked with the badge of the Strategic Air Command.

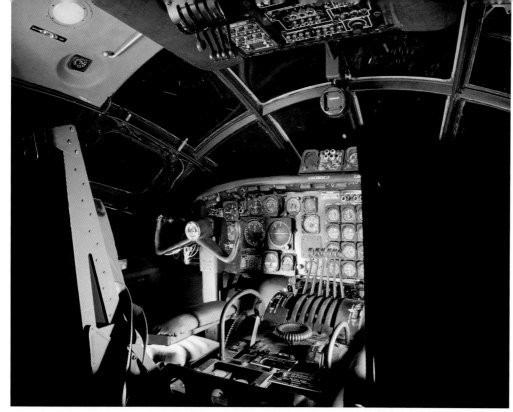

B–36—not readily suggestive of the size of the monster behind it. One clue lies in the width of the throttle quadrant and the positioning of the throttles. Six in the familiar place close to the captain's right hand are for the huge Pratt & Whitney radial engines, but there are four more in the roof controlling General Electric jet engines.

B–36 engineer's panel. A dazzling array of dials, switches, buttons, and levers confronted the B–36's flight engineer. From his seat he had his finger on every system that brought the aircraft to life. A handily placed clip over his head made notes and check lists readily available.

B–36 bomb bay. The aircraft's cavernous four-section bomb-bay could accommodate up to 84,000 pounds of conventional bombs. Alternatives included such giants as the Mark 17 nuclear weapon, right, which alone weighed 41,400 pounds. The Goblin, left, crouches close by. More usual defensive armament consisted of no fewer than sixteen 20-mm cannon fired from nose and tail positions and from six retractable turrets.

including an RB–50 and four RB–29s, and an ERB–47H of the 55th Strategic Reconnaissance Wing shot down by MiG–19s over the Barents Sea on 1 July 1960.

To remove the risk from strategic reconnaissance, the USAF sought aircraft of such high performance that they could operate over any location in the world with impunity. In the 1950s and 1960s two remarkable aircraft came from Lockheed's famous Skunk Works to meet the need. The first, the U–2, looked like a jet-powered sailplane. Even in its earliest form, the U–2 could operate up to 70,000 feet; later versions have pushed this up to 90,000 feet. For a while, at 70,000 feet it seemed out of Soviet reach, and in the late 1950s USAF pilots temporarily released to the Central Intelligence Agency (CIA) overflew the Soviet Union and gained much invaluable information about such things as bomber deployment, air defense systems, and submarine development. However, on 1 May 1960, a U–2 flown by Francis Gary Powers was shot down near Sverdlovsk by SA–2 missiles. Chairman Nikita Khrushchev used the incident to embarrass President Dwight Eisenhower and wreck

a summit meeting, and American penetrations of Soviet airspace were brought to a halt, at least for a time. At Lockheed the Skunk Works was already at work on an even more challenging aircraft. By the mid-1960s it gave the United States the SR–71 Black-bird, a strategic reconnaissance vehicle that could match the U–2's performance for range and altitude while adding the ability to sustain flight at more than three times the speed of sound.

Missiles on the Doorstep

When Fidel Castro seized power on 2 January 1959, Cuba joined the list of countries under occasional surveillance by the strategic reconnaissance eyes of the United States. After the fiasco of the 1961 Bay of Pigs invasion by United States-based Cuban exiles, the Soviets stepped up the supply of arms to their client, Castro, and by 1962 it was clear from photographs taken by U–2s that these included surface-to-air missiles (SAMs). Further, it seemed that the SAMs were placed to defend other sites intended for mobile medium-range ballistic missiles (MRBMs). Comprehensive high-altitude U–2 coverage of the island confirmed the

B–36 navigator's seat. The navigator sat in the bowels of the machine, unable to see out, relying on radar and navigational equipment to keep the B–36 on track.

XF–85 Goblin. The extraordinary little McDonnell XF–85 Goblin was to have been the B–36's defender, launched and recovered by a trapeze from a section of the huge aircraft's bomb-bay during operations. The hook on which this daring act depended sprouted from just in front of the XF–85's cockpit. The effort was a failure. The two XF–85's built achieved only 2 hours and 19 minutes flying time between them before their program was terminated in 1949.

assessment and revealed other sites being prepared with fixed launching pads for intermediate-range ballistic missiles (IRBMs). With these in place, the Soviets could launch nuclear warheads against American targets from the east coast to Wyoming. In mid-October, America's fears were confirmed when a U–2 mission photographed a site with MRBMs deployed. Low-level reconnaissance by RF–101s and USN RF–8s followed, and President John Kennedy was handed incontrovertible photographic evidence of both the presence of missiles in Cuba and Soviet involvement in placing them there. On 22 October Kennedy reported to the American people on the threat and the countermeasures being taken and announced a blockade of the island. Three days later he warned the Soviets directly against continuing to deploy missiles.

Meanwhile, the USAF packed its bases in Florida with combat aircraft—F–100s, F–104s, F–105s, and F–106s. At SAC, B–47s went to their dispersal bases; B–52s adopted a nuclear-armed airborne alert; and missile crews came to instant readiness. Tension rose on 27 October when Major Rudolf Anderson's U–2 was shot down over Cuba and he was killed. Matters worsened the next day when a U–2 on an Arctic mission inadvertently strayed over Siberia's Chukotski Peninsula and the Soviets readied their missiles. The United States accompanied its apology for the transgression with a steely assurance that its forces were now ready to take military action in Cuba and elsewhere, if necessary. Khrushchev took the hint and agreed to withdraw both the offending missiles and a number of Il–28 bombers already in place. The Cuban Missile crisis was over, having

imparted a salutary lesson on the value of strategic reconnaissance in an age of global confrontation. One fire had been put out, but another was already smoldering on the other side of the world.

Notes

1. This design, Boeing's Type 464–35, bore a striking resemblance to the Soviet strategic bomber, the Tupolev Tu–95 Bear, which entered service in 1956 but seems set to continue into the 21st century. Like the Type 464–35, the Tu–95 is also a four turbo-prop swept-wing aircraft, developed by the builders of the Tu–4, the Soviet copy of the B–29.

2. The air war in Korea was generally regarded as unique and of limited value as an influence on operational doctrine for any kind of conflict. Thomas K. Finletter, Secretary of the Air Force during the conflict, wrote: "[The Korean War] was a special case, and air power can learn little from there about its future role in United States foreign policy in the East."

3. On 7 May 1958, Major H.C. Johnson reached 91,243 feet in an F–104A. Nine days later, Captain W.W. Irwin recorded 1,404 miles per hour. On 14 December 1959, Captain J.B. Jordan, in an F–104C, raised the height record to 103,389 feet. Rocket-boosted F–104s were flown higher at the astronaut training school at Edwards Air Force Base, Chuck Yeager reaching an unofficial 108,000 feet in 1963.

4. American aircraft came from the USAF, USN, and CIA. Also lost were a number of British, Swedish, and Chinese Nationalist aircraft.

I won't let those air force generals bomb the smallest outhouse without checking with me.
(President Lyndon Johnson on his control of Operation ROLLING THUNDER, 1965)

We are swatting at flies when we should be going after the manure pile.
(General Curtis LeMay on the targeting restrictions in North Vietnam.)

The pilot hit by a surface-to-air missile whose site he was not permitted to bomb does not fall halfway out of the sky or spend seven years as a limited prisoner of war.
(Admiral U.S. Grant Sharp, CINCPAC, on tactical bombing restrictions, 1968.)

... the amount of fire power put on that piece of real estate exceeded anything that had ever been seen before in history by any foe and the enemy was hurt, his back broken by air power.
(General William Westmoreland, U.S. Army, on the role of B–52s at Khe Sanh, 1968.)

I have determined that we should go for broke .... I intend to stop at nothing to bring the enemy to his knees.
(President Richard Nixon to Secretary of State Kissinger, 30 March 1972)

Thank God for the U.S. Air Force!
(U.S. Army survivor rescued under fire by HH–53 helicopter at Quang Tri, 1972)

Chapter 10
Limited War Learning Curve

Veterans of an Asian War

Fanatics for logical progression who follow the trail of the USAF through the 1950s into the museum's Modern Flight Hangar and then outside onto the ramp have to retrace their steps to stand again in the shadow of the B–36. It is here that the story of the Vietnam War begins. Among the aircraft found overhead, flying in formation with the SAC monster's tail, are a couple too often overlooked. Lacking the speed and power of their more exotic jet cousins, the Cessna O–1 Bird Dog and O–2 Skymaster nevertheless deserve respectful attention; their forward air controller (FAC) role was among the most hazardous of the Vietnam War. Beneath the O–1 is another in the Cessna family, the YA–37A, an early counterinsurgency (COIN) aircraft.

In a pugnacious stance nearby is a rare bird, indeed. Aircraft whose crew members attain the nation's highest award for gallantry seldom survive the experience, but this is the Douglas A–1E Skyraider flown by Major Bernard Fisher in 1966 when he landed under fire in South Vietnam to rescue a fellow pilot and so earned the Medal of Honor. It is mightily hung with a typical weaponload and surrounded by an impressive collection of other possibilities—"Bullpup," "Rockeye," and an assortment of cluster bomb units dispensing such varied items as tear gas bomblets and land mines. Almost unnoticed in a corner, the slim shape of the opposition reaches upward—the Soviet SA–2 Guideline surface-to-air missile.

Potent symbols of air power in the Vietnam War—F–4Cs taking turns to refresh themselves from a KC–135 tanker, 1966.

Vietnam montage. USAF Museum artifacts from the Vietnam War include many items contributed by prisoners of war—manufactured sandals, a T-shirt, a bowl, and a spoon among them. Shown with them are an airman's shirt and dog tags (Airman 1st Class Pitsenbarger gave his life for comrades in Vietnam and was awarded a posthumous Air Force Cross) and Steve Ritchie's flight jacket (Ritchie scored five aerial victories over Vietnam while flying the F–4 Phantom).

On a wall close by, the progress of the Vietnam War is traced year by year. Beginning with the activities of American advisers in South Vietnam, the story unfolds in words and pictures, showing the changing fortunes of the opposing combatants and their allies from 1961 to 1973. Displays of rescue and survival gear, uniforms, and unit flags and insignia lie alongside Viet Cong booby traps. There are tales of courage, such as that of Captain Dethlefsen's Medal of Honor, and of achievement, like those of the USAF's Vietnam aces. In more somber mood is the section on prisoners of war (POWs), their near starvation diet, and primitive medical treatment. Their ingenuity is brought out by a display of items they manufactured during their incarceration. Perhaps the saddest Medal of Honor is here, that earned by Captain Lance Sijan who died in captivity after torture in 1968. An epilogue tells of treaties ignored by the North Vietnamese in their Southeast Asian conquests and sets out the bald figures of the cost of the Vietnam War to the United States. The story ends with a display of the last USAF flags flown in Southeast Asia. Tucked away at the bottom is an American flag that was carried by an American who served with the Royal Flying Corps in World War I, and was subsequently flown in a Lancaster over Germany in World War II, in a B–29 over Korea, and in a MAC aircraft into Vietnam. Before moving on,

visitors may notice that, in an undoubtedly unconscious gesture, the rest of the USAF Museum has turned its back on what happened in Vietnam. All of the aircraft in the gallery are facing away from the story on the wall.

The majority of the aircraft associated with the Vietnam War are in the Modern Flight Hangar. The walk there is interesting in itself. The evolution of the USAF's aircraft insignia is shown in color, revealing that the first national identifying mark, from the "Jennies" of 1916, was a single red star! A comprehensive aircraft model collection is followed by examples of aviation art, and aero-engine spark plugs and jet engine igniters are arranged in patterns to delight the eye. The corridor leading to the Modern Flight Hangar is lined with uniforms worn by members of the USAF and their predecessors.

The Modern Flight Hangar is very large, as it must be to accommodate its outsize treasures. The floor area here is greater than the other two hangars (the Early Years and Air Power Galleries) combined, yet it contains far fewer aircraft. Many of them are at the imposing end of the aircraft scale. Imposing to say the least is the massive shape of a Boeing B–52D. As the representative of a design rapidly approaching its half century and still in service, this aircraft is a phenomenon in military aviation. Having seen considerable action in Southeast Asia and survived a close encounter with an SA–2 missile, it is even more remarkable.

The B–52 is in good company. It is surrounded by others who bear the scars of combat in Vietnam. There are two Republic F–105 Thunderchiefs, D and G models. The F-105D carries nose art naming it Memphis Belle II. It shot down two MiGs in battle, and, like its illustrious B–17 predecessor, it proved a combat survivor. The F–105G served as a Wild Weasel in Vietnam and went one better than its brother, claiming victories over three MiGs. A tiny enemy, dwarfed by the Americans, is a MiG–17 nearby. Visitors eager to see its more potent cousin, the MiG–21, must cross the airfield to the museum's Annex. While there, they should note the Fairchild C–123K, a tubby old warrior that flew defoliant missions in Vietnam and received over 1,000 holes in its skin for its trouble. It earned the nickname "Patches," and it carries seven Purple Hearts as a reminder that seven crewmen were wounded during its many operations.

The museum's Martin B–57 is disguised as an EB–57B. Before its conversion to electronic countermeasures (ECM), it flew combat as a tactical bomber for over two years. An aircraft that performed regular ECM duty in Vietnam is the Douglas RB–66B skulking in the background. Menacing in its dark camouflage, the General Dynamics F–111A sits with wings partly swept, looking very much as it did for its part in LINEBACKER II, the campaign that closed the Vietnam War. Some of its associated hardware is also represented—a Pave Tack laser designator, a 20-mm Vulcan cannon, AGM–130A stand-off weapons, and a 3,000-pound "smart" bomb. Around the hangar walls and clustered among the aircraft on the floor are other smart weapons.

Smaller aircraft of the Vietnam War displayed include the North American Rockwell OV–10A Bronco, the Air Commandos' Helio U–10D Super Courier, and a Bell UH–1P Iroquois (more commonly Huey) helicopter, used for psychological warfare. Even smaller than these is the

MiG–21. The most potent enemy aircraft facing the United States in Southeast Asia was the MiG–21 Fishbed. Short ranged, but fast and agile, the MiG–21 was armed with Atoll air-to-air missiles. The intake for its Tumansky turbo-jet engine includes a fixed conical center body containing airborne intercept radar.

F–4 cockpit. The pilot's scope for APQ–100 radar peeks from beneath the shroud at the top of the F–4's front cockpit instrument panel. The main flight instruments are centrally placed below that; engine instruments are paired to the right; and weapon switches are hidden off to the left. To the right of the seat are the hoses that carry air for G-suit inflation and oxygen.

Teledyne Ryan AQM–34L Firebee drone, unique in the museum's collection for having been shot down over North Vietnam. At the other end of the hangar are two unusual aircraft. The Grumman HU–16B Albatross was a welcome sight to downed airmen in the Gulf of Tonkin. The one displayed became a star when it set an amphibian altitude record of 32,883 feet in 1973. Ominous in its all-black paint, the Sikorsky CH–3E close by is typical of the big helicopters so beloved for their "Jolly Green Giant" rescue work, but this one is black (and named Black Maria) because it was used for clandestine operations.

Scattered around the hangar are a number of special displays. An F–105 sits inside a typical revetment, and the canvas Lyles Poison Pub Cookhouse is handily alongside. USAF humor of the Vietnam era is celebrated in cartoons, and there is a service "Misery" communications intercept van, which earned its keep by monitoring American transmissions to ensure that they did not offer too much of

value to the enemy. There is an F–4 cockpit for visitors to sit in, and a display describing the work of Spooky, the AC–47 gunship, and the Medal of Honor earned by Airman First Class John Levitow in an AC–47 hit by a mortar shell on 24 February 1969.

Three more "fast movers" round out the Vietnam era. Northrop's YF–5A is a prototype of the Freedom Fighter, a few of which saw brief service with the USAF in Southeast Asia. The museum's LTV A–7D Corsair II is one flown by Major Colin Clarke on 18 November 1972. On that day he was airborne for nine hours on a rescue support mission for which he was awarded the Air Force Cross. Finally, there is the McDonnell Douglas F–4C Phantom in which Colonel Robin Olds and Lieutenant Stephen Crocker, his back-seater, shot down two MiGs in one day on 20 May 1967. It had been over 20 years since Robin Olds had gained his string of victories in World War II.

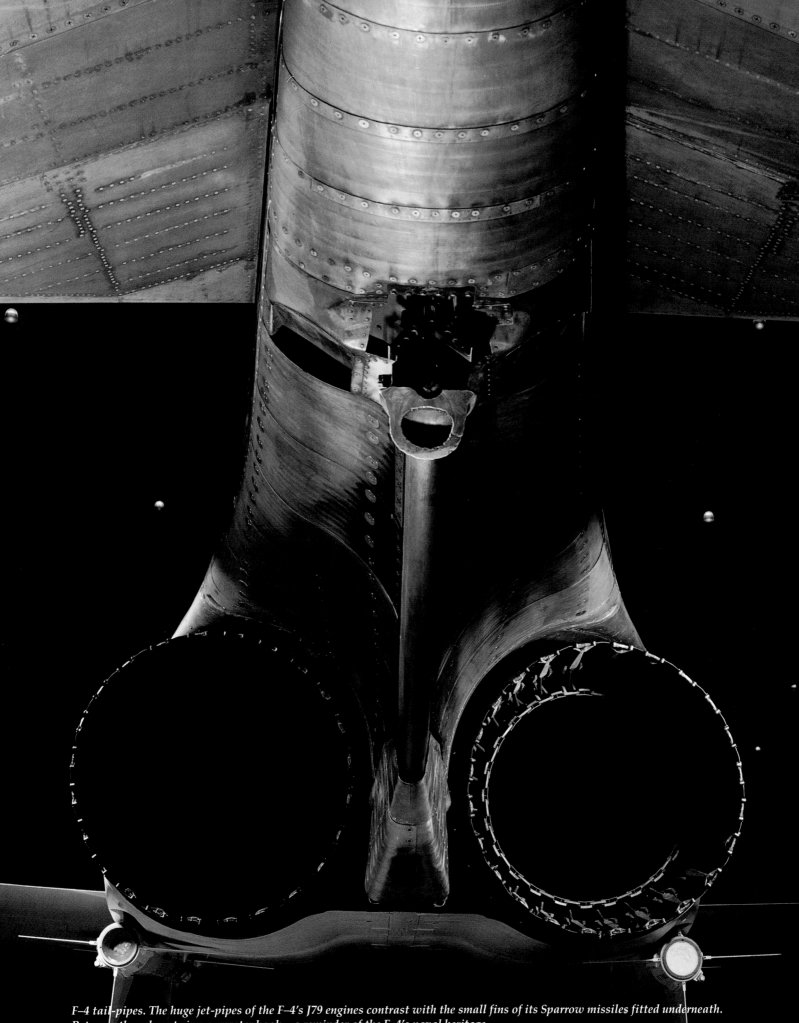

F–4 tail-pipes. The huge jet-pipes of the F–4's J79 engines contrast with the small fins of its Sparrow missiles fitted underneath. Between the exhausts is an arrester hook—a reminder of the F–4's naval heritage.

The First Small Step

Although the United States certainly took notice when the North Koreans burst across the 38th parallel in June 1950, it still managed to find the time to involve itself in events 20 degrees farther south. It had not smiled on France's attempt to regain its colonial grip on Indochina after World War II, but it regarded the threat of communist expansion in the area as a greater evil. Ho Chi Minh had established himself in North Vietnam and was engaged in a guerrilla war to unite all of Vietnam under a communist government and his leadership. According to the "Domino Theory," success by Ho Chi Minh in Vietnam would lead inevitably to communist domination of Laos and Cambodia, then Burma and Thailand soon thereafter. To the United States, resisting the fall of the first domino was essential, and in July 1950 it sent a few American military personnel to Saigon to form a Military Assistance Advisory Group (MAAG), offering help and advice to the beleaguered French. Thus, in a first small and deceptively innocuous step, the United States began its decades-long ordeal in Vietnam.

France's will to persist in Southeast Asia was effectively broken by its defeat at the hands of Viet Minh troops at Dien Bien Phu in May 1954. At an international conference in Geneva, France accepted the inevitable—the recognition of Vietnam, Cambodia, and Laos as independent countries and the temporary division of Vietnam at the 17th parallel pending nationwide elections to be held in 1956. A demilitarized zone (DMZ) partitioned North and South. Meanwhile, Ho Chi Minh in Hanoi and Ngo Dinh Diem in Saigon set up separate political administrations. The United States emphasized its partiality by offering the Saigon regime economic and military assistance and sponsoring the eight-nation Southeast Asia Treaty Organization (SEATO) to be the region's cloak of security against communist expansion. President Eisenhower supported Ngo Dinh Diem's plans to strengthen South Vietnam's military, and, from 1955 on, the MAAG took over training responsibility for most South Vietnamese forces, although USAF instructors for the Vietnamese Air Force (VNAF) did not arrive until 1957. In 1956 President Diem chose to ignore the requirement for a national election on the grounds that a solidly communist vote in the North would be overwhelming and could only lead to a government under Ho Chi Minh for Vietnam.

In 1957 communist guerrillas in South Vietnam stepped up their overt activities, instigating civil war. They increased their attacks during 1958 and 1959, and in April 1959 helped to form the South Vietnamese

Communist Party (Lao Dong), whose armed members were known as the Viet Cong. From May 1959, after Ho Chi Minh announced his intention to unify Vietnam by force, the Viet Cong were openly supported by the North. The United States reacted to this escalation initially by sending to Saigon more advisers and military equipment. Special Forces teams arrived in the South to train Army of the Republic of Vietnam (ARVN) rangers in counterinsurgency operations. As 1960 ended there were 800 or so American servicemen on duty with the MAAG in South Vietnam.

By 1961 the communist insurgency in the South had grown to critical proportions and Soviet Premier Nikita Khrushchev announced that the Soviet Union was wholeheartedly behind "wars of national liberation," including "the armed struggle waged by the people of Vietnam." Two weeks later, John Kennedy became President of the United States and made it clear that he was determined to meet the communist challenge head on. American involvement in Southeast Asia now began an inexorable climb toward a major regional war and the longest armed conflict in American history.

An RF–101C over Vietnam in 1967 after camouflage requirements had led to a reduction in size of American national symbols. The RF–101s' tactical reconnaissance responsibilities in Vietnam included providing pathfinder and damage assessment services for the strike forces.

The air war fell broadly into five phases. The first, from 1961 until mid-1964, was ostensibly covert, as the USAF flew reconnaissance sorties over Laos, sending whole units with their aircraft to undertake combat training duties with the VNAF. The USAF replaced the VNAF's aging F–8 Bearcats with A–1 Skyraiders and T–28s. Phase two, covering the five years from mid-1964 on, saw the large-scale deployment of USAF units into Southeast Asia and their continuous engagement in air operations over South Vietnam, with frequent forays into the North and Laos. The third phase, from mid-1969 until spring 1972, was a time of retrenchment as the USAF withdrew many units and handed over bases to the VNAF. During the fourth phase, following the 1972 North Vietnamese spring offensive and lasting until early 1973, the USAF conducted intense strike operations, including concentrated attacks on the Hanoi-Haiphong area. In phase five, from mid-1973 to May 1975, the USAF began its final withdrawal from Vietnam.

The Covert USAF

Regular USAF units were operating in Southeast Asia before the end of 1961. RF–101Cs of the 15th and 45th Tactical Reconnaissance Squadrons began flying missions over Vietnam and Laos from Tan Son Nhut Air Base near Saigon in October, and F–102As were later detached from the Philippines to carry out occasional patrols against unidentified intruders over the border between South Vietnam and Cambodia. Although these were operational missions, the first experience of actual combat was reserved for detachments of a different kind.

Responding to President Kennedy's expressed concern about America's military capability to fight limited wars or to engage in counterinsurgency operations, in April 1961 General LeMay arranged for the establishment of the 4400th Combat Crew Training Squadron at Eglin Air Force Base, Florida. Nicknamed "Jungle Jim," the unit would develop tactics and select aircraft for the counterinsurgency role. By November the USAF had deployed a Jungle Jim detachment under the codename Farm Gate to Bien Hoa, near Saigon, and directed it to train the VNAF. The detachment's first aircraft in Vietnam were four suitably modified T–28s, four SC–47s adapted for rough field operations with strengthened landing gear and JATO rockets, and four B–26 Invaders taken out of storage. For diplomatic reasons, the aircraft were flown in VNAF markings and American pilots were allowed to take part in operational sorties only if accompanied by Vietnamese. In effect, USAF "instructors" trained their students by example while flying the missions. The official line put out for the benefit of the press was: "No USAF pilot has ever flown in tactical missions except in the role of tactical instructor." These cosmetics did not entirely hide the fact that before the end of 1961 a USAF unit had become involved in a shooting war.

Two other USAF units moved to Vietnam early in 1962, both of them equipped with C–123 Providers. Operation MULE TRAIN brought the 346th Troop Carrier Squadron to Vietnam to provide tactical airlift support. More controversial was Operation RANCH HAND. UC–123Bs of the Special Aerial Spray Flight arrived at Tan Son Nhut to see whether they could defoliate the tropical jungle that hid the Viet Cong and their trails. On 2 February 1962, RANCH HAND unfortunately, became known for suffering the first USAF casualties of the war when a UC–123B crashed without survivors.

The Farm Gate detachment acquired more B–26s and T–28s, but these aircraft were showing their years. Corrosion was among the problems in elderly airframes now carrying far more than their originally designed weights of ordnance. In February 1964 a B–26 lost a wing during a combat sortie, and a T–28 suffered the same fate soon thereafter. In recognition of its increasing responsibilities, the Farm Gate detachment became known as the 1st Air Commando Squadron and soon acquired ex-U.S. Navy A–1E Skyraiders to replace its disintegrating aircraft. The service's choice of one aging prop-driven aircraft for another did not seem sensible. However, the venerable A–1E proved ideal for its role. Pilots praised its capacity to absorb battle damage and swore by the accuracy of its weapons delivery. Troops were gratified to find that the A–1E could provide support in weather which grounded the jets, and they admired both its weight of fire and its ability to loiter overhead for long periods. Although these piston-engined warriors were very valuable, by 1964 it had become clear that the jets could not be long denied.

An Operation RANCH HAND UC–123 spraying defoliant on Vietnam's jungle in an attempt to uncover trails used by the Viet Cong.

A–26 nose. The A–26 delivered powerful punches with both guns and bombs. On the aircraft here, eight .50-caliber machine guns are mounted in the nose, but other variants fitted four 20-mm cannon. Six .30-caliber machine guns fired from the wings, and bombs could be carried on wing pylons or internally.

A–1E nose. Leading the A–1E into the fray was a Wright R–3350 18-cylinder two-row 2,700-horsepower radial engine. It gave the Skyraider a maximum speed of over 300 miles per hour and the strength to lift four tons of external stores.

The Douglas A–26 Invader, one of the piston-engined aircraft resurrected for the Vietnam War. Because of its long legs and weapon-carrying capacity it was ideal for interdicting the Ho Chi Minh trail.

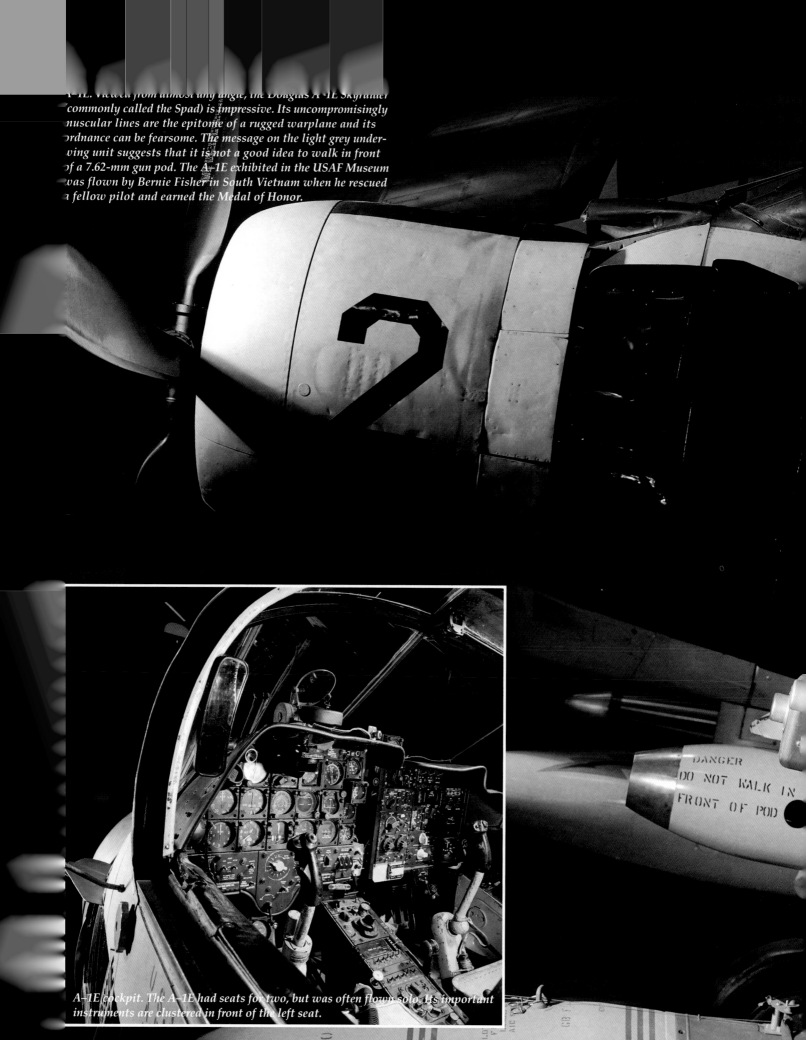

A–1E. Viewed from almost any angle, the Douglas A–1E Skyraider (commonly called the Spad) is impressive. Its uncompromisingly muscular lines are the epitome of a rugged warplane and its ordnance can be fearsome. The message on the light grey under-wing unit suggests that it is not a good idea to walk in front of a 7.62-mm gun pod. The A–1E exhibited in the USAF Museum was flown by Bernie Fisher in South Vietnam when he rescued a fellow pilot and earned the Medal of Honor.

DANGER DO NOT WALK IN FRONT OF POD

A–1E cockpit. The A–1E had seats for two, but was often flown solo. Its important instruments are clustered in front of the left seat.

M117 GENERAL PURPOSE BOMB

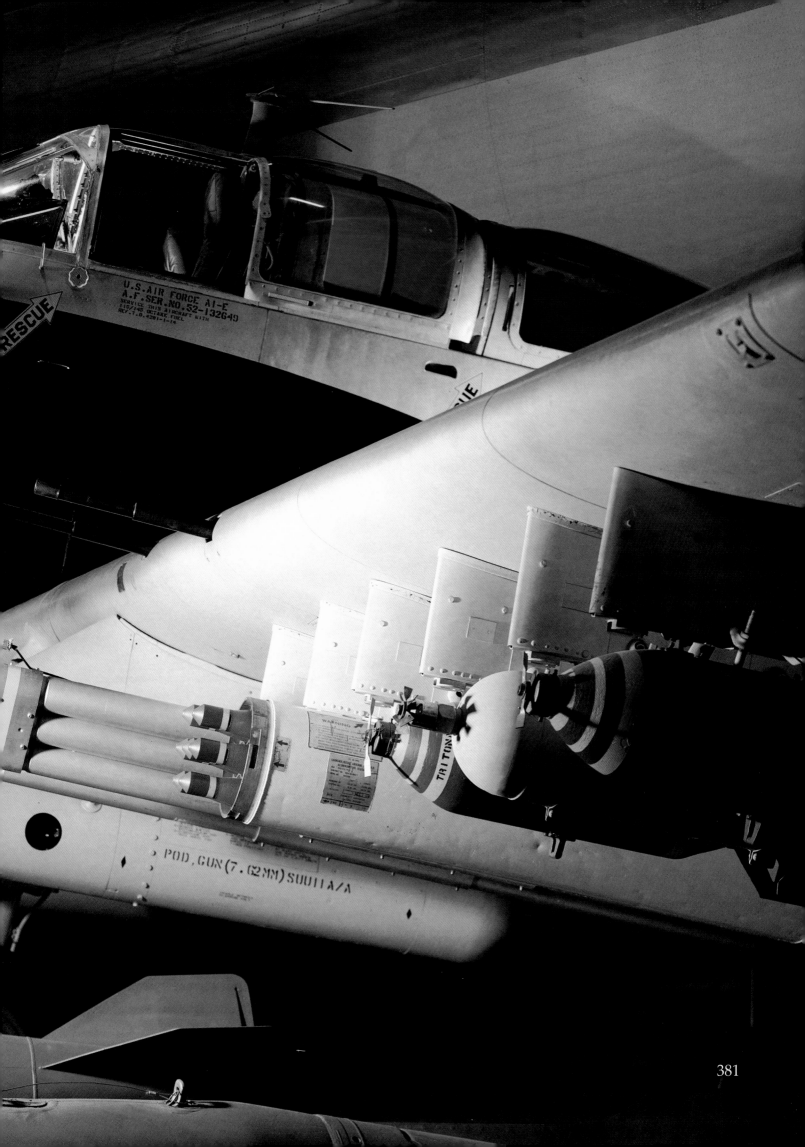

U.S.AIR FORCE A1-E
A.F. SER.NO.S2-132649
SERVICE THIS AIRCRAFT WITH
115/145 OCTANE FUEL
REF.T.O.4291-1-14

RESCUE

POD,GUN (7.62MM) SUU11A/A

The U–2, invaluable in Southeast Asia. Its high altitude capability and excellent passive defense systems allowed it to fly reconnaissance missions almost unmolested over even the most difficult areas.

Overt Steps

From the beginning of America's involvement in Vietnam intelligence gathering was an important activity. A variety of aircraft operated regularly out of Tan Son Nhut and Bien Hoa from mid-1962. EC–54s, EC–97Gs, RB–57Ds and Es, and U–2s photographed likely targets and tracked Viet Cong radio traffic. USN reconnaissance aircraft also participated and, when a Vought RF–8A was shot down by North Vietnamese anti-aircraft artillery (AAA) over Laos on 6 June 1964 and an F–8D was lost in the same area the following day, retaliation followed. On 9 June, eight F–100Ds of the 511th Tactical Fighter Squadron, supported by tankers, struck at AAA targets in Laos. The gloves had finally come off; the United States had taken action, officially acknowledging its effective engagement in open warfare, albeit limited and selective, with the communists in Southeast Asia.

USN ships were part of intelligence operations, too, deployed in the Gulf of Tonkin. On 2 August 1964, North Vietnamese torpedo boats attacked the destroyer *Maddox* as it cruised in international waters; two days later they gave a repeat performance. Immediate retaliatory American air strikes against the torpedo boat bases were followed by firm political action in Washington. President Lyndon Johnson sought sweeping powers to use American forces in Southeast Asia and won near unanimous support from Congress. On 7 August the Gulf of Tonkin Resolution gave the President authority to use armed force as necessary to assist South Vietnam against aggression and to repel attacks on American forces, which were, within days, massively reinforced. TAC deployed a Composite Strike Force and SAC sent more tankers. Aircraft from PACAF (Pacific Air Forces) included B–57s, F–100Ds, and F–105Ds. A U–2 found that MiG–15s and 17s had been moved forward to Hanoi from training bases in China. General Hunter Harris, Commander, PACAF, thus requested permission to destroy the new threat. At the same time, General Maxwell Taylor, U.S. Ambassador to South Vietnam, recommended "…a carefully orchestrated bombing attack" against North Vietnam. Rejecting their ideas, President Johnson still hoped that a mere show of force would be sufficient and that further escalation of the conflict could be avoided.

The "show of force" had little effect on the communists. Serious political instability in South Vietnam[1] encouraged the Viet Cong to intensify their efforts, and the flow of men and supplies down the Ho Chi Minh Trail through Laos from North Vietnam steadily increased. On 1 November the Viet Cong were confident enough to strike directly at the USAF with a mortar attack on Bien Hoa airfield that destroyed 5 B–57s and damaged 15 others. The USAF withdrew some of its deployed units to PACAF bases for safety. The U.S. Joint Chiefs of Staff urged that a riposte should be swift and tough. They had no faith in State Department arguments that the United States should follow a scale of graduated response. They believed that an escalating campaign would be taken by the North Vietnamese as a sign of weakness and would hand them the initiative, allowing them to choose the time and place of the next step. General LeMay, USAF Chief of Staff, believed that North Vietnam should be subjected to a punishing bombardment campaign, with the promise of more to come if negotiation was refused.[2] The JCS agreed. The President rejected their proposals, preferring the State Department's "tit-for-tat" option. However, acknowledging the deteriorating political and military situation, he agreed that American forces should launch some limited action immediately. In December 1964 the USAF, in a less-than-direct response, began Operation BARREL ROLL, conducting bombardment missions in Laos to assist Laotian forces against communist insurgents. President Johnson felt that the operation would serve to signal his determination to counter mounting communist aggression against South Vietnam.

However, the communists only increased their aggression, often targeting it specifically against Americans. On Christmas Eve 1964, they planted a bomb in the Brink Hotel in Saigon, which was being used as American officers' quarters. It exploded, killing 2 and wounding over 70. On 7 February 1965, the Viet Cong infiltrated a U.S. Army base and raided a nearby American advisers' compound at Pleiku, in the central highlands. They destroyed U.S. Army aircraft and inflicted over 130 American casualties, killing 8. Washington reacted by ordering raids on North Vietnamese barracks areas, President Johnson remaining concerned about "sending the right signal to Hanoi." In his turn, Ho Chi Minh signaled the Viet Cong to increase their efforts, and on 10 February they blew up another American hotel, this time in Qui Nhon, killing 23 Americans and wounding 21. The United States retaliated with further strikes on North Vietnamese barracks, but it would soon do more.

As the Viet Cong attacked Americans directly they raised the pace of their offensive elsewhere very sharply. They were often found operating as large, organized units, and they were achieving notable successes against the ARVN in the field. In the face of these unpalatable facts—the weakness of the Saigon regime, the consistent success of the Viet Cong, and the willingness of Hanoi to meet American challenges head on—the mood in Washington hardened; military leaders recognized that a turning point had been reached. They swept aside any talk of negotiated withdrawal by warning that American prestige was at risk and by demanding that military deployments to Southeast Asia be increased. The JCS believed that bombing the North was essential to halting communist erosion of the South, and they persisted in advocating a short, unrestrained air campaign to force Hanoi out of the war. President Johnson remained fearful that such a drastic step might bring Chinese or Soviet forces into the struggle. He, therefore, authorized limited air operations against the North, which he wanted kept within well defined and closely controlled parameters. His decision was announced in a cable to Ambassador Taylor: "We will execute a program of measured and limited air action against selected military targets in North Vietnam remaining south of the nineteenth parallel…. These actions will stop when the aggression stops." The program was to be carried out under the evocative codename ROLLING THUNDER.

ROLLING THUNDER

The conduct of the air war against North Vietnam was always a source of intense frustration to those local American commanders responsible for carrying out operations. President Johnson insisted on retaining such close control of the campaign that no significant target in the North could be struck without his personal approval. His targeting decisions were passed through Secretary of Defense Robert McNamara to the JCS, and were then issued as directives to the Commander in Chief, Pacific, who allocated targets and routes to the USAF, USN, and VNAF. Local air commanders responded to these orders, but had also to bear in mind their responsibilities to the Commander, Military Assistance Command, Vietnam (MACV), and to the American ambassadors in Saigon and Vientiane. This routing was necessarily inflexible and made quick reactions to developing situations almost impossible. It also created safe havens for the North Vietnamese within which their assets could not be attacked.

Initially ROLLING THUNDER selected objectives from a fixed list of 94 targets, principally bridges, railways, and roads. It authorized which could be struck during a given week and the number of sorties to be flown. It imposed copious restrictions to minimize local civilian casualties, although it seemed to make Soviet and Chinese citizens equally sacrosanct. It designated Hanoi, Haiphong, and a buffer zone along the Chinese border as protected areas. It spared ports from bombing and mining because of the danger to neutral (including Soviet) shipping. To avoid damaging crops it even designated dikes around rice paddies off limits; they, naturally, became favorite sites for anti-aircraft batteries. Worse still, for fear of hurting Soviet and Chinese advisers, it inflicted nothing more intrusive than reconnaissance against MiG bases and SAM sites being built and equipped; USAF pilots had to watch as they were completed and their crews trained, knowing that they would soon become lethal threats.

ROLLING THUNDER began on 2 March 1965, delivering an attack just 35 miles north of the Demilitarized Zone (DMZ). It sent 44 F–105Ds, 40 F–100Ds, 20 B–57Bs, and 7 RF–101Cs, supported by tankers and rescue helicopters, against the Xom Bong ammunition storage area. In post-flight debriefing, aircrews suggested that they had dropped the force's 120 tons of bombs on target, but indicated that anti-aircraft fire had been unexpectedly fierce. Many of the attacking aircraft bore scars of battle and six had been shot down. Sterling work by helicopters had saved five of the pilots, but one, Lieutenant Hayden Lockhart, had ejected from his blazing F–100 to become the first USAF prisoner of war in Vietnam.

As the weeks went by, ROLLING THUNDER intensified and North Vietnamese air defenses stiffened. American strikes moved farther north to the Dragon's Jaw Bridge across the Song Ma River at Than Hoa, half-way between Hanoi and the start of the Ho Chi Minh trail on 3 April. It was North Vietnam's sole north-south road and rail bridge and the only available route for rapidly moving military supplies heading south. It was thus high on the priority list of interdiction targets. The 3 April attack was to be the first

of many in a frustrating series lasting through seven years, until 1972.

Led by Lieutenant Colonel "Robbie" Risner of the 67th Tactical fighter Squadron, it was intended to be decisive. The mission's force was composed of 46 F–105s, 21 F–100s, 2 RF–101s, and 10 KC–135 tankers. The F–100s were to provide top cover and flak suppression for the main strike force of F–105s, 16 of which carried Bullpup missiles while the rest were loaded with eight 750-pound bombs each. Although it was well planned and executed, the mission was the first of many failures. It scored good hits on the bridge, but its 250-pound Bullpup warheads appeared to bounce off and the bombs merely punched easily repairable holes in roads and rail lines. The mission left the robust main structure of the bridge unaffected. To suffer this disappointment, pilots faced intense flak, which claimed an F–100 and an RF–101 and damaged many others.

ROLLING THUNDER aircraft re-struck the bridge the following day. It left the lightweight Bullpups behind and sent all 48 F–105s, each carrying eight 750-pound bombs. Although aircraft hit the bridge and its approaches with over 300 bombs, it still it stood, badly scarred but basically intact, a massive monument to overengineering. One F–105 was lost to flak before MiGs claimed their first victims of the war. In a high-speed attack, four MiG–17s burst out of low clouds and swept through a formation of heavily-laden F–105s waiting their turn at the target. Firing their 20-mm cannon, the MiGs shot down two on the first pass and kept going to ensure their escape.

The MiG's unwelcome intervention on a murky day suggested two things—that they intended to use hit-and-run tactics and that they were under radar control for interceptions. American countermeasures included the positioning of EC–121s over the Gulf of Tonkin to control traffic and to warn of approaching MiGs and the deployment to Southeast Asia of McDonnell F–4C Phantoms. For their part, the North Vietnamese understood the importance of bridges as choke points and quickly made the approaches to each of them a briar patch of anti-aircraft guns. Nevertheless, by late April USAF and USN attacks had destroyed 26 bridges and 7 ferries. American leaders were encouraged to believe that such disruption in what was a rudimentary transportation system must have a crippling effect on the struggle in the South and must weaken the determination of the North to continue the war. The bitter lessons of Korea seemed already to have been forgotten.

The F–105 Thunderchief, the primary strike aircraft in North Vietnam from 1965 until 1970, suffering in that time nearly 20 percent of the U.S. Air Force's total fixed-wing losses in the process. F–105D 58–1173, here loaded with 16 500-pound bombs, was used for armament trials in 1962.

In March 1965 U.S. Marines landed at Da Nang to secure American installations there. Their deployment to South Vietnam and ROLLING THUNDER's attacks on the North served to heighten public nervousness about the conflict throughout not only the United States but much of the world as well. To dispel this international unease, President Johnson made a speech in which he promised to engage North Vietnam in unconditional discussions. He further offered a $1 billion economic development program for North Vietnam to Ho Chi Minh if he stopped the aggression in South Vietnam. Hanoi's strident response left no doubt that it was not interested and suggested that its attitude had hardened because of the bombing

EC–121. Giving early warning of approaching MiGs was the primary role of the Lockheed EC–121 Warning Star in Southeast Asia. Other duties, undertaken by the EC–121R, included tracking likely targets through sensors sown along the Ho Chi Minh trail.

and increasing public criticism of government policy in the United States. Hanoi insisted on America's withdrawal from Southeast Asia and Vietnam's solving of its own problems.

In Washington there were two views—that the United States could meet such obduracy only by intensifying the bombing and committing more American combat troops to South Vietnam or that it should pause its bombing to pursue the possibility of negotiations, if only, in Secretary of State Dean Rusk's words, "…to meet criticisms that we haven't done enough." On 10 May the President cabled Ambassador Taylor, telling him that the forthcoming bombardment pause was intended to "clear a path toward peace or toward increased military action."

The pause was announced on 12 May 1965, but the North Vietnamese were not tempted. A series of diplomatic rebuffs led President Johnson to order the

bombing resumed and the second phase of ROLLING THUNDER opened after only five days. The operation authorized new targets, including some as far north as the rail lines linking Hanoi with China. American offensive sortie rates against the North rose steadily, reaching 4,000 for the month of May. More frequent armed reconnaissance missions attempted to harass targets of opportunity, such as trains and trucks. As such missions had been in Korea, these were unrewarding since the North Vietnamese increasingly abandoned movement by day or on main roads.

The first USAF loss to a surface-to-air (SAM) missile occurred on 24 July 1965 when an F–4C flying MiGCAP (top cover) for F–105s northwest of Hanoi was struck by what one of the pilots described as "a flying telephone pole." It was a Soviet SA–2, a two-and-a-half-ton missile guided by "Fan Song" radar. The

SA–2 could reach 60,000 feet and travel at Mach 2.5. By the end of 1965, 180 missiles had shot down 11 American aircraft, 5 of them from the USAF. Although not the most destructive of North Vietnam's defensive systems, the SAMs did force American attackers into a number of countermeasures—violent evasive maneuvers to defeat the missiles' ability to correct their tracking, and low-level missions in SAM areas to stay below the SA–2s effective envelope. Unfortunately, low-flying aircraft came within reach of the often lethal light anti-aircraft guns that proliferated everywhere in Vietnam. The USAF introduced a number of technological measures against SAMs such as Douglas EB–66s to detect and jam enemy radars and the more aggressive response of finding, engaging, and destroying SAM sites with specially equipped fighter-bombers, a method which came to be known as Wild Weasel.

Four two-seat F–100Fs initiated the seek and destroy operations. Using aircraft fitted with the Radar Homing And Warning (RHAW) system, a detachment from the USAF's Tactical Warfare Center arrived in Vietnam and began flying combat trials alongside F–105s. They were not only able to warn strike aircraft of imminent SAM firings, but also to home on the Fan Song radar's signals and either carry out or direct strikes against enemy sites. Later, modified EF–105F/Gs took over as principal Wild Weasels in missions to deliberately draw SAM fire. They then reacted with AGM–45 Shrike missiles, which followed the Fan Song beam to its source.

In their turn, the North Vietnamese showed their adaptability. They built SAM sites in profusion, many of which were either unoccupied or fake. They showed how quickly they could move from one site to another after a reconnaissance aircraft had seen them, and they developed sophisticated camouflage to make the sites look like villages or clumps of trees. Fake sites, equipped with dummy missiles and transmitting Fan Song signals to draw in American pilots, were surrounded by dense concentrations of guns known as flak traps. On 16 September 1965, a flak trap claimed the F–105 of one of the USAF's most celebrated airmen, Robbie Risner, condemning him to over seven years as a prisoner of war. Sadly, Risner's rank and reputation[3] ensured that he would

The unmistakable triple fins of the Lockheed EC–121 Constellation and the additional shark's fin of the upper radome in the background. The USAF Museum's EC–121D, named Triple Nickel *because of its 555 serial number, was the first ever to direct a successful aerial attack on an enemy aircraft—a North Vietnamese MiG–21 on 24 October 1967.*

EB–66 and F–105s. A Douglas EB–66 Destroyer acts as ECM (electronic countermeasures) escort for F–105s releasing their bombs over North Vietnam. EB–66s provided threat warnings and jamming protection against gun-laying radars and SAMs.

be singled out by his captors for special treatment. He was forced to endure the pain of physical torture and the deprivation of solitary confinement during his long incarceration.

By the end of 1965, so-called "fast-mover" squadrons of the USAF in Southeast Asia were spread among bases at Takhli, Korat, Ubon, and Don Muang airport in Thailand, and Tan Son Nhut, Da Nang, Bien Hoa, and Cam Ranh Bay in South Vietnam. Six squadrons had F–4Cs, which had begun to make their presence felt in the air-to-air war on 10 July 1965 when the combination of Phantoms and Sidewinder heat-seeking missiles accounted for two MiG–17s in a brief dogfight. Five more squadrons were equipped with F–105s,

four with F–100s, one with F–102s, one with B–57s, and one with F–5As. Other jet aircraft operating in support included RF–101s, KC–135s, RB–66s, and Wild Weasel F–100s. Special detachments were flying the RB–57E and the U–2C. Added to all these were USN squadrons flying from three carriers stationed in the South China Sea.

The air environment above Vietnam was growing increasingly hazardous. Of 273 American fixed-wing aircraft lost to enemy action in 1965, 158 belonged to the USAF. No fewer than 139 of the USAF's losses, including 54 F–105s, were attributed to AAA and small arms fire, a reflection in part of the fact that there were now more than 2,000 radar-directed AAA guns in North Vietnam.

F–4. Nothing about the McDonnell Douglas F–4 Phantom II is subtle. It is big, weighing up to 58,000 pounds loaded, and powerful, urged along by two General Electric J79s engines producing 17,000 pounds of thrust each in afterburner. It was the most significant Western combat aircraft to appear in the 1960s and was used to great effect during the Vietnam War for air superiority, strike, reconnaissance, and Wild Weasel missions. The USAF Museum's Vietnam veteran F–4C stands ready for air-to-air combat with a load of AIM–9 Sidewinders. Its two red stars identify it as the aircraft flown by Colonel Robin Olds, Commanding Officer, 8th Tactical Fighter Wing, and Lieutenant Stephen Crocker on 20 May 1967, when they destroyed two MiG–21s.

On 24 December 1965, President Johnson ordered a Christmas period cease-fire, which, for air operations, was extended into a prolonged bombardment pause. A "peace offensive" offered the withdrawal of American forces from Vietnam but refused the acceptance of Viet Cong participation in a coalition government in Saigon. Ho Chi Minh's rejected the offer as "deceitful," and on 31 January 1966, President Johnson opened the third phase of ROLLING THUNDER. Johnson was unwilling to accede to JCS requests for a marked increase in the tempo of the bombing and for the mining of enemy harbors. Still wanting to leave the door open for the North Vietnamese, he kept a tight grip on air operations, and phase three was less intense than phase two had

F–4 intake. Robin Olds' two victory stars decorate the plate that prevents turbulent boundary layer air from entering the engine. Bombs and Sidewinder missiles cluster under the port wing.

F–105 intake. The intakes on the Republic F–105 Thunderchief were unique. Their narrow reverse angle openings were designed to provide a double shock wave at supersonic speeds, to slow the air entering the compressor to an acceptable velocity. The Pratt & Whitney J75 engine could produce 24,500 pounds of thrust in afterburner, hurling the "Thud" along at speeds above Mach 1 at low-level or Mach 2 at 40,000 feet. The USAF Museum's Thunderchief served with the 357th Tactical Fighter Squadron, 355th Tactical Fighter Wing, based at Takhli, Thailand, in 1969. The two red stars record two aerial victories against MiGs. Memphis Belle II nose art is painted below the cockpit. The original Memphis Belle, a B–17, could not have carried the 12,000-pound bombload of an F–105.

F–105 cockpit. The second Thunderchief at the USAF Museum is an F–105G. It served in Southeast Asia from 1967 until the end of the Vietnam War, in the process flying numerous Wild Weasel missions and claiming three aerial victories over MiGs. It has two rear view mirrors, possibly to let the pilot keep an eye on the back-seater acquired by this late model aircraft, and it has the linear flight instruments fashionable at the time. The radar provided air search, automatic tracking, and terrain avoidance information.

F–105 tail. Aerials and electronic equipment caused the F–105's fin to grow lumps and irregularities on its smoothly swept surfaces. A ram air unit at the base of the fin provided cooling air for the rear of the aircraft. Clover leaf air brakes form the last three feet of the fuselage before the jet pipe.

RU

AF
60 504

391

MiG–21 tail. Although recognizably a MiG–21F (which flew with the Czech Air Force), the USAF Museum's Fishbed is marked as a MiG–21PF of the North Vietnamese Air Force.

been. However, by the end of March, the intransigence of Hanoi led Secretary of Defense McNamara to recommend that the bombing should be intensified and that the targets should include oil. Reluctantly, the President agreed, and phase four of ROLLING THUNDER began in June 1966, now under the operational control of Seventh Air Force, commanded by General William Momyer.

MiG–21 cockpit. Apart from the turquoise surroundings, the interior of the MiG–21's cockpit bears a marked similarity to its Western counterparts. Note the unusual canopy—hinged at the forward end.

For the remainder of 1966, American aircraft flew extended armed reconnaissance missions throughout the North (always excepting the Hanoi-Haiphong sanctuaries), attacked rail links with China, and made a determined effort against oil targets and the infiltration routes north of the DMZ. The pace of the air offensive increased sharply as American aircraft reached a peak of 12,000 sorties over North Vietnam in September. In spite of frequently poor weather and concentrated defenses, they inflicted substantial damage, demolishing countless trucks and railway wagons and hundreds of bridges, and cutting road and rail networks everywhere. An estimated two thirds of the North's oil storage capacity no longer existed. These considerable efforts forced the North Vietnamese to improvise. They stored oil in barrels rather than in large tanks, dispersing them in hundreds of minor dumps. They diverted perhaps 300,000 people into repair work and moving supplies, on foot or by bicycle if necessary. This they were evidently prepared to do as the ground war in South Vietnam gave no sign of slackening.

By the end of 1966 there were at least 150 SAM sites operating in North Vietnam, and the first MiG–21s had made their appearance carrying infra-red homing missiles. They could be seen flying from five airfields in the Hanoi area, but their bases were not on the list of targets for American aircraft. A typical execution order of the time included the instruction: "Not, repeat not, authorized to attack North Vietnamese air bases from which attacking aircraft may be operating." At least a partial answer to the MiG problem came in Operation BOLO. Colonel Robin Olds, who commanded of the 8th Tactical Fighter Wing flying F–4Cs, planned a mission to lure the MiGs into battle. On 2 January 1967, he and a force composed predominantly of F–4Cs approached the Hanoi area in a formation normally associated with a standard

A pair of thirsty F–4s waiting for a drink off the wing of a KC–135.

F–105 strike package. Cloud covered Hanoi and Olds had to trail his coat over the enemy airfields three times before MiG–21s began popping up on all sides. In the frenetic combat of the next few minutes, the Americans shot down seven MiGs for no loss. An extract from Colonel Olds' report of the action describes one success:

> [I] fell in behind and below the MiG–21 at his seven o'clock position at about .95 Mach. Range was 4,500 feet, angle off 15. The MiG–21 obligingly pulled up well above the horizon and exactly down sun. I put the pipper on his tail pipe, received a perfect growl, squeezed the trigger once, hesitated, then once again. The first Sidewinder leapt in front and within a split second turned left in a definite and beautiful collision course correction…. The missile went slightly down, then arced gracefully up, heading for impact. Suddenly the MiG–21 erupted in a brilliant flash of orange flame. A complete wing separated and flew back in the airstream, together with a mass of smaller debris. The MiG swapped ends

"Air Force Colonel Robin Olds Commander, 8th Tactical Fighter Wing," Fred Mason, 1970, USAF Art Collection.

immediately, and tumbled forward for a few instants. It then fell, twisting, corkscrewing, tumbling, lazily toward the top of the clouds. No pilot ejection occurred...

Determined enemy air defense efforts in 1966 drove up American fixed-wing combat losses to 465, of which 296 were USAF. Anti-aircraft artillery and small arms accounted for 265 USAF aircraft, and again the F–105s had suffered most heavily; no fewer than 103 Thunderchiefs had fallen to the guns.

A six-day truce on the occasion of the 1967 Lunar New Year (Tet) marked the end of ROLLING THUNDER, phase four. Phase five began on 14 February and lasted until Christmas 1967. During the year it took in the previously forbidden Hanoi-Haiphong area in which significant new targets were located, among them an industrial complex at Thai Nguyen, site of the country's only steel mill. Ringed with 96 AAA batteries and several SAM sites, it was a formidable challenge. Leading the first raid on 10 March were four F–105s, two of them equipped as Wild Weasels. On the run in, the lead aircraft was shot down and his wingman severely damaged. The remaining pair, led by Captain Merlyn Dethlefsen, set about the job of eliminating a SAM site that was threatening the strike aircraft bombing the steel mill. MiGs closed and attacked; Dethlefsen dived into the intense flak barrage to brush them off. The F–105s were hit repeatedly, but turned back into the flak twice more to drop their bombs and finish off the site with 20-mm cannon. Dethlefsen's fierce determination was rewarded with a Medal of Honor. He made light of his gritty persistence under fire: "All I did was the job I'd been sent to do," he said. "I expected to get shot at a lot." Following a similarly courageous action only a month later, a second F–104 Wild Weasel pilot earned a Medal of Honor. On 19 April 1967 Major Leo Thorsness braved heavy flak to hit two SAM sites, shot down one MiG, and damaged another while covering F–105 crewmen who had been forced to eject. He further engaged the attention of several other MiGs before the lack of ammunition and almost dry fuel tanks dictated his high-speed escape at low level and diversion to a forward base.

American aircraft hit other targets successfully in and around the Hanoi-Haiphong area in 1967— power plants, the provoking MiG airfields, and the Paul Doumer bridge across the Red River in Hanoi. They dropped several spans of the bridge at the first attempt with the help of 3,000-pound bombs. Elsewhere, Americans expanded their strike operations into the buffer zone with China and began mining rivers, but only south of the 20th parallel.

In stepped-up offensive operations, the air-to-air war moved increasingly in favor of the United States. The F–4D model of the Phantom and the AIM–4 Falcon missile arrived at the 555th Tactical Fighter Squadron, the combination scoring its first victory over a MiG on 26 October. By the end of the year, American aircraft had shot down 75 MiGs for the loss of 25 (a USAF ratio of 59 to 22), and American airmen had gained virtual air supremacy over North Vietnam. The year as a whole had seen American fixed-wing combat losses peak at 515; 325 of them were USAF; 252 of those were attributable to AAA and small arms fire.

In 1967 a number of studies closely scrutinized the results of ROLLING THUNDER, crediting the bombardment campaign with having hurt Hanoi's military-industrial base (such as it was) severely. Nevertheless, to Washington, Ho Chi Minh's strategy appeared to be unwavering, so did the North Vietnamese people's willingness to resist and carry on the war. What was more, in the balance account terms of Secretary McNamara, the bombing was costing the United States at least ten dollars for every dollar of damage inflicted. Even so, what might conceivably have made the difference, the mining of Haiphong and other harbors and thus the severance of North Vietnam's principal lifeline to the Soviet Union was still denied to American military leaders by President Johnson. He believed that the possible damaging of Soviet shipping was an unacceptable risk.

Following the 1967 Christmas bombardment pause, ROLLING THUNDER entered its sixth phase. It did so without McNamara, who was replaced as Secretary of Defense by Clark Clifford early in 1968. On 31 March 1968, Lyndon Johnson suspended all bombing north of the 20th parallel and announced that he would not be seeking a second term as President of the United States. To almost everyone's surprise, the North Vietnamese reacted by announcing that they would be willing to engage in peace talks. Later in the year, as the talks were underway in Paris and on the eve of the Presidential elections, Johnson halted the bombing of North Vietnam altogether. Forty-four months and over 300,000 sorties after it began, ROLLING THUNDER rumbled away into history.

The In-Country War

As the United States moved inexorably toward open involvement in Vietnam in 1964, it reconsidered the requirement for VNAF personnel to fly on all USAF operational sorties. On 18 February 1965, it rescinded the requirement, and the government of South Vietnam officially requested the USAF to fly in-country combat missions. B–57s struck at a guerrilla concentration the

O–1. Low-level FAC (forward air controller) missions in the slow, unarmored Cessna O–1E Bird Dog were hazardous operations, but the presence of a FAC to call in air strikes was often the difference between life and death for American or South Vietnamese ground forces in contact with the enemy.

next day. Other American combat aircraft became engaged in operations soon thereafter because a threatened coup in Saigon kept the VNAF otherwise occupied, standing by to intervene. By 6 March Washington accepted the inevitable and removed all restrictions on the use of American aircraft for combat in South Vietnam.

The restrictions lifted, USAF aircraft poured into the country under a crash program of airfield construction. By the end of 1965 the USAF had more than 500 aircraft and 21,000 men stationed at eight major air bases in South Vietnam. American ground forces had risen to over 200,000. Command arrangements for this massive military influx were labyrinthine. The general conduct of the air war in the South fell under the aegis of General William Westmoreland, MACV Commander, but, as 1966 dawned, the management of the air units was the direct responsibility of Major General Joseph Moore, MACV Air Deputy and Commander of the 2nd Air Division of the Thirteenth Air Force. (Later in the year, the 2nd Air Division became Seventh Air Force.) Moore answered to MACV for air operations over the South, but also looked after out-of-country missions for CINCPAC (Commander in Chief, Pacific). Not infrequently, the

two superior headquarters had urgent needs for the same squadrons at the same time. Answering to Major General Moore's Tactical Air Control Center in Saigon for operations within South Vietnam were four USAF-VNAF manned Direct Air Support Centers, one to each of four corps areas, which did their best to cooperate and assign air assets for tasks in support of the ground war. Complicating the picture was the fact that Moore's system had no control over aircraft belonging to either the Army or Marines.

Whatever juggling of air units was going on at staff levels, the control of combat aircraft once airborne was often in the hands of forward air controllers (FACs). Mostly former jet pilots, FACs spent much of the war flying the Cessna O–1 Bird Dog, a single-engined light plane capable of 115 miles per hour flat out and unarmed except for target marking rockets. Bird Dogs lacked even the minimal protection of armor and self-sealing fuel tanks. Since FACs had to make visual contact with the enemy and then hang around marking targets and directing strikes, their missions were among the most challenging flown by the USAF. Later, the O–1 was supplemented by the larger, twin-engined Cessna O–2 and the more capable North American OV–10, which had both armor and

OV–10 from the nose. Sponsons project from each side of the OV–10 with weapons attachment points. In this case, a rocket pod is fitted. The OV–10's power comes from two 715-horsepower Garrett T–76 turbo-prop engines, which were enough to make the Bronco a lively and extremely maneuverable aircraft.

OV–10 cockpit. The seat pan sits level with the cockpit rail, giving the pilot of the OV–10 the maximum amount of canopy to look through. A gunsight hangs down above the instrument panel.

OV–10. The North American Rockwell OV–10 Bronco was used by the U.S. Air Force primarily as a forward air control aircraft. Its large cockpit gave exceptional all-around visibility to both pilot and observer, who were placed in tandem on ejection seats. Additional fuel in the center-line tank allowed the OV–10 to offer extended time on station.

Major Bernard Fisher's A–1E Skyraider on the ramp in Pleiku, South Vietnam.

self-sealing tanks and carried powerful armament of its own. The job, however, was always hazardous. As one Skyraider pilot put it: "You've got to hand it to those guys…just a light plane, a pair of good eyes, and guts." During the war the USAF lost 122 O–1s, 82 O–2s, and 47 OV–10s in combat. Two FAC pilots, Captain Hilliard Wilbanks and Captain Steven Bennett, earned posthumous Medals of Honor for persistence and self-sacrifice in the face of heavy fire.[4]

FACs controlled a formidable array of strike aircraft and weapons. Fast movers like F–100s, F–4s, and B–57s could between them respond to calls for support with general-purpose bombs of up to 2,000 pounds, fragmentation bombs, cluster bomb units, a variety of rockets and missiles, gunfire, and the ground forces' weapon of choice—napalm. Soldiers liked napalm not only because it could be guaranteed to penetrate thick jungle foliage, but also because, since it created no shrapnel, it could be used very close to hard-pressed friendly troops. If the ground forces had a favorite aircraft, it was not among the jets. It was the prop-driven A–1 Skyraider. It could carry an incredible amount of ordnance, over four tons on 15 attachment points beneath the wings and fuselage, and it could stay in contact for long periods while its thirsty jet cousins came and went. Four 20-mm cannon made for lethal strafing attacks, and heavy

armor plating made the A–1 resistant to small arms fire. It was particularly suited for giving covering fire during rescue missions for downed aircrews, a task known as Rescue Combat Air Patrol (RESCAP). It operated under the call sign Sandy. By the end of the war, Sandies had assisted in the rescue of over 1,000 airmen.

On 10 March 1966, an outpost in the A Shau valley manned by 375 Montagnard irregulars and 20 American Green Beret advisers called for help against a force of 2,000 North Vietnamese. Flying extremely difficult close air support, four A–1Es led by Major Bernard Fisher faced thick, low clouds covering the rugged terrain, but they found a way into the valley through a gap in the overcast. Running the gauntlet of AAA and small arms fire coming from the valley slopes, they heard radio calls alerting them that the camp was being overrun. As they strafed the attackers, two of the Skyraiders were hit hard by enemy fire. One pulled up and made for home, but the other, piloted by Major "Jump" Myers, lost its engine and burst into flames. Myers bellied the aircraft onto the camp landing strip, exploding his external fuel tank in the process. He leaped clear into a ditch as flames enveloped his A–1E. Seeing that Myers was alive, Fisher called for a rescue helicopter before joining his wingman and two other newly arrived Skyraiders to strafe enemy troops trying to reach the downed pilot. However, the helicopter was at least 20 minutes away; the A–1Es were out of ammunition; and Fisher realized that the North Vietnamese would probably reach Myers before he could be rescued. Rather than run that risk, he decided to do the job himself. As the others made dummy runs overhead to distract the enemy, he landed his aircraft under fire on the shell-torn strip. Myers sprinted from the ditch and dived into the cockpit as Fisher opened up and roared away, dodging debris on the runway and climbing into the safety of the clouds. Fisher's Skyraider bore the scars of many hits, but made it back to base. For this breathtaking exploit, Bernard Fisher was awarded the Medal of Honor.

On countless occasions, close-support aircraft answered desperate calls for help from besieged troops and made the difference between survival and destruction. However, more than half of all operational sorties flown over South Vietnam were planned attacks on suspected guerrilla strongholds and supply routes. Such strikes were intended to deny the communists safe havens and storage areas, and they were carried out both day and night. In 1966 ground-based Combat Skyspot MSQ–77 radar was introduced. It guided bombers to precise release points, so allowing tactical strikes on selected targets at any time and in any weather.

The firepower for tactical operations was vastly increased in June 1965 when SAC made its B–52s available to MACV to fly combat missions under the codename ARC LIGHT. It was a surprising shift, but one which underlined the flexibility of air power. Fighter-bombers conducted strategic operations against the North while aircraft designed to promote the strategy of nuclear deterrence met tactical needs in the South. The B–52Fs flying the first ARC LIGHT missions from Guam were modified to carry 27 750-pound bombs internally and 24 more on external racks. Later, B–52Ds went through a "Big Belly" modification which allowed them to load the astonishing number of 84 500-pound bombs in the bay, while retaining the external capacity for 24 750-pound bombs. It was often claimed ARC LIGHT missions were wasteful, since the target intelligence on which they were based was in many cases less than certain and, in view of the B–52s' understandably slow reaction to a situation, seldom timely. Nevertheless, although the B–52s sometimes struck at empty forest, they were the most feared aircraft of the war, according to captured Viet Cong soldiers, whose morale had suffered terribly as they wondered when and where the earth would next erupt under attack. Because the B–52s operated so high, at 30,000 feet, unseen and unheard below, their hundreds

Bernie Fisher and "Jump" Myers after the astonishing rescue under fire in South Vietnam's A Shau valley on 10 March 1966 for which Fisher was awarded the Medal of Honor.

of bombs arrived as a complete surprise, obliterating nearly everything over a huge area. For anyone who had seen the awesome results of a B–52 raid, or had survived one, wondering when the heavens would open again concentrated the mind and weakened the spirit.

In 1967 part of the B–52 force was moved to Thailand. From there the big bombers could reach their targets much more quickly and without having to refuel. By then the B–52's contribution to the war had become considerable. Nearly two years after ARC LIGHT began, it launched its 10,000th B–52 combat sortie and was being increasingly relied on to break up enemy troop concentrations threatening American bases. For example, at the time of the Tet offensive in 1968, the enemy launched a major assault on the U.S. Marines' base at Khe Sanh, 6 miles from Laos and 14 miles south of the DMZ. General Westmoreland believed that "…the enemy hoped at Khe Sanh to obtain a climacteric victory such as he had done in 1954 at Dien Bien Phu." In January 1968, 20,000 North Vietnamese regulars attacked and surrounded the American base, keeping it under siege for 77 days. The USAF devised Operation NIAGARA to provide the Marines with air support, and General Momyer received temporary command of all American air assets operating at Khe Sanh. The USAF flew hundreds of sorties every day against enemy concentrations as

B–52 bombing. Its devastating rain of bombs made the high-flying B–52D, more commonly known as the Buff, the U.S. Air Force weapon most feared by the Viet Cong.

a C–130 command center handed off incoming fighter-bomber sorties to one of up to 30 FACs in good weather and let Combat Skyspot radar guide them in when clouds were heavy.

Although these missions were vital, the B–52s impressed the enemy most. A formation of three B–52s arrived over Khe Sanh every 90 minutes to bomb at Combat Skyspot's direction. Initially, NIAGARA established a buffer zone which allowed the B–52s to bomb no closer than 3,000 yards from the forward Marine positions. However, when it became apparent that enemy troops were developing extensive bunker complexes much closer in, the Marine commander nervously agreed to reduce the buffer to as little as 1,000 feet. Ensuing close-in strikes devastated enemy positions and exhilarated the Marines. A captured North Vietnamese soldier estimated that one strike alone had killed 75 percent of a 1,800-man regiment. His story rang true. By the time the siege was broken, the countryside around Khe Sanh had been transformed

into a wasteland and scarred by endless overlapping bomb craters. During NIAGARA American aircraft had dropped almost 100,000 tons of bombs, and two thirds of them had fallen from B–52s. Intelligence estimates suggested that two North Vietnamese divisions had been effectively destroyed as fighting units. It was hardly surprising that General Westmoreland later gave credit to the B–52s for preventing the large-scale build up of forces needed by the enemy to overrun Khe Sanh.

On the Trail

Although combat operations against the enemy's fighting forces, both North Vietnamese and Viet Cong, were essential to the war, they did not deprive communist insurgents in South Vietnam of their lifeblood. From the outset the vast network of rough roads and tracks through Laos, known collectively as the Ho Chi Minh Trail, had sustained the Viet Cong with a flow of supplies which grew steadily over the years to the proportions of a flood. The prime movers

B–52 nose. The looming presence of a Boeing B–52D Stratofortress dominates the USAF Museum's Modern Flight Gallery. The longest-lived combat aircraft ever produced, the B–52 has been in the front line since 1955 and will continue well into the 21st century. In Vietnam the B–52 was the weapon most feared by the enemy, particularly the big-belly B–52D with its internal capacity for carrying 84 500-pound or 750-pound bombs. The Buff in the USAF Museum saw action over Vietnam and was severely damaged by a surface-to-air missile on 9 April 1972.

B–52 cockpit. For all the complexity of the B–52, the cockpit is neatly and simply arranged. Flight instruments and radar scopes are in front of each pilot, and engine instruments run down the center in rows. At the top of the panel red warning light buttons signal engine fires and initiate extinguishers.

employed were thousands of Soviet ZIL–157 trucks. Stopping their movement became a paramount concern of American leaders.

Supplies from North Vietnam usually crossed into Laos and entered the Ho Chi Minh Trail through two passes—Mu Gia, about 75 miles north of the DMZ, and Keo Neua, which was twice as far. Much of the trail offered its users the natural concealment of a thick forest canopy, but its open spaces provided opportunities for reconnaissance aircraft to detect movement and for tactical aircraft to make visual attacks. Once American aircraft began operating over the trail, traffic moved at night through vulnerable areas. The first operations aimed specifically at interdicting the trail in southern Laos were codenamed STEEL TIGER. They began in April 1965, using roving F–100s and F–105s by day, and B–57s accompanied by C–130 flareships by night. The poor flying weather associated with the monsoon badly restricted operations until October, but STEEL TIGER sorties averaged over 1,000 per month, nevertheless. Even with the help of covert ground reconnaissance

A fistful of throttles. Each B–52 engine's throttle lever has two white knobs that allow the easier control of engines singly once the general setting for all eight has been made. To the left of the quadrant is the elevator trim wheel, and in front is the rotary control that allows the main undercarriage trucks to be offset before landing in a crosswind.

Re-arming an AC–47 Spooky. A broadside from three Gatling guns, each firing at rates of up to 6,000 rounds per minute, was spectacular.

teams to plot traffic on the trail, results did not match efforts expended and it became obvious that the USAF would have to greatly improve its interdiction methods.

It first had to prepare a systematic plan against areas of the trail in Laos contiguous with South Vietnam. The plan, codenamed TIGER HOUND, combined U.S. Air Force, Navy, Marine, and Army air resources with those of the small Royal Laotian Air Force. The USAF deployed UC–123s to spray defoliants on the forest obscuring the trail and established an airborne command post using C–47s and C–130s to control strike operations. FACs roamed the area, and RF–4Cs, equipped with infra-red sensors and side-looking radar, combed the trail for targets. F–100s, F–105s, B–57s, A–1Es, American carrier-borne aircraft and Laotian T–28s were on call for strikes; night operations added C–130 flareships and Army OV–1 Mohawks. Later, a few resurrected A–26Ks took on the night interdiction role, just as they had in Korea, and even some C–123s carried special detection devices and dispensed cargo-hold loads of bomblet canisters. By 1966, B–52s had joined in, operating with the aid of Combat Skyspot radars, and later came the sophisticated B–57Gs, fitted with low-light television, infra-red sensors, forward-looking radar and laser target-marking.

An electronic anti-infiltration system sometimes aided aircrews in their search for targets. It used small, air-dropped sensors which were sown along the trail and could detect the movement of troops and trucks. It transmitted information to a monitoring aircraft, like the EC–121R, which made assessments and recommended targets. Weaponry used against the trail was also unusual. Besides the conventional array of bombs, rockets, and guns were land mines, incendiary clusters, fuel-air explosive munitions, and even canisters of riot control gas.

This remarkable combination of air power instruments seemed impressive enough, but the most effective truck killers were found elsewhere, drawn from the unlikely ranks of tactical transports modified into forms that Admiral Nelson would have understood— gunships capable of firing broadsides of terrifying destructiveness. The first of the gunship line was the AC–47, Douglas's venerable "Gooney Bird" in yet another role. Known to the media as Puff, the Magic Dragon but to ground forces by the callsign Spooky, AC–47s were armed with three 7.62-mm mini-guns, which fired sideways from cargo-doors and windows. They attacked targets simply by flying an orbit around them and holding them centered in a sight placed to the left of the pilot in the cockpit window. Later, more sophisticated gunships included the AC–119K Shadow and several variants of the C–130 Hercules, the most advanced of which was the AC–130E Spectre. The Spectre was heavily armored and equipped with a multitude of sensors, including one which could detect running truck ignition systems. Its battery consisted of paired mini-guns and Vulcan 20-mm cannon, a 40-mm cannon and a 105-mm howitzer, all fired with the aid of a computer. A broadside from a Spectre was memorably devastating.

Gunships were as useful in South Vietnam against the Viet Cong as they were on the trail, giving timely aid to hard-pressed ground units on many occasions, their murderous fire destroying the cohesion of countless enemy attacks on Army bases and outposts. Impressive as the statistics of their destructive powers were, however, with literally thousands of trucks wrecked each year, even the mighty gunships could

not halt the flow of supplies along the Ho Chi Minh Trail completely, and the Viet Cong resolutely continued to increase their capability to operate in the countryside of South Vietnam throughout the 1960s.

Fetchers and Carriers

As is always the case in war, it was the men and machines engaged in front-line combat which caught the eye and monopolized the headlines. Behind them and their activities were a host of specializations without whose services the armed warriors could not have operated.

The contributions made by transport aircraft in World War II and Korea were essential to the conduct of the various campaigns, but in Southeast Asia their work was perhaps even more significant. The airbridge built across the Pacific by the Military Air Transport Service (Military Airlift Command from

C–141 medevac. A C–141 loads a medical vehicle at Cam Ranh Bay in April 1969. From 1965 Lockheed C–141s played a major role in the airlift of personnel and supplies within Southeast Asia and across the Pacific. Between 1965 and 1972 they flew over 6,000 aeromedical evacuation missions out of Vietnam.

A C–123 disgorging U.S. Marines at Calu, South Vietnam, in June 1968.

1965) was massive. In the absence of adequate ports and infrastructure in South Vietnam, it needed to be. In the early days the bulk of trans-oceanic traffic was handled by C–124s. MATS had 21 squadrons of them, backed up by 3 squadrons of C–133s, 7 of C–130s, and 3 of C–135s. The limitations of this force were soon exposed, and were emphasized by the fact that MATS had also to provide services elsewhere in the world. Only the C–124s and C–133s had the capacity to cope with such large items of equipment as tanks and bulldozers, but the C–124s were agonizingly slow and the C–133s technically temperamental.[5] Although help came from aircraft of the Air Force Reserve and Air National Guard, mostly aging C–97s and C–119s, the airbridge did not gain enough strength to take the strain fully until the appearance of the Lockheed C–141 Starlifter in 1965. The C–141A's ability to carry

its maximum payload of 67,000 pounds for 4,000 miles cruising at 440 knots was a quantum jump over the C–124's 25,000 pounds for 2,300 miles at 200 knots. Even so, the C–141's cargo bay was neither as high nor as wide as the C–124's, and it was not until Lockheed's giant C–5A Galaxy started operations into Southeast Asia in 1971 that the United States had a true strategic airlifter capable of handling the bulkiest military loads.

MAC did more than acquire new aircraft to improve its airlift capacity. Forced by the demands of the Vietnam War, it developed a whole new air transport system. It enlarged its established trans-Pacific routes to more than a dozen and equipped its airfields both en route and in Southeast Asia with longer runways and sophisticated facilities. It used more aircraft

404

and introduced freight priority categories; its "Red Ball" Express system guaranteed shipment of vital spares within 24 hours of receiving the request. MAC demonstrated an impressive capacity to react quickly in an emergency. For example, in 1967 C–141s and C–133s moved 10,335 paratroopers of the 101st Airborne Division, plus 5,118 tons of equipment (including 37 helicopters), from Fort Campbell, Kentucky, to Bien Hoa between 17 November and 29 December. It averaged an aircraft unloading time for this operation of just seven and a half minutes. MAC responded even more to the Tet offensive in February 1968, when it deployed a brigade of the 82nd Airborne Division at Fort Bragg, North Carolina, and a regiment of the 5th Marine Division at Camp Pendleton, California, together with 3,500 tons of equipment, to South Vietnam in only 12 days.

Outbound from Vietnam, MAC transports performed equally essential services. They took troops on rest and recuperation leave, evacuated the wounded, and carried the sad coffins of the dead. When it was all over, they went back to fetch those who had survived as prisoners of war and flew them home.

For tactical transports employed within the theater of operations, war had always held its hazards. In Vietnam, the risks were vastly more severe. In a country where there were no front lines and the enemy could appear almost anywhere, tactical transports operated at all times in a combat zone for American and ARVN troops who relied on them for supply in scattered outposts. They carried men and equipment quickly into areas for search and destroy operations, and they were involved in paratroop assaults. To keep the soldiers supplied, they landed on makeshift airstrips under fire or delivered loads using either the Low Altitude Parachute Extraction System (LAPES) or the Ground Proximity Extraction System (GPES) while flying through just above the runway. They also made deliveries by parachute, even when the drop zone was obscured, using either on-board or ground-based radar.

At first, C–47s and C–123s operated, but the immensely capable Lockheed C–130 Hercules began to appear in 1964, and in 1967 the U.S. Army transferred its force of de Havilland C–7 Caribous to the USAF. Small as it was, the C–7 proved invaluable. It was

Troops and vehicles of the 1st Cavalry Division and a C–130 of the 834th Air Division. C–130s showed incredible versatility during the Vietnam War, filling roles as strategic and tactical transports, tankers, gunships, command posts, rescue aircraft, drone controllers, and, occasionally, even as bombers.

simple and rugged, and it could get in and out of very short, rough strips. Its sortie rate under primitive conditions was remarkably high. In the 70 months after its transfer from the U.S. Army in January 1967 the Caribou flew over 773,000 sorties, an average of more than 11,000 per month. (Monthly averages for other types in theater during the same period were 6,651 for the C–123s and 8,597 for the C–130s.) In terms of lifting capacity, however, the C–130 had no competition. It was the most important theater transport aircraft for bulk movement, registering a high figure of 69,499 tons transported in one month. (The highest totals for other types were 16,643 for the C–123 and 10,264 for the C–7.) The ubiquitous C–130 was also involved in many other missions besides those in which it functioned as a gunship or aerial command post. It started forest fires by dropping oil drums (Operation BANISH BEACH), to sow anti-personnel mines during the interdiction of the trail in Laos, and it cleared instant helicopter landing zones in the forest with huge weapons like the 15,000-pound BLU–82 bomb (Operation COMMANDO VAULT).

On 12 May 1968, Lieutenant Colonel Joe Jackson answered a call for help from a special forces camp at Kham Duc. C–130s and C–123s had carried out an evacuation of the garrison under heavy fire earlier in the day, losing two C–130s and flying a third badly damaged in a desperate operation. Unfortunately, they had inadvertently left behind three members of a USAF control team who were in imminent danger of being overrun by enemy infantry swarming over the camp. Joe Jackson was flying a C–123 unsupported by attack aircraft. However, he judged that the Americans on the ground could not afford to wait. Approaching at 9,000 feet, he made a steep descent and slammed the C–123 down on the runway. Braking to a halt, he reversed the props and backed up to a point opposite the men taking cover. Guns, rockets, and mortars engaged the aircraft, but the control team managed to scramble on board and Jackson took off without being hit. For the daring rescue Joe Jackson was awarded the Medal of Honor, in a rare recognition of a "trash hauler" pilot.

Joe Jackson's exploit was extraordinary, but it was not unusual for unarmed trash haulers to face dangers or to brave enemy fire. During the siege of Khe Sanh, they supplied the surrounded Marine garrison entirely by air throughout, the C–123s and C–130s making 601 parachute drops and 460 landings between them. Transport crews operated daily into the besieged base, knowing that they would be exposed to anti-aircraft fire on the approach and over the field and to mortar fire on the ground. They reduced their

exposure time as much as possible by being unloaded on the move, so that their average touchdown to takeoff time was three minutes. Including those shot down or destroyed in attacks on Khe Sanh and other bases, the USAF lost 55 C–130s, 53 C–123s, and 20 C–7s during the Vietnam War.

Other Helping Hands

The combat aircrews who delivered the weapons and fought the enemy directly were only too well aware of the debt they owed to those in supporting roles, without whom their task would have been much more difficult and their chances of survival considerably reduced. The labor of the technicians who serviced the aircraft was especially close to their hearts, but the work of logisticians, air base defense teams, medical personnel, and many others was equally essential, though not often fully recognized. In the air, there were reconnaissance crews who sought out enemy defenses and likely targets, those who detected and countered enemy electronic trans-missions, the ever present tankers with their life-saving fuel, and the courageous men of the search and rescue squadrons.

Throughout the war, the USAF gathered copious information from many sources—visual observation, aerial photography, electronic surveillance and infra-red detection. Its aircraft were as varied as its intelligence activities. At one extreme was the Lockheed SR–71 Blackbird; at the other was the Cessna O–1. In between were jet aircraft like RF–101Cs, RF–4Cs, RB–57Es, RC–135s and U–2s, plus an assortment of remotely piloted vehicles (RPVs). Even for faster aircraft, gathering information was not a risk free exercise. In all, the USAF lost 33 RF–101s and 76 RF–4s in combat. Their task was not simple. Visual and photographic reconnaissance were often foiled by triple layer jungle, bad weather, and the preference of the enemy for movement by night. Emergencies, such as the siege of Khe Sanh, placed almost overwhelming demands on the reconnaissance forces. As a measure of the effort, fewer than ninety days of Operation NIAGARA at Khe Sanh involved almost 1,400 reconnaissance sorties.

Units like the 4025th Reconnaissance Squadron, responsible for a variety of RPVs or drones such as the Ryan BQM–34 series, performed much valuable reconnaissance work. RPVs, launched from C–130s, were capable of covering a very wide range of missions, including photography, television (with real-time transmission), ELINT (electronic intelligence), SIGINT (signals intelligence), jamming, and leaflet-dropping. Although programmed for a particular profile, their progress was monitored and could be adjusted by the C–130 controller as necessary. On return to a friendly

A low-flying C–123 over South Vietnam, escorted by an AC–47, in 1965.

area, the drone deployed a parachute and was snared by a recovery helicopter. The 4025th flew a total of 3,435 drone missions. It lost 578 RPVs.

Electronic support and electronic countermeasures (ESM and ECM) aircraft became increasingly important as the war went on. As North Vietnamese defenses became more electronically sophisticated, so the Americans responded with more competent electronic warfare systems. Most specialized of the USAF's aircraft in this role were the EB–66s, which were large enough for four radar receiver positions for detecting and identifying enemy signals and nine jammers for deceiving and disrupting enemy defensive systems.

Any doubts about the value of a tanker force were entirely dispelled in the skies over Southeast Asia. Whenever there were combat aircraft in action, there were tankers on station. They proved their worth repeatedly both as force multipliers and as aerial

lifeguards. Because tankers would be waiting, aircraft could take off with maximum weaponloads and then fill up with fuel at the top of the climb. On the way home after a strike, the tankers would refresh those that might otherwise die of thirst.

The KB–50Js that were originally in Southeast Asia were permanently grounded at the end of 1964. From then on, SAC took over aerial refueling and deployed its KC–135s in support of PACAF. It positioned tankers in Okinawa, Guam, Taiwan, and the Philippines, principally to look after deployments from the United States and to aid B–52 operations. SAC moved others forward into Southeast Asia to support the fighter-bombers. Since it regarded the tankers as highly valued assets, it based them not in South Vietnam but in Thailand. It spread as many as 172 KC–135s across the region between Kadena and Bangkok in 1972 and established 28 regular refueling stations over the countries of Southeast

KC–135 and drogue. A tanker streams a drogue from its boom prior to receiving a customer equipped with a probe. Air operations on the scale of those conducted by American military forces during the Vietnam War would not have been possible without the KC–135 tanker. Apart from enabling offensive operations to carry the maximum amount of ordnance to their targets, KC–135s were on hand to save countless aircraft leaving the combat area with low fuel or battle damage.

Asia and 7 more tracks in the area of the Philippines. In a little more than nine years of operating in support of the air war in Vietnam, SAC tankers gave away almost 9 billion pounds of fuel in the course of 813,878 refuelings.

These figures are spectacular, but they cannot begin to tell the whole story. On countless occasions, tankers were there to aid damaged or fuel-starved aircraft which would otherwise have been lost. Pilots often left the tanker with the heartfelt message: "Thanks, tank, you can count this a save." Some saves were often dramatic. Fighters could lose fuel so fast from battle-damage that they had to stay hooked-up and be towed back to base at the end of the tanker's boom. Others were stunningly complex, particularly one flown by a crew from the 902nd Air Refueling Squadron off North Vietnam on 31 May 1967. While engaged in refueling two F–104Cs, the tanker crew was asked to help a number of USN aircraft in dire straits. The first to arrive were two A–3s, both themselves equipped as tankers but

desperately short of fuel. As the A–3s each took a quick drink, two F–8s arrived, equally poorly placed. One latched on to the first A–3, while the other, so short of fuel that he could not afford to wait, hooked up with the second A–3, which was still attached to the KC–135. Further refuelings from the KC–135 took place in a complicated shuffle, including more for the original pair of F–104Cs, before two USN F–4s were taken on. The KC–135's own fuel supply was now so depleted that it was forced to divert into Da Nang, having transferred nearly 50,000 pounds of fuel in 14 contacts and saved eight aircraft in one sortie. In recognition of this remarkable achievement, Major John Casteel and his crew were awarded the 1967 Mackay Trophy for the most meritorious USAF flight of the year.

There were other airmen who regularly saved lives, but in a different way. The motto of the search and rescue (SAR) squadrons was "So That Others May Live." In pursuing this goal they routinely risked their own skins for anyone downed in enemy territory.

In the course of the war, all aircrews generally grew to understand that, if they were shot down, SAR teams would make every effort to get them out, regardless of location or risk. Such a policy did wonders for the morale of crews being asked to face some of the most effective air defense systems in the world. Unfortunately, once the opposition recognized what was happening, it used any downed flier as a lure around which it could gather a flak trap. Rescue missions therefore tended to increase in danger as time went by. Before it was all over, three Medals of Honor were earned in the course of rescue operations, two by helicopter pilots (Captain Gerald Young and Lieutenant James Fleming) and one by the pilot of a RESCAP A–1H (Lieutenant Colonel William Jones III).

In the early days of the war the few helicopters available for rescue in Southeast Asia were provided by Air America. It was not until mid-1964 and the open commitment of American forces to combat that the USAF deployed twin-rotor Kaman HH–43Bs and a few Grumman HU–16B amphibians specifically for rescue duties. Designed for local rescue in the United States, the HH–43B was not ideal for a combat area. It lacked armor, armament, and self-sealing fuel tanks, and it was short-ranged. As an interim solution, the USAF introduced armored HH–43Fs, but the range problem remained. In 1965 the arrival of Sikorsky HH–3Es, large, well-armored helicopters with a range of over 600 miles, improved matters. Fitted with a refueling probe, they could reach anywhere in Southeast Asia. Before long, the jungle camouflage of the HH–3E had gained it the nickname Jolly Green Giant. Two years later, the even more capable HH–53C Super Jolly Green made its debut and proved to be one of the great successes of the war. Nearly twice as large as the HH–3E, the Super Jolly was also faster,

Air rescue. On 23 February 1968, Captain Bernard Flanagan of the 355th Tactical Fighter Squadron had to eject from his F–100 after being hit by ground fire over South Vietnam. Within an hour he was rescued by an HH–3E helicopter of the 3rd Air Rescue Reconnaissance Group.

The Sikorsky CH–3, a big helicopter with an all-up weight of more than 22,000 pounds. Powered by two 1,500-horsepower General Electric T–58 engines, it had a maximum speed of nearly 180 miles per hour. In one form, the HH–3E, it became the "Jolly Green Giant" of Vietnam rescue missions. The USAF Museum's black CH–3E was used by the 20th Helicopter Squadron in Southeast Asia for clandestine operations, acquiring the nickname Black Maria in the process.

CH–3 cockpit. The hint that this is the cockpit of a big helicopter, a CH–3, is given by the glimpse of a cyclic control lever, just showing between the seats.

CH–3 detail. The combat record of this CH–3 is written in bullet hole patches.

more heavily armored, and formidably armed with three 7.62-mm miniguns.

As it developed, the SAR business became a highly organized operation. In 1967 it was renamed the Aerospace Rescue and Recovery Service (ARRS) and conducted missions into enemy territory by a rescue package of aircraft. By 1969 the mission commander was usually flying in an HC–130P equipped as a tanker and carrying an aerial tracker system for locating downed airmen. Escort was provided by A1E/H Sandies (later A–37Bs or A–7Ds could be included), and top cover by F–4s. Gunships might provide additional help. The Jolly Green carried a para-rescue jumper, trained as a scuba diver and medic, who was ready to jump or be winched down to the assistance of grounded aircrews. The helicopter's winch had 240 feet of cable ending in a heavy jungle penetrator to bring up its quarry through the jungle canopy.

The helicopter's crowning glory should have been a daring, well-planned, and brilliantly executed rescue of POWs from a camp outside Hanoi on 21 November 1971. One HH–3E full of U.S. Rangers deliberately crash-landed inside the prison compound while five CH–53Cs waited outside. Sadly, the cupboard was bare. The prisoners had been moved to another site

CH–3 winch. A vital resource for any combat helicopter is its winch. The CH–3 had a winch of 2,000-pound lifting capacity. Beyond is the rear cabin, which could accommodate up to 30 troops or 5,000 pounds of cargo.

A–1E. Stained with the grime of many combat missions and loaded with assorted weaponry, an A–1E Skyraider of the 1st Special Operations Squadron at Nakhon Phanom Royal Thai Air Force Base rumbles forward, with plenty of punch, on another escort and fire suppression sortie in support of rescue helicopters.

some time before. Out-of-date intelligence had led the rescuers to a rare failure. However, in this attempt and in more conventional rescues, the rescue teams proved clearly dedicated to their task. An example of their determination not to abandon aircrews to their fate was the rescue of Lieutenant Colonel Iceal Hambleton, the sole survivor from an EB–66 shot down on 2 April 1972. Hambleton avoided capture by the enemy for 12 days under an umbrella of A–1Es, OV–10s, and an assortment of jet fighters and heli-copters. His rescue cost several aircraft, but his rescuers never considered giving up on him as long as he was free.

From almost any point of view, the creative inno-vation demanded by the rescue challenge and the massive effort expended were worth it. No service was more respected, and perhaps none was more rewarding. By the end of the war the ARRS had successfully recovered 3,883 men—but not without cost. In the process, 45 rescue aircraft were lost and 71 men gave their lives.

The Beginning of the End

The bombing halt ordered by President Johnson as he came to the end of his term of office in 1968 was confirmed by President Nixon in January 1969. At that time the personnel strength of American forces in Vietnam had reached 536,000. Before the year was out Nixon announced a program of Vietnamization and initiated a steady American withdrawal from Southeast Asia. In April 1970 American troops joined with the South Vietnamese in an invasion of Cambodia to attack enemy bases and supply routes, but within months the U.S. Congress had banned the use of American ground forces in Laos or Cambodia, greatly encouraging the North Vietnamese. In addition, for more than three years after taking office, President Nixon maintained the ban on bombing the north. The North Vietnamese took advantage of the respite to build up their forces and prepare for an invasion of the south. They revived their industries and rebuilt their power stations, bridges, roads, and railways. The Soviets and Chinese poured supplies into the country and the North Vietnamese Army undertook exhaustive training exercises. American reconnaissance aircraft, which continued to fly over North Vietnam and continued to suffer losses, in spite of agreements made at the Paris talks supposedly guaranteeing them safe passage, continued to watch all of this. American tactical aircraft made tit-for-tat strikes, which targeted air defense sites. They carried out a series of strikes at the end of 1971 aimed at airfields, SAM sites, oil storage areas, and truck parks intended to deter the build-up of Hanoi's forces, but having little effect.

On 30 March 1972, the North Vietnamese invaded the South, sending large forces across the DMZ and developing other thrusts out of Laos and Cambodia to cut the country in half. With American military strength now down to less than 100,000, they hoped to overwhelm Saigon's forces, and Hanoi banked on Nixon's reaction being limited by anti-war feeling in the United States. Really effective response from the USAF was no longer possible. Fewer than 100 USAF combat aircraft remained in South Vietnam, and the total in the whole of Southeast Asia was down to 375. In any event, the North Vietnamese launched their invasion during the cloudy northeast monsoon, and the weather kept most aircraft from interfering with the ground battle. Those pilots who did make contact with North Vietnamese troops found that they were well covered by anti-aircraft systems. Large numbers of AAA guns and mobile SAMs were evident, and there was a new threat in the form of the shoulder-launched SA–7, a portable heat-seeker which could reach out to 8,000 feet. FACs and the A–1s of the VNAF, operating at relatively slow speeds and low levels, were particularly vulnerable.

Since the United States would not return ground forces to Vietnam, it recognized that American assistance to South Vietnam in repelling the invasion would have to come from the air. Accordingly, the USAF, USN, and USMC redeployed substantial numbers of aircraft to Southeast Asia. By mid-year, the USAF had almost 900 strike aircraft available, and the total number from the three services was up to 1,380. To begin with, strike operations against the North, conducted under the codename FREEDOM TRAIN, were restricted to areas south of the 20th parallel, but the alarming success of the invading forces led President Nixon to abandon the peace talks in Paris and authorize operations on a much more ambitious scale. These, at last, called for mine laying in and around North Vietnam's harbors and, on 8 May 1972, Nixon cleared a comprehensive campaign against a wide range of targets in the north called LINEBACKER.

LINEBACKER was not ROLLING THUNDER revived under a different name. It is true that there were still

OV–10. The North American-Rockwell OV–10 Bronco was a third generation forward air controller aircraft in Southeast Asia. Unlike its predecessors, the much faster OV–10 had armor plating, self-sealing fuel tanks, and carried substantial fire power.

A boomer's eye view of a 17th Bombardment Wing B–52 taking on fuel—an endlessly repeated activity in Southeast Asian skies during the Vietnam War. The bringing together of two very large aircraft close to each other became routine, but was always a challenge, demanding steadiness and high levels of skill from the aircrews involved.

some restrictions on target selection. LINEBACKER could not deliberately attack sensitive targets, such as anything close to the Chinese frontier or in densely populated areas of Hanoi. However, American air power generally was no longer micro-managed from the White House. Air Force commanders were able to use their judgement in seeking to destroy the transportation system, air defenses, and stocks of military supplies in the North. Immensely adding to the weight of the campaign, B–52s were allowed north of the 19th parallel for the first time, and, from September, F–111s were available to add their 24-hour all-weather capability. Operationally, the crews of the fighter-bombers were greatly aided in their offensive by "smart" bombs, which markedly increased the effectiveness of their strikes.

F–4s carrying Mk 84 2,000-pound and Mk 118 3,000-pound bombs fitted with laser-seeking heads and control surfaces made systematic attacks on the bridges of North Vietnam. The results were spectacular. On 13 May, 16 F–4s delivered twenty-four smart bombs between them against the infamous Than Hoa bridge, wrecking a target which had defied American airmen for years.[6] By the end of June American aircraft destroyed or badly damaged more than 400 bridges in North Vietnam. North Vietnamese use of more basic forms of transport, such as bicycles and small boats, ensured that the supply system did not grind to a complete halt. Nevertheless, the flow south became a trickle and, with the effective mining of North Vietnam's harbors, LINEBACKER was hurting the enemy's attempts to maintain the scale and pace of the offensive in the South.

For the USAF, LINEBACKER provided a serious challenge. The air defenses of North Vietnam had stiffened in the years since ROLLING THUNDER, and by 1972 the Hanoi-Haiphong region was one of the best defended areas in the world, bristling with AAA and SAM sites. Nearby, North Vietnam's air force had well over 200 MiG 17s, 19s, and 21s, and many of its pilots were old hands and the survivors of earlier battles. By contrast, USAF aircrews were generally younger than they had been in the 1960s, and the majority had never been in aerial combat. The MiGs now represented a formidable threat and, for a while, the kill-loss ratio swung in their favor. During ROLLING THUNDER, 85 percent of American aircraft downed were lost to AAA fire. Of the 44 USAF aircraft lost on LINEBACKER operations, 27 were shot down by MiGs.

Instrumental in turning the situation around was the establishment of "Teaball," a control center based in Thailand that coordinated all available information on enemy air force operations from radar and an assortment of intelligence-gathering sources. Teaball passed its information via various command aircraft to airborne missions to give them up-to-the-minute warning of enemy activities. Thus prepared, USAF crews began to give a better account of themselves, positioning their aircraft to meet approaching threats, and using the F–4's radar and its greater speed and power to advantage in countering the MiG's superior agility. In this environment, the USAF gained its only aces of the war. On 28 August 1972, Captain Steve Ritchie of the 555th Tactical Fighter Squadron, piloting an F–4E, shot down his fifth MiG–21. In the weeks that followed, two weapon systems officers, both F–4 back-seaters, also became aces. Captain Charles De Bellevue of the 555th Tactical Fighter Squadron raised his score to six MiGs (four with Ritchie), and Captain Jeffrey Feinstein of the 13th Tactical Fighter Squadron claimed five.

The LINEBACKER offensive was massive. Between April and October 1972, 155,548 tons of bombs fell on North Vietnam. Technology ensured that most of them were delivered with considerable accuracy. Although it was successful in the end, the campaign did not have any immediate effect on the invading North Vietnamese forces in South Vietnam. They had built up huge stockpiles of supplies to ensure that they could sustain their invasion. For the first few weeks, the NVA maintained relentless pressure on its ARVN opponents, threatening to provoke their complete collapse and so succeed in overrunning the country. Quang Tri fell, and the cities of Hue, Kontum, and An Loc seemed about to follow. On

all fronts, it was air power that blunted and then smashed the communist offensive, giving the ARVN time to recover and launch its own counteroffensive. Tactical transports repeatedly supplied besieged garrisons undergoing reinforcement, and fighter-bombers and gunships flew thousands of sorties against the NVA forces. The number of fast-mover sorties flown jumped from 247 in March to 7,516 in May. However, it may have been the B–52 attacks that proved decisive. Unlike the elusive Viet Cong, the NVA offered plentiful, recognizable targets—concentrations of troops and armor and lengthy truck convoys. On numerous occasions, B–52s caught the enemy in the open and effectively destroyed whole units, sometimes breaking up attacks less than half a mile in front of friendly forces. General John Vogt, Commander, Seventh Air Force, said that facing regular mechanized army units "…permitted air to put fire-power in on good, worthwhile targets instead of little huts in the jungle and a few scattered guerrilla bands…. After a good dose of [American air power] for several months, enemy ranks were so badly decimated that they lost all their offensive punch…"

By the middle of June the North Vietnamese invasion had stalled. The ARVN went over to the offensive, and on 13 July the Paris talks resumed. The last American ground forces left Vietnam in August, and, on 8 October, after North Vietnam had suffered a particularly concentrated period of bombing, Hanoi's representatives in Paris put forward new proposals. Within days the prospects for an agreement seemed promising, and on 23 October President Nixon terminated LINEBACKER. All bombing north of the 20th parallel was brought to a halt. Unfortunately, North Vietnam once more engaged in delaying tactics and used the time to restore its forces. When its representatives walked out of the talks on 13 December, Nixon ordered a resumption of the bombing. There followed an 11-day campaign, codenamed LINE-BACKER II, the most intense aerial assault of the war. It was intended to bomb North Vietnam back to the negotiating table.

The Way Out
From 18 to 29 December 1972, by day and night, American aircraft pounded airfields, military bases, oil storage, power stations, rail yards, and port facilities in and around the Hanoi-Haiphong area. In a significant development B–52s joined the attacks on the North Vietnamese capital. For the first time, Hanoi's leaders felt the crushing weight of conventional strikes from the big bombers for themselves, and the B–52s were exposed to the serried ranks of SA–2s defending the city.

F–4E. All brute power and awkward angles, F–4 Phantom IIs, in aerial combat with MiGs, scored 145 kills and achieved a kill-to-loss ratio of 3.73 to 1. The U.S. Air Force lost 33 F–4s to MiGs, 17 of them in 1972.

Ahead of the first B–52 raid, F–111s hit the MiG airfields and F–4s sowed chaff corridors to screen the bombers. Their protective effort was not entirely successful. High winds dispersed the clouds of chaff and the SAM sites fired over 200 missiles, shooting down three B–52s and damaging three more. After three days, B–52 squadrons had flown 300 sorties, but had lost 9 aircraft. Although a 3 percent aircraft loss was judged acceptable in World War II, it could not be long supported in a limited war. B–52s were too valuable. It was also ominous that six aircraft had been shot down on the third night, suggesting that worse might come. SAC took a close look at tactics being employed and realized the need for a change. It decided that B–52Gs not yet fitted with the upgraded ECM of the B–52Ds were to be kept away from Hanoi. B–52s would bomb from varying heights and different directions as raids became more concentrated in time, and they would avoid steep escape turns after bombing because they produced large radar returns. Their crews were authorized to make random altitude changes to confuse the SAM operators. Using these new tactics on the four remaining nights up to Christmas Eve, the B–52s suffered only two losses.

After a pause for Christmas Day, LINEBACKER attacks resumed all out, this time on Hanoi's air defenses. Most other targets had already been hard hit, but the North Vietnamese still gave no indication that they were ready to sign an agreement. If they hoped to shoot down more B–52s and so make the cost of continuing too high for the American public to bear, the destruction of their air defenses would remove that possibility and leave them vulnerable to whatever further operations American air power chose to undertake. On 26 December B–52s and F–111s blasted MiG airfields, SAM and radar sites, and command and control centers, but in perhaps the decisive blow, F–4s used the LORAN technique to destroy the main SAM assembly area in Hanoi. At the end of the day, the North Vietnamese condemned the "extermination bombing" but let Washington know that they were ready to renew talks. The bombing continued until the arrangements were finalized, but on 29 December LINEBACKER II was over. The B–52s had flown 729 sorties in 11 days and had dropped over 15,000 tons of bombs. The fighter-bombers added another 5,000 tons. The North Vietnamese had fired 1,242 SAMs and the USAF had lost 26 aircraft, including 15 B–52s.

416

There can be little doubt that the LINEBACKER campaigns together were instrumental in bringing the North Vietnamese back to the conference table in a frame of mind to sign an agreement. Peace talks were resumed on 8 January and the ceasefire document was signed on 23 January 1973. That took care of American combat activities in Vietnam, but not in Laos or Cambodia. The USAF continued bombardment operations against communist forces there in response to requests from the beleaguered governments. It flew its last sorties in Laos in mid-April and in Cambodia in mid-August, when Congress reacted to an escalation of the bombing by cutting off all funds for the air war.

The sad aftermath came in April 1975, when North Vietnam brought a whirlwind campaign of conquest in the South to its conclusion, and the United States set in motion its emergency evacuation plan, FREQUENT WIND. On 1 April USAF C–130s and C–141s began airlifting Americans and South Vietnamese refugees out of Tan Son Nhut Airport, Saigon. The USAF removed load restrictions on 20 April and the transports began setting records. A C–141 recorded 316 people on board, and C–130s took as many as 260. (Normal limits were 94 and 75.) As the airfield came under fire in the final days, the operation shifted to helicopter evacuation from the American Embassy compound. Fighters and gunships provided escort and were forced to attack enemy radars and gun batteries to preserve the American lifeline. With the triumphant North Vietnamese on the doorstep, the last helicopter lifted away from the embassy on 30 April, ending an operation in which American aircraft had brought out over 57,000 people from Saigon.

The Final Cost
In terms of the expenditure of national treasure, the air war in Southeast Asia was an expensive exercise for the United States. Combat over Southeast Asia between 1962 and 1973 cost the USAF alone 1,679 fixed-wing aircraft and 58 helicopters. It cost a further 495 fixed-wing aircraft and 18 helicopters in accidents, bringing the total USAF loss to 2,250 of all types.[7] Over six million tons of air munitions were expended, which was about three times the amount for all theaters in World War II.

By far the most successful of the enemy's defenses were AAA and small arms fire, which accounted for 1,459 of the USAF aircraft; 112 fell to SAMs and to MiGs. A further 103 aircraft were lost during enemy attacks on air bases. Of USAF aircraft involved, the fast-movers understandably provided most of the combat losses, with 379 F–4s (plus 76 RF–4s) and 334 F–105s at the top of the list. Some way behind were 198 F–100s and 153 A–1s.

Out of more than five million sorties, it could be claimed that casualties suffered were not too excessive; 2,118 airmen were known to have been killed and 3,460 wounded. The number of prisoners was never established with such precision. At the end of the war the North Vietnamese acknowledged holding 588 Americans in captivity, plus another three in China. Of those, 472 were airmen from all services. A longer list of airmen fell into the "missing" column, leaving an open wound of uncertainty that has never satisfactorily healed.

American prisoners had lived under stark conditions and had endured often barbaric treatment. It was a tribute to their collective spirit that so many survived their ordeal and emerged unbroken. To them, the sound of B–52s over Hanoi in 1972 was a message of hope. Colonel Risner, incarcerated for over seven years, felt that his lengthy trial was about to end: "We saw a reaction in the Vietnamese that we had never seen under the attacks from fighters. They at last knew that we had some weapons they had not felt, and that President Nixon was willing to use those weapons to get us out." Colonel Jon Reynolds agreed: "For the first time, the United States meant business. We knew it, the guards knew it, and it seems clear that the leaders of North Vietnam knew it."

Notes

1. President Diem had been assassinated in November 1963 and a struggle for power had ensued.
2. During Pentagon war games on the situation in Southeast Asia, General LeMay reportedly complained about civilian-imposed restraints on military action. He believed that the United States should use every available resource against North Vietnam. With typical bluntness, he summed up views by stating that, if necessary, "…we should bomb them back to the Stone Age."
3. Lieutenant Colonel Risner had been featured on the cover of *Time* magazine just a few months before he was shot down.
4. There were also Super FACs. F–100Fs were used to mark targets in North Vietnam. George "Bud" Day, Medal of Honor recipient and the most decorated American military man since Douglas MacArthur, became a POW in 1967 after his F–100F was shot down during a Super FAC mission.
5. The C–124 took almost two weeks to make the round trip between the United States and Southeast Asia, accumulating 95 flying hours in the process.
6. By contrast, during the attack against the Than Hoa bridge on 3 April 1965, despite 638 750-pound bombs dropped and 298 rockets fired, the bridge remained standing.
7. Fixed-wing losses for all American services in combat were 2,561; losses in accidents were 1,158. Helicopter losses for all services were a dramatic 4,869, a figure reflecting in part the hazards of the U.S. Army's operations in troop support. However, it should be noted that 2,282 of these were recorded as "operational (non-combat) losses."

Our superiority in the latest types of technology is a fact, comrades, and one cannot escape facts.

(President Leonid Brezhnev, U.S.S.R., July 1968)

The Soviet Union has military superiority over the United States. Henceforth the United States will be threatened. It had better get used to it!

(N. Ogarkov, U.S.S.R., to U.S. Congressman, 1979)

Our principal adversary, the Soviet Union, disposes military power to a dangerous degree, but otherwise is adrift in a sea of troubles.

(Alexander Haig, Caveat, 1984)

All of a sudden a 130 exploded. It was one hell of a fire—a huge, mammoth fireball.

(Colonel Charlie Beckwith, U.S. Army, after the disaster at Desert One, April 1980)

Far better it is to dare mighty things to win glorious triumphs, even though checkered by failure, than to take rank with those poor spirits who neither enjoy much nor suffer much, because they live in the grey twilight that knows not victory or defeat.

(President Theodore Roosevelt)

Chapter 11

Resurrection

Awesome Capabilities

After seeing the flood of material dealing with the Vietnam War, USAF Museum visitors enter drier territory in seeking for the artifacts of the 1970s and 1980s. The relative drought is in part an indication that the present is on the horizon. More treats await, but the journey through the history of air power is approaching its final stages. The story of the post-Vietnam era is both important and interesting, but many of its characters have outlived its challenges and continue to perform in the front line. Their future place in the USAF Museum may be assured, but they still have many miles to travel before retirement.

Among the most dramatic exhibits in the museum's Modern Flight Hangar is the Lockheed SR–71 Blackbird, a strategic reconnaissance aircraft spectacular both in appearance and achievement. Although a product of the 1960s, it still reigned supreme in the 1990s, its accomplishments unsurpassed. In 1976 an SR–71 established world records for speed (2,193 miles per hour) and for height in sustained horizontal flight (85,069 feet). The aircraft on display flew the first operational SR–71 sortie in 1968 and went on to accumulate 2,981 flying hours—more than any other SR–71.

Another aircraft with its genesis in the 1960s is the Rockwell B–1A Lancer. It is the direct ancestor of the B–1Bs now in service and so can claim that its test flying laid the foundation for a strategic bomber force of awesome capability. Nevertheless, it stands as a reminder that vacillations in defense policy and operational requirements can bedevil the production of major military aircraft. This B–1A, the fourth and last built, represents the midway point in a turbulent span of more than 20 years that stretched between the origin of an idea for the aircraft and its appearance as an operational reality.

The U.S. Air Force's new age dawned with the appearance of the McDonnell Douglas F–15 Eagle. First flown in 1972, the F–15 was the answer to a Vietnam fighter pilot's prayers. The value of the Eagle to the modern USAF is such that few can yet be retired from operational service. The museum's example is a special pre-production aircraft, with basic differences in systems and structure from those of the fighter squadrons. Named the Streak Eagle, it was used as a record

General Charles Gabriel, eleventh U.S. Air Force Chief of Staff from 1982 to 1986. General Gabriel flew combat missions both in Korea, in F–51s and F–86s, and in Vietnam, in F–4s, and was Chief of Staff during the critical re-equipment period of the early 1980s.

breaker. In 1975, flying from Grand Forks, North Dakota, it set eight time-to-height world records on the way to reaching 98,425 feet (30,000 meters) just 3 minutes and 28 seconds after brake release. The flight profile, flown by Major Roger Smith, read as follows:

> Release from hold-down cable at full afterburner with 7,000 pounds of fuel.
> Gear up and rotate at 70 knots, 3 seconds after release.
> At 420 knots, rotate into an Immelman and hold 2.65G.
> Expect to arrive level, upside down, at 32,000 feet and Mach 1.1.
> Rotate to right side up and accelerate to 600 knots while climbing to 36,000 feet.

419

*Accelerate to Mach 2.25 and pull 4Gs to a
60-degree climb angle. Hold 60-degree climb.
Shut down the afterburners when they quit.
Shut down the engines when they flame out.
Ride ballistically over the top at 55 knots and
103,000 feet.
Descend at 55-degree dive angle. When below
55,000 feet, try to start the engines.
Go home.*

*The museum does not, on the USAF's 50th anniversary,
own a truly representative General Dynamics F–16 Fighting
Falcon. Fighter squadrons still have too much to gain from
hanging on to their F–16 assets. The one on display is an
early pre-production F–16A sheep masquerading in the
colors of a DESERT STORM wolf. It is painted to represent
an F–16A of the 169th Tactical Fighter Group, South
Carolina Air National Guard, which took an active part
in DESERT STORM.*

After Vietnam

The USAF came out of the Vietnam War with
mixed feelings, believing that while it had generally
performed well and done the job it was asked to do,
it could have done more, and that a truly effective
use of air power had been frustrated by political
constraints. At an individual level, the American
serviceman generally experienced relief and pleasure
that the war was over, but those sweet sensations
were soured as he also experienced resentment toward
the large proportion of the American people who
had turned their opposition to the war into a lack
of sympathy for those who had done the fighting.
Even more uncomfortable to the American serviceman
was the realization that so many lives and so much
effort had been expended over more than a decade
to achieve political and diplomatic defeat for the
United States in Southeast Asia.

The open wound of Vietnam was slow to heal,
but the pain and irritation it engendered forced the
American military into a critical examination of the
nature of the war and the way it was fought. Doctrine,
methods, and equipment all changed in the aftermath
of Vietnam, but perhaps no transformation was more
profound than the move that led to the creation of all
volunteer services backed by strong reserves. Terms
like "conscription" and "the draft"' were cast aside,
and the standing forces of the United States were
made professional in every sense of the word. For
an increasingly technical service like the USAF, it
was especially welcome. Rates of pay increased to
match more closely those of the civilian world, and
talented people could be attracted by the prospect
of a rewarding career. The resulting air force might
be smaller, but it brought the promise of being better
trained and more competent than ever before.

*Teeth for the U.S. Air Force of the 1980s—the McDonnell Douglas F–15 Eagle and the General Dynamics F–16 Fighting Falcon, immensely
capable successors to the F–4, both superb as air superiority or ground attack aircraft.*

The USAF in particular was active in evaluating its performance in Vietnam and thereby seeking radical improvements in equipment, organization, and training. Not all of the news was bad, and a great many lessons had been learned, ranging from how (and how not) to use an air force as a political instrument to the inestimable value of "smart" weapons. The USAF had shown that it had the power to stop determined ground assaults in their tracks and, during LINEBACKER II, to influence an opposing leadership decisively. It had developed gunships and had gained an understanding of operating aircraft in high-threat environments. It had emphasized the vital importance of teamwork, whether it was in "strike packages," working with FACs, attempting rescues, or carrying out any other mission in the face of the enemy. Notably, a new generation of USAF officers and men had been tested in combat and had come away with firm ideas about the way their service should meet the challenges of the future.

In the first instance, recoiling from its open conflict with communism in Vietnam allowed the USAF to focus all of its attention on its principal concern—the direct Cold War confrontation with the Soviet Union. While contributing its B–52s to Southeast Asia, Strategic Air Command had not forgotten its deterrent role, nor had USAFE dropped its guard in Europe. This was fortunate, since the Soviet Union seemed to be gaining in strength and expanding its influence in the world at a time when the United States was depressed by its failure in Vietnam and upset by political turmoil at home. In Asia, Africa, and Central America, Soviet interests were prospering, and they were backed by impressive military power. Soviet armed forces had a personnel strength of 3.5 million, and its front-line equipment appeared to be a match for anything produced in the West. Over 1,500 land-based ICBMs (intercontinental ballistic missiles), 600 submarine-launched missiles, and 600 IRBMs (intermediate range ballistic missiles) targeted the NATO (North Atlantic Treaty Organization) countries. The Soviet Union was defended by 10,000 SAMs and 3,000 manned interceptors operating under comprehensive radar coverage. Moscow was ringed by an ABM (anti ballistic missile) system. There were 600 medium-range and 140 long-range air force bombers, and news of a supersonic, swing-wing strategic bomber—the Tu–160 Blackjack—close to operational service. The Soviet Army's massive and heavily armored ground forces were supported by 4,500 tactical aircraft. Added to these were the 6,000 plus aircraft of various types operated by the Soviet Navy. As time went on, Soviet weaponry got even better, with an apparently endless succession

of new missiles and combat aircraft from the Mikoyan and Sukhoi factories that posted remarkable performance figures. In the 1970s, Khrushchev's earlier boast that the Soviet Union would bury the West held the frightening prospect of becoming reality.

Confronted by the Soviet challenge, the USAF had to find ways of providing an effective counter while coping with a post-Vietnam reduction in strength and the fact that personnel costs in their all-volunteer force would consume around 40 percent of a shrinking budget. To the USAF's considerable credit it recognized the importance of maintaining spending on research and development on weapons and aircraft systems and on services supporting the operational squadrons. It recognized that even aging airframes could have their useful life extended by the incorporation of new radar, avionics, and weapons, and that new aircraft would be hamstrung if their state-of-the-art aerodynamics could not be matched by equally advanced systems. The 1970s saw explosive developments in electronics. Computers and software began to make a real impact on USAF equipment as aircraft essentially became powerful computers surrounded by engines, fuel, and weapons, and aircrews. Some unstable fighters could not be flown by the pilot without the computer's aid, but the electronic brains were quite capable of flying an operational profile, at night and in all weathers, untouched by human hand. At the same time, with opposing air defense systems posing a much greater threat, the science of electronic countermeasures became ever more important. To make best use of new equipment, air force training had to ensure competence at every level. Logistics administration had to become much more efficient, reducing staff and avoiding the trap of keeping in stock more spares and supplies than were absolutely necessary.

Aircraft Made to Measure
In reviewing its combat power, the USAF had to take account of deterring (and, if necessary, fighting) the Soviet Union and of retaining a capability to intervene in small wars wherever they affected the interests of the United States. Here, at least in part, the lessons of Vietnam were invaluable. Aircrews that had been in combat usually had specific ideas about what was needed in the front line. Much as they had appreciated the capabilities and toughness of aircraft like the F–4 and A–7, they knew their limitations, too. When the F–4 first appeared in Southeast Asia, it was fast, but it was also large, not very agile, gunless, and trailed the signature of smoking engines. A strap-on cannon and the later addition of leading edge slats had helped it a bit, but it needed something better. (Besides, it was time the Air Force had really capable fighters that had not been designed for the Navy.)

The Corsair II, which began its career as a Navy attack bomber before being brought into Air Force service.

The perfect answer came in the McDonnell Douglas F–15 Eagle, an aircraft intended to make the most of the electronics revolution of the 1970s. It was designed from the outset as an air superiority fighter. The F–15 first flew in 1972 and reached squadron service by the end of 1974. Even larger than the F–4, the F–15 is immensely powerful, its two 24,000-pound thrust Pratt & Whitney turbofans giving a clean aircraft a thrust-to-weight ratio of better than one at sea level. Its astonishing agility is born of this great power and the generous area of its delta-shaped wing. F–15 pilots revel in the splendid all-around visibility from the high bubble canopy and in the systems that simplify the business of flying and fighting—notably the head-up display and the hands-on-throttle-and-stick (HOTAS) arrangement of essential switches. The F–15's size accommodates the most comprehensive avionics and weapons control systems, an integral Vulcan cannon, plus a wide variety of external stores. It also made the Eagle an obvious candidate for development as a long-range, all-weather interdiction aircraft—the two-seat F–15E, capable of carrying 24,500 pounds of ordnance.

If the F–15 has a drawback it is unit cost. Even while the Eagle was still being developed, proposals were made for a lighter, cheaper fighter to complement the F–15 and allow the building of a larger front-line. The USAF needed enough aircraft to meet emergencies wherever in the world they occurred. After a fly-off with the Northrop YF–17 (subsequently produced for the USN as the McDonnell Douglas F/A–18), it selected General Dynamics' YF–16 for development as its lightweight fighter. In the years that followed, the F–16 Fighting Falcon grew in capability until it was neither as light nor as cheap as the Air Force had wanted, but there is no doubt that it has become a superbly adaptable fighter. It is an electronic masterpiece, with a head-up display and a side-stick controller operating fly-by-wire flying controls. Its computer-driven cockpit features a reclining seat, the better to help the pilot cope with the stresses of sustained 9G turns, and its wings are equipped with an array of hard points which allow for the carriage of over 20,000 pounds of external stores, a load exceeding its original empty gross weight! The F–16's dramatic performance, advanced systems, and its capacity to handle a wide range of weapons have made it an admirable all-weather, multirole aircraft, capable of excelling in roles as diverse as air superiority, close air support, or deep interdiction.

Although it was overshadowed by its younger cousins, the F–4 was too valuable an asset to waste. The Phantom's aging airframe was considerably modified and updated with new systems, and continued to give sterling service in the specialized roles of reconnaissance and defense suppression.

F–16s. The 388th Tactical Fighter Wing at Hill Air Force Base, Utah, was the first unit to be equipped with the F–16A in January 1979.

In Vietnam, the problem of taking on guerrillas in rugged, forested country was only partly solved by the resurrected A–1 Skyraider. Intense debate on the requirement for a modern specialized counterinsurgency-close support aircraft led to the production of the brutally angular Fairchild Republic A–10. Officially called Thunderbolt II, it quickly acquired a name more suited to its looks and personality—Warthog. Flying at speeds not much greater than its piston-engined predecessor, the A–10

is extremely maneuverable and built to withstand a high degree of battle damage. The pilot sits in what is effectively a "bathtub" of titanium armor. All systems are protected and duplicated, and the aircraft is designed to survive even if half its tail and an engine are blown away. Eleven pylons give the Warthog the capacity to carry many different combinations of external stores, but the most memorable feature of its offensive armament is "the gun." A seven-barrel 30-mm GAU–8A Avenger, this mighty cannon can fire at rates

423

*F–15 intakes. The USAF
Museum's McDonnell Douglas
F–15 is not a representative
operational aircraft. It is the Streak
Eagle, a special pre-production
aircraft used as a record breaker.
It set eight time-to-height records
in 1975, including a peak of
98,425 feet, reached 3 minutes and
28 seconds after brake release. It
exceeded Mach 2 during the climb
as its two 25,000-pound-thrust
Pratt & Whitney F100 turbofans
gulped air in huge quantities
through sharply angled engine
intakes. The intake ducts stand
clear of the fuselage to avoid
turbulent boundary layer air, and
they pitch up and down through
a limited range to adjust airflow
to meet the requirements of the
engine at various speeds.*

The F–15's two huge raked fins reaching a height of over 18 feet above the ramp. They are topped by various electronic counter-measure aerials.

of up to 4,200 rounds per minute and its depleted uranium ammunition is capable of destroying battle tanks.

At the other end of the offensive scale, the B–52 outlasted efforts to find a replacement. Since the "Buff" had been flying since 1952, it seemed only rational from time to time that the USAF propose its retirement. Well before the Vietnam War the service had made plans more than once to let the B–52 fade away, but the essence of a great military aircraft lies in its adaptability. As new threats appear, it is found that there is life left in the old airframe and, with a little modification, it rises to each challenge and soldiers on. The exotic B–58 and B–70 proved too specialized and died in their evolutionary blind alleys, while the Buff changed its spots and kept going. However, a determined effort to find a new strategic bomber

began in the mid-1960s under the Advanced Manned Strategic Aircraft (AMSA) program, and in 1970 the USAF chose a Rockwell International proposal for development.

Few aircraft can have had such an agonizing gestation as the Rockwell B–1. Specification changes, vacillation over the future of the manned bomber as the third element of the deterrence triad, and abrupt shifts in the direction of defense policy resulted in more than 20 years passing between the initiation of the project and the delivery of the first B–1B Lancer to an operational squadron. A major stumble occurred in 1977 when President Jimmy Carter cancelled the B–1A on the grounds that it was too expensive, that there were doubts about its ability to penetrate Soviet defenses, and that Air Launched Cruise Missiles (ALCMs) carried by the B–52 would be a better bet.

A–10. There is no doubting the ability of the A–10 Thunderbolt II to deliver a hefty punch. The awesome 7-barrel 30-mm cannon is backed up by the capacity to deliver up to 16,000 pounds of assorted ordnance from 11 pylons.

Use of prototypes for test flying continued, however, and President Ronald Reagan agreed to revive the B–1 in 1981. The USAF ordered 100 bombers under the Long Range Combat Aircraft (LRCA) program. Engineers had taken advantage of years of flight testing to produce a much improved aircraft, slower than the B–1A but much more capable. They applied principles of "stealth" technology to give the B–1B a radar cross-section only 1 percent of that of the B–52 and designed its variable geometry to produce an aircraft which, with its wings swept back, is very much at home at high speed and low level. Advanced terrain-following radar, sophisticated navigation equipment, and comprehensive defensive avionics make the Lancer a formidable all-weather bomber, capable of penetrating enemy defenses and delivering a massive nuclear or conventional blow. The 4,000-pound average combat load of a B–17 in World War II seems pathetic when compared to the B–1B's enormous capacity—an internal carriage of 8 ALCMs, 24 SRAMs, or 84 500-pound conventional bombs, plus 8 external hardpoints for an additional 14 ALCMs/SRAMs, or another 44 500-pound bombs.

By the beginning of the 1980s the character of the post-Vietnam USAF had taken shape. All of the major new items of equipment were on hand or well on

the way, and old stalwarts like the B–52 were still performing effectively in their roles. The swing-wing FB–111, christened the Aardvark, had survived a difficult baptism of fire in Southeast Asia and was serving as a potent interdiction aircraft, with the capacity to fly missions blind at 200 feet and high subsonic speeds, placing its weapons automatically within yards of the target. Updated U–2/TR–1s and Mach 3 SR–71s, a listening and looking combination unmatchable elsewhere, were carrying out strategic reconnaissance. In air transport the invaluable C–141, enhanced by an extended fuselage, doubled its usable cargo-hold volume, and the immense Lockheed C–5 Galaxy added the ability to lift 250,000 pounds of cargo and move such awkward loads as the Army's biggest tanks by air. The McDonnell Douglas KC–10 Extender gave the USAF a tanker of enormous capacity. Equipped with both the boom and probe-and-drogue refueling systems, it proved able to fly a round trip of 4,400 miles, transferring 200,000 pounds to receivers in the process. In the complex arena of command, control, and communications (C^3), Boeing aircraft held the reins. The E–3 Sentry Airborne Warning and Control System (AWACS), sprouting an outsize mushroom from its back, became the ultimate airborne military command post. In many ways even

"Operation Red Flag," Dick Kohfield, 1976, USAF Art Collection.

more sophisticated, the larger E–4B, originally operated as the National Emergency Airborne Command Post (NEACP, or "Kneecap") and flown by USAF crews, was provided to carry the President during an emergency. Now known as the National Airborne Operations Center (NAOC), it is hardened against the effects of nuclear explosions, and has the mystic ability to contact almost anyone available to listen, reaching out to military agencies or breaking into telephone networks and media frequencies at will.

Smaller but Stronger

There was no doubting that the USAF, even before the Reagan boom years of the 1980s, was a tremendously powerful and capable force. It was also smaller than it had been since the early 1940s. In World War II aircraft strength had risen to nearly 80,000. Just after Korea, it was 28,000, and during the Vietnam War it hovered around 12,000. By 1980 it was down to less than 7,000. The World War II figure of almost 2.5 million personnel contrasted with 900,000 in 1968, and 560,000 in the diminished USAF of 1980. In the process, the advance of technology had allowed the Air Force to do far more with much less, although at steadily rising cost.[1] At the same time, rates of airframe

procurement and replacement slowed dramatically. Almost 20,000 B–24s were produced in World War II and most of those served the Air Force between 1941 and 1950, an operational life of only nine years. The production run of the durable B–52 was 744; it entered service in 1955 and will be operational into the 21st century, having successfully absorbed extensive modifications in the course of its long career. Similarly, the P–40 was in the front line for nine years and even the outstanding P–51 lasted only fourteen. The F–4 joined the USAF in 1963 to begin well over thirty years of operational service.

With its major aircraft programs already underway, the USAF took advantage of President Reagan's defense build-up of the 1980s to acquire more of the most modern types, so ensuring that all aircraft systems and weapons were as close to the state of the art as possible. Not forgetting training and support services, the Air Force significantly improved living conditions for its personnel and their families. It further transformed the Air Force Reserve and the Air National Guard, raising them from their former status of second-class citizens flying USAF cast-offs and operating outdated equipment, to a position of equality.

427

The C–5A. Although beset by troubles at the start of its service, notably serious wing cracks, the C–5 Galaxy seemed destined for difficulty, but it quickly proved an indispensable element of America's strategic mobility. It offers the most ton-miles at the fastest speed of any American airlifter and its cavernous hold accepts even the bulk of the U.S. Army's M1 tank.

The SR–71, a stealthy aircraft long before the term was commonly used. It was designed to keep the radar cross-section as low as possible and was covered with a paint containing billions of microscopic iron balls that reduced radar reflectivity. The power required to provide the SR–71 with its stellar performance came from two Pratt & Whitney J58 afterburning turbo-jet engines of 32,500 pounds of thrust each. The large inlet cones were computer controlled, steadily retracting as Mach numbers increased.

SR–71 nose. The Lockheed SR–71A Blackbird combines sculptured lines with dramatic performance. Heights of up to 85,000 feet and speeds above Mach 3 were part of its operational reconnaissance profile. Equipped with a variety of sensors, the Blackbird could monitor an area of 100,000 square miles in an hour. (At its cruising speed, the SR–71 covered a mile in under two seconds, about the same velocity as a round fired by an A–10 cannon.) Skin temperatures reached 280 to 300 degrees Centigrade in flight, causing the 107-foot long aircraft to stretch by almost a foot. Its pilot and reconnaissance systems officer sat in separately hatched tandem cockpits, their small windows made of heat-resistant glass. The SR–71's fuel was JP–7, a special kerosene that doubled as a sink to absorb excessive heat loads.

SR–71 in flight. The USAF Museum's SR–71A, shown arriving at Dayton in March 1990, was flown by Majors Jerome O'Malley and Edward Payne in the aircraft's first operational SR–71 sortie on 21 March 1968. It became the most productive of the SR–71 fleet, flying 942 sorties, of which 257 were operational missions.

SR–71 tail. A ring of suck-in doors cooled and reduced the size of the SR–71's tail-pipes at low speeds. At normal flight speeds, the tail-pipes were the hottest exterior part of the aircraft, glowing white. The SR–71's airframe was built almost entirely of titanium and alloys to withstand the heat of Mach 3 cruising. Even so, the skin crinkled. The sharply canted fins were solid flying surfaces with no separate rudders.

SR–71 cockpit. The glass area allowing the SR–71's pilot a forward view was not generous, and, although made in heat resistant layers, it became noticeably warm during flight. Toward the top of the pilot's instrument panel the artificial horizon is backed up by another immediately above. To the left of the stand-by horizon is an angle-of-attack indicator, and a combination instrument near the compass shows a read-out of airspeed, altitude, and Mach number. On the console to the pilot's right are the auto-pilot controls, and at center-left in front of him is a yellow handle for deploying the drag-chute and a red warning light bearing the comforting message "RSO ejected."

In 1970 Secretary of Defense Melvin Laird promulgated the Total Force Policy, which set out the requirement by which Reserve and Guard units became combat-ready forces, immediately available for mobilization in support of the Regular Air Force and equipped accordingly. By the early 1980s the modernization program was readily apparent. The last F–100s and F–101s (which many of the world's air forces might have been delighted to have) were gone from the Guard's squadrons, and its aircraft inventory was little different from that of the USAF. Such aircraft as F–4Ds, RF–4Cs, A–10s, F–16As, KC–135Es, C–130Hs, F–15As, and C–5As began joining the Guard from the mid-1980s. The Air Force Reserve was similarly blessed, flying an equally impressive lineup. In celebration of their elevation to the premier league, Air Force Reserve and Guard squadrons excelled themselves by consistently gaining high marks in USAF Operational Readiness Inspections and in such exercises as Red Flag and Maple Flag. Guard units recorded several successes in air-to-air and air-to-ground gunnery meets and tactical reconnaissance competitions, flying against USAF squadrons.

In taking a long, critical look at the lessons of Vietnam, the USAF concluded that aircrews needed more preparation for combat. Believing that there was no substitute for actual experience, General Robert Dixon, Commander, Tactical Air Command, from 1973 to 1978, wanted aircrews to undergo combat training that was as close as possible to the real thing. This line of thought led to the establishment of the Red Flag exercises, the first of a series simulating combat conditions for air and ground personnel in a variety of roles.

The "Flags"
Nellis Air Force Base, Nevada, home of the USAF's Weapons and Tactics Center, was chosen as the base for Red Flag. With its combat ranges, totalling some

431

3.5 million acres, and an associated area of 12,000 square miles lying under military airspace, Nellis was ideal. The USAF invited its own squadrons and those of the other American services and NATO air forces to deploy to Nellis in rotation to join in six-week wars, flying against a convincing enemy and attacking realistic targets. The service formed a permanent enemy air force (the Aggressors), initially flying F–5s to simulate MiG–21s, to provide an air superiority challenge over the battlefield and to assist visiting air defense squadrons in opposing strike missions. The ground environment was designed to simulate enemy radars, SAMs, and AAA, and targets included airfields, aircraft, tanks, SAM sites and guns, some genuine and some mock-ups. From the start, the attackers used live ordnance. An Air Combat Maneuvering Instrumentation system recorded aerial combats and allowed them to be reviewed in three dimensional detail on the ground. The benefits of Red Flag (and other Flags) were almost immediately apparent. Standards of professionalism rose perceptibly, and the tendency to uninformed arrogance among inexperienced fighter pilots was curbed to confident enthusiasm and justified self-assurance in the heat of Red Flag's fiery combats.

Skirmishes

Regional disturbances and Cold War skirmishes involved the USAF in relatively limited ways during the 1980s. It was unfortunate that the first of them, a joint operation with the other American services, should carry the same sense of unnecessary failure which lingered after Southeast Asia. In November 1979 Islamic militants in Iran, protesting the sanctuary being given the deposed Shah in the United States, occupied the American embassy in Teheran and took 66 hostages. As tedious and fruitless diplomatic negotiations dragged on, plans were made for American forces to attempt a rescue.

After a period of planning and training, special forces assembled on two principal operating bases—the aircraft carrier USS *Nimitz* at the mouth of the Persian Gulf, and Masirah Island airfield, off the coast of Oman. The operation began on 24 April 1980 when eight USN RH–53D helicopters left the *Nimitz* for an abandoned airstrip southeast of Teheran, codenamed Desert One. There they were to join six USAF C–130s² bringing the 132-man rescue team and all the necessary equipment from Masirah. Ill luck dogged the mission from the start. Only six helicopters managed to reach Desert One more than 90 minutes late after struggling through a sand storm. Of the missing two, one made it back to the carrier, but the other had to be left in the desert. Another helicopter then

developed hydraulic failure at Desert One, leaving five for the operation. Since six was the minimum number required, the mission was aborted. The five serviceable RH–53Ds began refueling for the return flight from the EC–130H tankers. Lifting away to make room for the next in line, one helicopter allowed its rotor to strike a tanker's rear fuselage. Fire and explosions followed, and flying debris damaged the remaining RH–53Ds. Eight men were killed and a number of others burned. The survivors boarded the C–130s and withdrew, leaving the helicopters behind. At a cost of seven RH–53Ds, one EC–130H, eight dead and many wounded, it was a failure dearly bought and a savage reminder that the unexpected can defeat even the best equipped forces. The hostages were not released until the following year.

Another joint operation met with more success in October 1983 on the Caribbean island of Grenada. Reacting to a flagrant attempt by Cuba to usurp the government and turn Grenada into a satellite and transit base for Soviet aircraft, the United States intervened to eject Cuban forces and restore democratic rule. On 24 October Operation URGENT FURY began with MC–130Es dropping small detachments of SEALS and Delta Force into Grenada to reconnoiter key areas. In the early hours of 25 October more MC–130Es dropped two Ranger battalions onto the main airport at Point Salines under covering fire from AC–130H gunships. With the airfield secured, C–141s and C–130Es brought in elements of the 82nd Airborne Division, and American forces moved out to capture enemy strong points and ensure the safety of about 1,000 American students at the university. AC–130Hs and naval attack aircraft suppressed enemy fire. At the same time, C–5As flew into nearby Barbados with heavy equipment, including Army UH–60A helicopters. An E–3A and an EC–130E cruised over the Caribbean to monitor the situation. Although resistance was often stiff, the Cuban headquarters at Calvigny was overcome on 27 October. Minor mopping up operations continued for several more days. URGENT FURY proved more costly than had been hoped, with 19 American servicemen dead, 116 wounded, and at least seven Army helicopters lost, but it was a success. The American military had prevailed, Cuban prestige had suffered, and communism had been handed a setback in the Caribbean.

After a series of incidents between Libyan forces and the U.S. Navy in the Mediterranean in early 1986, a bomb exploded in a Berlin discotheque used by American servicemen. There was evidence of Libyan involvement, and President Reagan decided to retaliate. Operation EL DORADO CANYON was a combined USAF-USN strike against military and terrorist targets in Libya, the USAF being responsible for those near Tripoli and the USN for others in the Benghazi area. Initial USAF intelligence sorties were flown by SR–71s, TR–1As, U–2Rs, and RC–135s operating from bases in the United Kingdom, Greece, and Cyprus.

On the evening of 14 April 1986, 18 F–111Fs of the 48th Tactical Fighter Wing, based at Lakenheath in England and led by Lieutenant Colonel Arnie Franklin, set off for Libya. They had to fly an exhaustingly long and circuitous route via Gibraltar because French authorities had denied them the right to overfly France. They were supported by KC–10 and KC–135 tankers, an E–3A AWACS, an EC–135E tactical command center, and EF–111As for the electronic suppression of Libyan defenses. After four refuelings on the outbound leg, the F–111Fs crossed the Libyan coast west of Tripoli just before midnight to sweep around and approach their targets from the south. Using their Pave Tack laser marking system, they aimed their 2,000-pound Paveway bombs at the military side of Tripoli airport and at Al Aziziyah barracks, where the Libyan leader Gaddafi had his quarters. They did considerable damage to the barracks and destroyed a number of Libyan aircraft. Unfortunately, several Western embassies also suffered. One F–111F was lost in the Mediterranean after the attack. Although at the time EL DORADO CANYON was judged only a qualified success, the performance of the USAF aircrews was acknowledged as praiseworthy. Their completion of a round trip of 5,500 miles with multiple refuelings to attack pinpoint targets at night was a considerable challenge, and the achievement gained respect from military aviators world-wide. As time passed and Libya's terrorist excesses were seen to have been restrained, the accomplishments of the operation were appreciated in their true light.

Confrontations between warring factions in Central America attracted a good deal of concern in the United States during the 1980s, but American involvement was generally limited to military assistance in the form of training and equipment to those opposing the spread of communism, whether they be governments or rebels. USAF reconnaissance aircraft kept a close watch on events in Nicaragua and El Salvador, and AC–130Hs occasionally set out to track down arms smugglers, but overt intervention by American forces in the region did not occur until 1989, when Manuel Noriega went too far to be ignored in Panama. In December 1989 after Noriega had installed himself

as dictator and directed some bellicose remarks at the United States, Panamanian soldiers murdered a U.S. Marine Corps officer. Operation JUST CAUSE was launched in response. Before dawn on the morning of 20 December, USAF AC–130 gunships attacked Panamanian positions in support of an assault by Navy SEALS and Army Rangers. Other USAF aircraft participated—MC–130s and two very capable helicopters, the MH–53 Pave Low and the MH–60G Pave Hawk, both fitted with all of the electronic magic necessary to operate in all weather, by day or night, at low level. Later, when the first dust had settled, C–141s flew in troops of the 82nd Airborne Division. Effective resistance was ended within 48 hours. Noriega sought sanctuary in the Vatican Embassy for a while, but surrendered on 3 January 1990. A USAF MC–130 crew had the pleasure of flying him to Florida to stand trial on drug-related charges.

Almost unnoticed, an extraordinary aircraft made its operational debut during JUST CAUSE. Rio Hato airfield was attacked by a pair of Lockheed F–117 Nighthawks. Their efforts were not particularly noteworthy, but their mission provided merely a muted prelude. The complete Nighthawk work with full *fortissimo* orchestration was to follow only two years later in the Middle East.

Winning Combination

President Reagan and his Secretary of Defense, Caspar Weinberger, took office in 1981 with the firm intention of increasing the size of the defense budget. More money for the military had a dual purpose. In the first place, it was a deliberate escalation of the Cold War, meant to challenge the Soviet Union to an armament race which could leave the loser facing bankruptcy. As an additional benefit, it was aimed at reversing the decline in the status and perceived competence of America's armed forces following the depressing experiences of Southeast Asia and the attempted hostage rescue in Iran. It was perhaps serendipitous that the name of the Chief of Staff of the USAF during much of this resurrection was Gabriel. General Charles Gabriel was an officer who had flown hundreds of combat missions in both Korea and Vietnam. While he was Chief, he oversaw the introduction of all manner of new weapons and systems into service, including those belonging to the revolutionary world of stealth technology. With the arrival of the F–117 in the front line in 1983, the USAF took a leap forward in the science of air power that could not be matched elsewhere. It is a measure of the scale of the achievement that, unlike other great developments in aviation, such as metal monoplanes, jet engines, radar, swept wings, and missiles, all of which

"The Lesson," Keith Ferris, 1987, USAF Art Collection.

quickly became international, American stealth technology remains unmatched as the 21st century approaches.

By the mid-1980s the Reagan defense build-up had increased USAF strength to over 8,200 aircraft and 630,000 personnel. It also led to the historic period of the late 1980s and early 1990s, a time of unparalleled change in international relationships, with such tumultuous events as the fall of the Berlin Wall, the collapse of the Warsaw Pact, the defeat of the Soviet Communist Party, the disintegration of the Soviet Union, and the decline of communism world-wide.

In organizing itself for this final triumphant chapter of the Cold War, the USAF retained in its structure much that was familiar, but added and adjusted elements and commands as necessary to meet the demands of new circumstances and challenges. Much had changed, yet much had stayed the same since the days of Tooey Spaatz and the birth of the USAF. As the decade of the 1980s ended, the combat commands of TAC and SAC still dominated the front line, with TAC owning by far the largest aircraft inventory of almost 3,000. When reinforced by Air National Guard and Air Force Reserve aircraft in an emergency, the total rose to over 44 percent of all USAF aircraft.

Tactical Air Command (TAC), situated at Langley Air Force Base, Virginia, commanded three numbered air forces and three other units. The First Air Force was principally concerned with the air defense of the continental United States (F–15s), the Ninth Air Force with tactical fighter operations (F–15s, F–16s,

F–4s, A–10s, OV–10s, EC–135s, and UH–1s), and the Twelfth Air Force with an assortment of roles, including air superiority, interdiction, reconnaissance, and close air support (F–15s, F–16s, F–4s, F–111s, F–117s, A–10s, OV–10s, and OA–37s). The direct reporting units were the 28th Air Division (E3s, EC–135s, EC–130s), the Tactical Warfare Center at Eglin Air Force Base, Florida, and the Tactical Fighter Weapons Center at Nellis Air Force Base, Nevada. Besides playing host to Flag exercises, Nellis was also the home of a unique TAC squadron, the USAF's Thunderbirds aerial demonstration team. First formed in 1953, the team began by flying the F–84G and then moved successively to the F–84F, F–100, F–105 (briefly), F–4, T–38, and F–16. The Thunderbirds gave demonstrations in more than 50 countries, but their primary responsibility lay

in public relations at home, reinforcing the confidence of the American people in their Air Force, and supporting USAF recruiting and retention programs.

Strategic Air Command (SAC), located at Offutt Air Force Base, Nebraska, outnumbered by TAC in terms of aircraft, was still the USAF's largest command, controlling two elements of the nation's strategic triad. It had a personnel strength of 119,000, with another 15,000 gained from the Air National Guard and the Air Force Reserve. The strike force consisted of 1,000 ICBMs (Minuteman and Peacekeeper) and over 400 bombers (the B–52, FB–111, and B–1), supported by more than 600 tankers (the KC–135 and KC–10). Reconnaissance and airborne command aircraft completed the lineup (the U–2/TR–1 and RC–135). Most

MH–53. At the outset of Operation JUST CAUSE in December 1989, MH–53 Pave Low helicopters were used to drop U.S. Navy SEALS into Panama.

of SAC's assets were organized under two numbered air forces, the Eighth and Fifteenth, both with World War II backgrounds in strategic bombardment.

Military Airlift Command (MAC), located at Scott Air Force Base, Illinois, was a command whose role hardly varied from peace to war. It was constantly involved in lifting people and supplies around the world and was on call to help in natural or man-made emergencies. It was comprised of 90,000 personnel and 1,000 aircraft, and was massively supported by the Air National Guard and the Air Force Reserve, gaining an additional 71,000 personnel and 400 aircraft from them when needed. MAC was organized into three air forces and several separate units. The Twenty-first and Twenty-second Air Forces were the combat-ready theater and strategic airlift elements of MAC, flying a vast and varied array of aircraft, such as the C–5, C–141, C–130, C–9, C–12, C–20, C–23, C–135, C–137, C–140, T–39, T–43, and UH–1. The Twenty-third Air Force undertook special operations with such exotic machinery as variously equipped AC–130s, MC–130s, HC–130s, MH–53s and MH–60s. Other units included the Air Rescue, Air Weather, and Defense Courier Services. It was part of MAC's tradition that its aircraft were always available for humanitarian purposes.

Starting with the shining example of the Berlin Airlift, there was hardly a time when MAC was not involved somewhere with bringing relief to hard-pressed people. In the United States, MAC aircraft had delivered snow ploughs to Buffalo to aid recovery from blizzards, airlifted water filtration systems to Harrisburg after the Three Mile Island nuclear emergency, and rescued victims of the Mt. St. Helens eruption and a cruise ship sinking in the Gulf of Alaska. Earthquakes, hurricanes, floods, drought, and famine drew MAC assistance year after year, both in the United States and world-wide. The command's unique ability to react quickly and provide immense airlift capacity and its unrivalled professionalism earned the respect and gratitude of countless thousands of people on every continent.

Top Cover for North America was the motto of the Alaskan Air Command (AAC), located at Elmendorf Air Force Base, Alaska. A relatively small command with little more than 9,000 personnel, its principal responsibility was the defense of Alaska, and its fighter squadrons flew F–15s and A–10s. AAC answered to North American Air Defense Command (NORAD) for air defense purposes, and its F–15s frequently escorted probing Soviet aircraft north of

F–16s of the USAF's aerobatic display team in arrowhead formation, showing off their celebrated Thunderbird paint scheme.

the Arctic Circle. A large part of the command's hardware included minimally attended radar sites, linked into a highly automated warning system feeding information back to the operations center at Elmendorf Air Force Base.

Overseas, the USAF ran its affairs through the Pacific Air Forces (PACAF), located at Hickam Air Force Base, Hawaii, and the United States Air Forces in Europe (USAFE), located at Ramstein Air Base, Germany. PACAF covered almost half the globe, with an assigned area stretching from the west coast of the United States to the east coast of Africa, and from the Arctic to the Antarctic. Almost 300 fighter aircraft were on PACAF's strength, with support coming as necessary from the other major commands. Resident aircraft in the region included the F–15, F–16, F–4, A–10, and EC–135. Three numbered air forces, the Fifth, Seventh, and Thirteenth—all with historic links to the Pacific—served PACAF, with headquarters based in Japan, Korea, and the Philippines. USAFE was the air component of U.S. European Command

and a vital part of NATO, with its Commander in Chief also wearing the hat of Commander, Allied Air Forces Central Europe. USAFE consisted of three air forces, the Third in the United Kingdom, the Sixteenth in Spain (with units in Italy, Greece, and Turkey), and the Seventeenth in Germany (plus a base in the Netherlands). Their combat assets included various models of F–111s, F–15s, F–16s, and A–10s, as well as a number of ground-launched cruise missiles in the United Kingdom, Italy, and Germany. Aircraft of the other commands were constantly rotated through USAFE's bases in Europe.

Behind the combat commands were ranged a series of others without which the front line would have found it difficult to survive. Air Training Command (ATC), located at Randolph Air Force Base, Texas, provided the foundation on which the Air Force was built. Besides flying training, it was responsible for all basic and technical training, plus recruiting, and most specialized military education. In the USAF's world of training and education, only the Air Force

A C–9A Nightingale medevac aircraft.

Academy at Colorado Springs and the post-graduate schools of the Air University at Maxwell Air Force Base, Alabama, did not fall under ATC's wing. The scale of ATC's daily task can be seen from the fact that in 1989, over 46,000 Americans joined the USAF, seeking training in specializations as varied as aircrew, nurse, supply clerk, computer operator, or various kinds of technician. Ongoing career training brought the total figures up to 300,000 students graduating from 2,800 courses annually. Pilot training was a 49 week course and included 500 hours of ground instruction and 175 hours of flying, 74 in the T–37 and 101 in the T–38. Basic navigator training took 28 weeks, with the flying done aboard T–37s and T–43s.

The business of Air Force Systems Command (AFSC), located at Andrews Air Force Base, Maryland, was delivering the future to the USAF. AFSC was charged with identifying and acquiring emerging technologies to help define future USAF systems. It developed and tested high-technology hardware ranging from aircraft and avionics to spacecraft and missiles. Among its more exotic assets were the Air Force Flight Test Center at Edwards Air Force Base, California, the Electronic Systems Division at Hanscom Air Force Base, Massachusetts, the Armament Division at Eglin

Air Force Base, Florida, and the Aeronautical Systems Division at Wright-Patterson Air Force Base, Ohio.

The Air Force Logistics Command (AFLC), located at Wright-Patterson Air Force Base, Ohio, bought, supplied, maintained, repaired, and transported everything necessary to keep the Air Force both combat ready and satisfied. The command stocked or managed nearly 900,000 individual items, processing about five million requisitions each year, including articles as diverse as nuclear weapons and light bulbs, or jet engines and church organs. The combined floor space of the AFLC Logistics Centers was said to exceed the area of Rhode Island. Two unique Air Force establishments belonged to AFLC. One was the Military Aircraft Storage and Disposition Center at Davis-Monthan Air Force Base, Arizona, more commonly called the Boneyard, where over 3,000 aircraft retired from front-line service were mothballed in case of future need. The other was the USAF Museum at Wright-Patterson Air Force Base.

Two other commands, newly raised to that status in 1979, linked all the others with their global services. The Air Force Communications Command (AFCC), located at Scott Air Force Base, Illinois, provided all

The Cessna T–37B Tweet, first brought into service at the end of 1959. It will still be training U.S. Air Force pilots at the start of the 21st century.

T–38A Talons arriving at their U.S. Air Force units in March 1961. Structural renewal and avionics upgrades will extend their useful life until 2020. After over half a century of being handled by students, they should by then have more than earned their retirement. This Talon is seen over Randolph Air Force Base, San Antonio, Texas. Compare the background here with that in the photograph of the BT–9 at the end of Chapter 4.

kinds of communications for the USAF. In peace or war, whether by telephone or radio, cable or satellite, it was AFCC's business to see to engineering, installation, maintenance, and evaluation. AFCC was also responsible for the USAF's computers and air traffic control service.

The Electronic Security Command (ESC), located at Kelly Air Force Base, Texas, was formed to look after electronic warfare. ESC concerned itself with such esoteric subjects as cryptology and computer security programs, but its principal responsibilities were in both offensive and defensive electronic warfare. The command fielded equipment to confuse, jam, or destroy enemy C^3, and provided protection for the USAF's equivalent systems. Working with the combat commands, ESC's divisions took particular interest in the jammers, protective equipment, and weapons carried in such aircraft as the EF–111A, intended primarily for close-in jamming and escorting attack aircraft in enemy airspace, and the EC–130H Compass Call, designed to stand off and disrupt enemy C^3 over large areas. ECM pods for combat aircraft and EW RPV drones also came under ESC's scrutiny.

The story of the USAF's interest in the military uses of space and the hardware to exploit it had its roots in World War II, and its subsequent growth and development involved more than one Air Force command. However, the various threads were at last drawn together in 1982 with the birth of another member of the Air Force family—Space Command at Peterson Air Force Base, Colorado.

With this proven framework in place and functioning well, the USAF celebrated the end of the Cold War and set itself to face the new challenges of the 1990s.

Notes

1. The $80,000 P–47 of World War II had become the $12 million F–15 by the late 1970s.
2. MC–130Es with the special forces, AC–130Es for fire support over Teheran, and EC–130Hs to provide communications and helicopter refueling.

Part IV
Supremacy

Attempt the end, and never stand to doubt. Nothing's so hard, but search will find it out.

(Robert Herrick, 1591–1674)

To strive, to seek, to find, and not to yield.

(Alfred, Lord Tennyson, 1809–1892)

In research the horizon recedes as we advance . . .

(Mark Pattison, 1813–1884)

Engines of war have long since reached their limits, and I see no further hope of any improvement . . .

(Frontinus, 90 A.D.)

We crashed not because we ran out of gas, but because we ran out of knowledge.
   (Inscription on cup awarded to accident survivors, McCook Flight Test Section, 1920s)

Chapter 12

Frontiers of Flight

The Xs Mark their Spots

From the moment visitors enter the USAF Museum, they see the fruits of research and development. Most of the artifacts displayed are the end products of painstaking calculation and persistent trial and error. References to the research and development process itself go back to the work of Leonardo da Vinci, Langley, and the Wright brothers, for instance, or the inter-war experiments with air-to-air refueling and stratospheric flight. For the most part, however, the topic is so vast and all-encompassing that it is merely hinted at or taken for granted. Nevertheless, although most of the aircraft in the galleries are either seasoned veterans of front-line service or dressed up to look as if they are, a few were produced for the benefits of research alone, or led down evolutionary blind alleys and were overtaken by events. Others are prototypes or testbeds that gave birth to greater things. It is worth taking time to seek them out.

Among the more bizarre of the museum's offerings are some of the X planes. Several of them are clustered at one end of the Modern Flight Gallery. They huddle in the protective shadow of the largest member of their exotic fraternity, the North American XB–70 Valkyrie, an elegant Mach 3 monster conceived in the days when high-altitude penetration of Soviet defenses seemed feasible. Nearly 200 feet long and more than 30 feet high, it would have weighed well over half a million pounds when fully loaded. The one displayed is the sole survivor of the breed, its only sibling having been destroyed in a mid-air collision in 1966.

Several X planes are rocket-powered and were dependent on a mother-ship—a bomber such as the B–50 or B–52— to carry them aloft. Once released at high altitude, the pilot lit the rocket engines and surged away, often to previously undreamed of heights and speeds. The Bell X–1B was one of a series specifically intended to probe the realm of transonic and supersonic flight. A much improved version of the X–1 immortalized by the first supersonic flight in 1947, the X–1B was capable of reaching twice the speed of sound and was instrumented for research into the effects of kinetic heating during high-speed flight. It flew just 27 times before being retired to the museum in 1959.

Major General Albert Boyd, "the test pilots' test pilot." He accumulated over 23,000 flying hours in more than 700 types and models of aircraft.

Nearby are three of the later X planes, all designed to study different solutions to aerodynamic problems posed by the coming of the jet age. With its long, blade-like fuselage and improbably stubby wings, the Douglas X–3 was aptly named Stiletto. Its airframe was supposed to sustain supersonic speeds, but engines then available were not up to the task and the Stiletto achieved Mach 1 only in a dive. Hung above the Stiletto are Northrop's X–4 and Bell's X–5. The X–4 gave convincing evidence that the transonic stability problems of swept-wing aircraft without tailplanes were too difficult to be overcome by the technology of the time, and the X–5 became the first aircraft in the world to vary the sweep of its wings while in flight.

Most awesome of the museum's highest and fastest aircraft is the North American X–15A–2. This was the second of three X–15s built to reach an altitude of 50 miles and a speed approaching Mach 7. It was, however, the first to feel the thrust of a rocket engine and it became the fastest of the three. Rebuilt after a landing accident and modified to give improved performance, it was flown to Mach 6.72 by Major Pete Knight, USAF, on 3 October 1967. Going very fast with rockets is one thing; coming to a stop is another. The museum owns Northrop's "Gee Whiz" deceleration sled. It could accelerate on rails to 200 miles per hour and then come to rest in 45 feet, simulating the forces encountered in aircraft crashes. Compared to later achievements in deceleration research, these are not excessive figures, but they certainly bugged the eyes of those brave enough to endure the brief ride.

The USAF museum has two lifting bodies, wingless rocket-powered vehicles that simulated the unpowered approach and landing of a space shuttle after re-entry. They are a confusing pair. The Martin X–24B near the XB–70 was originally the X–24A, but, after being rebuilt with improved handling characteristics in 1972, it was redesignated. The X–24A (in the Space Gallery under the port wingtip of the B–36) was originally known as the Martin SV–5J, but was never flown and has been converted to the appearance of the X–24A for display purposes. In a glass case at the end of the Space Gallery are models of the proposed X–30 National Space Plane shown soaring clear of Earth's atmosphere.

Experiments with vertical fixed-wing flight are represented by three quite different aircraft. Two of them are situated in the Museum Annex hangars on the other side of Wright Field. The Hawker Siddeley XV–6A Kestrel vertical takeoff and landing fighter, forerunner of the better known Harrier, was one of six received from the United Kingdom for testing in the United States. The LTV XC–142A is at first sight little more than a chubby, medium-size transport. However, its four huge propellers, each 15 feet and 6 inches in diameter, give a clue to its true nature. It is a tilt-wing, intended to behave both like a conventional aircraft and a helicopter. The XC–142A first flew in 1964, and in its prime its portly body achieved some startling results, managing to record speeds of 400 miles per hour forward and 30 miles per hour backwards. It also succeeded in operating from an aircraft carrier. As impressive as all of that was, its program was cancelled before the end of the 1960s.

The third member of this vertical flight group is the Ryan X–13 Vertijet, shown in its unnatural pre-takeoff attitude, its nose pointed hopefully at the roof of the Modern Flight Gallery. The X–13 on display made the first full cycle through vertical takeoff to horizontal flight to vertical landing on 11 April 1957.

Hidden away in one corner of the Museum Annex is the ungainly Fisher P–75 Eagle. It was an unlovely hybrid from its conception, and it did not improve with age. Although not exhibited with an X designation, it was certainly an experiment, and one that failed. The Fisher Body Division of General Motors designed it in 1942, attempting to create a fighter with an assortment of readily available parts from existing aircraft and, to overcome any shortcomings, hanging those parts around a 2,885-horsepower Allison engine and dragging them along behind an impressive pair of contra-rotating propellers. With World War II production fever raging, the U.S. Army Air Forces placed an order for 2,500 P–75s before discovering during testing that the project was a disaster. The USAAF then cancelled the P–75 after only six had been built. Three were lost in crashes, two of them fatal.

Far more attractive and deserving of success was the North American YF–107A, the last fighter to bear its famous maker's name. Originally designated the F–100B, it was an all-weather fighter-bomber based on the F–100. Supersonic on its first flight and apparently trouble-free, it nevertheless lost out in competition with the F–105 and its program was cancelled after only three YF–107As had been built.

The museum's remaining X aircraft are diverse. A Republic XF–91 Thunderceptor stands in the annex and is loaded with unusual features. It has inverse taper on variable incidence wings, and it is powered by both an after-burning jet engine and a rocket motor. It was the fastest thing around in 1950, but it had a problem staying airborne for even half an hour. Eventually determined to be impractical as an operational aircraft, the XF–91 was retired in 1951. Further along the flight line, in the museum's restoration area, are the makings of a Convair XF–92A, the world's first jet aircraft with a delta wing and a useful testbed for the later F–102. Two more X planes can be found back in the Air Power Gallery, both from the creative minds of the McDonnell Corporation. The ugly little XF–85 Goblin parasite fighter squats beside its intended B–36 host, and the world's first ram-jet helicopter, the spidery XH–20 Little Henry, hovers not far away.

Outside on the museum's ramp is a fascinating blue and white F–4 Phantom. This particular aircraft (62–12200) had a varied career as a prototype and testbed. Taken from the U.S. Navy's production line, it became a USAF prototype, first as a YRF–4C and later as a YF–4E. In later life it served in the Agile Eagle program to test leading edge slats, evaluated a fly-by-wire system with a sidestick controller, and was the principal agent in the Precision Aircraft Control Technology (PACT) program, which involved the fitting of canards below the rear cockpit.

A lighter-than-air intervention drawing a crowd at McCook Field, 1921. The assembly hangar is on the right, and the test hangars of the Airplane Engineering Division are on the left.

Most recent of the museum's acquisitions from the research world is an aircraft known as Tacit Blue. Slab-sided and with a dull grey finish unrelieved by markings of any kind, Tacit Blue is not an appealing sight, looking hardly capable of flight. Nevertheless, uncompromisingly unattractive though it is, Tacit Blue was a considerable success story. It proved the concepts of stealth technology and laid the groundwork for its operational offspring, the F–117A Nighthawk and the B–2 Spirit.

USAF Research in the 1990s

At the beginning of the 1990s the responsibility for research and development in the USAF rested with Air Force Systems Command (AFSC). The command tested and developed everything from aircraft and air-to-air missiles to avionics and spacecraft. This vast range of activities was spread among a number of divisions. The lion's share of AFSC's budget went to the Aeronautical Systems Division at Wright-Patterson Air Force Base, Ohio, which had oversight of all development work on aircraft, their engines

and avionics, as well as missiles and such supporting systems as flight simulators. The Air Force Flight Test Center at Edwards Air Force Base in California's Mojave Desert looked after the evaluation of manned and unmanned aircraft and spacecraft for the USAF and a number of other agencies. At Eglin Air Force Base, Florida, the Armament Division tested and procured all of the USAF's non-nuclear weapons and related equipment. The Electronics Systems Division at Hanscom Air Force Base, Massachusetts, was the primary agency for the Air Force's command, control, communications, and intelligence (C^3I) systems. Among other AFSC subordinate formations were Space Division, the Ballistic Missile Office, the Directorate of Laboratories, the Aerospace Medical Division, and the Arnold Engineering Development Center, which managed the world's largest complex of wind tunnels, engine test cells, and space simulation chambers. The efforts of all these divisions were interwoven with work done by other services and by

Curtiss Jennies dominating the floor of the McCook Field hangar, 1918.

corporations of the commercial aerospace industry to maintain the USAF as the world's premier air force. It had not always been so organized or so comprehensive.

Links with Dayton

In the earliest days aviation research was largely a matter of individuals proceeding by "guess and by God." It was not until the Wright brothers turned their minds to the challenge of manned flight that a genuinely systematic approach was devised. They read and thought a great deal and worked things out methodically, calculating and experimenting as they went along and recording their results for further study. Much of their work was done on Huffman Prairie, near Dayton, Ohio, an area now part of the present Wright-Patterson Air Force Base, which can therefore lay claim to being the birthplace of aeronautical research and development.

The U.S. Army did not become formally involved in aeronautical research until after the United States had declared war on Germany in April 1917. The realization that the European powers had left the United States far behind in terms of military aviation forced the issue. In July 1917 the Army decided to open an aeronautical research and development facility at North Field, just north of downtown Dayton. Renamed McCook Field after a renowned Civil War family, the installation began operations in December 1917. It was a principally grass airfield with a 1,000-foot long hard surface runway available for use when the ground was wet. Testing at McCook was at first a fairly basic affair, instrumentation being rudimentary and results depending almost entirely on the pencilled jottings of pilots during flight. Just how basic it was may be judged from a remark made by one of McCook's most celebrated pilots, Jimmy Doolittle, who recalled: "I never flew without a pair of pliers, a screwdriver, and a crescent wrench in my pocket so I could fix things on the airplane."[1]

The work at McCook grew quickly to encompass everything that excited the curiosity of airmen. Engines cooled by liquid or air, fuel systems, turbo-superchargers, variable pitch propellers, machine guns, self-sealing fuel tanks, night flying techniques, aerial cameras, radio beam navigation, parachutes, and very much more. Two wind tunnels were built to test aircraft characteristics on the ground with

A McCook test pilot and record breaker in the 1920s, Jimmy Doolittle beside one of his favorite aircraft, a Curtiss Hawk.

DH–4. Having done sterling work for the U.S. Air Service in World War I, DH–4s soldiered on behind their Liberty engines throughout the 1920s. The aircraft illustrated is the one in which Lieutenant Frank Patterson died during gunnery trials in 1918. His name survives in today's Wright-Patterson Air Force Base, home of the USAF Museum.

McCook wind tunnel. Early wind tunnels were often considerable works of art and craftsmanship. The tunnel designed and built at McCook Field, Dayton, Ohio, in 1918 was wonderfully shaped in wood. Its 60-inch fan has 24 blades that can propel air through the 14-inch throat at speeds of up to 450 miles per hour.

McCook wind tunnel throat. Access to the McCook wind tunnel throat is gained through a small window. Aerofoils and models placed in the throat could be observed during tests. Smoke released into the tunnel revealed the streamlining (or otherwise) of the airflow around a model at various speeds.

A smiling John Macready in riding breeches with the Flight Test Section at McCook Field, 1926. From left: R.G. Lockwood, George Tourtellot, William Amis, Jimmy Doolittle, H.A. Johnson, Macready, Hoy Barksdale, James Hutchinson, R.C. Moffat, and Louis Meister. In front of Macready are two of several trophies awarded for misdemeanors—the Quacking Duck and the Flying Ass, the latter carrying the inscription "Trophy of Stupidity."

models. Aircraft were designed and built at McCook, too, including the Packard-Le Pere LUSAC 11 flown to over 33,000 feet by "Shorty" Schroeder in 1920 during supercharger tests.[2] Schroeder's narrow escape from death on that occasion was generally accepted as part of the job. Accidents were frequent and a number of McCook test pilots were killed when they pushed their aircraft through the known boundaries of aviation.[3] Acknowledging the hazards of what they were doing, the pilots created several idiot awards for survivors of crashes. There were the Alibi, Bonehead, Dumbbell, and Flying Ass trophies, and an award introduced by Schroeder himself—the Cup of Good Beginnings and Bad Endings.[4]

Basic and hazardous it might have been, but the volume of test flying grew so quickly that McCook airmen sought an overflow at Wilbur Wright Field, eight miles away and next to the Huffman Prairie

area used by the Wrights. Tests on the disappointing Barling bomber were among those conducted from Wilbur Wright Field. As McCook's small airfield and wooden buildings proved ever more constricting, however, the Air Service looked around for a permanent home for their testing operations. It selected a site northeast of Dayton, which it dedicated as Wright Field on 12 October 1927 in honor of both brothers. Wilbur Wright Field was absorbed and by 1930 the last of McCook's operations had been transferred to the new installation.

From its inception, the pioneering work carried out at Wright Field covered an enormous range of activities. Airmen investigated airframes, engines, and instruments—and their interaction—as well as the conflicting demands of range, speed, and load-carrying capacity. They derived standards and specifications for the new aeronautical technologies, worked out

449

LUSAC 11 nose. Powered by a Liberty engine, the LUSAC 11 proved to have a remarkable performance. Suitably modified, it was used as a high altitude research aircraft at McCook Field during the 1920s, several times breaking the world altitude record.

The LUSAC 11, designed in 1917 by Georges LePere, a French aeronautical engineer working for the United States. (The acronym LUSAC stands for LePere U.S. Army Combat.) It was originally intended as a combination fighter and reconnaissance aircraft, carrying a crew of two.

testing methods for aircraft both on the ground and in the air, and screened all innovations exhaustively before they cleared them for flight. In the 1930s the evolution of American air power could be followed from events at Wright Field. More prototypes came and went during this period than at any other time in American military aviation; some, like the B–17, moved on to far greater things, while others disappeared into well deserved obscurity. As aircraft went higher and faster, the problems with the effects of aviation extremes on the human body needed solving, and Wright Field acquired a Physiological

Research Laboratory, complete with pressure chambers that could simulate altitudes of up to 80,000 feet.

Despite the almost limitless military aviation interests being pursued there, Wright Field operated at a fairly modest scale because of pre-World War II spending restrictions until 1940, with about 60 buildings on site. World War II changed all that. By 1945 the installation contained over 300 buildings and its former grass airfield now boasted a triangle of three hard surface runways. It housed the largest wind tunnel in the world and a structural test building capable of handling the complete fuselage and wing section of a B–36.

Wartime urgency almost eliminated prototype testing. Instead, both test and squadron pilots put early production models of each type through their paces, flying them through every conceivable maneuver in a concentrated program to reveal weaknesses. They also suggested improvements as the production of the aircraft got under way. Wright Field's failures under this method, like the unlovely and inaptly named Fisher P–75 Eagle, were more than offset by aircraft which went on to compile illustrious combat records (the B–24/25/26/29, P–38/39/40/47/51/61, among others), plus a host of worthy transport and training aircraft. Notable milestones included one set by Lieutenant Colonel Laurence Craigie, Wright Field's Aircraft Projects Branch Chief, who was the first Air Force pilot and second American to fly the XP–59A, the first American jet, when it made its 1942 debut in the California desert. Later, the XP–59A arrived at

Wright Field, and in October 1944 Ann Baumgartner, a Women's Airforce Service Pilot (WASP), flew it to become the first American woman jet pilot.

As the Air Force continued to increase the range and scale of military aircraft testing it needed more space but had to look to other places to get it. Wright Field was too close to Dayton's expanding metropolitan area for comfort. Besides, the Air Force was having to confront safety and security, concerns that could be dealt with satisfactorily only in a more remote area. For this reason, beginning in 1942, it moved some of its flight testing to Muroc, California, and so laid the foundations for the later Edwards Air Force Base. A man who was instrumental in building up what would become the Air Force Flight Test Center at Edwards, Colonel Albert Boyd, arrived at Wright Field in 1945 to become chief of the Flight Test Division. His appetite for flying was insatiable. He tested nearly every aircraft that came to Wright Field but found time in June 1947 to fly the Lockheed P–80R Shooting Star to a new world speed record of 623.7 miles per hour over Muroc's wide open spaces. In 1949 Boyd moved to Muroc to take over as commander and was there to see the base renamed in honor of Captain Glenn Edwards, who had been killed in the crash of a YB–49 the year before.

As the Air Force expanded its facilities at Muroc-Edwards, it increasingly confined its testing in Dayton to more specialized areas, such as components, systems, and instruments. Bad-weather flying was tested there by the All Weather Flying Group after its establishment in 1945. Later designated a division,

this unit operated what became known as the All Weather Air Line (AWAL) between Clinton County Army Airfield (a satellite of Wright Field) and Andrews Air Force Base, Maryland, from August 1946 to September 1948. The AWAL provided a regular air transport service on five days every week. Flying a regular scheduled service, it completed 1,128 flights in all weather without cancellation or accident, and with an average error in takeoff and landing times of less than one minute. The lessons learned from this operation about the use of radar in air traffic control brought great rewards during the Berlin Airlift of 1948–1949.

After 1950 the USAF continued to conduct a great variety of specialized but, nonetheless, invaluable testing activities at Wright Field (and later at Wright-Patterson Air Force Base). It examined the effects of icing and lightning strikes on aircraft, the removal of rain from windshields, and improved traction on slippery runways. It also investigated sonic booms, found weightlessness in zero-G maneuvers, tried an air cushion landing system, refueled helicopters in flight, mated low-light television sensors with a Gatling gun hung under a B–57, and so on in bewildering diversity.

From the 1970s the 4950th Test Wing at Wright-Patterson primarily operated large research aircraft, mainly variants of the C–135 and C–141. Among the first were bulbous-nosed EC–135Ns, which became the Advanced Range Instrumentation Aircraft (ARIA), used to support world-wide missile and space testing. The 4950th also tested Identification Friend or Foe

XB–35 and P–61. Perhaps the most striking of post-World War II bombers, the Northrop XB–35, is chased by a P–61 in 1946. Northrop never abandoned the flying wing idea and it reappeared when the B–2 first took to the air more than 40 years later.

(IFF) systems in other aircraft, tail warning radars, infra-red seekers, electronic countermeasures (ECM) equipment, laser weapons, and satellite navigation systems. Testing in Dayton may have changed in character and scope since the days of the Wrights, but the urge to solve the problems associated with manned flight has remained as strong as ever.

Research in the Desert

The remote airfield at Muroc, deep in the Californian desert, began its long association with flight testing in December 1941 when a full-scale mock-up of the proposed Curtiss XP–55 first took to the air in an auspicious start. An ugly little flying wing with canard foreplanes and a pusher propeller, neither the mock-up nor the XP–55 ever overcame serious stability problems and only three XP–55s were made, two of which were destroyed in crashes. Matters improved the following year when Muroc saw a top secret project unveiled. On 2 October 1942, Bell test pilot Bob Stanley coaxed the XP–59A off the surface

of the dry lake-bed and so ushered the United States into the jet age. Lieutenant Colonel Laurence Craigie from Wright Field flew the aircraft later that same day.

For most of World War II, the urgent need for aircrews in front-line squadrons determined that most of the flying done at Muroc would involve aircrew training. However, flight testing also continued, and a number of first flights were recorded, among them Northrop's XP–56 and XP–79, both early elements of the flying-wing tradition that would see its culmination in the B–2 nearly 50 years later.[5] Testing was also completed on such exotics as Lockheed's XP–58 Chain Lightning (a massive escort and anti-shipping fighter), Bell's diminutive XP–77 (an all-wood lightweight fighter), and Convair's XP–81 (a compound jet and turbo-prop fighter), but none of these went further than the experimental stage. More significant was Lockheed's XP–80, nicknamed *Lulu Belle*, which first flew at Muroc in January 1944 and was an instant success, quickly establishing itself as the progenitor of a line of Shooting Star fighters and trainers which would survive to the end of the century.

The post-World War II period saw a rush of activity at Muroc as the technologies of the jet age offered dramatic improvements in performance. Republic's XP–84 Thunderjet, the USAF's first 600-mile-per-hour fighter, which flew in February 1946, was followed by the Hughes XF–11 reconnaissance aircraft and a succession of bombers. Douglas produced the prop and jet XB–42 Mixmaster and its pure jet cousin, the XB–43, the first American jet bomber. From Northrop came a huge flying wing, the prop-driven XB–35, later modified for jets as the YB–49, and Consolidated delivered the immense and more successful XB–36. These were trailed by the North American XB–45 Tornado (the first operational USAF jet bomber), the Convair XB–46 (one of the most aesthetically pleasing aircraft ever built), and the revolutionary Boeing XB–47 Stratojet. In the late 1940s the list of aircraft designed for the USAF and tested at Muroc-Edwards grew to include a string of fighters—the McDonnell XF–85 Goblin parasite, the Curtiss XF–87 Blackhawk all-weather interceptor and its rival the Northrop XF–89 Scorpion, the McDonnell XF–88 and Lockheed XF–90 penetration fighters, the Republic XF–91 Thunderceptor and the Convair XF–92A, the world's first piloted true delta. Of all the fighters tested, the

X–1B tail. This aircraft made just 27 flights in all before being retired in January 1959, with its assorted components still in the "almost new" category.

The XP–55, an imaginative Curtiss attempt to produce a pusher-driven fighter in the early 1940s. Never able to overcome serious stability problems, its further development was cancelled in 1945 after a fatal crash at a Wright Field air show.

X–1B. Bell X–1 rocket-powered aircraft were designed to investigate flight at transonic and supersonic speeds. The USAF Museum's X–1B was instrumented to research the effects of kinetic heating in high-speed flight. X–1s were carried aloft by a "mother" B–29 or B–50 and dropped at 25,000 feet or more before lighting up the rocket engine and surging away. The subsequent dash to supersonic flight was invariably followed by a "dead-stick" landing.

most successful was the North American XP–86 Sabre, first flown on 1 October 1947 by the same George Welch who had distinguished himself six years earlier by shooting down four Japanese aircraft during the attack on Pearl Harbor. The Sabre was a winner from the start, and over 7,000 were built in seven major variants before production ended in 1956.

The long association of Muroc-Edwards with the highly specialized X-series aircraft began in 1946 with a whisper, when the Bell X–1 was first air-launched without power. It picked up pace with a bang in October 1947 as Chuck Yeager fired all four rocket chambers to push the X–1 *Glamorous Glennis* beyond the speed of sound for the first time.[6] One other X-plane program was under way before the Korean War broke out. In December 1948 the Northrop X–4 Bantam began an investigation of the characteristics of semi-tailless aircraft at transonic speeds. In a quite different approach to the challenges of the trans-sonic region in 1951, Major John Stapp rode a sled with a 4,000-pound rocket motor and mounted on a track with a hydro-mechanical brake at the end. Riding this sled and another at Holloman Air Force Base, New Mexico, he participated in a series of tests to find out just what forces the human body could withstand. Before he was finished, Stapp had been brought to a halt from over 620 miles per hour in just 1.4 seconds, experiencing peak decelerations of

X–1B cockpit. For a pilot perhaps the most significant difference between more conventional aircraft cockpits and that of the X–1 was the absence of a throttle. Power came from four switches at the top left of the instrument panel that controlled the rocket motor chambers, and they were either on or off. In the X–1B the Machmeter below the rocket switches reads only to Mach 1, which is ungenerous for an aircraft known to be capable of far greater speed.

XB–51. First flown in October 1949, Martin's XB–51 proved to be an impressive performer. However, it was overtaken by political events and Martin was left with a license to manufacture the British-designed Canberra instead.

X–3. Aptly named Stiletto, the Douglas X–3 never lived up to its appearance. It could be induced to go supersonic only in a dive.

over 40 Gs and exposing himself to a windblast that approached Mach 1.

The Air Force Flight Test Center

On 25 June 1951, an official ceremony formally activated the Air Force Flight Test Center (AFFTC) at Edwards Air Force Base. The motto of the new unit was particularly appropriate: *Ad Inexplorata* (Toward the Unkown).

During the 1950s several other X planes made their mark at Edwards. Bell's X–5 probed the secrets of wings that could be variably swept in flight, and the Douglas X–3 Stiletto promised blazing speed but its airframe had outrun the capabilities of its engines. Designed for sustained supersonic flight, the X–3

could exceed Mach 1 only in a dive. Even so, it provided valuable data for such later aircraft as the F–104 and the X–15. The X–1 series (three X–1s, plus the X–1A, 1B, 1D and 1E, the latter a modified X–1) did much better and continued to push back the boundaries of manned flight. Before the program ended in 1958, Chuck Yeager had taken the X–1A to Mach 2.435 and demonstrated conclusively that it could not be flown any faster. At that speed, Yeager said, the aircraft went "divergent" on all three axes and tumbled down through 51,000 feet in less than a minute before he regained control. Bell's swept-wing successor, the X–2, went still higher and faster than the X–1, reaching 126,000 feet and Mach 3.2 in 1956. Captain Milburn Apt was the first man to fly at more

455

Joe Engle and the X–15. In the two years starting October 1963, Joe Engle flew the X–15 a total of 16 times, reaching Mach 5.71 on his tenth flight and an altitude of 271,000 feet on his fifteenth. He later joined the Space Shuttle program, commanding Columbia *in 1981 and* Discovery *in 1985.*

than three times the speed of sound, but he did not live to enjoy his celebrity. Just after Apt had set the record, the X–2 succumbed to the inertia coupling which had overtaken Chuck Yeager. Apt attempted to eject from the tumbling aircraft but was fatally injured.

Captain Apt was not the only Air Force test pilot at Edwards to pay with his life in the 1950s for the privilege of operating at the limits of aeronautical knowledge. On 9 May 1952, Major Neil Lathrop died when a Martin XB–51 came apart during a high-speed structural test. The second Bell X–5 failed to recover from a spin in October 1953 and Major Raymond Popson was killed in the crash. One year later North American's chief test pilot, George Welch, paid the penalty for taking an F–100A to its G-limit at Mach 1.4. The aircraft suffered the dreaded inertia coupling phenomenon and disintegrated. Although not a serving officer at the time, George Welch was well known in the Air Force as a World War II ace with 16 victories to his credit. Such losses were grievous, but, considering the amount and nature of the testing

done at Edwards during the 1950s, the number of serious accidents was lower than might have been expected. At the same time, there was little doubt that the achievements of the AFFTC had made it the world's leading aviation testing and research facility. Thus established at the forefront of aeronautical research, AFFTC sought new frontiers and, before the decade was out, it initiated a program that carried manned flight to the edge of space.

The North American X–15 was built to meet a 1952 specification for an aircraft that could reach an altitude of fifty miles and speeds up to Mach 7. Such figures presupposed an airframe with the capacity to withstand an extraordinary range of temperatures, from a friction-induced 650 degrees to an ambient minus 180 degrees Centigrade. North American thus built the aircraft principally from titanium and stainless steel, covering the whole with a skin of nickel alloy steel. In March 1959 the first of three X–15As made a captive flight from Edwards under the wing of its "mother," a specially modified B–52A.

X–15 tail. On the uncompromisingly blunt end of the X–15A–2, the exhaust cone is on the receiving end of a throttled Thiokol XLR 99 liquid-propellant rocket engine with a rated thrust of 57,000 pounds at 45,000 feet. Above it towers the foot-wide trailing edge of the wedge section dorsal fin, pivoted for directional control and fitted with split air brakes. The spherical tank contains helium to pressurize the liquid hydrogen tanks. A conventional nose-wheel was used, but the rear of the X–15 was supported on landing by steel skids.

457

Between that date and 24 October 1968, there were 199 X–15 flights. In the course of the program, the X–15 became the first aircraft to fly above 200,000 and 300,000 feet and the first to exceed four, five, and six times the speed of sound. The pilot passing each of these marks was Major Bob White, USAF. The X–15 went on to record maximum figures of 354,200 feet (Joe Walker, NASA, 22 August 1963) and Mach 6.72 (Major Pete Knight, USAF, 3 October 1967).[7]

B–52-assisted flights of the rocket-powered X–15 were the most obviously spectacular of those conducted from Edwards in the 1960s, but they were a small proportion of tests actually completed. Jet aircraft, taking off under their own power, made great progress, expanding their performance flight envelope enormously. At the outer edge came aircraft like the Convair B–58 Hustler, a Mach 2 bomber that in 1962 lifted a payload of more than 11,000 pounds to over

X–15A–2. The USAF Museum's aircraft was flown by Major Pete Knight to Mach 6.72 on 3 October 1967. The three-layered windscreen includes a fused silica outer pane and an alumino-silicate middle pane. The airframe is covered with a skin of nickel alloy steel. A spherical device in the nose senses angles of attack and sideslip during upper atmosphere flight. Around the nose are eight of a dozen small rocket nozzles used to control aircraft attitude above the effective atmosphere. One of two 22-foot-long tanks attached to the fuselage contained anhydrous ammonia, and the other, liquid oxygen. This allowed the engine to run for 150 seconds or more, up from less than 90 seconds on internal fuel. (The X–15A–2 burned almost 16 tons of fuel in two and a half minutes.) The tanks were jettisoned and recovered by parachute.

X–15 cockpit. Flying in atmospheric air, the X–15 was controlled by means of the normal stick in the center of the cockpit. However, since there were no ailerons, its pitch and roll were induced by the all-moving tailplane, whose two halves could be moved together or differentially. The small rockets which controlled the aircraft outside the atmosphere were operated by a small stick hidden from view beneath the left cockpit rail. On the panel, instruments are almost outnumbered by red warning captions.

458

XB–70 cockpit exterior. A retractable visor smoothed out the slight bump of the XB–70's cockpit for flight at high speeds. In the cockpit, the fuselage was built mainly of titanium. A two-man crew's seats became pressurized ejection capsules in an emergency; thus, pressure suits were not worn, despite very high operating altitudes.

The XB–70 in level flight. The XB–70's wingtips fold down, 25 degrees in sub-sonic low altitudes, and 65 degrees in high altitudes and Mach 3.

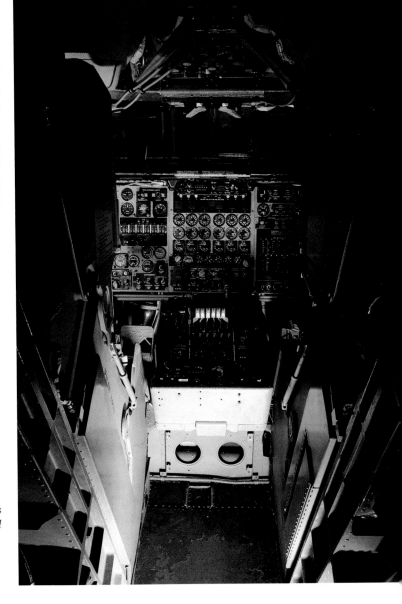

XB–70 cockpit interior. Entered between the pilots' seats, the XB–70 cockpit appears orderly and well laid out. Engine instruments and controls dominate the center. In the foreground are throttle levers controlling six General Electric YJ93 engines producing 31,000 pounds of thrust each in afterburner, sufficient to drive the half-million pound XB–70 forward at more than Mach 3 to altitudes over 70,000 feet. Just above the throttle quadrant are the landing gear lever and a rotary control for the movable wingtips, which could be drooped as much as 65 degrees to ensure stability for Mach 3 high-altitude flight.

Two huge tailpipes from the imposing row of six at the rear of the XB–70. The outer one is angled away from its neighbor to reduce the mutual disturbance of jet exhaust shock waves.

85,000 feet, and the amazing Lockheed YF–12A, the predecessor of the SR–71 Blackbird, which showed that it could sustain Mach 3 plus at 80,000 feet. Just as astounding was the North American XB–70 Valkyrie, a bomber weighing half a million pounds, which achieved Mach 3 at 70,000 feet in 1965. Overtaken by developments in Soviet radar and missile technology, only two XB–70s were built and both were flown in the interests of pure research. Sadly, the Valkyrie was at the center of one of the worst tragedies ever experienced at Edwards. In 1966 during a public relations photographic flight in formation with four fighter aircraft, the second XB–70 was struck by NASA pilot Joe Walker's F–104. Al White, NASA, ejected from the stricken Valkyrie, but Walker and Major Carl Cross, USAF, were killed and both aircraft destroyed. In 1969 the surviving XB–70 was flown to the USAF Museum.

Other projects of the 1960s included several which led to major acquisitions for the USAF's front line. The McDonnell YF–4C Phantom II (formerly the YF–110A Spectre) began flying from Edwards in 1963 and was followed by the reconnaissance version (YRF–4C) the following year. Intensive evaluation of the General Dynamics swing-wing F–111A started in 1965, and by the end of the decade Lockheed's gigantic C–5A was demonstrating its huge capacity by setting a world takeoff weight record of 789,200 pounds in 1969.

XB–70 intakes. The intake area of the XB–70 suggests a machine from a futuristic movie. The flying wedge shape under the fuselage kept boundary layer air from spilling into the intake ducts, which themselves were sensitive to shock wave formation and were adjusted automatically to ensure that smooth airflow reached the engines. The intakes are situated almost halfway back along the underside of the almost 200-foot-long fuselage.

The XB–70 sweeping upward. Over 180,000 pounds of thrust hurl the half-million-pound XB–70 into the air. The folding tips on the 65-degree sweep delta wings are set level for takeoff, and the Valkyrie appears to need the help of extended ears to lift its nose skyward.

The LTV–Hiller–Ryan XC–142A, an imaginative attempt to produce a transport with vertical takeoff and landing capability in the mid-1960s. Four General Electric T64 turbo-prop engines of 3,080 horsepower driving four bladed propellers of 15 feet 6 inches in diameter were hung on wings that were tiltable through 100 degrees. A small vertically-mounted tail rotor ensured longitudinal control during vertical and hovering flight. All engines were interconnected by cross-shafting. The spacious main cabin could accommodate 32, and flight tests showed that the aircraft had a speed range of plus 400 miles per hour to minus 35 miles per hour. Of five XC–142As built, only one, on display at the USAF Museum, is left.

Among more specialized programs was a study of boundary layer control, completed in the Northrop X–21A (a modified Douglas WB–66D). The future demands of space flight were met with astronaut training in Lockheed NF–104As, which were rocket-assisted to boost them to heights above 120,00 feet, and, from 1963 on, with tests on a series of lifting bodies from Northrop and Martin Marietta, wingless aircraft that examined problems likely to be encountered by space shuttles returning from orbit for unpowered landings.

Post-Vietnam

The 1970s and 1980s Edwards test pilots became less involved in pushing at the outer edges of the performance envelope for sheer height and speed and more taken up with exploiting both old knowledge and new systems technologies to develop more capable aircraft. After Vietnam the USAF was sorely in need of new equipment and Edwards was necessarily at the forefront of filling the service's requirements. In 1972 Fairchild Republic's YA–10A and Northrop's YA–9A began competing to succeed the venerable A–1 Skyraider; the Warthog eventually came out on top. That same year the McDonnell Douglas F–15A Eagle made its debut, impressing everyone from the start. Its testing progressed rapidly and, a year later, the Eagle was flying at Mach 2.5 and 60,000 feet. It was also quickly apparent that it was the most powerful and agile fighter aircraft yet built, and that it would handily meet the USAF's need to field an unmatched air superiority fighter.

Anxieties about the F–15's size and cost led to another fierce competition in the mid-1970s, this time for a lightweight fighter, between the General Dynamics

X–24A. The Martin Marietta X–24A PILOT (Piloted Low-speed Test) was one of a series of lifting-bodies designed to examine problems associated with manned re-entry vehicles being designed to perform as both spacecraft and conventional aircraft. The X–24A was launched from a B–52 and accelerated under rocket power to Mach 2 and 100,000 feet before completing a rapid glide recovery to Edwards Air Force Base. It successfully completed 28 powered flights. The USAF Museum's aircraft was originally the SV–5J, a jet-powered derivative of the X–24A, which never flew. It has been restored as an X–24A for display purposes.

YF–16 and the Northrop YF–17 Cobra. The YF–16 first flew at Edwards in 1974 and it subsequently went on to win selection by the USAF and to initiate the long production run of the F–16 Fighting Falcon, the world's first fly-by-wire fighter. Disappointment in the YF–17 camp was eased somewhat by its subsequent success as the USN's FA–18 Hornet and by the passing of a significant milestone at an early stage of the flight test program. On 23 June 1974, the YF–17 became the first jet aircraft to exceed the speed of sound in level flight without the help of afterburning.

Prominent among the larger aircraft tested at Edwards during this period were the Rockwell B–1A, which arrived in 1974, and a pair of Advanced Medium STOL (short take off and landing) Transports (AMSTs)–the McDonnell Douglas YC–15 and the Boeing YC–14. None of these managed to get past the testing phase, but at least some of the work done on them bore fruit some years later in the B–1B Lancer and the C–17A. The McDonnell Douglas KC–10A Extender made its first appearance at Edwards in 1980 and went on to enjoy a successful career in its own right.

Most of the significant investigations at Edwards in the 1980s involved new concepts and technologies. Test aircraft acquired add-on designations which described their special functions or hid them in confusing acronyms. There was the fly-by-light A–7D, which had fiber optic links to flight controls, and the Advanced Fighter Technology Integration (AFTI) F–16, one of the most capable research aircraft ever constructed. As it developed it incorporated such diverse and sometimes strange attributes as direct lift and pitch-pointing control, direct sideforce and yaw-pointing control, digital flight control, an advanced cockpit with multi-function displays, a voice actuated command system, integrated weapon firing/flight control, an automated maneuvering attack system, and an enhanced night attack helmet mounted display.

Another aircraft involved in the AFTI program was the F–111. In 1985 it flew fitted with Boeing's Mission Adaptive Wing (MAW). By operating leading and trailing edge flaps, a computer adapted the camber of the wing to ensure that its shape was always optimal for varying phases of flight. Further studies into

X–29. A forward sweep technology, Grumman's remarkable X–29 is a demonstrator made largely from parts of other aircraft, among them the forward fuselage and nose gear from an F–5 and the engine and main gear from an F–16. Like many modern fighter aircraft, the X–29 is so unstable that it cannot be flown by human hands alone, and must rely on computers to sense and correct, almost instantaneously, deviations from a chosen flight path.

Tacit Blue. Looking more like a Greyhound bus with wings than a flying machine, Tacit Blue is a unique aircraft that validated many of the concepts of stealth technology. The $165 million program, which ran from 1978 to 1985, provided invaluable information that led to the B–2 and other stealth systems.

improved performance and maneuverability were undertaken by the laboriously captioned F–15 Short Take Off and Landing Maneuver Technology Demonstrator (STOL/MTD). This was an F–15B modified with thrust vectoring nozzles, canard controls, and rough-field landing gear. During intensive testing it demonstrated dramatic improvements in landing and takeoff distances and impressive controllability at high angles of attack. It also used an Autonomous Landing Guidance system to make precision night landings on a blacked out Edwards runway without ground-based aids.

Among other notable newcomers to the Edwards flightline as the 1980s ended was the Grumman X–29, designed to probe the possibilities of forward-swept wings. It was followed by an aircraft that drew the mind back irresistibly to the early days of desert flight testing. Northrop's B–2 seemed to be a resurrected YB–49, back at center stage after waiting in the wings for forty years.

By 1989 Edwards had long been unparalleled as a flight test center, but in September of that year its capabilities were increased even further. The USAF opened the Air Force Anechoic Facility to test the integrated avionics systems of large aircraft within a protected and secure environment. The facility's shielded central chamber measures 264 feet by 250 feet, with a 70-foot high ceiling and was first used to assist in the development of the B–1B's defensive avionics system.

Flight testing at Edwards has never stopped moving forward in its pursuit of improvements in aerospace vehicles. As the 1990s dawned, the continued development of the B–2 Spirit, with its remarkable stealth technology and its complex systems, was accompanied by the introduction of state-of-the-art aircraft in both transport and fighter roles. The McDonnell Douglas C–17 Globemaster III promised to simplify the handling of heavy cargo and function as the only transport capable of carrying the largest U.S. Army equipment into restricted runways in severe weather. The fighters of the 21st century appeared in the forms of the Lockheed-Boeing YF–22 and the Northrop-McDonnell Douglas YF–23. At the end of another close competition, the USAF selected the YF–22 as the advanced tactical fighter to replace the F–15.

Flair and imagination have never been in short supply at Edwards, where more aviation milestones have been set than anywhere else on Earth. Even more dramatic creations than those already seen can be expected to arrive for testing during the USAF's second half century. Among them new multi-service aircraft may be prominent, and the hydrogen-fueled X–30 may succeed in demonstrating air-breathing single-stage-to-orbit flight, and in bringing Mach 25 speeds into the realm of the routine. Whatever possibilities emerge, one thing is certain. Edwards will remain at the forefront of aerospace research, establishing new frontiers with each passing year.

Notes

1. Instructions to test pilots were pretty basic, too. Among those issued by the commander of McCook Field, Colonel Thurman Bane, was the following: "Pilots will make sure that they thoroughly understand the operation of all controls, especially the motor controls, before taking off."
2. See Chapter 3.
3. Lieutenant Frank Patterson died in the crash of a DH–4 during gunnery trials in 1918. Patterson Field was later named in his honor, and his name survives in today's Wright-Patterson Air Force Base.
4. See the quotations at the beginning of Chapter 12.
5. The XP–79 Flying Ram was unique in that it was intended to be both rocket-powered and capable of slicing off parts of enemy aircraft with its sharp and extremely strong wing.
6. See Chapter 8.
7. Mach 6.72 equals a ground speed of 4,534 miles per hour or 6,650 feet per second, a velocity approximately twice that of a shell from the GAU–8 cannon in an A–10 Warthog.

It is difficult to say what is impossible, for the dream of yesterday is the hope of today and the reality of tomorrow.

(Robert Goddard, American rocket pioneer)

Our national space effort represents a great gain in and a great resource of our national strength.

(President John Kennedy, 1961)

Intercontinental air power and missiles are the new double-edged sword of destruction, hanging by a hair over us all.

(Trevor Gardner, Assistant Secretary of the Air Force, 1956)

We are confident that weapons like the ICBM and IRBM will help the Air Force to enable the free world to maintain deterrent forces which no aggressor in his right mind would dare to challenge.

(Major General Bernard Schriever, USAF, 1958)

Sputnik came along in October of 1957 and all hell broke loose!

(General Bernard Schriever, USAF)

Several decades from now, the important battles may be … space battles, and we should be spending a certain fraction of our national resources to ensure that we do not lag in obtaining space supremacy. The mission is to maintain the peace.

(General Bernard Schriever, USAF)

They really wanted to send a dog, but they thought that would be too cruel.

(Alan Shepard, before becoming the first American in space, May 1961)

The Earth from orbit is a delight — alive, inviting, enchanting — offering visual variety and an emotional feeling of belonging "down there."

(Michael Collins, Apollo 11 astronaut)

Chapter 13

Wild Black Yonder

Jovian Thunderbolts, Olympian Views

Tucked away in one corner of the museum's Air Power Gallery, with the port wingtip of the giant B–36 serving as a partial roof, is the Space Gallery. Entering from the Air Power Gallery end, visitors leave behind the familiar wings and engines of atmospheric flight and confront a world dominated by the intertwining tubes and flaring nozzles of rocket engines. Gondolas, capsules and space suits combine to create an impression that space can be inhospitable and uncomfortable. An Aerojet Aerobee rocket exhibit near the entrance creates the impression that some of the earliest space travelers seem to have found it so. A cutaway nose-cone shows the less-than-generous accommodations provided for monkeys Patricia and Mike and white mice Mildred and Albert when they were launched into space as part of preparations for manned space flight. Fortunately, all four survived the experience apparently none the worse for wear.

Nearby is a display on balloon ascents of the 1950s and early 1960s. The champion of high-altitude balloons was Captain Joe Kittinger, who rode in both of the gondolas exhibited, reaching a height of 82,200 feet in Stargazer and 101,516 feet in Manhigh II. Photographs show that in August 1960 he also rode an open gondola named Excelsior to 102,800 feet and then stepped out of it! His free-fall descent of 84,700 feet lasted more than four and a half minutes, during which he reached Mach 0.93. Slowed by the atmosphere to less than 200 miles per hour before his parachute opened, he reached the ground 13 minutes and 45 seconds after leaving the gondola.

The exposed plumbing of various rocket engines can be seen on both sides of the Space Gallery. There is the XLR–99 motor from an X–15 and there are engines from rockets like the Jupiter IRBM and the Titan II ICBM. The story of rocket propulsion—from the experiments of Robert Goddard and the V–2s of Wernher von Braun to the Saturns that launched men to the Moon—adorns the walls. Above hang research satellites designed by Lockheed and Northrop. The X–24A lifting body is banked over against one wall, near an experimental boost-glide reentry vehicle and a display about the manned orbiting laboratory. Photographs of U.S. Air Force astronauts are mounted above examples

General Bernard Schriever, Commander, Air Force Systems Command from 1961 to 1966. No officer was more responsible for the creation of the second (land-based ballistic missile) leg of America's strategic triad.

of the Mercury and Gemini spacecraft, and nearby is the Apollo 15 capsule that in July 1971 carried the USAF crew of Colonel David Scott, Lieutenant Colonel James Irwin, and Major Alfred Worden to the Moon. A piece of Moon rock offers evidence of their visit.

Ranged around Apollo 15 are various exhibits of space memorabilia. Several figures, their visored helmets staring blankly, reveal the evolution of the space suit, beginning with one from 1958 that carries more than a hint of an ancestry in medieval armor. There is a space sled intended for expeditions away from the parent craft and the more practical maneuvering unit that the astronauts finally chose for their space-walks. Space foods are there to tempt the curious palate. The hardware of space displayed is prolific.

Joe Kittinger taking the biggest step of his life from more than 102,000 feet above the Earth on 16 August 1960.

There are magnetic boots, a space can-opener, and a zero-G razor. Items that have bestowed added benefits on the more Earth-bound population include cordless drills, solar-powered calculators, thermal blankets, Velcro fastenings, computer chips and compact discs. They are all useful as reminders that the human adventure in space has already changed the way we live on Earth.

The Cold War was an agent of change, too, and some of its most powerful implements stand outside the museum buildings—slim, metal shapes in gleaming silver and white, some towering skyward, others straining forward on launching ramps, all seemingly eager for release—a sculpture park dedicated to deterrence. Dominating the display are the ballistic missiles, many of them named in recognition of their awesome power—Atlas, Thor, Titan, Jupiter. The names of later weapons chose to emphasize peaceful intent allied with instant readiness—Minuteman I, II, and III.

Elsewhere, both inside and out, the museum houses a variety of winged missiles, ranging from strategic weapons with intercontinental range to very high speed interceptors. Boeing's CIM–10A Bomarc was the world's first active-homing surface-to-air missile, and it was as fast as it looks, achieving speeds of Mach 3 plus. At the other end of the scale, the Northrop SM–62 Snark was the first American intercontinental nuclear missile. It plugged the gap in the late 1950s and early 1960s until ICBMs became available. Tactical cousins of the Snark are two Martin pilotless aircraft, the TM–61A Matador and its successor, the CGM–13B Mace. An American replica of the weapon which inspired the Matador, the German V–1 buzz-bomb, hangs in the Air Power Gallery.

In the mid-1950s the future of American strategic striking power appeared to lie with very fast cruise missiles; thus North American Aviation began development of the Navaho. To prove the concept and solve some of the problems, it built and flew several smaller pilotless aircraft designated X–10s. The one in the museum is the only X–10 survivor. Examples of two later cruise missiles bring to mind strong images of their respective operational deployments. The General Dynamics-McDonnell Douglas ground-launched cruise missile (GLCM) became notorious for generating fierce localized opposition when based in Europe, while the Boeing air-launched cruise missile (ALCM), carried by B–52s and B–1s, served as the very essence of deterrence with Strategic Air Command.

Two weapons with significant teeth—a Martin Matador and a German Shepherd guard dog tasked with keeping inquisitive intruders at bay.

The Rockets' Red Glare

The stories of mankind's early steps in the exploitation of space and the development of missiles as weapons of war are inextricably interwoven. For both enterprises, rockets, guidance systems, complex avionics, and a host of other particulars had to be perfected. The technology that built deterrence with ICBMs also placed satellites in orbit around the Earth and carried men to the Moon. These dramatic achievements were not born of new ideas. The Chinese are known to have had rockets around 1,200 A.D. and the Greeks were speculating about peaceful voyages in space nearly 2,000 years ago. In more modern times it was perhaps inevitable that the first measures in practical rocketry would be initiated with military aims.

American military aviators first showed a serious interest in guided missiles in World War I. Beginning in 1917, aeronautical scientists conducted experiments in the United States with pilotless aircraft known as Bugs. Their efforts continued only fitfully between the wars, but they became much more serious in June 1944, when the Germans launched the world's first operational strategic guided missile against London. The Fieseler 103 (the *Vergeltungswaffe Eins*, or V–1)

was a small pilotless flying bomb powered by a pulse jet engine. It was inaccurate and could be caught by the better Allied fighters. Militarily of little consequence, it was politically significant because of the alarm it caused civilian populations. Worse followed in September 1944 with another German first, the A–4 (V–2) ballistic missile. Although no more accurate than the V–1, the supersonic V–2 rocket was immune from interception and added the psychological impact of a "bolt from the blue" weapon to the destructive force of its one-ton warhead. Answering the cry for the United States to match the enemy's technology, the USAAF funded the JB (jet bomb) series of studies. From these came the JB–2, an American copy of the V–1 manufactured by a consortium of automobile companies. Northrop developed a pilotless flying wing, produced as the JB–1/JB–10. None of the JB weapons programs generated great enthusiasm, however, and they did not long survive the war.

By the end of World War II, General Hap Arnold had become convinced that technological and scientific advances, particularly in atomic energy and guided missiles, would revolutionize military doctrine, and he believed that the future of the Air Force depended

Kettering Bugs, built by the Dayton-Wright Company during World War I, the nearest two on their detachable trollies. The Bug was intended to carry a 180-pound warhead for 40 miles at 55 miles per hour. The number of propeller revolutions turned determined its mission range. At that point, cams withdrew bolts attaching the wings and the fuselage became a bomb.

on how well it adjusted to the new realities. In the immediate post-war period, however, the prevailing attitude was that guided missiles as practical weapons were many years away and that more pressing problems needed solving. This attitude, combined with a shortage of funds and endless interservice bickering over the issue of who would do what with which missile, reduced progress in American missile technology to a crawl.

The first practical American intercontinental missile program was Northrop's SM–62A Snark, begun in January 1946. It did not proceed with any particular haste and did not reach flight-test stage until 1951. The Snark was a pilotless aircraft in the mold of the V–1, but it was much more powerful and capable. It cruised at high subsonic speeds and had a range of over 6,000 miles. Its inertial guidance was updated by a star tracker, ensuring reasonable accuracy, and its warhead was multi-megaton, which took care of any lingering errors at the receiving end. Even more remarkable was the North American Navaho, another winged vehicle. Begun in 1947, the Navaho flew successfully in June 1958. It was highly imposing at nearly 100 feet and 290,000 pounds. When hurled off its ramp by rocket engines delivering 415,000 pounds of thrust, Navaho climbed to over 60,000 feet before its rockets were jettisoned and ram jets took over to drive it to Mach 3.25. Although it was impressive, the missile never became operational. By the time they were ready, Navaho and Snark had been overtaken by events.

The United States attempted to initiate an ICBM program in 1946. Commissioned from Wright Field, Convair undertook Project MX–774B to develop an ICBM capable of carrying a 5,000-pound warhead over a distance of 5,000 miles to strike within one mile of its target. So soon after World War II this was a startling requirement, given the one ton for 200 miles or so of the V–2. Funding soon became a problem, and in July 1947 the project was cancelled, programs for Snark and Navaho being given a higher priority because they were expected to reach operational status more quickly. Some Air Force officers were not particularly enthusiastic about missiles, anyway. General Curtis LeMay, Commander in Chief, Strategic Air Command, was among the skeptics. Until he could be shown that missiles performed reliably and accurately, he would believe that they were useful only as "political and psychological weapons," or "penetration aids" for his manned bombers.

Handicapped by a lack of urgency and direction in its missile development, the United States received a series of wake-up calls in the 1950s. The shocks of the Soviet atomic bomb test of August 1949 and the Korean War were followed by news in 1953 that the Soviet Union had detonated a hydrogen bomb and by alarming intelligence reports that it was developing rockets of enormous power. By 1955 the Air Force had a crash program running to produce an ICBM—the Atlas—and had appointed the dynamic Brigadier General Bernard Schriever to drive it forward.[1] It soon added two new projects to develop another ICBM—the Titan—and an IRBM—the Thor. However, the problem of limited funding had returned and the missile programs were already suffering severe cuts when the Soviet Union took the world by surprise again. On 4 October 1957, it launched a small artificial satellite named Sputnik into orbit from the Baikonur Cosmodrome in Kazakhstan. The effect of its persistent beeping signals on the United States was electrifying.

Soon after World War II Stalin had approved an ambitious long-term program of rocket development in the Soviet Union to deploy an ICBM force. The West knew of the Soviet Union's successful fielding of several ballistic missiles and the distinct threat that they posed to NATO forces in Europe by the time of Sputnik's launch. In 1957 the Soviet Union added an immense rocket (later designated the SS–6 by the West) to its arsenal with much greater range and lifting power than anything conceived in the United States. The West's suspicions of the rocket's existence proved correct; an SS–6 had placed Sputnik in orbit. Within a month another SS–6 had carried a dog named Laika into orbit inside a capsule weighing more than half a ton. The military implications were obvious, and there was much talk in the United States about the West's having conceded a technological lead to the Soviet Union and of the emergence of a "missile gap." The United States soon deferred any spending cuts in its missile development programs.

Alarm over the missile gap subsided relatively quickly as American programs gathered speed and had largely evaporated by the time of the 1962 Cuban missile confrontation between the United States and the Soviet Union. By then the United States had deployed 126 Atlas and 54 Titan I ICBMs and squadrons of both Thor and Jupiter (inherited from the Army) IRBMs to operate in Europe. In 1962 it also placed on alert ten Minuteman Is, the first of the solid propellant rockets which would come to form the backbone of America's land-based nuclear deterrent. In the mid-1960s the United States was phasing out of service liquid propellant Atlas and Titan Is, leaving only 54 of the more powerful Titan IIs in the front line with the Minutemen.[2] By the end of the decade, the

A Northrop SM–62A Snark blasting away from its launch ramp.

Atlas launch. Liquid-fueled Atlas ballistic missiles were rushed into service during the late 1950s to provide an interim deterrent while more capable systems were developed. By the mid-1960s, the Atlas was being phased out of the front line but has since been useful as a launch vehicle for satellites.

Minuteman force had grown to 20 squadrons of 50 missiles each (450 Minuteman II and 550 Minuteman III), scattered across America's plains states and along its northern rim.

As ICBMs go, Minuteman in all three of its forms is a small missile, less than 60 feet long and with a launch weight of under 80,000 pounds.[3] Its small size was part of its appeal, as were its relative simplicity,

the stability of its solid propellant, and the speed of its reaction time. Most important, Minuteman was cheaper to acquire, deploy, and operate than liquid propellant missiles. At first, Strategic Air Command envisaged placing at least some Minutemen on trains, and successful trials took place, but disagreement on the details of such a mobile version limited its deployment to silos. Here, too, Minuteman held a

Titan engine. Given the job it has to do, the Aerojet General LR 87 rocket engine, which provides first-stage power for the Titan II intercontinental ballistic missile and launch vehicle, is surprisingly small. Burning liquid propellants, the nozzles of the LR 87 project a massive 430,000 pounds of thrust to hurl the Titan clear of Earth's atmosphere. They are gimbal-mounted to control the trajectory of the Titan during the boost phase of flight.

clear advantage over Atlas and Titan, its silos being little more than simple holes in the ground, with no efflux ducts and none of the plumbing associated with liquid propellants. Every Minuteman fired is preceded out of its silo by a distinctive smoke ring, followed soon after by the flame and smoke of the first of its three stages and then by the missile itself, rising unharmed through rolling clouds. In its most potent form, Minuteman is capable of striking targets up to 8,000 miles distant with deadly accuracy, and its destructive power has been varied to include a

single warhead in the megaton range (Minuteman II), and three maneuverable independently-targeted reentry vehicles (MIRVs) of 335 kilotons each (Minuteman III)[4]. Ten of these terrifying weapons are controlled from each two-man command bunker, which is a manpower to destructiveness ratio of impressive proportions.

The build-up in ICBMs and enormous strategic striking power they represented did not come easily. Their development was at the frontiers of technology;

A 330,000-pound Titan II standing in its silo at McConnell Air Force Base, Kansas. Since their retirement from service as intercontinental ballistic missiles, Titans have retained their importance as launch vehicles for many military space programs.

"The First Silo Shot, Vandenberg AFB, May 1961," Nixon Galloway, 1961, USAF Art Collection.

Minuteman I, the first of the solid-propellant intercontinental ballistic missiles to go into service in 1962. Much smaller than its predecessors, Minuteman was more reliable and easier to handle.

their costs strained defense budgets, and the debate they sparked between the services was often acrimonious. The USAF saw missiles of all kinds as aerial vehicles that were essentially air power components and therefore natural extensions to its responsibilities. The older services did not agree, but the USAF persisted in promoting itself as the principal aerospace agent for the employment of air-breathing aircraft (manned and unmanned), ballistic missiles, spacecraft and satellites. Once the USAF was assigned responsibility for land-based ICBMs in 1950, and for IRBMs in 1956, this view came in large part to prevail and the USAF was forced to re-examine its role as a major element of national defense. The integration of missiles into the service entailed considerable reorganization and some hard thinking about Air Force doctrine, which now had to expand to include concepts of warfare both within and outside the atmosphere. New bases, new training programs, new career paths, and new logistical problems all added to the turmoil, and everyone had to adjust to the sobering thought that air power had finally matched the apocalyptic notions of the early

theorists. Once launched, the ICBMs were the bombers that really would "always get through,"[5] and with dreadful effect.

Since the deployment of Minuteman, only one other ICBM has reached operational status with the USAF. In the 1970s Soviet missile guidance had become so advanced that it enabled newer Soviet ICBMs to kill hard targets. Thus the Minuteman was increasingly vulnerable, and a more survivable American system was called for. Work on a new missile (MX) began as did a number of elaborate schemes for making the weapon as invulnerable as possible. Proposals included an underground rail system to keep the MX both hidden and mobile, a "shell game" in which 300 missiles moved about among 8,500 shelters, and Dense Pack, which put all the missiles in one vast field with the hope that some would survive an onslaught. In the end, none of these was found acceptable, and the MX Peacekeeper was deployed in former Minuteman silos beginning in 1986. Much larger than Minuteman at a launch weight of 195,000 pounds, the Peacekeeper can carry ten half megaton

Minuteman control room. Minuteman launch control centers are sunk approximately 50 feet underground. The blast-resistant, shock-mounted capsules are manned by two officers who control ten minuteman launch sites. On display at the USAF Museum is a Minuteman launch control center training facility. The two officers are seated at consoles placed well apart from each other. Since two keys must be used to launch a missile and they must be turned almost simultaneously, it is not possible for one man to initiate a launch.

MIRVs. In response to dramatic changes in the world situation, President Bush announced in his 1992 State of the Union address that MX production was being halted. Only 50 Peacekeepers reached the front line to become operational with the 90th Strategic Missile Wing at Francis E. Warren Air Force Base, Wyoming.

Gaining Space

The beepings of Sputnik did more than warn of a potential missile gap; they produced other effects, both positive and negative. On the positive side, the Soviet Union had done the United States a favor by unilaterally establishing the concept of freedom of space. It had not sought permission from the United States (or any other nation) for its satellite to pass over non-Soviet territory, but the Eisenhower administration was happy to keep quiet and accept the international precedent. On the other hand, there was something disturbing about the opposition's hardware passing unhindered over the United States at regular intervals, even if it was little more than a simple transmitter. President Eisenhower was quick to pursue the possibility of placing an American reconnaissance satellite into orbit.

The United States had made considerable efforts since the onset of the Cold War to unravel the secrets of military strength and nuclear capability that lay hidden in the vastness of the Soviet Union's interior; aerial reconnaissance missions around the periphery of the Soviet empire began immediately and yielded useful information about ports and coastal areas. However, it could only obtain deeper intelligence from overflights. In early 1956 the United States released over 400 camera-carrying balloons and allowed them to drift across the Soviet Union on the prevailing winds. Forty were recovered, some snatched in mid-air by specially modified C–119s before they could splash into the Pacific. Over 13,000 photographs resulted, but the operation irritated the Soviets and was not very successful in terms of intelligence gained. Since they meandered over endless fields and forests at the whim of the weather, the balloons did little more than add frustration to ignorance.

From July 1956 the U–2 overflights of the Soviet Union were vastly more successful, but they came to an abrupt end when Gary Powers was shot down near Sverdlovsk in 1960. It was more obvious than ever that the only satisfactory solution to the problem of surveillance of the Soviet Union lay with satellites. It may have been less immediately apparent that competition in the field of satellites was the first stage of a struggle for leadership in space.

The United States conducted studies into possible uses for satellites throughout the 1950s. Although thinly funded, they considered weather forecasting, communications, and navigation, but the Soviet threat made reconnaissance top priority. In 1956 the USAF awarded Lockheed a contract (WS–117L) to provide a reconnaissance satellite with cameras that could "detect objects no more than twenty feet on a side." The launch vehicle was to be an Atlas fitted with a Lockheed Agena upper stage. Lack of an adequate budget ensured that the project would proceed at a leisurely pace. Sputnik changed all that, agitating the smooth waters of American complacency and sweeping American policy along in its wake. In January 1958 the National Security Council assigned the greatest importance to the development of an operational reconnaissance satellite, and by October President Eisenhower had introduced the National Aeronautics and Space Administration (NASA) to oversee a national space program. An Advanced Research Projects Agency (ARPA) through which the services reported on military space matters followed shortly thereafter.[6]

Within the new framework, the USAF was instructed to drop the WS–117L (Weapon System) designation for its satellite. According to ARPA, the change was intended to "…reduce the effectiveness of possible diplomatic protest against peacetime employment." Development continued under the title Sentry, and later as the Satellite and Missile Observation System (SAMOS). Since SAMOS, designed to take pictures and radio them back to a ground station, could not become operational until the early 1960s, an interim system was devised. This was Eisenhower's Project CORONA, known publicly as Discoverer, a simple satellite using a Thor as the launching booster, intended to return its film to Earth in reentry capsules.

In a sequence of discouraging perversity, the first 12 Discoverers failed. Boosters exploded; satellites tumbled out of control; film turned brittle and broke; and reentry (if achieved) occurred anywhere but at the planned time and place. The capsule from Discoverer 13 was recovered after a successful reentry on 12 August 1960, and six days later Discoverer 14 delivered the first images of Earth taken from space. From then on, the system steadily improved. When SAMOS arrived, it had an almost equally painful birth, as did another satellite known as the Missile Detection and Alarm System (MIDAS). In light of CORONA's continued success, SAMOS was cancelled in 1962. Failures were commonplace, and years were to pass before satellite operations could with any assurance be described as reliable.

Matador, an early American winged missile, silhouetted against the skyline outside the USAF Museum. Matador was the first American unmanned bomber. A time capsule buried near the foot of the sunlit flagpole is to be opened in 2076.

USAF Museum visitors passing Missile Row on the way to the main entrance. Shown here are Minuteman III, Minuteman I, Jupiter, and Titan I.

Under the Kennedy administration, the USAF's part in the nation's space program became more closely defined. Among its principal responsibilities, the service embraced the defense support missions of early warning and space defense. The first of these demanded automated satellites equipped with infra-red sensors to spot Soviet missile launches. The other included the development of satellites that could detect nuclear explosions on Earth or in space. Associated activities involved the tracking of satellites (both friendly and hostile) from ground bases. Then there were other established defense support tasks, such as the provision of satellite communications facilities, weather information, and navigation aids.

In the 1970s and 1980s the disappointments and poor performances of earlier years faded to little more than distant memories. Electronic intelligence and photographic reconnaissance were routinely carried out, the latter by such large satellites as those commonly called Big Bird, combining high resolution pictures with area coverage. The keyhole camera in Big Bird, which could resolve objects as small as one foot across, returned its film to Earth by capsule, but a 20-foot dish antenna could transmit wide area images to ground stations. Later digital systems do not use film at all. They use computers that look for signs of change, scan images, and then transmit the results to the surface by radio. This successful program was brought to the edge of impotence in 1985 and 1986 by the failure of two Titans in succession and the loss of the space shuttle as a launch vehicle following the *Challenger* disaster. The United States was left with a single reconnaissance satellite in orbit, a precarious situation that lasted for 18 months. In the event, the USAF chose to order more Titan launchers and abandon the use of the space shuttle for military missions. By the late 1980s, the crisis was over.

For the detection of Soviet missiles, the temperamental MIDAS system was succeeded by the far more capable and reliable Defense Support Program (DSP) satellites. At the heart of the DSP was a large infra-red telescope that proved remarkably sensitive to rocket launch flares generated by ICBMs from land or sea or by much smaller vehicles. Hovering in geosynchronous orbit, DSPs gave instant warning of launches and provided information from which the number of missiles, their azimuth, and projected impact points could be determined. DSP satellites eliminated the possibility of an undetected surprise ICBM attack against the United States.

The problem of detecting nuclear explosions in the atmosphere was tackled with a series of Project Vela satellites. These were placed in orbits 70,000 miles above the Earth and, replaced at intervals, served successfully from 1963 to 1984. Since then, similar but improved detection devices, known as the Integrated Operational Nuclear Detection System (IONDS), have been carried aloft as passengers in other vehicles, notably the Navstar satellites.

Following several false starts and changes in policy, the Defense Satellite Communications System (DSCS, or "Discus") appeared in the 1960s. It was intended to provide a military communications network capable of handling voice, imagery, digital data, and teletype information. DSCS I satellites were linked to fixed bases, but the more flexible DSCS II and III series were capable of orbit repositioning and communication with small portable ground stations. DSCS III was also more survivable because of its resistance to Electro-Magnetic Pulse (EMP) damage. Another development was the Air Force Satellite Communications System (AFSATCOM) channels on board a number of U.S. Navy and Satellite Data System (SDS) satellites in both equatorial and polar orbit. AFSATCOM ensured efficient transmission of messages between strategic bombers and missile silos on the one hand, and ground and airborne command posts on the other. The even more advanced Milstar satellites followed in the 1990s. Operating in Extremely High Frequency (EHF) bands, Milstars avoided the prolonged radio black-out after high-altitude nuclear explosions.

The development of weather satellites was originally entrusted to NASA, but in the early 1960s the USAF designed one to meet specific military needs. Polar orbiting, low-altitude Defense Meteorological Satellite Program (DMSP) vehicles gave vital service during the Vietnam War. General Momyer at the time was unstinting in his praise: "This [satellite] weather picture is probably the greatest innovation of the war." Subsequently, even more capable DMSP satellites proved just as important in combat operations like those in Grenada, Panama, and Libya, and in the equally challenging missions of SR–71s, U–2s, and space shuttles.

In the early 1970s the USAF acquired the additional responsibility of leading the development of a space-based navigation system. Known as the Navstar Global Positioning System (GPS), it quickly showed that it could provide positional information to an accuracy of 30 feet or better. Even so, its funding and therefore its launches were delayed in favor of other items. By 1991 only 16 were in operation and the originally planned constellation of 24 satellites was not in place until 1994.

The construction of a system to track all satellites (and space debris) in orbit was a complex business. It involved combining the efforts of the USAF, USN, and Canadian Armed Forces into a network called the Space Detection and Tracking System (SPADATS), operated by the North American Aerospace Defense Command (NORAD) at Colorado Springs. Sensors feeding SPADATS were scattered around the world. They included radars from the Aleutians to Turkey, and Baker-Nunn cameras as far apart as New Zealand and Norway. Later, in the 1980s, the system's name was changed from SPADATS to the Space Surveillance Network (SSN), and it was upgraded with the Ground-based Electro-Optical Deep Space System (GEODSS), with sites in New Mexico, Hawaii, South Korea, and Diego Garcia. Other improvements included the passive receivers of the Deep Space Tracking System (DSTS) and a number of upgraded radars, such as those of the BMEWS and Pave Paws systems. The combination of all of this data allowed NORAD to ensure that the growing numbers of objects in Earth orbit were identified and constantly tracked. Among the thousands regularly watched, only about 5 percent are operational satellites. The rest are mere spacecraft debris or inactive payloads, enduring orbital monotony while awaiting the merciful release of blazing re-entry to the atmosphere.

American efforts to exploit space for military purposes came together and paid off handsomely during the Gulf War. This was the first conflict in which information from communications, weather, early warning, navigation, and reconnaissance satellites was regularly employed at all levels of planning and operations. In curious confirmation of an ancient principle of battle, American space systems gained the Coalition forces the high ground during the struggle against Iraq. Satellites were invaluable, and their services were combined quickly and effectively. A particularly dramatic demonstration of their immense reach and swiftness was given in response to the menace of the Iraqi Scuds. DSP satellites, designed to catch much bigger fish, were equally capable of detecting Scud liftoffs. In Colorado Springs the impact point was determined, and warning messages flashed via communications satellites to the Middle East. Alarms were sounded and Patriot missile batteries were alerted before the Scud could complete its seven-minute flight to Tel Aviv. The experience of the residents there was a far cry from the bolt-from-the-blue one of Londoners under V–2 attack in 1944.

Although the complete Navstar constellation was not in place in 1991, and there were times during each day when GPS information was limited in the Gulf area, the navigational advantages of the system were wonderfully apparent. It guided Coalition aircraft accurately to their targets day and night in all weather, and directed artillery fire with invariable precision. Special forces roamed deep behind enemy lines,

The main battle staff position in the Combat Operations Center, North American Aerospace Defense Command.

confident that they knew their position exactly. When Coalition ground forces finally advanced, they did so secure in the knowledge that units on either side of them were navigating along planned routes and that there was little chance of confliction, even though they were all moving through flat, featureless terrain in the dark. The weather satellites, too, proved their worth repeatedly. The Gulf region suffered the worst recorded weather in fourteen years during DESERT STORM, and the DSMPs eased the problems of target selection and prevented the launching of many sorties which would have been aborted or recalled. When DESERT STORM was over, Lieutenant General Donald Cromer, Commander, Space Division, asserted that the operation would be seen as "…a watershed for recognizing that space is as much a part of the Air Force and the military infrastructure as airplanes, tanks, and ships. All future wars will be planned and executed with that in mind."

Air Force Astronauts

In the early 1950s it was apparent that manned space flight was only a matter of time. To the USAF, it was only reasonable to assume that when it came it would do so as a logical extension of Air Force activity, following an unbroken line of progression from the Wright Flyer to the stars. While the U.S. Army took an interest in the German V–2 and busied itself with large rockets, the USAF held to more traditional forms flown by pilots and operated like conventional aircraft, at least within the atmosphere. The X–15 was a step along that road and was the first aircraft to break through the arbitrary frontier of space fifty miles up. In doing so, it earned astronauts' wings for many of its pilots, including the USAF's Bob White, Bob Rushworth, Joe Engle, and Pete Knight.

The X–15, however, was not a spacecraft. In 1958 the USAF moved closer to the goal of flying its own space plane when Boeing was commissioned for Dyna Soar, a program later designated X–20. As expressed by the USAF, the X–20 program was intended to produce an aircraft capable of space-based reconnaissance and bombardment missions. Political discomfort with the idea of offensive weapons in space and competition for funds with NASA's programs eventually doomed the X–20. Much to the chagrin of the USAF, Secretary of Defense Robert McNamara announced its cancellation in December 1963, just as the first aircraft was nearing completion.

The blow of the X–20's cancellation was somewhat softened by the allocation of the Manned Orbiting Laboratory (MOL) program to the USAF. The program was to deploy small orbiting space stations serviced by Gemini space capsules produced for the USAF

The Ballistic Missile Early Warning System station at Clear, Alaska.

"Astronaut," Bob McCall, 1972, USAF Art Collection.

by extensions of the existing McDonnell production line. After a great deal of effort, however, the MOL followed the X–20 into the graveyard of promising ideas. It was cancelled by Defense Secretary Melvin Laird in June 1969, when American priorities were being set by the Vietnam War and, in space, by NASA's drive to land men on the Moon. Official reasons given for terminating the MOL were the need to trim the defense budget and the improving reliability of unmanned vehicles. The USAF's dream of creating a separate Air Force-manned space program died with the MOL.

While suffering through the failures of its X–20 and MOL projects, the USAF had necessarily become involved in NASA's space capsule program. President Eisenhower was satisfied that plans for manned space flight should remain under civilian control, but he directed that potential astronauts be drawn from the existing ranks of military test pilots. In 1959 seven men chosen to endure the rigors of the cramped confines of Mercury space capsules were announced. There were three USAF captains (Deke Slayton, Virgil Grissom, and Gordon Cooper), three USN lieutenant commanders (Walter Schirra, Alan Shepard, and Scott Carpenter), and a USMC lieutenant colonel (John Glenn). On 5 May 1961, Shepard became the first American in space, just three weeks after Yuri Gagarin had been successful for the Soviet Union. Grissom went next, like Shepard, fired down range into the Atlantic in a sub-orbital shot. Glenn made the first earth orbit for the United States in his Mercury capsule *Friendship 7* on 20 February 1962. In the last of the six manned Mercury missions, the USAF's Gordon Cooper spent over 34 hours in space and then gave the lie to insinuations that the astronauts were mere passengers in the capsules. An electrical

Michael Collins, left, *Command Module pilot for Apollo 11, the first Moon landing mission, being helped into his pressure suit.*

failure forced Cooper to control his reentry manually, which he did with precision, bringing the capsule to a splashdown in the Pacific only four miles ahead of the recovery ship.

As America's space program developed into the Gemini and Apollo series, more astronauts were selected, 9 in 1962 and 14 more in 1963. From 1963 on, the requirement that candidates be test pilots was dropped, but most were still military personnel. USAF pilots were involved in many of the most memorable events, both intrepid and tragic, during the rush to honor President Kennedy's pledge to land a man on the Moon before the end of the 1960s. In June 1964 Ed White climbed out of Gemini IV to become the first American to walk in space. The world's first space rendezvous was achieved in December 1965 with Tom Stafford and Frank Borman as members of the crews of Geminis VI and VII. In a sharp reminder that the technology of spaceflight was far from perfect, a fire on board an Apollo spacecraft

at the Kennedy Space Center in January 1967 killed all three astronauts, including Virgil Grissom and Ed White. Frank Borman and William Anders were on board Apollo 8 for the first manned orbit of the Moon in December 1968, and Mike Collins and Buzz Aldrin were teamed with Neil Armstrong for the climactic Apollo 11 mission, which put the first man on the Moon in July 1969.

Moon landings continued until Apollo 17 in December 1972. With the exception of the near disaster of Apollo 13, the complex and hazardous enterprise was brought to an almost flawless conclusion. Astronauts spent more time on the Moon's surface with each landing, conducting experiments and collecting rock samples. Apollo 15's crew was all USAF—David Scott, James Irwin, and Alfred Worden. The lunar module *Falcon* moved away from the relatively safe flat areas previously used and touched down in the more rugged Hadley-Apennine region of the Moon in July 1971, after which Scott and Irwin spent a total of more than

Apollo 15. An all-U.S. Air Force crew landed the lunar module Falcon *on the Moon on 30 July 1972. Next to* Falcon *is the Moon's first car, a lunar rover, which was driven 17 miles at speeds of up to 8 miles per hour.*

Apollo 15's crew after its safe return to Earth—David Scott (commander, saluting), Alfred Worden (command module pilot), and James Irwin (lunar module pilot).

19 hours outside on the Moon's surface, deploying an Apollo Lunar Surface Experiments Package (ALSEP) and accumulating nearly 169 pounds of rocks. Scott also had the privilege of becoming the first to drive a four-wheeled vehicle, the electric-powered lunar rover, on the Moon. The California Institute of Technology subsequently paid tribute to Apollo 15 as "one of the most brilliant missions in space science ever flown."

Later Apollo contributions to the space program involved the Skylab missions and, in 1975, the remarkable Apollo-Soyuz Test Project (ASTP) cooperative venture with the Soviet Union. Commander for the ASTP mission was Tom Stafford and, participating at last, was Deke Slayton, the only one of the original seven Mercury astronauts not to fly. Grounded in the early 1960s because of a suspected heart condition, Slayton had been medically reinstated and, at 48, was the oldest man to have flown in space. It was noticeable, however, that experience counted for more than youth on missions like the ASTP. All five members of the American and Soviet crews were more than 40 years old. With the successful joining of American and Soviet hands in space in July 1975, the United States entered a long winter of absence from space. Americans did not leave the Earth's atmosphere again until April 1981.

The Space Shuttle was intended to do much more than take up where previous space programs left off. It was conceived of as flexible enough to undertake an almost limitless variety of space operations and thereby to serve as a universal, and reusable, replacement for all that had gone before. Although the Shuttle was a NASA program, the USAF helped fund the effort and therefore influenced the design of the spacecraft, taking account of the fact that military space operations would be dependent on its capabilities. It was confidently predicted that the Shuttle, while still on the drawing board, would perform like a space-age DC–3, a workhorse running regular missions to and from space and handling its multifarious tasks as routine. In the event, it did not. The inevitable unforeseen problems and delays and a backlog of missions soon accumulated. The first Shuttle did not get into space until April 1981; thereafter, consistently unable to meet its scheduled launch rate, the four-Shuttle fleet concentrated on research and development. NASA had planned for 100 launches up to the end of 1985, but only 23 actually took place.

As they were in the Mercury, Gemini, and Apollo programs, USAF personnel were regularly involved as Shuttle crew members; it was originally intended that up to a third of the Shuttle's missions would be devoted to military tasks. In 1983 the USAF, as problems and delays continued, sensibly renewed its interest in expendable boosters, which were under threat of being phased out. By early 1985 it had selected the Titan 34D (later Titan IV) as the Shuttle back-up system. That year, the first military Shuttle missions were successfully flown, and several more were planned for 1986. Then, in January 1986, just as things appeared to be going well, they were stopped dead by the *Challenger* disaster, which killed seven astronauts in an explosion shortly after liftoff from the Kennedy Space Center. Two Titan failures and the loss of a Delta booster during the same period effectively grounded America's entire space program for many months.

Although the Titan and Delta losses suggested problems, it had become obvious that sole reliance on the Shuttle for military space missions was unwise and the idea of expendable launch vehicles returned to favor. Several post-*Challenger* military Shuttle flights helped make up ground lost while the program was in abeyance, but the emphasis for the future had shifted to unmanned launches. The seventh military mission after the Shuttle returned to space in September 1988 flew in December 1992. It was the ninth and last military Shuttle mission overall and its successful conclusion marked the end of the USAF's direct involvement with manned space flight.

Notes

1. General Bernard Schriever was a visionary in the fields of ballistic missiles and space. In 1957 he appeared on the cover of *Time* magazine as the man who directed the nation's ballistic missile research and development programs and who helped provide their launching sites, tracking facilities, and ground support systems. No single officer was more responsible for creating the second leg of America's strategic triad than was Schriever. When Air Force Systems Command was formed in 1961 he was made its leader and promoted to four-star general.

2. Titan IIs used storable liquid propellants and were more easily handled than Titan Is.

3. This compares with the Titan II's 103 feet and 330,000 pounds and the Soviet SS–18's approximately 121 feet and 485,000 pounds.

4. In his 1992 State of the Union address, President Bush announced the planned removal of two of the three warheads from each Minuteman III.

5. British Prime Minister Stanley Baldwin stated in 1932: "I think it is well for the man in the street to realize that there is no power on Earth that can protect him from being bombed. Whatever people may tell him, the bomber will always get through."

6. In early 1958 the President also approved a secret project for a reconnaissance satellite known as CORONA, entrusting its management to a select CIA-USAF team.

You cannot lose a war with air supremacy, and you cannot win one without it.

(Carl Vinson, Chairman, House Committee on Armed Services)

The fireball from my kill was incredible. It completely lit up the sky and I could see the [Iraqi Air Force Mirage] break up or explode into millions of pieces . . . . There was AAA everywhere, SAMs were being shot . . . bombs were dropping, and the Wild Weasels were shooting their HARMS at all the SAM sites. Needless to say, it was very stressful.

(Captain Steve Tate, F–15C, 1st Tactical Fighter Wing)

We were allowed by the national command authorities to conduct the war the way the war was supposed to be conducted.

(Colonel Tom Lennon, F–111F, 48th Tactical Fighter Wing)

Air technology has finally caught up to air theory.

(Lieutenant General Charles Horner, USAF, Joint Force Air Component Commander, Desert Storm)

. . . by God, we've licked the Vietnam syndrome once and for all.

(President George Bush on the conclusion of Desert Storm)

The military has the best and brightest people it has ever had, the highest quality equipment, and the best training. The dollars spent in the 1980s made all this possible. For the future, we need to fund the right tools for the next century.

(Lieutenant General Charles Horner, USAF, Joint Force Air Component Commander, Desert Storm)

Chapter 14

Air Power Master Class

Smart and Stealthy Hardware

Having followed the story of American air power from its earliest days to the end of the 1980s, visitors to the USAF Museum at Dayton now near the end of their journey. From this point on, most of the aircraft among the stars of the museum's galleries in the 21st century are better seen still doing their jobs in operational squadrons or performing at air displays. F–15Es, B–2s, KC–10s, C–5s, C–17s, C–141s and their like will be serving in the front line for many years to come and are unlikely to grace Dayton's halls in the near future. However, representatives of the dramatic events of 1990–1991 in and around the Persian Gulf are at Dayton. There are two, both prominent in the combat arena of DESERT STORM.

The F–111F version of the swing-wing Aardvark thoroughly deserves its place in aviation's hall of fame. Among the least well publicized of the Gulf War's performers, it was perhaps the most successful in terms of sorties flown and ordnance delivered on target. The type was showing its age as the 21st century approached, but, in the 1990s, it could still be argued that it could be considered the best all-around attack aircraft in the world.

More obviously fascinating and with much greater star quality in the public eye is the startling Lockheed F–117A Nighthawk, generally referred to as the Stealth fighter. As visitors enter the museum's Modern Flight Hangar, its magnetic personality demands attention. It stands slightly to the left and in front of the monstrous B–52. It is not at all overawed by the looming Buff. For an aircraft designed to escape detection, it assumes astonishing prominence as an exhibit. Its multi-faceted blackness absorbs visitors and compels their presence. Wonder and astonishment are not inappropriate reactions to its menacing weirdness. Questions hover in the air around it: Is that a real warplane? Does it really fly? Can it actually make itself invisible? Iraqis who experienced the Nighthawk's capabilities first hand in 1991 might have no difficulty answering all three questions in the affirmative.

As might be expected, the F–117A on display is not a combat aircraft. It is the second of the type built and was used exclusively for testing. Nevertheless, its angular other-worldly appearance is genuine enough, and it really did fly.

Lieutenant General Charles Horner, Commander, Central Air Forces, during the Gulf War.

Another little known aspect of the DESERT STORM epic appears in a corner of the Modern Flight Hangar in the display of the Aerospace Rescue and Recovery Service. In telling of a desert rescue, it offers a glimpse of the often harsh realities of war. Lieutenant Devon Jones of the U.S. Navy, an F–14 pilot, was shot down deep inside Iraq in January 1991. He has every reason to be grateful for the determined professionalism of the U.S. Air Force's rescue teams, who saved him from capture by plucking him from the desert in the face of his enemies. Visitors will be rewarded if they spend a few moments to read the story of the Aerospace Rescue and Recovery Service, a vital but largely unsung element of the USAF.

Cold War's Close

The Cold War was over and there was much to celebrate, but, as the USAF entered the 1990s, it was uncomfortably aware that post-war fruits often bear the seeds of other problems. Its principal adversary no longer able to take the field, the USAF's force structure and the solid template against which it had been designed and shaped over many years faded markedly. Consequently, the Air Force's role for the post-Cold War era became less simple to define. Given the previous experiences of politically limited war in Korea and Vietnam, predictions of possible future employment in trouble spots around the world were not encouraging. However, the USAF was equipped to meet any global challenge, and in 1990 it was ready when the world witnessed flagrant aggression on the shores of the Persian Gulf. Saddam Hussein of Iraq launched an invasion of Kuwait, thereby setting the scene for a limited conflict in which air power advocates would see their cherished convictions amply vindicated.

DESERT SHIELD

Early in the morning of 2 August 1990, the Iraqi Army burst across its frontier with Kuwait in considerable strength. More than 100,000 troops and several hundred tanks brushed aside such little resistance as they encountered and within hours the tiny Gulf emirate was firmly in Saddam's grasp. The world's fourth largest army now stood on Saudi Arabia's doorstep, and Saddam Hussein appeared poised to become the man dominating Middle East oil.

Reverberations shook the world's economic foundations and international reaction was immediate. The United Nations Security Council condemned the invasion and President George Bush ordered U.S. Navy units into the region. By 6 August the UN had authorized worldwide economic sanctions against Iraq, and President Bush had announced the movement of U.S. Army and U.S. Air Force units to the Middle East in Operation DESERT SHIELD. Initially, the aim of American forces was to defend Saudi Arabia

C–5A. The whole of the U.S. Air Force C–5A Galaxy fleet was committed to the DESERT SHIELD-DESERT STORM strategic airlift. On their own, in the first three weeks, the Galaxies exceeded the achievements of the entire 1948 Berlin Airlift.

Stretched C–141s, vital elements of strategic airlift during DESERT SHIELD-DESERT STORM. As many as 265 of them flew routes between the United States and the Persian Gulf region.

against the further ambitions of Saddam Hussein. Communications and surveillance satellites were maneuvered into positions from which they could better support any American operations, and Military Airlift Command (MAC) got ready to undertake the largest airlift in history.

On 7 August, within 18 hours of the President's order, MAC C–141s and C–5s had begun the deployment of the 82nd Airborne Division's "Ready Brigade" and supporting elements of 1st Tactical Fighter Wing F–15 squadrons. The 48 F–15Cs of the wing were on their way, too, flying non-stop from Langley Air Force Base, Virginia, to Dhahran, Saudi Arabia, refueling 7 or 8 times during a flight averaging 14 to 15 hours. In welcome confirmation of allied solidarity, the United Kingdom deployed Royal Air Force Tornados the following day. By the middle of the month, other USAF squadrons of F–15C/Es, F–4G Wild Weasels, A–10s, and F–16s had joined these trailblazers in Saudi Arabia, and E–3 AWACS aircraft had begun a continuous patrol over the troubled area. On 21 August 22 F–117 Nighthawk stealth aircraft took off from their base in Nevada to exchange the desert surroundings

of one continent for those of another. While all this was happening, USAFE (United States Air Forces in Europe) F–111s and F–16s arrived at bases in Turkey, and Strategic Air Command (SAC) deployed its U–2R/TR–1A reconnaissance assets and moved B–52s forward to Diego Garcia in the Indian Ocean.

Looked at in terms of scale, rate, or distance, the American military buildup in Saudi Arabia was impressive. The air bridge was particularly remarkable. Once established, it spanned nearly half the globe and saw a cargo aircraft landing somewhere in the Middle East every ten minutes or less. By the end of the campaign, the USAF's strategic airlift had recorded 20,500 missions (a mission being a completed movement from origin to destination, regardless of intermediate stops), carried 534,000 passengers, and hauled 542,000 tons of cargo. The airlift totalled 4.65 billion tons, which compared to just under 700 million for the 65 weeks of the Berlin Airlift in 1948.

To the USAF, the operation was a timely vindication of its case for maintaining a truly balanced air force, capable of accomplishing tasks across the whole wide

491

MH–53J Pave Low helicopter. This formidably armed aircraft was one of a team that led the Gulf War's first strike, guiding U.S. Army Apaches to two vital radar sites in the Iraqi defensive screen.

spectrum of air power and of responding swiftly to an emergency anywhere in the world. It could not have projected global power without its fleet of large-capacity cargo and tanker aircraft in inventory, nor without the ready availability of well trained Reserve and National Guard personnel to fill gaps in the front line. Given Iraq's considerable forces and aggressive intent, the USAF had to provide good reconnaissance too, and, on the assumption that Saddam was not going to back down and withdraw from Kuwait, it needed aircraft for every combat role, from air superiority through conventional bombing to tank busting. Behind its aerial armada were the essential supporting services that enabled it to fight—command and control facilities, maintenance, armaments, food, accommodation, medical services, and administration, among others. In the months following the President's launching order, the personnel and equipment to make such a force function were uprooted from their American bases, transported many thousands of miles to work in unfamiliar (and

often basic) surroundings, and asked to create an instantly combat-ready air force, capable of defeating any opposition it met. That they did all this superlatively well, is a tribute to the professionalism which the USAF had achieved in the 1980s.

After August, the momentum in the Gulf changed hands. From posing an offensive threat to Saudi Arabia, Iraq had become more concerned with the defense of its ill-gotten gains. By mid-January 1991, Iraqi troops were well dug in, but the coalition opposing them had so built up that it was confident of a successful assault to recover Kuwait. Twenty-two nations had answered the UN call for troops, and the American contingent had risen to more than 400,000. The overall commander of the Coalition forces was General Norman Schwarzkopf, U.S. Army, although all Arab national forces remained under the operational control of the Saudi Chief of Staff, Prince Khalid. Deputy to Schwarzkopf and theater air forces commander was Lieutenant General Charles Horner,

U.S. Air Force. From the beginning, it was apparent that there would be no repeat of the mistakes of Vietnam. There would be no micro-managing from Washington. The President, the Secretary of Defense, and the Chairman of the Joint Chiefs of Staff would decide policies and set goals. They would leave the planning and execution of operations to the discretion of the theater commander.

On 29 November 1990, the UN adopted a resolution that approved the use of "all necessary means" to remove Iraqi forces from Kuwait if they did not leave voluntarily by 15 January 1991. Saddam remained recalcitrant. He would not leave what he now called his 19th province, and he assured the Coalition that he would order the use of chemical weapons in repulsing any attack on his forces. On 12 January, as the UN's deadline approached and Iraq's leaders remained unmoved by universal condemnation of their aggression, the U.S. Congress gave President Bush the authority to go to war. In the desert nearly one million soldiers and airmen faced each other and prepared themselves for what Saddam had promised would be the "mother of all battles." The Coalition's

generals had every reason to believe that he was right, and that the recovery of Kuwait would not be easy. Iraqi forces had spent five months preparing a defensive line in Kuwait that included bunkers, berms, minefields, masses of razor wire, and oil-filled ditches ready for burning. General "Tony" McPeak, USAF Chief of Staff, described Iraq's protection against air attack as "...a first class air defense, not a featherweight opponent..." It was indeed formidable, with advanced aircraft like the MiG–29 among those equipping the Iraqi Air Force's 39 fighter squadrons, and ground defenses that included perhaps 9,000 AAA guns and 17,000 SAMs, all backed by modern radars and computer data links.

If Saddam Hussein had hoped for an early commitment of ground forces in an assault on his fortress, he was disappointed. The first blows, and most of those that followed, were struck from the air. By mid-January 1991, the 690 combat aircraft of the Iraqi Air Force were outmatched in both quality and quantity by those of the Coalition air forces. Ten countries had contributed units to raise the front-line Coalition strength in the Gulf to almost 2,500 fixed-wing aircraft.

AWACS. Boeing E–3 Sentry AWACS aircraft were involved in the 1990–1991 Persian Gulf confrontation with Iraq from the beginning. Their all-seeing eyes closely monitored Iraqi activity during DESERT SHIELD, then maintained a continuous picture of the battle zone throughout DESERT STORM, warning and controlling Coalition aircraft as necessary.

F–117A. The surreal shape of modern air warfare was unveiled in Iraq when F–117A Nighthawks led the attack on command and control facilities in Baghdad. Making the most of their stealthy design and smart weapons, F–117As struck with impunity and great precision.

Of these, the USAF provided 50 percent, the USN 16 percent, the USMC 7 percent, and allied air forces 27 percent. The campaign air plan was split into four phases. In Phase 1, Coalition airmen were to gain air superiority over Iraq and Kuwait, destroy Iraqi strategic attack capability, and disrupt the enemy command and control system. Phase 2 would suppress the air defenses around Kuwait, and Phase 3 would shift the weight of attack to the Iraqi Army deployed around Kuwait, while continuing to pursue the objectives of Phases 1 and 2 as necessary. Phase 4 was concerned with air support for ground operations as and when they took place. As it happened, air strength available to the Coalition commanders was such that it was possible to run the first three phases concurrently.

DESERT STORM

To Iraqi early warning radar operators, the returns on their screens during the early morning hours of 17 January looked at first no different from those they had grown used to seeing for months. AWACS aircraft and F–15 combat patrols were orbiting just inside Saudi Arabian airspace as usual. But 17 January would not be just another quiet night. What the

operators could not see were hundreds of aircraft forming into strike packages outside the range of their early warning cover. Nor did they realize that their units were at the top of the Coalition target list. The first shots of the DESERT STORM campaign were fired at two radar sites by a special team of U.S. Army AH–64 Apache helicopters, led into position by MH–53J Pave Low helicopters of the U.S. Air Force. The helicopters' Hellfire laser-guided missiles and 2.75-inch rockets destroyed the sites, punching a hole in Iraq's air defense screen through which the initial waves of strike aircraft could flow unseen.

At about 1:00 a.m. local time, as the Apaches made their way to their targets, tankers from the USAF, USN, and RAF got airborne to establish their refueling stations. Combat air patrols were strengthened with more USAF F–15s, USN F–14s, Canadian CF–18s, and RAF Tornado F–3s. Strike aircraft began taking off from bases in Saudi Arabia and Turkey and from aircraft carriers in the Persian Gulf and the Red Sea. At 3:00 a.m., all hell broke loose over Iraq. From the ships in the Gulf came the first of a barrage of Tomahawk missiles. They led the attack on Saddam

Hussein's capital of Baghdad. Seven B–52Gs reached the climax of a 35-hour mission from Barksdale Air Force Base, Louisiana, the longest bombing raid ever, launching AGM–86C ALCMs at power stations and communications facilities. Confusing the issue for the defenders in the early stages of the attack were almost 200 pilotless decoys. These drew the attention of anti-aircraft radars, which thereby exposed themselves to the HARMs (High-speed Anti-Radiation Missiles) of predatory Wild Weasels.

At about the time that the Apaches were turning away from reducing their targets to rubble, the F–117A Nighthawks made their surreptitious entrance, first attacking radars close to Baghdad and then a communications center in the city itself. Before the night was out, the Nighthawks had hit 34 targets, using a variety of laser-guided bombs with dramatic effect. Their low observable technology (commonly called stealth) allowed them to operate with impunity in Iraqi airspace at night. They used it to attack high-value targets, especially in heavily defended areas where, for precision, they had to orbit while identifying the aiming point. The aircraft struck command centers, control bunkers, chemical-nuclear facilities, critical bridges and the like with startling accuracy. The Nighthawks' contribution on the first night of DESERT STORM was remarkable. Flying only 2.5 percent of the Coalition's sorties in the first 24 hours, they took on over 30 percent of the targets and achieved hit rates of better than 80 percent.

As follow-up raids approached their targets, it was apparent that Iraq's defensive system was crumbling from the effects of the earlier strikes. F–111s, F15Es, F/A18s, and RAF and Saudi Tornados went after air bases, Scud missile sites, and more radars. They were supported by EF–111 Ravens, jamming whatever electronic emissions survived the onslaught. One EF–111 scored a defensive victory after dodging a missile fired by an Iraqi Mirage. The Ravens' tight diving turn behind a screen of chaff and infrared decoys finished just above the desert, but the chasing Mirage did not pull out. As the EF–111's crew reported: "We got so low, he couldn't hack it and smeared into the ground behind us." It was the first Iraqi aircraft destroyed during DESERT STORM air combat.

EF–111A. The Sparkvark, an extremely sophisticated electronic warfare aircraft, was a vital factor in the DESERT STORM air war, using its powerful avionics to jam and confuse Iraqi defenses.

F–15Cs dominating the skies over Iraq during DESERT STORM. U.S. Air Force Eagles shot down 31 of the 35 Iraqi aircraft destroyed in aerial combat.

The first conventional air-to-air "kill" was achieved by an F–15C pilot, Captain Steve Tate of the 1st Tactical Fighter Wing. Alerted by AWACS to the presence of a bogey approaching his flight, Tate confirmed it as not friendly and loosed off an AIM–7 Sparrow at twelve miles range. The weapon struck an Iraqi Mirage, which disappeared in a huge fireball. It was a rare encounter. Not many Iraqi Air Force aircraft got airborne and Coalition contacts with those that did were few and far between. For their part, the ground-based defenders fired copious quantities of AAA and SAMs, but got little return for their efforts. Coalition aircraft flew over 670 sorties that first night, without loss.[1]

By midnight on the first day, they had flown over 2,100 sorties, degrading Iraqi air defenses severely. During the day the Coalition had suffered its first losses—an F/A–18 and an A–6E of the USN, a Kuwaiti A–4, and three Tornados, one Italian and two British. Since the Iraqi Air Force had flown only 24 fighter sorties, it was not surprising that none of the Coalition losses came in air-to-air combat. The Iraqis, however, lost eight fighters, five of them to the F–15Cs

of the 33rd Tactical Fighter Wing from Eglin Air Force Base, Florida. The almost clinically impersonal nature of late 20th century air warfare was summarized by one of the victorious F–15C pilots, Captain Charles Magill, a Marine exchange officer flying with the 33rd Tactical Fighter Wing: "When you get down to the bottom line, everything was incredibly basic. [Set up your] weapon system…just right, shoot your ordnance at the first opportune moment, watch the MiG blow up, and get the hell out."

Unable to withstand the Coalition's aerial onslaught, Iraq hit back in the only way guaranteed to cause international alarm. After dark on 17 January, it fired a Scud ballistic missile at the Dhahran air base. The missile was claimed destroyed by a U.S. Army Patriot SAM before reaching the ground. Soon afterwards, however, Iraq fired several more Scuds at Tel Aviv and Haifa in Israel, causing casualties and some local damage. Militarily, the Scud was of little consequence. With its small warhead, limited range, and lack of accuracy, it was a minimal threat to Coalition operations. Even with chemical warheads, it could not have affected the outcome of the struggle. However,

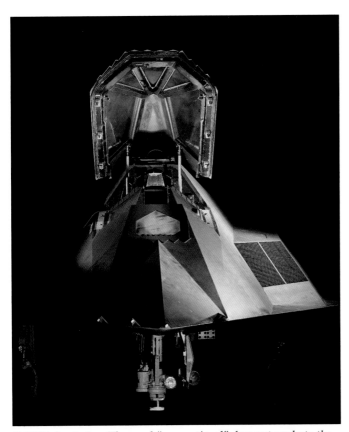

F–117A front view. The word "conventional" does not apply to the Lockheed F–117A Nighthawk. Even its F designation is surprising, since the aircraft is in no sense what is generally understood to be a fighter. Head on, the many-faceted exterior of this arrowhead-shaped aircraft is readily apparent, made so to reflect inquisitive radar signals at a variety of angles. Its few raised edges are jagged for the same reason and much of its surface is manufactured from radar-absorbent materials. The intakes for the aircraft's two General Electric F404 engines (10,800 pounds of thrust; no afterburner) are on either side of the nose, on the upper surface, and each is covered by a grill whose strips are closer together than the opposition's radar wavelengths. Directly in front of the cockpit, a fine mesh covers a forward-looking infra-red sensor. The USAF Museum's F–117A is the second one built. It was specially modified as a test aircraft and was retired when its development program was completed in 1991.

fired at non-combatant Israel, the ineffective Scud became a political instrument of disturbing power. Saddam was attempting to provoke Israel into striking back. He wanted to break up the fragile Coalition, since the Arab allies would not wish to be seen fighting on the same side as their traditional enemy. Intense American political pressure and the rapid deployment of Patriot batteries to Israel defused the crisis he had caused, and Israelis gritted their teeth to suffer in silence through a barrage of 40 Scuds in the course of the conflict. Iraq fired 46 more Scuds at Saudi Arabia, one of which demolished an American barracks and killed 28 U.S. Army reservists.

The Scuds posed such serious political danger that the Coalition was forced to divert its strike aircraft from other tasks to find and destroy them and effectively

extended the planned period of DESERT STORM air operations from 30 to 39 days. It dealt quickly with fixed Scud sites, but had more difficulty with mobile launchers. The "Great Scud Hunt" began on the night of 18 January by F–15Es of the 4th Tactical Fighter Wing from Seymour Johnson Air Force Base, North Carolina. They flew in pairs at about 15,000 feet, their leader generally carrying four GBU–10 laser-guided bombs and their wingman carrying six CBU–87 cluster bombs. Sweeping ahead with their LANTIRN (Low-Altitude Navigation and Targeting Infra-Red for Night) equipment, they searched for signs of mobile Scud missile launchers, attacking in sequence when they found a site.

Another significant weapon against the Scuds was Boeing's E–8A Joint STARS (J-STARS), two proto-types of which were rushed to the Gulf to boost the Coalition's surveillance effort. Still involved in the development stage of the J-STARS battlefield control system, the E–8As were a great success. Their huge side-looking radars could detect stationary armored vehicles and provide an accurate plot of slow-moving objects. Much in demand as a controlling agency for

F–117A LGB. High-explosive bombs have been vastly increased in effectiveness by fitting the Paveway series of laser-guidance units to their noses. Internal bays keep the F–117A's smart bombs hidden away until just before release. During the Gulf War Nighthawks used the GBU–27 (a modified form of the third generation GBU–24, called Paveway III) as the guidance system for their bombs with considerable success. Note the faceted radar-dispersing edges on the weapons bay and nose-wheel doors.

A–10 gun. As Iraqi troops discovered, the GAU–8 Avenger multi-barrel cannon is a mighty instrument of destruction. The gun fills the lower forward fuselage of the A–10, the rear of the ammunition drum reaching nearly 21 feet back from the muzzle. A GAU–8 fully loaded with 1,350 rounds of 30-mm ammunition weighs nearly two tons.

tactical aircraft generally, the E–8As were particularly valuable in locating mobile Scuds for the roving F–15Es.

Up to 26 January the Coalition air offensive was principally concerned with ensuring air supremacy and with the destruction of Iraq's command and control system; the Scud hunt was an unlooked for complication. The USAF struck some Iraqi troop concentrations in the early stages with A–10s and B–52s, but after 26 January it stepped up its pace, striking more as other attack aircraft joined in. Its F–16s and A–10s were the most numerous types deployed to the Gulf, around 200 of each seeing combat, and they were heavily employed against Iraqi troops and vehicles. In close encounters, the A–10s used their awesome 30-mm cannon to fearsome effect. One pair of Warthog pilots from the 23rd Tactical Fighter Wing claimed twenty-three tanks between them in one day, and two others, from the 10th Tactical Fighter Wing and the 926th Tactical Fighter Group, Air Force Reserves, destroyed enemy helicopters, claiming the first ever air-to-air successes for the A–10.

Initially, the B–52s flew from the island airfield of Diego Garcia in the Indian Ocean, but they came from other bases in the United Kingdom, Spain, and Saudi Arabia as the conflict wore on. All of them were B–52Gs, carrying loads of 51 750-pound bombs used in the saturation bombing of soft targets, particularly the Republican Guard troop concentrations in the desert, west of Basra. Flying in flights of three, they achieved coordinated releases of 153 bombs at a time, carpeting an area one and a half miles long by a mile wide. Such a weight of explosive had as shattering an effect on the morale of the troops as it had on the landscape and was probably instrumental in persuading large numbers of soldiers to surrender as soon as the Coalition ground offensive was launched.

In addition to carrying out direct attacks on Iraqi Army units, Coalition aircraft turned their attention to military storage areas and the interdiction of supply routes to weaken the enemy's fighting capability before the ground offensive. This did not mean that they left earlier targets. They still made raids deep

A–10 front view. Commonly called the Warthog, Fairchild Republic's A–10A was more formally named Thunderbolt II. It was designed as an in-fighter, a highly maneuverable aircraft that gave effective close support to troops. Besides the crushing power of its mighty multi-barrel GAU–8 cannon, the A–10 has the capacity to carry up to 16,000 pounds of all kinds of ordnance on eight hard points under the wings and three more under the fuselage. (Note that the nose-wheel is offset to make room for the gun on the aircraft's center-line.) Heavy armor, multiple aircraft systems, and widely separated engines set high above the fuselage increase the A–10's probability of survival against intense ground fire. The USAF Museum's A–10 was flown by Captain Paul Johnson during Operation DESERT STORM. For his performance during an eight-hour rescue support mission, Johnson was awarded the Air Force Cross.

into Iraq, searching out command and control centers and ensuring that the comatose air defense system did not get a chance to rise again. Many surviving elements of the Iraqi Air Force were fleeing to safe havens in Iran, but Coalition aircraft still made occasional contact with enemy fighters in the air. On 27 January two F–15Cs of the 36th Tactical Fighter Wing from Bitburg Air Base, Germany, were vectored toward an enemy formation by a patrolling AWACS. In the hectic seconds after finding and closing to firing range, they launched a rapid combination of AIM–7s and AIM–9s to shoot down three MiG–23s and one Mirage F–1.

On the night of 27 January the USAF struck an important blow for environmental causes. The Iraqis had seriously damaged Kuwaiti oil fields and were deliberately allowing two pumping stations to spill large quantities of oil into the Persian Gulf. Three F–111Fs of the 48th Tactical Fighter Wing, RAF Lakenheath, United Kingdom, made a precision attack on the pumping stations involved. The weapons

they used were GBU–15 laser-guided bombs, tossed from two of the F–111Fs flying supersonic at 20,000 feet. The third Aardvark, tracking parallel with the coast 50 miles out to sea, guided the bombs onto their targets. They scored direct hits on both stations and the flow of oil stopped. Success in such a newsworthy effort offered a rare moment of recognition to the crews of the F–111Fs. Dogged by their sometimes checkered past and overtaken in the public eye by younger and more glamorous types, the Aardvarks in the Gulf quietly went about compiling the most impressive record of any strike aircraft in the war. By the time it was over, F–111Fs had been everywhere and had attacked everything. They flew around 2,500 combat sorties and provided video-tape confirmation that they had destroyed 2,203 targets, including at least 920 tanks, 252 artillery pieces, 245 hardened aircraft shelters, 13 runways, and 12 bridges. (They seriously damaged another 52.) Of the more than 8,000 precision guided munitions dropped by USAF

A–10 cockpit. The inside of a bathtub is not usually like this. The A–10 cockpit fits within a protective titanium bathtub shield capable of withstanding a 23-mm shell. The windscreen is bullet-proof glass, and the pilot sits on a zero-zero Douglas ejection seat—one that could eject a pilot safely with the aircraft stationary on the ground. The trigger fires the GAU–8 cannon and releases 30-mm depleted uranium rounds at a rate of up to 4,200 per minute, the heaviest weight of fire ever from an aircraft gun.

F–111F. The combat record of the F–111F Aardvarks from the 48th Tactical Fighter Wing at Lakenheath, England, was among the most impressive of any in the Gulf War. Aardvarks delivered over half of the precision guided weapons aimed at Iraqi targets.

F–111A cockpit. In the F–111 the crew stayed together whatever happened, making emergency escape in a McDonnell Douglas zero-zero module fired from the aircraft by a 40,000-pound-thrust rocket. A parachute lowered the module to the ground with the crew members still strapped in their seats. Airbags cushioned the impact and acted as flotation gear in water. (The module's rocket could be fired under water, too.) The module was also a survival shelter.

F–111F tail. The F–111F at the USAF Museum was the first fixed-wing combat aircraft to penetrate the opposition's airspace both in Libya and Iraq. Then an aircraft of the 48th Tactical Fighter Wing at Lakenheath, England, it now carries the markings of the 27th Fighter Wing, Cannon Air Force Base, New Mexico, the unit with which it flew until the end of its career.

The F–111F. The F model was the most potent all-weather attack version of the General Dynamics F–111, commonly known as the Aardvark. In 1967 the F–111 was the first variable geometry combat aircraft to enter service. The wing sweep (here fully swept) could vary between 16 and 72 degrees, reducing the span from 63 to 32 feet. The snout of the F–111F covers nav-attack and terrain-following radars, and the most common combat load included electronic countermeasure and Pave Tack laser designation pods, plus four 2,000-pound laser guided bombs.

F–111F nose. The main wheels of the F–111 retracted into the fuselage and were covered by a single door that could be extended as an air brake in flight. The F model was powered by two 25,100-pound-thrust Pratt & Whitney TF30 turbofan engines, a considerable improvement over previous variants. Full-span slats and flaps adorned the wings; the all-flying tail surfaces moved symmetrically or differentially to provide both elevator and aileron functions.

The Lockheed's C–130 Hercules, one of the most adaptable and durable aircraft ever designed. First flown in 1954, it has served in many roles—transport; freight carrying; maritime patrolling; mine-laying; electronic countermeasure, command and control, special operations, weather reconnaissance, search and rescue; aerial refueling; capsule recovering; and airborne medical. This aircraft flew in the Gulf War and was retired to the USAF Museum in 1995. From front to rear, on the left side of its fuselage, the AC–130A carried an AN/ASQ–5 Black Crow vehicle ignition sensor, an AN/ASQ–24A stabilized tracking set, two M–61 six-barrel 20-mm cannon, an AN/AAD–4 FLIR, two 7.62-mm machine guns, two 40-mm Bofors guns, an AN/APQ–133 beacon tracking radar, and an AN/AVQ–17 searchlight.

aircraft, no fewer than 4,660 were entrusted to F–111Fs.[2] As if to confirm their status, the Aardvarks finished the war in style, winning a fly-off with the F–15Es for the distinction of delivering the special GBU–28/B Deep Throat bomb, a weapon capable of penetrating over 100 feet of earth or 22 feet of reinforced concrete. On the last night of the war, two F–111Fs guided their new bombs into the hardened high command bunkers north of Baghdad, letting Iraq's leaders know that they were at personal risk even deep below ground.

As February passed and the Coalition kept up its relentless aerial assault on Iraq's military machine, the backbone of the USAF's front line aircraft flew combat sorties by the thousand, and some of the more specialized types got the chance to demonstrate their true value. Among them were a number of variants

AC–130. On Azrael, Angel of Death, *the USAF Museum's AC–130A, 40-mm cannon muzzles reach out under the wing. Above are square-ended Hamilton Standard propeller blades on the port engines. Four Allison T56 turbo-prop engines gave the C–130A a range of almost 2,000 miles with an 18-ton payload. At shorter ranges the AC–130A could spend many hours on call over the battle area.*

of the ubiquitous C–130. The EC–130H Compass Call added the final touches to the campaign to close Iraqi eyes and ears. With their batteries of communications jammers and their computerized frequency scanning ability, Compass Call aircraft swamped the airwaves throughout Iraq, rendering reliable enemy radio communication almost impossible. First cousins to the

EC–130Hs are the EC–130Es of the Pennsylvania Air National Guard. They transmit over both commercial and military radio and television frequencies, and during DESERT SHIELD-DESERT STORM they blanketed Iraq with broadcasts to demoralize both troops and civilians, simply by telling the truth about what was happening. Like those of the B–52s, their missions made an impact, convincing large numbers of the enemy to surrender.

Hail Mary

With the Iraqi Air Force reduced to impotence and the enemy incapable of monitoring Coalition activities, General Schwarzkopf was able to set the stage for the final act of the Gulf War drama, secure in the knowledge that Saddam's forces were blind and deaf to his preparations. While maintaining a strong presence in front of Kuwait and trailing the coat of the U.S. Marines assault ships as a distraction off shore, Schwarzkopf moved a huge force of American, British, and French armored units westward into the desert, setting up a monstrous left hook to outflank the Iraqi Army and cut across its escape routes. As he did so, Coalition air forces continued to pound away at targets of all kinds, although they intensified their attacks on enemy airfields for a while to prevent the Iraqi Air Force from attempting a desperate concerted effort to respond to a ground offensive with chemical weapons.

At 4:00 a.m. on the morning of 24 February 1991, strong Coalition ground forces, backed up by overwhelming air support, thrust forward from their holding positions into Kuwait and southern Iraq in the largest combined offensive since World War II. It involved more than half a million troops. The frontal assault on Kuwait engaged the attention of the bulk of the Iraqi Army while the Coalition's armored columns raced across the desert far to the west. A–10s, helicopter gunships, and Marine AV–8B Harriers came into their own, playing havoc with the enemy's armor. To the west the inestimable value of plentiful tactical airlift was being shown. The wettest weather for many years had turned extensive areas of the desert into a morass and was bogging down the Army's supply convoys. C–130s, which had been heavily occupied already in moving troops and equipment to forward staging areas, now airdropped tons of supplies to the rapidly moving spearheads, enabling them to maintain the momentum of their advance deep into enemy territory.

Their defensive plans unhinged by the crushing weight of the air campaign and by the speed and power of Schwarzkopf's armored left hook, most Iraqi troops either withdrew from their positions in confusion or surrendered in thousands. Those few who chose to stand and resist were comprehensively outgunned and outfought. Flushed from their carefully prepared bunkers and revetments, Iraqis attempting to scramble out of the battle area and escape were harried unmercifully by the Coalition's ever present close air support. The road from Kuwait to Basra became a river of death and destruction, with the wreckage of hundreds of vehicles of all kinds scattered along it and in the desert nearby. By 27 February Coalition ground forces had advanced to place themselves across the escape routes from Kuwait as the Iraqi Army's resistance had effectively ceased. President Bush declared a ceasefire starting from 8:00 a.m. Baghdad time on 28 February, exactly 100 hours after the ground assault began.

GBU–12 Paveway II 500-pound bombs, used to great effect by various American attack aircraft against Iraqi targets during DESERT STORM.

The Air Power Achievement

The Gulf War had lasted six weeks, all but four days of which was taken up by an air offensive against Iraq that was unrelenting in its severity. The Coalition air forces had flown 110,000 sorties, with the USAF claiming the lion's share. Losses had been remarkably light, totalling only 35 fixed-wing aircraft, 14 of which came from the USAF. All were attributable to ground fire.[3] The Iraqi Air Force also lost 35 fixed-wing aircraft during combat sorties, but all of them were shot down in air-to-air engagements, 31 of them by F–15s of the USAF. Many more Iraqi aircraft were destroyed on the ground by air attack, and well over 100 others fled to the dubious haven of Iran.

DESERT STORM was a crushing military victory, built on the often spectacular achievements of Coalition air power. From the speed of the initial response to Saddam's aggression and the creation of an air bridge thousands of miles long, to the imposition of air supremacy over Iraq and the effective destruction of the Iraqi Army as a fighting force, the Coalition's air forces demonstrated that air power *properly used* is a dominating factor in any major clash of arms. The USAF shouldered by far the greatest burden of any of the air forces involved in the Gulf War and saw its dedication to advanced technologies justified in the performance of its newest and most complex systems. Teamed with AWACS, the untried J-STARS provided unprecedented airborne battle control capabilities. The F–117As, F–15Es and EF–111As proved to be both effective and, to the surprise of some, extremely reliable, with serviceability rates approaching, and occasionally exceeding, an average of 90 percent. Precision guided munitions revolutionized the air campaign. Less than 8 percent of the 88,500 tons of bombs dropped were "smart," but they accounted for almost 80 percent of the targets known to have been destroyed by bombardment. The Navstar Global Positioning System (GPS) and the Low Altitude Navigation and Targeting Infra-red for Night (LANTIRN) equipment were prominent among those which enabled USAF attack aircraft to maintain an around-the-clock, all-weather campaign against Iraq with astonishing (and, for their enemies, disturbing) accuracy.

None of this would have led to the remarkable results achieved if available air power had not been properly used. The USAF's post-Vietnam insistence on recruiting the right people and giving them the best possible training paid off handsomely. In DESERT STORM the USAF's personnel were notable for their professionalism. Perhaps just as significant was the political decision which, more than any other, exorcised the ghosts of Vietnam. Once the United States determined that it was necessary to commit the military to action in the Gulf, the conduct of the campaign was left to the theater commander. He, in turn, had the advantage of dealing with a single air commander who was able to use his air assets to the best possible effect. For once, it all came together for the airmen, who grasped their advantage and laid the foundations of a great victory. Wherever he is, Billy Mitchell must have been smiling.

Notes

1. Initially, Iraq claimed considerable success, reporting that it had shot down over 100 Coalition aircraft. Its claims might not have been entirely imaginary. Over 100 decoys went down in or around Baghdad and might have either fallen or been shot down. It was not the first time that defenders had claimed small aircraft falling to Earth in the middle of intense anti-aircraft barrages. The same thing happened during the first night of the German V–1 attack on London in 1944. The gunners did not initially understand that the V–1 was accomplishing its mission if it fell to Earth.

2. One senior American commander reportedly said during a raid briefing: "I want this target hit. Give it to the F–111s."

3. Two F–15Es, one F–4G, five F–16Cs, five A–10s, one EF–111A, one AC–130H. A total of 20 aircrew killed, 14 of them in the AC–130H. Non-combat fixed-wing USAF accidents during the period of DESERT STORM claimed a B–52G and two F–16Cs.

Our real problem is not our strength today; it is rather the vital necessity of action today to ensure our strength tomorrow.

(President Dwight Eisenhower)

Don't hit at all if it is honorably possible to avoid hitting, but never hit soft.

(President Theodore Roosevelt)

If a nation values anything more than freedom, it will lose that freedom; and the irony of it is that if it is comfort or money that it values more, it will lose that, too.

(Somerset Maugham)

Forces that cannot win will not deter.

(General Nathan Twining, USAF)

Air power has become predominant, both as a deterrent to war, and — in the eventuality of war — as the devastating force to destroy an enemy's potential and fatally undermine his will to wage war.

(General Omar Bradley, U.S. Army)

The air ocean and its endless outer space extension are one and indivisible and should be controlled by a single homogeneous force.

(Alexander de Seversky)

Chapter 15

21st Century Air Force

Global Reach, Global Power

In 1991 the U.S. Air Force was on the crest of a wave, carried along by a surge of euphoria in the wake of a Gulf War victory solidly built on the achievements of air power. After such a crushing demonstration of professionalism and effectiveness, it was widely held that a service that had performed so efficiently and served national interests so capably must surely have reached a state approaching perfection in its personnel, organization, equipment, and training. However justified that view may have been, it was overridden by a number of other, more pressing realities, in response to which the USAF was already being committed to a process of fundamental change even as the Gulf War was being fought.

Faced with the need to rethink national defense policy in the aftermath of the Cold War, and having to tackle the problem of recurring budget deficits, the United States chose to cut defense spending and reduce the size of its armed forces to levels not seen since the brief period of massive demobilization following World War II. Before the Berlin Wall came down, the USAF's uniformed personnel strength approached 600,000 and there was a total active inventory of over 6,700 aircraft. As it prepared to celebrate its 50th anniversary as an independent service

USAF Academy cadets, leaders of the United States Air Force of the 21st century, raising their flag in front of the chapel at Colorado Springs.

in 1997, those figures were down to 400,000 and 4,700. At an early stage of the service's shrinkage, USAF leaders recognized that if they were to avoid serious operational impairment as they reduced by one-third they would have to considerably restructure and redeploy its forces. Commitments in various parts of the world might continue to arise, but the USAF would find the costly option of manning and maintaining numerous overseas bases no longer feasible. Although a few major facilities, in Europe and Korea for instance, would remain outside the United States, the leaner USAF would have to feature the idea of composite task forces—multi-role packages able to deploy quickly from home bases to wherever they were needed in an emergency.

Before the alarms and diversions of the Kuwait crisis, Secretary of the Air Force Donald Rice was already engrossed in the challenge of shaping the USAF to operate within a diminishing budget in a world of great instability and only one superpower. In 1990 he issued a paper entitled Global Reach-Global Power, which broke out of the mental straitjacket imposed by the words "strategic" and "tactical," and concentrated attention on key attributes of air power—speed, range, flexibility, precision, and lethality. Global Reach-Global Power emphasized the extraordinary capabilities of a force equipped with state-of-the-art jet aircraft, precision weapons, massive air refueling and airlift capacity, and space-based information, communications, and navigation systems. It suggested that these technological developments had revolutionized the ability of the United States to influence world events and to project military power when necessary.

Not everyone agreed with the views of Global Reach-Global Power. Some argued that the USAF's expensive systems were no longer affordable. Others even questioned whether a separate air force was needed at all in the post-Cold War world. Lengthy debate on the subject was overtaken by events when Iraq invaded Kuwait. In a dramatic demonstration of what a modern air force could accomplish, the USAF silenced the doubters and confirmed its long-term future while assuring victory in the Gulf War. In mid-1991, taking account of lessons learned, USAF leaders resisted the temptation to rest on their laurels, accepted the inevitability of change, and began to build an Air Force for the 21st century.

The most traumatic restructuring measure they undertook was the merging of the long established Strategic and Tactical Air Commands. Since its birth, the USAF had been characterized by the contrasting identities of its combat arms. At its most basic level,

this resolved itself into a simple rivalry between bomber and fighter pilots, but it had gone deeper than that. In Curtis LeMay's time, SAC had grown into an almost independent service, an air force within the Air Force, and the strategic mission dominated USAF policy and doctrine. Then, and in later years when tactical concerns arose, the USAF was not the "single homogeneous force" promoted by air power theorists. Its various arms cooperated, but they did not always share common points of view or accept each others' priorities. The 1992 merger of the tactical and strategic worlds under one roof at what had been TAC Headquarters therefore came as something of a shock to traditionalists.

Air Combat Command
The new Air Combat Command (ACC), established at Langley Air Force Base, Virginia, absorbed the assets of TAC and SAC and became the headquarters of by far the largest USAF organization. Problems of scale were eased somewhat when SAC's tanker aircraft were classed as support aircraft and therefore moved to the second new command, Air Mobility Command (AMC), which replaced the old Military Airlift Command (MAC). Later, ACC was further reduced when responsibility for ICBMs was allocated to Air Force Space Command (AFSPC). In its final form, ACC comprises four numbered air forces (the First, Eighth, Ninth, Twelfth, and the Air National Guard [ANG]) and a direct reporting unit (the Air Warfare Center). Between them, they are primarily concerned with combat aircraft, ranging through the inventory from B–2s to F–16s. It is ACC's task to train its units in peacetime so that they are fully prepared for combat, but in an actual emergency ACC assets would normally be transferred as required to the commander in chief of the forces selected to tackle the problem.[1]

Although the threat from a monolithic Soviet Union has faded into history, nuclear arsenals that pose a threat to the United States remain. ACC's heavy bombers, therefore, retain their nuclear strike capability as one leg of America's strategic triad. However, the new command is a more flexible force than its predecessors, better able to respond easily and rapidly to threats and contingencies at all levels and in any region of the world. Composite wings have been created—mini-air forces equipped with several aircraft types together comprising a self-sufficient rapid deployment force with a mix of the combat tools needed to contain burgeoning emergencies or defeat an aggressor. Alternatively, the Air Expeditionary Force (AEF) concept has been gaining favor. AEFs have been put together and deployed on several occasions to the Middle East since the Gulf War.

A grey-painted B–52 of the 5th
Bombardment Wing, Minot Air
Force Base, North Dakota. As old
as the basic design is, with the help
of equipment upgrades and new
engines it is confidently expected
that the wing's Buffs will still
be operating through the first
quarter of the 21st century.

B–52 cockpit. As might be expected
in such a long-serving aircraft,
the B–52 carries elements of old
and new technologies. Video
displays sit alongside instruments
from an earlier generation. Grand-
fathers of today's B–52 pilots would
find the cockpit recognizable and
the throttle levers familiar under
their hands.

At the level of nuclear deterrence, the long established strategic role of ACC's heavy bombers remains unchanged. Delivery of nuclear weapons would be achieved either by penetrating enemy defenses or by standing off to fire air-launched cruise missiles (ALCMs). The venerable B–52 is still extremely valuable in the latter role, carrying up to 20 ALCMs for launching as far as 1,500 miles from the target. Penetration is better performed by B–1B Lancers, now the mainstay of the bomber fleet, and the relatively small force of B–2A Spirits.

Northrop's B–2 is a unique "flying wing" advanced technology aircraft, employing stealth techniques in its construction and powered by four non-afterburning turbofans. Included in its sophisticated design are digital flight controls, a new electronic warfare system, a low-probability-of-intercept radar, and a GPS-Aided Targeting System (GATS). At takeoff, the B–2 might weigh up to 400,000 pounds, and its armament could include a wide variety of nuclear or conventional weapons. The GPS-Aided Munitions (GAM), used in combination with GATS, gives the B–2 the ability to strike multiple targets on a single pass. The addition of flight refueling to its already considerable range gives the bomber its global reach. The extraordinary capabilities of the B–2 are managed by a crew of only two, who sit side-by-side in a cockpit smoothly blended into the wing's center section. If any aircraft, by its appearance alone, can be said to epitomize the USAF for the 21st century, it is surely the B–2. The enormous cost of the futuristic bomber necessarily limits the number acquired for front-line service, but, in terms of precise destructive capacity per unit, the B–2's power is unprecedented.

Although the B–2 is capable of carrying as many as 80 500-pound high-explosive bombs, so valuable an asset would not likely be risked on a tactical mission. If used with conventional weapons, the B–2's precise destructive powers would surely be aimed at strategic objectives. As became apparent both in Vietnam and the Gulf, however, the formerly simple separation of aircraft into strategic and tactical roles, almost arbitrarily by size, is no longer appropriate. B–52s were used tactically against Iraqi troop concentrations, for example, while fighters took on strategic targets, like national command centers. This blurring of distinctions between roles will continue as weapons systems take on tasks for which they are most suited, depending on circumstances.

B–1B. The smooth blending of the Rockwell B–1B's wings and small cross-section fuselage contrast with the boxy engine pods, which appear to have been added almost as an afterthought. Nevertheless, the radar cross-section of the B–1B is a fraction of the B–52's, and the four General Electric afterburning turbofans can together produce the very respectable total of 120,000 pounds of thrust, enough to give the 400-ton plus Lancer a low-level penetration speed in excess of 600 miles per hour.

B–1B. The aircraft's center section is a massive titanium box capable of bearing the loads of turbulent low-level flight and of carrying the heavy wing-sweep mechanism and main undercarriage. The wings, set fully forward at 15 degrees can be swept to 67 degrees for high-speed high-altitude flight. The small vanes on each side of the nose provide yaw and pitch damping in rough conditions.

Most of ACC's front-line aircraft impressed themselves on the public consciousness during the Gulf War. Their designs are no longer new, but they are far from being outdated. The newest of them, the F–117A Nighthawk, first flew in 1981, while the oldest, the B–52, dates in its earliest form from the mid-1950s. Even so, in the mid-1990s, all of them are either preeminent or among the best in the world for their particular roles. As strike-attack aircraft, the F–117A and the F–15E Strike Eagle are equipped to deliver precision guided munitions in any weather, day or night, and to operate in highly threatening environments.

The stealthy F–117A is nearly impossible to detect on radar and the F–15E retains the superior air-to-air combat capabilities of its breed once its external load is dropped. Indeed, the F–15E may be the 20th century's ultimate all-around combat aircraft. Equipped with APG–70 synthetic aperture radar and a full all-weather night fit, including infra-red sensors and terrain-following radar, the Strike Eagle can attack targets with over 24,000 pounds of assorted ordnance, including Maverick missiles, CBUs, and both "dumb" and "smart" bombs. While doing so it retains the ability to destroy enemy aircraft beyond

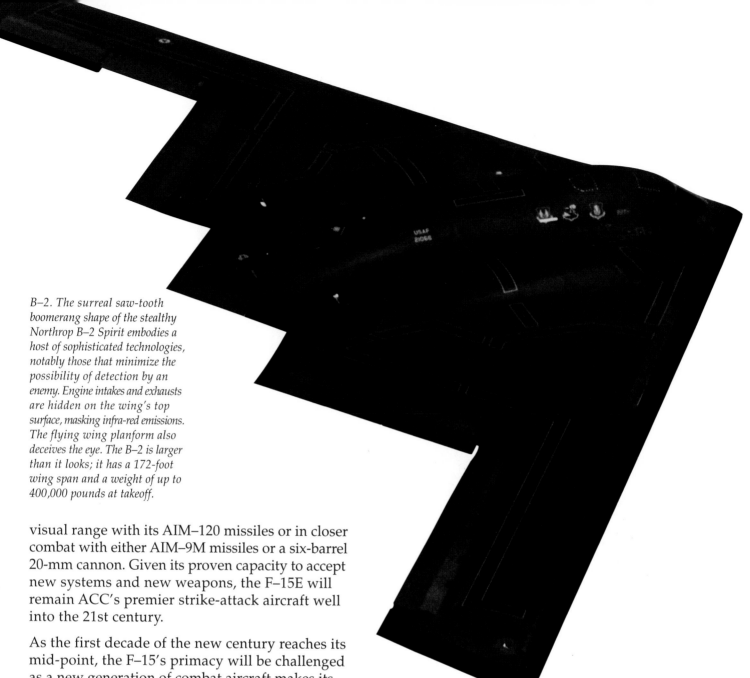

B–2. The surreal saw-tooth boomerang shape of the stealthy Northrop B–2 Spirit embodies a host of sophisticated technologies, notably those that minimize the possibility of detection by an enemy. Engine intakes and exhausts are hidden on the wing's top surface, masking infra-red emissions. The flying wing planform also deceives the eye. The B–2 is larger than it looks; it has a 172-foot wing span and a weight of up to 400,000 pounds at takeoff.

visual range with its AIM–120 missiles or in closer combat with either AIM–9M missiles or a six-barrel 20-mm cannon. Given its proven capacity to accept new systems and new weapons, the F–15E will remain ACC's premier strike-attack aircraft well into the 21st century.

As the first decade of the new century reaches its mid-point, the F–15's primacy will be challenged as a new generation of combat aircraft makes its appearance. The Lockheed Martin F–22 will be able to penetrate enemy airspace and engage multiple aircraft targets simultaneously at long range before being detected. It will take advantage of stealth technology and will be highly maneuverable when either subsonic or supersonic. Two Pratt & Whitney engines, rated at 35,000 pounds of thrust each in afterburner, will have vectored thrust to allow maneuvering at high angles of attack. The F–22 will not need such thrust for supersonic flight, however, achieving a cruising speed of Mach 1.5 without afterburner. Its superb aerodynamics will be backed up by avionics systems of astonishing capability feeding information to the pilot through a head-up display and six flat multi-function cockpit display panels. It will use Very High Speed Integrated Circuits (VHSIC) and fiber optics data transmission and include a voice command facility. The F–22 is not a small aircraft, weighing up to 60,000 pounds at takeoff, a reflection of a twin-engined design

that provides weapons storage and ample fuel internally. Intended to handle a wide range of both air-to-air and air-to ground weapons, the F–22 will also act as a multi-role aircraft, adding in time strategic strike, interdiction, reconnaissance, and defense suppression to its air supremacy function.

Although not quite as capable as the F–15, the smaller and cheaper F–16 has proved itself an extremely adaptable multi-role fighter whose all-around cost-effectiveness has made it the most represented aircraft in ACC's front line. It will remain so distinguished for many years to come. Specialized variants include the F–16 ADF (Air Defense Fighter), the F–16CG (LANTIRN capable), and the F–16CJ with the HARM Targeting System (HTS) for air defense suppression missions. Some squadrons are already using F–16C/Ds modified for close air support and air defense suppression roles. A–10 Warthogs soldier on, giving way

F–15s. The sun is far from setting on the career of the magnificent F–15 Eagle. In its various forms the F–15 provides the U.S. Air Force with superlative performance in air defense, mission escort, intercept, battlefield support, defense suppression, interdiction, and nuclear strike roles.

gradually to F–16s over the battlefield, but still contributing in OA–10 form as the mounts of forward air controllers (FACs) and elements of air rescue teams.

ACC's defensive responsibilities are met by the First Air Force, an administrative command possessing no aircraft of its own. All American air defense commitments for the foreseeable future will be entrusted to F–15/F–16 squadrons of the Air National Guard, which is required to train its crews for combat roles in peacetime. In the event of an air threat developing to the United States, ACC becomes the gaining command for the ANG's air defense assets.

ACC's other aircraft include the unmatched EF–111 for electronic warfare, the HH–60 Pave Hawk helicopter, and an assortment of C–135 variants for command and control duties, range instrumentation, intelligence gathering, and weather reconnaissance.[2] E–3B/C Sentries and E–8 J-STARS bring their all-seeing eyes to the battlefield, and the E–4B NAOC (National Airborne Operations Center) is always ready to serve should the threat of nuclear war become real. In peace or war, ACC's strategic reconnaissance aircraft are engaged in actual operations daily. RC–135s and U–2Rs keep watch on the world's trouble spots, helped

out by three incomparable SR–71 Blackbirds, brought out of premature retirement in 1995 to give the USAF back its capability for wide-area reconnaissance at speeds above Mach 3.

Air Mobility Command

In the USAF's reshaping of 1992, Military Airlift Command (MAC) rearranged more than its initial letters when it became Air Mobility Command (AMC). The headquarters remains at Scott Air Force Base, Illinois, but units and equipment have been reshuffled. AMC controls two numbered air forces, as did MAC— the Fifteenth (a SAC number) and Twenty-First, the Twenty-Second having gone to the Air Force Reserve. AMC's losses of assault transports to ACC in 1992 were more than offset by its acquisition of the tanker force, and, in any event, in 1996 the USAF decided that the transports should be returned.

The newest aircraft in AMC's fleet is the McDonnell Douglas C–17 Globemaster III, which was declared operational in 1995 and is destined to be at the core of USAF airlifting for decades to come. Designed to provide both inter- and intra-theater lifting capacity for all classes of military cargo, the C–17 owns a hold roomy enough to carry as much as four times

SR–71. More than 30 years after it first flew, the SR–71 remains the fastest, highest flying manned reconnaissance vehicle in existence. Retired because of their demanding maintenance requirements and high operating costs, three were restored to the front line in the 1990s.

The U–2R of the 1990s, a much larger and more capable aircraft than the original Lockheed Dragon Lady of the 1950s. Intelligence gathering systems can include synthetic aperture radar, a SIGINT (signals intelligence) suite, infra-red sensors, optical cameras, and a PLSS (Precision Location Strike System). The U–2R's detachable nose cone helps to make it a most adaptable vehicle, allowing variously equipped alternative cones to be fitted when a reconnaissance role change becomes necessary.

the maximum payload of a Hercules and to handle items too awkwardly bulky even for its strategic partner, the gigantic C–5A. Primarily intended to replace the most aged of the C–141 fleet in long-range strategic airlift, the C–17 is nevertheless, like the C–130, able to move tactically from small, austere airfields.[3] Its normal crew of three, two on the flight deck plus a loadmaster, operate the aircraft with the benefit of state-of-the-art systems, ranging from the first fly-by-wire controls and head-up displays seen in a military transport to powered equipment that greatly simplifies the handling of large cargo items.

Air Force Materiel Command

Recombining functions that were separated in the 1950s, the USAF formed Air Force Materiel Command in 1992 from the merger of Air Force Systems Command and Air Force Logistics Command. AFMC's responsibilities can be summed up as developing, testing, acquiring, delivering, and sustaining USAF weapon systems and equipment. From its headquarters at Wright-Patterson Air Force Base, AFMC oversees the work of a network of four major product centers, four superlaboratories, three test centers, five air logistics centers, and five specialized centers. Overall, these units employ over 100,000 military and civilian personnel and are concerned with obtaining and managing equipment used in every aspect of Air Force life, from B–2s to kitchen sinks.

Air Force Space Command

In 1993, following the major USAF reorganizations of 1992, Air Force Space Command (AFSPC), Peterson Air Force Base, Colorado, acquired the ballistic missile force from ACC, so adding operational responsibility for nuclear weapons (530 Minuteman IIIs and 50 Peacekeepers) to its other, wide-ranging duties in the fields of radars and satellites. The command splits its responsibilities between two numbered air forces, the Fourteenth and Twentieth. In an era of increasing world turbulence, the value of Space Command's daily work cannot be overstated. Since the break up of the Soviet Union, the importance of the nuclear deterrent may have become less starkly obvious, but the maintenance of a credible ultimate deterrent as an element of national policy is just as vital as it ever was. As was demonstrated during the Gulf War, the specialized field of Command, Control, Communications, and Intelligence (C³I) is hardly less significant. Mastery of C³I is an essential part of combat readiness today and is likely to be more so tomorrow, accentuating the crucial nature of the role to be played by AFSPC and its satellites in the years ahead.

Air Force Special Operations Command

Air Force Special Operations Command (AFSOC), Hurlburt Field, Florida, was formed in 1990 from the forces of Twenty-Third Air Force in MAC. It serves as the Air Force component of the U.S. Special Operations Command, working in the fields of unconventional warfare, clandestine operations, and counter-terrorism with a unique collection of aircraft, including exotically equipped C–130 variants and heavily armed helicopters of great sophistication.

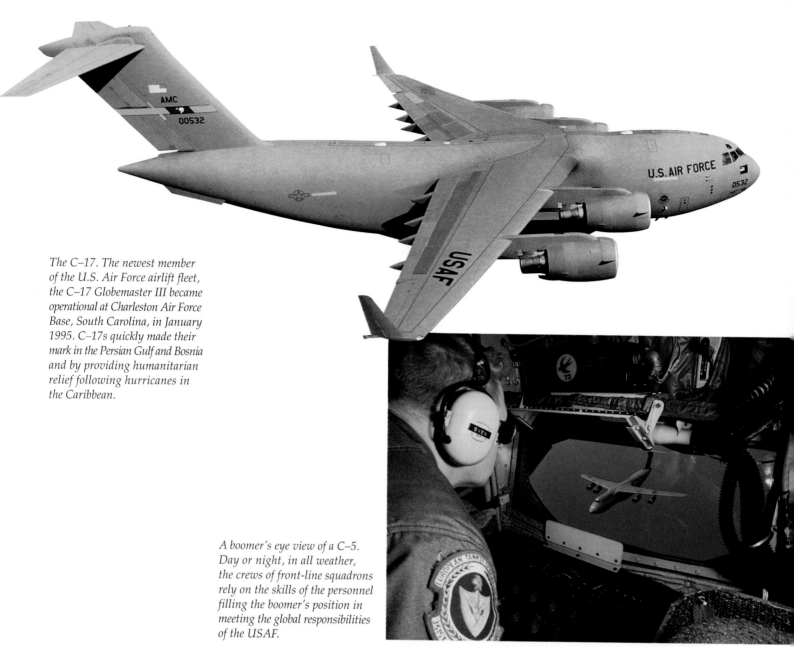

The C–17. The newest member of the U.S. Air Force airlift fleet, the C–17 Globemaster III became operational at Charleston Air Force Base, South Carolina, in January 1995. C–17s quickly made their mark in the Persian Gulf and Bosnia and by providing humanitarian relief following hurricanes in the Caribbean.

A boomer's eye view of a C–5. Day or night, in all weather, the crews of front-line squadrons rely on the skills of the personnel filling the boomer's position in meeting the global responsibilities of the USAF.

C–5 loading. Bearing its post-Gulf War Air Mobility Command label on its visor, a C–5 Galaxy gapes to swallow another outsize load.

Besides its units in the United States, AFSOC controls special operations groups based in the United Kingdom and Japan. In a crisis AFSOC is the gaining command for additional EC/AC–130As from the Air National Guard and Air Force Reserve.

Air Education and Training Command

In the restructuring of 1992, Air Training Command was given both ACC's crew training task and the Air University at Maxwell Air Force Base, becoming in the process Air Education and Training Command (AETC). Two numbered air forces answer to AETC— the Second at Keesler Air Force Base, Mississippi, and the Nineteenth at Randolph Air Force Base, Texas. AETC's responsibilities include recruiting and training all new Air Force personnel, career education for those of all ranks already established in the service, and training foreign air force personnel in assorted skills. With a staff of 60,000 and units spread across the United States from coast to coast, AETC is both complex and large.

MC–130H. The clown's nose on this Hercules identifies it as an MC–130H Combat Talon II variant, developed for use by special forces. Its enlarged radome contains a multi-mode radar that enhances low-level navigation and provides terrain following and avoidance.

Sikorsky M/HH–60G Pave Hawk helicopter, whose extensive special features enable it to undertake special operations and combat search and rescue duties.

AETC's flying training aircraft are among the longest serving in the Air Force; most are at least a quarter of a century old. Prospective pilots, however, get their first taste of Air Force flying in a new aircraft. The little Slingsby T–3A Firefly replaced the T–41 Mescalero in 1992 to weed out those candidates judged unsuitable for pilot training. After successfully surviving the T–3A, student pilots move on to primary training in the Cessna T–37B, which has given yeoman service since 1959. Nearly 500 T–37Bs are still flying and have been modified to extend their service life into the next century. From 1999 on, they will be progressively replaced by the winner of the Joint Primary Aircraft Training System (JPATS) competition, a turbo-prop powered trainer based on the Swiss Pilatus PC–9 and built in the United States by Raytheon. AETC envisages no such replacement for the next step in its training program, at least for those intended to fly combat aircraft. The T–38 Talon has been the USAF's advanced trainer since 1961 and has undergone major structural renewal and avionics upgrades that together should extend its service life to

the year 2020. By then, the T–38 will have outlived many of those who earned their wings in its cockpit during the 1960s and will have thoroughly earned retirement.

Until 1993 all USAF pilots in advanced training flew the T–38. After that, the Air Force went to Specialized Undergraduate Pilot Training (SUPT) and those selected for transport and tanker types moved from the T–37B to the new T–1 Jayhawk, a version of the Beechjet 400A, a twin-engined executive aircraft specifically modified for military multi-engined pilot training. USAF navigators complete their training in the Boeing CT–43, derived from the 737–200 airliner. AETC units also operate some of the newer USAF aircraft in inventory, including the F–15, F–16, and C–17.

The USAF Overseas

The United States Air Forces in Europe (USAFE) are hardly what they once were. USAFE's numbered air forces (the Third in the United Kingdom, the Sixteenth in Italy, and the Seventeenth in Germany) had 12 wings operating when the 1990s began. Reflecting the dramatic change in the political situation, these

Female pilot. In the modern U. S. Air Force, the faces in the cockpit might be those of men or women.

520

shrank to five operational wings by 1996, equipped with 108 fighters (F–15Cs/Ds and F–16Cs/Ds), 60 attack aircraft (F–15Es and A–10s), 6 observation aircraft (OA–10s), and an assortment of 47 others (tankers, reconnaissance, and transports). The Seventeenth Air Force was inactivated in September 1996, leaving the Third Air Force responsible for operations north of the Alps and the Sixteenth Air Force covering everything farther south.

The Pacific Air Forces (PACAF) have always been generously provided with numbered air forces. The Fifth (Japan), Seventh (South Korea), Eleventh (Alaska), and Thirteenth (Guam) have all survived with a total of eight wings operating. They have 246 F–15, F–16, and A–10 fighter-attack aircraft, 4 E–3 AWACS, 18 OA–10s, 15 KC–135 tankers, 38 transports and 11 helicopters—all of which is little enough to cover an operational area extending from the west coast of the United States to the east coast of Africa and from the Arctic to the Antarctic.

The reductions in strength experienced by USAFE and PACAF in the 1990s were the inevitable result of post-Cold War defense cuts. The realities of the draw-down serve to emphasize the importance of the principles embodied in Global Reach-Global Power that underpinned the Air Force reorganization.

While forces in place overseas may be sufficient to maintain a presence and perhaps cope with minor contingencies, the 21st century USAF must be able to react to a serious crisis by deploying from its home bases in numbers and with speed. If necessary, it must also be capable of imposing itself decisively on the situation once it arrives.

The Agencies

The restructuring of the USAF did not stop with the major commands. Many supporting functions were realigned and others were disestablished entirely. Those that remained, including a few with previous command status,[4] were formed into functionally arranged Field Operating Agencies (FOAs) reporting to offices in USAF Headquarters. Three Direct Reporting Units (DRUs) were retained to report directly to the Chief of Staff—the USAF Academy; the 11th Wing, which is largely concerned with ceremonial functions and includes the USAF Band and Honor Guard; and the Air Force Operational Test and Evaluation Center, which undertakes testing of such critical items as the B–2, C–17, and many command and control systems. Collectively, 27 FOAs cover the myriad supporting activities that ensure the smooth day-to-day running of the Air Force. Their titles indicate the enormous range of their interests—

C–130s taxiing. Air Combat Command C–130Es line up, ready to go on a paradropping exercise. The long-serving Hercules, in its various forms, is set to continue serving as the U.S. Air Force's premier tactical transport well into the 21st century.

E–3. The USAF describes the E–3B/C Sentry as a mobile, flexible, survivable, and jam-resistant surveillance and C³ system capable of all-weather, long-range surveillance of all air vehicles above all kinds of terrain. With capabilities like these, E–3s are national assets, serving in their deployments as early indicators of American national interests and at the forefront of any subsequent projection of American force.

Upgrades for the MH–53J Pave Low helicopter. Improvements in the helicopter's already impressive capabilities blend information gained from on-board systems (FLIR, terrain-following radar, GPS, INS, secure communications, comprehensive ECM, etc.) with graphically displayed over-the-horizon intelligence. The MH–53J and MC–130P partnership gives the U.S. Air Force a formidable capability for rescue and special operations.

auditing, flight standards, civil engineering, real estate, special investigations, personnel management, news, legal services, environmental excellence, weather, and many more, including Air Force history.

Reserve Forces

Listed among the USAF's FOAs are the Air Force Reserve (AFRes) and Air National Guard (ANG), although as operators of combat aircraft they bear

Technicians finding out what it is like to work while encumbered with clothing designed to protect them from the effects of nuclear, biological, and chemical warfare. Hardships and discomfort are commonplace in warfare, and modern war can be particularly demanding.

little resemblance to the other 25. The AFRes has the primary responsibility of providing the USAF with immediately available combat-ready forces in a national emergency. It is organized into three numbered air forces—the Tenth (Bergstrom Air Force Base, Texas), which looks after fighters and tankers, and the Fourth (McClellan Air Force Base, California) and the Twenty-Second (Dobbins Air Force Base, Georgia), which are primarily responsible for transports. Close to 80,000 personnel man 37 flying wings, which operate almost 500 assigned aircraft in all roles, including F–16s, B–52s, KC–135s, C–5s, C–141s, and a varied collection of C–130s and helicopters. Reserve crews also serve under an associate program that gives them experience with regular USAF units in front-line aircraft like the KC–10 and C–17.

The ANG inherits an honorable tradition closely linked with the birth of the United States as an independent nation—that of the volunteer, the Minuteman willing to fight in times of national crisis. Every one of the 50 states, plus the District of Columbia and Puerto Rico, has at least one ANG unit assigned, all of which operate under state government jurisdiction except in times of national emergency. With a personnel strength of over 111,000 operating 88 flying wings with more than 1,200 modern aircraft, the ANG represents an increasingly important element of American air power. In the USAF's 50th anniversary year, the ANG provides 100 percent of air defense fighters, 33 percent of multi-role fighters, 43 percent of KC–135 air refueling, 28 percent of air rescue, 45 percent of tactical airlift, and 8 percent of strategic airlift. In other duties, the ANG's tasks include 100 percent of aircraft control and 80 percent of Air Force communications. ANG units have made major recent contributions to operations in Central America, the Gulf region, and Bosnia and have been identified on many occasions with disaster relief both worldwide and in the United States after hurricanes, floods, and earthquakes.

In the years ahead, as the USAF is compelled by budgetary constraints to meet its global responsibilities while restricting the size of its front line, its ability to call on additional forces of the size and professionalism of the ANG and the AFRes will be a considerable advantage. American military intervention in any future world crisis would not be practicable without their involvement.

The 21st Century
The USAF begins its second 50 years and will enter the 21st century as the world's most powerful air arm. Although its strength in both personnel and aircraft has fallen significantly in recent years, its effectiveness has nevertheless increased dramatically. In terms of simple numbers, the USAF may actually

F–22. The Lockheed-Martin F–22 will become established as the U.S. Air Force's air superiority aircraft with the dawn of the 21st century. State-of-the-art avionics and superb aerodynamics will combine to make the F–22 a combat aircraft of extraordinary capabilities.

Without their supporting cast of technicians, aircrew actors in combat's drama could not perform. Here, armorers of the 48th Tactical Fighter Wing Maintenance Loading Team guide a LGB on its way to an F–111 during Operation DESERT STORM, 1991.

be smaller than the air forces of Russia and China, but in its ability to assure air supremacy, strike hard and precisely, and to move aircraft, people, and heavy equipment quickly to anywhere in the world, the USAF has no rivals.

America's lead in aerospace technology has been growing, and should continue to do so for the foreseeable future. No other nation or group of nations has yet demonstrated a capacity to produce military aircraft that match the F–117A, the B–2, the C–17, and the F–22, or much of their weaponry and equipment. In space the United States is equally dominant, particularly in navigation, communications, and intelligence gathering of all kinds for military purposes. It should remain so provided it correctly anticipates future challenges and continues to invest in further developing its capabilities. Space is the high ground of the 21st century battlefield and the USAF must secure its pre-eminent place there.

KC–10 and A–10. A tanker of huge capacity, the KC–10 Extender can transfer 200,000 pounds of fuel at a radius of 2,200 miles from base. On overseas deployments, it doubles as an escort tanker for combat aircraft and as a transport carrying personnel and ground equipment.

Symbols of the U. S. Air Force's Global Reach-Global Power—the power and stealth of a B–2 linked with the force-multiplying capability of the KC–10 tanker force.

If the USAF's superiority in aerospace technology is unparalleled, it is equally the case that the quality of its personnel is better than ever. The Air Force has the most highly educated work force in its history and takes advantage of that force's professionalism by delegating decision making and accountability to the lowest practicable level throughout the service. It has sharply reduced the size and number of head-quarters staffs and placed the responsibility for the day-to-day activities more firmly in the hands of its operators. The Air Force of the future may have to ask fewer to tackle more, and United States-based units will face the prospect of even more overseas deployments than in the past, but given the caliber of its personnel, there is no reason to suppose that the USAF will not meet any challenges that arise.

At various times in this first century of air power, the United States allowed its strength or its technological advantages in aviation to evaporate as public attention focused on seemingly more immediate problems than those of national security. Somerset Maugham's penetrating observation on freedom at times appeared to fall on deaf ears.[5] The United States squandered the priceless lead gained by the achievements of the Wright brothers before World War I, and it cut funding for America's military aviation to recklessly low levels after both World War I and World War II. In the aftermath of the Cold War and the disintegration of the Soviet Union, it was inevitable that a technologically advanced (and therefore very expensive) service like the USAF would have to justify its existence to a public searching for a peace dividend. From that point of view, the Gulf War may have been providential in that it allowed the USAF to demonstrate the value of a modern air force in countering the dangers of the post-Cold War world. Having created a positive image for itself, the USAF was able to complete its reorganization and look to the future with confidence.

As it celebrates its 50th anniversary, the United States Air Force is laying the foundations for a 21st century service in terms of plans, structure, personnel, aircraft, weapons, and supporting equipment. Americans can be assured that they have invested wisely, and that the USAF will indeed be a force with global reach and global power in the years to come.

Notes

1. As it did in DESERT STORM the USAF's combat came under General Schwarzkopf's command. However, since ACC is a component of USACOM, it is conceivable that it could have a war-fighting role in an emergency directly threatening the United States homeland.
2. Between 1992 and 1996 ACC also operated C–130s in all of their various forms, but they were then returned to their original owners in AMC.
3. A C–17, operating with a payload of 44,000 pounds, close to the maximum for a C–130, has taken off and landed in less than 1,400 feet.
4. For example, Air Force Intelligence Command is now an agency, and Air Force Communications Command became the Air Force C^4 (Command, Control, Communications, and Computers) Agency. Where there were 13 major commands before 1992, there are now only 8.
5. See quotation at the beginning of this chapter.

Appendix A
The United States Air Force Museum

This book contains passages describing what visitors might expect to see, and perhaps feel, when walking through the various galleries and annexes of the United States Air Force Museum. Not covered in the main text is a brief history of the museum itself, the work it does, and its aims for the future.

In 1923 the Aeronautical Engineering Center at McCook Field, Dayton, Ohio, set up a small display in the corner of a hangar known as the Engineering Division Museum, where both American and foreign aviation technology from World War I were exhibited. By 1927 the collection had been much reduced by a combination of natural deterioration, pilferage, and fire. The remnants were then moved, as the Army Aeronautical Museum, to a new home at Wright Field, where they occupied about 1,500 square feet of a laboratory building. More securely housed, the collection was, nonetheless, so severely cramped that most of its aircraft had to be shown without wings. Even then, the fuselages were so close together that many were difficult to view.

In 1935 the need for a separate and properly organized museum was finally recognized when the collection was moved to a new structure specifically designed to house and display aviation artifacts. The new museum, offering an array of over 2,000 items, was opened to the public in 1936. With World War II on the horizon, however, different priorities arose and the new building was needed for other things. In 1940, therefore, the exhibition was closed to the public and its collection was placed in long-term storage.

After the Allied victories over Germany and Japan in 1945, several months elapsed before the museum program began to revive, and in 1946 Mark Sloan was appointed as curator of the Air Force collection. In an engine overhaul building at Patterson Field set aside as the museum's new home, Sloan began to collect artifacts both for the National Air Museum of the Smithsonian Institution and for what was then described as the Air Force Technical Museum.

By April 1954 the collection was once more opened to public view, and at first there were no complete

USAF Museum. A 52nd Fighter Group memorial has a Spitfire and a Mustang curving upward.

aircraft on display. When aircraft did arrive, most were left outside exposed to the weather. The interior of the museum was hardly ideal. It was neither fire-proofed nor air-conditioned, and it had supporting pillars every 16 feet in one direction and every 50 feet in the other. By the early 1960s even the outdoor area was over-crowded. It became clear that a solution to the problem

Presidential planes. On the far side of Wright Field from the USAF Museum's main buildings is the Museum Annex, consisting of two hangars open to the public. These house varied aircraft, including two used by U.S. presidents. The VC–121E Columbine *carried Eisenhower, and* Independence *is a VC–118 that saw service with both presidents.* Independence *flew Truman to Wake Island in 1950 for his meeting with General Douglas MacArthur.*

of housing and protecting the USAF's uniquely valuable and growing collection was badly needed.

Help came from the Air Force Museum Foundation, chartered in 1960 by a group of private citizens led by Eugene Kettering. Launching a fund drive in 1964, they raised over $6 million for the construction of a new museum complex. Work began in 1970 and the USAF Museum opened its doors in August 1971. A large building with floor space almost 800 feet long and 240 feet wide allowed for the inside display of more than 80 aircraft—everything from an original Wright B Flyer to Century-Series jet fighters and even a Convair B-36, surely the largest aircraft anywhere under cover.

In 1976 a building expanding the administrative center and adding various visitor facilities was opened, and in 1985 ground was broken on a third, much larger hangar, which was completed in April 1988. By then total floorspace available for exhibits had grown to over ten and a half acres, making the USAF Museum the largest aviation museum in the world. Within it were stored thousands of drawings, photographs, magazines, books, microfilm images, tape recordings, press clippings, and films. Annexes on the other side of Wright Field

USAF Museum. An outdoor statue of a bronze eagle honors American prisoners of war.

USAF Museum. A memorial park, dedicated to over 250 units and individuals and containing placques, granite monuments, and trees, invites contemplation.

USAF Museum. Visitors are welcomed by the impressive presence of the Rockwell B–1A Lancer. In the background, the F–15 Streak Eagle stands in front of the museum entrance hall, with a display hangar on the left and the IMAX theater on the right.

held additional aircraft, major restoration projects, and shelves and cabinets for artifacts of all kinds. Outside the main buildings, large missiles and aircraft still looking for shelter clustered on extensive concrete aprons, adding their nostalgic appeal to the museum's surroundings.

In the 1990s aviation museums have continued to live with the pressure of constant and appreciable growth. As the USAF celebrates its 50th anniversary, it is exhibiting aircraft and equipment from the 1980s and will incorporate more from each passing decade. It is also laying plans for further extensions to allow space for both new acquisitions and restorations and to accommodate some of the aircraft at present braving the weather. The museum has improved amenities by remodeling the restaurant and adding a 500-seat IMAX theater where visitors, confronted by a six-story-high screen and wrapped in sound from dozens of speakers, can experience vicariously the thrills and

enjoyment of flying powerful aircraft or walking in space. Gifts and books are available in the excellent shops operated by the Air Force Museum Foundation near the entrance to the main buildings.

There have been other additions to the area surrounding the main museum—an air traffic control tower and a group of Nissen huts that recall the great days of the Eighth Air Force in Europe during World War II and a memorial park that commemorates the service of well over 250 units and individuals. The memorials—simple plaques, granite monuments, and trees—have been donated by family members, group associations, and other benefactors. Another addition honors the past, but nods toward the future. For the benefit of generations yet unborn, a time capsule, filled with documents, prints, and microfilm of aircraft developed at Wright-Patterson Air Force Base and with articles covering contemporary events, lies buried in front of the museum.

F–16. The USAF Museum's red, white, and blue F–16 is no stranger to admiring crowds. It is instantly recognizable as an aircraft that once flew with the internationally recognized U.S. Air Force aerobatic display team, the Thunderbirds.

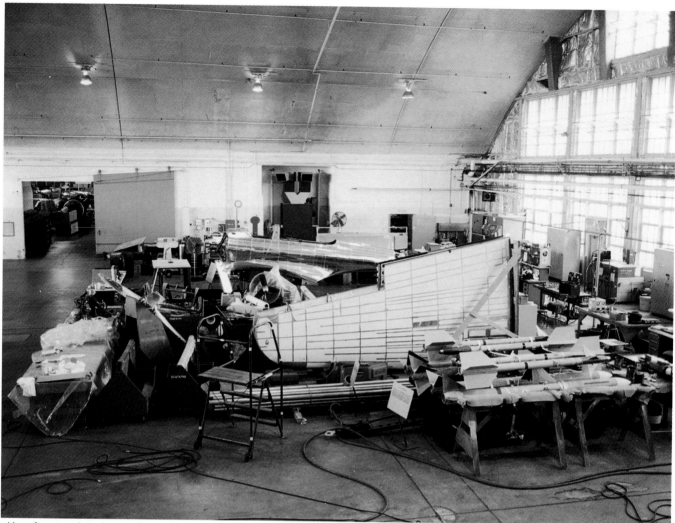

Aircraft restoration. Among the most important of the USAF Museum's activities is aircraft restoration. It is undertaken by dedicated craftsmen with painstaking care. Whenever possible, original parts are refinished to exhibition standard, but, where necessary, missing or badly worn items are manufactured, preferably from company drawings. The photograph shows the restoration of a museum aircraft and gives some idea of the extremely high quality of work done.

As comprehensive as its coverage of air power history is at Dayton, the USAF Museum supports Air Force and Department of Defense Museums in every part of the United States and abroad. It lends them vast quantities of items, including thousands of aircraft.

As it approaches the 21st century, the USAF Museum is a far cry from the relatively minor affair of the 1920s and 1930s. Its 2,000-item collection has mushroomed to more than 50,000 objects, from the minute to the colossal, not much more than 10 percent of which can be exhibited at any one time. The collection's and the museum's prodigious escalation in size has been matched by their equally impressive growth in international status and popularity. In the 1950s they received only about 10,000 visitors annually. In each year of the 1990s they have received more than one million.

To look after the rising flood and to ensure that the collection is maintained in impeccable condition, the museum employs a professional staff of almost 100 and is able to rely on the dedicated service of more than 300 volunteers.

In 1971 Secretary of the Air Force Robert Seamans was present for the dedication ceremony of the new museum buildings, as were Preesident Richard Nixon and members of the Wright family. In his speech, the Secretary summarized the purpose of the USAF Museum, and his words ring true today:

> The new Air Force Museum will serve as a tribute to all Americans who have contributed so much to the field of aviation. It will also serve as an inspiration to future generations of Americans to increase their knowledge and awareness of the United States Air Force and the history of flight.

Appendix B
Leaders of the USAF

Secretaries of the Air Force

W. Stuart Symington
18 September 1947–24 April 1950

Thomas K. Finletter
24 April 1950–20 January 1953

Harold E. Talbott
4 February 1953–13 August 1955

Donald A. Quarles
15 August 1955–30 April 1957

James H. Douglas, Jr.
1 May 1957–10 December 1959

Dudley C. Sharp
11 December 1959–20 January 1961

Eugene M. Zuckert
24 January 1961–30 September 1965

Harold Brown
1 October 1965–15 February 1969

Robert C. Seamans, Jr.
15 February 1969–14 May 1973

John L. McLucas (acting)
15 May 1973–18 July 1973

John L. McLucas
18 July 1973–23 November 1975

James W. Plummer (acting)
24 November 1975–1 January 1976

James W. Plummer
2 January 1976–6 April 1977

John C. Stetson
6 April 1977–18 May 1979

Hans Mark (acting)
18 May 1979–26 July 1979

Hans Mark
26 July 1979–9 February 1981

Verne Orr
9 February 1981–30 November 1985

Russell A. Rourke
9 December 1985–7 April 1986

Edward C. Aldridge, Jr (acting)
8 April 1986–8 June 1986

Edward C. Aldridge, Jr
9 June 1986–16 December 1988

James F. McGovern (acting)
16 December 1988–29 April 1989

John J. Welch, Jr. (acting)
29 April 1989–21 May 1989

Donald B. Rice
22 May 1989–20 January 1993

Michael B. Donley (acting)
20 January 1993–13 July 1993

Merrill A. McPeak (acting)
14 July 1993–5 August 1993

Sheila E. Widnall
6 August 1993–31 October 1997

USAF Chiefs of Staff

Carl A. Spaatz
26 September 1947–29 April 1948

Hoyt S. Vandenberg
30 April 1948–29 June 1953

Nathan F. Twining
30 June 1953–30 June 1957

Thomas D. White
1 July 1957–30 June 1961

Curtis E. LeMay
30 June 1961–31 January 1965

John P. McConnell
1 February 1965–31 July 1969

John D. Ryan
1 August 1969–31 July 1973

George S. Brown
1 August 1973–30 June 1974

David C. Jones
1 July 1974–20 June 1978

Lew Allen, Jr.
1 July 1978–30 June 1982

Charles A. Gabriel
1 July 1982–30 June 1986

Larry D. Welch
1 July 1986–30 June 1990

Michael J. Dugan
1 July 1990–17 September 1990

John M. Loh (acting)
18 September 1990–29 October 1990

Merrill A. McPeak
30 October 1990–25 October 1994

Ronald R. Fogleman
26 October 1994–1 September 1997

Ralph E. Eberhart (acting)
2 September 1997–

Michael E. Ryan
* Confirmed 24 September 1997

Appendix C

Medals of Honor

World War I

Rickenbacker, Captain Edward V.
25 September 1918, Billy, France

Luke, 2nd Lieutenant Frank, Jr.
29 September 1918, Murvaux, France

Bleckley, 2nd Lieutenant Erwin R.
6 October 1918, Binarville, France

Goettler, 2nd Lieutenant Harold E.
6 October 1918, Binarville, France

World War II

Doolittle, Lieutenant Colonel James H.
18 April 1942, Tokyo, Japan

Pease, Captain Harl, Jr.
7 August 1942, Rabaul, New Britain

Craw, Colonel Demas T.
8 November 1942, Port Lyautey, French Morocco

Hamilton, Major Pierpoint M.
8 November 1942, Port Lyautey, French Morocco

Walker, Brigadier General Kenneth N.
5 January 1943, Rabaul, New Britain

Mathis, 1st Lieutenant Jack W.
18 March 1943, Vegesack, Germany

Smith, Sergeant Maynard H.
1 May 1943, St Nazaire, France

Sarnoski, 2nd Lieutenant Joseph R.
16 June 1943, Buka, Solomons

Zeamer, Major J., Jr.
16 June 1943, Buka, Solomons

Morgan, 2nd Lieutenant John C.
28 July 1943, Kiel, Germany

Baker, Lieutenant Colonel Addison E.
1 August 1943, Ploesti, Romania

Hughes, 2nd Lieutenant Lloyd H.
1 August 1943, Ploesti, Romania

Jerstad, Major John L.
1 August 1943, Ploesti, Romania

Johnson, Colonel Leon W.
1 August 1943, Ploesti, Romania

Kane, Colonel John R.
1 August 1943, Ploesti, Romania

Cheli, Major Ralph
18 August 1943, Wewak, New Guinea

Kearby, Colonel Neel E.
11 October 1943, Wewak, New Guinea

Wilkins, Major Raymond H.
2 November 1943, Rabaul, New Britain

Vosler, Technical Sergeant Forrest L.
20 December 1943, Bremen, Germany

Howard, Lieutenant Colonel James H.
11 January 1944, Oschersleben, Germany

Lawley, 1st Lieutenant William R., Jr.
20 February 1944, Leipzig, Germany

Mathies, Staff Sergeant Archibald
20 February 1944, Leipzig, Germany

Truemper, 2nd Lieutenant Walter E.
20 February 1944, Leipzig, Germany

Michael, 1st Lieutenant Edward S.
11 April 1944, Brunswick, Germany

Vance, Lieutenant Colonel Leon R.
5 June 1944, Wimereaux, France

Kingsley, 2nd Lieutenant David R.
23 June 1944, Ploesti, Romania

Pucket, 1st Lieutenant Donald D.
9 July 1944 Ploesti, Romania

Lindsey, Captain Darrell R.
9 August 1944, Pontoise, France

Bong, Major Richard I.
10 October–15 November 1944, SW Pacific

Carswell, Major Horace S., Jr.
26 October 1944, South China Sea

Femoyer, 2nd Lieutenant Robert E.
2 November 1944, Merseburg, Germany

Gott, 1st Lieutenant Donald J.
9 November 1944, Saarbrucken, Germany

Metzger, 2nd Lieutenant William E., Jr.
9 November 1944, Saarbrucken, Germany

Castle, Brigadier General Frederick W.
24 December 1944, Liege, Belgium

McGuire, Major Thomas B., Jr.
25—26 December 1944, Luzon, Philippines

Shomo, Major William A.
11 January 1945, Luzon, Philippines

Erwin, Staff Sergeant Henry E.
12 April 1945, Koriyama, Japan

Knight, 1st Lieutenant Raymond L.
25 April 1945, Po Valley, Italy

Korea

Sebille, Major Louis J.
5 August 1950, Hamch'ang, South Korea

Walmsley, Captain John S., Jr.
14 September 1951, Yangdok, North Korea

Davis, Major George A., Jr.
10 February 1952, Sinuiju-Yalu River, North Korea

Loring, Major Charles J., Jr.
22 November 1952, Sniper Ridge, North Korea

Vietnam

Fisher, Major Bernard F.
10 March 1966, A Shau Valley, South Vietnam

Wilbanks, Captain Hilliard A.
24 February 1967, Dalat, South Vietnam

Dethlefsen, Major Merlyn H.
10 March 1967, Thai Nguyen, North Vietnam

Thorsness, Lieutenant Colonel Leo K.
19 April 1967, North Vietnam

Young, Captain Gerald O.
9 November 1967, Da Nang, South Vietnam

Jackson, Lieutenant Colonel Joe M.
12 May 1968, Kham Duc, South Vietnam

Jones, Colonel William A., III
1 September 1968, Dong Hoi, North Vietnam

Fleming, 1st Lieutenant James P.
26 November 1968, Duc Co, South Vietnam

Levitow, Airman 1st Class John L.
24 February 1969, Long Binh, South Vietnam

Bennett, Captain Steven L.
29 June 1972, Quang Tri, South Vietnam

Day, Colonel George E.
Prisoner of War, Hanoi, North Vietnam

Sijan, Captain Lance P.
Prisoner of War, Hanoi, North Vietnam

Appendix D

The Mackay Trophy

Established before World War I by Clarence H. Mackay, publisher of *Collier's* magazine and aviation enthusiast, the Mackay Trophy is presented annually by the National Aeronautic Association in recognition of the most meritorious United States Air Force flight of the year.

1912 *2nd Lieutenant Henry H. Arnold*
First successful aerial reconnaissance of U.S. Army maneuvers, Wright biplane

1913 *2nd Lieutenant Joseph E. Carberry and 2nd Lieutenant Fred Seydel*
Reconnaissance exercises, Curtiss biplane

1914 *Captain Townsend F. Dodd and Lieutenant Shapler W. Fitzgerald*
Reconnaissance exercises

1915 *Lieutenant B.W. Jones*
First U.S. Army officer to loop an aircraft

1916 Not awarded
1917 Not awarded

1918 *Lieutenant Edward V. Rickenbacker*
American ace of aces, SPAD

1919 *Lieutenant Belvin W. Maynard, Lieutenant Alexander Pearson, Jr., Lieutenant R.S. Worthington, Captain John O. Donaldson, Captain Lowell H. Smith, Lieutenant Harold E. Hartney, Lieutenant E.H. Manzelman, Lieutenant R.G. Bagby, Lieutenant D.B. Gish, Captain F. Steinie*
Performance in Brigadier General William Mitchell's trans-continental endurance and reliability test

1920 *Captain St. Clair Streett, Captain Howard T. Douglas, 1st Lieutenant Clifford C. Nutt, 2nd Lieutenant Erik H. Nelson, 2nd Lieutenant C.H. Crumrine, 2nd Lieutenant Ross C. Kirkpatrick, Sergeant Edmund Henriques, Sergeant Albert T. Vierra, Sergeant Joseph E. Englis*
Alaskan flight, DH–4s

1921 *Lieutenant John A. Macready*
World altitude record of 34,509 feet, LePere biplane

1922 *Lieutenant John A. Macready, Lieutenant Oakley G. Kelly*
World endurance record of 35 hours, 18 minutes, 30 seconds, Fokker T–2

1923 *Lieutenant John A. Macready, Lieutenant Oakley G. Kelly*
First non-stop trans-continental flight (Roosevelt Field, New York, to Rockwell Field, California), 26 hours, 50 minutes, Fokker T–2

1924 *Captain Lowell H. Smith, 1st Lieutenant Leigh Wade, 1st Lieutenant Leslie P. Arnold, 1st Lieutenant Erik H. Nelson, 2nd Lieutenant John Harding, Jr., 2nd Lieutenant Henry H. Ogden*
First flight around the world, Douglas World Cruisers

1925 *Lieutenant Cyrus Bettis, Lieutenant James H. Doolittle*
Winners of the Pulitzer and Schneider Trophy races

1926 *Major Herbert A. Dargue, Captain Ira C. Eaker, Captain Arthur B. McDaniel, Captain C.F. Wolsey, 1st Lieutenant J.W. Benton, 1st Lieutenant Charles McRobinson, 1st Lieutenant Muir S. Fairchild, 1st Lieutenant Bernard S. Thompson, 1st Lieutenant Leonard D. Weddington, 1st Lieutenant Ennis C. Whitehead*
Pan-American goodwill flight, Loening OA-1A amphibians

1927 *Lieutenant Albert F. Hegenberger, Lieutenant Lester J. Maitland*
First flight from California to Hawaii, Fokker C–2

1928 *1st Lieutenant Harry A. Sutton*
Research into the spinning characteristics of aircraft

1929 *Captain Albert W. Stevens*
High altitude photography

1930 *Major Ralph Royce*
1st Pursuit Group's mid-winter cross-country flight from Selfridge, Field, Michigan, to Spokane, Washington.

1931 *Major General Benjamin D. Foulois*
Leadership of the 1st Air Division

1932 *1st Lieutenant Charles H. Howard*
Testing of cosmic rays at various altitudes,
11th Bombardment Squadron, Condors

1933 *Captain Westside T. Larson*
Contributions to aerial defense; blind landings
and takeoffs

1934 *Lieutenant Colonel Henry H. Arnold*
Flight from Washington, D.C., to Fairbanks,
Alaska, Martin B–10s

1935 *Major Albert W. Stevens, Captain Orville Anderson*
World record balloon ascent to 72,395 feet

1936 *Captain Richard E. Nugent, 1st Lieutenant Joseph
A. Miller, 1st Lieutenant Edwin G. Simenson, 2nd
Lieutenant William P. Ragsdale, Jr., 2nd Lieutenant
Burton W. Armstrong, 2nd Lieutenant Herbert
Morgan, Jr., Technical Sergeant Gilbert W. Olsen,
Staff Sergeant Howard M. Miller, Corpsman
Frank B. Conner*
Bad weather bombing exercise, Martin bombers

1937 *Captain Carl J. Crane, Captain George V. Holloman*
First fully automatic landing, Wright Field,
23 August 1937, Fokker C–14B

1938 *2nd Bombardment Group*
Goodwill flight to Buenos Aires, 15–27
February 1938

1939 *Major Caleb V. Haynes, Major William D. Old,
Captain John A. Samford, Captain Richard S.
Freeman, 1st Lieutenant Torgils G. Wold, Master
Sergeant Adolph Cattarius, Technical Sergeant
Henry L. Hines, Technical Sergeant William J.
Heldt, Technical Sergeant David L. Spicer, Staff
Sergeant Russell E. Junior, Staff Sergeant James
E. Sands*
Earthquake relief mission to Chile, B–15

1940 Not awarded

1946 Not awarded

1947 *Captain Charles E. Yeager*
First supersonic flight, Bell X–1

1948 *Lieutenant Colonel Emil Beaudry*
Greenland rescue

1949 *Captain James G. Gallagher and crew*
First non-stop flight around the world, 94
hours, 1 minute, B–29 *Lucky Lady II*

1950 *27th Fighter Escort Wing*
Trans-Atlantic deployment, F–84Es

1951 *Colonel Fred J. Ascani*
100-km closed circuit speed record of 635.686
miles per hour, F–86

1952 *Major Louis H. Carrington, Jr., Major Frederick W.
Shook, Captain Wallace D. Yancey*
First jet non-stop trans-Pacific flight, RB–45

1953 *40th Air Division, Strategic Air Command*
Non-stop trans-Atlantic fighter deployment
with flight refueling, F–84Gs

1954 *308th Bombardment Wing*
Leapfrog intercontinental exercise, B–47s

1955 *Colonel Horace A. Hanes*
First supersonic world speed record, 822 miles
per hour, F–100C

1956 *Captain Iven C. Kincheloe, Jr.*
Reaching 125,907 feet in the Bell X–2

1957 *93rd Bombardment Wing, Strategic Air Command*
First non-stop jet flight around the world,
45 hrs 19 mins, B-52s

1958 *Tactical Air Command Composite Air Strike Force*
Rapid deployment to the Far East

1959 *4520th Aerial Demonstration Team*
Goodwill tour of the Far East

1960 *6593rd Test Squadron*
Aerial recoveries of space capsules, C–119

1961 *Lieutenant Colonel William R. Payne, Major William
L. Polhemus, Major Raymond R. Wagener*
New York to Paris, 3 hours, 19 minutes,
41 seconds, B–58

1962 *Major Robert G. Sowers, Captain Robert McDonald,
Captain John T. Walton*
New York—Los Angeles—New York, 4 hours,
41 minutes, 15 seconds, B–58

1963 *Captain Warren P. Tomsett, Captain John R.
Ordemann, Captain Donald R. Mack, Technical
Sergeant Edsol P. Inslow, Staff Sergeant Jack E.
Morgan, Staff Sergeant Frank C. Barrett*
Evacuation of wounded under fire in Vietnam

1964 *464th Troop Carrier Wing, Tactical Air Command*
Evacuation of refugees from the Republic
of Congo

1965 *Colonel Robert L. Stephens, Lieutenant Colonel
Daniel Andre, Lieutenant Colonel Walter F. Daniel,
Major Noel T. Warner, Major James P. Cooney*
Nine world records, including sustained
speed of 2,070 miles per hour and altitude
of 80,258 feet, YF–12A

1966	*Colonel Albert R. Howarth* Courage and airmanship in Southeast Asia
1967	*Major John R. Casteel, Captain Dean L. Hoar, Captain Richard L. Trail, Master Sergeant Nathan C. Campbell* Emergency multiple flight refuelings off Vietnam, KC–135
1968	*Lieutenant Colonel Daryl C. Cole* Conspicuous gallantry in Southeast Asia, C-130
1969	*49th Tactical Fighter Wing* Deployment of 72 F–4Ds from West Germany to New Mexico
1970	*Captain Alan D. Milacek and crew* Destruction of targets in Vietnam with a severely damaged aircraft, AC–119K
1971	*Lieutenant Colonel Thomas B. Estes, Lieutenant Colonel Dewain C. Vick* Record-breaking flights, SR–71
1972	*Captain Richard S. Ritchie, Captain Charles B. DeBellevue, Captain Jeffrey S. Feinstein* Vietnam War aces
1973	*Military Airlift Command aircrews* Return of POWs from Southeast Asia
1974	*Major Roger J. Smith, Major David W. Peterson, Major Willard R. MacFarlane* Project Streak Eagle test pilots, F–15
1975	*Major Robert W. Undorf* Outstanding performance during the *Mayaguez* crew rescue
1976	*Captain James A. Yule* Gallantry while an instructor in a B–52D
1977	*Captain David M. Sprinkel and crew* United States-Union of Soviet Socialist Republics energy research project, C–5
1978	*Lieutenant Colonel Robert F. Schultz and crew, Captain Todd H. Hohberger and crew* Airlift to Zaire, C–5
1979	*Major James E. McCardle* Helicopter rescue of 28 Taiwanese seamen
1980	*Crews from 644th Bombardment Squadron* Location of Soviet naval units in Arabian Sea during non-stop flight around the world
1981	*Captain John J Walters* Rescue mission in Alaskan waters
1982	*Crew in E–21, 19th Bombardment Wing* Emergency landing of B–52

1983	*Crew in E–113, 42nd Bombardment Wing* Emergency refueling and towing of F–4E
1984	*Lieutenant Colonel James L. Hobson, Jr.* Grenada assault, MC–130
1985	*Lieutenant Colonel David E. Faught* Emergency landing, KC–135
1986	*Crew from 68th Air Refueling Group, Strategic Air Command* Emergency trans-Atlantic refueling of Marine A–4s, KC–10
1987	*B–1B System Program Office* 72 record B–1B flights
1988	*Crew from 436th Military Airlift Wing* Mission to Semipalatinsk, Union of Soviet Socialist Republics, as part of Intermediate-range Nuclear Forces Accords, C–5
1989	*Crew from 96th Bombardment Wing* Emergency landing of B–1B
1990	*Crew from 16th Special Operations Squadron* Operations in Panama
1991	*Crew from 20th Special Operations Squadron* Rescue of USN F–14 pilot inside Iraq, MH-53
1992	*Captain P.B. Eunice and crew from Air Combat Command* Emergency landing of C–130H severely damaged in international airspace by Peruvian fighters.
1993	*Crew from 668th Bombardment Squadron* Emergency landing of B–52 following loss of four engines
1994	*Crew from 56th Rescue Squadron* Rescue of Icelandic sailors from foundered merchant vessel, HH–60G
1995	*Crew from Dyess Air Force Base* Flight around the world, 36 hours, 13 minutes, 36 seconds, B–1B

Bibliography

Books

Air Force Museum Foundation. *United States Air Force Museum.* Dayton, Ohio: Air Force Museum Foundation, 1992.

Ambrose, Stephen E. *D-Day.* New York: Simon & Schuster, 1994.

Anderson, Clarence "Bud," and Joseph Hamelin. *To Fly and Fight.* New York: St. Martin's Press, 1990.

Anderton, David A. *History of the U.S. Air Force.* New York: The Military Press, 1981.

———. *Aggressors.* Vol. 3. Charlottesville, Virginia: Howell Press, 1991.

Angelucci, Enzo. *The World Encyclopedia of Civil Aircraft.* New York: Crown Publishers, 1982.

———. *The Rand McNally Encyclopedia of Military Aircraft.* New York: The Military Press, 1983.

Apple, Nick, and Gene Gurney. *The Air Force Museum.* Dayton, Ohio: Central Printing, 1991.

Arnold, H.J.P. *Man in Space.* New York: Smithmark, 1993.

Avery, N.L. *B–25 Mitchell.* St. Paul, Minnesota: Phalanx Publishing, 1992.

Aymar, Brandt. *Men in the Air.* New York: Crown Publishers, 1990.

Ball, John D. *Edwards: Flight Test Center of the USAF.* New York: Duell, Sloan and Pearce, 1962.

Beck, Alfred M., ed. *With Courage: The U.S. Army Air Forces in World War II.* Washington: Air Force History and Museums Program, 1994.

Bendiner, Elmer. *The Fall of Fortresses.* New York: G.P. Putnam's Sons, 1980.

Berger, Carl. *The United States Air Force in Southeast Asia.* Washington: Office of Air Force History, 1977.

Biddle, Wayne. *Barons of the Sky.* New York: Simon & Schuster, 1991.

Bidwell, Shelford. *The Chindit War.* New York: MacMillan, 1979.

Bilstein, Jay, and Roger Miller. *Aviation in Texas.* San Antonio, Texas: Texas Monthly Press, 1985.

Bodie, Warren M. *Lockheed P–38 Lightning.* Hiawassee, Georgia: Widewing Publications, 1991.

Bowen, Ezra. *Knights of the Air.* Alexandria, Virginia: Time-Life Books, 1980.

Bowers, Peter M. *Boeing B–17 Flying Fortress.* Seattle: Museum of Flight, 1985.

Boyne, Walter. *Boeing B–52.* London: Jane's Publishing Company, 1981.

———. *Phantom in Combat.* Washington: Smithsonian Institution Press, 1985.

———. *The Leading Edge.* New York: Stewart, Tabori & Chang, 1986.

———.*The Smithsonian Book of Flight.* Washington: Smithsonian Institution Press, 1987.

———. *Silver Wings.* New York: Simon & Schuster, 1993.

———. *Clash of Wings.* New York: Simon & Schuster, 1994.

———, and Donald Lopez. *The Jet Age.* Washington: Smithsonian Institution Press, 1979.

Braybrook, Roy. *Air Power: The Coalition and Iraqi Air Forces.* London: Osprey, 1991.

Brown, David, Christopher Shores, and Kenneth Macksey. *The Guinness History of Air Warfare.* Enfield, Middlesex, England: Guinness Superlatives, 1976.

Bryan, C.D.B. *The National Air and Space Museum.* New York: Harry N. Abrams, 1979.

Caine, Philip D. *Eagles of the RAF.* Washington: National Defense University Press, 1991.

Calvorcoressi, Peter, and Guy Wint. *Total War.* London: Pelican Books, 1974.

Campbell, Christy. *Air War Pacific.* New York: Crescent Books, 1990.

Christy, Joe. *American Air Power, the First 75 Years*. Blue Ridge Summit, Pennsylvania: Tab Books, 1982.

Clancy, Tom. *Fighter Wing*. New York: Berkley Books, 1995.

Cloe, John Hailie. *Top Cover for America*. Missoula, Montana: Pictorial Histories, 1985.

Coffey, Thomas M. *Decision over Schweinfurt*. New York: David MacKay, 1977.

——. *Hap*. New York: Viking Press, 1982.

Coffman, Edward M. *The War to End All Wars*. Madison, Wisconsin: University of Wisconsin Press, 1986.

Cole, Alice, Alfred Goldberg, Samuel A. Tucker, and Rudolph A. Winnacker. *The Department of Defense. 1944–1978*. Washington: Office of the Secretary of Defense Historical Office, 1978.

Comer, John. *Combat Crew*. London: Leo Cooper,1988.

Constable, George. *World War II*. New York: Prentice Hall Press, 1989.

Cooling, Benjamin Franklin. *Case Studies in the Development of Close Air Support*. Washington: Office of Air Force History, 1990.

Copp, DeWitt S. *A Few Great Captains*. New York: Doubleday, 1980.

——. *Forged in Fire*. New York: Doubleday, 1982.

Corneliesse, Diana. *Against the Wind*. Dayton, Ohio: Aeronautical Systems Center, 1994.

Cortesi, Lawrence. *Pacific Siege*. New York: Zebra Books, 1984.

Costello, John. *Pacific War 1941–1945*. New York: Quill, 1982.

Craven, Wesley Frank, and James Lea Cate eds. *The Army Air Forces in WWII*. 7 Vols. Chicago: University of Chicago Press, 1948–1958. Reprint, Washington: Office of Air Force History, 1983.

Cross, Robin. *The Bombers*. London: Bantam Press, 1987.

Davis, Larry. *Air War over Korea*. Carrollton, Texas: Squadron/Signal Publications, 1982.

——. *Wild Weasel*. Carrollton, Texas: Squadron/ Signal Publications, 1986.

Dean, David J. *The Air Force Role in Low Intensity Conflict*. Maxwell Air Force Base, Alabama: Air University Press, 1986.

Dear, M.R.D., and I.C.B. Foot. *The Oxford Companion to World War II*. Oxford: Oxford University Press, 1995.

Donald, David. *U.S. Air Force Air Power Directory*. London: Aerospace Publishing, 1992.

Doolittle, James H., and Carroll V. Glines. *I Could Never be so Lucky Again*. New York: Bantam Books, 1991.

Dorr, Robert F., and David Donald. *Fighters of the USAF*. New York: Military Press, 1990.

Dorr, Robert F. *Vought A–7 Corsair II*. London: Osprey, 1985.

Drury, Richard S. *My Secret War*. Fallbrook, California: Aero Publishers, 1979.

Duerksen, Menno. *The Memphis Belle*. Memphis, Tennessee: Castle Books, 1987.

Dupuy, Trevor, Curt Johnson, and David Bongard. *The Harper Encyclopedia of Military Biography*. New York: Harper Collins, 1992.

Dyson, Emma, Dean Herrin, and Amy Slaton. *The Engineering of Flight*. Washington: U.S. Department of the Interior, 1993.

Edmonds, Walter D. *They Fought with What They Had*. Washington: Center for Air Force History, 1992.

Ellis, John. *Brute Force*. New York: Viking, 1990.

Elstob, Peter. *Bastogne*. London: MacDonald & Company, 1968.

Ethell, Jeffrey, and Robert T. Sand. *Fighter Command*. Osceola Wisconsin: Motorbooks International, 1991, and Alfred Price. *Target Berlin*. London: Jane's Publishing, 1981.

Ethell, Jeffrey, and Alfred Price. *Target Berlin*. London: Jane's Publishing, 1981.

Finney, Robert T. *Air Corps Tactical School 1920–1940*. Washington: Center for Air Force History, 1992.

Fletcher, Eugene. *Fletcher's Gang*. Seattle: University of Washington Press, 1988.

Flintham, Victor. *Air Wars and Aircraft*. London: Arms & Armour Press, 1989.

Ford, Daniel. *Flying Tigers*. Washington: Smithsonian Institution Press, 1991.

Foxworth, Thomas G. *The Speed Seekers*. Newbury Park, California: Haynes Publications, 1989.

Francillon, Rene J. *The United States Air National Guard*. London: Aerospace Publishing, 1993.

———. *Vietnam: The War in the Air*. New York: Arch Cape Press, 1987.

Frank, Richard B. *Guadalcanal*. New York: Random House, 1990.

Frankland, Noble. *Bomber Offensive*. New York: Ballantine Books, 1970.

Freeman, Roger. *B–17: Fortress at War*. New York: Charles Scribner's Sons, 1977.

———. *Combat Profile: Mustang*. London: Ian Allan, 1989.

———. *The Mighty Eighth in Color*. Stillwater, Minnesota: Speciality Press, 1992.

———. *The American Airman in Europe*. Osceloa, Wisconsin: Motorbooks International, 1991.

———. *The Mighty Eighth*. New York: Doubleday, 1978.

———. *The Mighty Eighth War Diary*. Osceola, Wisconsin: Motorbooks International, 1990.

———. *The Mighty Eighth War Manual*. Osceola, Wisconsin: Motorbooks International, 1991.

Futrell, Robert F. *The United States Air Force in Korea, 1950–1953*. Washington: Office of Air Force History, 1982.

———., et al. *Aces and Aerial Victories: The United States Air Force in Southeast Asia, 1965–1973*. Washington: Office of Air Force History, 1976.

Galland, Adolf. *The First and the Last*. London: Methuen, 1955.

Garfield, Brian. *The Thousand Mile War*. New York: Bantam Books, 1982.

Gibbs-Smith, Charles H. *Aviation*. London: Her Majesty's Stationery Office, 1985.

———. *Early Flying Machines 1799–1909*. London: Methuen, 1975.

Gilster, Herman L. *The Air War in Southeast Asia*. Maxwell Air Force Base, Alabama: Air University Press, 1993.

———. *Round the World Flights*. New York: Van Nostrand Reinhold, 1982.

Glines, Carroll V., *Compact History of the USAF*. New York: Hawthorn Books, 1963.

Glines, Carroll V., Harry M. Zubkoff, and F. Clifton Berry. *Flights*. Montgomery, Alabama: Community Communications, 1994.

Goldberg, Alfred. *A History of the United States Air Force*. Princeton: Van Nostrand, 1957.

Graham, Dominich. *Cassino*. New York: Ballantine Books, 1971.

Green, William. *Warplanes of the Third Reich*. New York: Galahad Books, 1986.

———, and Fricker, John. *Air Forces of the World: Their History, Development, and Present Strength*. London: Hanover House, 1958.

Green, William, and Gordon Swanborough. *The Complete Book of Fighters*. New York: Smithmark, 1994.

Greenwood, John T. *Milestones of Aviation*. New York: MacMillan, 1989.

Greer, Thomas H. *The Development of Doctrine in the Army Air Arm, 1917–1941*. Washington: Office of Air Force History, 1985.

Grinsell, Robert. *Aces Full*. Grenada Hills, California: Sentry Books, 1974.

Grintner, Lawrence E., and Peter M. Dunn. *The American War in Vietnam*. New York: Greenwood Press, 1987.

Gunston, Bill. *Rockets and Missiles*. New York: Crescent Books, 1979.

———. *American Warplanes*. New York: Crescent Books, 1986.

———. *The Illustrated Encyclopedia of Aircraft Armament*. New York: Orion Books, 1988.

———. *Chronicle of Aviation*. Liberty, Missouri: J.L. International, 1992.

Hall, Grover C., Jr. *1,000 Destroyed*. Fallbrook, California: Aero Publishers, 1978.

Hallion, Richard P. *On the Frontier: Flight Research at Dryden, 1946–1981*. Washington: National Aeronautics and Space Administration, 1984.

———. *Strike from the Sky*. Washington: Smithsonian Institution Press, 1989.

———. *Storm Over Iraq: Air Power and the Gulf War*. Washington: Smithsonian Institution Press, 1992.

Halpern, John. *Early Birds*. New York: E.P. Dutton, 1981.

Hammel, Eric. *Aces Against Germany*. New York: Pocket Books, 1995.

———. *Aces Against Japan*. New York: Pocket Books, 1995.

Hansen, Chuck. *U.S. Nuclear Weapons*. New York: Orion, 1988.

Hastings, Max. *Overlord*. New York: Simon & Schuster, 1984.

——. *The Korean War*. New York: Simon & Schuster, 1987.

Haugland, Vern. *The Eagle Squadrons*. New York: Ziff-Davis Flying Books, 1979.

Haulman, Daniel. *The High Road to Tokyo Bay*. Washington: Center for Air Force History, 1993.

Hawkins, Ian L. *B–17s over Berlin*. Washington: Brassey's, 1990.

Hennessy, Juliette. *The United States Army Air Arm, April 1861 to April 1917*. Washington: Office of Air Force History, 1985.

Hess, William N. *American Fighter Aces Album*. Dallas, Texas: Taylor Publishing, 1979.

——, and Thomas G. Ivie. *Fighters of the Mighty Eighth*. Osceola, Wisconsin: Motorbooks International, 1990.

——. *P–51 Mustang Aces*. Osceola, Wisconsin: Motorbooks International, 1992.

Higham, Robin, and Abigail T. Sidall. *Flying Combat Aircraft of the USAAF/USAF*. Vols. 1 and 2. Ames, Iowa: Iowa State University Press, 1975, 1978.

Howard, Fred. *Wilbur and Orville*. New York: Alfred A. Knopf, 1987.

Hoyt, Edwin P. *War in the Pacific*. New York: Avon Books, 1991.

Hudson, James J. *Hostile Skies*. New York: Syracuse University Press, 1968.

Hughes, Thomas Alexander. *Over Lord*. New York: Free Press, 1985.

Huttig, Jack. *1927: Summer of Eagles*. Chicago: Nelson-Hall, 1979.

Inoguchi, Rikihei, and Tadashi Nakajima. *The Divine Wind*. New York: Bantam Books, 1978.

Jablonski, Edward. *Air War*. New York: Doubleday, 1979.

——. *America in the Air War*. Alexandria, Virginia: Time-Life Books, 1982.

——. *Flying Fortress*. New York: Doubleday, 1965.

Jenkins, Dennis R. *McDonnell Douglas F–15*. Arlington, Texas: Aerofax, 1990.

Jerram, Michael G. *Incredible Flying Machines*. London: Marshall Cavendish, 1980.

Johnson, J.E. *The Story of Air Fighting*. London: Hutchinson & Co, 1985.

Josephy, Alvin M. *The American Heritage History of Flight*. New York: American Heritage, 1962.

Kaplan, Philip, and Andy Saunders. *Little Friends*. New York: Random House, 1991.

Karnow, Stanley. *Vietnam*, New York: Viking, 1983.

Keegan, John. *The Times Atlas of the Second World War*. New York: Harper & Row, 1989.

——. *The Second World War*. New York: Viking, 1990.

Kelsey, Benjamin S. *The Dragon's Teeth*. Washington: Smithsonian Institution Press, 1982.

Kennett, Lee. *The First Air War 1914–1918*. New York: Free Press, 1991.

Kinzey, Bert. *The Fury of Desert Storm*. Blue Ridge Summit, Pennsylvania: Tab Books, 1991.

Knaack, Marcelle Size. *Encyclopedia of U.S. Air Force Aircraft and Missile Systems*. Vol. 1. Washington: Office of Air Force History, 1978.

Lande, D.A. *From Somewhere in England*. Osceola, Wisconsin: Motorbooks International, 1991.

Larrabee, Eric. *Commander in Chief*. New York: Harper & Row, 1987.

Leuthner and Jensen. *High Honor*. Washington: Smithsonian Institution Press, 1989.

Liddell-Hart, Basil H. *History of the Second World War*. London: Cassell, 1970.

Longstreet, Stephen. *The Canvas Falcons*. New York: Barnes & Noble, 1995.

Lopez, Donald S. *Fighter Pilot's Heaven*. Washington: Smithsonian Institution Press, 1995.

——. *Into the Teeth of the Tiger*. New York: Bantam Books, 1986.

Lucas, Laddie. *Wings of War*. London: Hutchinson & Company, 1983.

Macksey, Kenneth. *The Penguin Encyclopedia of Weapons and Military Technology*. New York: The Viking Press, 1993.

Magoun, F. Alexander, and Eric Hodgins. *A History of Aircraft*. New York: Arno Press, 1972.

Manchester, William. *American Caesar*. Boston: Little, Brown & Company, 1978.

Mark, Eduard. *Aerial Interdiction in Three Wars.* Washington: Center for Air Force History, 1994.

Markman, Steve, and Bill Holder. *One-of-a-Kind Research Aircraft.* Atglen, Pennsylvania: Schiffer Publishing, 1990.

Marshall, Chris. *The World's Great Interceptor Aircraft.* New York: Gallery Books, 1989.

Mason, David. *Breakout.* New York: Ballantine Books, 1969.

Mason, Francis K. *Aces of the Air.* New York: Mayflower Books, 1981.

———. *Battle over Britain.* London: McWhirter Twins Ltd., 1969.

———. *War in the Air.* New York: Crescent Books, 1985.

Mason, Herbert, A., Jr., Randy G. Bergeron, and James A. Renfrow. *U.S. Army Air Forces in World War II: Operation Thursday.* Washington: Air Force History and Museums Program, 1994.

Mason, Herbert Molloy, Jr. *The U.S. Air Force: A Turbulent History.* New York: Charter, 1976.

Maurer, Maurer. *The U.S. Air Service in World War I.* Washington: Office of Air Force History, 1978.

———. *Aviation in the US Army 1919–1939.* Washington: Office of Air Force History, 1987.

———. *Air Force Combat Units of World War II.* Edison, New Jersey: Chartwell Books, 1994.

McAulay, Lex. *Battle of the Bismarck Sea.* New York: St. Martin's Press, 1991.

McCullough, David. *Truman.* New York: Simon & Schuster, 1992.

McFarland, Stephen L., and Wesley Philips Newton. *To Command the Sky: The Battle for Air Superiority over Germany, 1942–1944.* Washington: Smithsonian Institution Press, 1991.

McKay, Ernest A. *A World to Conquer.* New York: Arco Publishing, 1981.

Micheletti, Eric. *Air War over the Gulf.* London: Windrow & Greene, 1991.

Middlebrook, Martin. *The Schweinfurt-Regensburg Mission.* London: Allen Lane, 1983.

Middleton, Drew. *Air War Vietnam.* New York: Bobbs-Merrill Company, 1978.

———. *Crossroads of Modern Warfare.* New York: Doubleday, 1983.

Miller, Roger G., ed. *Seeing off the Bear: Anglo-American Air Power Cooperation during the Cold War.* Washington: Air Force History and Museums Program, 1995.

Mitcham, Samuel W. *Eagles of the Third Reich.* Shrewsbury, England: Airlife, 1989.

Momyer, William W. *Air Power in Three Wars.* Washington: Government Printing Office, 1983.

Mondey, David. *The Illustrated Encyclopedia of the World's Aircraft.* New York: A & W Publishers, 1978.

———. *Aviation.* London: Octopus Books, 1980.

———, and Lewis Nalls. *USAF at War in the Pacific.* New York: Scribners, 1980.

Morocco, John. *The Vietnam Experience.* Boston: Boston Publishing Company, 1984.

Morrison, Wilbur H. *Fortress Without a Roof.* New York: St. Martin's Press, 1982.

Morse, Stan. *Gulf Air War Debrief.* Westport, Connecticut: Airtime Publishing, 1992.

Murray, Williamson. *Strategy for Defeat.* Secaucus, New Jersey: Chartwell Books, 1986.

Nalty, Bernard C. *Pearl Harbor and the War in the Pacific.* New York: Smithmark, 1991.

Neufeld, Jacob. *Ballistic Missiles in the United States Air Force.* Washington: Office of Air Force History, 1990.

———. *Research and Development in the United States Air Force.* Washington: Center for Air Force History, 1993.

Nevin, David. *Architects of Air Power.* Alexandria, Virginia: Time-Life Books, 1981.

Nicholls, Jack C., and Warren E. Thompson. *Korea: The Air War, 1950–1953.* London: Osprey, 1991.

Office of Assistant Chief of Air Staff, Intelligence. *Condensed Analysis of the Ninth Air Force.* Washington: Office of Air Force History, 1984.

———. *The AAF in the Invasion of Southern France: An Interim Report.* New imprint, Wings at War Commemorative Edition, No. 1. Washington: Center for Air Force History, 1992.

———. *Sunday Punch in Normandy: The Tactical Use of Heavy Bombardment in the Normandy Invasion: An Interim Report.* New imprint, Wings at War Commemorative Edition, No. 2. Washington: Center for Air Force History, 1992.

———. *Pacific Counterblow: The 11th Bombardment Group and the 67th Fighter Squadron in the Battle for Guadalcanal: An Interim Report.* New imprint, Wings at War Commemorative Edition, No. 3. Washington: Center for Air Force History, 1992.

———. *Airborne Assault on Holland: An Interim Report.* New imprint, Wings at War Commemorative Edition, No. 4. Washington: Center for Air Force History, 1992.

———. *Air-Ground Teamwork on the Western Front: The Role of the XIX Tactical Air Command during August 1944: An Interim Report.* New imprint, Wings at War Commemorative Edition, No. 5. Washington: Center for Air Force History, 1992.

———. *The AAF in Northwest Africa: An Account of the Twelfth Air Force in the Northwest African Landings and the Battle for Tunisia: An Interim Report.* New imprint, Wings at War Commemorative Edition, No. 6. Washington: Center for Air Force History, 1992.

Ogden, Bob. *Great Aircraft Collections of the World.* New York: Gallery Books, 1988.

Overy, R.J. *The Air War 1939–1945.* New York: Scarborough Books, 1982.

Pace, Steve. *X-Fighters.* Osceola, Wisconsin: Motorbooks International, 1991.

———. *Edwards Air Force Base.* Osceola, Wisconsin: Motorbooks International, 1994.

Pape, Ronald C., and Garry R. Harrison. *Queen of the Midnight Skies.* Westchester, Pennsylvania: Schiffer Military History, 1992.

Patterson, Dan, and Paul Perkins. *The Lady.* Charlottesville, Virginia: Howell Press, 1993.

———. *The Mustang.* Charlottesville, Virginia: Howell Press, 1995.

———, and Michelle Crean. *The Soldier.* Charlottesville, Virginia: Howell Press, 1994.

Peacock, Lindsay T. *Strategic Air Command.* London: Arms & Armour Press, 1983.

Pimlott, John. *Strategic Bombing.* New York: Gallery Books, 1990.

Pitt, Barrie. *Military History of World War II.* New York: Military Press, 1989.

Platt, Frank C. *Great Battles of World War I in the Air.* New York: Weathervane Books, 1966.

Polmar, Norman. *Strategic Air Command.* Annapolis, Maryland: Nautical & Aviation Publishing, 1979.

Prange, Gordon E. *At Dawn We Slept.* New York: McGraw-Hill, 1981.

Price, Alfred. *Luftwaffe.* New York: Ballantine Books, 1969.

———. *The Bomber in World War II.* New York: Charles Scribner's Sons, 1979.

———. *Aircraft versus Submarine.* London: Jane's Publishing Company, 1980.

———. *Spitfire at War.* London: Ian Allan, 1985.

Redding, Robert, and Bill Yenne. *Boeing: Planemaker to the World.* New York: Crescent Books, 1983.

Rickenbacker, Eddie. *Fighting the Flying Circus.* New York: Avon Books, 1967.

Rickenbacker, Edward V. *Rickenbacker.* Englewood Cliffs, New Jersey: Prentice-Hall, 1968.

Robinson, Anthony, and Michael J.H. Taylor. *In the Cockpit.* Secaucus, New Jersey: Chartwell Books, 1991.

Rooney, D.D. *Stilwell.* New York: Ballantine Books, 1971.

Scutts, Jerry. *Lion in the Sky.* Wellingborough, England: Patrick Stephens, 1987.

Seagrave, Sterling. *Soldiers of Fortune.* Alexandria, Virginia: Time-Life Books, 1981.

Sherry, Michael S. *The Rise of American Air Power.* New Haven, Connecticut: Yale University Press, 1987.

Shores, Christopher. *Air Aces.* Greenwich, Connecticut: Bison Books, 1983.

———. *Duel for the Sky.* New York: Doubleday, 1985.

Shultz, Richard H., Jr., and Robert L. Pfaltzgraff, Jr. *The Future of Air Power in the Aftermath of the Gulf War.* Maxwell Air Force Base, Alabama: Air University Press, 1992.

Speer, Albert. *Inside the Third Reich.* London: Sphere Books, 1971.

Spick, Mike. *Milestones of Manned Flight.* New York: Smithmark, 1994.

Steijger, Cees. *A History of USAFE.* Shrewsbury, England: Airlife Publishing, 1991.

Strategic Bombing Survey Team. *United States Strategic Bombing Surveys.* Maxwell Air Force Base, Alabama: Air University Press, 1987.

Sweetman, Bill, et al. *The Great Book of World War II Airplanes*. Bonanza Books, 1984.

Sweetman, Bill. *YF–22 and YF–23*. Osceola, Wisconsin: Motorbooks International, 1991.

Taylor, John W.R. *Jane's All the World's Aircraft*. London: Jane's Publishing Company, Annually.

———. *Combat Aircraft of the World*. New York: G.P. Putnam's Sons, 1969.

———. *A History of Aerial Warfare*. London: Hamlyn, 1974.

———, and Kenneth Munson. *History of Aviation*. New York: Crown Publishers, 1972.

———, Michael J.H. Taylor, and David Mondey. *The Guiness Book of Air Facts and Feats*. Enfield, Middlesex, England: Guinness Superlatives, 1977.

Taylor, Michael J.H. *Jane's Encyclopedia of Aviation*. New York: Portland House, 1989.

———. *Jane's Fighting Aircraft of World War I*. New York: Military Press, 1990.

Thomas, Gordon, and Max Morgan Witts. *Enola Gay*. New York: Stein and Day, 1977.

Thompson, R.W. *D-Day*. New York: Ballantine Books, 1968 .

Tibbets, Paul, with Clair Stebbins and Harry Franken. *The Tibbets Story*. New York: Stein & Day, 1978.

Tilford, Earl H., Jr. *Setup*. Maxwell Air Force Base, Alabama: Air University Press, 1991.

———. *United States Air Force Search and Rescue in Southeast Asia*. Washington: Center for Air Force History, 1992.

Tuchman, Barbara W. *Stilwell and the American Experience in China*. New York: MacMillan, 1971.

Vader, John. *New Guinea*. New York: Ballantine Books, 1971.

———. *Pacific Hawk*. New York: Ballantine Books, 1970.

van der Vat , Dan. *The Pacific Campaign*. New York: Simon & Schuster, 1991.

Wagner, Ray. *Mustang Designer*. New York: Orion, 1990.

Walker, Bryce. *Fighting Jets*. Alexandria, Virginia: Time-Life Books, 1983.

Walker, Lois, and Shelby Wickam. *From Huffman Prairie to the Moon*. Washington: Government Printing Office, 1986.

Warnock, A. Timothy. *The Battle Against the U-Boat in the American Theater*. Washington: Center for Air Force History, 1993.

Weigley, Russell G. *Eisenhower's Lieutenants*. Bloomington, Indiana: Indiana University Press, 1981.

Weinberg, Gerhard L. *A World at Arms*. Cambridge University Press, 1994.

Wilkinson, Roy. *The World's Great Attack Aircraft*. New York: Gallery Books, 1988.

Willmott, H.P. *B–17 Flying Fortress*. London: Arms & Armour Press, 1980.

Wohl, Robert. *A Passion for Wings*. New Haven, Connecticut: Yale University Press, 1994.

Wolfe, Martin. *Green Light*. Washington: Center for Air force History, 1993.

Wood, Tony, and Bill Gunston. *Hitler's Luftwaffe*. New York: Crescent Books, 1979.

Yeager, Chuck, and Leo Janos. *Yeager*. New York: Bantam Books, 1985.

Yenne, Bill. *History of the U.S. Air Force*. Stanford, Connecticut: Longmeadow Press, 1992.

Magazines and Periodicals

Air Force Magazine, Air Force Association

Air Power History, Air Force History Support Office and the Air Force Historical Foundation

Air & Space, Smithsonian Institution, Washington

Desert Storm, Military History Magazine. Leesburg, Virginia: Empire Press, 1991.

Military History, Empire Press, Leesburg, Virginia

Military History Quarterly, American Historical Publications and the Society for Military History

Wings of Fame, Aerospace Publishing, London

Unpublished Papers and Articles Prepared in the Air Force History Support Office, Washington, D.C.

Hallion, Richard P. *The New Air Force.*

———. *Out of the Past, Into the Future.*

Peebles, Curtis. *The United States Air Force and the Military Space Program.*

Glossary

AAA	Anti-Aircraft Artillery	ALCM	Air Launched Cruise Missile
AAC	Alaskan Air Command	ALSEP	Apollo Lunar Surface Experiments Package
AAF	Army Air Forces	AMC	Air Materiel Command
AAFAC	Army Air Forces Anti-Submarine Command	AMSA	Advanced Manned Strategic Aircraft
ABM	Anti-Ballistic Missile	ANG	Air National Guard
ACC	Air Combat Command	ARDC	Air Research and Development Command
ACSC	Air Command and Staff College		
ADC	Air Defense Command	ARIA	Advanced Range Instrumentation Aircraft
AEF	American Expeditionary Force	ARPA	Advanced Research Projects Agency
AETC	Air Education and Training Command	ARRS	Aerospace Rescue and Recovery Service
AFB	Air Force Base	ARS	Air Rescue Service
AFCC	Air Force Communications Command	ARVN	Army of the Republic of Vietnam
AFFTC	Air Force Flight Test Center	ASTP	Apollo-Soyuz Test Project
AFLC	Air Force Logistics Command	ATC	Air Transport Command (USAAF)
AFMC	Air Force Materiel Command	ATC	Air Training Command (USAF)
AFRes	Air Force Reserve	AVG	American Volunteer Group
AFROTC	Air Force Reserve Officer Training Corps	AWACS	Airborne Warning and Control System
AFSATCOM	Air Force Satellite Communications System	AWAL	All Weather Air Line
AFSPC	Air Force Space Command	AWC	Air War College
AFSC	Air Force Systems Command	AWPD	Air War Plans Division
AFSOC	Air Force Special Operations Command	AWS	Air Weather Service
AFTI	Advanced Fighter Technology Integration	BMEWS	Ballistic Missile Early Warning System
AIM	Air Intercept Missile		

C³I	Command, Control, Communications and Intelligence		GATS	GPS-Aided Targeting System
CAP	Combat Air Patrol		GEODSS	Ground-based Electro-Optical Deep Space System
CATF	China Air Task Force		GHQ	General Headquarters
CBI	China-Burma-India Theater		GLCM	Ground Launched Cruise Missile
COMAIRSOLS	Commander Air Solomons		GPES	Ground Proximity Parachute Extraction system
CONAC	Continental Air Command			
CrewTAF	Crew Training Air Force		GPS	Global Positioning System
DEW	Distant Early Warning		H2X	Designation for World War II bombing radar
DMSP	Defense Meteorological Satellite Program		HARM	High-speed Anti-Radiation Missile
DMZ	Demiltarized Zone		HOTAS	Hands on Throttle and Controls
DRU	Direct Reporting Unit			
DSCS	Defense Satellite Communications System		IBS	India-Burma Sector
DSP	Defense Support Program		ICBM	Intercontinental Ballistic Missile
DSTS	Deep Space Tracking System		IFF	Identification Friend or Foe
			IONDS	Integrated Operational Nuclear Detection system
EAC	Eastern Air Command		IRBM	Intermediate Range Ballistic Missile
ECM	Electronic Counter-Measures			
EHF	Extremely High Frequency		JAC	Joint Aircraft Committee
EMP	Electro-Magnetic Pulse		JATO	Jet-Assisted Take-Off
ESC	Electronic Security Command		JCS	Joint Chiefs of Staff
ESM	Electronic Support Measures		JPATS	Joint Primary Aircraft Training System
			JSTARS	Joint Surveillance and Target Attack Radar System
FAC	Forward Air Controller			
FAI	Federation Aeronautique Internationale		JSTPS	Joint Strategic Planning Staff
FEAF	Far East Air Force			
FlyTAF	Flying Training Air Force		LANTIRN	Low Altitude Navigation and Targeting Infra-Red for Night
FOA	Field Operating Agency		LAPES	Low Altitude Precision Extraction System

LORAN	Long Range Aid to Navigation	RAF	Royal Air Force
LRCA	Long Range Combat Aircraft	RESCAP	Rescue Combat Air Patrol
		RFC	Royal Flying Corps
MAAG	Military Assistance Advisory Group	RHAW	Radar Homing and Warning
		RNZAF	Royal New Zealand Air Force
MAC	Military Airlift Command	ROK	Republic of Korea
MACV	Military Assistance Command Vietnam	RPV	Remotely Piloted Vehicle
MATS	Military Air Transport Service		
MAW	Mission Adaptive Wing	SAC	Strategic Air Command
MIDAS	Missile Detection and Alarm System	SAGE	Semi-Automatic Ground Environment
MIRV	Maneuverable Independently Targeted Re-entry Vehicle	SAM	Surface to Air Missile
MOL	Manned Orbiting Laboratory	SAMOS	Satellite and Missile Observation System
MRBM	Medium Range Ballistic Missile	SAR	Search and Rescue
MTD	Maneuver Technology Demonstrator	SDS	Satellite Data System
		SEATO	Southeast Asia Treaty Organization
NAAF	Northwest African Air Forces	SIOP	Single Integrated Operational Plan
NASA	National Aeronautics and Space Administration	SPADATS	Space Detection and Tracking System
NATAF	Northwest African Tactical Air Force	SRAM	Short Range Attack Missile
NATO	North Atlantic Treaty Organization	SSN	Space Surveillance Network
NAOC	National Airborne Operations Center	STOL	Short Take-Off and Landing
		SUPT	Specialized Undergraduate Pilot Training
NEACP	National Emergency Airborne Command Post		
NKAF	North Korean Air Force	TAC	Tactical Air Command
NORAD	North American Air Defense Command	TAF	Tactical Air Force
		TechTAF	Technical Training Air Force
OKW	Oberkommando der Wehrmacht (German Army High Command)	UN	United Nations
		USAAF	United States Army Air Forces
PACAF	Pacific Air Forces	USAF	United States Air Force

USAFE	United States Air Forces in Europe
USASTAF	United States Army Strategic Air Forces
USMC	United States Marine Corps
USN	United States Navy
USSBS	United States Strategic Bombing Survey
V–1	Vergeltungswaffe Eins (German flying bomb, WW II)
VHSIC	Very High Speed Integrated Circuits
VLR	Very Long Range
VNAF	Vietnam Air Force
WASP	Women's Airforce Service Pilots

U.S. Military Aircraft Designations

Three systems have been used to designate American military aircraft since World War I. The first was adopted in 1924 after wartime experience had shown the need for an organized system of reference. The second came in 1948 following USAF independence. At that time the American services had no commonality in their aircraft designations. In 1962 they decided to design a single system for U.S. military aircraft and to restart type numbering. The primary role designations for the three periods are as follows:

	1924	1948	1962
A	Attack	Amphibian	Attack
B	Bombardment	Bomber	Bomber
C	Cargo	Cargo	Cargo
F	Photographic (1930–1947)	Fighter	Fighter
G	Gyroplane	Glider	–
H	—	Helicopter	Helicopter
L	Liaison	Liaison	–
O	Observation (1942–1947)	—	Observation
P	Pursuit	—	Patrol
Q	Drone	Drone	Drone
R	Rotary Wing (1941–1947)	Reconnaissance	Reconnaissance
S	Supersonic (1946–1947)	Sailplane (1960)	Anti—submarine
T	Trainer	Trainer	Trainer
U	—	Utility	Utility
V	—	V/STOL	V/STOL
X	—	Experimental	Experimental
Z	—	—	Airship
FB	—	—	Fighter Bomber
TR	—	—	Tactical Reconnaissance
SR	—	—	Strategic Reconnaissance

Secondary role designations were also allocated. These appeared as a prefix to the primary designation letter.

	1924	1948	1962
A	Advanced; Assault	Calibration	Attack
B	Basic; Bomber	Bomber	—
C	Cargo	Cargo	Cargo
D	—	Drone Director	Drone Director
E	—	Electronics (Exempt to '55)	Electronics
F	Photographic (1944–1947)	Fighter	Fighter
G	Glider (1942–1947)	Parasite Carrier	Grounded
H	Heavy (1925–1927)	—	Search & Rescue
J	Jet (1943–1947)	Temporary Test	Temporary Test
K	Ferret (1944–1947)	Tanker	Tanker
L	Light (1925–1932)	Liaison	Cold Weather
M	—	MedEvac	Missile Carrier
N	—	Permanent Test	Permanent Test
O	Observation	—	Observation
P	Pursuit	Passenger	—
Q	—	Drone	Drone
R	Restricted (1942–1947)	Reconnaissance	Reconnaissance
S	—	Search & Rescue	Anti–submarine
T	Trainer (1943–1947)	Trainer	Trainer
U	Utility (1941–1947)	Utility	Utility
V	—	VIP Transport	VIP Transport
W	—	Weather	Weather
X	Experimental (1928–1947)	Experimental	Experimental
Y	Service Test (1928–1947)	Service Test	Service Test
Z	Obsolete (1928–1947)	Obsolete	Project

Plans & Operations Mentioned in Text

WW II

ANVIL/DRAGOON	Allied invasion of Southern France, 15 August 1944
ARGUMENT	Air attacks on industries supporting the Luftwaffe
BOLERO	Planning and build-up stage for Allied invasion of France
CLARION	Allied air attacks on communications in Germany, 22–23 February 1945
COBRA	Breakout of U.S. forces from Normandy, 25 July 1944
CROSSBOW	Allied air attacks on V–1 launching sites
DIADEM	Allied offensive in Italy, Spring 1944
FRANTIC	USAAF shuttle missions against distant European targets, turning around on Soviet bases
GYMNAST	Proposed Allied invasion of North Africa
MARKET/GARDEN	Operations aimed at capturing Rhine bridge at Arnhem, September 1944
MATTERHORN	USAAF bombing offensive against Japan
OVERLORD	Allied invasion of Normandy, 6 June 1944
POINTBLANK	Combined Bomber Offensive against Germany
RAINBOW	Pre-war U.S. operational plans
ROUNDUP	Proposed 1943 Allied invasion of northern France
SLEDGEHAMMER	Proposed Allied landing on coast of northern France in late 1942
STRANGLE	Air attacks on enemy communications in Italy, March 1944
TORCH	Allied invasion of North Africa, 8 November 1942

Berlin Airlift

VITTLES	Supply of West Berlin by air during Soviet blockade, 1948–1949
LITTLE VITTLES	Delivery of candy to children during Berlin Airlift

Korean War

STRANGLE	Interdiction of enemy communications in North Korea, 1951
KIDDIE CAR	Airlift to rescue Korean War orphans

Vietnam War

ARC LIGHT	B–52 bombing missions against the Viet Cong
BANISH BEACH	C–130 missions to start forest fires by dropping oil drums
BARREL ROLL	USAF campaign in support of Laotian ground forces
BOLO	F–4 decoy mission aimed at bringing MiGs to battle, 2 January 1967
COMMANDO VAULT	C–130 missions aimed at blasting out helicopter landing areas in heavy jungle with weapons weighing up to 15,000 pounds
FARM GATE	USAF training detachment to VNAF, 1961

FREEDOM TRAIN	Strike operations against North Vietnam below 20th parallel, 1972	

Abbreviations of Air Force unit designations are derived from a few initial letters. Simply combining them as appropriate decodes a unit's primary role:

W:	Wing
G:	Group
S:	Squadron
AR:	Air Rescue
B:	Bombardment
C:	Composite
F:	Fighter
I:	Interceptor
N:	Night
P:	Photographic
R:	Reconnaissance
S:	Strategic
T:	Tactical
TC:	Troop Carrier
CCT:	Combat Crew Training

FREQUENT WIND — U.S. plan for emergency evacuation from South Vietnam, 1975

LINEBACKER I — Comprehensive bombing campaign against North Vietnam, 1972

LINEBACKER II — Intense aerial assault on North Vietnamese targets, December 1972

MULE TRAIN — Tactical airlift support in South Vietnam, 1962

NIAGARA — Air support for U.S. Marines at Khe Sanh, 1968

RANCH HAND — Defoliation operations

ROLLING THUNDER — Campaign of limited air attacks against selected military targets in North Vietnam

STEEL TIGER — Limited interdiction of Ho Chi Minh Trail in Southern Laos

TIGER HOUND — Extensive operations against Ho Chi Minh Trail

Grenada

URGENT FURY — Operation against Marxist forces on Grenada

Panama

JUST CAUSE — Operation against Panama Defense Force troops of dictator Manuel Noriega

Libya

ELDORADO CANYON — Air strike against targets in Libya

Iraq

DESERT SHIELD — Build-up of forces in the Persian Gulf region following Iraqi invasion of Kuwait

DESERT STORM — Campaign against Iraqi forces to restore independence to Kuwait